STUDIES IN
CONTEMPORARY
JEWRY

The publication of *Studies in Contemporary Jewry* was made possible through the generous assistance of the Samuel and Althea Stroum Philanthropic Fund, Seattle, Washington.

INSTITUTE OF CONTEMPORARY JEWRY
THE HEBREW UNIVERSITY
OF JERUSALEM

JEWS AND MESSIANISM IN THE MODERN ERA:

Metaphor and Meaning

STUDIES IN
CONTEMPORARY
JEWRY
AN ANNUAL
VII

————1991————

Edited by Jonathan Frankel

Published for the Institute by
OXFORD UNIVERSITY PRESS
New York • Oxford

Oxford University Press

Oxford   New York   Toronto
Delhi   Bombay   Calcutta   Madras   Karachi
Petaling Jaya   Singapore   Hong Kong   Tokyo
Nairobi   Dar es Salaam   Cape Town
Melbourne   Auckland
and associated companies in
Berlin   Ibadan

ISBN 0-19-506690-1
ISSN 0740-8625
Library of Congress Catalog Card Number: 84-649196

2 4 6 8 10 9 7 5 3 1

Printed in the United States of America
on acid-free paper

Preface

The theme of the symposium in this volume of *Studies in Contemporary Jewry*, messianism as a factor in modern Jewish history, is one that is unusually well suited to a publication of The Hebrew University of Jerusalem. This, after all, is a subject that was held to be of key importance by many of the most remarkable scholars associated with this university. The names of Martin Buber, Ben-Zion Dinur, Gershom Scholem and Jacob L. Talmon come to mind immediately, but a far more extensive list could be compiled without any difficulty. It is, thus, not surprising that most of the articles in the symposium have been contributed by scholars at Israeli universities.

However, it is certainly worth noting that a number of the authors (most notably Janet Aviad, Eli Lederhendler and Yaacov Shavit) insist on the need to adopt what can perhaps best be called a minimalist approach in estimating the political significance of messianic terminology. When are the "Days of the Messiah" to be understood as metaphor and when as an article of faith?

While this volume was in preparation, we had a changing of the guard on the staff of the annual. Dr. Eli Lederhendler, who has served as the managing editor since the publication first went into its planning stage some ten years ago, decided to leave in order to concentrate full time on his own research. Throughout his editorship, he proved the ideal colleague on whose excellent judgment, unstinting dedication and great goodwill we could always depend. At the same time, and for the same reason, our book review editor, Hannah Koevary, also left us. In recent years, she had become a much-valued and respected member of the editorial team. This volume was prepared jointly by them and by their replacements, Laurie Fialkoff and David Rechter, who had the thankless task of taking over as the manuscript of Volume VII was being completed and the galleys of Volume VI were being read. They have survived the experience undaunted.

J.F.

Contents

Symposium
Jews and Messianism in the Modern Era:
Metaphor and Meaning

Essays

Review Essays

Book Reviews (by subject)

Political and Communal History   331

Social Sciences, Social History and Politics ... 347

Religion, Thought and Education   362

Antisemitism, Holocaust and Genocide   414

Language, Art and Literature   432

Symposium

Jews and Messianism
in the Modern Era:
Metaphor and Meaning

The Messianic Idea
and Zionist Ideologies

Jody Elizabeth Myers
(CALIFORNIA STATE UNIVERSITY, NORTHRIDGE)

It is commonplace to note the close relationship between the messianic idea and
Zionist thought. Still missing is a clarification of the essential distinctions between
messianism and Zionism. For example, in his classic essay on the Zionist idea,
Arthur Hertzberg describes the differences in the broadest of terms:

> What marks Zionism as a fresh beginning in Jewish history is that its ultimate values
> derived from the general milieu. . . . The scheme of Jewish religion had seen the
> messianic problem as one of resolving the tension between the Jew and his Maker—the
> Exile is punishment and atonement for sin; for the new doctrine [Zionism], at its
> newest, the essential issue is the end of the millennia of struggle between the Jew and
> the world.[1]

Hertzberg characterizes this transformation as the "secularization of the messianic
ideal." Jacob Katz also does little more than assert the this-worldly turn of religious
belief: "In [modern Zionism] Jewish messianic belief was, so to speak, purged of its
miraculous elements, and retained only its political, social and some of its spiritual
objectives."[2]

However, these observations do not pinpoint the particular sense in which
Zionism departed from religious messianism. "Secularized messianism" is, after
all, a term that has also been appropriately applied to eighteenth-century Haskalah
patriotism, nineteenth-century liberalism and twentieth-century Zionist Revisionism.[3] A careful articulation of the distinctions between traditional messianism and
Zionism is important for several reasons. First, it is essential for an appreciation of
the tremendous change in consciousness heralded by the advent of Zionism. Second, it ought to highlight the complexity of the philosophical and religious choices
involved by illustrating that the messianic idea in Judaism is broader and more
flexible than it is usually portrayed. Third, the prevalent assumptions that the
transition from messianism to Zionism meant a shift from religion to secularism
exclude from consideration a crucial group of modern Jewish nationalists: religious
Jews who adopted their own form of Zionism. Certainly, the link between messianism and Zionism was different for them than it was for secular Jews. And
because they, more than other Jews, struggled to maintain their messianic faith,

3

their ideological choices will best reveal which of the traditional beliefs could be successfully incorporated within the new movement, and which could not.

My task, then, will be to define the different types of Jewish nationalist ideology in relation to messianism, paying particular attention to the positions adopted by religious Jews.

One way to accomplish this task is to construct a typology of the Jewish ideologies that call for a return to Zion.[4] Such ideologies can be classified according to their attitude toward three key issues. These particular questions have been singled out because they are of essential importance in each ideology and because the varied answers given to them immediately distinguish one approach from the other.[5] The first of these major issues is the historical outlook, specifically, whether or not (and, if so, to what extent) could the Exile of the Jews from their land be terminated by human action. The second is the question of the means to be used in ending the Exile; and the third involves the varied ways in which the postexilic era was visualized. Using these three indications as a guide, two ideologies can be isolated within—and two outside—the messianic tradition. These are ideal types—I do not imply that they necessarily or always exist in reality as pure forms. Instead, they should be envisaged as points along a spectrum.

Jewish messianism, in all its permutations, is a belief in God's ultimate responsibility for the Exile of the Jews and in the certainty that God, through a redeemer, will restore His people to greatness, inaugurating a new era in accordance with biblical prophecies.

Despite the extraordinary variation within messianic literature with regard to the specific details of the Redemption, the dominant approach has been a commitment to passivity. An analysis of what is thus commonly called passive messianism yields, in accordance with the key issues discussed above, the following pattern of beliefs. First, there is a belief in maximal divine and minimal human control over history. The fate of the Jews is not in their own hands. As a punishment for their sins, God decreed their exile from the land of Israel and subjugated them to the nations of the world. Only God can reverse this decision. In response to the second question (how to end the Exile), the passive messianist sees human options as quite limited; opinions range from the belief that the Redemption is wholly independent of human behavior (e.g., as part of an irreversible predetermined plan) to the conviction that the fulfillment of the mitzvot and acts of repentance can bring God to end the Exile.[6]

All passive messianists agree, though, that more demonstrative or directed actions—for example, "rebelling against the nations of the world," conquering Palestine, emigrating en masse to the land of Israel or taking the injunction to pray for the return to Zion to extremes—constitute illegitimate attempts to "force the End." The classic expression of messianic passivity is a talmudic teaching pegged to the thrice-uttered oath from the Song of Songs (2:7, 3:5, 8:4), "I adjure you, O daughters of Jerusalem, not to stir, neither to awaken love, until it pleases." The rabbis taught that implied here are the three (some say six) oaths that God imposed on Israel and the gentiles, preserving the Exile until God alone decrees its end.[7] Consistent with the passive messianists' emphasis on God's omnipotence and human passivity is their insistence that the Exile will end supernaturally through God's sudden abrogation of historical laws; apocalypticism flows logically from the doctrine of human powerlessness. A messianic figure and miraculous events also figure prominently in their descriptions of the redemptive process.[8]

Finally, passive messianists envision the postexilic era as the messianic age that they imagine, for the most part, as a radically transformed and perfect world. The antinomianism implicit in this outlook—specifically, the notion that in the new era Jewish law will be fundamentally transformed or rendered obsolete—has been held in check by the conservative teachings of the rabbis. Even those who imagine a messianic age as one of supernatural change also include in their visions the restoration of the Temple, a sovereign Davidic king ruling over the land of Israel and a complete ingathering of the Jews. This Redemption, then, is a combination of restorative and eschatological elements.[9]

The second messianic ideology, active messianism, is not diametrically opposed to passive messianism; instead, it shares similar assumptions. Its historical outlook is more rational, and it allows greater latitude for natural law, chance and human initiative in determining the end of the Exile. God controls history, but this control is subtle and in conformity with natural laws. Thus, although it is acknowledged that God decreed the Exile, there is a tendency to note that the departure from the land of Israel was partly a voluntary step taken by the Jews who, furthermore, did not return to that land when opportunity arose.

Accordingly, active messianists insist that the redemptive process is an *interactive* dynamic of divine and human deeds. When Jews perceive the finger of God in history (and the message from on high can be deciphered with the help of a correct reading of biblical texts), they are to take concrete actions to hasten the messianic age. Now is the time to initiate the restoration of the preexilic conditions of life, such as rebuilding the Temple. The model for this was the restoration following the Babylonian Exile that occurred gradually, naturally and with the assistance of the gentiles.

The activism advocated is still circumscribed by the religious tradition: by the inhibiting influence of the three oaths. Thus, active messianists feel compelled to assert that the time has come "to awaken love" or that the oaths do not apply to the proposed activity.[10] Adherents of this view believe that God desires their activism. Theirs is not a faithless impatience with God's saving power but rather a praiseworthy demonstration of their faith that, as a loving partner, He will respond favorably to their overtures. They believe that God will assist and enhance their initiatives; thus, the Redemption will evolve in a gradual and natural manner over an extended period. The emphasis on human initiative precludes apocalypticism. The miraculous is not central to this scheme: some maintain that the miracles foretold in biblical prophecies will occur at the later stages of the messianic process, whereas others insist that supernatural events do not constitute an essential element in this scheme of things at all.[11]

The third component of this ideology, its vision of the postexilic era, largely corresponds to that of the passive messianists: a messianic age that is a fulfillment of the biblical prophecies. It differs only in that the Redemption unfolds gradually and, at least in its initial stages, appears natural.

Chronologically, active messianism developed prior to the passive variant, but the latter eventually became the dominant outlook. For some time after the destruction of the Second Temple, Jews retained the hope that their defeat would prove to be a brief interval reversible through their own efforts. That much is suggested by the widespread support among the Jews of Palestine for the Bar Kokhba Revolt (132–135 C.E.).[12] However, in the wake of the disastrous failure of the revolt and with the transference of the center of Jewish life to Babylonia over the next few centuries, messianic passivity developed into one of the mainstays of rabbinic Judaism.[13] The rabbis criticized active messianism as false messianism or as dangerous and foolish rebelliousness.

Nevertheless, though passive messianism had stabilizing functions, it could not fully overcome the authentic religious tensions of exilic life; indeed, it was a reminder of these tensions. Passive messianism constituted a theodicy that justified God's temporary abandonment of the Jews, yet maintained the hope that God would be responsive to their pleas for reconciliation and renewal. It encouraged obedience to postdestruction institutions and authorities, yet preserved the belief that God would restore the royal dynasty and the Temple cult in the messianic age. It encouraged the Jews to defend their political interests and better their conditions of life in the Diaspora, their long-term home, yet it taught that the Exile was an unnatural condition.[14] These tensions were epitomized in Diaspora Jews' relation to the land of Israel. Although they believed that it was their natural home, they endowed it with cathartic powers and contributed material support only for maintaining it as a holy site outside the normal framework of life.

When these contradictions became difficult to sustain, active messianism was bound to surface.[15] This occurred *not* at times of sheer desperation and despair, but at times of political flux in Palestine: when, for example, a new regime took over the country or when the ruling power enacted reforms; during pivotal years of the Roman period in Palestine; after the start of Crusader rule; at the high point of Ottoman power during the sixteenth century.[16] At such junctures, Jews would suspect that God was signaling the end of the Exile and awaiting their enthusiastic cooperation. They found support for their convictions scattered throughout halakhic and aggadic literature, and more systematic presentations could be found in medieval rationalist philosophy and Kabbalah.[17] It is important to emphasize that this pragmatic and realistic approach predates the modern era. This outlook is as deeply rooted in the Jewish messianic tradition as is passive messianism, and it is incorrect to argue otherwise.[18]

Active messianism apparently underwent a revival among religious Jews during the first two-thirds of the nineteenth century. Seeking a more rational religion, moderate *maskilim* (proponents of Enlightenment) turned to the medieval Jewish rationalist philosophers in their attempt to restate the tenets of Judaism in modern form. Some of them preferred the activist tradition, finding it more attractive than the dominant passive outlook, saddled as it was with miraculous and apocalyptic elements.[19] Furthermore, the notion that the world was slowly moving toward a higher state of being in the messianic age was compatible with, and probably reinforced by, the modern belief in progress. The popularization of kabbalistic literature in early modern Central and Eastern Europe also contributed to the acceptance of active messianism.

But all this would not have been sufficient to revive activist messianic ideas had it not been for political improvements, particularly in the Middle East, that were bound to stimulate Jewish hopes. Among these developments particular mention should be made of the Egyptian conquest of Palestine; the more favorable attitude of the Turkish regime to the Jews; the intercession of the European consuls on behalf of the Jewish community in the Holy Land; the improved civic status of the Jews in Europe; and the increasing number of Christians who supported (albeit for their own religious reasons) a Jewish return to Zion.

Several mid-nineteenth-century rabbis, all operating independently of one another, perceived some or all of these phenomena as signals that God was about to initiate the Redemption or that, indeed, the Redemption had already begun. Some of the disciples of the Vilna Gaon, Yehudah Alkalai, Zvi Hirsch Kalischer, Eliyahu Guttmacher, Nathan Friedland and others felt that the Jews ought to respond by taking concrete action, most notably a mass migration to the land of Israel. In addition, Kalischer and Guttmacher called for a program of agricultural settlement and for the restoration of sacrificial worship at the rebuilt altar. All of them believed that once their projects were under way, God would ensure the messianic process its triumphal conclusion.[20] For several decades their optimistic outlook lent new energy to the longstanding philanthropic involvement of European Jews in the Yishuv. However, in both its scope and motivation, active messianism deviated from the traditional philanthropy.

Not included within the messianic tradition are two other ideologies that call for a return to Zion. The first of these is characterized by its unequivocally secular outlook; for this, the term "Zionism" (*tout court*) is reserved here. Zionist ideology stands in contrast to messianic thinking when measured by all three components of the typology. The Exile is perceived as a phenomenon shaped solely by political, cultural and economic forces. History is made entirely by people; God has no role in it whatsoever. This denial of the historical outlook central to traditional Judaism results in divergence on the other two counts as well. The means to end the Exile reside entirely in human hands and a pragmatic approach is therefore demanded. The methods adopted may be tempered by moral or cultural concerns, but the religious self-restraint imposed by Jewish tradition (e.g., the three oaths) is no longer relevant.

Similarly, the concept of the postexilic era is an entirely natural one: the Jewish people will be transformed from an object to a subject of history, living on their own land where they can guarantee their material well-being and free self-expression. The restoration of preexilic institutions is not deemed desirable, except insofar as these correspond to the goals of modern nationalism. Thus, on each of the three points—the historical outlook, the means and the goal—the religious principles of messianic thought are denied.

It is important to keep in mind that, even though Zionists occasionally utilize messianic language and concepts, their rejection of the theocentric worldview is paramount here. They often identify Zionist goals with traditional messianic expectations such as the Ingathering of the Exiles, the centrality of Jerusalem, the confrontational wars to come, peace in nature, or international harmony.[21] The use of messianic language by secular Zionists, though, must be regarded as a tactic designed to show that Zionism and messianism are not opposed to, but are compatible with, one another—or else to show that Zionism has continued and renewed, not replaced, traditional messianic beliefs. In short, it is a strategy for minimizing the radical break with tradition. On the other hand, the secular outlook denies God's influence—however minimal—on history and leaves humanity to its own resources. From varying perspectives, this denial can appear as liberating or as terrifying.

Be that as it may, the vision of, say, the confrontational wars to come, is bound to appear radically different to the secular than to the religious Jew: for the former there can be no absolute guarantee of the outcome. It has been plausibly argued that familiarity with the messianic tradition in many cases made the acceptance of similar secular ideals easier. However, it is probably also true that this familiarity often made the shift from messianism to Zionism all the more painful.[22]

The fourth ideology does not fit neatly into the framework of either secular Zionism or religious tradition. It is held by Jews who accept passive messianism on a theoretical level—they believe that God is the ultimate power responsible for the Exile; they reject human efforts to hasten the redemptive process; and in their prayers and rituals, they call for the coming of the messianic age—but they abandon this viewpoint when it comes to what they define as the realm of practical politics. There, they accept the three assumptions of secular Zionism: that the Jews have control of their national fate, that pragmatic means for the return to Zion be adopted and that the goal is the establishment of a Jewish commonwealth in Palestine. The establishment of a Jewish commonwealth is seen as a solution to immediate religious, social and economic problems. Their motives are decidedly nonmessianic; they do not claim to be hastening the messianic age, nor do they regard signs of success as part of the redemptive process. They have faith that God alone will bring the Messiah, but they feel compelled to adopt active political measures to settle Palestine in the meantime. In other words, they have compartmentalized their religious outlook in order to deal most rationally with the problems at hand.[23] This hybrid ideology is best referred to as nonmessianic religious Zionism.

Nonmessianic religious Zionism first appeared in the 1840s in the writings of the Hungarian Rabbi Yosef Natonek, who explicitly called for the conquest of Palestine and the establishment of a Jewish state.[24] His position was exceptional among religious Jews, since even the active messianists did not call for conquest or rebellion of any kind. Only in the 1870s—when a significant number of religious Jews finally began to press for mass emigration to Palestine, as well as land purchase and economic development there—did these Jews go beyond the bounds of traditional philanthropism. Rabbis Shmuel Mohilever, Yitzhak Elhanan Spector, Naftali Zvi Yehudah Berlin and Yaakov Reines were the best known exponents of this outlook.[25]

Why did they not simply adopt a thoroughgoing, active messianist ideology? Essentially, two reasons were involved. The first was the widespread Jewish accep-

tance of a secular outlook in the second half of the century. Secular ideas undermined and ultimately negated the traditional coherence of the messianic doctrine.
Furthermore, the fact that religious ideals were no longer quite so important to an
increasing number of Jews meant that some religious Jews, concerned about preserving Jewish unity, had to seek a new common basis for Jewish identity. Zionism,
it was sometimes believed, could serve this function, whereas religion could not.[26]

The second reason for the rejection of active messianism was the problematic
Jewish situation. I have argued that active messianism appeared during the first two-
thirds of the nineteenth century primarily because events occurred then that could be
interpreted as positive, divine signals of the Redemption. The events of the last third
of the century did not lend themselves as well to this optimistic interpretation.
Indeed, the emergence of Zionism was a direct outgrowth of the severe problems
then facing the Jewish people.

Zionism presumes a threat to Diaspora Jewry so dangerous that, for a solution,
national displacement is required. By the 1870s and 1880s, religious Jews, too,
increasingly perceived themselves to be living in a time of crisis: they saw widespread
disregard of mitzvot, the waning culture of Torah study (even among the Orthodox)
and the growth of antisemitism. To many of them a Jewish national home in Palestine
looked initially as if it could provide a solution to all these problems. The Yishuv
could serve as a refuge from antisemitism; but more important, because pious rabbis
were still a dominant influence there and irreligious Jews were still in the minority, it
offered an opportunity to build a rejuvenated Torah-centered Jewry. Religious
Zionists saw the movement as a way to reclaim their authority over the Jews and to
reclaim from the gentiles some modicum of control over the future of their nation.
However, once secularized Jews began to dominate the Zionist movement and the
new Yishuv, the optimism of active messianism began to seem more implausible. On
the other hand, the nonmessianic religious solution was also problematic, even for
those Orthodox Zionists who propounded it.[27]

The harsh criticism leveled at the religious Zionists by their Orthodox opponents,
and the former's defensive apologetics, served to underline the overwhelming loyalty of the religious camp to passive messianism and the weakness of the religious
Zionist position. Religious Zionists tried valiantly to demonstrate their faithful
adherence to the passive messianic tradition. This involved finding alternate interpretations of the oaths. Some argued that the oaths only prohibited the establishment of a Jewish government, and they had no intention of going that far. When
religious Zionists accepted the Basel Program with its call for a legally guaranteed
Jewish homeland, they rationalized their decision by the argument that the oaths
prohibited only illegal and rebellious activities—a condition that was not violated
by a search for an internationally recognized charter. They emphasized the nonmessianic nature of their specific goal, but, of course, the Jewish tradition had always
regarded an Ingathering of the Exiles and restoration of Jewish sovereignty as
messianic events. For this reason, nonmessianic religious Zionists were denounced
by many of their rabbinic peers as adherents of a false messianism, despite their
protestations to the contrary.[28]

Another defensive strategy was to emphasize how great a mitzvah it was to settle
and build up the land; this, too, was controversial as halakhic opinion proved to be

divided on the issue.[29] A third tactic was to justify their rejection of the traditional constraints on higher, religious grounds. Mohilever, for example, defended the activities of Hibbat Zion as *pikuah nefesh* (necessary to prevent the endangerment of lives), describing the Jewish people as trapped in a house on fire. In such a case, he argued, one has an overriding duty to dispense with theological niceties and such principles as nonassociation with freethinkers.[30] This was perhaps the weakest approach, because better places of refuge (e.g., America), were available that did not entail the violation of the three oaths. Such an argument, moreover, bore an uncomfortable similarity to the secular Zionists' impatience with religion.

During the course of the twentieth century, active messianism reemerged and began to dominate the rhetoric employed by many religious Zionists, both in Israel and elsewhere. The two factors that had led to its decline in the latter years of the nineteenth century—the dire situation of the Jews and the growing Orthodox receptivity to secular culture—appear to have been reversed. First, many religious Jews came to regard political developments in the Middle East as unusually promising. Rabbi Avraham Yitzhak Kook, who taught a mystical version of active messianism, encouraged this outlook and gave it new legitimacy and a wider following. Many Jews interpreted such events as the issuing of the Balfour Declaration, the partial ingathering of the Jews, the victorious Israeli wars and the reunification of Jerusalem as divine signals that the Redemption was approaching, or indeed had already begun. Some have even interpreted the most terrible event of the century, the Holocaust, as the birth pangs of the imminent messianic age. It is this determination to regard all events in a positive light that makes this ideology so attractive and dynamic, especially in contrast to the more sober and balanced secular Zionist ideologies.

A second factor in the revival of active religious messianism is that a growing number of Orthodox Jews, confident that they have successfully emerged from the crisis of secularism, have sought to express and to justify their nationalism with rhetoric that is distinctly religious and that is not indebted to secular Zionism. Active messianism provides them an all-encompassing worldview that is deeply rooted in tradition. It gives expression to a religious triumphalism, empowering them, as it were, to determine, with God, the future of the nation.

Notes

The writing of this article was made possible by a grant from the Northridge Foundation, California State University, Northridge.

1. Arthur Hertzberg (ed.), *The Zionist Idea: A Historical Analysis and Reader* (New York: 1960), 18.

2. Jacob Katz, "The Jewish National Movement: A Sociological Analysis," in *Jewish Society Through the Ages*, ed. Hayim Hillel Ben-Sasson and Shmuel Ettinger (New York: 1971), 269. Elsewhere, Katz notes that messianism bequeathed to Jewish nationalism the striving for a future utopia and a return to Zion (276–277), and he attributes the Jews' quick acceptance of Herzl's leadership to their religious expectation of a personal redeemer (283).

3. On messianism during the Haskalah, see Baruch Mevorach, "Haemunah bamashiaḥ befulmusei hariformah harishonim," *Ẓiyon* 34 (1969), 191–208; and David Biale, *Power and Powerlessness in Jewish History* (New York: 1986), 103–109. On liberalism's debt to messianism, see Katz, "The Jewish National Movement," 275–277. Gershom Scholem's critique of Revisionism is discussed in Biale's *Gershom Scholem: Kabbalah and Counter-History*, 2nd ed. (Cambridge, Mass.: 1982), 100–105.

4. "Ideology" is perhaps too definitive a characterization of the fragmented comments typical of messianic literature. Beginning with the rabbinic period, however, a crystallization of attitudes occurred that formed the basis for later systematized approaches to the messianic process.

5. Aviezer Ravitzky, "Haẓafui vehareshut hanetunah," in *Yisrael likrat hameah ha'esrim veaḥat*, ed. Aluf Hareven (Jerusalem: 1984), 139–197, uses messianic determinism as a major demarcation of messianic ideologies. I have not found this to be decisive, because it appears in all types of religious as well as secular ideologies.

6. A discussion of the Tannaitic debate over the power of repentance versus the predestined Redemption can be found in Ephraim E. Urbach, *The Sages: Their Concepts and Beliefs*, trans. Israel Abrahams (Cambridge, Mass.: 1987), 668–684. Sanhedrin 97b is the classic rabbinic expression of the belief that, because the predestined dates for the Redemption have passed, the only valid human activity to hasten the end of the Exile is repentance, "R. Eliezer said: If [the people of] Israel repent, they will be redeemed. R. Joshua said to him, If they do not repent, will they not be redeemed?! But the Holy One, blessed be He, will set up a king over them, whose decrees shall be as cruel as Haman's, whereby Israel shall engage in repentance, and He will thus bring them back to the right path."

7. Ketubot 110b–111a. The historical context of this passage is discussed later; see n. 13.

8. On passivity and powerlessness, see Yonina Talmon, "The Pursuit of the Millenium," *Archives européenes de sociologie* 3, no. 1 (1962), 136. The sudden arrival of Redemption does not preclude the possibility that it will not be complete for quite some time. For a variety of rabbinic statements on this subject, see Raphael Patai, *The Messiah Texts* (Detroit: 1979), 54–64.

9. For a discussion of the tension between antinomianism and the rabbinic mentality, see Gershom Scholem, "Toward an Understanding of the Messianic Idea in Judaism," in his *The Messianic Idea in Judaism, and Other Essays on Jewish Spirituality* (New York: 1971), 17–24. The rabbinic tradition consistently treated the restoration of Jewish sovereignty over Palestine as a messianic possibility only. This will be a problem for the fourth type, discussed later. There are a number of excellent anthologies and surveys of messianic literature available in English, among them Patai, *The Messiah Texts;* Joseph Klausner, *The Messianic Idea in Israel*, trans. W. F. Stinespring (New York: 1955); Abba Hillel Silver, *A History of Messianic Speculation in Israel* (New York: 1927, repr. Boston: 1959).

10. The first response, the claim that the messianic moment is at hand and the oaths no longer apply, was bound to be received with adamant protest. The second response was safer and more frequently proffered. It usually amounted to the claim that the oaths prohibit only violent or rebellious activity, but not peaceful and legal actions. A useful prooftext for this was Yaakov Emden's emendation of the Talmud's version of the oath "do not emigrate to the land of Israel *in a wall*"—the word *baḥomah* explained by Rashi to mean "together, in force"—to "do not emigrate to the Land of Israel *like a wall*"—in force. In other words, mass emigration was permitted, but not violence. Emden elsewhere discussed the desirability of conquering Palestine, concluding his suggestion with the problem of the oath; see his letter to Aaron Gomperz, as quoted in Azriel Shohet, *'Im ḥilufei tekufot* (Jerusalem: 1960), 247. On Emden's decision permitting the premessianic restoration of sacrificial worship, see Jody Elizabeth Myers, "Attitudes Toward a Resumption of Sacrificial Worship in the Nineteenth Century," *Modern Judaism* 7 (February 1987), 33–55.

11. Maimonides's messianic theory is an example of this latter type. See Scholem, "The Messianic Idea in Judaism," 24–33. The moderate nature of this type of messianic hope is excluded from Yonina Talmon's "Millenarian Movements," *Archives européenes de*

sociologie 7, no. 2 (1966), esp. 166, 174, where she stresses the image of the millennium as total perfection divorced from reality.

12. In a later and less activist era, this support was reduced in talmudic sources to Rabbi Akiva's lone belief in Bar Kokhba's messiahship. See Gedalyahu Alon, "The Attitude of the Pharisees to Roman Rule and the House of Herod," in his *Jews, Judaism, and the Classical World*, trans. Israel Abrahams (Jerusalem: 1977), 45–46. Aharon Oppenheimer, "Meshihiyuto shel bar-Kokhva," in *Meshihiyut veeskhatalogiah*, ed. Zvi Baras (Jerusalem: 1983), 153–156, reviews the statements attributed to Rabbi Akiva and shows that those originating closest to the time of the Bar Kokhba Revolt clearly indicate that Akiva harbored only moderate and realistic goals for the "messianic movement." This echoes the viewpoint of Urbach, *The Sages*, 672–676.

13. It is significant that the classic expression of passive messianism, the talmudic discussion of the thrice-uttered oaths in the Song of Songs (Ketubot 110b–111a), is structured as a debate between a Palestinian and a Babylonian rabbi. The Babylonian, with a greater vested interest in the maintenance of postexilic institutions, argues against the permissibility of individual emigration to Palestine. The Palestinian reduces this extreme messianic passivity to prohibitions against conquest of, and en masse emigration to, the land of Israel, rebellion against the nations and excessively hastening the end of the Exile. [For further discussion of the three oaths, see Aviezer Ravitzky herein, pp. 34–67]

14. Passive messianism should not be confused with political passivity. According to the ideology of passive messianism, political activism is valid until the point at which it encourages rebellion against the gentiles and the ending of the Exile. See Amos Funkenstein, "Hapasiviyut kesimanah shel yahadut hagolah: mitos umeziyut," Zalman Aranne Lecture, Tel-Aviv University, 1982.

15. The way in which these contradictions are connected to messianic activism, particularly the problem of sacrificial worship, is explored in greater detail in Myers, "Sacrificial Worship," 29–50.

16. By nature this ideology will not be well documented, because it challenges the norm. However, the following show evidence of active messianic sympathy that arose during these junctures. During the rule of Judah the Patriarch, see Oppenheimer, "Meshihiyuto shel bar-kokhva," 164; and Urbach, *The Sages*, 678. On Jewish messianic enthusiasm during the reign of Emperor Julian (the Apostate) and the Persian conquest of Palestine, see Michael Avi-Yonah, *The Jews of Palestine* (New York: 1976), 191–198, 265–268. On the messianic ideas of Estori ha-Farhi, the medieval geographer of Palestine, see the critical edition and introduction by A. M. Luncz in *Kaftor vaferah*, 2 vols. (Jerusalem: 1897). On the Safed ordination controversy in the sixteenth century, see Jacob Katz, "Mahloket hasemikhah bein rabbi Ya'akov Berab veha-Ralbah," *Ziyon* 17 (1959), 28–45.

17. The desire for a rationalistic messianic belief predated the medieval era, though that is where it was most obviously coupled with philosophical rationalism. Oppenheimer, "Meshihiyuto shel bar-Kokhva," 154, suggests that the realistic conception of the messianic figure reflected in Akiva's messianic stance was motivated by the desire to distance Jewish beliefs from the competing Christian belief in a supernatural, miracle-performing Messiah figure. Maimonides's messianic theory is an example of medieval active messianism. See Amos Funkenstein, "Maimonides: Political Theory and Realistic Messianism," *Miscellanea Mediaevalia* 11 (1977), 81–103; and Aviezer Ravitzky, "'Kefi koah haadam': yemot hamashiah bemishnat haRambam," in Baras, *Meshihiyut veeskhatologiah*, 191–220. On messianism and the Kabbalah, see the other articles in Baras.

18. For instance, it is inaccurate to claim that the messianists insisted on a miraculous Redemption, whereas the modern Zionists posited a self-achieved one. This has been Jacob Katz's position, though in his recent writings he has modified it by arguing that premodern active messianism allowed only "spiritual" or "ritualistic" devices for "hastening the End," in contrast to the modern messianists who pursued practical means, such as the agricultural renewal of the land of Israel; cf. his articles, "Tzevi Hirsch Kalischer," in *Guardians of Our Heritage*, ed. Leo Jung (New York: 1958), 209–227, and "Israel and the Messiah," *Commentary* 73 no. 1 (January 1982), 35. I find this distinction to be artificial; by

this reasoning, Nahmanides's advocacy of the Jewish settlement, buildup and farming of the land of Israel in the thirteenth century was also modern and out of sync with tradition.

19. The connection between the revival of active messianic thought and the growth of rationalism is explored in Jody Elizabeth Myers, "Zevi Hirsch Kalischer and the Origins of Religious Zionism," in *From East and West: Jews in a Changing Europe,* ed. Frances Malino and David Sorkin (Oxford: 1989), 267–294.

20. Jody Elizabeth Myers, *Seeking Zion: The Messianic Ideology of Zevi Hirsch Kalischer,* Ph.D. diss., UCLA (Los Angeles: 1985). On messianic activism and the students of the Vilna Gaon, see Aryeh Morgenstern, *Meshiḥiyut veyishuv ereẓ yisrael bamaḥaẓit harishonah shel hameah hatesh'a 'esrei* (Jerusalem: 1985), 13–37.

21. Israel (Yisrael) Kolatt has catalogued the Zionist use of messianic concepts; see "Ẓiyonut umeshiḥiyut," in Baras, *Meshiḥiyut veeskhatologiah,* 419–432.

22. Katz, "The Jewish National Movement," 277, argues the former point. The tension between the religious and secular outlook seems missing from the discussion of messianism and Zionism in Shmuel Almog, *Zionism and History: The Rise of a New Jewish Consciousness,* trans. Ina Friedman (New York: 1987), 58–66. The transformation is wonderfully evoked in Shmarya Levin's autobiography, *Forward from Exile,* ed. and trans. Maurice Samuel (New York: 1967), 196.

23. Yosef Salmon has pointed out that this quasi-secular approach of the early religious Zionist parties enabled the Orthodox to claim successfully for themselves a space within the Zionist enterprise; see his "Masoret umoderniyut bamaḥshavah haẓiyonit-datit bereshitah," in *Ideologiah umediniyut ẓiyonit* (Jerusalem: 1978), 32.

24. B. Frankel, *Reshit haẓiyonut hamedinit hamodernit* (Haifa: 1956).

25. Representative writings in translation can be found in Hertzberg, *The Zionist Idea. Shivat ẓiyon,* ed. Abraham Sluzki (Warsaw: 1891), is a collection of testimony (mainly rabbinic) in support of the Hibbat Zion movement that contains an excellent sample of letters by religious Jews. Religious Zionists tend to ignore these distinct types of religious thought. For example, Shmuel Ha-Cohen Weingarten, a religious historian of the movement, has explained that "among the [early religious Zionists] were those who omitted mentioning their primary objective—bringing the Redemption; they were content to mention in their writings only the objective of working for the settlement of the land"; cf. his "Atḥalta degeulah," in *Sefer haẓiyonut hadatit,* 2 vols., ed. Yitzhak Rafael and S. Z. Shragai (Jerusalem: 1977), vol. 1, 112. This statement is a distortion: Mohilever and his colleagues were familiar with the writings of the active messianists, but they carefully and deliberately chose another route.

26. Ehud Luz, *Makbilim nifgashim* (Tel-Aviv: 1985), 55–95.

27. *Ibid.,* 69–79.

28. Mordechai Breuer, "Hadiyun beshalosh hashevu'ot badorot haaḥaronim," in *Geulah umedinah: Hakinus hashenati lemaḥshevet hayahadut* (Jerusalem: 1979), 49–57. (No ed. named.)

29. For an example of this argument, see the booklet published by the State of Israel Ministry of Immigrant Absorption, "The Duty of Aliyah to Eretz Israel" (Jerusalem: 1977). A summary of the halakhic problem can be found in J. David Bleich, *Contemporary Halakhic Problems* (New York: 1977), 7–8.

30. From his message to the First Zionist Congress (1897), as quoted in Hertzberg, *The Zionist Idea,* 402.

Interpreting Messianic Rhetoric in the Russian Haskalah and Early Zionism

Eli Lederhendler
(TEL-AVIV UNIVERSITY AND THE HEBREW UNIVERSITY)

THE SEMANTIC CONUNDRUM: WHEN IS MESSIANISM NOT MESSIANISM?

What constitutes a genuine messianic movement in post-mishnaic Judaism? This seemingly simple question is difficult to answer because messianism is a paradoxical idea that contains its own negation. Given the fact that all such movements occur in history—that is, in the unredeemed "present"—they are, in theological terms, "false," and have, indeed, been referred to as "antimessianic." They are "false" in the sense that they fail, by definition, to actualize their redemptive vision. And they are antimessianic insofar as they challenge and reject the classical, "passive," theurgic approach to Redemption as it appears in the rabbinic tradition. Hence, they are often related to antinomian impulses and may be fairly described as heretical in and of themselves.

Indeed, messianic movements in Judaism may be characterized as unorthodox attempts to choose one component of Jewish eschatology—or set of components—over another, and thus undermine or override a delicate dialectical balance that classical rabbinic Judaism has left unresolved. These components may be expressed as pairs of antitheses, all of which are, paradoxically, included in the Jewish messianic tradition. As a result, there is tension between universalism and particularism: Redemption embraces all humanity; but it also pertains primarily to the Redemption of Israel. Thus, the people of Israel become, as it were, God's agents for salvation in this world. Second, apocalypticism coexists with restorationism. There is no definitive answer to the question of whether the messianic era is essentially beyond human experience, human history as we know it, and human comprehension or is, rather, a theocratic restoration within the natural realm.

Finally, there is the question of divine control as against human responsibility. The Redemption is variously understood as having to be accomplished through God's direct and miraculous intervention in the course of history according to a predestined plan whose existence is predicated on the implausibility of an unredeemed, tragically flawed universe created by a perfect and omnipotent God. At the

14

same time, Redemption is also contingent on the deeds and religious integrity of man, and of the Jew in particular, so that its timing, its inception and even its very substance depend on human acts.[1]

Millenarian movements in Jewish history typically reduced these polarities to a simpler conception of the End of Days. They departed from and rejected the rabbinic-Judaic norm in that they adopted a unidimensional understanding of Redemption to a greater extent than was sanctioned in the classical tradition as such. The impulse to "force the End" is a revolutionary one, roundly condemned throughout history by most Jewish spiritual and civic authorities as an essentially erroneous approach, the product of false consciousness, a doctrine gone awry.

If it is difficult to decide whether such bona fide millenarian movements as that of Shabbetai Zvi are messianic or antimessianic, the semantic-conceptual thicket becomes virtually impenetrable when we attempt to categorize a modern social and political movement such as Zionism in relation to messianism. Zionism resembled the radical messianic movements in Jewish history in the sense that it, too, was reductionist in its definition of Redemption. Taking our three sets of antitheses, Zionism—though it incorporated elements of a universalist vision—was committed, first of all, to a particularist program; it took restoration to be the real meaning of Jewish messianism through the ages, firmly rejecting apocalypticism; and, in its secular forms as well as in mainstream religious Zionism, it unequivocally opted for human responsibility and human action over passive expectations of miraculous divine intervention. In fact, it may be considered a rebellion against the quietest approach.

Jacob Neusner has written about the analogous, if different, characteristics of the seventeenth-century Sabbatian movement and Herzlian Zionism:

> The contrast between the two is instructive. Sabbateanism phrased its message in strictly theological, Kabbalistic terms. Shabbatai Zvi was not merely "the Messiah," but rather played a central role in the metaphysical drama created by tensions within the Godhead itself. Zionism spoke in political and thoroughly worldly terms, identifying the Jewish problem with sociological, economic and cultural matters. Herzl was never "the Messiah," though Zionism unhesitatingly utilized the ancient Messianic scriptures and images of Jewish messianism. The contrast is, therefore, between theological and ideological messianism, and it is rendered significant by the fact that *the spiritual experience, apart from the verbal explanations associated with it, in each case exhibits strikingly similar features: an emotional millenarian upheaval, dividing friend from friend, leading some to despair and others to unworldly hope, and leading a great many to act in new ways.*[2]

Yet how far can we press this functional resemblance of Zionism to messianic heresies without ourselves being reductionist to the point of the absurd? May one speak at all of messianism where there is no guiding Messiah-ideology (to say nothing of a messianic figure as such) and little eschatological content other than the very loosely defined goal of national redemption and the pursuit of a radical solution to the Jewish question?

Both early Jewish nationalists and Zionist historians indulged in a form of anachronistic analysis when they identified the Jewish messianic tradition with national consciousness and political restorationism. Modern nationalists certainly made this identification and, perhaps understandably, attributed the same underlying motives to premodern Jews. But seen within the religious context of its time, traditional messianism was not so much a political or nationalist–restorationist ideology as a theodicy.[3] It was a consoling mechanism that, on the one hand, played a key role for premodern Jews in their ongoing polemic with, and defense against, Christian conversionism and, on the other hand, served the internal purpose of countering and restraining the more radical and heretical beliefs promoted by Jewish messianic movements. It was not intended to be a realistic program for reshaping the Jewish political condition. "Next year in Jerusalem" is not a statement of geographical intent, but of spiritual aspiration.

The issue is clouded by the messianic rhetoric or allusions to Redemption employed by the Jewish nationalists, and it is further complicated by the accusation of false messianism leveled at the Zionists by their early Orthodox detractors:

> [We cry out] against the delusions of the new false messiah, that appears in somewhat different garb than [the] messianic pretenders of the past, and that calls itself "Zionism."
>
> Activity faithfully undertaken for the public welfare has always been respected and held sacred among our people. . . . But public service and public servants have always stayed within strict limits. First, such activities have only been directed toward achieving the modicum of improvement in the material and religious life of the Jews that would permit them to live according to their faith. And they retained their faith in an everlasting salvation that would come only in the End of Days. [Jewish leaders] never violated those limits by seeking complete and perfect Redemption, which is the proper task of the Messiah. . . . And now the Zionists have come and have broken the age-old rules. They have replaced the efforts to win improvement in the material and spiritual status and conditions of our lives with an effort to achieve a complete and perfect Redemption. . . . They intoxicate the masses with the heady wine of eternal salvation and thereby deflect their attention from daily needs . . . and mislead them with . . . the lie that Redemption is here at hand.[4]

Translated into historical terms, this charge (voiced, in this instance, in 1900) amounts to a perception—by some contemporaries, at least—that the Zionists were would-be, although grossly misguided, messianists of the first order. Thus, the charge of antimessianism or false messianism makes for a complex, almost insoluble, semantic problem.

Some scholars, who do not wholeheartedly subscribe to the thesis (most closely associated, perhaps, with Ben-Zion Dinur or Josef Klausner)[5] that ties Zionism directly to the age-old Jewish yearning for Redemption and for the return to the land, nevertheless, often speak of Zionism as a modern sequel to religious messianism that transformed, adapted or otherwise derived from the messianic heritage. Jacob Katz, for example, maintains:

> [The Zionists] were inspired by the conviction that a Jewish society, rebuilt in its ancient land, would somehow reestablish a direct link with its pristine past. This was an obvious and conscious adaptation of a basic feature of Jewish messianism, and was reflected in particular in the symbolic vocabulary employed by the Zionist movement. . . . Zionism's deep involvement with the messianic expectations of the Jewish people served as its driving force . . . given the obvious historical link between the two. For without the messianic hopes of restoration to its ancient homeland, why should

the Jewish people have chosen this spot of all places on which to reconstruct a national state?[6]

[Zionism was] Jewish messianic belief . . . purged of its miraculous elements.[7]

Yet others have argued—none better than Gershom Scholem—that messianism is actually an escape into myth, an antipolitical and ahistorical impulse that inevitably remains unfulfilled: "a life lived in deferment [in which] nothing can be done definitively, nothing can be irrevocably accomplished, . . . nothing concrete . . . can be accomplished by the unredeemed."[8] In that sense, Zionism was profoundly antimessianic. To Scholem a messianism shorn of miraculous elements is no longer messianism at all. The politicization of Redemption in Zionism created the precise antithesis of the messianic idea, a conscious rejection of its mythic worldview and, therefore, something quite unidentifiable with Sabbatianism.

Dinur and Scholem operated with diametrically opposed definitions of religious messianism and, not surprisingly, held opposite convictions regarding the relationship between Zionism and the messianic tradition. Thus, any attempt to come to grips with these questions must first seek to reach some understanding of the relationship between traditional Jewish messianism and political action.

Beyond that, there is the issue of the rhetoric or symbols used by the Zionists in stating their case. Why did they do this? And what did it mean to them?

Finally, there is the problem of subliminal messianism: the possibility that a movement such as Zionism elicited support or aroused opposition in Jewish society because it struck a familiar chord or resonated with older traditions and yearnings, even if the movement as such was not explicitly messianic in either form or content. Whether or not this perception was sound and whether or not allusive rhetoric that conjured with prophetic promises was just that and nothing more, the "messianic" or "false messianic" label itself had social consequences that are significant historical data. Some Jews probably determined their attitude to Zionism on the basis of their ideas about messianism. Thus, Stephen Sharot argues, "While Zionism in Eastern Europe was not a direct product of religious millenarianism, part of its appeal was that it presented a secular solution that had similarities to millenarianism."[9] Yet how sound, historically, is the contention that Zionism, regardless of its stated positions, was able to tap a subterranean source of messianic inspiration in the popular Jewish imagination?

It is quite possible that there are no conclusive answers to any of these questions. The present examination of a small group of pre-Herzlian nationalists is insufficient as a basis for comprehensive conclusions. Nevertheless, I will try to suggest why an examination of early Jewish nationalism in nineteenth-century Russia tends to weaken the case for a strong nexus between Zionism and messianism.

EARLY JEWISH NATIONALISM: HASKALAH AS CONTEXT

In trying to understand why early Jewish nationalists said what they did, I proceed from the assumption that it is more fruitful to see them not primarily as proto-Zionists but as part of a certain social group and as products of a certain intellectual tradition. Their social position helped to determine how they expressed their convictions, and rhetorical norms that were prevalent in mid-nineteenth-century Jewish intellectual discourse certainly affected the way certain words were employed in the 1870s and 1880s.

In analyzing the processes of political modernization and secularization within the Russian Haskalah, a key question relates to legitimation. Secular political ideologies were first articulated and developed within limited circles of the Jewish intelligentsia (primarily, *maskilim* [modernists] and students). Unlike the politics practiced by Jewish spokesmen and notables in premodern times, the new politics of the middle and late nineteenth century did not command widespread assent and authority. Lacking the legitimacy of an age-old political tradition, such new political creeds as nationalism and socialism, when applied to the Jewish situation, required explanation and justification. Their adherents, a minority within the preponderantly traditionalist Jewish population, were inevitably defensive. They verbally assaulted their opponents with the kind of polemics that attested, deep down, to their relatively weak position. Rhetorical aggressiveness hid apologetic motives.

The search for legitimacy led the *maskilim* to appeal to a new source of political authority—the will of the people.[10] Appeals to public opinion and the people's interests served the modern intellectuals as effective surrogates for the more traditional underpinnings of Jewish politics: the authority of rabbis and other leading figures and the cultivation of stable relations with the organs of state government.

Yet the immanent and inchoate historical force represented by the people's will could not so easily provide the transcendant, fixed purpose that in traditional politics was played by God's guidance, by Providence. In traditional society, political activity was undertaken by Jews to sustain the well-being, security or integrity of their communities, and it was invested with religious legitimacy and purpose. In theological terms, survival in Exile—maintained through the efforts of Jewish political and spiritual leaders—both reflected and justified God's continuing Covenant with Israel. The belief that the surviving remnant would someday be redeemed by a messiah–king lent consolation, purpose and confidence to the life of an embattled minority. Politics in this system expressed on the temporal plane the Jews' conviction that their existence retained ultimate meaning not only for themselves but also for humankind, for the cosmos and for God. Along with the performance of mitzvot (in the sense here of religious ordinances), politics made the Jews partners with God in the unfolding drama of their own salvation.[11]

The sense of purposiveness in the march of time and the sense of the Jews' unique place in history with which the redemptionist faith endowed traditional Jews could not be adequately replaced by "the people" as the basis of the new Jewish politics. Populist or nationalist ideas tended toward a reconciliation between "the masses" and the intellectual elite and reflected a fundamental reorientation in Jewish politics—a new democratic consciousness and a desire to reconstruct a Jewish political community.[12] But by themselves, such propositions indicated no direction, purpose or agenda that transcended short-term goals. In order to express transcendant values and fixed purpose, the adherents of the new cultural and political trends pressed into service another myth—in addition to the myth of "the people"—namely, the national "destiny" of the Jews, their historical singularity and their "prophetic" mission.[13] Recourse to terms laden with messianic symbolism allowed the expression, in Hebrew, of contemporary romantic and utopian ideas.

True, the linguistic difficulty faced by *maskilim,* who found few apt Hebrew equivalents for modern social and political concepts, was surely another and an important factor in their use of traditional terms. In and of itself, however, the lexicographic problem does not exhaust the issue. (One might point to the way in which Polish romantic nationalism was also expressed in messianic terminology.)

Jewish nationalism, in particular, has so often been linked by historians to the Jewish messianic tradition in part because of the rhetoric and symbolism that accompanied the early development of the Hibbat Zion and Zionist movements.[14] I suggest that messianic rhetoric had no specific eschatological referents for late nineteenth-century Russian Jewish intellectuals and that such rhetoric embodied a code—that is, a vocabulary that made it possible for nationalists to enhance their effectiveness and legitimacy by hitching their star to a transcendant purpose—in order to pose both a romantic challenge to the liberal rationalism of the Enlightenment and to explain to *themselves* (even more than to others) that they were heirs, in a new form, to an older tradition.

In their struggle to gain recognition and support, they brandished certain evocative words—*geulah* (Redemption), *yeshu'ah* (salvation), *ye'ud* (destiny), *kibbuẓ galuyot* (the Ingathering of the Exiles), *ḥazon* (prophetic vision), *ẓiyon* (Zion) and *ereẓ avoteinu* (the land of our fathers)—that they knew were central to religious meaning in Judaism. By using such terms they were declaring their intention to decipher and proclaim their contemporary significance. Previously the sign and scepter of rabbinic dominance, the invocation of such consecrated words was intended to carry political weight in Jewish society. The nationalists used them to assert their claim to be a new national priesthood who could read the Urim and Thummim of history.

THE RHETORIC OF NATIONAL SALVATION

David Gordon's programmatic essay of 1863, "In Peace and Tranquility Shall Ye Be Redeemed," lamented the fact that some Jews and "self-anointed scholars" (those, primarily, of the Reform movement) had abandoned the traditional belief "that the time would come for [Jews] to return to the land of their fathers." Those who denied Israel's future hopes were lacking in

> Jewish national pride [but] thank God, most of our brethren still yearn for their ancestral land, their holy city, their sacred Temple. . . . This hope is an axiom of our faith [that] has no parallel in any other nation. . . . The mission [*te'udah*] of the Jew is and always has been to be a full participant in all civic affairs and especially in the search for wisdom and knowledge, and to demand the rights that he deserves as a human being, without slavishly subordinating himself to others, but rather standing up for his holy Torah. He should not sell his birthright for a mess of pottage.[15]

Recent history had shown that nations could attain marvelous achievements and could restore their ancient glory. In the light of such developments, "Redemption for Israel, too, is awaiting its fulfillment in our time."[16] Thus, the progress and direction of history itself pointed the way to a Jewish national renaissance and possible restoration (with the help of an enlightened Europe).

Although such hopes proved premature, the nationalist Hebrew press continued to emphasize the essential identity between the Jewish people, their religious faith, their national spirit (*Volksgeist*) and their national destiny, particularly in the wake of the Reform rabbinic conferences of 1868–1869 (in Kassel and Leipzig). Responding to the decision of the Reform rabbis to de-emphasize the messianic theme in the prayer book, Gordon contended:

> The ultimate destiny of the Jews never was and never can be this life of Exile. [It can never mean] that the Jews will remain dispersed and simply melt away among the nations of the world.[17]

> With all our love for knowledge, for science and for the land of our birth, the Jews should also be entitled to raise their eyes to the holy mountain—that is, to Zion—and to recall the holiness of their people in days of old, to take courage from the beautiful hope for an Ingathering of the Exiles.[18]

Mordechai Ben-Hillel Hacohen, warning of the dangers of assimilation facing young, Russian-educated Jews, emphasized the supreme importance of national unity:

> [The leading Jewish thinkers] do not mourn simply the rejection of ritual practices by the youth, or their abandonment of certain customs . . . but, rather, the progressive weakening of the *spirit* of Israel. . . . What fate awaits Israel when the new generation will no longer understand the tongue of their ancestors, no longer cleave to the Torah, and no longer recall that they are scions of an ancient stock . . . ? The language and Torah of our ancestors were what kept Israel united until now.[19]

Dr. Yitzhak Kaminer, of Kiev, wrote in his poem, "The Nationhood of Israel":

> Our breath of life, God's Messiah,
> the spirit that animates all our history,
> the faith in Israel's Redemption . . .
> This is the positive touchstone,
> the elixir of light and life
> for those who bear the bitterness of the Exile.

Shorn of this faith, the poet warned, Jewish survival itself would be endangered in an age of waning religious observance.[20]

But perhaps the most systematic exposition of romantic nationalist ideas and their presentation in terms of the Jewish traditions of messianism was that of Peretz Smolenskin. In his essay of 1871–1872, "A Time for Deeds," Smolenskin marveled at the Jewish people's ability to survive while more powerful nations rose and fell. The Jews owed their survival neither to physical power nor to bravery as such, "Rather, God's angel was always leading [them] to pave the way. . . . That angel is the destiny [of the Jews], for which [they] were created and which has been [their] constant aim."[21]

All these writers couched their appeal for national pride and national unity in terms that defined Jewish peoplehood as a powerful organic bond (to use the romantic terminology) in which religion, generally, and the messianic-redemptive vision, specifically, had once performed a cementing and guiding function. For "religion" the nationalists read "national spirit," clearly subordinating theology to national ideology. Under the impact of modernity, the cement of religion was crumbling, threatening to bring down the entire edifice unless it could be shored up by a modern appreciation of peoplehood and destiny. In short, their argument represented a post-traditional celebration of tradition, not so much as a way of life for the contemporary Jew but as a national asset that ought not to be heedlessly squandered.

Smolenskin expanded on this thesis at great length in his rather long-winded manifesto, '*Am 'olam* (The Eternal [or Universal] People), in which the nationalist polemic was explicitly aimed against the Reform rabbis and the trend toward assimilation.[22]

The prophecies of eventual salvation, he averred, had "struck deep roots in the heart of the people and had given it something to live for during times of sorrow and persecution." And he continued:

> This faith—the faith in a Messiah or future Redemption—became the cornerstone of all [Jewish] thought and practice. . . . A nation cannot live without such hope to raise its spirits . . . and forge its collective existence. But if a nation [believes that it] has achieved all it can possibly hope to accomplish, and disavows all further ambition for its people and its land [the way the Reformers have done], then the customs of the nation will cease to unite it. Each individual will live for his own welfare alone, and the collective life of the nation will, without intention, diminish to the point of complete disintegration. . . . As each of them goes about his own business, the life of the nation will end, and a generation will arise that has no knowledge of that life, for the nation will have died, its severed limbs will have been grafted onto other nations.[23]

But this is not so, Smolenskin maintained, with a people that retains a healthy spirit of hope that safeguards it from the perils of complacency amid plenty and against the grievous wounds that history can visit on nations. Even under the worst conditions, a guiding hope has the capacity to galvanize a nation. Some nations had indeed succumbed and disappeared, but Israel had survived because of what he termed its "life-spirit." The Torah and its message of hope, he continued, had therefore been the Jews' "salvation and comfort . . . , a shelter and a fortress that united them as much as country and statehood."[24] The two (Torah and salvationist hope) were intertwined; the waning of one or the other had always led to a period of stagnation, disintegration or assimilation.

Given the hope of integration into European society raised by the emancipation, the Jews of the West were denying the national hope of Redemption and editing it out of their Judaism. Were the Reformers to succeed in snuffing out the messianic belief ("that keeps Israel's spirit alive . . . and still today has the power to unite them"), this would threaten the entire existence of the Jewish people. Hope for a future Redemption was all the more necessary because religious observance was lax and Torah study no longer widespread. Without the messianic hope nothing at all would be left to stand in the way of the Jews' complete disappearance.[26]

Moreover, everyone understands that this hope is just that: a creed, a point of subjective consciousness that in no way interferes with or denies the Jews' ability to function at every level of civic life in the Diaspora. "Our obligation is, nonetheless, to preserve that faith [in the Messiah], because for us it is a bond of unity," even more than religion as such; for the religion of a Jew in Vilna is quite unlike the religion practiced in Berlin.[27]

For Smolenskin, then, it is the gravitational weight of the messianic idea that counts most. It is a distillation of the historical consciousness of Jewry, the emblematic basis for a community of *fate* even when a community of *faith* has become impossible. Neither the exact content of messianism (with its attendant eschatological features) nor the expectation of its actual fulfillment explains its true force and real value. Rather, its affirmation alone is enough to create unity out of diversity and to prevent the egoistic, materialistic and perhaps transitory successes of individual Jews from sapping the vigor of the collective. When Smolenskin referred to the messianic idea, then, it was his way of reasserting the nationalist idea in his debate with the Reform movement and with Berlin Haskalah generally.[28]

Just how the nationalist–Zionist idea might be promoted—and a more activist dimension added—was illustrated in nationalist writings of the late 1870s and early 1880s that employed rhetorical catchphrases lifted directly from the messianic tradition.

Thus, the Society for Redeeming the Land, established in Palestine in 1876 to purchase land for Jewish settlement, declared in its statement of purpose:

> By this we hope to bring closer the ultimate and true Redemption that will surely come . . . ; for, despite the dark and sad times [we live in] . . . and the poverty we see around us here . . . we, nonetheless, can perceive the glimmerings of a new day that is slowly dawning and the signs of a salvation that is drawing nigh.[29]

David Gordon, writing in the early winter of 1880, declared:

> The sacred and noble idea of settling the land of Israel is bound up with our national destiny and the hopes we harbor for the future. . . . [Assimilated Jewish notables] and the Reformers would have us believe that Israel's destiny is only to be dispersed among the nations! . . . [Their error] can only smother in the hearts of our youth any feeling for our national destiny and the sacred hope of Jeshurun, the hope for the future that will see an end to our dispersion.[30]

> The political situation in the Orient [has afforded us the opportunity] to establish a sizeable area for Jews to till the land of our ancestors. That would mark, God willing, a first step toward our future hope [*tikvateinu ha'atidah*] toward the ultimate hope of Israel [*mikveh yisrael*] for salvation.[31]

In *Hashahar* of 1883, one writer expressed the nationalist impulse with the following fantasy, filled with messianic motifs:

> Were Ezra and Rabbi Akiva alive today, their joy over our unprecedented national self-awareness would be boundless. . . . Were Nehemiah and Bar Kokhba to be brought before the people, they would proclaim: Behold your gods, O Israel, who will go forth before you to take you up to the land that God swore to your fathers![32]

Or, to take another striking example from the same year:

For the sake of the Torah and their hope of Redemption, Jews were prepared to suffer death at the hands of their oppressors. . . . Survival is an instinct of every living thing and is implanted in every person. The people of Israel sensed that the Torah and the memory of their [lost] homeland were the foundation of their very existence, on which their lives [as a people] depended. Just as other nations go to war to defend their country against their foes, so, too, did the Jews battle for their spiritual homeland—that is, the Torah and the hope for Redemption—as in a war for survival. . . . [The people] sensed that they themselves, their Torah and their hope for Redemption were indivisible, and they have made that [perception] a principle of life and death.[33]

Yet references to the organic and spiritual bonds of nationhood (i.e., the indissoluble union of martyrs' blood and the symbolic soil of the cherished homeland) and messianist terminology were tempered by an important disclaimer, one that indicated to the reader the essential distinction between myth and reality, metaphor and meaning.

Thus, David Gordon argued that Jewish settlements in Palestine would serve the limited, nonmessianic and perfectly legitimate purpose (in the theological sense) of providing "cities of refuge" to be available to the Jewish people should their enemies attempt to disturb their peace and security in Europe.[34]

Alexander Zederbaum (publisher of *Hameliz*) stated his support for Jewish agricultural colonies in Palestine by invoking the prophetic visions of Daniel, but he preceded his statement with this caveat:

It does not enter our minds at all today to involve ourselves in calculations of the End of Days [in the manner of Daniel]. . . . But we should bear in mind what Daniel heard in his vision [about the return to Jerusalem], as the word of God in heaven that has guided Israel throughout its history, and we should pay close attention to the significance of the events of our time.[35]

Smolenskin, too, pointed out the essential distinction between messianists of the past and nationalists of his own day. The latter, in looking forward to a time when the Jews might take their place among the nations of the world, were not in the least bit interested in calculating the time of the *eschaton;* neither were any of them hoping to rebuild the Temple and restore the sacrificial cult.[36]

And Mordechai Ben-Hillel Hacohen spoke of the general nonmessianic tenor of the times, even as he issued a stirring biblical call to "Rise up and go unto Zion":

Among the present generation there are many who do not believe in all those miraculous events that are supposed to accompany the Ingathering of the Exiles. And yet, their gaze is still fixed on Zion and on a Redemption there in time to come, and they retain their hope for a rebirth of our nation on the holy mountain in Jerusalem. . . . Those among the new generation of Jews who love their people and look to its future embrace the hope that if Jewry will accurately read the portents of what lies ahead, then the hope of Redemption can serve as its beacon, just as this century has brought salvation to the Greeks and to the peoples of the Balkans. . . . There are many today who believe that the salvation of Israel also lies this way. To the extent that such believers increase—and those who wish to witness [salvation by means of] miracles and wonders decrease—the day of our national Redemption will draw ever closer. . . . My people, your salvation lies within you. . . . Our own eyes should tell us that the present moment calls to us from out of the whirlwind: Rise up and go unto Zion![37]

The drive to establish Jewish settlements in Palestine and to organize Hibbat Zion societies throughout the Pale of Settlement (and abroad) received added impetus after 1881. Romantic nationalist ideology—and the rhetoric that it inspired—became an important aspect of Jewish modernism in Eastern Europe at the end of the nineteenth century. Nationalist ranks swelled in reaction to the wave of anti-semitism that hit Central and East European Jews during those years—the pogroms in Russia, in particular.

Most of the nationalist positions, however, had been adumbrated by Jewish intellectuals during the 1860s and 1870s. Indeed, although such men as Moshe Leib Lilienblum and Leon Pinsker were profoundly shaken by the pogroms, others, such as David Gordon, Mordechai Ben-Hillel Hacohen and Eliezer Ben-Yehudah, did not perceptibly alter their basic convictions because of the pogroms. (Smolenskin, previously opposed to a territorial definition of Jewish nationalism, was more disposed after 1881 to accept a Palestinocentric point of view. Despite this new operative conclusion, his basic nationalist ethos remained largely as before.) Instead, the Palestinophile movement they had helped to create merely took on added urgency and greater organizational coherence as efforts were turned to mobilizing supporters and funds.

ECLIPSE OF THE MESSIAH

I have argued that the employment of rhetoric possessing metahistorical and even messianic undertones in the service of Jewish nationalism ought to be understood within the context of the Russian Haskalah as a code—a kind of developed meta-phor—that is meant to suggest a link between romantic ideals of nationhood and a higher purpose or to establish a living tradition retrospectively.[38] The manipulation of significant passwords was also a way to suggest that the moral claim to national leadership advanced by the nationalists was more than mere chutzpah or hubris.

What sort of support could they hope to rally, what sort of legitimacy could they hope to gain on this basis? Was it an appeal made to a messianically attuned audience, and therefore clothed in messianic rhetoric? Is this, then, an indirect form of proof that Zionism tapped into a reservoir of messianic yearnings or was fueled by an undercurrent of messianic tension?

To explore these questions we will have to consider briefly some background issues in East European Jewish society in the course of the nineteenth century. I will contend, first, that the level of messianic tension in that society was remarkably low; second, that the rhetorical conventions of the Russian Haskalah had already paved the way for the use of messianic vocabulary emptied of all eschatological meaning; and, third, that the fact of the massive Jewish emigration westward from all parts of Southern and Eastern Europe, during the very years in which nationalist writers appealed for the Jewish resettlement of Palestine, tends to undermine claims that most Jews had been primed to prepare for a redemptive return to Zion.

This is not to say that there was a total absence of messianic consciousness in East European Jewish society in the nineteenth century, only that, in the post-Sabbatian period, messianic language was often used in ways that tended to ease or obscure tensions with the gentile world rather than express them apocalyptically, and that more radical messianist positions did not elicit a widespread response, whether positive or negative.

In the first instance, this thesis is applicable to Hasidism. In the formulation proposed by Gershom Scholem, Hasidism neutralized the messianic-apocalyptic element in the Lurianic kabbalistic tradition, replacing it with an accent on the inner spiritual life of the individual.[39] Scholem argued:

> Redemption of the soul without redemption of the social body, i.e., of the nation from its historical exile . . . has never had a messianic meaning in Judaism. . . . Hasidism, with the destructive consequences of [Sabbatianism] before its eyes, renounced the idea of messianic revolt and made its peace with exile.[40]

The acute messianic tension was removed by altering the redemptive timetable: the process of *tikkun,* the restoration of the holiness in the universe, which in Lurianic Kabbalah was considered to be all but complete, was seen in Hasidic thought as only just having begun. The end was far indeed from imminent realization.[41] The essence of early Hasidism, Scholem asserted, concurring with Hillel Zeitlin, was that "every individual is the Redeemer, the Messiah, of his own little world."[42]

Scholem further observed that Hasidic homiletic literature took to its logical extreme the device of spiritualizing and allegorizing such terms as "Zion," "*galut*" and "*geulah,*" thus revaluing such concepts in terms of the inner life of the soul.[43]

Yet another observer has put the case somewhat differently, namely, that Hasidism sought to revive the faith and the willingness of the Jews to await the Messiah's coming without the excessive impatience of the discredited Sabbatians.[44]

From a sociological point of view, the most important element in this neutralization of millenarian potential is probably to be found in the multicentered and "routine" nature of the charismatic leadership that emerged within Hasidism and that prevented messianic expectations in one Hasidic court from spilling over into others.[45]

The most sustained counterargument against this trend of thought is that advocated by Dinur, to whom Hasidism represented a messianic movement par excellence. He maintained that Hasidism consciously set out to pave the way for Redemption by replacing the rabbinic-bureaucratic communal leadership, which had failed, with a renewed prophetic leadership.[46]

And yet for all the messianic consciousness that pervaded Hasidic thought, it would seem that Hasidism did not turn into a sectarian movement precisely because of its sublimation of millenarian impulses.

As for the non-Hasidic, "Lithuanian" wing of East European Jewry, it has been suggested that it gave birth to a truly millenarian movement in the first four decades of the nineteenth century.[47] According to this rather controversial thesis, advanced by Aryeh Morgenstern, the disciples of the Vilna Gaon carried on a living tradition—derived from the oral teachings of their master—that enjoined them to spearhead the collective return to, and colonization of, the land of Israel. This was an active, this-worldly preparation for the Final Redemption that was based on the belief that the time had now come to abrogate the time-honored "three oaths," the rabbinic formula proscribing rebellion against gentile rule or "forcing the End" through mass settlement in the land of Israel.[48]

The circle of disciples (five leading rabbinic figures), their students and their families brought 511 settlers to Palestine by 1812; other organized groups followed in 1819 and 1826.[49] They constituted a distinctive stream within a larger wave of immigrants, many if not most of whom were apparently inspired by the belief that the Messiah's advent would take place in the year 5600 (1840)—a belief shared by other Jews in various parts of the world and by Christian millenarians.[50]

The disciples of the Vilna Gaon, Morgenstern argues, coupled this belief with a messianic doctrine of specific content, including the assignment of responsibility for initiating the Redemption to the Jews themselves. Settlement of the Holy Land was one aspect of this activist approach; another was an attempt to restore the line of ancient rabbinic ordination and, through it, a functioning Sanhedrin. They also introduced liturgical innovations to accord with the spiritual Sabbath eve of time (i.e., the eve of the Redemption). Finally, the failure of the Messiah to arrive on schedule led to what Morgenstern calls a crisis of faith, an ideological retrenchment, and even two cases of conversion to Christianity—all expressions of an authentic millenarial trauma.[51]

The validity of this thesis has been contested by those who question the messianic nature of the Lithuanian movement and charge Morgenstern with a tendentious reading of the sources. At any rate, it remains clear that this group had relatively little impact outside its own fairly limited ranks. It appears to have acted with a certain degree of circumspection and thus no more than a flurry of attention was attracted by the events in Jerusalem in 1840, which were considerably overshadowed by the Damascus blood-libel affair of that year.[52]

A similarly feeble response greeted the proto-Zionist messianic ideas propagated by rabbis Zvi Hirsh Kalischer and Yehudah Alkalai who, independently of one another, reached similar conclusions concerning Jewish settlement of the Holy Land as a precondition for God's final deliverance of Israel. Both men were more or less ignored insofar as their messianic ideas were concerned. Kalischer developed his theories connecting the emancipation of Western Jewry with a providential scheme of Redemption, unfolding by stages, during the 1830s and 1840s.[53] As Yosef Salmon has suggested, however, some of Kalischer's messianic rhetoric had more to do with the Orthodox campaign against religious reform in Central Europe than with millennial restoration.[54]

Both Kalischer and his Southern European counterpart, Alkalai, were active on behalf of their ideas until the 1870s, but neither one succeeded in establishing a following in traditional circles (although David Gordon, as well as Moses Hess, seem to have been influenced by them).[55]

The atrophy of radical messianism—its reduction from a historical force of some potency to the preserve of isolated groups and individuals, as well as the shrouding of the idea of the Messiah in layers of spiritual metaphor—can also be illustrated by the way in which the Russian *maskilim* used the term *mashiaḥ* (messiah) to designate the Russian tsar as a God-anointed ruler.[56] This unconventional usage combined elements of the divine right of kings, maskilic *melizah* (flowery rhetoric and hyperbole) and the implied dismissal of more traditional ideas about a messiah–redeemer.[57]

A similar device appears in some poems of Avraham Ber Gottlober, who depicted the coronation in heaven of Alexander II as performed by none other than King Solomon; he also had God address Nicholas I as "my dear son."[58] Adam Hacohen Lebenson, in his *Kelil yofi*, wrote that the tsar must have unlimited power on earth just as God is the "autocrat of Heaven." The tsar is "the heavenly king on earth."[59] Such rhetoric matched the political agenda of the Russian Jewish intelligentsia that, at mid-century, made much of the benevolence of the enlightened, absolutist state.

Maskilim of the late 1850s and early 1860s also heaped scorn on the attempts to calculate messianic years. Shortly before the new Hebrew year of 5620 (September 21, 1859), one such writer pilloried those who suggested that the new year was numerically auspicious; he reminded his readers that such dabbling in eschatological guesswork had had only deleterious results in the past.[60]

Others proposed that the messianic era was to be identified with the emancipation of Jewish communities from their medieval status. Basing himself on both the Babylonian talmudic sage, Shmuel, and on the teachings of Maimonides, a *maskil* from Ekaterinoslav wrote:

> In the messianic age, nothing of the natural order that we know today will change. Only the yoke of oppression will be removed from us. All the words of the prophets [about the miraculous End of Days] are meant only metaphorically. . . . [Shmuel did not mean that the gentile rulers would cease to rule but rather meant that] in the fullness of time, the burden of oppression and persecution that Israel suffered in his day will be lifted, . . . the reign of the wicked will cease . . . , those who hate Judah will be cut off and all men will call on the name of the Lord, Creator of the world, and they will offer the gift of brotherly love on the altar of peace, without distinction of religion or faith: those will be the days of the Messiah. . . . Our era is truly [like the messianic age] a time of freedom [from oppression] because of the spirit of truth and peace that pervades all peoples of the earth. The elated voice of brotherhood and fellowship resounds all around us. Anyone with human feeling in his breast [observing all this], must have a sense of holiness, a sense of the Divine, and will want to say: Oh Lord, Your name is great, for You have passed Your arm of holiness in blessing over all mankind, bringing peace and showing us all the great goodness that You promised us in Isaiah's vision of the End of Days.[61]

Another contemporary *maskil*, urging the Jews to love Russia, the land of their birth, counseled them against taking messianic promises too literally to heart. Even Jeremiah, he reminded his readers, had encouraged the Jews to build homes in their land of Exile and to pray for the welfare of that country, even though he also prophesied that the Exile would end after seventy years. We do not (he continued) live in the hope of returning and regaining our land by force; we merely pray for God's salvation. Moreover, "the concept of the advent of the Messiah is, in essence, meant only to raise the morale of the Jews, lest they lose heart under the burden of their sorrows."[62]

In an article entitled "A Word for Our Time: Footsteps of the Messiah," a *maskil* from Warsaw argued that the messianic salvation promised by Scripture was not a matter of restoring the Jewish people to the land of Israel, but of elevating the status of the Jews. The saviors of the nation are those who act to achieve this, including the men of the Alliance israélite universelle and "all the Jewish newspapers and their writers and supporters, writing in Hebrew and the various languages of the other nations," as well as "the men of wise heart and courage who wage God's [i.e., the Jews'] battles against their enemies [and] our protectors, those in high positions and wise in matters of state."[63]

Finally, we have the example of Judah Leib Gordon, one of the foremost figures of the Russian Haskalah, whose own conceptualization of the messianic Redemption was couched in rationalistic terms of progress, enlightened reform and the victory of civilization. As Michael Stanislawski has pointed out, Gordon demythologized the concept of Redemption and gave it a new meaning when he asserted that the Jews, through their entry into modern European society, could determine their own fate.[64] He admitted that his references to a messianic future were a "polemical device," part of a critique of Orthodox obscurantism, and he insisted that modern "right-thinking" Jews hope only for "redemption by means of the universal recognition of their human rights."[65]

Gordon's recasting of the messianic doctrine in the service of the Haskalah was undoubtedly an important step in the effort of East European Jewish intellectuals to invoke for their emerging new strategies for redemption the most profound and evocative chords in Jewish consciousness, while at the same time subverting traditional Judaism, its politics, and its culture.[66]

The sublimation of messianic activism within Hasidism, the lack of popular enthusiasm for messianic speculations and the emergence of a group of Europeanized rationalists who were willing to use messianic language as a political symbol are very different phenomena, each with its own sociocultural context. Yet each would appear to be related, if not to one another then to a common perception of the Dispersion that did not include its imminent demise. By and large, Russian Jewry did not succumb to the temptation to narrow the gap between "this world" and the "days of the Messiah." *Maskilim* who did so had first to empty messianism of its eschatological and supernatural content. Their metaphorical use of messianic terminology was in reality a way of fostering a this-worldly consciousness, not a breakthrough to Redemption through universal salvation.[67]

Last but not least there is the matter of the mass emigration of East European Jews to the West, conventionally dated from 1881 (although it had its beginnings in the 1870s). Here we have sociological evidence that may help us identify the position of the inarticulate masses of Jews with regard to the issue of messianism. Over a forty-year period, two and a half million Jews literally turned their backs on Palestine as they uprooted themselves to improve their lot abroad, causing the greatest mass migration in Jewish history.

This circumstance casts doubt on any assumption that most Jews were imbued with a messianic yearning for a Jewish national rebirth and that the Zionist appeal was overtly or subliminally directed to stimulate those yearnings. Granted, some of the immigrants were undoubtedly Orthodox in their beliefs, including beliefs about the Messiah, and their rejection of the Zionist program possibly rested on traditional messianic teachings. Thus, their choice of destination does not imply any negation of religious messianic faith. By the same token, however, it hardly attests to deep stirrings of an intensely messianic nature. (It would be more accurate to speak of their conventional, low-energy faith in a final Redeemer, expressed in their daily devotions.)

It may also be contended that the emigration fever of 1881–1882 may well have produced a greater stream of Zion-seekers had it not been for objective political and economic factors that blocked a mass immigration to Palestine at the time. In addition, there were tremendous social forces at work that directed emigrants to the New World (e.g., aid rendered to Russian Jewish emigrants by West European Jewish organizations). Yet, again, we simply have no positive evidence that the Jewish populace as a whole or the emigrants themselves were in the grip of a messianic upheaval. In the absence of any evidence of this nature, the mute facts of the mass emigration to the West must speak for themselves.

Nationalist rhetoric that justified Zionism in terms borrowed from the prophetic– messianic tradition was as likely to offend the staunchly Orthodox as appeal to them—if not more so. That consideration, in fact, typically led religious Zionists in Eastern Europe to disavow any messianic intentions, and Yaacov Shavit has cogently argued that the Hibbat Zion groups were careful to select symbols and historical analogies (primarily the return to Judea led by Ezra and Nehemiah) that de-emphasized eschatological elements.[68]

What benefit or legitimacy, then, could those early nationalists discussed earlier have hoped to gain by deliberately invoking the messianic heritage? The primary advantage lay in the chance to call on history as witness and support for their arguments. Jewish survival, Jewish unity, the loyalty of the Jews to their unique religious culture and their continued status as outsiders in European society pro- vided evidence to support nationalist claims—evidence that lent weight and authori- ty to otherwise ad hoc theses based on populism or doctrines of self-determination.

Although this cannot be proved conclusively, I am persuaded, too, that their readers were attuned to the fact that David Gordon, Peretz Smolenskin and those who followed after them were using messianic rhetoric as a code; that such words as ''Redemption'' were neither meant nor taken to convey what they had conveyed to earlier generations; and that such writers were (and were understood to be) simply translating into Hebrew terminology and communicating in terms of Jewish cultural referents the romantic concepts of nationhood: national pride, national struggle, national destiny and national homeland.

They affirmed the messianic tradition but only in a strictly limited sense, constru- ing it as a historical instrument for the preservation of Jewish nationhood. They fostered an intense attachment to the land of Zion, but only in the same sense that Poles, Greeks, Italians and Ukrainians raised ''homeland'' to a quasi-sacred status. They attracted a following, but not nearly as numerous a constituency as that of their Orthodox opponents or as broadly based as the mass emigration. Moreover, there were good reasons—other than any that might have been connected to mes- sianist passion—for joining Hibbat Zion societies, reasons that had much to do with the social appeal of such groups.[69]

I, therefore, interpret the use of messianic rhetoric by Jewish nationalists as evidence not of the *continuity* of messianism within Judaism, but of *discontinuity*. Allusions to prophetic scriptural passages and liturgical phrases were used because of their recognition value. Redemption through one's own efforts was a concept that could be readily transmitted to a constituency who had lost faith in eschatological visions but who were still firmly rooted in the Hebraic cultural idiom. References to the constancy of the age-old messianic faith or to the national destiny of the Jews lent depth to a nationalist conceptualization of Judaism. Such references created a perfect platform from which one could launch critical barbs at antinationalists of various stripes: against Reformers, assimilationists and Orthodox messianists alike. Words such as "Redemption" and "destiny" raised the decibel level of nationalist propaganda, amplifying the otherwise reedy voice in which early Jewish nationalists addressed their fellow Jews. They created an illusion of historical justification for the nationalist position, without which the case of the Zionists would have appeared woefully out of touch with reality.

In short, messianism was a mythic factor that provided romantic nationalists with a much richer dimension of oratory and conviction than anything that could be derived (negatively) from the rise of modern antisemitism or (positively) from the fluctuating will of the people.

Notes

Research for this essay was generously supported by the Herzl Fellowship at The Hebrew University of Jerusalem.

1. Jacob Neusner explains the paradox of divine control and human responsibility as follows: salvation (according to the rabbis of the talmudic era) could only be achieved through becoming holy, and this meant absolute submission to the rule of God, including a humble acceptance of gentile rule in Exile.

> Israel has the power to save itself by giving up its arrogant claim to be able to do anything to save itself. . . . Since the spiritual condition of Israel governs [the fulfillment of salvationist hopes], Israel itself holds the key to its own redemption. But this it can achieve only by throwing away the key (*Messiah in Context: Israel's History and Destiny in Formative Judaism* [Philadelphia: 1984], 185, 210).

Cf. *ibid.*, 114–115, 152, 211, 224, 231.

2. Jacob Neusner, "From Theology to Ideology: The Transformation of Judaism in Modern Times," in *Churches and States: The Religious Institution and Modernization*, ed. Kalman H. Silvert (New York: 1967), 14, emphasis added.

3. See, e.g., Jacob Talmon:

> The salvationist hope was desperately needed by the Jews to explain to themselves and to others why the chosen people had been abandoned by God. The very idea of providential justice hinged upon it. The [Jews'] stubborn will to retain [their] uniqueness and the refusal to merge with the peoples around lacked all rationale without the sustaining vision of choice, sin, trial, atonement and salvation (*The Myth of the Nation and the Vision of Revolution* [Berkeley, Los Angeles and London: 1980], 175).

On theodicy, see Peter Berger, *The Social Reality of Religion* (London: 1969), 53–80.

4. Shlomo Zalman Landa and Yosef Rabinowicz (comps.), *Sefer or layesharim* (Warsaw: 1900), 8, 23–25.

5. See, e.g., Ben-Zion Dinur, *Sefer haẓiyonut: mevasrei haẓiyonut* (Tel-Aviv: 1938), vol. 1, bk. 1, 4ff.; Yisrael Klausner, *Hara'ayon hameshiḥi beyisrael mereishito ve'ad ḥatimat hamishnah* (Tel-Aviv: 1950), 229ff.; idem, *Behitorerut 'am, ha'aliyah harishonah mirusiah* (Jerusalem: 1962); cf. David Myers, "History as Ideology: The Case of Ben Zion Dinur, Zionist Historian 'Par Excellence,'" *Modern Judaism* 8, no. 2 (May 1988), 167–193.

6. Jacob Katz, "Orthodoxy in Historical Perspective," in *Studies in Contemporary Jewry*, vol. 2, *The Challenge of Modernity and Jewish Orthodoxy*, ed. Peter Y. Medding (Bloomington: 1986), 11, 16.

7. Jacob Katz, "The Jewish National Movement: A Sociological Analysis," in *Jewish Society Through the Ages*, ed. Hayim Hillel Ben-Sasson and Shmuel Ettinger (New York: 1971), 269.

8. Gershom Scholem, "Toward an Understanding of the Messianic Idea in Judaism," in his *The Messianic Idea in Judaism and Other Essays on Jewish Spirituality*, trans. M. A. Meyers (New York: 1971), 35.

9. Stephen Sharot, *Messianism, Mysticism and Magic: A Sociological Analysis of Jewish Religious Movements* (Chapel Hill: 1982), 221.

10. See Eli Lederhendler, *The Road to Modern Jewish Politics: Political Tradition and Political Reconstruction in the Jewish Community of Tsarist Russia* (New York: 1989), ch. 5.

11. See Eli Lederhendler, *From Autonomy to Auto-emancipation: Historical Continuity, Political Development, and the Preconditions for the Emergence of National Jewish Politics in Nineteenth-century Russia* (Ph.D. diss., Jewish Theological Seminary of America, 1987), 61–63, 91–101.

12. Lederhendler, *Road to Modern Jewish Politics*, ch. 5.

13. On a parallel use of rhetoric to create new myths, see Lynn Hunt:

Certain key words served as revolutionary incantations. Nation was perhaps the most universally sacred, but there were also *patrie*, constitution, law, . . . regeneration, virtue, and vigilance. . . . Revolutionaries placed such emphasis on the ritual use of words because they were seeking a replacement for the charisma of kingship (*Politics, Culture, and Class in the French Revolution* [Berkeley, Los Angeles and London: 1984], 21).

My thanks to Richard I. Cohen for bringing Hunt's book to my attention.

14. For discussion, see, e.g., Shmuel Almog, "Hameshiḥiyut keetgar laẓiyonut," in *Meshiḥiyut veeskhatologiah*, ed. Zvi Baras (Jerusalem: 1983), 433–438; Israel (Yisrael) Kolatt, "Ẓiyonut umeshiḥiyut," in Baras, *Meshiḥiyut veeskhatologiah*, 419–432; Azriel Shochat, "Shemot, semalim, vehavai beḥibbat ẓiyon," *Shivat ẓiyon* 2–3 (1952), 228–250; Yaacov Shavit, "Shivat ẓiyon beḥibbat ẓiyon," *Haẓiyonut* 9 (1984), 359–372.

15. David Gordon, "Beshuvah venaḥat tevashe'un," *Hamaggid*, no. 14 (1863), 105–106.

16. *Ibid.*, 106.

17. David Gordon, "Davar be'ito," *Hamaggid*, no. 27 (1869), 214; cf. Yosef Salmon, "David Gordon ve'iton hamaggid: ḥilufei 'emdot laleumiyut hayehudit, 1860–1882," *Ẓiyon* 47 (1982), 153; and Isaac Barzilay, "'Hamaggid' vereishit hatenu'ah haleumit," *Biẓaron* 37 (1957–1958), 179–182.

18. David Gordon, "Davar be'ito," *Hamaggid*, no. 28 (1869), 222.

19. Mordechai Ben-Hillel Hacohen, "Dor holekh vedor ba," *Hashaḥar* 9 (1876–1877), 124.

20. Yitzhak Kaminer, "Leumiyut yisrael," *Hamaggid*, no. 38 (1879), 299.

21. Peretz Smolenskin, "'Et la'asot," *Hashaḥar* 4 (1872–1873), 72 (repr., idem, *'Am 'olam* [Vienna: 1873], 130).

22. Smolenskin, "'Am 'olam," *Hashaḥar* 3 (1871–1872); repr., idem, *'Am 'olam*.

23. Smolenskin, "'Am 'olam," 206–207 (repr. 44–45).

24. *Ibid.*, 207 (repr., 45).

25. *Ibid.*, 665 (repr., 97).

26. *Ibid.*, 670–671 (repr., 102–103).

27. *Ibid.*, 671–673 (repr., 103–105).

28. On Smolenskin's attitude toward Berlin Haskalah and German Jewish intellectuals, see Isaac Barzilay, "Smolenskin's Polemic Against Mendelssohn in Historical Perspective," in *Proceedings of the American Academy for Jewish Research* 53 (1986), 11–48.

29. Alter Druyanov (ed.), Shulamit Laskov (rev. and ed.), *Ketavim letenu'at ḥibbat ẓiyon veyishuv ereẓ yisrael* (Tel-Aviv: 1982), vol. 1, 49–51, doc. 2.

30. David Gordon, "Yishuv ereẓ yisrael," *Hamaggid,* no. 46 (1880), 386.

31. *Ibid.* (article in installments), no. 47 (1880), 396.

32. S. H., "Hadat vehaleumiyut," *Hashaḥar* 12 (1883), 40.

33. "Brit 'am," *Hashaḥar* 12 (1883), 205–206.

34. David Gordon, "Yom livnot gedarayikh," *Hamaggid,* no. 18 (1881), 143.

35. Alexander Zederbaum, "Bin badavar vehaven bamareh," *Hameliẓ,* no. 20, (1881), 405.

36. Peretz Smolenskin, "Mishpat 'ami," *Hashaḥar* 12 (1883), 11.

37. Mordechai Ben-Hillel Hacohen, "Kumu vena'aleh ẓiyon!" *Hamaggid,* no. 24 (1881), 197. And see the comment by "Ben-Shem," in *Knesset yisrael* 1 (1886), 922, "The fundamental idea of those who preach for Love of Zion is not to [promote the idea of] miracles and wonderful acts, not to bring the End closer, and not to revel in fantasies; nor do they seek for themselves the crown of Providence."

38. On the use of historical analogies, see Shavit, "Shivat ẓiyon," *Haẓiyonut* 9 (1984), 359–372.

39. Gershom Scholem, *Major Trends in Jewish Mysticism* (New York: 1941), 329–330; idem, "The Neutralizations of the Messianic Element in Early Hasidism," in his *Messianic Idea in Judaism,* 176–202; cf. Rivka Shatz, "Hayesod hameshiḥi bemaḥshevet haḥasidut," *Molad,* n.s., 1, no. 1 (1967), 105–111; idem, *Haḥasidut kemistikah* (Jerusalem: 1968), 52, 168–176.

40. Scholem, *Messianic Idea in Judaism,* 194–195.

41. *Ibid.*, 195–196.

42. *Ibid.*, 202; Hillel Zeitlin, *Haḥasidut* (Warsaw: 1910), 29; cf. Yaakov Hisdai (ed.), *Sifrut haderush kemakor histori biyemei reishit haḥasidut* (Jerusalem: 1984), 106 (passage from *Meor 'einayim* by Rabbi Nahum of Czernowitz).

43. Scholem, *Messianic Idea in Judaism,* 200–201; Shatz, "Hayesod hameshiḥi," 105–106.

44. Meir Orian, "Ḥazon hageulah vehagshamato bemishnat haḥasidut," in *Geulah umedinah: Hakinus hashenati lemaḥshevet hayahadut* (Jerusalem: 1979). 35–36. (No ed. named.)

45. Sharot, *Messianism, Mysticism and Magic,* 155–188.

46. Ben-Zion Dinur, "Reishitah shel haḥasidut," in his *Bemifneh hadorot,* (Jerusalem: 1972), vol. 1, esp. 159, 170, 181–188, 207–227.

47. Aryeh Morgenstern, *Meshiḥiyut veyishuv ereẓ yisrael bamaḥaẓit harishonah shel hameah hatesh'a 'esrei* (Jerusalem: 1985).

48. *Ibid.*, 32–35, 66–113; cf. Dinur, "Hayesodot haideologiim shel ha'aliyot bishnot t"k-t"r [1740–1840]," in *Bemifneh hadorot,* vol. 1, 69–79; Mordechai Breuer, "Hadiyun beshalosh hashevu'ot," in *Geulah umedinah,* 50.

49. Morgenstern, *Meshiḥiyut,* 71–72, 74–78.

50. *Ibid.*, 38–65; Jacob Katz, "'Al shnat t"r keshanah meshiḥit vehashpa'atah 'al pe'ilut haperushim lekiruv hageulah," *Kathedra* 24 (1982), 73–75; Abraham Duker, "The Tarniks (Believers in the Coming of the Messiah in 1840)," in *Joshua Starr Memorial Volume* (New York: 1953), 191–201. Published by *Jewish Social Studies*.

51. Morgenstern, *Meshiḥiyut,* 122–132, 156–159, 212–215, 220–240.

52. This entire thesis, as outlined by Morgenstern, is the focus of much scholarly dispute. On doubts raised about the impact of the "Lithuanian" group, their special character and their messianist motivation, see Menahem Friedman, "Lesheelat hatefisah hameshiḥit shel talmidei haGra be'ikvot keriah bamekorot," *Cathedra* 24 (1982), 70–72; Israel (Yisrael)

Bartal, "Zipiyot meshihiyot umekoman bameziut hahistorit," *Cathedra* 31 (1984), 159–181.

53. Jacob Katz, "Demuto hahistorit shel harav Zvi Hirsh Kalisher," in his *Leumiyut yehudit* (Jerusalem: 1982), 291–298 (first published in *Shivat ziyon* 2–3 [1952]); *idem*, "Meshihiyut uleumiyut bemishnato shel harav Yehudah Alkalai," in his *Leumiyut yehudit*, 310–328, (first published in *Shivat ziyon* 4 [1956]); *idem*, "The Jewish National Movement," 271–275; Sharot, *Messianism, Mysticism and Magic*, 218.

54. Yosef Salmon, "'Aliyatah shel haleumiyut hayehudit bemerkaz eiropah uvema'aravah," *Haziyonut* 12 (1987), 8–9.

55. See David Vital, *The Origins of Zionism* (Oxford: 1980), 12–15; Katz, "Demuto hahistorit," 297; *idem*, "Orthodoxy in Historical Perspective," 10; Michael Graetz, *Haperiferiah haytah lamerkaz* (Jerusalem: 1982), 281–287.

56. The phenomenon has been noted by Azriel Shochat in "Hitrofefut hazipiyot hameshihiyot ezel rishonei hamaskilim berusiah vehahathalot lesheifat hishtalvut bahevrah harusit," *'Iyun uma'as* 2 (1981), 205–211.

57. Isaac Ber Levinsohn, *Te'udah beyisrael* (Vilna: 1828), dedication; *idem*, *Efes damim* (Vilna: 1837), 15; *idem*, *Beit yehudah* (Vilna: 1839), 333, 364.

58. Avraham Ber Gottlober, *'Anaf 'ez avot* (Vilna: 1858), 12, 61; *idem*, *Mizmor letodah* (Zhitomir: 1866), 10.

59. Adam Hacohen Lebenson, *Kelil yofi* (Vilna: 1856), 28.

60. "'Ikva demeshiha," suppl., *Hamaggid*, no. 37 (1859).

61. Yaakov Shmuel Halevi Trachtman, "Maamar me'ein yemot hamashiah," suppl., *Hamaggid*, no. 42 (1862).

62. *Hameliz*, no. 20 (1869), 228–229.

63. "Davar be'ito: 'ikva demeshiha," *Hamaggid*, no. 24, (1863), 189.

64. Michael Stanislawski, *For Whom Do I Toil? Judah Leib Gordon and the Crisis of Russian Jewry* (New York: 1988), 73; cf. 71–73, 100–102, 120–121.

65. *Ibid.*, 121.

66. *Ibid.*, 102.

67. This attitude typified many illustrious Russian maskilim and writers, including Isaac Ber Levinsohn, Avraham Mapu, Israel Aksenfeld, Ayzik Mayer Dik, Avraham Ber Gottlober, Joachim Tarnopol and Alexander Zederbaum. See, Mordecai Levin, *'Erkei hevrah vekhalkalah baideologiah shel tekufat hahaskalah* (Jerusalem: 1975), 228–231; Azriel Shochat, *Mossad harabanut mita'am berusiah* (Haifa: 1975), 69–70.

68. Shavit, "Shivat ziyon," and see Shavit's essay in this volume, pp. 100–127.

69. Shochat, "Shemot, semalim, vehavai," 243–245.

"Forcing the End": Zionism and the State of Israel as Antimessianic Undertakings

Aviezer Ravitzky
(THE HEBREW UNIVERSITY)

THE SATAN WHO CHOOSES JERUSALEM

In S. Y. Agnon's "A Whole Loaf," the narrator introduces us to two of his oldest and closest friends. One is Dr. Yekutiel Ne'eman, who clearly represents Moses, the Faithful One (*neeman*) of the House of the Lord; the other, Mr. Gressler, is the very image of Satan, the embodiment of the Evil Urge and its seductions.[1] The narrator experiences many personal reversals and finds himself buffeted back and forth repeatedly between these two. But when Gressler, the demonic friend, causes the narrator's home and all his possessions to go up in smoke, he decides to put an end to Gressler's seductive mischief. He breaks off the friendship, "buries himself in the book of Yekutiel Ne'eman" and finally packs up and leaves for Eretz Israel (Palestine).[2]

"As soon as I set off for Eretz Israel," he continues, "who should I run into first but Gressler; for he was traveling on the same ship, albeit on the upper deck, which is reserved for the rich, whereas I rode on the lower deck with the poor." The two characters thus carry their flirtation with them even to the Holy Land, where their paths frequently cross. Sometime later, the two are traveling in a carriage (an allusion to that of Mephistopheles) that overturns, casting them to the ground. Rolling in the dirt, they soil the important letters that Yekutiel Ne'eman had asked the narrator to deliver.

"As soon as I set off for Eretz Israel, who should I run into first but Gressler." Even in the Holy Land there is no respite from the unceasing struggle between the two giants, the Torah of Moses and the chariot of Satan. It is not only the Shekhinah (divine presence) that, as tradition would have it, dwells in Eretz Israel; the Sitra Aḥra (force of evil), too, is there, ready to pounce on a Jew as soon as he sets foot on the sacred soil; and sometimes this force proves more virulent there than it ever was in the alien land from which the Jew came.

Agnon appears to have made use here of a parable from an early source. In fact, the same motif had once been used by the Rebbe of Munkacz, Rabbi Hayim Elazar

34

Shapira, in a letter to his followers in Jerusalem, after his visit there in 1930. In an ironical and penetrating passage, he wrote:

> When I journeyed to the Holy Land I said to the Adversary before embarking at Stambul, "A berth costs a great deal of money. . . . You decide: either you go to the Holy Land and I stay here . . . or you stay here and I go alone to the Holy Land. . . . And he chose to stay there. . . . And I rejoiced in my voyage. But when I reached the Holy Land, I immediately caught sight of the Adversary standing there in the port, and I cried out in anguish, "What are you doing here? Did I not leave you in Stambul with the understanding that you would stay there?" And he . . . answered, saying, "You ask me what I am doing here? 'The fellow came here as an alien, and already he acts the ruler' [Gen. 19:9]. Why, this is my regular abode, and the one . . . with whom you spoke in Stambul was . . . just my overseas emissary!"[3]

Here, too, the narrator has boarded a ship bound for Eretz Israel, imagining that he is leaving Satan and his temptations behind; but he is in for a rude surprise, for his old tempter is to latch onto him there with even greater vigor and tenacity.

Yet unlike Agnon, Shapira goes on to spell out the meaning of the parable. Today's Satan, who makes his home in the Holy Land, is none other than the new Zionist settlement movement. Zion (Shapira argued) has always been the focus of a great struggle between light and darkness, between God, on the one hand, and the Evil Urge on the other. So it is, too, in our own time with its dreadful events. It is not only God who delights to dwell in the Holy Land and the Holy City, but also "the new ones, who came but lately" (Deut. 32:17), those who seek to force Zion to submit to them and make it the center of their sacrilegious enterprise. In this spirit, Shapira goes on to interpret the sense of the verse in Zechariah 3:2. It is not "May the Lord who has chosen Jerusalem rebuke you, O Satan" but rather "May the Lord rebuke you, O Satan who chooses Jerusalem."[4]

This severe condemnation of the modern settlement movement runs as a constant thread throughout the Munkaczer Rebbe's writings and sermons. As might be expected, he launches his critique with the question of the settlers' relationship to religion, to the Torah and its precepts. But he goes on to question the Zionist enterprise as a whole in terms of its larger theological meaning in relation to traditional messianic beliefs. On both these levels, Shapira's criticism is far-reaching, going well beyond the customary anti-Zionism of the haredi (more correctly spelled ḥaredi [God-fearing or ultra-Orthodox]) leadership of his day and, indeed, of our own.

As to the first point, Shapira naturally takes a stand against any upbuilding of the Holy Land by secular means or at the hands of sinners. But beyond this, he is consistent in his view that Eretz Israel is no place for ordinary pious Jews, either. Here he is elaborating on a much earlier tradition, going back to the Middle Ages, that sought, on halakhic and ideological grounds, to discourage people from settling there.[5] This trend of thought stresses the heavy religious demands that the land makes upon its inhabitants: the extra degree of spirituality required and the extra punishment attached to violating the commandments there. Living in Eretz Israel entails a spiritual risk that the simple Jew, however pious, may not be able to withstand. As one of the thirteenth-century Tosafists put it, "There is no commandment at the present time to live in Eretz Israel, for there are a number of precepts that apply only there and a number of punishments [for violating them] that are too much for us."[6] Shapira, too, emphasizes the spiritual dangers of living in the land, the possibility that it may prove the downfall of those of insufficient mettle. This is particularly the case, he argues, in view of the new reality created there by the Zionists.

> He who rebels against the kingdom from within the king's palace is not the same as one who rebels outside it. This is the meaning of "a land that consumes its inhabitants" [Num. 13:32]. And as for those who go there and think they can get away with levity and reckless contentiousness, I would invoke the verses, "But you came and defiled My land" [Jer. 2:7] and "Who asked of you to trample My courts?" [Isa. 1:12].[7]

This passage is cited by Shapira from the writings of Rabbi Meir of Rothenburg (twelfth century), but he applies it to the new settlers. If living in the land is fraught with spiritual danger, if it is meant to be the dwelling place of the righteous alone and a place of doom for the unworthy, how much less should the new Zionist heretics and unbelievers, those who openly proclaim their undertaking to be a rebellion against God and His Torah, be permitted to set foot there?

The crux of Shapira's polemic, however, is the question of faith and Redemption, the theological meaning of the Zionist enterprise. For him, any merely human attempt to bring the Jews collectively to Eretz Israel and settle them there represents a forcing of the End and a usurpation of the role of the Messiah. Here it is even clearer that the argument applies not only to secular movements, but also to those Jews who, out of a religious or even an ultra-Orthodox ideology, presume to settle en masse on the holy soil. For, whatever the motivation, such action implies an abandonment of the belief in "the miraculous coming of the Righteous Redeemer." The inevitable result of such activity is thus not physical construction but "spiritual destruction."[8] It threatens to bring upon the people of Israel a new Exile, even harsher than the preceding ones.

But what of the commandment to settle Eretz Israel? In his volume of halakhic responsa, *Minḥat El'azar,* the Munkaczer Rebbe argues that this precept applies only to the messianic era, not to our own time. What is more, even in the time to come, the responsibility for bringing about the return to Zion will be entirely in the hands of the Messiah; he alone, acting in miraculous ways, will bring Israel back to conquer and settle the land. In other words, the Jewish people are to play no active role, either collectively or as individuals, in the process of return, "For it will not be up to them to conquer [the land]; this will come rather from a commandment and an order imposed upon the holy King Messiah, who alone will do it. . . . It will not be done by natural means, but through strange and marvelous signs and wonders."[9] The question of settling in Eretz Israel is thus removed from the normative realm altogether, and there is no possible historical case in which the Jewish people as a collective would be obligated to go there. On the contrary, any merely human effort in this direction, even if undertaken by pious Jews, would betray a lack of faith and the beginnings of heresy.

The Munkaczer Rebbe represented the conservative extreme of haredi thinking in his day. It should come as no surprise, then, that his wrath was directed not only at the Zionists, but also—and perhaps primarily—at Agudat Israel, the more middle-of-the-road haredi group that took part in the settlement of ultra-Orthodox Jews in Eretz Israel. Such Jews might take pride in their beards and piety, but they were, in effect, tacit partners of the Zionists, and "in their hypocrisy they have done us more harm than all the wicked of the earth."[10] Indeed, Shapira waged a vigorous struggle against them all his life.

This struggle reached its height in 1922 at a protest meeting of haredi leaders held in Csap, Slovakia. Those in attendance, the leaders of the radical ultra-Orthodox wing of "Hungarian" Jewry (the reference, of course, being to Hungary in its pre-1918 frontiers), sought to stem the tide of secularization and "sacrilege" that seemed to threaten religious education throughout Eastern Europe and Jewish life in the Holy Land. But on this occasion, their criticism was not aimed directly at the *maskilim* (proponents of Enlightenment), the Zionists or the Reform movement; it was primarily aimed at Agudat Israel, whose rabbis and leaders they perceived as compromisers, accommodationists and, ultimately, collaborators with the secular adversary. The Munkaczer Rebbe, who had called the meeting and chaired it, rose to enumerate, one by one, the sins of the Aguda and its leaders: from the way they conducted yeshiva education to the way they related to Zionism and the settlement of Eretz Israel.[11]

First, he charged, the Agudists were allowing themselves to be influenced by the new, suspect currents of thought sweeping West European Orthodoxy. In their schools, they were permitting the purity of genuine sacred study to be tainted with "admixtures of secular learning," combining Torah and worldly knowledge. Thus, the yeshiva newly established in Warsaw by the Gerer Rebbe deviated gravely, in Shapira's view, from what was acceptable. It was nothing more than an imitation of the misguided modern rabbinical seminaries set up by the German "doctor-rabbis" (university-trained rabbis) and "ra'- banim" (lit., evil sons—a play on the Hebrew word *rabanim,* or rabbis—used to designate the errant Reformers). This development might spread to other places, including the holy city of Jerusalem, where these people might presume to establish a world rabbinical seminary, a technical school and the like: "a stock sprouting poisonous weed and wormwood [Deut. 29:17]."[12]

Second, although the Agudists pretended to fight the Zionists, their actions and even their words revealed a growing similarity of behavior and thinking. Like the Zionists, the Aguda was trying to develop Eretz Israel physically and preaching settlement "through [the tilling of] fields and vineyards," contrary to the tradition that the Holy Land is intended only for prayer and sacred study.[13] In the final analysis, they were collaborating with the Zionists and even infecting innocent schoolchildren with the Zionist ethos and style, "They are defiling the children's minds and hearts with foolishness that leads to levity and heresy, God forbid—songs that speak of the settlement of the Land, the fields and vineyards of Eretz Israel, like [those of] the Zionist poets."[14] Moreover, the Agudists were sabotaging the economic basis of Torah study in the Holy Land, for by their words and deeds they were causing the diversion of funds from the academies and yeshivot of Eretz Israel to agricultural settlement and material development. In this way, they were taking food from the mouths of the students of Torah. "Sages and saints who were spending their lives in holiness and purity in our Holy Land have now suddenly and unaccountably fallen prey to the wickedness of the Zionists, the Mizrachi [religious Zionists], and the Agudists."[15]

Third, Shapira found the Aguda literature to contain statements that could be construed as directly challenging the traditional belief in the Messiah and subverting the traditional Jew's simple, passive expectation of divine salvation. He cited expressions that, in his view, clearly showed the influence of the false Zionist doctrine that Israel would inherit the land through its own physical efforts—aided by the other nations—rather than through profound penitence and exclusive devotion to the study of Torah. He concluded that the Agudists "are for all practical purposes Zionists. . . . They pour fuel on the fire, claiming they are trying to put it out, but in the end the Agudists and the Zionists will be joined together arm in arm."[16]

Of course, this was not an objective reflection of the views or activity of Agudat Israel at the time. In fact, the Aguda came into being in a struggle against the Zionist movement; from the outset, it declared all-out war on secular Jewish nationalism and its new ideas about revival and Redemption. Although the Aguda ideologues did approve of settling the land, they meant that only the faithful should undertake such activity under conditions conducive to piety, and they forbade any collaboration with the Zionist enterprise. Likewise, when they sometimes allowed the limited introduction of secular studies into the curriculum of their schools, they did so solely on the basis of the students' practical needs as future jobholders rather than out of any enthusiasm for the notion of a secular national revival.

Nevertheless, the dispute between the Munkaczer Rebbe and his camp, on the one hand, and Agudat Israel, on the other, must be taken seriously. However inaccurate the description of the Aguda voiced at the rabbinic meeting, it amply illustrates the image the radical group had of itself, its sense of being deeply at odds with the great majority of ultra-Orthodox Jews in Poland and Lithuania and, certainly, in Western Europe.[17] Indeed, other speakers on that occasion agreed with the views expressed by the Munkaczer Rebbe, and the meeting ended with a unanimous ban on association of any kind with Agudat Israel.

The first name on the list of signatories to the ban was that of a young rabbi, scion of one of the Hasidic dynasties, who was presiding at that time over the small community of Orsova. Of all the speakers, he was the most vehement in his support of Shapira's separatist, antisettlement views. This man, Rabbi Yoel Moshe Teitelbaum, was in time to become the Satmarer Rebbe, the adored leader of tens of thousands of hasidim and the most vigorous opponent that Zionism and the state of Israel were ever to know in the haredi camp.[18] The ideas and principles first voiced in the Munkaczer court were to be developed into a full-fledged doctrine in Teitelbaum's sermons and writings.

Thus, the opposition to mass aliyah and settlement that had existed all along grew over the years into an uncompromising struggle led by Teitelbaum against the sovereign Jewish state and all its works. Under his guidance, the time-honored call for the establishment of separate "holy communities" turned into an insistence on total self-segregation by the new "remnant of Israel" and the delegitimation of all those who continued to falsely consider themselves part of the Jewish people—from the secularists to Agudat Israel. Moreover, the fear of "forcing the End" and undermining faith in divine Redemption, a fear that had emerged at the turn of the century, grew in Teitelbaum's doctrine into a metahistorical demonization of the Zionist enterprise as the ongoing antimessianic work of Satan himself.

Teitelbaum's reading of the verse from Zechariah echoed that of the Munkaczer Rebbe ("May the Lord rebuke you, O Satan who chooses Jerusalem"). He saw it as referring to actual events in the Holy Land that were endowed by him with both historical and metaphysical meaning. He wrote:

> May the Lord rebuke Satan, for [the latter] has chosen Jerusalem in order better to overcome those who dwell there . . . to seduce and corrupt the entire world wrapped in the mantle of Jerusalem's glory. . . . And "outrages [have been] committed by the enemy against the Sanctuary" [Ps. 74:3] in the hallowed land . . . for vicious people have come there and defiled it with their heretical government, may God protect us.[19]

In Teitelbaum's view, the Holocaust and the establishment of the state of Israel were not contrary developments, destruction and construction, but a single continuous process: the final eruption of the forces of evil as a prelude to Redemption.

THE GUARDIANS OF THE WALLS

The extreme anti-Zionists in the Diaspora who chose to split off from the rest of the haredi camp found faithful allies in the Holy City itself. This alliance has endured for two generations.

The old Ashkenazic Yishuv (the pre-Zionist Jewish community) in Jerusalem had long been a stronghold of the most conservative attitudes on education and religious practice. It served as a kind of refuge, particularly for Hungarian Jews, from the winds of change sweeping Europe. But at the turn of the century, this stronghold itself seemed to be threatened by the new waves of aliyah. The latter brought together in Jerusalem people of widely diverse beliefs and practices. More than in any other place, it was at this crossroads of the Jewish world that one could find the full spectrum of secularists, traditionalists, moderate Orthodox, ultra-Orthodox and self-styled zealots—and all had to live together in close quarters. What is more, they had to deal with the question of institutional cooperation, a matter that was particularly troublesome for the non-Zionist ultra-Orthodox, and which came up repeatedly in a variety of settings: the city council, the Jewish Agency, the National Council (that among other things, collected voluntary taxes), the Chief Rabbinate, the prestate militia and, later, the Israeli Knesset, government and army.

It is no wonder that the conservative forces in the face of this social and political reality should feel the need to barricade themselves behind an ideology that would permit them to attack the mounting threat at its root. And, of course, the extremists kept a close watch on their own camp for any signs of cooperation with the enemy institutions—cooperation that, if exposed, was promptly vilified. The most zealous would enter into conflict with the rabbinic leadership of the ultra-Orthodox community itself whenever it seemed insufficiently resolute in pursuit of its own stated values and goals.[20] It was, thus, natural that Munkacz and Satmar should find allies in these circles in Jerusalem.

With the death in 1932 of Yoseph Hayim Sonnenfeld, rabbi of the Edah Haredit (Jerusalem's organized ultra-Orthodox community), the radicals pressed for the election of Teitelbaum (who had not yet become the Satmarer Rebbe) as his successor. The leaders of the community were frightened by Teitelbaum's close ties to the zealots, however, and the effort came to naught.[21]

Three years later, in the wake of severe disagreements over matters of education and self-segregation, a group of radicals led by Rabbi Amram Blau and Rabbi Aharon Katzenellenbogen split off from the Edah Haredit and formed a separate group, later to become the Neturei Karta (Guardians of the City). In 1945, this group obtained a majority in the Edah Haredit council and thus took control. The circle was closed in 1953 when the Satmarer Rebbe was chosen as the rabbi of the Edah. To be sure, the Rebbe continued to live in Williamsburg, Brooklyn, where tens of thousands of his followers were concentrated, and he never exercised direct control over the lives of the Jerusalem zealots. Nevertheless, he placed his distinctive stamp on their emerging ideology along with his halakhic backing.

Thus, all three interlocking groups—the Satmarer hasidim, the Neturei Karta and the Edah Haredit—could henceforth be considered one ideological camp, which we will refer to as the "guardians of the walls," despite the obvious sociological differences among them. (We shall consider later the schism that has taken place in this community in recent years).

It was only after the Holocaust and the founding of the state of Israel that the worldview of this group was fully crystallized in written form. Nevertheless, note should be taken of a significant contribution made to this process by the Jerusalem community in the preceding period. This contribution is well represented in the works of Rabbi Yeshayahu Asher Zelig Margolis, "one of the leaders of the hosts of the zealous Hasidim in Jerusalem,"[22] who wrote in the 1920s and 1930s.[23]

Margolis, a rabbinic scholar well versed in the Kabbalah, sought to give depth to the ideology—one might even call it a *theology*—of zealotry and self-segregation and to ground this doctrine in early sources. A creative thinker in his own right, he also had a gift for anthologizing, editing and polemics, and he knew how to tap the potential for radicalism long dormant in his comrades. Indeed, Teitelbaum was later to eulogize him as "the great luminary who fought the Lord's battle and was zealous for the faith, [the man] who was long close to my soul."[24]

What follows is a summary of the principle components of this ideology.

1. *Conservatism.* An extremely conservative attitude is taken toward all aspects of the Jewish way of life. Innovation is forbidden in all areas, from education and study to the details of dress, the cut of the beard, and the "impurity of waving the hair."[25] Seemingly external details take on a deep, inner and often symbolic and mystical significance. Thus, the slightest departure from accepted patterns is forbidden, "Care should be taken that the right lapel overlaps the left, so that the right hand of the Most High, 'the right hand of the Lord uplifted' in its exalted Love, predominates over the left side, which represents Power, the strength of the Evil Impulse." Whoever makes changes is presumed guilty; better that there be fewer yeshiva students than that boys be admitted whose "dress and deportment" deviate in the slightest from established custom.[26]

2. *An Embattled Minority.* According to the worldview of the Jewish people as an embattled minority, it is the zealot, he who fights the Lord's battles, who is the normative Jew. Those few who are prepared to step into the breach and stand fast against the tide are the bulwark of Jewish survival down through the ages. Thus, Jewish history is not mainly the story of the people of Israel as such but rather that of the repeated encounters between the "guardians of the walls" and the benighted masses. Similarly, the true leader is portrayed not as one who leads the people but rather as one who is prepared to oppose them without fear. In other words, Margolis's is a kind of counterhistory pivoted entirely on the heroism of the zealous minority fighting for its Torah.

For example, the true distinction of the tribe of Levi was not its service in the Temple but rather its zeal in the Lord's cause—slaying the multitudes of sinners—after the building of the Golden Calf.[27] Moses was first and foremost the one who stood up to his fellow Hebrews—the one who intervened in the fight between the two Jews ("And he said to the offender, 'Why do you strike your fellow?'" [Exod. 2:13]) and who met single-handedly the challenge of Korah, Dathan and Abiram. Even Aaron, portrayed in rabbinic sources as the archetypal "lover of peace and pursuer of peace," is seen by Margolis in a new light. To "pursue" does not necessarily mean to seek; rather, "sometimes [Aaron] would drive peace away, for 'pursue' [peace] [Ps. 34:15] can also mean to drive something away." Similarly, to say that Aaron was a "lover of peace" does not necessarily mean that he would make peace among his fellow men. On the contrary, he would reprove Israel for its sins and thus "make peace between Israel and its Heavenly Father."

Thus, zealotry, protest and controversy for the sake of Heaven are not particular or exceptional responses but rather the perennial Jewish norm. Moses and Phinehas ben-Eleazar, the leader and the zealot, respectively, are no longer viewed as contrasting models of Jewish behavior; they belong to the same end of a continuum.[28] Moreover, it makes no difference whether the battle must be fought against Jews who violate the Covenant, and thus bear falsely the name of Israel, or against the gentile enemies of the Jewish people—it is all one battle.

> Thus all those "who have not taken a false oath by My life" [Ps. 24:4] or indulged in deceit should go forth like the tribe of Levi. Moses our Teacher, of blessed memory, did not praise the Levites for the holiness and exaltation of their singing in the Temple but for "[saying] of [their] fathers and mothers, 'I consider them not'" [Deut. 33:9], at the time of the sin of the [Golden] Calf, when they gave their full devotion to the sanctification of the Divine Name, may it be blessed. . . . From this we conclude that the Holy One, blessed be He, considers [such devotion] more important and precious even than the Temple service.
>
> And thus would our forefathers always act when the wicked arose in the land. . . . At the time of the Hasmoneans, the blessed Lord came to [their] aid, "delivering the mighty into the hands of the weak and the many into the hands of the few." . . . [from the prayer book] Even if there be but one [righteous person] in the city, the Tanna says, [Avot 5:23] "let him be strong as a tiger and light as an eagle, swift as a deer and courageous as a lion'; this is the true heroism that every God-fearing person should display. . . . Thus did Elijah stand up to Ahab and the 450 prophets of Baal and the whole generation that followed them. And Hananiah, Mishael and Azariah stood up to

the wicked Nebuchadnezzar, a tryant who made the great powers of the world tremble. And thus did the righteous Mordecai stand up to the evil Haman without quavering. . . . It is therefore a sacred obligation for every Israelite to take up this holy war, as it is written, "The Lord will be at war with Amalek throughout the generations" [Exod. 17:16].[29]

3. *Social and Metaphysical Separation.* Margolis's ideology naturally demands that the "remnant of Israel" separate itself completely from the community of the nonobservant and (in his view) incompletely observant. This demand, one that originally arose out of the purely pragmatic need to protect the faithful and shelter their children from the "evil winds" of the time, now takes on greater depth and is given a mystical grounding.

By joining forces with evil, the Jewish heretic proclaims that he is "not rooted in the soul of Israel" but rather belongs to "the external souls, the Amalekite spirits. . . . These are descended from the mixed multitude [who came with Israel] out of Egypt."[30] The way such people end up proves their origins. Thus, one must define boundaries to separate the sacred and profane, light and darkness, Israel and so-called Israel.

Nor, in fact, can these Jewish infidels be expected to repent and truly change their ways. A Jew who transgresses as a result of momentary transgression can, of course, correct and atone for his transgression. But the wicked have made sin a positive ideology rather than just a lapse; their heresy is a faith in its own right. Thus, their very personality and inner being are bound up with evil and impurity and, as a result, the gates of penitence are utterly closed to them.[31] (This distinction, it should be noted, does have a sound basis in halakhic and philosophical sources). As for Zionism, then, "none who go to her can return" [Prov. 2:19]. The rebel who throws off the yoke can never go back. "If the Lord is God, follow Him; and if Baal, follow him!" [1 Kings 18:21]. An ontological gulf has opened between those who continue to keep the embers of the faith glowing, on the one hand, and the apostate seducers and corrupters on the other, "the mixed multitude who mingled with the people of Israel. . . . These, the offspring of Pharaoh, arise in every generation and every age in a different guise and with different names, seeking to undo us."[32] Any attempt to win these renegades back into the fold can only result in a blurring of boundaries and a confusion of value systems. Let them rather carry on as before, and let this lead to the final parting of the ways between good and evil, pure and impure, on the eve of the ultimate Redemption. "For the pruning of dead wood improves the tree"; and "When Israel is rid of these people, the Son of David will come."[33] Hence, social self-segregation comes to symbolize, at bottom, a metaphysical separation. As in so many other instances in the history of religions, the embattled few come to see themselves as the "children of light," the elect, who take their stand against a fallen society that is fundamentally debased.

Of course, such sharp formulations result at times from the heat of debate as the speaker gets carried away with his own rhetoric. However, as Yehuda Leibes has pointed out, these particular ideas do have a basis in the kabbalistic tradition, including the polemics of that self-styled "zealot and son of a zealot," Rabbi Yaakov Emden, against the Sabbatians.[34]

4. *Redemption and Its False Substitutes.* Margolis repeatedly stresses the profoundly subversive effect of Zionism on traditional messianic beliefs, replacing as it does the supernatural with the natural, the religious with the secular, the passive with the active. In this, he adds little of substance to the views of the Munkaczer and Lubavitcher schools; he is only more sharply polemical. Like them, he warns against "forcing the End" by mass aliyah in advance of the final Redemption, and he, too, goes to great lengths in his demonization of Zionism:

> Samael [Satan] himself and all his host have come down to mislead and intoxicate the whole of Israel throughout the world. . . . And this is the substitute they offer for [true] Redemption: false idolatry, *żarat Ba'al-Pe'or* [lit., the troubles of Ba'al Pe'or—a play on *hażharat Balfour* (Balfour Declaration)] that, through our sins, has darkened the vision of Israel; and blind [*'iverim*] Hebrews [*'ivrim*] have arisen . . . saying, "Redemption is coming," . . . and verily, since the time of the first Golden Calf, Satan has never had such an opportunity to blind Israel (God forbid) as he has now.[35]

Most noteworthy in this context is that in Jerusalem at this time (the interwar period) a doctrine of redemptive religious Zionism was being developed by Rabbi Avraham Yitzhak Hacohen Kook. Margolis took note of this development and damned it in the strongest terms. His principal grievance was with Kook's defense of secular Zionists, his readiness to accord the contemporary Return to Zion a religious meaning:

> He takes the Lord's sanctuary and recasts it in the idolatrous image of their national revival. . . . He accords [the latter] all the traditional [*mesorsi (Ashkenazic transliteration)*], albeit emasculated [*mesorasi*], splendor[36] and depth. . . . "And he dreamed a dream" [Gen. 37:5] and "prophesied to you delusion and folly" [Lam. 2:14], [a vision] in which the angels of Redemption—wicked people called angels—"were ascending and descending upon it" [Gen. 28:12].[37]

A detailed examination of this polemic would carry us beyond the bounds of the present discussion. The gist of it is, according to Margolis, that what was taking place was neither Redemption nor "the beginning of Redemption," but the work of Satan, pure and simple.

Thus far we have been examining the radical haredi viewpoint as articulated by Asher Zelig Margolis. More than any other figure, he represents the alliance between the zealots in Jerusalem and those in Hungary and Slovakia. Margolis corresponded regularly with the Munkaczer Rebbe, and in 1930, he arranged for Shapira to visit Jerusalem.[38] He was (as already noted) less successful in his efforts two years later to have the Satmarer Rebbe appointed rabbi of the Edah Haredit. But he kept up contact with Teitelbaum over a period of years,[39] and after the state of Israel was established, it was Margolis who encouraged him to publish a comprehensive tract explaining his opposition to the state and the boycott of the Knesset elections.[40] It was at this time that Teitelbaum's major work, *Vayoel Moshe,* began to take shape.

It is interesting that Margolis was also a close disciple of the elderly Sephardic sage Rabbi Shlomo Eliezer Alfandari, known as "the Holy Grandfather" (he lived past one hundred).[41] He often quoted Alfandari, and he received the latter's *haskamah* (imprimatur) for his book. Margolis was certainly more extreme than his mentor, but Alfandari, too, took a radical position in regard to self-segregation. He wrote a tract attacking Kook, and the zealots attributed to him such acerbic sayings as, "The Mizrachi [religious Zionists] and the Aguda differ in name alone, and what binds them all together is money and power rather than [concern for] the honor of Heaven."[42]

Of all the sages of the land of Israel, Alfandari was the one revered by the Munkaczer Rebbe as the leading saint of his generation. Shapira's whole pilgrimage to Eretz Israel, attended by a considerable entourage, centered around Alfandari. Indeed, it seemed as though it was on this man's stature and mystical virtues that Shapira pinned his hopes for a speedy Redemption. Those of his companions who were privy to his meeting with Alfandari later reported it as follows. Basing himself on the rabbinic dictum, "What the righteous decree, the Holy One, blessed be He, fulfills,"

> the Rebbe pleaded with the Holy Grandfather, as the leading saint of his generation, that he decree irrevocably, for the glory of the Shekhinah and the well-being of all Israel, that the Messiah, son of David, come quickly in our own time, for we could no longer bear our plight. . . . And the Holy Grandfather, in his humility, said, "I am not a righteous man." And our Rebbe stayed and pleaded with him for a long time.[43]

It was as if the Holy Grandfather were the very antithesis of the "Satan who chooses Jerusalem."

JEWISH PASSIVITY, THE THREE OATHS AND THE HOLOCAUST

The Holocaust and the rise of the state of Israel led the Neturei Karta, the Edah Haredit, and the Satmarer hasidim to formulate their views in a more systematic way. These dramatic events had caused theological uneasiness in many quarters, raising fundamental questions about messianic Redemption, Jewish passivity, political sovereignty and the role of the Jewish people in the world. But the radical ultra-Orthodox groups were among the first to articulate a direct religious response.

There were important haredi factions who tended to avoid these questions, denying that the events had any theological meaning. The Holocaust, on the one hand, was seen as an instance of *deus absconditus,* of an unfathomable mystery from which no conclusions could be drawn concerning the revealed ways of God in the world. The state of Israel, on the other hand, was viewed as a purely secular, religiously neutral phenomenon with no bearing on the relation between the Jew and his Creator or between the people of Israel and their Torah.

The self-segregated extremists, however, tended to view the concrete events of the day in a highly religious light, indeed, as being altogether of a metaphysical and demoniacal rather than historical nature. The concrete occurrences represented for them the very hand of God, the higher Providence that hovers over history, judging all in order to reward and punish.

Statistically speaking, the phenomenon we are concerned with is a marginal one. The extremists all told number perhaps ten thousand in Israel today and several tens of thousands in the United States.[44] But their indirect influence, the challenge posed by their radical views, is widely felt in the haredi mainstream.[45] They project an image of consistency and unswerving faith, like some kind of avant garde whose demands disturb the self-satisfied bourgeois complacency of others. Though the views of the radicals are vehemently rejected by most of the ultra-Orthodox community, the former serve a kind of gadfly function, warning the community of the dangers of too much cooperation with the Zionists and their state. And they, no doubt, succeed in drawing the larger community into repeated confrontations with Israeli society and its institutions. It is a universal phenomenon that extreme, absolutist ideologies, untainted by complexity or ambivalence, frequently have an influence far beyond the circle of their own followers.

The same might have been said of the radiating influence within the extremist camp itself, where the miniscule Neturei Karta, for example, long exerted an impact on the thinking of a larger group. But a change has taken place of late, and the most unbridled of the extremists have been expelled from the Edah Haredit. This development is related to a split within Neturei Karta itself: the most militant faction, which numbers less than a hundred families, no longer accepts the authority of the Edah Haredit rabbinic court (*BaDaẒ*).

It is this faction that expresses political affinity for the P.L.O. and that refuses to take part in demonstrations that have police permits because doing so would amount to an indirect recognition of the authority of the state. In 1988, the dissension reached such a pitch that a leader of the most extreme faction, Rabbi Hayim Katzenellbogen, was formally excommunicated by the Edah Haredit court. The remaining faction, led by Rabbi Uri Blau, cooperates with the Edah, which continues to represent most of the radical groups.

Despite some internal variations, the radical camp has taken a consistent ideological line for nearly two generations. We will now look at the intellectual and spiritual roots of this ideology.

We begin with the key issue: the (antimessianic) theological import of the Zionist enterprise and Jewish sovereignty.

In 1938, the Yishuv imposed a head tax, called *kofer hayishuv,* on all the Jewish residents of the country in order to pay the cost of organized defense against Arab attacks. The Jerusalem separatists refused on principle to contribute to the military effort, taking their watchword from the Palestinian Talmud (Hogigah 2:7):

> Rabbi Yehudah Hanasi sent Rabbi Hiyah, Rabbi Assi and Rabbi Ammi to appoint scribes and teachers in towns throughout Eretz Israel.[46] They came to a certain place where they could find neither a scribe nor a teacher. They said to [the townspeople]: Bring us the guardians of the city [*neturei karta*]. They brought them the town watchmen. They said to them: Are these then the guardians of the city? In fact, they are its destroyers! They said to them: Who then are the guardians of the city? They said to them: Scribes and teachers, as the Scripture states: "Unless the Lord builds the house . . . its builders labor in vain; unless the Lord watches over the city, the watchman keeps vigil in vain" [Ps. 127:1].

The name "Neturei Karta," which is used to this day by the most radical of the ultra-Orthodox groups, was thus intended to connote a challenge to the new values, the new definitions of Jewishness and Jewish history that were introduced by the Zionists. The separatists emphasized that the people of Israel, God's people, had stepped out of the stream of ordinary history when they entered the realm of the Torah. Israel had been commanded to show indifference and passivity toward all things political and military and active devotion to things of the spirit. But now the Zionists sought to upset this divinely established order and entice the people of Israel into a double betrayal of their destiny. They were calling on the Jews to force their way into the realm of earthly history and to abandon the yoke of the Torah and the Kingdom of Heaven.

Furthermore, in seeking the normalization of the Jewish people on a purely mundane, historical level, the national movement deliberately called into question the transcendent law that had governed all of Jewish history; the ahistorical law of divine reward and punishment, Exile and Redemption; the Providence that had delivered Israel from the laws of nature and from "normal" human affairs. The covenant between Israel and the Creator had placed Jewish destiny on a purely religious plane. The catastrophes that had befallen the people had resulted not from the aggressive intentions of its enemies, but, as the prayer book puts it, "because of our sins." Similarly, the future restoration of Jewish life would not be a matter of mere bricks and mortar, instead, in Maimonides's words (in the *Mishneh Torah, Hilkhot teshuvah* 7:5), "Israel is to be redeemed by penitence alone." The political attempt to bring the Eternal People into the history of the nations was blasphemy, an act in brazen defiance of Providence.

What is more, the Zionists and those who had fallen under their spell were exposing the Jewish population to serious physical danger. Their nationalistic pretentions and arrogant political machinations were provoking the animosity of the Arabs, with whom the old Yishuv had learned to live in peace over many generations. The passage cited earlier, "Are these then the guardians of the city? In fact, they are its destroyers!" seemed now to have a double significance, both physical and spiritual, and the guardians of the walls felt called upon "to rescue both our bodies and our souls from the rule of these wicked people." In the harsh words of Rabbi Amram Blau, leader of the Neturei Karta during the immediate prestate period:

> Over Israel there have arisen Zionists who adopt gentile notions in an attempt to force the End, using a false idea of this-worldly Redemption through power and the kindness of the other nations. . . . They have come to the Holy Land and raised the flag of rebellion against the Kingdom of Heaven. . . . They have connived by the most horrendous means to uproot our holy Torah, as well as all human morality. . . . They have become entangled with our Arab neighbors to the point where the Yishuv is being subjected to riots and Jewish blood is being shed, Heaven forfend. . . . Our Holy Torah teaches that, while in Exile, we should take no interest in the political realm, until the coming of the Messiah, may he come speedily and in our own day, and there is nothing in this position to antagonize our Arab neighbors. While in Exile we wish only to live and to fulfill the commandments of our Creator, may His Name be blessed; and we have no interest in living in our Holy Land except to inbibe its holiness and fulfill the commandments which can only be fulfilled here.[47]

"Exile" (in this context) is, of course, an expression of time and condition rather than one of place, and those living in Eretz Israel are as much in Exile as Jews anywhere else.

The closer Zionism came to realizing its goals, the more sharply focused became the ideology and historiosophy of Jewish passivity in opposition to it. Inactivity in regard to mundane political matters was turned into the essential feature of Jewishness in the premessianic era. It is the Jews' patient expectation of complete Redemption, a miraculous occurrence unconnected with any worldly effort on their part, that captures the fundamental nature of Judaism itself: acknowledgment of divine rule, of prophetic destiny, of the chosenness of Israel and of the special laws governing Israel's fate.[48] It is no longer just the Jew's unique way of life that has religious significance; the very fact that he lives in Exile becomes a declaration of faith. His very passivity represents a heroic decision that must daily be reaffirmed.

The exact opposition is expressed in the Zionist claim that it can bring about salvation and national rebirth in advance of the messianic age. Any attempt to realize messianic expectations—the conquest of the Holy Land, political liberation, the Ingathering of the Exiles—by human means is tantamount to blasphemy. For, "in all that pertains to Redemption, the holy Torah forbids us to make the slightest effort to force the End, and whoever does so is in complete opposition to the true faith and has no portion in the Torah of Moses."[49]

A sovereign Jewish state would be a new Tower of Babel, an insolent human attempt to usurp the prerogative of the Creator Himself. It is antimessianic hubris— in Yerahmiel Domb's words, "absolute apostasy, brazen arrogance, dreadful heresy that shakes the foundations of the world and hacks at the very root of the Covenant linking [the Children of] Israel and their Father in Heaven."[50]

It is in this context that a theological "explanation" is given for the Holocaust, an explanation that in its categorical and oversimplified character is unparalleled among Jewish reactions to this event: it is seen as a collective punishment for a collective offense, the Jewish people's rebellion against the rule of Heaven, as reflected in the Zionist effort to "force the End"!

These notions are grounded in the well-known doctrine of the midrashic oaths. A talmudic midrash takes as its point of departure the recurrent verse from the Song of Songs, "I adjure you, O maidens of Jerusalem, by gazelles or by hinds of the field: Do not wake or rouse love until it please."[51] The midrash enumerates various oaths that God exacted from Israel: in effect, rules to guide the behavior of the Jewish people while in Exile. The first is that "Israel should not go up *beḥomah* (lit., the wall—but in Rashi's interpretation, "in force"). The second is that "Israel should not rebel against the nations of the world." A third adjuration, according to one version of the text, is that "they should not force the End." At the same time, the Lord foreswore the nations of the world as well "that they not subjugate Israel overmuch." And Rabbi Eleazar adds, "The Holy One, blessed be He, [in this verse] was saying to Israel, 'If you keep the oath, all will be well; but if you do not, I shall strip away your flesh like that of gazelles or hinds of the field [who fall prey]!' "'"[52]

The midrash of the three oaths appears to have had no significant impact on subsequent halakhic literature, nor was it used as the basis of any generally applicable legal norm.[53] But in recent times it did come into vogue in certain circles as part of the polemic over aliyah and the rebuilding of the land. Thus, Rabbi Samson Raphael Hirsch, the leader of German Orthodox Jewry in the nineteenth century, interpreted the injunction against going up *"baḥomah"* to mean "they should never try to reestablish their state on their own" [1837].[54]

Likewise, Shalom Dov Baer Schneersohn, the Lubavitcher Rebbe at the time when the Zionist movement was founded, understood the injunction against "forcing the End" as a firm prohibition against "leaving the Exile by main force or any physical contrivance."[55] Similar views were expressed by other contemporary sages, including, as we have said, Hayim Elazar Shapira and Yishayahu Asher Zelig Margolis.[56] Yet it was only with the Holocaust and the establishment of the state of Israel that the three oaths were given primary importance and made the cornerstone of the anti-Zionist doctrine of Exile, the great declaration of Jewish passivity as the expression par excellence of fealty to God.

It was the Satmarer Rebbe, Rabbi Yoel Teitelbaum, who made the three oaths the summation of a whole way of thinking and a binding halakhic norm. In his view, this norm was of such gravity that a Jew should be prepared to endure martyrdom rather than violate it! Teitelbaum scoured the literature looking for support for his notion of the special significance of the adjurations, demonstrating in the process how creatively the midrashic techniques of reinterpretation can still be used.[57] For example, having failed to find any mention of the three oaths in so fundamental a halakhic work as Maimonides's *Mishneh Torah,* he does not conclude that Maimonides meant to be lenient in the matter, but just the opposite: "forcing the End" was of such gravity that it did not do simply to list it as one prohibition among many. "To force the End prematurely is worse than all other transgressions, even the most serious in the Torah!"[58] An act such as this that undermines the very foundations of the faith and contradicts essential principles of Torah cannot be adequately dealt with among ordinary halakhic prohibitions.

(A surprising mirror image of this claim is the messianic religious Zionist notion of the commandment to resettle the Holy Land. The fact that this commandment is missing from Maimonides's enumeration of the 613 commandments is explained in terms of its being an overarching principle rather than a mere detail of law.[59])

From here Teitelbaum turned to the terror of the Holocaust, giving it, too, a theological interpretation. (He himself had escaped from the Nazis in Hungary aboard Rezsö Kasztner's evacuation train.) His discussion of the midrashic oaths is marked throughout by a far-reaching radicalism. The discussion actually proceeds from a single point of departure: the ultimate human experience, that of death. Thus, speaking about the seriousness of the prohibition, he writes, "These Adjurations may not be violated even on pain of death; even if they threaten you with the cruelest torture, it is no less forbidden to leave the Exile [en masse] than to commit apostasy!"[60] Or in regard to the punishment for violating the prohibition, "Nowhere in the Scriptures do we find so dreadful a punishment as [that which is

threatened here] for the sin of [forcing] the End and violating the adjuration—
[namely] stripping away the flesh."[61]

Earlier instances in which Jews collectively betrayed their faith and destiny are
seen in the same light. First and foremost is the classic case of the Bar Kokhba
rebellion, in which Jews living in a time of "Exile" seized freedom and sovereignty
for themselves. Teitelbaum sees this episode as a clear instance of the violation of
the three oaths; hence, the catastrophic consequences were inevitable, "When [Bar
Kokhba] was slain, the enemies of Israel slew more Jews than they did at the time of
the Destruction [of the Temple]. . . . It was then that the horn of Israel was cast
down, never to be raised up again until the coming of the Son of David."[62]

One theme emerges clearly from this whole fabric of extreme statements: the
Jewish tradition offers ample resources for coming to grips with the mass murder
and collective destruction of our own day. For Teitelbaum, the Holocaust should be
interpreted within the same classic categories of reward and punishment, sin and
repentance, guilt and reckoning as have all the past trials that Jews and other human
beings have endured. The Holocaust should also be seen in light of Jewish experience down through the ages, from the Golden Calf to Bar Kokhba and Shabbetai
Zvi. It was not an "eclipse of God" or an unintelligible chaos, but a revelation of
divine judgment. The Nazi Auschwitz, with its bottomless evil, may have been on
another planet, but the *Jewish* Auschwitz took place in *this* world; thus it must be
understood in terms of traditional beliefs and the transcendent law that has always
determined the fate of the people of Israel. Thus, in contrast to the belief of some
modern religious thinkers, the Holocaust does not require a new religious orientation or usher in a new era in the convenantal relationship between God and His
people as Irving Greenberg would have it,[63] nor does it give rise to a new "614th
commandment," as Emil Fackenheim argues.[64] On the contrary, it confirms the
traditional norms and patterns of faith. The appropriate religious response to these
events is thus the classic one, and the teachers of our day are duty-bound to reprove
the people and call them to repentance:

> Because of our sinfulness we have suffered greatly, suffering as bitter as wormwood,
> worse than any Israel has known since it became a people. . . . In former times,
> whenever troubles befell Jacob, the matter was pondered and reasons sought—which
> sin had brought the troubles about—so that we could make amends and return to the
> Lord, may He be blessed. . . . But in our generation one need not look far for the sin
> responsible for our calamity. . . . The heretics have made all kinds of efforts to violate
> these adjurations, to go up by force and to seize sovereignty and freedom by them-
> selves, before the appointed time. . . . [They] have lured the majority of the Jewish
> people into awful heresy, the like of which has not been seen since the world was
> created. . . . And so it is no wonder that the Lord has lashed out in anger. . . . And
> there were also righteous people who perished because of the iniquity of the sinners and
> corrupters, so great was the [divine] wrath.[65]

This is the gist of the argument that lays the blame for the Holocaust at the doorstep
of Zionism. It is noteworthy that as early as the Second World War harsh accusations were made by some ultra-Orthodox radicals about direct Zionist responsibility

for what was happening: it was the Zionists' declarations that provoked the anger of the oppressor to the point of bloodshed; it was they who hindered rescue efforts; it was they who disturbed the tranquility of the Jews in the lands of their dispersion. Even the claim we are concerned with here, involving sin and punishment, was voiced as early as the 1940s by the Neturei Karta, and since then it has been repeated in many of their attacks.[66] But it was only in the writings of Teitelbaum that this idea became an entire doctrine supported in detail by references to Jewish law and lore.

Actually, Teitelbaum's aim was to defend tradition and faith against a double assault: the theological incongruity of the Holocaust and the theological heresy implicit in Zionism. Both posed difficult challenges to the traditional passivity of the Exile,[67] and by way of reaction, that passivity was then turned into the very essence of Jewish faith and identity. It was not that the Exile had become untenable and brought about its own destruction but rather that the Zionist betrayal of the Exile had brought catastrophe on the Jewish people. The Zionists having "gone up by force," rebelling against the nations and "forcing the End," the nations, in turn, rose up and violated the one oath to which they had been adjured, "not to subjugate Israel overmuch"; so Israel's flesh was stripped away and left to be devoured by wild beasts.[68] And just as the sin had been a collective one, involving the masses of the Jewish people, so was the punishment collective: once the assailant was given free rein to kill, he no longer distinguished between the righteous and the wicked. Thus was Teitelbaum's demonization of Zionism rendered complete. "Satan and the Angel of Death are one and the same" (Baba Batra 16a).

It is difficult here to avoid questioning not only the image of Zionism reflected in this analysis, but also the image of God and of divine Providence. Clearly, the God who had revealed Himself to Teitelbaum—a survivor of Bergen-Belsen whose family, community and people were annihilated at Auschwitz—was the God of Judgment.

"THE TORAH STATE": A CONTRADICTION IN TERMS

The successful realization of the Zionist aim to create a Jewish state posed a painful dilemma for the haredi camp. Up to that point, the confrontation had been with a mere idea or vision; now, there was the reality to contend with. It had been one thing to steer clear of a voluntary ideological movement, but it was quite another to remain separate from a living, comprehensive social structure with the full range of political, legal, economic and military institutions. In fact, the majority of ultra-Orthodox Jews chose to recognize the new historical reality, if only de facto, and were able to find ways of tolerating it and even cooperating with it to a limited degree.

The radicals, on the other hand, rejected outright any compromise with, or reconciliation to, the new polity, stubbornly refusing to accept the yoke of "the spirit of heresy armed with the power of the state."[69] The success of the evildoers on the material, political or military level did not legitimate their iniquity. "The

Amalekites, the 'mixed multitude,' take many forms," warned Rabbi Elyakim Schlezinger, head of the Ramah Yeshiva in London, "What was once called Zionism and ostracized as such by all faithful Jews is now called a state. What was once the treasury of the Jewish National Fund is now the state treasury [*sic*]. The so-called pioneers, who were always considered beyond the pale, are now members of the Knesset." Even the apparent success of the evildoers in winning over observant Jews to their cause has no bearing on the essence of what they are about. "There are times when the 'mixed multitude' is clean-shaven and times when it is bearded, times when it seems boorish and ignorant and times when it takes the guise of the sage and the saint."[70] In other words, political or institutional cooperation between the Zionists and the ultra-Orthodox does not legitimate the former but rather delegitimates the latter.

The guardians of the walls were determined not to budge from their fortress. Immediately after statehood was proclaimed, they imposed a ban on participation in elections to the Knesset, swore never to set foot in government institutions and prohibited the acceptance of any funds whatsoever from the state or its representatives, even for such sacred purposes as the support of yeshivot and communal activities. They redoubled their criticism of Agudat Israel, which ostensibly carried on its tradition of opposition to the Zionist movement yet accepted the benefits, financial and otherwise, of the Zionist state.[71] The separatists were particularly harsh in their condemnation of the Aguda's political "realism." Its leaders, they said, "were given the Torah of realism by the Evil Urge." Lacking in principle, the Aguda "used 'reality' and 'after-the-fact' [arguments] to make the criminal activities [of the Zionists] seem kosher."[72]

In the separatists' view, Agudat Israel represented treacherous pragmatism and opportunism, "[a bunch of] hypocrites and flatterers, latter-day renegades who are turning the world to lawlessness." Their deviance illustrated clearly the dangers that lay in wait for all God-fearing people now that Zionism had taken on a new, politically powerful, economically seductive guise. Both logic and experience taught, as Rabbi Amram Blau put it, "If [we] let up even to the slightest degree, God forbid, from our hatred of evil, of seducers and corrupters, [if we breach] the separateness to which our holy Torah obliges us, . . . then the way is open to every forbidden thing, for we will have left the straight and narrow path for a crooked one."[73]

The consolidation of the state thus led to an intensification of separatist protest and a deepening of the gulf between the "Remnant of Israel" and "the regime that calls itself Israel." The more the Zionist enterprise took root in the Holy Land and the clearer it became that it was not merely a passing episode, the more inimical toward one another did external reality and internal principle seem. The former, the work of Satan, was utterly opposed to the latter, the word of God, and had to be totally ignored by the faithful. The radical position makes none of the pragmatic distinctions between *ab initio* and *ex post facto*, tactics and strategy or short- and long-term objectives. It rejects concepts such as partial realization, step-by-step progress or accommodation to circumstances. It knows nothing of tacit consent, only of vocal protest.

As noted, the opposition of these groups to Zionism was directed not so much against the secular character of the movement as against its deeper theological meaning: the human attempt to "force the End" and usurp the messianic prerogative. The same logic was now at work in the castigation of the state of Israel: it is not that the state is secular or that it passes offensive laws but rather that it exists at all; not that it behaves in one way or another but rather that its very creation—by human, this-worldly, political initiative—is an affront. Yerahmiel Domb, the most extreme contemporary ideologue of the guardians of the walls, author of a dozen books and pamphlets, wrote the following in an article in their newsletter, *Hahomah* [The Wall]:

> The Zionists profane the holy Sabbath, but that is profanation of the Sabbath, not Zionism, and there would be profaners of the Sabbath without them. The Zionists eat forbidden food, but that is not Zionism; there are many people in this world who eat forbidden food aside from the Zionists. The Zionists transgress and violate all [the teachings of] the Torah, but that is not Zionism; there were sinners in this world before Zionism came along. Zionism is one thing and one thing only: the state! The idea of a Jewish state is the great defilement and the profound heresy that the Zionists have introduced. . . . In its very essence Zionism utterly denies the essentials of our faith, and it is in an absolute denial that reaches down to the very depths, the very foundations, the very roots.[74]

And Domb wrote in his wide-ranging work, *Kuntres 'et nisayon* (*Tract for a Time of Trial*):

> Zionism in and of itself represents a negation of faith in the holiness of the Torah and the holiness of Israel, in the coming of the Messiah and the resurrection of the dead, in reward and punishment, in all things divine. . . . Zionism, i.e., the notion that we [ought to] have *a state, freedom, and independence,* does not ostensibly contradict any explicitly [revealed] precept, positive or negative, yet it represents a dreadful heresy. The heresy of Zionism—leaving aside that of the Zionists themselves—amounts to a negation of all the principles of our faith. . . . This Zionism, [the idea] that we [ought to be] a nation and have a state, is a pollution that encompasses all other pollutions, a complete heresy that includes all other heresies.[75]

Ironically, the author's view dovetails with that of a particular school of thought within the Zionist movement, the one known as political Zionism. In his view, what is essential to Zionism is not cultural or social revival or even the Ingathering of the Exiles but rather the achievement of Jewish self-rule.

The upshot is that any form of Jewish historical (i.e., premessianic) existence that has the trappings of statehood is *ipso facto* invalid, whatever its aims and however it conducts itself. Even if the state were to adopt the halakhah as its legal system and all its inhabitants became religious Jews, its fundamental nature would not be affected, for there would still be the original sin of its having been established at all, as Teitelbaum notes, "The very idea of the people of Israel achieving independence before the coming of the Messiah represents heresy against the ways of the Lord, may He be blessed, for it is He alone who enslaves and redeems."[76]

Thus, the faithful should not strive for "religious legislation" or seek to remake public life and institutions in the spirit of the Torah, as Israel's religious parties boast of doing. The notion of a "Torah state" or a "halakhic state" achieved by human beings is likewise no more than an obscene slogan and a falsehood. Indeed, a "Torah state" would be a contradiction in terms, a vain attempt to realize the Torah by uprooting it.

These radical haredi circles would seem, then, to be the most fervent advocates of the separation of religion and state in Israel. Yet they call for separation not because the two realms have nothing to do with one another but rather because they are in direct conflict. "It is not possible for one person to adhere to both faith in the state and faith in our holy Torah, for they are complete opposites and cannot share a single crown."[77] Teitelbaum put it most incisively:

> Even if the cabinet ministers were "all beloved [of God], all pure," even if they were all talmudic sages, nevertheless, because they have seized freedom and sovereignty before the appointed time, they have forced the End and thus committed heresy against our holy Torah and faith. The kingdom of [Bar Kokhba] was, after all, ruled by the Torah, . . . and his contemporaries were all saints, . . . yet see how grievously they were punished, Heaven spare us the like, for [their actions, in rebelling against Rome] amounted to a forcing of the End before the appointed time.
>
> Even if the members of the Knesset were saints, it would be a terrible crime to seize deliverance and statehood before the appointed time, for as we have already shown, the prohibition against violating the adjuration and trying to advance the End applies to all Jews, however righteous.[78]

In sum, the state of Israel amounts to a perversion that cannot be rectified. It was conceived and born in sin, and the sole remedy is for the Jewish people as a whole to disengage themselves from collective political activity and forego entirely the sovereignty it so illicitly seized.

The guardians of the walls are also contemptuous of the efforts made by the religious parties to pass "religious legislation" for another reason: the Torah and the commandments would be desecrated by the very fact of having been discussed and decided on by a secular legislature. We shall examine this argument more closely, since it has important implications for public controversies now raging in Israel that are far beyond the confines of the radical haredi community in Jerusalem. In fact, the argument involves three interrelated claims.

The first claim concerns the source of authority. According to the radical view, all legislation regarding religious matters that is adopted by a secular body (e.g., the Knesset) makes the divine commandments seem human, thus undermining the unique authority of the Torah as transcendent, revealed Law. A citizen who obeys a Sabbath ordinance passed by the Knesset is obeying a "Zionist Sabbath law" rather than observing the holy Sabbath, even if the Knesset adopts the religious precepts of the Sabbath in their entirety. A religious law would, thus, have been converted into "a human, earthly, gentile law of Zionism" that must be viewed as "a high-handed annulment of the Torah, by legal means, in favor of a human religion."[79] Secularization of the halakhah through its enactment into legislation is, in fact, desecration of the halakhah.

There is an interesting analogy between this argument and Kant's well-known distinction between the moral imperative—which is rooted in an inward sense of duty—and the legal imperative, which is rooted in external authority. Here, too, what is decisive is not the resulting behavior but rather the intent, not the content of the law but rather the motivation for observing it. Of course, our concern is with *religious* motivation rather than with the autonomous categorical imperative—thus, what is at stake in the enactment of secular legislation is not just a downgrading but a profanation.

Second, even from a purely formal point of view, making questions of Torah and halakhah a matter of bargaining and voting in the legislature amounts to subjecting the commandments—the word of God—to secular human authority. Whatever the outcome, precedence is clearly given to the decisions of the legislature over the rulings of the halakhic codes, making for a "subversion of the Torah."[80] When the religious parties take part in such voting, they are implicitly accepting the right of the legislature and the electorate to accept or reject the Torah.

In the words of Rabbi Shimon Israel Posen, a leading halakhic authority of the Satmarer community in New York:

> Woe unto them for the shame of it, that people who put on phylacteries every day sit in that assembly [*kinus*] of the wicked called the "Knesset" and, signing their names to falsehoods, forge the signature of the Holy One, blessed be He, Heaven forfend; for they think they can decide by majority vote whether the Torah of truth will be trampled upon even further or whether God's Torah will be granted authority; and they accept a reward from the enemies of the Lord, who embrace falsehood with all their might.[81]

Finally, even when it yields to the religious parties and passes such laws as a Sabbath ordinance, the Knesset adopts the laws selectively, and thus not in their halakhic form. It picks and chooses among the regulations and symbols as it sees fit, in reality creating its own version of the Sabbath. The public as a result is grievously misled, for many innocent and seemingly innocent people take the "Sabbath ordinance" as an indication of what is permitted and forbidden by the Torah. The same criticism applies to a distinction made by the religious parties between the public domain, which should be governed by Jewish tradition, and the private domain, in which each person should be free to do as he or she chooses. The guardians of the walls see this distinction as making a mockery of the Torah by depriving it of its authority in the private realm. In their polemical tract *Lehasir masveh* (Stripping Away the Mask), the Neturei Karta condemn Agudat Israel and its legislative initiatives:

> According to the laws of our holy Sabbath, there is no difference between the severity of violation in private and that in public (except for the commandment to separate the violator from the community of Israel, which refers to the public realm), and it is no less forbidden to light a cigarette than to drive a train. . . . [But once such a "Sabbath ordinance" is passed,] everyone who obeys it will be considered a "Sabbath observer," even though he may commit violations [of the Sabbath] so serious that [in biblical law] capital punishment was ordained for them.[82]

The conclusion of these three arguments is that observant Jews should not accept the rules of the parliamentary game or have any truck with such mischief. Their participation in the voting can only give a seal of religious approval to the decisions of the Knesset, thus precluding any future opposition. On the one hand, Teitelbaum argues "the pious who enter the house of heresy enter into compromises regarding fundamentals of our holy Torah." On the other hand, "[their] power is thereby diminished": they forego the right of protest, for their enemies can then claim, "the pious have their representatives in the Knesset, but they are only an inconsequential minority who, as it were, have not a leg to stand on, especially since they themselves are willing to concede essential points of the Torah."[83]

These arguments are all of a piece. Furthermore, they go hand in hand with the basic tenet of the guardians of the walls, that denies legitimacy to the Jewish state and to its appropriation of the name "Israel." Let us be more concrete. Were the Edah Haredit, the Neturei Karta or the Satmarer hasidim to accord the Israeli regime and the Israeli public the standing associated in religious tradition with *malkhut* (the kingdom), *nasi* (the prince), *kahal* (the community) or *klal yisrael* (the Jewish people), would they then have to draw such a firm line between the religious and the political realms? They would then be halakhically in a position to grant juridical and religious authority to a consensus of the people or its representatives; to recognize the renewed validity of the classical distinction in Jewish tradition between, for example, individual and communal transgressions.

But such thinking, which characterizes many of the religious Zionists, is alien to them. Their demand that the Knesset keep out of matters of halakhah and religion is grounded not only in a fear of secularization, but also in theological denial of the legitimacy of the state itself, viewing it, instead, as an antimessianic attempt to "force the End." It would not matter what form of government it had—democratic, monarchical or even purely theocratic—the state cannot be improved. The only thing to do is to eliminate it.

Why, one might well ask, if the state is beyond repair, do the radical separatists continually mount street demonstrations rather than simply stay home? What point is there in sounding alarms and issuing denunciations if the effort is defined from the outset as being meaningless and futile? Indeed, if the Zionist public has, in effect, excluded itself from the historic Jewish people, are not the Lord's faithful released from all responsibility for its actions? To be sure, these demonstrations are avowedly not attempts to redress, but mainly expressions of protest, declarations to all the world that the faithful Remnant of Israel has no part in the machinations of the Zionists but instead utterly dissociates and separates itself from them.[84] The demonstrations call into question the right of the state and the majority of its people to use the name Israel or—at the very least—to monopolize it for themselves. This is the message for external consumption. At the same time, within their own community, the demonstrations function to "make the heretics smell bad," especially to the younger generation. A distinction is drawn, loudly and clearly, between the sacred and the profane, and all possible rapprochement with the unbelievers is ruled out. In this sense, confrontation per se, doing battle with the wicked, has a religious and educational value in its own right, "The duty to hate the wicked and combat them is a major principle of the Torah."[85] Or, in the words of the psalmist, "O Lord, You know I hate those who hate You, and loathe Your adversaries" (Ps. 139:21).

Of course, such ideological considerations do not exhaust the motivations that bring people into the streets. A Jew who cries "*Shabbes! Shabbes!*" in the streets of the Holy City is presumably doing more than making a symbolic gesture and is not only concerned with the world's reaction or the education of his own children; no doubt, he himself is actually pained by a concrete violation of the Sabbath he has witnessed. He is turning directly to the violators—typically, those who drive on the Sabbath—and demanding that they change their ways. He is motivated by the religious duty of reproof and the sense of responsibility all Jews are supposed to feel for one another, in spite of the oft-repeated assertion that the Zionists have excluded themselves from the Jewish people. Yet (as we have seen) the avowed purpose of these public demonstrations is to symbolize dissociation and withdrawal rather than involvement.

FAITH, REALITY AND DETERMINISM

When the Munkaczer Rebbe some two generations ago called the Zionist settlement movement the "Satan who chooses Jerusalem," he was speaking about the religious transgressions of the new settlers and their initial attempts to build the Holy Land by physical, secular means. But when the Satmarer Rebbe spoke, after the establishment of the state, about the "Satan who chooses Jerusalem to seduce and corrupt the entire world wrapped in the mantle of Jerusalem's glory," he was no longer addressing himself to the unexpected historical successes of the Zionists and their audacious political endeavors. Rather, he was speaking in demonological terms. The manifest success of the collective rebellion against divine rule now manifest in the Holy Land testifies, in his view, to the workings of very real powers of evil that have arisen to challenge the Shekhinah in its own sanctuary. Only the literal intervention of Satan himself could have given the Zionists the strength to overcome holiness and drag an entire world down in their net.

The demonological interpretation of Zionist history reached the height of its development following the Six Day War, when the Zionists, saved from dire peril, stormed Judea and Jerusalem and entered the Temple Mount and the place of the Holy of Holies. This astounding military victory, seen by many Jews as miraculous deliverance on a biblical scale, was a source of great embarrassment to the radicals. After years of confidently awaiting the demise of the rebellious state, they were forced to bring their heightened religio-historical sensitivity to bear on a completely reverse situation. The Neturei Karta's Rabbi, Hayim Katzenellbogen, said some time later:

> Who can forget the darkness of the six days in [1967], when under the pretext of the [closing of the] Straits of Tiran the Zionists arose, surveyed the earth, and declared war. And in the end they conquered all of Eretz Israel from the Arabs, reaching the place of our glorious Temple. And the thing led to confusion and uncertainty, which grew apace. During the first week after the conquest, the sages forgot their wisdom; the trail of successes and the [ostensible] miracles, as well as [their own] blindness, led them to dance around the [Golden] Calf. Perfectly pious Jews looked catastrophe in the face and could not cope with it.[86]

The religious mind has always wondered "why . . . the wicked prosper,"[87] why divine Providence fails to intervene in the natural order and defeat them. In this, there is nothing new. But that the triumph of evil should actually be assisted by miracles? That fortune actually smile on those who would force the End? Such a situation could only lead to what the social psychologists call cognitive dissonance.[88] On the one hand, there were the events themselves, which in the religious imagination evoked associations of the miraculous, "the deliverance of the Lord in the blink of an eye" and entry into the sacred precincts; yet, on the other hand, there was the unworthiness of "the saved," the heretics and destroyers of the Covenant who should by all rights have been spurned rather than favored by Providence.

The Satmarer Rebbe, who viewed this problem with the utmost gravity, "spoke out with a voice that 'kindles flames' [Ps. 29:7]"—according to one of his admirers—"calling out in the assembly of the believers, 'Whoever is for the Lord, come to me!' [Exod. 32:26], but as for him who believes [the Zionist] successes are 'miraculous,' he has no place among us."[89] Teitelbaum understood very well which aspect of the new reality would be most seductive, and he strictly forbade his followers to go to the Western Wall, now made accessible by the Israeli victory. In Jerusalem, Amram Blau, leader of the Neturei Karta, seems to have issued such a ban even earlier. The God-fearing had to refrain from enjoying the forbidden fruits of the Zionist conquest. They were duty-bound to stay well out of earshot of the shofar blasts on the Temple Mount that defiled the holy places with a nationalistic, military myth.

Teitelbaum was urgently concerned with offering the public more systematic guidance as well; within a short time, he published a book entitled (On Redemption and Its [Illegitimate] Substitutes '*Al hageulah ve'al hatemurah*). In it he explains the deeper meaning of the events, calling on the remnant of Israel to summon all its strength for that fateful—perhaps final(?)—stand against the forces of evil that must precede the Redemption. "[As for] the conquest of the Old City and the place of the Temple, . . . how could anyone imagine that the Holy One, blessed be He, would perform miracles for idolators? [Such a notion] is pure heresy. The only possible explanation is that this is the work of [Satan] and his minions. . . . [Satan] is sparing no effort to deceive the world [through these events], for in this trial our Redemption is at stake."[90]

In other words, the people of Israel now faced the greatest test of faith they had ever encountered. It is no longer the classic situation in which Jews, confronted with the gray reality of Exile in an unchanging world, are asked to persevere in their belief in miraculous deliverance. The present trial is a more difficult one, a test of the faith that true Redemption is yet to come in the face of a reality that has only the appearance of Redemption but is, in fact, the work of the Devil. It is this test that will separate the wheat from the chaff, purifying the God-fearing for their messianic destiny.

Teitelbaum had the wisdom to instil in his followers a sense of the momentous, heroic nature of their task so as to counterbalance the feelings of heroic, historic achievement then current among the Zionists, "For we know from the sages and the holy books that each time thought is given on high to our [true] Redemption, Satan conspires to produce a mere semblance of Redemption in its stead."[91]

The heady feeling in Israel following the Six Day War was short-lived. The Yom Kippur War of 1973 and the Lebanon War of 1982, as well as the peace accords with Egypt, all brought about a measure of realism: the excitement was tempered by doubt and restraint.

These historic turns have not been without their effect on the Neturei Karta and their polemics, eliciting in recent years a certain ambivalence on their part. To be sure, these people have remained alienated from political and military power and have continued to stress the demonic character of the state's victories and successes. At the same time, one also begins to detect an opposite focus that is reminiscent of views expressed by the Neturei Karta spokesmen in the early years of Israel's independence: a focus on the retreats, material failures and political weaknesses of the state as decisive proof of its false and transitory character. In this view, external reality no longer appears as dissonant with but rather, in many respects, as confirming deeply held beliefs and expectations about the future. Indeed, a number of writers in this camp (in its periodical press in particular) implicitly acknowledge this change when they speak about "the rise of the Zionist state" and "its decline" in various periods of recent history.[92]

But whether current events favor the Zionist cause or not, the radicals are expected to stand aside and watch from the sidelines in utter passivity. Their assigned role is that of the spectator and critic, not the shaper and mover. In this sense, their approach differs profoundly from Western and latter-day Muslim[93] radicalism, as well as from that of contemporary Jewish political messianism. The zealotry of the haredim entails protest and withdrawal, not an attempt to seize power. Indeed, the more militant this radicalism becomes, the less likely it is to use political power or physical force to achieve its ends.

It is unthinkable, for example, that the guardians of the walls would ever organize underground paramilitary activity against the state of Israel. This would turn them into "Zionists" themselves, as they see it, for they would then be furthering the normalization of the Jewish people. What do the Zionists want, after all, but to turn the Lord's people into a nation like all nations, to determine its fate through earthly means and by force? To fight them with their own "gentile" weapons would be to concede the Zionists' victory, an act of surrender by the Remnant of Israel.

The argument of the archmilitant Domb may be summaried as follows:

> We have no alternative political program to that of Zionism, nor do we have bombs or other weapons. We shall take no action against the heretical Jewish state, any more than against the Vatican or the Communist states. We are bound to oppose and protest, but responsibility for the course of history rests in the hands of God alone. Whether the Zionists are for the moment successful or not, we put no faith in them. They could build an empire and we would still deny their legitimacy and refuse their favors.[94]

The more extreme faction of the Neturei Karta has achieved notoriety by going so far as to profess affinity for the enemies of the state of Israel. Some have even professed support for the P.L.O. (or in an earlier period, for the Kingdom of Jordan) and have made symbolic gestures of solidarity with it. Does this not contradict the principle of political passivity? In their view, it is simply an assertion of religious principle, not an attempt to change the course of political history. Jewish sovereignty in the age of Exile must be negated, and the adherence of the Jewish people to its solemn oath to God must be publicly reaffirmed. God Himself has ordained that, for the time being, Jews should be ruled by gentiles, and the Zionists have rebelled against this decree. The latter must, therefore, not be allowed to appear as the sole representatives of the Jewish people.

Moreover, this position is seen as being very much within the classic tradition of submission to the powers that be, a pattern that reflects the Jewish instinct for survival in the age of Exile. Assuming that the designs of the Devil are short-lived and the Zionist regime not long for this world, is it not wise to begin now to cultivate its successor? Should steps not be taken now to prevent this new ruler from seeing the Jewish people as his mortal enemy? The guardians of the walls are, as it were, simply safeguarding long-range Jewish interests. Hence, what we have is both a declaration of religious conviction and an act of *shtadlanut* (diplomacy that curries favor with the authorities) in perfect accord with the requirements of Jewish existence in the exilic age and in perfect opposition to the Zionist attempt to bring that age to an end.

For all its passivity, this position, they believe, will ultimately win out. The Remnant of Israel will triumph, and the Jewish people as a whole will be reshaped in its image. Like radical groups everywhere, the haredi extremists see themselves as the vanguard of the future, only temporarily biding their time as a deviant, separatist minority. Now on the margins of history, they are the true harbingers of history's promised and long-awaited fulfillment. The guardians of the walls are, thus, those who remain true not only to the past but also to the future, those who leave the camp, as it were, to scout ahead. "While yet under the rule of darkness, we shall know no victory, only struggle," Domb writes in another of his pamphlets. "We shall not triumph today, but it is crystal clear that triumph will ultimately be ours. . . . The future belongs not to the [Golden] Calf or the dancing [around it] but rather . . . to the Lord."[95]

Whatever their numerical weight, it is the faithful who provide the nucleus around which events are destined to unfold. Contemporary writers, like Margolis before them, point to the inner struggles in Jewish history in which those few who keep the spark alive muster the strength of spirit to stand up to the many who betray the Covenant; and it is the former that history vindicates, from the biblical instances of Joshua and Caleb, in their dissent from the other ten scouts, or Elijah, in his challenge to the prophets of Baal, to the later struggles of Rabbi Yaakov Sasportas against the Sabbatians and of Rabbi Yaakov Emden, "who commanded his son never to be afraid, but to stand his ground, even if he be the last surviving adherent of his luminous teachings."[96]

Clearly manifest in these ideas is a deterministic view of the future of the state of Israel. In its antimessianism, Zionism represents an obstacle on the inevitable path of history, one standing in the way of Redemption. The rebellious Jewish state is doomed to destruction in the process. Teitelbaum wrote following the 1967 victory:

It is clear beyond all shadow of a doubt that the buildings put up by the heretics and apostates in our Holy Land will all be burned to the ground by the Messiah, leaving not a trace behind, and in their place the Lord, may He be blessed, will raise up for us other buildings sanctified by supernal holiness; and then "all the nations shall know that I the Lord have rebuilt the places that were destroyed" [Ezek. 36:36], but they will not be as they were [before].[97]

It is as if the prophecies and midrashim concerning the cataclysm to preceed the Redemption, the terrible birth pangs of the Messiah, all referred to the eventual fate of Zionism.[98] The Jewish state was conceived and born in sin; there can thus be no gradual process of evolution, improvement or purification in its case, only a complete uprooting, with the structure of the future to be erected on the ruins of the past.

Ironically, a sense of Jewish solidarity is often a prominent feature of such discussions. The guardians of the walls say, "May the state be destroyed without a single Jew getting hurt!"[99] The Lord will find ways of clearing a path for the Messiah without shedding Jewish blood. Thus Teitelbaum, predicting the downfall of the "heretical kingdom" as a necessary precondition for the Redemption, is careful to add, "Divine mercy will be needed so that the kingdom is destroyed entirely by divine means and not by the other nations, because if the nations were responsible there would of course be a great danger to the Jewish people."[100]

Even after the Six Day War, which he saw as a manifestation of the demonic, he wrote, "While the war was underway there was no choice but to pray in earnest for the Jewish people that they not be devoured by [the gentiles] and not meet a horrible end, God forbid."[101] And apparently his concern was not confined to the fate of those few thousand Jews in the Holy Land whom he saw as the Remnant of Israel.

The same could not be said for the sovereign Jewish state, that Tower of Babel erected by the Zionists. For it, there could be no escape from the sentence of a deterministic messianism.

Notes

1. Shmuel Yosef Agnon, "Pat shelamah," in *Kol sipurav shel S. Y. Agnon,* vol. 6, *Samukh venireh* (Jerusalem and Tel-Aviv: 1960); Baruch Kurzweil, *Masot 'al sipurei Agnon* (Jerusalem and Tel-Aviv: 1963), 86–94.

2. The Agnon family home in Homburg burned down in 1924, destroying Agnon's library and manuscripts. He emigrated to Eretz Israel in that year. On the theme of the disaster of fire in a sinful land, see Hillel Barzel, *Bein Agnon leKafka* (Ramat-Gan: 1973), 44, 112, 301; and Shmuel Yosef Agnon, *Kol sipurav shel S. Y. Agnon,* vol. 7, *'Ad hena,* 141. On the motif of the house and its biographical background, see Dov Sadan, *'Al Shai Agnon* (Tel-Aviv: 1967), 105–121.

3. See Moshe Goldstein (ed.) *Tikun 'olam* (Munkacz: 1933), sec. 97 (151).

4. The source of this interpretation is to be found in Azariah of Pano's "Ḥakor din," *'Asarah maamarot,* 2:7.

5. See Aviezer Ravitzky, "Haẓivi lakh ẓiyunim," in *Ereẓ yisrael behagut hayehudit bimei habeinayim,* ed. Moshe Halamish and A. Ravitzky (Jerusalem: 1990).

6. Tosafot on Ketubot 110b. In the early part of this century, this passage was used as a prooftext against the new settlement movement by Shalom Dov Baer Schneersohn of Lubavitch, in *Iggeret bidvar . . . kupat Rabbi Meir Ba'al Hanes* (1907), 19. See Yosef Salmon, "'Emdat haḥevrah haḥaredit berusiyah-polin laẓiyonut," *Eshel beersheva* 1 (1976), 395. In *Teshuvot Maharit* and in the *Pitḥei teshuvah* commentary on *Even ha'ezer* 75:6, the

statement is attributed to "an erring student." In any event, this was not an unusual point of view in Ashkenazic Jewry at the time. See also Ephraim Urbach, *Ba'alei hatosafot* (Jerusalem: 1968), 108–109; Yisrael Tashma, "'Inyenei ereẓ yisrael," *Shalem* 1 (1974), 81; Mordechai Breuer, "'Erkhei geulah bemivḥan hadorot," in *Geulah umedinah: hakinus hashenati lemaḥshevet hayahadut* (Jerusalem: 1979), 151–155. (No ed. named.) Yishai Yuval, "Hitnaḥalut: ya'avor veal yehareg," *Morashah* 9 (1977), 26–36.

7. Meir ben-Baruch of Rothenburg, *Sheelot uteshuvot Maharam* (Berlin: 1891), secs. 14–15. Shapira cites Rabbi Meir, who adds, "But whoever goes for the sake of Heaven and lives there in holiness and purity shall enjoy unlimited reward, provided he can make a living there." See also Ephraim Urbach, *'Al ẓiyonut veyahadut* (Jerusalem: 1985), 151. For other sources, see *Sefer haredim* (Venice: 1591), 57–60; and Moses Nachmanides, sermon for Rosh Hashanah, in *Kitvei Ramban,* ed. Hayim Dov Chavel (Jerusalem: 1963), pt. 1 (250).

8. Goldstein, *Tikun 'olam,* sec. 3 (3). See also sec. 85 (146–147). The rebbe cites as authority Rabbi Jonathan Eybeschütz and others.

9. Hayim Elazar Shapira, *Sheelot uteshuvot minḥat El'azar,* pt. 5, sec. 16; Goldstein, *Tikun 'olam,* sec. 94 (129)—a disagreement with Rabbi Avraham of Sochaczew, the author of *Avnei nezer.* In Shapira's view, the commandment to settle the land applied to all Jews only during the first Jewish conquest (in the time of Joshua), and it was for this reason that Maimonides did not include it in his listing of the Commandments.

10. Goldstein, *Tikun 'olam,* sec. 97 (154).

11. *Ibid.,* secs. 26–29 (31–38).

12. *Ibid.,* sec. 26 (32). See the correspondence with the Gerer Rebbe, secs. 6–16 (7–17).

13. *Ibid.,* sec. 27 (34). The first general convention of the Aguda (1923) and the Gerer Rebbe's visit to Eretz Israel prepared the ground for haredi agricultural settlement. See also remarks by Shapira about the Gerer Rebbe, "How can I [keep silent] when I see . . . that he has written there [that it is praiseworthy] to engage in labor and material pursuits in all the trades in Eretz Israel, which is the Zionist way of building up the land by human means and contrary to what we have learned [in the holy books]" (in *ibid.,* sec. 17 [18]). Cf. Shapira's speech in Jerusalem (1930) in Moshe Goldstein, *Sefer mas'ot yerushalayim* (Munkacz: 1931), 105.

14. Goldstein, *Tikun 'olam,* sec. 26 (32). The text has probably undergone partial editing.

15. *Ibid.,* sec. 30 (36), sec. 17 (18). See Rivka Shatz, "'Imut hasifrut haḥaredit 'im haziyonut," *Nativ* 5 (1989), 48–52.

16. Goldstein, *Tikun 'olam,* sec. 28 (34–35), sec. 6 (6). See also Shapira's letters criticizing the Aguda in his *Divrei haiggeret* (Jerusalem: 1932) and his *Darkhei ḥayim veshalom* (Munkacz: 1940), 221.

17. B. R. Wilson, *Religious Sects* (New York and Toronto: 1970); *idem,* "An Analysis of Sect Development," in his *Patterns of Sectarianism* (London: 1967), 244–286. Shapira and his followers were the most militant of the ultra-Orthodox. The Lubavitcher school, who held similar views (see later discussion), refrained from such extreme and strident polemics. At this time, their circle included the martyred Rabbi Issahar Shlomo Teichtal, one of whose letters appears in Goldstein, *Tikun 'olam,* sec. 80 ("No human action or deed can help in the slightest to cause the horn of Zion and Jerusalem to be raised to the point where the Lord looks down from on high and pours over us a heavenly spirit of purity.") During the Holocaust, in which Rabbi Teichtal perished, he wrote a book, *Em habanim semeḥah* (Budapest: 1943), that reflects a change of heart.

18. See also the open letter signed by Hayim Elazar Shapira, Yoel Moshe Teitelbaum and others in the 1925 tract *Shim'u devar Hashem,* published in *Hakol Kol Yaakov* (Jerusalem: 1980), 2; the 1924 tract against the Zionists by Teitelbaum and others, published in Abraham Fuchs, *Haadmor misatmar* (Jerusalem: 1980), 228; Teitelbaum's 1927 broadside against Zionism, published in his *Divrei Yoel* (Brooklyn: 1980), vol. 1, secs. 62–63; and Teitelbaum's responsum condemning Agudat Israel in his tract *Shomer emunim* (Budapest: 1939). The fact that Teitelbaum's views were nurtured in radical circles that even then had

broken away from the ultra-Orthodox mainstream contradicts the thesis—put forth, e.g., in A. L. Nadler, "Piety and Politics," *Judaism* 31, no. 2 (1982), 135–152—that his position was in line with then-current ultra-Orthodox rabbinic opinion. On Teitelbaum's biography, see Fuchs, *Haadmor misatmar;* Aaron Rosmarin, *Der satmarer rebbe* (New York: 1967); I. Z. Rubin, *Satmar: An Island in the City* (New York: 1972), 34–40.

19. "Yishuv ereẓ yisrael," in Yoel Moshe Teitelbaum, *Vayoel Moshe* (Jerusalem: 1978), sec. 149; see also sec. 68.

20. For a sociological perspective on this subject, see Menahem Friedman, *Ḥevrah vedat: haortodoksiyah halo-ẓiyonit beereẓ yisrael, 1918–1936* (Jerusalem: 1978), and on zealotry, *ibid.*, 19–22; Yehoshua Kaniel, *Hemshekh utemurah* (Jerusalem: 1982), 190–210; Netanel Katzburg, "Hapulmus haruḥani ba'olam hayehudi vehayishuv birushalayim bameah hatesh'a-'esrei," in *Yerushalayim: mishivat ẓiyon 'ad layeẓiah min haḥomot* (Jerusalem: 1980), 168–172 (no ed. named); Menahem Friedman, "Religious Zealotry in Israeli Society," in *On Ethnic and Religious Diversity in Israel,* ed. Solomon Poll and Ernest Krausz (Ramat-Gan: 1975), 99–111; Charles S. Liebman, "Extremism as a Religious Norm," *Journal of the Scientific Study of Religion* 20 (1983), 75ff. On changes in the Jerusalem Jewish community, see Shmuel Ravitzky, "Lekorot hayishuv hayehudi birushalayim," *Measaf yavneh* 1 (1939), 154–172; Uziel O. Schmelz, "The Development of the Jewish Population of Jerusalem During the Past Hundred Years," *Jewish Journal of Sociology* 2 (1960), 57–73. On typical defenses against secularization and change, see Erich Voegelin, *The New Science of Politics* (Chicago: 1952), 122.

21. Friedman, *Ḥevrah vedat*, 345, 134–135, 141. In a handbill issued in the fall of 1933, the city's ultra-Orthodox people were asked to sign a manifesto in support of Teitelbaum (Fuchs, *Haadmor misatmar*, 154).

22. The language is that of Moshe Goldstein, a Munkaczer hasid, in his *Maamar ḥayot esh* (Munkacz: 1931). A Jerusalem handbill (1933) condemning the excitement in Agudat Israel over the Balfour Declaration bears the stamp of Margolis's thinking. And indeed, in *Tikun 'olam,* edited by the same Goldstein, these words are attributed to "God-fearing people, the leaders of the zealots in the cause of the Lord of Hosts and His Torah" (85).

23. See Yehuda Liebes, "Ha'edah haḥaredit birushalayim vekat midbar yehudah," *Jerusalem Studies in Jewish Thought* 1 (1982), 137–152.

24. See the beginning of Yishayahu A. Z. Margolis's *Beur hashir bar yoḥai* (Meron: 1974).

25. Yishayahu A. Z. Margolis, *'Amudei arazim* (Jerusalem: 1932), 38–47.

26. *Ibid.*, 31, 35. Dozens of pages are devoted to demonstrating the halakhic and kabbalistic importance of the various details of dress customary in the author's circle. See also Yishayahu A. Z. Margolis, *Ashrei haish* (Jerusalem, 1925), 71.

27. Yishayahu A. Z. Margolis, *Kumi ori* (Jerusalem: 1925). 24, cited in Friedman, *Ḥevrah vedat*, 135; Yishayahu A. Z. Margolis, *Kumi roni* (Jerusalem: 1925), 44; *idem, Ashrei haish*, 34.

28. Margolis, *Ashrei haish*, 10. The author also suggests classical sources for these ideas.

29. *Ibid.*, 61–64. Numerous examples are found throughout the book, e.g., 5, 24, 32, 69, 75. See also Margolis, *Kumi roni*, 44–45 and elsewhere.

30. Margolis, *Ashrei haish*, 65.

31. *Ibid.*, 23–25.

32. Margolis, *Kumi roni*, 39.

33. Margolis, *Ashrei haish*, 25; *idem, Maamarei rabbi El'azar* (Jerusalem; 1930) 22.

34. Yehuda Liebes, "Ha'edah haḥaredit," 143. See also *idem,* "Meshiḥiyuto shel rabbi Ya'akov Emdin veyaḥaso lashabtaut," *Tarbiẓ* 49 (1980), 125.

35. Margolis, *'Amudei arazim*, 6. The question of messianism and Zionism is treated at length in *idem, Kumi roni*, 38–41; *idem, Ashrei haish*, 41–50; and throughout his *Kumi ori*.

36. See Avraham Yitzhak Kook, *Ḥazon hageulah* (New York: 1974), 195.

37. Margolis, *Ashrei haish*, 56 (the book lambasts Rav Kook); *idem, 'Amudei arazim,*

5. See Liebes, "Ha'edah haḥaredit," 148. See also Rivka Shatz, "Reishit hamas'a neged harav Kook," *Molad,* n.s. 6, no. 32 (1974), 251–262.

38. See Goldstein, *Mas'ot yerushalayim,* 27–31, 319; Margolis, *'Amudei arazim,* 30, 53, 64 (drawn from the teachings of the Munkaczer Rebbe).

39. See nn. 21, 24. See also the reproduction of a letter from Teitelbaum to Margolis that is included in the latter's *Sefer middot Rashbi* (Meron: 1979).

40. See Yoel Moshe Teitelbaum, *Divrei Yoel,* vol. 1, sec. 88. The discussion here of the question of the elections was afterwards expanded into the main body of Teitelbaum's *Vayoel Moshe,* see the introduction to the Jerusalem edition of 1978, 11; and *Mishmeret ḥomatenu* 11 no. 41 (1959), 323.

41. Rabbi Shlomo Eliezer Alfandari, a halakhic and kabbalistic sage, taught in Turkey, Safed and Jerusalem. Margolis was influenced by him (see *Ashrei haish,* 14, 35, 38 and *'Amudei arazim,* 37, 68); he received Alfandari's imprimatur for his book *Kumi roni* (most of his books were written after Alfandari's death); and he tried to publish some of Alfandari's halakhic responsa (Goldstein, *Mas'ot yerushalayim,* 321). He complained that "strangers have trespassed upon [Alfandari's] patrimony, plundering his holy writings and the treasures of his teachings" (Margolis, *'Amudei arazim,* 53). On Alfandari, see Pinhas Grayevsky, *Miginzei yerushalayim* 19 (1931); Meir Benayahu, introduction to Raphael Bitran, *Middot tovot* (Jerusalem: 1988); and Goldstein, *Maamar ḥayot esh.* See also Y. Nissim (ed.), *Sheelot uteshuvot Maharsha* (Jerusalem: 1932), pt. 1; and D. Y. Weiss (ed.), *Sheelot uteshuvot saba kadisha* (Jerusalem: 1973–1974). On the nature of the Weiss edition, see the above-mentioned introduction by Benayahu to Bitran's *Middot tovot.*

42. Goldstein, *Mas'ot yerushalayim,* 308. See remarks attributed to Alfandari criticizing rabbis who "flatter the wicked" (302) and praising the Munkaczer Rebbe for knowing how to "tell the House of Jacob its iniquities" (313). See also Alfandari's letter concerning the chief rabbinate (308), "Rav Kook, may God preserve and protect him, must disavow the things he has written in his pamphlets, things that are not in accordance with the Torah, for this is the cause of the bitterness against him on the part of the God-fearing, because it is against our holy Torah, as I have shown clearly in a pamphlet especially devoted to this subject." (However harsh his criticism, Alfandari's style is far more moderate than that of Margolis's calumnies). See also Alfandari's responsum concerning prayer in the company of sinners as quoted in Goldstein, *Masot yerushalayim,* "Now, in these latter days, we are not dealing with Jewish transgressors [in general], but with emissaries and witnesses [of the Evil Impulse], and [the latter] seek only to overwhelm the God-fearing, using tokens of purity that make it [appear to be] the will of God." (There can be little doubt that it is the religious Zionists who are the objects of this attack.) This observation is relevant to Yosef Toby's article "Shorshei yaḥasah shel yahadut hamizraḥ el hatenuah haẓiyonit," in *Temurot bahistoriah hayehudit haḥadashah* (Jerusalem: 1988), 169–192, esp. 189–192.

43. Goldstein, *Mas'ot yerushalayim,* 121. The Rebbe's "Jerusalem journeys" of the year 1930 as described in this book revolved around the charismatic personality of Alfandari. It was on the basis of the latter's explicit invitation and blessing that Shapira made the trip, and he described his meeting with Alfandari as the journey's high point (*ibid.,* 20). See also his characterization of Alfandari as the leading saint of his generation (*ibid.,* 24). Hayim Beer has recently portrayed the episode in literary form in *'Et hazamir* (Tel-Aviv: 1987), 200–225.

44. On contemporary Satmarer Hasidism, see Solomon Poll, *The Hasidic Community of Wiliamsburg* (New York: 1962); Rubin, *Satmar;* and Harry Gresh and Sam Miller, "Satmar in Brooklyn: A Zealot Community," *Commentary* 28 (1959), 389–399.

45. For appreciations of Teitelbaum and examples of his influence, see, e.g., R. R. Grozovsky (at one time, the head of the Council of Torah Sages in the United States), *Be'ayot hazeman* (Bnei Brak: 1960), 36; Binyamin Mendelssohn (rabbi of Komemiyut), *Kuntres igrot harav* (Komemiyut: 1973), 42–43; Moshe Scheinfeld, *Niv hamoreh* (Tishrei, 5735 [1975]); *Hashkafatenu* (Bnei Brak: 1978), pt. 1 (no ed. named; unpaginated); and *Kuntres mesit umediaḥ,* published by the Braslaver hasidim (Jerusalem: 1987), 9. See also the eulogy

by Rabbi Eliezer M. Schach in his *Mikhtavim umaamarim* (Bnei Brak: 1980) and eulogies of, and articles about, Teitelbaum in the memorial work, *Sheki'at haḥamah* (New York: 1980). More reserved assessments and outright attacks are even more numerous. See, for instance, the Agudat Israel pamphlet *Lehasir hamasveh* (Jerusalem: 1951). See also S. Z. Abramov, *Perpetual Dilemma* (Rutherford, Madison and Teaneck: 1976), 157.

46. See *Eikhah rabbati*, petiḥta 2 (Solomon Buber ed., 2). As early as the turn of the century, the Jerusalem extremists were referred to tauntingly as "Neturei Karta," see *Haẓevi* 7 (1887); *Haor* 11 (1893); Kaniel, *Hemshekh utemurah*, 192. On the other hand, the Agudat Israel leader Rabbi Elhanan Wasserman also used this talmudic passage to criticize the Zionists: see *Koveẓ maamarim* (Tel-Aviv: 1986), 130. See also the essay on the settlement of Eretz Israel in Teitlebaum, *Vayoel Moshe*, sec. 125.

47. Amram Blau, *Ṭorat rabbi Amram*, ed. Y. L. Frank and Mordechai Weiss (Jerusalem: 1977), 20. See Blau's remarks at the outbreak of the War of Independence (*ibid.*, 17):

> Their defamation and conniving against our holy Torah have placed the whole Jewish population in mortal danger, one percent against ninety-nine, plunging the surviving remnant of the people of Israel in the Holy Land into a war against powerful forces both within and without. . . . We shall not be drawn into exposing ourselves, our wives, and our children to them, heaven forfend, to die for the sake of the Zionist idolatry. It is inconceivable that wicked, unbelieving, ignorant, utterly irresponsible heretics should come along and drag the entire population, several hundred thousand Jews, like sheep to the slaughter, God forbid, because of their false, insane ideas, and that the entire population, like an innocent dove, should allow them to lead it away to be killed, God forbid.

On this question, cf. Y. M. Teitelbaum, *'Al hageulah ve'al hatemurah* (Brooklyn: 1967), 85; *idem, Divrei Yoel,* 87.

48. See Teitelbaum, *Vayoel Moshe,* essay on the midrashic oaths, secs. 10–25, 45, 75–78; *ibid.,* essay on the settlement of Eretz Israel, sec. 109; A. Y. Epstein, "Divrei hesped," in *Sheki'at haḥamah,* 196; Yerahmiel Domb, *Kuntres 'et nisayon* (Jerusalem: 1972), 4–11; *idem, Kuntres 'al hanisim* (Jerusalem: 1957), 44, 52; *idem, Lo niẓaḥon* (London, n.d.), 7–8; *idem, The Transformation: The Case of the Neturei Karta* (London: 1958), 1–14. See Uriel Tal, "Jewish Self-understanding and the Land and the State of Israel," *Union Theological Quarterly* 26, no. 4 (1971), 357.

49. Teitelbaum, *Vayoel Moshe,* essay on the midrashic oaths, sec. 76.

50. Domb, *Kuntres 'et nisayon,* preface.

51. Song of Songs 2:7, 3:5, 8:4.

52. Ketubot 3a.

53. For detailed sources related to the question of the adjurations, see Shmuel Weingarten, *Hishb'ati etkhem* (Jerusalem: 1976); Breuer, "*Erkhei geulah,*" 49–57; Shlomo Aviner, "Beirurim be'inyan 'shelo ya'alu keḥomah'," *No'am* 20 (1980), 4–28; Meir Blumenfeld, "Bidvar hashevu'ah shelo ya'alu keḥomah," in *Shanah beshanah* (Jerusalem: 1974), (no ed. named) 148–153; Menahem M. Kasher, *Hatekufah hagedolah* (Jerusalem: 1969), 150, 174–178, 195–197, 221, 272–281; Ephraim Urbach, *Ḥazal: pirkei emunot vede'ot* (Jerusalem: 1971), 611; Israel Shchipanski, "Geulat miẓrayim, geulat bavel vehageulah ha'atidah," *Or hamizraḥ* 22 (1973), 200–225; Ehud Luz, *Makbilim nifgashim* (Tel-Aviv: 1985), 285–286; Aryeh Morgenstern, *Meshiḥiut veyishuv ereẓ yisrael bamaḥazit harishonah shel hameah hatesh'a 'esreh* (Jerusalem: 1985), 15, 104–107. It is noteworthy that Rabbi Y. J. Reines, the founder of the Mizrachi party, based himself on the adjurations in forbidding military conquest of the land, see his *Or ḥadash 'al ẓiyon* (Vilna: 1902), 19b. See also Israel Hildesheimer, *Gesamelte Aufsätze,* Meir Hildesheimer, ed. (Frankfurt); Issahar Shlomo Teichtal, *Em habanim semeḥah,* 177.

54. Samson Raphael Hirsch, *Ḥorev* (Jerusalem: 1965), par. 608–609; Breuer, "*Erkhei geulah,*" 53.

55. Shlomo Zalman Landa and Yosef Rabinovicz (comps.), *Sefer or layesharim* (Warsaw: 1900), 57. Cf. Avraham Levenstein, *Ẓeror Hamor* (Amsterdam: 1820).

56. Goldstein, *Tikun 'olam,* 4 (Shapira following Rabbi Jonathan Eybeschütz); Margolis, *Kumi roni,* 39–40; *idem, Ashrei haish,* 42.

57. See Urbach, *'Al ẓiyonut veyahadut,* 352; Norman Lamm, "The Ideology of the Neturei Karta According to the Satmer Version," *Tradition* 13 (1971), 39–53.

58. Teitelbaum, *Vayoel Moshe,* essay on the midrashic oaths, sec. 81; cf. sec. 78, "The adjuration not to try to win their own Redemption is much more severe than the adjuration made at the giving of the Torah!" For Maimonides's view, see *ibid.,* secs. 31–36, 78, 80–81. Teitelbaum follows the version of the story given in the Babylonian Talmud, according to which Bar Kokhba was killed by Jewish sages, whereas Maimonides takes the view of the Palestinian Talmud that it was the Romans who killed him (*Vayoel Moshe,* essay on the midrashic oaths, secs. 39, 52). See also Aviezer Ravitzky "'Kefi koaḥ haadam': yemot hamashiaḥ bemishnat haRambam," in *Meshiḥiyut veeskhatologiah,* ed. Zvi Baras (Jerusalem: 1983), 209.

59. Zvi Yehudah Kook, *Lehilkhot ẓibur* (Jerusalem: 1987), 133, 140.

60. Teitelbaum, *Vayoel Moshe,* essay on the midrashic oaths, sec. 81. Teitelbaum bases his argument here on Rabbi Yehudah Loew (the Maharal) of Prague. See also Rabbi Kasher's critique in *Hatekufah hagedolah,* 272–281. Cf. Rivka Shatz, "Torat haMaharal bein eksistenẓiah leeskhatologiah," in Baras, *Meshiḥiyut veeskhatologiah,* 305; Otto Dov Kulka, "Harek'a hahistori shel mishnato haleumit shel hamaharal miprag," *Ẓiyon* 50 (1985), 282.

61. Teitelbaum, *Vayoel Moshe,* preface (6).

62. *Ibid.,* sec. 139; cf. preface (6).

63. Irving Greenberg, "Cloud of Smoke, Pillar of Fire," in *Auschwitz: Beginning of a New Era?* (New York: 1977), 7–55; *idem,* "The Third Great Cycle of Jewish History," in *Perspectives* (1981), 40–42; *idem,* "Voluntary Covenant?" in *ibid.* (1984), 1–36. Cf. Andre Neher, *The Exile of the World* (Philadelphia: 1981).

64. Among recent publications, see Emil Fackenheim, *To Mend the World* (New York: 1982), 10; and *idem,* "Holocaust," in *Contemporary Jewish Religious Thought,* ed. Arthur A. Cohen and Paul Mendes-Flohr (New York: 1987), 399–408. Cf. Michael Wyschogrod, "Faith and the Holocaust," *Judaism* 20 3(1971), 286–294; and Jacob Neusner, *Stranger at Home* (Chicago: 1981), 65–81.

65. Teitelbaum, *Vayoel Moshe,* preface (5–7).

66. As early as 1940, the Neturei Karta published a proclamation pinning responsibility for the Nazi persecution of the Jews on Zionism. Such accusations multiplied after the Holocaust. "Everything is to be blamed," wrote one polemicist, "on the heretical, rebellious, seductive and corrupting Zionist leadership, which held sway over the congregation of Israel and [induced it] to rebel against the [true] King, the King of the Universe, and His rule over the Holy Land and the holy city of Jerusalem" (*Haḥomah,* Shevat 5706 [1946]). The adjurations were also invoked in this context as early as the 1940s, e.g., see Amram Blau, "'Al elil haleumiyut," in *Om ani ḥomah* (Jerusalem: 1949), 50–52; and Yizhak Ashkenazi, "'Al timredu baumot," in *ibid.,* 164.

67. See Amos Funkenstein, "Hapasiviyut kesimanah shel yahadut hagolah: mitos umeẓiyut," Zalman Aranne Lecture, Tel-Aviv University, 1982, 3–11.

68. There were rabbis sympathetic to Zionism who interpreted; the text to opposite effect: the Adjurations, they said, are interrelated; now that the gentiles have violated theirs, we are exempt from ours. Thus Yitzhak Herzog, "Hakamat medinah kodem biat hamashiaḥ," in *Sefer haẓiyonut hadatit,* ed. Yitzhak Raphael (Jerusalem: 1977), 62; Kasher, *Hatekufah hagedolah,* 176, 194; Aviner, "Beirurim," 16–17 (plus citations of classical prooftexts); Lamm, "Ideology," 42. Rabbi Yisrael of Shklov expressed a similar viewpoint earlier on: see Avraham Ya'ari, *Igrot ereẓ yisrael* (Tel-Aviv: 1943), 352; Morgenstern, *Meshiḥiyut,* 32; *idem,* "Nisyono shel rabbi Yisrael mishklov leḥadesh et hasemikhah," in *Yovel sinai* (Jerusalem: 1987), n. 36. In this view, the Diaspora survives because of a balance between Jewish passivity and the restraint of the gentiles, despite their subjugation of the Jews. Another argument has it that it is the gentiles' consent in recent times (Balfour, the United Nations) that has relieved the Jews of the fear of violating their oath not to rebel

against alien rule. See also the critique of Teitelbaum in Avraham Weiss, *Hamahaneh haharedi* (organ of the Belzer hasidim), 4 Elul 5748 (1988), 393, among others.

69. *Lehasir masveh* (publication of the Neturei Karta [Jerusalem: 1950]), 3.

70. See Elyakim Schlezinger, "Hesped," in *Sheki'at hahamah*, 171. Cf. Epstein in *ibid.*, 196; Teitelbaum, *Divrei Yoel*, vol. 1, secs. 68, 78, 89; A. Blau, *Torat rabbi 'Amram*, sec. 6; A. Z. Partigol (the Skolener Rebbe), open letter to the Council of Torah Sages, in *Shim'u devar Hashem*, published in *Hakol kol Ya'akov*, 30–34.

71. As explained earlier, such spiritual forebears of today's radicals as Hayim Elazar Shapira were already battling the Agudists of their own day. But it is not surprising that present-day radicals should place emphasis on the recent deviation of Agudat Israel from the teachings of its own forebears.

72. Eliyahu Porush, "Ha'ez vehabarzel bimedinat hazedukim," in A. Blau, *Torat rabbi 'Amram*, sec. 26.

73. A. Blau, *Torat rabbi 'Amram*, sec. 6.

74. Domb, *Hahomah* 25 (1975), 94–95.

75. Domb, *'Et nisayon*, 4. See also the supplement to *Mishmeret homatenu* (Jerusalem: 1966).

76. Teitelbaum, *Vayoel moshe*, preface, vii.

77. *Ibid.*, xiii.

78. *Ibid.*, essay on the midrashic oaths, secs. 77, 85. See the declaration of Hitahdut Harabanim Dearzot Habrit Vekanadah (an organization of Satmarer rabbis) in *Shim'u devar Hashem*, published in *Hakol kol Ya'akov*, 37. A similar position had been taken earlier (1948) in a Neturei Karta handbill entitled "Lifkoah 'einayim."

79. *Lehasir masveh*, 12; Domb, *'Et nisayon*, 142.

80. Domb, *The Transformation*, 288.

81. S. I. Posen, *Torat Elokim* (Brooklyn: 1966) vol. 1, letter 19. On Posen, see Abraham Fuchs, *Yeshivot hungariah bigedulatan uvehurbanan* (Jerusalem: 1987), 183–187.

82. *Lehasir masveh*, 12; Domb, *'Al hanissim*, 49.

83. Teitelbaum, *Divrei Yoel* vol. 1, sec. 79.

84. Y. B. Holzer, *Yelamed da'at* (New York: 1988), 500; a proclamation by a group of rabbis, in the volume *Milhamot Hashem* (Brooklyn: 1983), 110; Blau, *Torat rabbi 'Amram*, sec. 3.

85. Holzer, *Yelamed da'at*, 15. The book in its entirety is a polemic against the Lubavitcher Hasidic movement and its efforts to attract people to religion.

86. Eulogy of the Satmarer Rebbe, published by Yeshivat Torah Veyirah, 1979; in *Sheki'at hahamah*, 194.

87. Job 21:7; Jer. 12:1.

88. Leon Festinger, *A Theory of Cognitive Dissonance* (Stanford: 1957); Leon Festinger, Henry W. Riecken and Stanley Schachter, *When Prophecy Fails* (Minneapolis, 1956).

89. See Hayim Katznellbogen in *Sheki'at hahamah*, 161.

90. Teitelbaum, *'Al hageulah*, 7–9. See remarks by Richard Niebuhr on people who could have been expected to be "terribly unsure" but turned out, in fact, to be "doubly sure," in Willard B. Gatewood, *Controversy in the Twenties: Fundamentalism, Modernism, Evolution* (Nashville: 1969), 46. See Janet O'Dea, "Gush Emunim: Roots and Ambiguities," *Forum* 23 (1975), 47.

91. Teitelbaum, *'Al hageulah*, 20.

92. Blau, *Torat rabbi 'Amram*, preface.

93. Emanuel Sivan, *Kanaei haislam* (Tel-Aviv: 1986), 92–124.

94. Domb, *'Al hanissim*, 51–52.

95. Domb, *Lo nizahon*, 12; idem, *Kuntres 'et nisayon*, 254; I. M. Dushinsky, *Der Yid* (1980), issue for the portion "Emor."

96. Teitelbaum, *Hiddushei torah* (Brooklyn: 1960), chapter on the portion "Vayishlah," mentioned in the pamphlet *Dibrot kodesh*, included in the volume *Hakol kol Ya'akov*, 14; idem, *Vayoel Moshe*, essay on the midrashic oaths, secs. 158, 175; Domb, *The Transformation*, 68, 115, 120.

97. Teitelbaum, *'Al hageulah,* 133. For extreme deterministic formulations, see Domb, *The Transformation,* 142, 148, 126 (to be found in Aviezer Ravitzky, "Haẓafui vehareshut hanetunah," in *Yisrael likrat hameah ha'esrim veaḥat,* [Jerusalem: 1984], 140).

98. A handbill published by the rabbinic court of the Edah Haredit, chaired by Rabbi Yitzhak Yaakov Weiss, on the eve of Independence Day, 1980, states, "Dread the day of judgment and the day of reproof, for bitter and grievous will be the upshot of this great breach of faith and this rebellion against the rule of Heaven, God forbid."

99. *Der Yid* 9 (1984); issue for the portion "Behar" cited in a lecture by Menahem Friedman at The Hebrew University, 1987. See also his remarks in an interview by N. Golan in *Haẓofeh,* 26 Tishrei 5749 (1989).

100. Teitelbaum, *Vayoel Moshe,* sec. 8.

101. Teitelbaum, *'Al hageulah,* 13.

A Neglected Chapter in the History of Christian Zionism in America: William E. Blackstone and the Petition of 1916

Yaakov Ariel
(THE HEBREW UNIVERSITY)

In the last two decades, the evidence of American Christian evangelical support of Israel has become increasingly noticeable. Evangelicals have taken up the Israeli cause, as they see it, and have been numbered among the most vociferous champions of Israel in America. Leading evangelists in the United States have promoted in both their sermons and writings the idea that Israel fulfills a role and purpose in God's plans for the End of Days.

The support of Zionism on the basis of messianic expectations has a long history in American Christianity. Even before the rise of political Zionism, there were American Protestants who promoted in words and deeds the idea that a Jewish state should be established in Palestine. With the emergence of the Zionist movement in America, Christian protagonists of Jewish restoration extended their help and support.

An outstanding example was William E. Blackstone, who in 1916 organized a "memorial" addressed to President Wilson that urged him to convene an international conference that would call for the granting of Palestine to the Jews. In addition to the petition, Blackstone secured the endorsement of major Protestant churches for his plan. The petition was initiated in collaboration with Zionist leaders in America, who were working to secure Wilson's support for the Zionist cause and, more specifically, for the type of concrete measures that would soon be endorsed by the Balfour Declaration.

Blackstone's initiative is a neglected chapter in this history of both American Zionism and American Christian support for Jewish restoration.

WILLIAM E. BLACKSTONE AND PREMILLENNIAL DISPENSATIONALISM

William Eugene Blackstone was born in Adams, New York, on October 6, 1841.[1] His father was a tinsmith, and Blackstone described his origins as humble. His parents, Andrew and Sally Blackstone, were members of the local Methodist church, and their son was to remain a Methodist all his life. Although Blackstone never received any official training as a minister, he played an active part in church life, serving as a lay Bible teacher, a preacher and the superintendent of a Sunday school.

Blackstone never attended a college or a seminary, nor was he an intellectual or an academician. Nevertheless, he wrote, published and edited extensively, and he corresponded widely with prominent public figures, all in a style that would not have embarrassed someone with academic credentials. In his writings, Blackstone proved himself to have a thorough knowledge of the Scriptures. His reading (when he found time for it) covered many areas of interest.[2]

During the Civil War, Blackstone volunteered to serve in the Union army in the Christian Commission (an organization similar to the YMCA or the Red Cross), and he was assigned to General Grant's headquarters.

In 1866, Blackstone married Sarah Louise Smith. The Blackstones led a happy family life, making their home first in Rockford, Illinois, where Blackstone sold agricultural insurance, and from 1870 in Chicago, then very much the boom city. There, Blackstone engaged in building and property investments and proved to be a successful businessman. It was during his years in Chicago that he adopted his premillennialist-dispensationalist beliefs.

Premillennialism, the belief in the imminent return of Jesus and in the establishment of his reign on earth for a thousand years, was a common tenet of faith in the early stages of Christianity. However, in the fifth century, Western Christianity became mostly amillennial in its outlook, and biblical passages with eschatological overtones have usually been interpreted since then in symbolic terms. Nevertheless, nonconformist messianic movements emerged throughout the Middle Ages; and the Reformation, in the sixteenth century, was accompanied by a strong wave of eschatological expectations, particularly among some of the more radical sects. Some of these groups anticipated the return of the Jews to the Holy Land and the rejuvenation of Israel in the imminent messianic era.[3]

The English civil war of the seventeenth century took place in the context of a new wave of premillennialist expectations. Messianic hopes that stressed the role and place of the Jewish people in the events of the End of Time may have influenced English government policy toward the readmission of Jews. Certainly, such views were at least partially effective in counteracting negative public sentiment on the issue.[4]

In the early nineteenth century, there was a dramatic rise in messianic expectations among Protestants, especially in the English-speaking world. It became not uncommon to interpret the French Revolution and the Napoleonic Wars as a sign that an era was ending and that the predicted eschatological events had begun.[5]

The new premillennialist ferment brought about a renewed interest in the Jews in evangelical circles, specifically in the prospect of their national restoration and eventual conversion.[6] Messianic aspirations influenced, among other things, the discussion on Jewish liberties in Britain. And in 1840, at the urging of Lord Ashley Cooper (later Seventh Earl of Shaftesbury, leader of the evangelical party in Britain and an ardent premillennialist), Lord Palmerston (the British foreign secretary) ordered his ambassador in Constantinople to support the idea of large-scale Jewish settlement in Palestine. The geostrategic reasoning that accompanied this suggestion was that a Jewish Palestine would act as a buffer against the threat of a possible Egyptian invasion.[7]

It was in this atmosphere of intensified eschatological expectations in Britain that dispensationalism, a new school of belief in the Second Coming of Jesus, was born. Dispensationalism is not only an eschatological belief, but also a system of biblical hermeneutics and a philosophy of history. It was crystallized in the 1830s by John Nelson Darby (1800–1882) and the group he led, the Plymouth Brethren. Dispensationalists assert that human history is divided into a few ages or eras. The last age is the millennium, the thousand-year reign of Christ on earth, and the present era is believed to be the one before the last. God's plan for humanity in each successive age can be reconstructed from the biblical text.[8] As against the traditional claim of Christianity to be the new Israel, the Plymouth Brethren recognized the Jewish people to be both the historical Israel and the object of the biblical prophecies foretelling a restored Davidic kingdom in the messianic age. This belief thus assigned to the Jews a crucial role in the events of the End of Time.

Darby advocated a theory that has served as an ideological cornerstone for dispensationalists ever since: that the true Church of Christ has nothing to do with the actual and official Church establishment. It is defined, instead, as the body of true believers and is composed of persons who have undergone a genuine inner religious experience that enables them to live saintly lives. They alone will be saved at the time of final judgment and enjoy eternal life.

Although Darby and the Plymouth Brethren gathered followers in Britain, dispensationalism never became a mass movement there as it was later to become in the United States. The dispensationalist conviction started to spread in America in the 1860s, gaining support among members of major Protestant denominations: Presbyterians, Methodists, Congregationalists and Baptists.

Blackstone was among the early converts to the new messianic hope in the United States. His social circle, in general, was exposed to dispensationalism, and some of his close friends shared his convictions. He became associated with some of the leading protagonists of dispensationalism in America, such as Dwight L. Moody (1837–1899) and James H. Brookes (1830–1897), and he himself soon began to propagate his new belief. He lectured on the subject in churches and YMCA clubs; on his business travels, he tried to convince people he met of the imminence of Christ's return. In 1878, Blackstone decided to end his business activities altogether and to devote himself completely to his evangelical campaign. He explained this move in terms of a religious-mystical experience in which he responded to God's call.

In the years that followed, Blackstone published a series of books and pamphlets to help promote the premillennialist belief,[9] the most important being *Jesus Is Coming,* first published in 1878. It was translated over the years into forty-two languages, including Yiddish and Hebrew. By the 1920s, it had a circulation of more than six hundred thousand copies.

THE PLACE OF THE JEWISH PEOPLE AND OF ZIONISM IN BLACKSTONE'S ESCHATOLOGICAL UNDERSTANDING

Blackstone, as did all dispensationalists, considered the Jewish people to be both the true heirs of biblical Israel and the object of the prophecies that predicted the restoration of the Jews to the land of Israel.[10] The literal hermeneutics applied to the Bible by the dispensationalists resulted in the abandonment of the traditional claim by the Church to be the true Israel and in the recognition of the Jewish nation as still destined to play a central role in history.

Blackstone considered the Jewish refusal to accept Jesus as the Messiah to have been a tragic mistake, one that had devastating effects on their fate ever since.[11] It had, he wrote, "cost them centuries of sorrow."[12] Blackstone refers to the Jewish maltreatment of Jesus as well as to his crucifixion, suggesting that it was because the Jews had denied Jesus that his first appearance had not brought with it the establishment of the awaited kingdom.[13] Nevertheless, although the Jewish people had been scattered among the nations, he argued, they had not been abandoned by God.[14] In the current, sixth dispensation, "the Christian era" or "the times of the Gentiles," the Jewish people had played a passive role overshadowed by that of the Church.[15] The current age, however, was but a "parenthesis" in the progress of the ages. And in the very last stage of this era, the Jews had again resumed a major role in history, as demonstrated by the Jewish national revival and the new Jewish settlements in Palestine.[16]

In Blackstone's view, the millennial kingdom would be preceded by a period of seven years, which he termed "the Great Tribulation." The bodies of believers in Christ would be "raptured" from earth, that is, they would meet Jesus in the air and remain with him there until his descent to earth. Once this had occurred, Israel, the Jewish nation, would undergo a period of turmoil: the time of Jacob's trouble.[17] The Jews would return to the Holy Land in "unbelief " and would establish a state, but this would not yet be the desired kingdom. Except for a minority persecuted by their own brethren, the Jews would not accept Christ and would let themselves be ruled by Antichrist,[18] "Then the Lord shall come with His saints down to the earth and destroy this lawless Antichrist, deliver Israel, who will then look upon 'Him they have pierced. . . .' He will judge the living nations and establish His millennial kingdom."[19]

In the last dispensation, the millennium, the Jewish nation, or more precisely, that part of the Jewish nation (about one-third) that would survive the tribulation, would assume its place as the leading nation on earth, led by the son of David, Jesus the Messiah.

Blackstone occasionally published articles on Jewish religious themes in the *Jewish Era,* a magazine published by the Chicago Hebrew Mission. One finds in these articles a reflection of some of the ambivalence in Blackstone's attitude toward Judaism.[20] On the one hand, he believed that Judaism did not offer salvation and its adherents were doomed. Only in Christianity could Jews find true spiritual refuge and meaning. On the other hand, Jewish tradition—the beliefs, laws and rites of the Jewish people—had kept them waiting for the Messiah and for the reestablishment of their ancient national home in Palestine. Thus, they were willing to fulfill the role intended for them in God's plan for human history.

By the same token, Blackstone reacted negatively to Reform Judaism as well as to liberal or assimilated Jews in general. The major problem with Reform or liberal (non-Zionist) Jews, so it seemed to Blackstone, was that they had turned their backs on their role and duty regarding the divine plan for the End of Days. They refused to participate in the Jewish national restoration, which was to serve as a means and preparation for the great events to come.[21] As these groups of Jews were resistant to dispensationalist missionary efforts and would not accept Christ, they could be saved neither as Christians nor as Jews in the land of Israel who would eventually accept Jesus in the course of the Great Tribulation. They would perish. Blackstone considered evangelical Protestant Christianity to be the only religious belief that offered salvation to its believers. Atheists, heathens and non-Christians in general, as well as non-Protestant Christians or deviant Protestant groups such as the Seventh Day Adventists or the Mormons, were doomed to perish.[22] Orthodox and Zionist Jews were a partial exception to this rule because of their special function in the advancement of the millennial kingdom.

Blackstone was a central figure in the field of missionary work among the Jews in America, and it was on his initiative that the Chicago Hebrew Mission was founded in 1887. Among other concerns, Blackstone, with other dispensationlist missionaries, sought to save individual Jews from the fate that was awaiting them at "the time of Jacob's trouble."

Although Blackstone was a confirmed supporter of the Zionist cause (and in 1916–1917 worked closely with the Zionist leadership in America), his theoretical approach toward the Zionist movement was ambivalent. On the one hand, Blackstone rejoiced over the activity of the Zionist movement and the Jewish resettlement in Palestine. They were "signs of the time" that indicated the imminent coming of Christ. They were a proof that the end was at hand. Blackstone referred to these signs time and again in his many articles and tracts.[23] On the other hand, he perceived Zionism as no more than a tool, a means, for the fulfillment of the divine plan for the End of Days. When discussing the Zionist movement and its achievements, he was careful to note that it could by no means fulfill God's plan for humanity, that it was only a step in the process of the advancement of the ages. The Zionist movement, he observed, was a secular movement that did not understand itself as a realization of biblical prophecy but rather sought to find a home and refuge for the Jewish nation.[24] This, however, it could not really achieve. A true home and refuge for the Jews, he insisted, could be established only when they accepted their true Messiah, Jesus Christ, as their savior.[25] The "Jewish problem" was, thus, not a matter of refuge and national survival, but a religious issue.

Blackstone believed that the United States had a special task to carry out in God's plan for humanity. God had assigned to America the role of a modern Cyrus—to assist in the Jewish restoration of Palestine. God, he believed, would judge America, among other things, according to the way it carried out that assignment.[26] He developed this belief gradually; it assumed its final shape during the First World War, which Blackstone considered to be the beginning of the end of the age.[27]

The belief in the particular role assigned to the United States in helping prepare the stage for the arrival of Jesus was Blackstone's innovation and contribution to dispensationalist eschatological belief in America. It became part of premillennialist conviction in America, and it serves as the background for much of the support American fundamentalists have offered the Zionist cause.

THE PETITION OF 1891

In 1891, Blackstone organized a petition to U.S. President Benjamin Harrison. In it, Harrison was requested to take steps to obtain international consent for the restoration of Palestine to the Jews. The petition was signed by 413 eminent Americans: mayors, governors, congressmen, clergymen, judges, journalists, editors and publishers of leading newspapers and prominent businessmen.[28]

Blackstone based his 1891 appeal on the unfortunate condition of the Jews in Russia, who lived under severe legal restrictions and had recently been subjected to harassment and mob violence. Although he undoubtedly cared for the fate of the Jews around the world, Blackstone was motivated, first and foremost, by his premillennialist hopes. Most of those who signed the petition, however, were not premillennialists, and it was Blackstone's humanitarian call to solve the problem of the Russian Jews that elicited such a broad-based response. "A million of exiles, by their terrible suffering, are piteously appealing to our sympathy, justice and humanity," declared the petition (see Appendix 1).[29]

Blackstone's call to solve the humanitarian problem of Russian Jews by awarding them Palestine was couched in political, legal and economic arguments. On the political and legal level, he pointed out that his scheme had precedents, for new national states had been created in Europe with international consent and help in the nineteenth century. If the Congress of Berlin (1878) could decide in favor of the establishment of a Bulgarian state in what had been Turkish territory, the same could be done for a Jewish state in Palestine. As for the economics involved, Blackstone argued, world Jewry would help finance both the settlement of "their suffering brethren in their time-honored habitation" and compensate Turkey for "whatever vested rights by possession" it had in Palestine.

Although he based his plan for the restoration of Palestine to the Jews in large part on such rational and mundane factors, and although the petition contained no reference to premillennialist hopes, it nevertheless reflected a strong religious-biblical reasoning. The Jewish claim to Palestine, it asserted, was based on "God's distribution of nations." Blackstone saw it as the duty of "the Christian nations of Europe to show kindness to Israel." The Christian, biblical appeal of the petition, which was endorsed by so many notable Americans, reflected, among other things, the strength of the Bible as a factor in the thinking of Protestant America.

The 1891 petition was an impressive document that stirred a great deal of public interest at the time. However, the U.S. government did not then take up the cause of Jewish restoration to Palestine, and Blackstone's initiative soon faded into obscurity.

Blackstone, however, was not discouraged. He continued trying both to persuade the American government to reconsider, and also to promote his ideas among

American Protestants. In 1903, through his efforts, the Methodist Ministers' Meeting in Chicago issued a resolution that called upon the American government to accept his plan.

THE 1916 PETITION

In 1916, Blackstone organized the presentation to President Woodrow Wilson of a new petition concerning the restoration of the Jews to Zion. This petition was probably more significant than the earlier one because it seems to have had a greater impact. Whereas the petition of 1891 was Blackstone's own initiative, he coordinated his efforts in 1916 with the leaders of the Zionist movement in America.[30] In the twenty-five years that had passed between the first petition and the second, great changes had taken place in American Zionism. It had developed from an insignificant group of a few dozen proto-Zionists who had little standing in American Jewish public life into an organization that included many thousands of members, and it had won the ardent loyalty of some of the most outstanding personalities in American Jewry. Among its members was Louis D. Brandeis, who of all President Wilson's Jewish associates was closest to him and enjoyed his esteem. Brandeis was chairman of the Provisional Executive Committee for General Zionist Affairs[31] until July 21, 1916, when he became a Supreme Court justice. He continued to serve even then as the honorary president of the Provisional Executive Committee and remained its actual leader.

American Zionist leaders took an interest in, and responded favorably to, Blackstone's pro-Zionist activity. Nathan Straus (the owner of R.H. Macy and an active Zionist), Stephen Wise (the prominent New York rabbi and Brandeis's successor as chairman of the Provisional Executive Committee for General Zionist Affairs), Jacob de Haas (secretary of that committee) and Brandeis himself believed Blackstone's work to be of benefit to the Zionist cause. In 1916–1917, the American Zionist leaders were engaged in efforts to persuade the American government to support the Zionist cause, and they were eager to win Christian backing. They thus approached Blackstone with the idea of undertaking a new appeal similar to that submitted to President Harrison in 1891.[32] In their letters to Blackstone, Straus and Brandeis urged him to concentrate on collecting Christian signatures for this petition.[33]

The Zionist leaders were aware of Blackstone's premillennialist thinking from his books and pamphlets.[34] In his letters to them, he often discussed his religious convictions and his eschatological understanding of the role and fate of the Jewish people.[35] He even sent to Zionist leaders premillennialist material that was to be kept in a safe place and opened when the "rapture" took place.[36] His forecast that great turmoil awaited Israel in the wake of that event and that only a part of the Jewish people would survive the Great Tribulation was thus no secret. At a Zionist conference held in Los Angeles in January 1918, Blackstone explicitly stated his belief that those Jews who did not convert to Christianity or did not emigrate to Palestine were doomed to perish.[37]

Zionists dismissed Blackstone's doctrine but were nonetheless prepared to work with him, perhaps without realizing the scope of his involvement in actual missionary work among the Jews. That premillennialist hopes motivated much of the missionary work aimed at Jews was a fact they could hardly know in all its detail. They, after all, were no experts on the Christian missions to the Jews. In addition, it should be noted that, although Jews were irritated by evangelizing attempts, they believed for the most part that very few Jews converted to Christianity out of conviction. Jews had developed a cynical attitude toward conversions to Christianity, the general notion being that they were caused by financial or social considerations rather than religious persuasion.[38]

The Zionist leaders treated Blackstone as a desired and honored friend. He was invited to participate and speak at Zionist conferences.[39] Some Zionists, such as Nathan Straus, conducted a personal, albeit formal, correspondence with him, sending him holiday greetings and expressing concern when he was ill.[40]

Beyond that, however, the relationship between Blackstone and this group of Zionist leaders may be characterized as one of mutual trust. Stephen Wise, for example, confided to him his bitterness toward his rival, Judah Magnes.[41] Blackstone was entrusted with discreet duties as well;[42] he, in turn, assigned to Brandeis the execution of his will, leaving his estate to the Zionist movement.[43] Blackstone also donated $5,000 out of his own pocket to the emergency fund that was organized by the Provisional Executive Committee in order to help Jewish refugees and victims of the First World War in Eastern Europe and Palestine.[44] His gesture was almost unique among American dispensationalists of that period, who as a rule did not contribute money to Zionist efforts.

The 1916 petition differed in substance from that of 1891. The basic idea—that the government of the United States should initiate an international conference that would decide on the establishment in Palestine of a national home for the Jews— recurred in both documents. However, whereas the petition of 1891 took its point of departure from the plight of Russian Jewry, that of 1916 proceeded from the general proposition that the "civilized world seeks some feasible method of relieving the persecuted Jews" (see Appendix 2). The issue of Jewish emigration from Russia was not mentioned in the new petition. Between 1891 and 1916, almost two million Jewish immigrants from Eastern Europe had entered the United States. The return of Palestine to the Jews was not perceived at this stage as having so urgent a connection with the redirection of the massive Jewish emigration wave. Precedents for the creation of national states on former Turkish territory were also omitted. Instead, Blackstone hinted at his understanding that the First World War would serve as a significant step in the advancement of the ages.[45]

Blackstone, who was seventy-five in 1916, set out on a less ambitious task than in 1891, collecting only eighty-two signatures for the new petition. Its list of signatories, as before, included, among others, newspaper editors, bishops and bank presidents, though the collection of prominent names was much less impressive than that of the 1891 petition. An examination of the signatures reveals that Blackstone limited his efforts to four cities: Los Angeles, Chicago, New York and Ithaca, N.Y. He did not make a great effort to collect signatures and was not concerned this time with quantity. That the idea of the restoration of Palestine to the Jews enjoyed strong support from the American public had already been proven as far as he was concerned.[46]

More impressive than the actual signatures on the 1916 petition was the fact that it was officially endorsed by major Protestant organizations and presented to President Wilson by these church bodies as a proposal for solving the problem of Jewish suffering. On May 26, 1916, the General Assembly of the Presbyterian Church, U.S.A., adopted Blackstone's petition as its own resolution[47] and, as such, presented it to President Wilson, who accepted it "in a very kindly manner."[48] A series of ministers' meetings in Los Angeles, then Blackstone's hometown, also endorsed and adopted his petition, as did the Methodist Ministers' Meeting of Southern California on May 1, 1916;[49] the Presbyterian Ministerial Association of Los Angeles on May 8, 1916;[50] and the Los Angeles Baptist Ministers' Conference on May 1, 1916.[51] Blackstone was in close contact with the leaders of these major Protestant denominations, and the endorsements were to a large degree a result of his persuasion. An illustration of Blackstone's connections and influence with leaders of mainstream Protestant denominations is the fact that he organized a formal committee made up of distinguished Protestant churchmen to present the petition to President Wilson. The members of the committee were: Bishop J. W. Bashford of the Methodist Church; Dr. F. M. North, president of the Federal Council of Churches of Christ in America; Dr. Robert E. Speer, secretary of the Presbyterian Board of Foreign Missions; and Dr. John R. Mott, general secretary of the International Committee of YMCAs. (Dr. Mott received a Nobel Prize for Peace in 1946 for a lifetime's activity in the cause of Christian unity.) When Blackstone realized that he himself might not be able to participate in the presentation of the petition to the president, he authorized these church leaders to do so without him.[52] Bishop Bashford, in particular, identified himself with Blackstone's cause and was his confidant concerning the 1916 petition.[53]

Blackstone likewise negotiated for the support of the Federal Council of the Churches of Christ in America. (Many Protestant denominations in America participated in the Federal Council at the time, including some that did not endorse Blackstone's petition, among them the Lutheran General Synod, the Disciples of Christ and the Mennonite Church.) Blackstone's request, which was brought up in November 1916, was turned down by the Advisory Council of the Churches of Christ in America.[54] Although many of the church leaders who supported Blackstone were not dispensationalists, it seems that Blackstone's initiative found more willing and approving audiences among members of denominations that were, in general, part of the Reform tradition and had been influenced powerfully by nineteenth-century American revivalism, as was the case with Methodists, Presbyterians and Baptists.

Blackstone's connections with leaders of mainstream Protestantism in America and his ability to bring many of them and their churches to support the idea of the Jewish restoration of Palestine manifests one difference between the American Protestantism of then and that of today. Although the modernist–conservative debate had already emerged, the borderline between liberal and evangelical Protestantism was not yet fully defined early in the century. Blackstone was able to establish good connections with the leadership of the established Protestant churches in order to make them work for his cause. He had access to the heart of Protestant America and American culture in general. After the modernist–conservative debate reached its dramatic climax in the mid-1920s with the Scopes trial, evangelical Protestantism ceased to be an integral part of the mainstream of American culture, and it is doubtful if thereafter an evangelical activist could ever have mobilized liberal denominations to act to such an extent on behalf of his eschatological hopes.

Blackstone was ready to have his petition presented to President Wilson by October 1916,[55] but the Zionist leadership kept him from doing so, claiming that the time was not ripe for a public presentation and that it should be formally delivered to Wilson when he could give it his full attention.[56]

President Wilson not only knew about the petition, but saw it informally a few times. Blackstone sent him a copy of it for unofficial consideration. Wise had shown it to him twice "unofficially."[57] Wilson also received the petition with the endorsement of the three conferences of ministers in California and of the General Assembly of the Presbyterian Church in the U.S.A. The official presentation of the petition, however, was constantly delayed, and it never actually took place.[58] Blackstone was willing to leave the matter of the public presentation of the petition to the Zionist leadership, claiming that he had "no personal ambition nor desires in reference to [it]" and that his only concern was that "it may accomplish the best results for the Jewish people in all the world."[59]

It seems that Wilson was hesitant to accept Blackstone's petition publicly,[60] but he did treat it seriously. He suggested changes that he thought should be made in it.[61] Moreover, if he had considered it an unimportant, eccentric document, he could easily have given his consent to its presentation. The president of the United States was used to accepting petitions on various matters, including many he cared little about. Harrison had accepted Blackstone's petition solemnly in March 1891, although he had no intention of carrying out its suggestions. One should note that the United States was not then in a state of war with Turkey and an official, ceremonious acceptance of a public demand to deprive the Turkish Empire of part of its territory probably seemed undesirable to Wilson.[62] It was, it seems, at this time (1916–1917) that he developed a favorable attitude toward the Zionist movement and the idea of a Jewish national home in Palestine, but he did not publicly state his support of Zionism until September 1918. His pro-Zionist sentiments were kept hidden from his secretary of state, Robert H. Lansing, and from the State Department (and the American public), who knew little about Wilson's attitude and his consent to the Balfour Declaration.[63] It might be that his hesitation to accept the petition officially was due to his unwillingness to make his position public.

Although the petition was never formally presented, it nonetheless achieved its goal. It was intended, as far as the Zionist leadership was concerned, to show President Wilson that Protestant America favored the idea of the Jewish restoration to Palestine. Endorsed as it was by the Presbyterian Church and other church bodies, it served this purpose well. By the summer of 1917, the Zionist leaders were convinced of Wilson's support for their cause and saw no need to embarrass him by publicly presenting the petition.[64]

What exact effect the petition had on Wilson is almost impossible to determine.

The president left no clue as to what part it played in his decision to support the Zionist cause. Historians who have written about Wilson's role in the origins of the Balfour Declaration were not even aware of Blackstone's petition and the endorsement it received from Protestant bodies.[65]

Wilson was not a premillennialist,[66] and the eschatological reasoning Blackstone expressed in his private dispatches would hardly have impressed him. He was, however, a committed Protestant, the son of a Presbyterian minister, who had grown up in an evangelical atmosphere. Daily reading of the Bible was part of his routine. The Presbyterian Church that endorsed Blackstone's proposal was his own church. Wilson revealed his Christian feelings concerning the Jewish homeland in Palestine twice, though not in public. In a private talk with Rabbi Stephen Wise in June 1917, he remarked, "To think that I, the son of a manse, should be able to restore the Holy Land to its people."[67] In February 1920, when the issue of the borders of Palestine was discussed in Paris, a concerned Brandeis wrote to Wilson that it would be a betrayal of the promise of "Christendom" regarding a national Jewish home in Palestine if a decision was reached in favor of shrunken borders for Palestine. Wilson was moved and ordered Secretary of State Lansing to direct the American representatives in Paris to do their utmost to meet Brandeis's request.[68] However, if religious sentiment helped to shape Wilson's favorable attitude toward Zionism, he was careful not to reveal the fact publicly.

Not all the voices of Protestant America favored a national Jewish home in Palestine. A pro-Arab Protestant lobby was organized in 1919 and was active at the Peace Conference in Paris. It consisted of missionaries associated with the Syrian Protestant College in Beirut[69] who were committed to Arab nationalism and favored the idea of an Arab state in "Greater Syria," including Palestine.[70] In their view, the idea of a Jewish home in Palestine posed a threat to the Arab national hope and, perhaps, to their own interests in the Middle East as well. The pro-Arab Protestant group was one of the strongest and most energetic groups lobbying in Paris about the Palestine issue. One of its influential members was Cleveland H. Dodge, a close associate of Wilson who had backed him financially in his election campaign.[71]

Blackstone took no steps to create a lobby to counterbalance the pro-Arab one. He continued to write to Wilson and share his opinions with him. However, he regarded the fulfillment of the Balfour Declaration and the establishment of a Jewish home in Palestine as a fait accompli and did not see any need to fight on its behalf.[72] In addition, it should be noted that an examination of Blackstone's tactics reveals that they never included an attempt to establish a permanent lobby. In 1891, once the petition had been presented, his initiative had faded away; in 1916, he followed the same path. Although many in the dispensationalist camp were enthusiastic about the development of the Zionist movement and approved of Blackstone's activity, no pro-Zionist organization emerged in the dispensationalist camp in this period. Blackstone acted on his own.

For the most part, Blackstone's pro-Zionist initiatives were soon forgotten. Historians of the Zionist movement, for example, have rarely been aware of his efforts and contributions. A temporary revival of interest in Blackstone took place in 1966. On the occasion of Israel's eighteenth anniversary and the seventy-fifth anniversary of Blackstone's petition of 1891, the America-Israel Society in the United States organized memorial meetings for Blackstone and trees were planted in Israel in his memory.

CONCLUSION

William Blackstone's petitions were the earliest examples of a dispensationalist attempt to influence the American government to support the Zionist cause. In his political activity, Blackstone manifested goodwill toward the Jewish people and the Zionist movement. However, one should not mistake his primary motivation. He saw in the establishment of a Jewish state in Palestine a means to an end: the coming of the Messiah and the millennial kingdom. Although he showed concern over the fate of the Jews, the physical and national survival of the Jewish people was not his ultimate aim.

In his active promotion of the Zionist endeavor, Blackstone was not immediately followed by other premillennialists. Although American fundamentalist–premillennialists reacted with great enthusiasm to the Zionist movement and its success, their support of the movement for many years remained largely passive.

One reason for this was the blow dealt in the mid-1920s to fundamentalism in America by the famous Scopes trial and its aftermath, which caused the movement to recede from the public arena.

This reality changed drastically in the 1970s when American fundamentalists emerged again as a powerful force in American public life. As fundamentalists have resumed a higher public profile, their favorable attitude toward the state of Israel has been translated into deeds, and they have become politically active on its behalf.

Although the international political situation has changed radically since 1916–1917, the current fundamentalist-premillennialist attitude toward Zionism is very much in keeping with Blackstone's understanding of the role and place of that movement in God's plans for humanity. Today's fundamentalists, likewise, do not see the Jewish state in terms of the security and safety of the Jews. Rather, the establishment of Israel is perceived as merely one step toward the realization of the millennial kingdom. The existence of the new state is no more than a temporary stage in the advancement of the eschatological timetable, a vehicle predestined to prepare the ground for the messianic age.

APPENDIX 1

The Petition of 1891

What shall be done for the Russian Jews? It is both unwise and useless to dictate to Russia concerning her internal affairs. The Jews have lived as foreigners in her dominions for centuries, and she fully believes that they are a burden upon her resources and prejudicial to the welfare of her peasant population, and will not allow them to remain. She is determined that they must go. Hence, like the Sephardim of Spain, these Ashkenazim must emigrate. But where shall 2,000,000 of such poor people go? Europe is crowded and has no room for more peasant population. Shall they come to America? This will be a tremendous expense and require years.

Why not give Palestine back to them again? According to God's distribution of nations it is their home, an inalienable possession from which they were expelled by force. Under their cultivation it was a remarkably fruitful land, sustaining millions of Israelites who industriously tilled its hillsides and valleys. They were agriculturists and producers as well as a nation of great commercial importance—the center of civilization and religion.

Why shall not the powers which under the treaty of Berlin in 1878 gave Bulgaria to the Bulgarians and Servia to the Servians, now give Palestine back to the Jews? These provinces, as well as Roumania, Montenegro, and Greece, were wrested from the Turks and given to their natural owners. Does not Palestine as rightfully belong to the Jews? It is said that rains are increasing and there are many evidences that the land is recovering its ancient fertility. If they could have autonomy in government the Jews of the world would rally to transport and establish their suffering brethren in their time-honored habitation. For over seventeen centuries they have patiently waited for such a privileged opportunity. They have not become agriculturists elsewhere because they believed they were mere sojourners in the various nations, and were yet to return to Palestine and till their own land. Whatever vested rights, by possession, may have accrued to Turkey can be easily compensated, possibly by the Jews assuming an equitable portion of the national debt.

We believe this is an appropriate time for all nations, and especially the Christian nations of Europe, to show kindness to Israel. A million of exiles, by their terrible suffering, are piteously appealing to our sympathy, justice and humanity. Let us now restore to them the land of which they were so cruelly despoiled by our Roman ancestors.

To this end we respectfully petition His Excellency Benjamin Harrison, President of the United States, and the Honorable James G. Blaine, Secretary of State, to use their good offices and influence with the Governments of their Imperial Majesties—

> Alexander III, Czar of Russia;
> Victoria, Queen of Great Britain and Empress of India;
> William II, Emperor of Germany;
> Francis Joseph, Emperor of Austr[o]-Hungary;
> Abdul Hamid II, Sultan of Turkey;
> His Royal Majesty, Humbert, King of Italy;
> Her Royal Majesty, Marie Christiana, Queen Regent of Spain;

and the Government of the Republic of France, and with the Governments of Belgium, Holland, Denmark, Sweden, Portugal, Roumania, Servia, Bulgaria, and Greece, to secure the holding at an early date of an international conference to consider the condition of the Israelites and their claims to Palestine as their ancient home, and to promote, in all other just and proper ways, the alleviation of their suffering condition.

APPENDIX 2

The Petition of 1916

WHEREAS the civilized world seeks some feasible method of relieving the persecuted Jews, and

WHEREAS we recognize the difficulty of harmonizing the widely divergent races of the multitudinous population of Russia and other nations, and

WHEREAS the governments of these nations should properly resent any foreign interference with their internal affairs, and

WHEREAS each of many nations can consistently point to the others as evidence that the Jews are not in its dominion alone, oppressed and slaughtered, and

WHEREAS the Jewish question is worldwide and demands an international remedy, and

WHEREAS the environment of the Jews is so fraught with alarming danger in many quarters of the world that humanity and the Golden Rule demand speedy action, and

WHEREAS the Jews, when expelled from Spain, were given an asylum in Turkey and have, since then, until the breaking out of the present unprecedented war, received such comparatively kind treatment in the Sultan's dominions as to give assurance that some satisfactory arrangement can now be made for their permanent resettlement in Palestine, and

WHEREAS a Memorial, copy of which is attached hereto, was presented by Mr. Wm. E. Blackstone, in 1891 to Hon. Benjamin Harrison then President of the United States entitled "What shall be done for the Russian Jews" in which it was prayed that the good offices of this Government might be used to intercede with the Governments of Europe for an international conference to consider the condition of the Jews and their right to a home in Palestine, and

WHEREAS the remarkable endorsement of the Memorial by eminent statesmen, clergymen, philanthropists, financiers, the religious and secular press of our Country, as well as our most prominent Jewish citizens, cannot fail to emphasize the wisdom of the plan proposed, and

WHEREAS the records of the State Department at Washington since the presentation of said Memorial evidence the development of a remarkable benign activity on the part of our Government in behalf of the Jews, and

WHEREAS we deem the imminent outcome of the present sad and destructive war a most opportune time for calling such an international conference of the Powers,

NOW THEREFORE, we the undersigned, representative individuals, societies, organizations and public officers in the United States, most respectfully commend the Memorial aforesaid and the attached letter of presentation and document attached, pertaining thereto, to the Honorable Woodrow Wilson, President of the United States and officers of our government, for consideration of the action therein prayed and such measures as may be deemed wise and best for the permanent relief of the Jews.

Notes

1. On Blackstone's life, see "William E. Blackstone: The Friend of Israel," *Jewish Era* 1 (1892), 75–76; Culter B. Whitwell, "The Life Story of William E. Blackstone and of 'Jesus Is Coming'," *Sunday School Times*, 11 January 1936 (repr. *Jewish Era* 46 [1936], 64–67); "Their Works Do Follow Them," *Alliance Weekly*, 18 January 1936; Beth M. Lindberg, *A God-filled Life: The Story of William E. Blackstone* (Chicago: n.d.); Sandy Keck, "W. E. Blackstone: Champion of Zion" (a series of eleven articles), *American Messianic Fellowship Monthly* (1973–1974), 78–79.

2. E.g., Blackstone's letter to *Jewish Era* 11 (1901), 9.

3. See George H. Williams, *The Radical Reformation* (Philadelphia: 1970).

4. See David S. Katz, *Philo-Semitism and the Readmission of the Jews to England, 1603–65* (Oxford: 1982).

5. Clarke Garrett, *Respectable Folly: Millenarians and the French Revolution in France and England* (Baltimore: 1975); W. H. Oliver, *Prophets and Millennialists: The Uses of Biblical Prophesy in England from the 1790's to the 1840's* (Auckland: 1978); John F. C. Harrison, *The Second Coming: Popular Millenarianism 1780–1850* (London: 1979).

6. Franz Kobler, *The Vision Was There* (London: 1956); Meir Vereté, "Ra'ayon Shivat yisrael bamaḥshavah haprotestantit beangliyah bashanim 1790–1840," *Ẕiyon* 33 (1968), 145–179; Barbara W. Tuchman, *Bible and Sword* (London: 1983), 158–223; Mel Scult, *Millennial Expectations and Jewish Liberties* (Leiden: 1978).

7. Tuchman, *Bible and Sword*, 175–177.

8. On dispensationalism, see Clarence B. Bass, *Background to Dispensationalism* (Grand Rapids: 1960); Dave MacPherson, *The Incredible Cover Up: The True Story of the Pre-Trib Rapture* (Plainfield: 1975); Ernest R. Sandeen, *The Roots of Fundamentalism: British and American Millenarianism, 1800–1930* (Grand Rapids: 1978).

9. William E. Blackstone, *Satan, His Kingdom and Its Overthrow* (Chicago: 1900); *idem, The Millennium* (Chicago: 1904); *idem, The Heart of the Jewish Problem* (Chicago: 1905).

10. See, e.g., Blackstone, *Jesus Is Coming*, 3rd ed. (Los Angeles: 1908), 162–176.

11. *Ibid.*

12. Blackstone, *Heart of the Jewish Problem*, 16.

13. Blackstone, *Jesus Is Coming*, 84.

14. E.g., *ibid.*, 171, 234–235.

15. *Ibid.*, 222.

16. *Ibid.*, 236–241.

17. *Ibid.*, 174–176, 224–227.

18. Blackstone had thousands of copies of *Jesus Is Coming* in Hebrew, and other languages as well, stored in Petra in Transjordan. His intention was that Jews who would find refuge there at the "time of Jacob's trouble" would be able to discover the truth, accept Christ, and save themselves.

19. Blackstone, *Jesus Is Coming*, 226, 227.

20. E.g., William E. Blackstone, "The Jews," *Jewish Era* 33 (1924), 87.

21. E.g., William E. Blackstone, "Jerusalem," *Jewish Era* 1 (1892) 70–71.

22. William E. Blackstone, "Missions," in *Prophetic Studies of the International Prophetic Conference, Chicago, November 1886* (Chicago: 1886), 194–201; *idem, Satan, His Kingdom and Its Overthrow*, 36.

23. See, e.g., Blackstone, *Jesus Is Coming*, 208–209.

24. *Ibid.*, 240; William E. Blackstone, *The "Times of the Gentiles" and the Times of the End* (Chicago: n.d.) 18–19. There is no basis for Y. Malachy's claim that "in the last years of his life, disappointment at the secular character of Zionism and an intensification of his missionary strivings may be detected" (*American Fundamentalism and Israel* [Jerusalem: 1978], 141). Blackstone was an active missionary to the Jews and criticized the secular character of Zionism all along the way.

25. Blackstone, *Heart of the Jewish Problem*.

26. In a letter to President Wilson 4 November 1914, Blackstone wrote concerning Isaiah 18:

No nation in all past history, at all fits the prophecy, unless it be our own United States, which God has so wonderfully raised up, just before the harvest.

If our country is the prophecy's "Land shadowing with Wings," then the seventh verse indicates that we shall be specially used in the coming restoration of Israel to their God-given home in Palestine.

In a telegram to Warren C. Harding 30 December 1920, Blackstone wrote, "God has reserved our nation in special service in the impending crux of human history. Isaiah Eighteen." From copies in Blackstone's personal papers in the possession of the American Messianic Fellowship, Chicago [hereafter BPP/AMF].

27. See, e.g., *Jewish Era*, 26 (1917), 6. On Blackstone's interpretation of the First World War, see also the chapter "The War in the Light of Prophecy," in Carl F. Ehle, *Prolegomena to Christian Zionism in America: The Views of Increase Mather and William E. Blackstone Concerning the Doctrine of the Restoration of Israel* (Ph.D. diss., New York University, 1977), 290–302.

28. Among notable signers were Chief Justice Melville W. Fuller of the U.S. Supreme Court; Congressman (later president) William McKinley from Ohio; Governor William H. Russel of Massachusetts; Mayor Hugh J. Grant of New York City; Mayor N. Matthews, Jr., of Philadelphia; Congressman Robert R. Hitt, chairman of the House Committee on Foreign Affairs; Congressman T. B. Reed, speaker of the House of Representatives; James Cardinal Gibbons, Archbishop of Baltimore; and financiers J. Pierpont Morgan, John D. Rockefeller and Cyrus McCormick. From a copy in BPP/AMF.

29. The state of the Jews in Russia concerned the American public. The United States had intervened several times on behalf of Russian Jewry, and the House of Representatives passed a resolution in 1890 calling on the president to keep it informed about the persecution of Jews in Russia. See Cyrus Alder and Aaron M. Margalith, *With Firmness in the Right: American Diplomatic Action Affecting Jews, 1840–1940* (New York: 1946), esp. 217–221.

30. Blackstone did establish contacts in 1891 with Zionist activists such as Adam Rosenberg, the secretary of Shave Zion in New York.

31. The Provisional Executive Committee for General Zionist Affairs was established in August 1914 to coordinate the activities of all Zionist groups and parties in the United States. The committee virtually absorbed the Federation of American Zionists. See Melvin I. Urofsky, *American Zionism from Herzl to the Holocaust* (New York: 1975), 118–163.

32. See copy of Blackstone's letter to J. P. Tumulty, Wilson's secretary, 2 May 1916, BPP/AMF.

33. Straus's letter 16 May 1916 and Brandeis's letter 22 May 1916, BPP/AMF. "Your memorial would be most effective if it derives its support from non-Jews," Brandeis wrote.

34. See, e.g., a copy of Blackstone's letter to Brandeis 20 September 1918; Jacob de Haas's letter to Blackstone 7 March 1918; a copy of Blackstone's letter to Stephen Wise 25 February 1918, all BPP/AMF.

35. See, e.g., a copy of Blackstone's letter to Stephen Wise, 30 June 1917, BPP/AMF.

36. See, e.g., a copy of Blackstone's letter to Brandeis 20 September 1918 and his letter to Wise February, 1918, both BPP/AMF.

37. *Jewish Era* 27 (1918), 44; Lindberg, *A God-filled Life.*

38. See, e.g., David M. Eichhorn, *Evangelizing the American Jew* (Middle Village, N.Y.: 1978), 195.

39. Blackstone participated in Zionist meetings in Philadelphia in July 1916 and in Los Angeles in January 1918.

40. See, e.g., Nathan Straus's yearly telegrams to Blackstone congratulating him on New Year's Eve, BPP/AMF.

41. See Wise's letter of April 1918 to Blackstone, BPP/AMF.

42. At one time, e.g., Marvin Lowenthal, the director of the Provisional Executive Committee for General Zionist Affairs asked Blackstone to publish a Zionist propaganda article under his name. See Lowenthal's letter to Blackstone 2 March 1917, BPP/AMF.

43. The will was based on the assumption that the "rapture" would take place very soon. Blackstone believed that he and his family would be "raptured" from earth with all the true believers. In the meantime, until his return to earth, he wanted the Zionist movement to make use of his earthly possessions and commissioned Brandeis to be the trustee of the Milton Stewart Fund. Brandeis hesitated at first to accept Blackstone's will, but later consented. See copies of Blackstone's letters to Brandeis 18 April 1917 and 20 September 1918; Brandeis's letter to Blackstone 25 April 1917, BPP/AMF. See also Brandeis's letter to Blackstone 26 March 1917 in *Letters of Louis D. Brandeis*, 5 vols., ed. Melvin I. Urofsky and David W. Levy (Albany, N.Y.: 1971–1978), vol. 4, 278.

44. See Brandeis's letter 21 February 1917 to Blackstone thanking him for his contribution, BPP/AMF.

45. "Whereas we deem the imminent outcome of the present sad and destructive war a most opportune time for calling such an international conference of the Powers."

46. In a letter to President Wilson 16 November 1917, Blackstone wrote:

It would have been possible to have secured any number of signatures of the most representative character to the Memorial, but this was so evident that it was not necessary. The endorsement of the Presbyterian General Assembly, the Ministers' Meetings of the Methodists and Baptists, and many representative individuals and officials, evidence the general approval which the Memorial receives from our entire population (copy in BPP/AMF).

Cf. also the ninth clause of the 1916 petition, "WHEREAS the remarkable endorsement of the memorial. . . ."

47. *Minutes of the General Assembly of the Presbyterian Church in the United States of America,* n.s., vol. 16, August 1916 (Philadelphia: 1916), 185–186.

48. Letter of Rev. W. H. Roberts to John W. Baer, president of Occidental College, L.A., 28 August 1916, BPP/AMF.

49. See a copy of the resolutions of the Methodist Ministers' Meeting of Southern California in BPP/AMF.

50. See a copy of the resolution of the Presbyterian Ministerial Association of Los Angeles in BPP/AMF.

51. See a copy of the Los Angeles Baptist Ministers' Conference resolutions in BPP/AMF.

52. See a copy of Blackstone's letter to President Wilson 23 March 1917 in BPP/AMF. Later on, Dr. Arthur J. Brown replaced Dr. Speer as secretary of the Presbyterian Board of Foreign Missions and as a member of the committee for the presentation of the memorial to President Wilson. Dr. Mott's name was also deleted from the list of members of this committee. See a copy of Blackstone's letter to President Wilson, 14 June 1917, BPP/AMF.

53. See Blackstone's correspondence with Bishop Bashford in BPP/AMF, e.g., their exchange of letters 2–3 July 1917.

54. See Henry K. Carroll's letter to Blackstone 14 November 1916, BPP/AMF. Anita Libman-Lebeson and Timothy P. Weber were mistaken in naming the Federal Council of the Churches of Christ in America among the Christian bodies that endorsed the petition: Anita Libman-Lebeson, "Zionism Comes to Chicago," in *Early History of Zionism in America,* ed. Isidore S. Meyer (New York: 1958), 169; Timothy P. Weber, *Living in the Shadow of the Second Coming: American Premillennialism, 1875–1982* (Grand Rapids: 1983), 140.

55. The petition was ready in May 1916, but Blackstone continued to collect signatures for it. He was ready to have the committee of Protestant church leaders present it to President Wilson in October 1916, but Wilson, who was busy with his election campaign, was not in Washington, D.C.

56. See Wise's letters to Blackstone 30 June 1917 and 17 September 1918; Nathan Straus's letter to Blackstone 16 May 1916; de Haas's letter to Blackstone 26 December 1916; and Brandeis's letter to Blackstone 21 February 1917, all in BPP/AMF. See also Brandeis's letters to Jacob de Haas, 8 May 1917, 7 June 1917 and 6 December 1917, in Urofsky and Levy, *Letters of Louis D. Brandeis,* vol. 4, 289, 296, 327.

57. Stephen Wise had shown it to the president "in an unofficial manner" twice, in June 1917 and September 1918. See Wise's letters to Blackstone 30 June 1917 and 17 September 1918, BPP/AMF. Blackstone sent a copy of the petition to Wilson in May 1916.

58. Historians who have not gone through Blackstone's personal papers mistakenly thought that Blackstone submitted the petition. E.g., Libman-Lebeson, "Zionism Comes to Chicago," in Meyer, *Early History of Zionism in America,* 163; Malachy, *American Fundamentalism and Israel,* 139; Lawrence J. Epstein, *Zion's Call: Christian Contributions to the Origins and Development of Israel* (Lanham: 1984), 112.

59. See a copy of his letter to Stephen Wise of 9 July 1917, BPP/AMF.

60. In his letter to Blackstone 30 June 1917, Stephen Wise wrote:

I had the honor of presenting in informal fashion to the President at the White House yesterday a copy of your petition. The President accepted it, but he felt that this was not the best time for the public or private presentation thereof. I think I have the right to say that the President is prepared to leave to Justice Brandeis the decision with respect to the most opportune time in which formally to present the petition to him. (BPP/AMF).

Wise refers to his meeting with Wilson in his autobiography (*Challenging Years* [New York: 1949], 189) but does not mention Blackstone and his petition.

Bashford, one of the people to whom Blackstone entrusted the presentation of the petition, wrote to Blackstone two days afterward and told him, "The whole matter of a public hearing depends upon President Wilson. At times he seems to want the public hearing and at other times he requests it to be postponed" (BPP/AMF).

61. See Robert Speers's letter to Blackstone 23 May 1917 and Bashford's letter to Blackstone 1 June 1917, BPP/AMF. Wilson discussed his suggestions for changes with Brandeis. His specific request was to drop the suggestion to put the future Jewish commonwealth in Palestine under "international control" and leave the control "undesignated." Brandeis was in favor of the same changes. See Brandeis's letter to Jacob de Haas 8 May 1917 in Urofsky and Levy, *Letters of Louis D. Brandeis*, vol. 4, 289. Brandeis obviously discussed the petition in detail with Wilson.

62. At one point Wilson sent an emissary, Henry J. Morganthau, to the Middle East to try to persuade Turkey to sign a separate peace treaty with the Entente Powers. The British, who were eager to conquer Turkish territories, sent Chaim Weizmann to persuade Morgenthau to abandon his mission. Wilson was aware of Britain's attempt to use her promise to build a Jewish home in Palestine as a means of taking control of Palestine. Although he favored the Zionist idea, Wilson hesitated at first to give his approval to the issuing of the Balfour Declaration. See Leonard Stein, *The Balfour Declaration* (London: 1961), 529; Peter Grose, *Israel in the Mind of America* (New York: 1983), 61–62.

63. See Grose, *Israel in the Mind of America*, 60–63. Cf. Stein, *Balfour Declaration*, 30.

64. Cf. Ben Halpern, *A Clash of Heroes: Brandeis, Weizmann, and American Zionism* (New York: 1987), 168.

65. See, e.g., Stein, *Balfour Declaration;* Isaiah Friedman, *The Question of Palestine, 1914–1918: British–Jewish–Arab Relations* (London: 1973).

66. "He [President Wilson] never once mentioned the Second Coming, and he always said that we need not worry about heaven—that would take care of itself—but had to be concerned about the problems of this world." Arthur S. Link, Wilson's biographer and editor of his papers, in a letter to Yaakov Ariel 18 July 1984.

67. Wise, *Challenging Years,* 186–187.

68. Frank E. Manual, *The Realities of American-Palestine Relations* (Washington, D.C.: 1949), 256–257.

69. Founded in 1866, known today as the American University of Beirut.

70. Joseph L. Grabill, *Protestant Diplomacy and the Near East: Missionary Influence on American Policy, 1810–1927* (Minneapolis: 1971). Grabill deals mostly with the missionaries' attempt to influence the Wilson administration.

71. On Dodge's connection with Wilson, see *ibid.,* 80–93.

72. See, e.g., *ibid.,* 178. Wilson, in fact, was not impressed by the efforts of the pro-Arab lobby and remained fully committed to his pro-Zionist promises.

Birth Pangs of the Messiah: The Reflections of Two Polish Rabbis on Their Era

Gershon C. Bacon
(BAR-ILAN UNIVERSITY)

THE CONCEPT OF *ḤEVLEI MASHIAḤ*

It is a commonplace to state that traditional Judaism in its struggle against modernizing and secularizing forces inside and outside the Jewish community insisted on the continued relevance of the messianic idea. Orthodox spokesmen resisted any attempt to transform the messianic era into a metaphor, bereft of national content, for universal peace or economic justice.[1] Yet despite this virtual consensus, there was considerable debate within Orthodox ranks over the nature of the messianic era. The significance of the debate was not merely theological or intellectual; disagreement over these issues was directly related to differences in religious and political behavior. The multiplicity of responses to the issue of messianism reveals how wide a range of Orthodox perspectives concerning the bewildering modern era could exist side by side.

Among the many points of disagreement, those related to the "birth pangs of the Messiah" (*ḥevlei mashiaḥ*) or the "footsteps of the Messiah" (in Hebrew, *pa'amei mashiaḥ*; in Aramaic, *'ikveta demeshiḥa*) occupy a special place and strike us with particular poignancy. According to Jewish tradition, a catastrophic time of upheaval and suffering will precede the messianic Redemption. Rabbinic literature notes that myriad natural, economic and social disasters will strike the people of Israel at that time:

> The number of scholars will decline. Sorrow and pain will dull the people's eyes, and tribulations and harsh decrees will follow one on the other. . . . In the generation in which the Son of David is to come, the meeting place of scholars will be turned into a brothel, the Galilee will be destroyed . . . the young will humiliate the elderly, and the old will rise in honor of the young. Daughters will rebel against their mothers and daughters-in-law against their mothers-in-law. The generation will be "dog-faced," and sons will have no shame in front of their fathers. . . . In the [approaching] footsteps of the Messiah insolence will increase.[2]

86

This is only a sampling of the various omens that were to presage the impending messianic era. In addition, the age-old tradition of calculating the End—attempts to determine the date of the Redemption on the basis of biblical verses, numerology and the like—persisted despite the discouragement of noted rabbinic figures.[3]

The concept of *hevlei mashiah* lends history a strange, almost dialectical rhythm. When "many troubles wash over the people like a river, [you may] expect him [the Messiah]."[4] Thus, in a very concrete manner, the fulfillment of the direst prophecies contains an element of consolation. In perhaps the most striking example of this kind of reasoning, we are told that Rabbi Akiva laughed upon seeing foxes emerge from the ruins of the Temple in Jerusalem, in contrast to his colleagues, who burst into tears of anguish at the sight that recalled the worst predictions of Lamentations (5:17–18). Akiva explained to his shocked associates that the fulfillment of the prophecies of doom only strengthened his conviction that God would also fulfill His promises of future Redemption. The other rabbis responded, "Akiva, you have consoled us."[5] Nevertheless, many rabbis voiced the wish, "Let him [the Messiah] come, but let me not witness it," so great was their fear of the horrific events of the *hevlei mashiah*.[6]

Similarly, even in their darkest moments, Jews throughout the ages could find some measure of consolation by ascribing their tribulations to the dreaded *hevlei mashiah*, which implied that Redemption could not be far behind. Thus, Jewish chroniclers of the Chmielnicki uprising in the seventeenth century interpreted the bloody events as, inter alia, catastrophic harbingers of the End of Days, to the point that the very name of the Cossack leader was found to contain an allusion to an underlying significance: Chmiel [in Hebrew letters, Hmil] stood for *Hevlei Mashiah Yavou La'olam* (i.e., "the birth pangs of the Messiah will come upon the world").[7]

In the eighteenth century, the prominent Hasidic leader Rabbi Yaakov Yosef of Polonnoye explained the failure of religious leadership in his day in terms of the stresses and strains to be expected in the time of *'ikveta demeshiha*.[8] Nor did this concept necessarily lose its relevance in the modern era. Traditional Jews continued to find solace in it as they confronted new cataclysmic events. At least some of the Hasidic rebbes viewed Napoleon's eastward march as part of the premessianic upheavals.[9]

In the period of the First World War, hundreds of thousands of Jews were left homeless as the front lines crossed areas of dense Jewish settlement in Eastern Europe and as Jews were driven away from the front for fear they would aid the enemy. Poverty and starvation became the lot of many. The end of the First World War brought no relief as civil wars and territorial wars continued to ravage the area, leaving the Jews vulnerable to massive pogroms.[10]

In interwar Poland, Jews faced severe economic pressure, including discriminatory taxation, boycott and increasing poverty.[11] In addition, traditional Jewry was troubled by the fact that a considerable proportion of the Jewish people had abandoned religious observance to a lesser or greater extent. New parties and groups, usually inimical to Orthodoxy, vigorously pressed their claims to leadership of the entire community.[12]

The Zionist resettlement of the land of Israel, an effort laden with messianic overtones, confused and upset many traditionalists because of the decidedly secular nature of the Zionist enterprise. Religious Zionists had to develop a rationale for continuing to collaborate with secularists in order to defuse harsh criticism by anti-Zionist rebbes, local rabbis and heads of yeshivot.[13] And for their part, anti-Zionist Orthodox leaders and writers—usually to be found in the ranks of Agudat Israel—put forward positive explanations for current reverses in an effort to mobilize the largely apolitical Orthodox populace and bolster morale among their followers.[14]

These processes are reflected in the writings of two Polish rabbis who represented two contending Orthodox camps: Rabbi Yitzhak Nissenbaum[15] (born in 1868) of the religious Zionists and Rabbi Elhanan Wasserman[16] (born in 1875) of Agudat Israel. (Both men were killed by the Nazis during the Second World War.) Each in his own way tried to come to terms with the social and political conditions of the interwar period, and the concept of the birth pangs of the Messiah served them as an ideological anchor of sorts in their efforts to explain the problems of their time. They applied the concept in markedly different ways and came to strikingly different conclusions, although they drew on the same rabbinic sources. A comparison of their views thus sheds light on the vast ideological gap separating the Zionist and anti-Zionist streams in Polish Orthodoxy.

HEVLEI MASHIAH AS A CALL TO ACTION

Rabbi Yitzhak Nissenbaum served the Zionist movement for many years in various capacities, beginning in the 1890s, when he assisted Rabbi Shmuel Mohilever in the Hibbat Zion movement.[17] From then on, he made his mark as one of the most skilful and prolific exponents of the Zionist cause in the Orthodox community. In his sermons and articles, which drew on experience garnered as he traveled throughout Poland and Russia to propagate the Zionist idea, Nissenbaum combined his talents as a preacher with his broad knowledge of traditional sources. Even a casual perusal of Nissenbaum's writings reveals a remarkable facility with talmudic, midrashic and other rabbinic texts, all enlisted for the Zionist cause. With the artistry of a seasoned preacher, Nissenbaum wove the various elements into a single tapestry, a continuous narrative with a clear aim and objective. He scanned ancient texts with a practiced eye for their contemporary application and relevance and was able to move back and forth across the millennia, sometimes even in the course of a single sentence, with seeming effortlessness.

Nissenbaum's published works that dealt with the messianic idea neatly bracket the interwar period. His essay *"Shalosh tekufot"* ("Three Eras") appeared in 1920,[18] and his last work *Masoret veherut* (*Tradition and Freedom*)[19] appeared shortly before the outbreak of the Second World War. (The concept of "the footsteps of the Messiah" as presented in the latter work has merited brief treatment in an essay by the late Avraham Rubinstein.[20]) A comparison between Nissenbaum's views at the outset of Polish independence with those he held on the eve of catastrophe reveals some interesting developments and changes in emphasis and direction, along with obvious points of continuity.

In his earlier essay, Nissenbaum presents the conventional rabbinic scheme of

Jewish history and its epochal periodization: two thousand years of Chaos, two thousand of Torah and two thousand of the Messiah,[21] the title of each era reflecting its predominant theme. Although the transition between these eras may not be abrupt (the messianic idea did, of course, predate the year 4000 [corresponding to 239–240 C.E.]), only in the period after this date did the messianic idea come into focus as the central feature of the age. It then became one of the pillars of Jewish existence, one of the "suns" that drove away the darkness of the Exile.[22]

What comprises the essence of the messianic idea according to Rabbi Nissenbaum? Two elements dominate his discussion: faith and action. Together these represent the synthetic approach of the tradition, and only through both, in tandem, would the eventual Redemption come about. Moving deftly back and forth from his ancient sources to present-day conditions, Nissenbaum criticized the skeptics of long ago and of his own day, whatever their origin and status—Jews and non-Jews, scholars and uneducated alike. Sniping subtly at the rabbinic opponents of Zionism, Nissenbaum cited the talmudic dictum, "in the generation in which the Son of David will come, there will be a denunciation of scholars,"[23] taking this to mean that "many would criticize the sages who weaken the hands of the nation as it aspires to Redemption."[24] In other words, those leaders who should have been in the forefront of the struggle for Redemption stood aside.

Moreover, as the Talmud itself predicted, in the (messianic) future even the nonfruit-bearing trees in the land of Israel would produce fruit:[25] that is, the "barren trees" (the uneducated, even the nonreligious Jews) had started to bear fruit. They were rebuilding the land of Israel and performing the practical work that would draw the Redemption closer. Should not the "fruit trees" learn a lesson from this and at least do their share?[26]

To those who insisted that the land could only be recovered under the guidance of great pious men,[27] Nissenbaum quoted the Midrash[28] to argue that even the angels erred on occasion (as when they bemoaned the completion of the Tabernacle by human hands). However, once they realized their error, the angels joined in the work of building[29]—again, a rebuke to the anti-Zionist rabbis.

This activist doctrine also applied to the idea of the birth pangs of the Messiah. Nissenbaum stressed that throughout the era of the Exile every generation had believed in some sense that in its time the Son of David would come. If troubles and suffering increased, this was a sign that the Redemption was near, and any terrible suffering was considered *hevlei mashiah*. In his own day, when Jewish blood was shed with impunity on an unprecedented scale, the same messianic faith indicated that the time of a reestablished Jewish state was near.[30] Although this notion had always provided the Jews with psychological support and consolation, it also imposed on them a sense of obligation to the land of their forefathers, a duty to feel intimately connected to the land of Israel.[31]

The Jewish people had preserved this connection with the land in the many countries of its Exile, but exilic conditions had led, perforce, to an attenuation of that connection. As Nissenbaum saw it, the very process that had preserved a rarefied link to the land of Israel through synagogue rituals and the liturgy had, by the same token, robbed the Jews of any sense of the mundane, physical aspects of the land itself. The physical element had been reduced to hopes of eventual burial in the Holy Land, and finally to a tiny sack of imported soil placed in the coffin: soil gathered and packed by the energetic non-Jewish inhabitants and rulers of the Holy Land. The Jews had lost the healthy instincts of a nation living on its own soil, and those individuals who might on occasion express the need to revive such feelings were regarded with deep suspicion, as if they had uttered some heresy.[32]

What the Jewish people needed was no less than a revolution in its attitudes in order to transform the Jerusalem "of wailing and graves [into a Jerusalem where] the nation . . . would cease to mourn . . . and would rejoice in its life and celebrate in its land."[33] The work of the Zionist movement in Palestine breathed new values into Jewish national life; built agricultural settlements, libraries and schools; and was raising a new generation of physically fit, Hebrew-speaking farmers. In this, Nissenbaum saw a return to the original values evoked by the Torah when it spoke of a "land flowing with milk and honey."[34] In other words, the Zionists had drawn the proper conclusion from the tribulations of Diaspora existence and were creating the needed revolution in Jewish life. If in the course of its work, the Zionist movement attempted to impose "new mitzvot" on the Jewish nation—settling the land, learning Hebrew and becoming actively involved in the affairs of the nation— Nissenbaum saw all this as not only positive in its own right, but also as implicit in the most ancient sources of Judaism.[35]

With all his evident enthusiasm for the straight-backed, muscular new Jews growing up on the soil of the ancient homeland and for what he called the "song of Judaism," Nissenbaum took pains to stress the crucial role of the Torah and its commandments in the process of Redemption. Without knowledge of the Torah and the observance of its mitzvot, the generation of the Messiah would never arrive. Even on this point, though, Nissenbaum hastened to add that Torah and mitzvot by themselves were insufficient. They needed the added element of the "song of Judaism, the song of the Messiah, the exalted visions beheld by our prophets of the 'End of Days,' the days of Redemption of the Hebrew nation."[36]

Almost twenty years later, as storm clouds gathered over European Jewry, Rabbi Nissenbaum returned to the same themes of the Messiah and Redemption, this time with a sense of impending disaster. His basic approach, however, remained one of faith mixed with an even more urgent appeal for action. His last published work, *Masoret veḥerut* (1939), contains an extended discussion of the means to achieve Redemption for the Jewish people. He did include the caveat that the Torah and prophets provided no clear, unambiguous picture of the process of Redemption beyond the basic promise that it would, indeed, take place at some time in the future.[37] Having made this point, however, he proceeded in a long and moving meditation on the messianic process to present his view of the ideas implicit in the words of the biblical prophets.

Once again, the concept of *ḥevlei mashiaḥ* is extensively discussed. Nissenbaum remarked (almost parenthetically) that the persecutions of the past were indeed the birth pangs of the Messiah, at least potentially. Why then had the Redemption not already taken place? This calamity was due to the lack of action by the Jewish people. Clinging to the hope of Redemption, in which action would be initiated by God, the Jews failed to effect a general awakening of the entire nation.[38]

Nissenbaum produced a litany of missed opportunities and inaction. He grieved not only for lost time, but because the Jewish people had ignored the clear signs of Providence. As he saw it, only divine intervention could adequately explain the events of the previous one hundred years. Factors leading to an active change in Jewish and international attitudes toward the resettlement of the Jews in Palestine had fallen into alignment, seeming to recall the cry of the prophet Zechariah ringing across the centuries, "Strengthen the hands of the builders!"[39] The events of the past fifty-six years in the Holy Land, with the return of some four hundred thousand Jews who had established agricultural settlements and new towns and cities, had intrinsic value beyond the immediate moment. Here Nissenbaum saw "the footsteps of the Redemption, the hoped-for Redemption . . . slowly approaching."[40]

Nissenbaum interpreted the events of the 1930s as the clearest sign of all that the footsteps of the Messiah were now to be heard in history. On the one hand, the Jews were being persecuted and tortured in times and places that no one would have predicted. The cruelty exhibited toward them had reached levels that nobody had expected to encounter in an era of unparalleled human progress. On the other hand, a series of unpredicted obstacles had appeared in the seemingly steady process of the Ingathering of the Exiles and the upbuilding of the Jewish center in Palestine. To Nissenbaum only one answer was possible, "This is the path of Redemption, these are the footsteps of the Messiah, the birth pangs of the Messiah."[41]

Most important, he stressed that this was ultimately a positive development. The *hevlei mashiah* were not the death throes of the Exile, but the birth pangs of the Redemption. No birth is ever easy, and he could only surmise the suffering and difficulties to come. Nevertheless, Nissenbaum reminded his readers, whatever obstacles sprang up, this time the birth process had already started and would continue to its ultimate conclusion: the messianic Redemption.

Why, then, were the present travails so great? This was a fulfillment of the Torah's warning that God would exact punishment for the sins of the fathers unto the fourth generation.[42] In this case, the fathers' sin lay in the inadequate response to the first calls for the rebirth of Zion in the mid-nineteenth century. A generation later, the pogroms in Russia had partially awakened the nation from its lethargy but, again, far less than demanded by Providence. A third, and now a fourth, generation had reached maturity, and Providence still awaited the appropriate response. The hand of Providence depended on the new generation to fulfill its aims; hence, these youths were undergoing a dual "visitation": a wave of unprecedented wrath and punishment, but also an intimation of Redemption. In Nissenbaum's own chilling words,

These are the birth pangs of the Messiah and the footsteps of the Messiah. The more the footsteps of the Messiah are delayed through our own fault—the fault of the nation that stands aloof from the upbuilding of its land and the founding of its state—the more the birth pangs of the Messiah will intensify in order to awaken it, to pressure it, with a strong hand. In that way, it will rise up for the sake of its own Redemption.[43]

He quoted Rabbi Mordechai Gimpel Jaffe (one of the first nineteenth-century rabbis to call for the rebirth of the land of Israel), who had said that when the lovers of Zion failed to fulfill their duty, when the builders of the land of Israel tired, the Hand of Providence intervened.[44]

In his powerful essay of 1935 entitled "Doro shel mashiah" ("The Generation of the Messiah"), we already find in capsule form Nissenbaum's appeal to the religious youth of his day cast in terms of the eternal struggle between the Jewish people and its historical enemy, Amalek. As the time of Redemption drew near, Amalek would gather all its strength to assault Israel from every side. Here his timetable differed slightly, as he reckoned that the coming of the Messiah would take three generations—at that time the Jews stood in the first or second of the three. Difficult times awaited them, the dreaded *hevlei mashiah,* and hundreds of thousands of Jews had already felt their effect, but this should not be a cause for despair. On the contrary, suffering should rouse the Jewish people to new life; each member of the generation bore a special responsibility precisely because he belonged to the generation of the Messiah. From that perspective, the sacrifices and suffering seemed less daunting because they were birth pangs, "the birth of that holy and pure humanity foreseen by our prophets as 'the End of Days'."[45] The people of Israel stood on the threshold of a new era. Everything depended on their attitude and on their actions.

HEVLEI MASHIAH AS A REMINDER TO HOLD FAST

In the writings of Rabbi Elhanan Wasserman, we find the counterpoint to the generally optimistic views of Rabbi Yitzhak Nissenbaum. Within the ranks of Agudat Israel, Wasserman, head of the yeshiva in Baranowicz, was one of the few rabbis who even came close to formulating a systematic ideology. He, therefore, commands special attention. His message to the perplexed Orthodox Jews of his time was one of despair, of rebuke—but of ultimate hope if only the faithful would remain steadfast.

Wasserman published his views in the press of Agudat Israel, in yeshiva journals or in pamphlet form. Many years after his death at the hands of the Nazis, these scattered articles were translated (from Yiddish) into Hebrew and published in a single collection.[46] His simple and unremitting message of divine retribution and wrath, published so close to the events of the Nazi Holocaust, would in the eyes of later mythmakers turn Wasserman into a prophetic figure, even if he himself rejected such designations. He saw himself as merely spelling out the "simple meaning" (*peshat*) of Scripture in the modern context.[47]

The most striking statement of his views can be found in his essay "'Ikveta demeshiha," written by Wasserman toward the end of his sixteen-month stay in the United States in 1938–1939, where he had gone to raise funds for his yeshiva. The theme had been on his mind since Hitler's rise to power; in a short article he had published in the mid-1930s under the same title, he had already stated his position in outline form.[48] Like his contemporary, Nissenbaum, Elhanan Wasserman assured his readers and students that they were living in the era of the footsteps of the Messiah; but, he warned, no one knew how long this period might last.[49]

Like other rabbis and publicists active in Agudat Israel, Wasserman found in the concept of *hevlei mashiah* a fitting explanation for the disturbing changes that had rocked the twentieth century. If one began from the premise that the present era was that of *'ikveta demeshiha*, all of the seemingly confusing events of the time made sense and, indeed, were predicted long ago by the Bible and Talmud.[50] There was no need for undue despair, for the very success of the irreligious Jews in achieving political power was a sign of hope. If the biblical and rabbinic outline of history was unfolding in the present age, then these trying times would end in the promised messianic era.

In analyzing events of his own day, Wasserman told his audience that one need only look in the Torah in order to understand the otherwise baffling developments. In general, Wasserman asserted that he was expressing the plain sense of the words of the Torah, with an I-told-you-so attitude. The rabbis and Torah scholars struggling with modernity had warned of such troubles ever since the time of the Enlightenment (Haskalah).

The predicament of the Jewish people, he said, stemmed from two historical wrong turns over the past one hundred fifty years. The first of these was the Berlin Haskalah that had flourished at the end of the eighteenth century. The second was the development of Jewish nationalism in the nineteenth century. Both arose out of the mistaken and rebellious attempt by Jews to transform their people into a nation like other nations of the world and to reject their special role in the divine plan for the universe.[51] He cited the warning of the prophet Ezekiel that God would "reign over you with a strong hand and with an outstretched arm, and with overflowing fury," should the Jews persist in such rebelliousness.[52] The signs of divine anger increased daily as the nations began to react to the futile attempt by Jews to bridge the gap between the Jewish people and other nations. The more insistent Jews became in their attempts to resemble others, the more vehement would the opposition of the gentiles become.[53]

As he scanned his generation, Wasserman saw all the characteristic signs of *hevlei mashiah*. Scoffers and heretics led the Jewish people while religious scholars were ridiculed. Study of Torah declined, as did financial support for the yeshivot. Punishment for this neglect of Torah learning had not been long in coming: the amount of money and property looted and confiscated from Jews in Vienna alone came to $40 million.[54] Wasserman also pointed to the growing poverty of the Jewish masses. After all, had not the rabbis said long ago, "The Son of David will not come until the last penny is gone from the purse?"[55] For thousands of Polish Jews, this prophecy had the distinct ring of reality.[56]

Another sign of imminent Redemption was the phenomenon of Jewish wandering. The stability of communities had been undermined as families were split up and scattered across the globe. Wasserman quoted his teacher, Rabbi Yisrael Meir Kagan (known as the Hafetz Hayim), who had taught him the contemporary meaning of what the prophet Amos had predicted "I will shake the House of Israel— through all the nations—as one shakes [sand] in a sieve."[57] Grains of sand shaken through a sieve may land close by or far away, but none remain in the same place.[58] This would be the fate of the Jews in the time of *'ikveta demeshiha*.

This time of *hevlei mashiah* differed from earlier difficult periods of Jewish suffering in Exile in that there had always before been some safe refuge far from the gathering storm. Now things were different. Jews would be persecuted and expelled everywhere; they would find welcome nowhere.[59] The feeling that all these changes were taking place in frighteningly rapid succession added to the pain and perplexity felt by many Orthodox Jews. Societal and political upheavals that had formerly been spread over centuries now took only decades.[60]

Wasserman expressed his greatest pain and concern over the overwhelming changes within Jewry, which he also defined as *hevlei mashiah*. First and foremost this meant an increase in the "insolence" that was a sign of the premessianic age.[61] The clearest manifestation of this prophecy was the rise of new Jewish leaders who opposed the rabbis and rejected the religious tradition. These unbelievers waged an open battle against the Torah and did not recognize the rightful place of Torah scholars in the leadership of the community. No longer was the spirit of Amalek limited to the external enemies of the Jews; now an internal "Amalek" fought against traditional Jewry. The journalists and party leaders, with their "new Torah" and "new commandments," led people astray and instilled spiritual darkness in their minds and hearts. These "leaders" prevented the people from listening to the message of the genuine Torah.[62]

Nationalism stands out in Wasserman's view as one of the chief heresies and plagues of the modern era. It was especially reprehensible when it took the self-contradictory form (as he saw it) of religious nationalism. The very term "religious nationalism" implied that religion alone was insufficient; this was heretical in and of itself. Religious Zionists sowed confusion among the Jewish masses. Until the Zionists had come along, everyone knew that a good Jew was one who observed the commandments. But they had legitimized a leadership composed of nonbelievers in deference to their "national consciousness" and their fealty to the "national commandments" of Zionism.

In thus allying themselves with secular Jews, the religious Zionists had made a grave error. They were unable to influence the movement from within; on the contrary, they themselves had been infected with secular ideas.[63] Nor did claims of a new, vibrant Jewish center arising in the land of Israel impress Wasserman. How could one speak of a "Jewish land" when half the children there received a "Hellenist" education designed to alienate them from traditional Judaism?[64] The secular Zionists may have adopted customs and terms sanctified by tradition, such as the festival of the first fruits on Shavuot, but they had turned them into a sacrilegious parody of the commandments of the Torah.

Yet all these seemingly disastrous events portended a glorious future. As the prophet Zechariah had predicted, "I will refine them as silver is refined, and will try them as gold is tried."[65] These disturbing phenomena were all part of God's plan. In the period of *hevlei mashiah*, God would test the pious by raising to power those who had rejected God and His ways. If the righteous survived this test, salvation would quickly follow. The Hafetz Hayim had put it another way. It was in the nature of things to flare up like a candle just before they expired. In the same way, the powers of impurity were enjoying the last glow of their power in the world.[66]

What should the Jewish people do in this time of crisis? Wasserman does not counsel any revolution in Jewish life but rather a return to basic values through communal and individual acts of repentance. He invoked the advice offered long before by Rabbi Elazar in the Talmud: to be saved from the *hevlei mashiah* a person should engage in study of the Torah and perform acts of kindness.[67] Each Jew ought, therefore, to devote some time each day to study, to extra prayer and to deeds of altruism.

In their battle against the forces of Amalek, the only weapon that Jews had at their disposal was the Torah.[68] This meant that Jews had to avoid the political arena at all costs if they wished to survive this difficult period. The rabbis had compared the Jews to a lamb among seventy wolves; for the Jews, then, acting by the rules of the nations was like trying to measure a liquid in meters. Jews could not fight their enemies. The best advice was to cry out to God in prayer. Such appeals were effective only if directed to Heaven, not to the "civilized world" or to the League of Nations.[69] In this time of distress, he continued, the eternal advice of the Bible still held true: "to be solid like a wall in our faith and not to surrender to our surroundings."[70]

In summing up his words of rebuke and consolation, Wasserman adduced as the basic theme of *hevlei mashiah* that "God seeks out the persecuted."[71] As the measure of suffering increased, so would the chances of salvation. Wasserman saw his own time as the most difficult in the history of the Exile: surely the hour of birth pangs had arrived and the messianic era was near.[72]

COMPARISON AND CONTRAST

On several of the most salient points regarding the concept of *hevlei mashiah*, then, our two authors concur. First and foremost, they agreed that their own time fitted this concept. In this they were far from alone—East European rabbis in the Zionist camp, the Aguda camp, and in nonpartisan or antipolitical alignments all shared this messianic temper. Wasserman's revered teacher, the Hafetz Hayim, took the concept quite literally. Believing that the Redemption could come about suddenly, he urged Jews of priestly or Levitical ancestry to study the laws pertaining to the ancient sacrificial rites so that they would be able to officiate when the Temple in Jerusalem was rebuilt.[73]

Second, having assumed that the world had already entered the period of *'ikveta demeshiha,* both rabbis regarded the persecution of the Jews as something to be expected. Neither took upon himself the mantle of prophecy, but both hinted at a long spell of suffering, holding out the prospect of the ultimate Redemption at the end of the cycle of Exile, wandering and oppression.

Finally, both Nissenbaum and Wasserman, following an age-old Jewish approach, looked upon the internal Jewish arena as the crucial one in determining the course of history. All the phenomena in the "outside world"—the rise of Nazism in Germany and official antisemitism in Poland, the economic crisis with all its implications, the rise of the Soviet regime and its campaign against religion—were essentially a backdrop for the struggles within the Jewish community. What counted in the redemptive process, and what ultimately would accelerate or impede that process, would occur among Jews.

Beyond these points of consensus, however, the differences between the two men are significant and illuminating. First, we may point to their use of sources: Nissenbaum is more eclectic, drawing on a wide variety of talmudic and midrashic sources and using all sorts of rhetorical devices to point out the relevance to contemporary circumstances of the texts he cites. He systematically filters out negative references to internal upheavals within Jewry—the growth of "insolence," the generation being "dog-faced" and the like—that did not accord with his enthusiasm for the revolution wrought by the Jewish national movement. For his part, Wasserman devoted a great deal of his analysis to those very points, emphasizing internal strain and tension, the desertion of Torah study and the abandonment of traditional values.

This difference stems from their differing moods and aims. Wasserman attempted to speak for an embattled minority (he would probably have said an embattled silent majority) within Jewry who could find nothing positive about the accelerating loss of religious faith among the younger generation and the progressive weakening of the traditional leadership. Nissenbaum, however, spoke favorably of the "revolutionary" forces in Jewish life that he believed would eventually fulfill the ideals embodied in the tradition. It should not surprise us, then, if Wasserman is on the whole more descriptive—trying to explain the disconcerting evidence of major dislocations—whereas Nissenbaum's emphasis lay on the prescriptive—trying to enlist support for a new course of action.

Put most simply, the two rabbis diverged in their basic assessment of the situation. What Nissenbaum regarded as signs of rebirth and calls for action to hasten the Redemption, Wasserman saw as among the terrible *hevlei mashiah,* from which one could only pray to God for deliverance. What one saw as part of the solution, the other viewed as part of the problem. Ultimately, though, both men told their audiences to look beyond the suffering of the present to the glorious messianic future. Their reading of the difficult position of Polish Jewry, in particular, and world Jewry, in general, represents two divergent Orthodox views. In the case of Wasserman, at least, his views have been assigned prophetic import in the wake of the Holocaust and are frequently referred to in the writings of postwar Orthodox thinkers in Israel.[74]

CONCLUSION

Both rabbis, Wasserman and Nissenbaum, perished in the Holocaust. Available evidence indicates that in those years of horror they remained consistent in their different approaches to the notion of *hevlei mashiah.* Wasserman saw the unfolding events of the Second World War as further confirmation that the world had entered the final period of *hevlei mashiah.*[75] In his words from that time, as reported by students and colleagues, we encounter a feeling of inescapable fate to the point that at first he belittled any efforts to search for a safe haven, noting that the *hevlei mashiah* meant that the entire world, including America or Argentina, would be swept up in the conflict.[76]

Consistent in his views even in those trying times, Wasserman hesitated in 1940 to aid a rabbinical colleague in acquiring a visa to the United States, noting his fears for the spiritual health of the rabbi's young children.[77] Rabbi Wasserman himself, ignoring the pleas of friends and admirers to remain in the United States, was determined to maintain his yeshiva. He wandered with his students in Soviet-occupied Lithuania, parting from them, finally, only out of fear of imminent arrest by the NKVD.[78] Throughout this period, he preached his doctrine that Torah study was the anchor of Jewish existence, devoting himself to that end to the last; he was killed in the Ninth Fort in Nazi-occupied Kovno in the summer of 1941.[79]

We have less information about Rabbi Nissenbaum's activities in this period, but it appears that he continued his educational work in the Warsaw ghetto, speaking and writing under pseudonyms in various underground publications. He also continued to preach of the Redemption, even if he doubted that he himself would live to witness that day.[80]

For the purposes of our discussion, though, the most important testimony relates to Nissenbaum's views on how the Jews should behave in face of the Nazi threat. Once again, he demonstrated his innovative approach, and his appeal was to action stemming from faith. In the Warsaw ghetto, the subject of *kiddush hashem* (sanctification of the Divine Name, i.e., martyrdom) became a common item for lectures and private discussions as rumors and fragments of information about mass slaughter in other places filtered into the ghetto. It was in this despondent atmosphere that Nissenbaum reportedly said, "Now is time for sanctification of life [*kiddush hahayyim*] and not for Sanctification of the Name [*kiddush hashem*] through death. Once, when our enemies demanded our soul, the Jew martyred his body for *kiddush hashem*. Today, when the enemy demands our bodies, it is the Jew's obligation to defend himself, to preserve his life."[81]

Various observers testified to the sense of encouragement that Nissenbaum's words afforded them in their daily struggle to survive under inhuman conditions. To the very end, Rabbi Nissenbaum kept to his activist view, looking for a way for the individual Jew and the Jewish people to respond to the travails of the birth pangs of the Messiah—always with an eye to the ultimate Redemption.

Notes

1. See, e.g., the message of Rabbi Samuel Mohilever addressed to the First Zionist Congress—held in Basel, Switzerland, in 1897—in Arthur Hertzberg (ed.), *The Zionist Idea: A Historical Analysis and Reader* (New York: 1960), 403–404.

2. Sanhedrin 97a; Sotah 49b.

3. See, e.g., the extensive discussion in Abba Hillel Silver, *A History of Messianic Speculation in Israel* (New York: 1927, Boston: 1959).

4. Sanhedrin 98a.

5. *Sifre Deuteronomy*, ed. Louis Finkelstein (New York: 1969), 94–95; paralleled in Makkot 24a–24b.

6. Sanhedrin 98b.

7. See the introduction of Natan Neta Hanover to his *Yevein mezulah* reprinted in *Sipurei hagezerot bishenot tah vetat*, intro. Moshe Rosman (Jerusalem: 1982), 24.

8. Yaakov Yosef of Polonnoye, *Toledot Yaakov Yosef* (photo offset printing of Lemberg [Lvov] 1863 edition; Brooklyn: 1955), "Naso," 127d.

9. See the various traditions cited in Baruch Mevorach (ed.), *Napoleon utekufato* (Jerusalem: 1968), 183–189; one version is also cited in *The Golden Tradition*, ed. Lucy Dawidowicz (Boston: 1968), 95–96.

10. For details on this era, see Celia Heller, *On the Edge of Destruction: Jews of Poland Between the Two World Wars* (New York: 1977), 47–53; see also Abram Sachar, *Sufferance Is the Badge* (New York: 1958); S. Horak, *Poland and Her National Minorities* (New York: 1961).

11. Heller, *Edge of Destruction,* 98–109; see also Oscar Janowsky, *People at Bay* (New York and London: 1938).

12. Yisrael Meir Hakohen (Kagan), *Mikhtavei Ḥafeẓ Ḥayim* (Israel: 1969), vol. 2, 135.

13. The usual explanatory line centered on two main themes. First, in a time of emergency for the Jewish people, religious Jews should cooperate with all elements in the nation working for rescue of the nation as a whole. Second, if religious Jews—who constituted such a large percentage of the Jewish population in Eastern Europe—enlisted in sufficient numbers in the ranks of the Zionist movement, they would be able to exercise decisive influence on the nature and direction of the movement. See, e.g., the aforementioned message of Mohilever (n. 1), in Hertzberg, *Zionist Idea,* 402.

14. See Gershon C. Bacon, "Da'at torah veḥevlei mashiaḥ: lisheelat haideologiah shel agudat yisrael befolin," *Tarbiẓ* 52, no. 3 (1983), 497–508.

15. See Yitzhak Nissenbaum's autobiographical work *'Alei ḥeldi* (Jerusalem: 1969); Nurit Yizhar, *Mishnato haẓiyonit ufo'alo haẓiburi shel harav Yitzḥak Nissenbaum* (master's thesis, Bar-Ilan University, 1983).

16. On Wasserman, see Aharon Sorasky, *Or Elḥanan,* 2 vols. (Israel: 1978).

17. Nissenbaum, *'Alei ḥeldi,* 105ff.

18. In Nissenbaum's collection of essays, *Hayahadut haleumit* (Warsaw: 1920), 17–58.

19. Nissenbaum, *Masoret veḥerut* (Warsaw: 1939).

20. Avraham Rubinstein, "Pa'amei mashiaḥ veḥevlei mashiaḥ bemishnato shel harav Yizḥak Nissenbaum," in *Sefer Shragai,* ed. Mordechai Eliav and Yitzhak Raphael, (1981), vol. 1, 118–126.

21. Avodah Zarah 9a.

22. Nissenbaum, *Hayahadut haleumit,* 41.

23. Ketubot 112b.

24. Nissenbaum, *Hayahadut haleumit,* 44.

25. Ketubot 112b.

26. Nissenbaum, *Hayahadut haleumit,* 44.

27. An allusion to the Aguda-based concept of "da'at torah," whereby all party decisions and positions would be based on decisions of the Council of Torah Sages, the titular heads of the party.

28. Numbers Rabbah, ch. 12, par. 8.

29. Nissenbaum, *Hayahadut haleumit,* 53–54.

30. *Ibid.,* 45.

31. *Ibid.,* 45.

32. *Ibid.,* 48–49.

33. *Ibid.,* 50.

34. *Ibid.* Note that in the text, Nissenbaum refers to the physical aspect as "the value of our Torah."

35. *Ibid.,* 54–55.

36. *Ibid.,* 51.

37. Nissenbaum, *Masoret veḥerut,* 98.

38. *Ibid.,* 97. Cited in Rubinstein, "Pa'amei mashiaḥ," 122.

39. Based on Zech. 8:13.

40. Nissenbaum, *Masoret veḥerut,* 118.

41. *Ibid.,* 119.

42. Exod. 20:5. "For I the Lord your God am an impassioned God, visiting the guilt of the fathers upon the children, upon the third and upon the fourth generations of those who reject Me" (trans. Jewish Publication Society [Philadelphia: 1962]).

43. Nissenbaum, *Masoret veḥerut,* 122.

44. *Ibid.,* 120.

45. Nissenbaum, *Ketavim nivḥarim* (Jerusalem: 1948), 320–321, cited in Yizhar, *Mishnato haziyonit,* 133–134.

46. Elhanan Bunem Wasserman, *Sefer koveẓ maamarim* (Jerusalem: 1963). His key essay "'Ikveta demeshiḥa" also appeared in English under the title *Epoch of the Messiah* (Los Angeles: n.d.).

47. Sorasky, *Or Elḥanan,* vol. 2, 219–220, esp. n. 6.

48. *Ibid.,* 175, 218.

49. *Ibid.,* 221.

50. Wasserman, "'Ikveta demeshiḥa," introduction, in *Koveẓ maamarim,* 106.

51. *Ibid.,* 111–112 (par. 7).

52. Ezek. 20:33.

53. Wasserman, "'Ikveta demeshiḥa," 112 (par. 7).

54. *Ibid.,* 110–111 (pars. 4–6).

55. Sanhedrin 97a.

56. Wasserman, "'Ikveta demeshiḥa," 117 (par. 17).

57. Amos 9:9.

58. Wasserman, "'Ikveta demeshiḥa," 114 (par. 11).

59. *Ibid.,* 119–120 (par. 22).

60. *Ibid.,* 117–118 (par. 18); Elhanan Bunem Wasserman, "Omer ani ma'asei lemelekh," in *Koveẓ maamarim,* 101 (par. 22).

61. Mishnah Sotah 9:15.

62. Wasserman, "'Ikveta demeshiḥa," 113 (par. 9).

63. *Ibid.,* 126–127 (pars. 34–35).

64. Wasserman, "Omer ani ma'asei lemelekh," 101 (par. 21).

65. Zech. 13:9.

66. Wasserman, "Omer ani ma'asei lemelekh," 105 (par. 30).

67. Sanhedrin 98b, cited by Wasserman, 'Ikveta demeshiḥa," 120 (par. 24).

68. Wasserman, "Omer ani ma'asei lemelekh," 94–95 (pars. 9–10).

69. Wasserman, "'Ikveta demeshiḥa," 122–124 (pars. 27–28).

70. *Ibid.,* 121 (par. 25).

71. Eccl. 3:15.

72. Wasserman, "'Ikveta demeshiḥa," 122–124 (par. 38).

73. S. Greiniman (ed.) *Hafeẓ Ḥayim 'al hatorah* (Bnei Brak, n.d.), 198–199.

74. See the detailed study by Aviezer Ravitzky, "Exile in the Holy Land: The Dilemma of Ḥaredi Jewry," in *Studies in Contemporary Jewry* vol. 5, *Israel: State and Society, 1948–1988,* ed. Peter Y. Medding (New York: 1989), esp. 111–112.

75. Sorasky, *Or Elḥanan,* vol. 2, 240.

76. *Ibid.,* 239–240, esp. n. 6.

77. *Ibid.,* 246–247.

78. *Ibid.,* 273–274.

79. *Ibid.,* 281–284.

80. Yisrael Shapira, "Aḥarit davar," in Nissenbaum, *'Alei ḥeldi,* 358–359.

81. Natan Eck, *Hato'im bedarkhei hamavet,* 36, cited in Lucy Dawidowicz, *The War Against the Jews 1933–1945* (New York: 1976), 291–292.

Realism and Messianism
in Zionism and the Yishuv

Yaacov Shavit
(TEL-AVIV UNIVERSITY)

The concept of "messianism," almost always used in conjunction with that of "utopia," has accompanied the Zionist movement from its earliest days. On the one hand, messianism is seen as a kind of demiurge inspiring great changes and summoning up irrational but creative strengths. Drawing its power from the very depths of the nation's past, it confronts the present with the challenge of a golden age. On the other hand, the messianic force is also treated as dangerous in the extreme, and the mere use of the term is often meant to serve as a warning against the seductive fascination of unrestrained fantasies and empty visions.

Messianism is seen as a positive expression of the basic human longing for a better world in the future and of the drive to build such a world; at the same time, it is seen as a negative expression of the no less human craving for a single truth—absolute, all-encompassing and totalitarian—to be imposed on society in its totality. Thus, certain political movements were destined, according to this latter type of analysis, to manifest a character that would be at once messianic, revolutionary and totalitarian. Every revolutionary movement, then, becomes messianic and vice versa; and every messianic-revolutionary movement contains within itself a totalitarian impulse.

The employment of the term "messianism" to characterize and evaluate ideologies, social movements and political parties and events may be explained in a number of different ways. On one point, though, there can be no disagreement: messianism is a concept that has been used persistently and intensively throughout Zionist history. Taken up first by contemporaries, it was then adopted by historians. Thus, for example, the literature that deals with the climate of opinion and political culture of the Yishuv between the Balfour Declaration and the establishment of the state of Israel makes frequent and varied use of the concept. It has served to characterize states of mind, ideologies and concrete historical situations. On more than one occasion mention has been made of the "messianic expectations," or the "messianic fervor" that, at crucial moments, allegedly gripped the Yishuv, or certain circles therein. Various movements with their different social expressions and ideologies have been described as drawing on wellsprings of "messianic expectations" or displaying "messianic yearnings."[1]

Both in the literature of the day and in modern historiography, it has been claimed, for example, that messianic expectations in the Yishuv erupted immediately after the Balfour Declaration; that the messianic tidings of the Bolshevik revolution produced a powerful, albeit ambivalent reaction; and that the profound anxiety caused by the rise of fascism and Nazism in the 1930s strengthened the expectations of an actual messianic Redemption. The Third Aliyah, and especially the Gedud Ha'avodah (Labor Battalion) have been described as demonstrating messianic tension during the 1920s; and Revisionism has been seen as expressing either messianic realism (according to its supporters) or false messianism (according to its opponents). In addition, the desire to formulate a consistent messianic message has been ascribed to individual scholars, philosophers and poets, such as Joseph Klausner, Martin Buber and Uri Zvi Greenberg.

In sum, as the concept of messianism has become more commonplace in the characterization, definition and evaluation of various social phenomena, it has been less classified and analyzed in and of itself. Though the connection between Zionism and messianism has been discussed and debated a great deal, such arguments have generally been characterized by a vague and one-dimensional approach. In fact, as I shall try to demonstrate in this discussion, the concept of messianism provides a broad framework within which very different, even conflicting, ideas may find a place. "Messianism" has long served as a fashionable and flexible term, able to provoke an immediate reaction from its audience. However, it has not necessarily been a useful tool for either the social or the intellectual historian.

Interest in the history of Jewish messianic movements, the study of the messianic idea itself and the wide use of the concept of messianism in political and ideological contexts are all closely interlinked. However, the very fact that these different spheres have been so closely connected and that they have even stimulated one another's development makes it all the more important to distinguish between them. The academic research that has made collections of messianic texts and critical-historical studies available to the interested reader for the first time is not to be confused with attempts to formulate a philosophy of Jewish history that assigns a central role to the messianic idea and the various messianic movements. A second distinction is that which should be made between the use of the term "messianism" by ideologists and political figures and its use in society at large.

Historians make their task far too easy when they extract carefully selected phrases from key texts and then declare them to be typical of an entire worldview, or *mentalité*. True, in the analysis of earlier periods of Jewish history, individual texts often do have to serve as conclusive evidence to either illustrate the character of messianic thought or prove the existence of messianic fervor at one time or another. In fact, it is on the basis of a limited number of documents that historians have spoken of "messianic propaganda" or of "an irresistable wave of messianic fervor" in given historical contexts.[2] However, when it comes to the collective mentality of any modern social grouping to contemporary *anonyme Geistesgeschichte*, there is not a limited collection of texts to be examined but rather a flood of material. Because it is not just interest in the development of messianism per se that motivates the study of messianic tension—the real issue is the supposition that the messianic idea exerts great social and political power—the quotation of a limited selection of texts is no longer sufficient. Only the examination of a very broad range of sources can enable the historian to ascertain how far messianic concepts and messianic rhetoric really influenced the consciousness, language and outlook (cultural, political, social) of a given group or society.

However, the abundance of material by no means simplifies the task of the historian. The fact that messianic themes and concepts were popular or even that they were integrated into the weltanschauung of an individual or a movement does not necessarily explain what function they served. There is no doubt that in the modern period the history of Jewish messianism was increasingly made available to the educated reader and that "messianism" did become a convenient and legitimate term of discussion. It is by no means clear, however, precisely what those who used the term actually meant by it.[3]

As I see it, a clear distinction has to be drawn between *messianic ideas* (or ideology), *messianic metaphors* and *messianic rhetoric*. And it is one of the basic assumptions of this discussion that messianic ideas played only a peripheral role in determining political culture and action during the period under scrutiny. The most important use of messianism was simply as metaphor or rhetoric.

During the process of its politicization, the Zionist movement formulated new definitions of the concept of messianism and made them an integral part of its developing political culture. These meanings, quite different from any that had preceded them, were used to reinforce the message of the movement. Messianism was broken down into a series of precedents, symbols and images that answered the needs and psyche of the time. Thus, any investigation of this subject has to make a clear-cut distinction between the actual role of messianic belief systems in Jewish history—specifically in the rise of Jewish nationalism—and the widespread polemical use made of messianic motifs and symbols.

In his penetrating critique of Jacob L. Talmon's view of political messianism, which had a seminal influence on perceptions of Zionism,[4] Andrzej Walicki writes:

> It is possible to use the term "messianism" as a common name for the ideologies predicting and striving for an imminent regeneration of mankind, [but] if both Mickiewicz and Marx are labelled "messianists," this can only mean that the word "messianism" is used as a polemical device rather than as a scholarly, descriptive term.[5]

After all, if great expectations of the future are always to be equated with messianism, the result can only be trivialization. One could add that, even when used as a scholarly term, the concept messianism is all too often used vaguely, tendentiously or without distinguishing different shades of meaning. Thus, Anthony D. S. Smith, who recently came out strongly against "the millennialist theory of nationalism of both the conservative and radical varieties," has rightly proposed the use of clear definitions based on both structure and content to distinguish the national from the millenarian movements.[6]

However, when one examines the way in which modern Jewish intellectual history—and within it the history of modern Jewish nationalism—has been written, one finds that such careful distinctions have rarely been made. Various secular, nonnationalist or antinationalist ideologies are described as linked to traditional Jewish faith in the Redemption. Jewish nationalism, in contrast, is portrayed as often unwilling to accept national redemption alone and as determined to unite it with one form or another of universal millenarianisms (anarchist, Marxist).

The label messianic is applied by historians and sociologists in order to underline the urgency of expectations within a given movement and the degree to which it gives itself over to dreams of Redemption and seeks to realize them. Thus, messianism is used as little more than a synonym for radical revolutionism or political zealotry or even totalitarianism. But in descriptions of Jewish nationalism, these latter phenomena that exist in their own right are too frequently treated as merely secondary aspects of the messianic ethos. And Zionism, in turn, is reduced from independent to subordinate status—a reincarnation, as it were, of the traditional messianic faith in the people of Israel restored to the land of Israel (albeit with the addition of a modern utopianism).

There are thus, two issues here for an observer to define: first, the relationship (and even the continuity) between Zionist messianism and the messianic tradition in Jewish history; second, the precise nature of the messianism to be found within the Zionist movement.

It has justly been said that messianism constituted a great challenge to Zionism, which therefore adopted contradictory attitudes toward it.[7] Indeed, Zionist appraisals of the messianic movements in Jewish history serve less to illuminate the past than to reveal the self-perceptions characteristic of the Zionist movement at a given time and place. It would be no exaggeration, in fact, to say that certain groups within the movement actually used conflicting attitudes to messianism as the yardstick to mark themselves off from their opponents.

Modern Jewish nationalism, after all, found itself from the first in opposition to a whole range of messianisms: the stance of traditional rabbinic Judaism was characterized as passive messianism because it viewed the Redemption as dependent on divine intervention in history; the mission theology of Reform Judaism was seen as a form of messianism leading to assimilation and the loss of national identity; and Marxism and Communism were feared as forms of universal messianism likewise threatening the loss of nationhood.

On the other hand, of course, there were also many Zionists who were determined to define their own movement as a revitalization of the messianic faith. At the heart of this idea was a view of messianism as one of the fundamental concepts of Judaism—an integral part of both the faith itself and of its teachings. Jewish messianism was revered as a vital force in its own right, one providing a vision of the future in both national and universal terms.[8] At work here was the conscious desire to understand Jewish nationalism as a phenomenon immanent within, and emerging from, Judaism and Jewish history rather than as the product of pressure and influence from without. The urge to read into history a direct connection between messianism and nationalism was shared by many circles and commentators who otherwise held widely differing viewpoints.

In reality, though, the history of messianic thought and movements in Jewish history is such that it is clearly erroneous to speak of messianism in general.

Messianic thought and messianic movements have taken on a variety of forms. Bar Kokhba's messianism, for example, was different from that of Judah the Patriarch, and both were quite separate from that of Shabbetai Zvi. This being so, with precisely which type of messianism, if any, were Zionists to identify themselves?

Obviously, in very basic terms, they had first to distinguish between the "active" and "passive" forms of traditional messianism. The latter was seen as postponing the Redemption until some distant future; the former as convinced of its imminent approach. No less (perhaps more) important, Zionism had to secularize the concept of false messianism. It was no longer a question of whether great expectations would lead to heterodoxy, religious nihilism and conversion but rather whether they were feasible or else outside the realm of possibility. False messianism, therefore, became that messianism that was unrealistic. In this way, Communism could be defined as false messianism because its promise to redeem the Jews within a universal framework was held to be a delusion tempting them into self-destruction.[9] Zionist Revisionism could also be defined as false messianism by its rival—the Zionist labor movement—because it promised to bring about a revolutionary political breakthrough and mass aliyah from Eastern Europe within a few years.[10] Indeed, throughout the period discussed here, various groups hurled accusations and counteraccusations at each other, each claiming that its opponents were either passive messianists (minimalists, lacking in initiative and imagination) or else messianic adventurists (maximalists chasing their own fantasies).

Thus, messianism both as a concept and as a historical paradigm has played a role in Zionist thought since its earliest days. In a positive sense, it could symbolize a belief in the need to make an absolute break and find a total solution; more negatively, it connoted despair, adventurism, total ruin. It could symbolize both the popular activism that had declared war on the fossilized world of the traditional Jew and also the reckless substitution of fantasy for reality. It could be seen as preparing the way for the charismatic leader (made of the same miraculous stuff as the Redeemer himself) and, in general, as endowing Jewish history with a new and dramatic dimension of dynamism and sweeping romanticism. It could act as a restraining influence or exert an almost magical fascination.[11]

In short, those who viewed political nationalism as eminently realistic and grounded in the concrete analysis of the real world were wary of any identification with messianic delusions from the past. Those, however, who wanted to lay bare deeper spiritual layers in Jewish nationalism held that messianism imparted to nationalism a religious dimension and metaphysical profundity. Even Marxists could claim that messianism was "one of the ways in which national self-consciousness and national activism has revealed itself" and that it had exerted an impact "on the proletariat, too."[12]

As adopted by Zionist groupings, messianism was usually linked to utopianism (national redemption was allied to the redemption of society and mankind as a whole), but it could also act against utopianism. Whereas Zionist messianism sought an immediate and total, quantitative solution to the Jewish question (the redemption of the nation as a whole), Zionist utopias tended to be qualitative in nature, dependent on elite groups rather than on the masses. In fact, the masses were sometimes viewed as an actual barrier on the road of the elite to a utopian life.

All this said, we are left with four basic questions:

1. Did Zionism in any form constitute a continuation of the messianic tradition in Jewish history?
2. Was Zionism messianic, inasmuch as it set itself goals that embraced both national-political redemption and modern social utopianism?
3. Was Zionism messianic because of its revolutionary goals and its willingness to make great sacrifices to that end, demanding complete, even totalistic, loyalty from its followers?
4. Was the ideology of Zionism in general (and of its two major constituent movements, labor and Revisionism, in particular) totalitarian in nature because of its immanent messianic tendencies? And did the actual patterns of behavior manifested by these movements in the political and social spheres reveal the urge to impose a totalitarian uniformity on life in all of its aspects?

It is my thesis that a clear distinction has to be made between the historiographical interpretation of messianic phenomena in Jewish history[13] and the theory that interprets Zionism as itself messianic; between messianic ideas, a genuine messianic ideology, and messianism used as either a metaphorical or rhetorical device. Again, a distinction has to be made between Zionism as a total idea and its actual modus operandi in reality. Belief in an absolute break was (and is), of course, part of the Zionist weltanschauung, but more often than not this belief was balanced by empiricism and realism, by restraints both objective and subjective—even when they, in turn, were accompanied by messianic rhetoric. The Zionist use of the term "Redemption" embraced ideas, programs and aspirations that had formed no part of any previous messianic scheme: these included *geulat hakark'a* (the redemption of the soil), *'avodah 'azmit* (Jewish labor); modernization, social planning, the creation of a collective society, individual commitment, a cultural rebirth.

To repeat, then, messianism in Zionist usage constituted a structured credo only rarely; far more often, it served as a convenient tool to label extremism or, alternatively, as a way to inspire emotion or enthusiasm.

Messianism was already a well-established part of modern Jewish nationalism when the Palestine labor movement first made its appearance on the Zionist stage—and this was even more the case twenty years later when Revisionism began to take shape.

There is much evidence that can be used to argue that a messianic awakening took place among the Russian Jews in the early 1880s. The dramatic events of the time were often interpreted as messianic auguries, as the fulfillment of the ancient prophecies, as signposts on a predestined course. On a less exotic level, there were others who saw the events of 1881–1882 as a shock of historic proportions from which would arise a new future. Basically, however, the writings of the Hibbat Zion movement represented not a genuine messianic faith or mode of thought, but simply messianic rhetoric that was meant to explain the crisis and help find an answer to it.

True, the pogroms and the subsequent appearance of Hibbat Zion were, indeed, described as the long-awaited messianic breakthrough. As Peretz Smolenskin wrote to Eliezer Ben-Yehudah in 1881, "If you seek to clear the way for the Messiah by your efforts, then both the believers and the enlightened will rise up against you."[14] In reality, though, this eruption of expectancy simply reflected a profound but straightforward hope for change that was born out of the chaotic and dangerous circumstances.

For his part, Simon Dubnow produced a quick response to the new messianic mood with the publication in 1882–1883 of a series of articles on Sabbatianism and Frankism in the Russian Jewish monthly, *Voskhod*. These were clearly (and none too subtly) aimed against Hibbat Zion, which looked suspiciously (so the articles seemed to imply) like the pseudomessianic movements of the past.[15]

In fact, Hibbat Zion was not a messianic, but a protonational movement. If it was interested in any concrete form of historical messianism at all (and even this in very moderate terms), then it was the Return to Zion of the Persian period—a form that I believe should be termed nonmessianic messianism. The basis for the Return to Zion in the Persian period was the proclamation of the emperor Cyrus in 538 B.C.E. This was the most successful (perhaps, the only) messianic event in Jewish history. Though the talmudic tradition later adopted an ambiguous attitude toward it,[16] contemporary prophets went so far as to hail Cyrus as the Messiah ("Thus said the Lord to Cyrus, His anointed one [i.e., Messiah], whose right hand He has grasped, treading down nations before him, ungirding the loins of kings." [Isa. 45:1]).

This messianic metaphor became so powerful in the writings of Hibbat Zion that quite sane members of Hovevei Zion were capable of comparing so eccentric a figure as Laurence Oliphant with Cyrus the Messiah–Redeemer.[17] The Cyrus phenomenon can be called nonmessianic messianism because it represents a form of "natural" redemption made possible by the gracious permission of a foreign ruler, by politics and settlement and by a gradual process of restoration rather than by a single, miraculous, all-embracing event. For the religious members of Hovevei Zion, the example of Cyrus could thus legitimize both their active political support for the resettlement of Palestine and their cooperation with secular members of the movement.[18]

All this notwithstanding, a realistic and pragmatic tone was dominant in the political culture of Hibbat Zion. There were no signs of either eschatological-catastrophic or utopian-revolutionary messianism. Almost no use was made of metaphors drawing on messianic movements (the Persian period apart) from the distant or more recent past. Hibbat Zion, like the Second Aliyah after it, preferred symbols that were romantic, heroic and nationalist in nature—not miraculous. Thus, Judah the Maccabee and Bar Kokhba were perceived as archetypal national heroes rather than as messiahs.

True, if one is looking for messianic characteristics, it is easier to find them in the Zionist movement itself rather than in its protonationalist and protopolitical predecessor of the 1880s. Many observers have been impressed by the almost super-natural—hence messianic—force of Herzl's charismatic personality. Only such a personality, in their view, could have accomplished such great achievements in so short a time. Likewise, it is not surprising that "realistic" Zionists possessed of a positivist-evolutionist outlook (e.g., Ahad Ha'am) saw Herzl's political Zionism as the reincarnation of Sabbatian messianism, not as a normal political movement. In criticizing Herzl's alleged messianism, Ahad Ha'am made implicit use of messianic themes similar to those addressed by Rabbi Hiyah to Rabbi Shimon ben-Halafta at the time of Judah the Patriarch, "This is the way of Israel's Redemption: little by little at first; but once it is started, it will grow greater" (Palestinian Talmud, Berakhot 1:1).

Like Herzl—and because of him—Ahad Ha'am was very preoccupied with messianic phenomena. He saw messianism as a driving force within history, distinguishing between traditional messianism, which relied on transcendental forces, and modern messianism, which sought scientific explanations for the dynamics of history. Beyond this theoretical distinction, he was also troubled by something that would later trouble the Zionist movement as a whole: the question of chutzpah—the towering self-confidence, even hubris, of those who claimed to see the signs of the Messiah and were eager to announce his arrival. With more than a little sarcasm, he pronounced his "a generation of messiahs" and did not bother to conceal the fact that this barb was aimed at both the socialists and the Herzlian Zionists. "Happy are those," he declared, "at whose door the Messiah stands, Redemption knocks, and the truth is revealed." However, he argued, messianic faith should not be allowed to go beyond the realm of abstract and consoling hope and should not be a guide to action:

> Life in these times is hard indeed for anybody who cannot blindly follow the Messiah of one [group] or another; who cannot hear the sounds of the oncoming Redemption and Salvation, neither from near nor from afar, not for their own time, nor for the days when grass will grow over the graves of their children's children; for anybody who still sees knowledge and logic as "mighty gods," set as impartial judges above all parties, and not merely as trumpet-blowing, flag-waving slaves to some "Messiah."[19]

This passage, of course, contains a clear reference to the parallel between Herzl and Bar Kokhba, as it echoes the words addressed by Rabbi Yohanan ben-Tortah to Rabbi Akiva, "Grass will grow on your cheeks and still the Son of David will not have come" (Palestinian Talmud, Ta'anit 4:8). Here, incidentally, is an excellent example of how easily a messianic metaphor can create a false analogy: Herzl's aim, after all, was not to liberate the land of Israel by force of arms but rather to win a proclamation parallel to that issued by Cyrus to the Jews in Babylon. When the Uganda plan became a pressing issue, and it seemed to Ahad Ha'am that his direst warnings were about to be justified, he did not hesitate to compare Herzl—the man who was about to lead the Jews to their doom somewhere in darkest Africa—to Shabbetai Zvi.[20]

Herzl, as will shortly become apparent, was well aware of this comparison. Because he, no less (and perhaps more) than Ahad Ha'am, saw himself as a champion of knowledge and logic, free of irrational messianism in any shape or form, he must have felt such a comparison totally unjustified. Nevertheless, the storm of feeling over the Uganda plan was such that not only Ahad Ha'am, but many others, too, immediately saw it as a new form of Sabbatian nihilism. Perhaps the bitterest expression was given to these feelings by Hayim Nahman Bialik, who lampooned Herzl in a satirical verse called "Rabbi Zerah" that even Ahad Ha'am refused to publish.[21]

Remarkably enough, Bialik made another, much more favorable, reference to Sabbatianism in 1917, soon after the publication of the Balfour Declaration. At a mass meeting in Odessa on December 20, 1917, Bialik spoke of Shabbetai Zvi and Sabbatianism as forces that had "nurtured the hope of Redemption in the nation's soul" and had "fallen, crushed by the burden of their dreams." They had, therefore, earned the right to be remembered at such an historic moment.[22]

Of all the forms of messianism, in fact, it was Sabbatianism that had left the deepest mark on modern Jewish history and that now cast a long shadow over Zionism. Zionist attitudes toward Sabbatianism were complex and ambiguous. In the final analysis, it was seen as a "rebel" and popular movement unique in Jewish history. As such, Zionism could not easily condemn it outright. On the other hand, it had ended in failure and antinomianism, and any identification with this had to be utterly shunned.

Herzl himself, compared by his opponents to Shabbetai Zvi, can be found pondering his attitude toward this seventeenth-century messiah (he seems to have been unaware of any other form of Jewish messianism). Quite conscious of the fact that his own charisma was a central force in the Zionist movement and that this had led many to accept him as a Messiah, he asked himself whether Shabbetai Zvi had really been anything other than an astonishingly magnetic charlatan who had drawn the gullible masses in his wake. Herzl clearly understood the power of the slogans and symbolism that the masses attached to him. To the question of how the leader of a modern political party could be distinguished from a messianic leader in the Sabbatian mold, he answered that, though Shabbetai Zvi had drawn his power from the popular longing for Redemption, there was no place for miracle workers in the modern age. Needed now were political action and national planning. No supernatural leader was required, for the people would inspire themselves with the power of their collective will.

Herzl, then, could not view the dramatic outburst of messianic yearning in an entirely negative light. At the same time, however, he had to establish absolutely the fact that Zionism was not messianic in nature, just as it was not utopian. Zionism's purpose was to give new direction both to the nation's deeply rooted desire for Redemption and to its vision of an ideal society. The methods to be employed were far removed from those of Sabbatianism, which had relied on providential intervention and the overturn of the natural order. One must remember that the same Herzl whose premonition of catastrophe led him to propose his all-encompassing solution also propounded the moderate (and minimalist) Basel program and the Uganda compromise.

It was his grand vision of the Jewish state, though, that made him a "King of Israel." Did this program, however, really reflect the essence of his Zionism? Or was it perhaps only meant to startle Hibbat Zion out of its dead-end routine of clubs and societies?[23] In many respects, Herzl the politician and diplomat was the pragmatist par excellence and took his "messianism" firmly in stride.

If revolutionary ideals were, ipso facto, also messianic or at least transmutations of a messianic outlook, socialist Zionism in all its forms would have to be labeled as a classic case of political messianism. However, if we go beyond such broad generalities, we find that ideology and opinion during the Second Aliyah did not display specific messianic tendencies in any concrete way. It was a rational and essentially realistic outlook, albeit combined, and also in conflict, with nationalist and romantic tendencies, that characterized the labor movement in Palestine at that time.[24] Even the nationalist romanticism, which made much of real events and heroes from Jewish history (but reshaped them to fit the demands of a highly developed social as well as national consciousness),[25] lacked a genuinely messianic character.

This is also true of the Third Aliyah and its constituent radical movements. Social radicalism, with its roots in Marxist scientific socialism, realistic constructivism, romanticism and utopianism were all of much greater influence than any form of messianism. On the other hand, Communism at that time was taken to be a highly alluring form of (false) messianism that was enticing Jewish youth to its destruction. (This was the message of Yitzhak Lamdan's famous poem of 1927, *Masadah*). Berl Katznelson even tried (with only very limited success) to draw a distinction between socio-Zionist messianism, by which he meant the Marxist varieties of Zionist determinism, and pioneering, socialist-Zionist constructivism, or voluntaristic activism.[26] (In this context, the contrast between messianism and activism was clearly tendentious.)

In the period before the First World War, then, neither Poale Zion nor Hapoel Hazair were eagerly expecting any apocalyptic breakthrough to a new age of mass Redemption. Between the two World Wars, it is true, representatives of Hehalutz in independent Poland sometimes described it as a messianic movement whose pioneering spirit "is hastening the millennium; is capable of every sacrifice; and is marching toward the future on the edge of the abyss"[27]—but the reality was somewhat different. The terms in which Hehalutz characterized its messianic aspirations make it quite clear that here was a case of what might be called existential messianism—a rebellion against life in the Diaspora—rather than any form of political or religious messianism. In truth, constructivist Zionism, which rejected reliance on diplomatic activity ("the Messiah will not come in response to the yawns of politicians"), on party politics and on any single event or breakthrough was here making use of messianic rhetoric to give itself historical meaning and weight that was well beyond anything warranted by its real situation.

The Gedud Ha'avodah has also been described at times as messianic because of its concept of a fully egalitarian society. Its publications, however, reveal very little messianism.[28] All-embracing utopian schemes for the future, it should again be stressed, are not to be confused with a messianic world outlook. To be sure, Uri Zvi Greenberg did describe the Gedud Ha'avodah as a "messianic army" in his poetry, and he frequently used similar phraseology ("the preparation of the masses," a "directed spiritual dictatorship") in order to express his revolutionary Bolshevism. However, he was the exception that proved the rule, and his critics in the labor movement attacked in the strongest terms his "nostalgic calls for messianism, for Sabbatianism, for a movement of the spirit and for magic formulae—all of which simply obscure the fundamental principle of contemporary Zionism: it has to be rooted in action, in a determination to turn ideas into facts.'' Greenberg's messianic poetry was variously described as populism and chiliastic Zionism, the product of alienation and despair.[29]

Certainly, the intelligentsia of the labor movement were very strongly influenced both by the decline (as they saw it) of Western culture and equally by their utopian vision of a new world that would combine a new religion, honesty, sanctity and new ideals. At the same time, however, they were quite clearly aware of the great divide separating their ideal from their ability to achieve it for the foreseeable future on anything but the most limited scale.

David Horowitz, then a member of the Hashomer Hazair encampment at Betaniyah, asked in 1921:

> Would we have had the right to draw strength from the messianic dreams of millennia just in order to establish yet one more small townlet quite undistinguishable from any other in Poland, Lithuania or America? Our only reason for leaving the empty life of Europe was to create for ourselves a new life in our homeland, one that would offer us a rebirth as human beings.[30]

And somewhat similar thoughts were also voiced there in the same year by Natan Bistritzky:

> The Almighty marks out a people of many millions and destroys a few hundred thousand. Others, also in their hundreds of thousands, He drags by force of terror, nostalgia and human instinct to their own homeland, that they find already settled by strangers who also have their own rights there. And from among this great passive mass, He chooses a select few—hundreds, perhaps thousands—and entrusts them with the messianic hopes of the people, of mankind.[31]

Here, as in other such texts, the burden of messianism is seen as falling on the avant-garde, who were distinguished from the people, the rest of the Jews, by their character and destiny alike. The total change in the social order that they sought and saw as essential would remain within the confines of the avant-garde group—the people as a whole would remain unaffected. Moreover, the avant-garde, with few exceptions, thought in terms neither of great political (apocalyptic) coups nor of the military conquest of the land.

In short, political messianism was rarely to be found in the labor movement during the period of the Second and Third Aliyot, although messianic terminology was employed often enough. The thinking of the movement represented a development of Smolenskin's words from the very earliest days of Jewish nationalism: ''We do not seek to bring the Messiah by force, nor do we desire as of now to establish a kingdom. We wish simply for the bread of life in the land and tranquility for those who work it.''[32] Here was no eschatological attempt to bring the millennium, to ''force the End.''

On the face of things, it was the Balfour Declaration that, for a brief moment at least, revitalized those quasi-messianic hopes that had lain dormant since Herzl's last days. Zionist historiography has made much of the ''almost messianic [faith] in the accomplishment of the Zionist dream, of a Jewish state within a few years,''[33] that gripped the Yishuv in the wake of the declaration. Once again, though, this evaluation of the situation is based on a limited number of statements that are highly rhetorical in nature. Shmuel Yavnieli, for example, announced that the declaration represented ". . . the millennium! It is the magic word that we have not dared to utter. Let us speak it now." He went on, "Every Jewish military man in the camp of the Hebrews is doing his part to realize the messianic idea."[34] And there were those who saw in the events of late 1917 a repetition of history, comparing the Cyrus declaration, which had brought the Jews back from Babylon, with the Balfour Declaration delivered to Chaim Weizmann.[35]

Yosef Hayim Brenner, who viewed heroic romanticism and messianism as forms of escapism, as surrender to a burdensome historical mythology, ridiculed the excitement over the Balfour Declaration. With no little sarcasm, he described how, "on the table in front of me there are newspapers full of celebratory articles about Balfour–Cyrus and the dream that for millennia, etc. etc." Brenner maintained that the idea of Balfour as a new Cyrus was based on the blind, naive belief that international affairs were based on principles of good faith and idealism rather than on "the real interests of power."[36] He argued that the Jewish Legion ("the [*shofar*] of messianic Zionism") was a product of naivete and weakness, ever giving itself to meaningless rhetoric. This underlay his famous cry (based on Sanhedrin 99a) "Israel has no Messiah," and so "let us gather our strength in order to live without [him]."[37] He shared the stand of Hapoel Hazair that the Poale Zion party, with its support for the Jewish Legion and for the idea of "the historic leap forward," demonstrated a lack of realism: it had abandoned the ideas of organic growth, the conquest of labor and the conquest of the soil, and instead, had been caught up in self-destructive political messianism.

In actual fact, though, the use of messianic and antimessianic rhetoric and metaphor only masked the real intentions of those who employed them. The truth is that the Balfour Declaration (even when combined with the fateful events in Russia) did not arouse expectations of imminent national Redemption or of an immediate Jewish state. The excitement was caused by the decisive, even revolutionary, change in the standing of the Zionist movement both in the international political arena and also, of course, in Palestine. Zionism, it now seemed, had the chance to pursue its policy of settlement without outside interference. At the very most, the reactions can be said to have expressed something of the nonmessianic messianism defined earlier.

In any event, even the metaphorical and rhetorical use of messianic themes vanished soon enough—long before the utopian ideas went into decline. Both messianic and utopian language had almost completely gone out of fashion by the mid-1920s, except when employed in a pejorative sense. It was this sharp decrease in messianic (or, rather, quasi-messianic) tension within the labor movement and, in particular, within its pioneer avant-garde, that led Uri Zvi Greenberg to react to what he saw as betrayal with stark and biting criticism. He attacked the movement for denying its messianic essence and destiny. However, for its part, the labor movement saw Revisionism, born out of the crisis of the Fourth Aliyah, as nothing other than false messianism come to lead the people astray.

During the 1930s, messianic terminology was not infrequently used in polemics, particularly, for example, during the partition debate that followed the Peel Commission report of 1937. "You should not be the complete realist, the complete statesman," declared Menahem Ussishkin angrily to Weizmann, "Do not merely satisfy yourself with the hope that the Messiah will come—fight to ensure that he does so in our days."[38] In other words, he was accusing Weizmann of that egregious deviation, passive messianism. On the other hand, Ben-Gurion could write during that same debate that Zionist diplomacy should distinguish between realism and mysticism, or in his words, "messianic yearnings," an unbounded faith in Jewish power regardless of circumstances. The nation's statesmen, he argued, should not chase fantasies but see the truth for what it was:[39] the demand for Jewish sovereignty over the entire land of Israel west of the Jordan should be kept in the background until some later date; meanwhile, policy had to be based on what was possible.

In other words, messianism came to be used less and less as the labor movement adopted an overtly realistic and pragmatic stance. The symbols now most favored were drawn from the nation's political and military past (David's kingdom, the prophets, the Hasmonean revolt, the revolt of 66–73 C.E., and Bar Kokhba's war)[40] rather than from messianic mythology. In fact, the distinction drawn between the prophetic and the messianic ideals became particularly pronounced in this period. Generally speaking, in the prevailing political culture during the late 1920s and 1930s, there was a clear preference in the labor movement for a political terminology primarily "modern" in nature, whereas messianic imagery was very clearly associated with the (rejected) traditional world.

In sum, the term "messianism" increasingly became a synonym for "fantasy," that is, a lack of political realism. Even on the eve of, and during, the Second World War—the years of extreme tension and catastrophe—members of the labor movement tended to employ the messianic theme in a pejorative rather than a positive sense. This was not the case, however, at the other end of the political and ideological spectrum. From its very earliest days, Revisionism was described by its enemies on the Left as a romantic and irresponsible political movement. They, therefore, naturally identified it with the European Right and, in due course, even with fascism.[41] However, the fact is that neither messianic ideology nor even messianic metaphor and rhetoric played any significant role in Revisionist publications. They were conspicuously absent in Zev Jabotinsky's writings and in the historical vocabulary employed by other members of the Revisionist leadership.

On closer examination, the accepted opinion that Revisionism entered the political arena imbued with belief in the possibility of mass Redemption (the imminent Ingathering of the Exiles) or in the desirability of a totalitarian society appears to be fallacious. The truth is that Revisionism was an ultranationalist political party suffused with the spirit of romanticism. Even during the great debate of the late 1930s, the Revisionists did not usually summon the messianic ideal to buttress their position; and, of course, they vehemently rejected every attempt to compare their own ideology to Sabbatianism or Frankism.

Messianic metaphor was certainly to be found, however, in the belles lettres and in the historiography produced by members and supporters of the Revisionist movement, as we see in Yaakov Cohen's poem, "The Zealot Anthem" (1933):

The sun in our heart,
Rebellion in our eyes,
And the word of the Lord in our blood,
We,
The hosts of the Messiah,
Brigades of iron and flame.

Cohen's use of the phrase, "The hosts of the Messiah," in this poem (published in the monthly, *Betar*), was clearly intended to suggest that the ancient zealots, in their fight against the Romans, could legitimately be seen as performing a messianic role. The Zealots are described here not simply as archetypal freedom fighters but, more important, as men determined to prepare the way for the Messiah and the establishment of the kingdom of heaven and earth. The poet thus presents a mythological and highly allegorical view of a messianic past that he believes will one day return.

Moreover, a new dimension was added to the messianic vision at this time—the idea of territorial integrity, of the historic borders. Power over, and possession of, the land of Israel were not to be achieved by means of diplomacy or the plough; they could be won by conquest alone. Force of arms was necessary in order to redeem the land from foreign rule and alien claims. The universal and ethical messages so often associated with the messianic and prophetic idea were here supplanted by chauvinistic themes of war. Blood and the sword, the war of conquest, sacrifice: such were the images drawn from ancient eschatological visions and now presented as the inescapable messianic destiny of the Jewish people in the land of Israel.

Although these themes began to appear here and there in Revisionist publications following the Arab riots of 1929, it was only in the great ideological poetry of Uri Zvi Greenberg that any attempt was made to formulate them into a messianic system of thought, a philosophy of history, an active political ideology. The metamorphosis of Greenberg's eschatological outlook (related to changes in both his political affiliations and his poetry in general) as well as the source texts he drew on, deserve a much more detailed examination than can be provided here.[42] Suffice it to say that Greenberg's disciples viewed him as a messianic poet par excellence and believed that he had reached a profound understanding of Jewish history. In their eyes, he had demonstrated the most penetrating insight into the irreversible trends of the time and was thus vouchsafed a clear vision of the future.

On the other hand, Greenberg's critics saw him as the archexponent of a false messianism. In their view, he preached an eschatological vision of complete national redemption at a single stroke—the Diaspora would be brought to an end and the Kingdom of Israel would be established by a war of conquest. The second false element in Greenberg's outlook, as they saw it, was that he advocated a totalitarian society utterly dedicated to the messianic ideal. In this way, Greenberg was perceived, on the one hand, as a fantasist, on the other, as a fascist.

Greenberg was, perhaps, the only Zionist thinker of his day to seek not simply to *interpret* Jewish history in messianic terms but also to translate his ideas into a *concrete program* of immediate political relevance. He saw Zionism as a messianic movement in its very essence, and Herzl as the man, "born in the Holy Spirit," who had brought the messianic tidings. Aliyah, immigration to the land of Israel, whether individual or collective, should constitute a messianic act; not merely a physical change of place, it had to bring with it a complete, existential metamorphosis that gave the immigrant, the pioneer, a completely new spiritual outlook and made him literally a new man.

Thus, in the early 1920s, while still in the labor movement, Greenberg could describe the pioneers of the Third Aliyah both in poetry and prose as a messianic avant-garde. They were, in his opinion, bringing to life a new "total ideal," and so constituted the antithesis of the petit bourgeois ethos found not only in Exile but also in Palestine. For him they represented the renewal, in mythological and allegorical terms, of the heroic, superhuman life lived in ancient Palestine. To the Fourth Aliyah, with its openly bourgeois and "normal" values, he reacted with a horrified sarcasm, seeing it as devoid of any metaphysical or messianic ideology, ideals or ethos.

There was no place in his Zionism for a universal message. Particularly after the Arab rioting of 1929, the territorial theme began to replace the existential motif in his concept of messianism. No longer was he thinking in terms of building a new and perfect society on the ruins of a bourgeois (or Christian and antisemitic) Europe; he now developed instead a mystic Jewish nationalism to confront the brutality of Arab nationalism. And on another level, he confronted the Yishuv with the vision of a golden age when the Jewish people, a unique physical and metaphysical entity, a perfect and unchanging *Volksstamm*, would fulfill its ancient destiny.

In this messianic scheme of things, the nation's sovereignty over its entire historical homeland was of supreme significance. Like Martin Buber,[43] he, too, saw the union between nation and land as mystical and sacred—sanctified by history and endowed with existential and metahistorical import. However, Greenberg (here in contrast to Buber) was utterly convinced that this union could only be consummated by full possession of the land. For him, the spiritual and cultural renaissance of the Jewish people could be achieved by nothing less.

Greenberg's poetry of the 1930s applied an eschatological key to historic and contemporary events and was imbued with a messianic tension quite unlike anything produced by members of the labor movement. It was composed against the background of the Arab rebellion in Palestine (1936–1938) and the impending catastrophe faced by Polish Jewry. These developments heightened both the fear of apocalyptic cataclysm and the expectation of the Redemption to be brought about by human hands:

> And I have a Messiah,
> Perhaps still far off,
> Hidden in David's sword
> In his sheath.[44]

He gives a vivid (almost realistic) description of the Polish Jews crossing the seas, supported by the Messiah–Redeemer:

> And he will be as a lion arising in the Yishuv
> The Black Sea to his right and the Baltic Sea to his left

> Hasidim will rush to immerse themselves
> Hastily donning their Sabbath dress on an ordinary weekday.[45]

These hopes of the millennium presented (albeit in verse) as a concrete political program infuriated many. Among those angered was Nahum Sokolow, then president of the Zionist Organization, who wrote these harsh words in 1935, "A new Shabbetai Zvi-ism has appeared in the world—or more accurately a new Frankism, the later Polish version of this delusion—in the form of conspiracy . . . that captures young hearts by means of a militaristic mystique."[46]

Some two years earlier, Hayim Arlosoroff had acutely perceived the nature of the quasi-messianic expectations felt by the Polish Jews, who yearned desperately for charismatic leadership and grandiose plans—thus exerting pressure on the politics of the Yishuv. In a letter to his wife written from Włocławek, Poland, on May 28, 1933, he described the crowds at the railroad station who had greeted him as if he were the "redeemer" bearing tidings of salvation, "As I know too well, there are few points of contact between this dream and reality. The object of their adulation is a total figment of their imagination. However, even as such, he is of symbolic value to the movement and so may do some good."[47]

Although Greenberg's writings constituted the boldest attempt to articulate a non-religious messianic vision, he cannot be said to have produced a full-scale or consistent ideology. It was his apostles—led by Yehoshua Heshel Yeivin, a writer and member of the so-called maximalist trio [Yeivin, Greenberg himself and Abba Ahimeir], and Dr. Yisrael Sheib (Eldad), a leader of Betar in Poland and of the Lehi (Stern Group) in Palestine—who laid the mantle of messianic prophecy on Greenberg's shoulders, proclaiming him the herald of "realistic messianism" and even hailing him as the founder of a genuinely messianic movement. They managed to discount the possible theological heterodoxy contained in his assertion that the attainment of national sovereignty had to precede the return of the Jewish people to full religious observance by appealing to Rabbi Yehoshua's pronouncement that Redemption would precede repentance (Palestinian Talmud, Ta'anit 1:5). Greenberg's followers were also able to cite other classical messianic works (such as the early medieval *Book of Zerubbavel*) that likewise regarded Redemption as independent of repentance.[48] (It is worth noting that their stance on this issue was little different from that of members in the traditional religious camp who harbored activist messianic leanings. They, too, viewed religious revival as conditional on political and territorial renewal rather than vice versa.)[49]

The fact that Greenberg's poetry gave expression not only to intimations of looming catastrophe and apocalypse, but also to faith in imminent Redemption, was the source of the enormous inner tensions evident in his poetry. This response, however, was rarely reflected in the Revisionist ideology of Betar or the Irgun during the 1930s and 1940s: there radical but unadulterated nationalism reigned supreme even when messianic terminology was employed. When, for example, Ahimeir wrote, "Our Messiah will not come in the form of a poor man riding a donkey. The Messiah will come, as all messiahs do, riding on a tank and bearing tidings to the people,"[50] he was, for all the messianic rhetoric, simply using a straightforward metaphor inspired by revolutionary heroism and wars of independence. In general, it was the example of modern European revolutionary movements that had the most formative effect on the Zionist Right. It was only the desire to clothe this experience in Jewish metaphors that led to the frequent use of messianic imagery.

Moreover, for the radical Right, the use of such imagery was appealing because it seemed to emphasize that Jewish heroism was uniquely authentic (with itself as a prime example) and that national wars were immanent in Jewish history and, again, qualitatively unique. It was this desire to underline the degree of continuity between the Lehi and historical messianic movements that led Avraham ("Yair") Stern to write a series of articles, published under the title "The Messianic Movements in Israel," in the underground paper *Bamaḥteret* during the period 1940–1941. Here, indeed, an attempt was made to translate Greenberg's eschatological poetry into concrete political terms.

Stern argued forcefully that the messianic ideal, "the utter certainty that the Messiah will come, is not the creation of the Diaspora." Instead, this idea was born at the time when the nation suffered under Roman subjugation, although it grew stronger after the destruction of the Second Temple. It was able to console the people for their loss and give them hope for both a dramatic Redemption and vengeance against their enemies. Opposed to this nationalist, historical messianism, as Stern saw it, stood a passive, mystical, ahistorical messianism; in his view, the whole of Jewish history could be reduced to the eternal struggle between these two forces. The struggle for independence and Lehi's declaration of war on the British authorities thus became nothing less than the last link in the chain of messianic activism.

Following Stern's violent death, Yisrael Eldad took upon himself the task of organizing these fragmentary thoughts and ideas into a systematic and reasoned ideology. He did this in a series of articles entitled *"Avnei yesod"* ("Foundation Stones") that was published in 1943 in the movement's journal, *Heḥazit* (the successor to *Bamaḥteret*). Eldad described Zionism in entirely messianic terms: Jewish national aspirations were in no way the result of suffering in the Diaspora, and mere Jewish sovereignty was not the true goal. Zionism had to be understood as an expression of the Jewish destiny and of the immutable sovereignty inherent in the Jewish people, and its goal was the restoration of the golden age of the Davidic kingdom. This term took on a mythological and allegorical status in Lehi's messianic scheme of things[51] (the "Kingdom" forms one of the divine spheres in kabbalistic thought).

It is not easy to evaluate the impact that this militant messianic ideology had even on Lehi itself. The articles on this subject that were published during the years of the armed struggle only reflected the outlook of a small group of "prophets" and their disciples. They were not characteristic of the underground movement as a whole, which expressed its ideas primarily in classical national-revolutionary terminology. There is even disagreement regarding the extent to which the majority identified with the messianic program of the "Eighteen Principles of the Revival," supposedly the manifesto of the movement.

In the years prior to the establishment of the state, then, messianic ideology was employed systematically only by marginal groups. Even in the most intense period of drama and anticipation, from 1944 to 1948, it is almost impossible to find genuine declarations of messianic fervor in the mainstream.

Furthermore, the establishment of the state itself was rarely understood as the arrival of the millennium, despite the undoubtedly dramatic way in which it came about. The War of Independence, dissatisfaction with the country's truncated borders, disappointment with the developing character of the state and, above all, the marginal role played by messianic ideas and metaphors in symbolism and historical allusion acted together to deny to the establishment of an independent Jewish state—a revolutionary breakthrough that could well have been interpreted as a messianic event—any historic or metahistorical messianic significance.

However, the messianic theme can still be followed during the 1950s. First, David Ben-Gurion, who had previously avoided using messianic ideas or metaphors, now tried to confer on the state a new symbolism, portraying it not just as a regime, a political end in itself, but as a radically new means for the Jewish people to fulfill their historic mission. This "messianic destiny," as Ben-Gurion formulated it, was thoroughly bound up with the Ingathering of the Exiles, with making the desert bloom, with the ethical duties of the state. His critics, however, suspected that this form of messianic rhetoric masked an urge to endow the state with absolute power.[52]

Another possible example of messianism in the 1950s was to be found on the fringes of the political spectrum. The "Sulam" group was formed by past members of Lehi who refused to abandon their militant and messianic nationalist ideology. They were extremely critical of all aspects of the state as it had developed since 1948, and they continued to dream of the establishment of the Third Commonwealth that would, among other things, attain the nation's maximal historical frontiers.

Different fates were in store for these two types of messianic formula. Ben-Gurion's use of messianic terminology, which aroused much hostility, was already becoming rare by the mid-1950s. The messianism of the Sulam group, in contrast, survived on the periphery of Israeli political life only to be launched suddenly onto center stage by the events prior to, during and after the Six Day War of 1967. Since then, it has grown into a major force in Israeli political culture.

I have already noted that the widespread interest in the history of Jewish messianic movements was clearly linked to the urge to define the place of Zionism within Jewish history. And there is no question that both historians and writers did a great deal to familiarize the public at large with the major messianic episodes of the past. Such scholars as Joseph Klausner, A. Z. Aescoly, Yehudah Even-Shmuel Kaufman, Ben-Zion Dinur, A. Marmorstein, Gershom Scholem and Yitzhak Baer[53] made available to the Hebrew reader for the first time documentary collections and academic studies of the subject, while literary treatments of messianic themes often caught the public imagination.[54]

Though a wide-ranging corpus of messianic material was thus available to the general reader, it would seem that in the ideological polemics of the time little distinction was drawn between the different historical forms of messianism. Moreover, a particular interpretation of messianism as such and of its place in Jewish history did not necessarily match the political ideology of the scholar involved; at times, the opposite appeared to be the case. Academic research, after all, followed its own rules, at least to some extent. Messianism as a generalized category became a yardstick against which to measure the Zionist ethos as a whole, its relationship to Judaism and its place in the continuity of Jewish history. Messianism was widely seen as an expression of the life-force of the Jewish people—a source of dynamism and vitality in opposition to the mundane concerns of the halakhah.

The historiographical viewpoint represented on the Left by Rubashov (Shazar) and Dinur, for example, reveals a remarkable (though ultimately not surprising) similarity to the views held by some groups on the Right. The similarity is not unexpected, as there were many at both poles who shared the same strong romantic nationalist tendencies. In 1925, on the three-hundredth anniversary of Shabbetai Zvi's birth, Rubashov published an article in *Davar* in which he extolled the virtues of the man who had, "through the magic of messianic hopes, established a popular movement of dimensions hitherto unknown in the history of the Diaspora.''[55] Klausner (even though he stood much further to the Right) described Shabbetai Zvi more circumspectly as a man who had "claimed that he could bring the Redemption by means of the practical Kabbalah and miracles,'' and contrasted him most unfavorably with Don Yosef Nasi, who had tried to bring the Redemption nearer by the use of normal (including political) means.[56] Even Klausner, however, tended to attribute the various outbursts of false messianism to the national longing for Zion, regarding them therefore as genuine revolutionary movements.

Klausner divided the messianic movements of Jewish history into two classes: rational and irrational (mystical) movements (though he regarded both as expressing a negative urge to escape from history). He defined the irrational movements as those in which the yearning for Zion had become so intense that the everyday mitzvot were considered as no longer binding:

> This yearning at times gives the impression of having represented nothing but a pathological craving for something non-existent—an empty longing, expressive only of a religious romanticism. And yet, not infrequently, while watching, we see that this yearning became a mighty driving force, bursting its way into history and working wonders. Then the realization comes upon us that we have witnessed a total revolution in the life of the Jews.[57]

He argued that these irrational movements, with their new values drawn from within rather than from without (in contrast to those of the rational movements), set the land of Israel at the center of Jewish life and thought, thus transforming what had been simply religious sentiment into an explosive national force.

Klausner saw a dialectical process as built into the history of Jewish messianism that, on the one hand, was drawn toward heresy, heterodoxy and an escape from history and, on the other hand, was drawn to the land of Israel as the national territory, thus preventing a total divorce from reality. Historic— that is, rabbinic—

Judaism responded to this challenge by reemphasizing, in turn, the value and status of the national homeland.

In modern times, Klausner argued, secular Zionism, for all its opposition to tradition, found itself forced by a similar process to place an ever greater emphasis on the importance of the land of Israel. At the very heart of the contemporary transformation of Jewish "dehistoricism" into creative "historicism," Klausner argued, was a romanticism that saw the national heritage and collective memory as of intrinsic worth and that encouraged dreams of political renewal in the ancestral homeland.

Klausner's historical conception (*Geschichtskonstruktion*) shares a common denominator with that of Ben-Zion Dinur, who likewise described the magnetic pull of the land of Israel as a central (or perhaps, *the* central) factor in Jewish history. Dinur laid heavier emphasis, however, on the various forms of Jewish messianic excitement in medieval Europe, seeing them not merely as symptomatic of the past, but also as possessing long-term significance. The messianic urge at work in traditional society encouraged aliyah as a means to hasten the Redemption as well as fostering the search for new ways to establish contact with distant and lost Jewish communities (the Ten Tribes).

Dinur and his students claimed that not only was there no contradiction or break between the Jewish faith (and commandments) and active messianism, but that the two were even organically connected. He was, therefore, able to view Sabbatianism in a basically favorable light because, in his view, it had revived hope in the resettlement of Palestine, produced a literature to reinforce that hope and imbued the mass of the people with the idea that Redemption in the national homeland was a real and imminent possibility.[58] He was able to bypass the fact that Sabbatianism and Frankism were heretical by subsuming them under the general heading of messianism and by stressing that messianic movements in general were in the mainstream of Jewish history.

In contrast, those scholars who continued to view messianism as a heterodox phenomenon and to emphasize the dialectics of continuity and messianic crisis were now faced with a not inconsiderable problem. Their philosophy of history posited the organic unity of Jewish history; and they looked forward to a rebirth of the nation involving, inter alia, not just the attainment of the land of Israel, but also a revolution in Jewish law (halakhah). Messianism in this scheme of things could, it was hoped, serve as an overall ideal and as the basis of the national renaissance that would provide the new Hebrew culture with a metaphysical dimension. They were thus tempted to view false messianism in a positive light, conceiving it as a legitimate element both in their view of history and in their vision of Jewish destiny.

Klausner sought to harmonize the nationalistic and universal aspects of the Jewish messianic vision—to balance the messianic by the prophetic ideal. And he was anxious, too, to give some contemporary relevance to the ideas of Redemption implicit (in his view) in the Haskalah and in the nationalist forms of Judaism in the West. Others on the Right, however, dropped these universal ideas, as well as the concept of the mission theology, without a second thought. Their sole concern was the future destiny of the nation, not of humanity. If they expected a second revelation, it was destined for the Jewish people and not for the world as a whole.

The messianic thought of Klausner (and still more that of Dinur) was developed by Yehoshua Heshel Yeivin, who, in the late 1920s had partnered Uri Zvi Greenberg and Abba Ahimeir in founding the maximalist wing of the Revisionist movement. In 1928 Yeivin published an article entitled *"Minaftulei derekh hageulah"* ("The Twisting Road to Redemption") in the official Zionist weekly *Ha'olam*.[59] The article was accompanied by an editorial that described it as "an important essay on Zionist ideology," but as *"only partly"* reflecting the views of the editors."

Yeivin argued that no widespread messianic movement had arisen in the fourteen hundred years between the fall of Betar at the time of Bar Kokhba and the destruction of Spanish Jewry at the end of the fifteenth century (apart from the uprising of David Elroi, which did not impinge on the Jewish centers in Europe). In contrast to Klausner, Yeivin did not include the Karaite messianic movements in his discussion but, along with Dinur, he did see Jewish history from the sixteenth century on as "a series of almost unremitting attempts to attain Redemption." He sought the explanation for this development in, among other things, the influence of European nationalism, the new geographical discoveries of the day and the schisms in the Christian church.

The notion that Redemption would come in the wake of historical crises was, as he saw it, the major factor that had given rise to various messianic schemes and programs. He viewed sixteenth- and seventeenth-century messianic activity— David Reuveni's military fantasy, Rabbi Yaakov Berab's attempt to renew the ancient rabbinical ordination, the kabbalistic system of Rabbi Yitzhak Luria and Shabbetai Zvi's dreams of kingship—as being manifestations of a single revivalist movement "to turn the wheel of Hebrew history toward national liberation." In the hundred years between the mid-eighteenth and the mid-nineteenth century, however, Hasidism had succeeded in cooling down the messianic excitement and in finding a spiritual substitute for the magnetic pull of the land of Israel.

Herzl's role in Jewish history, Yeivin maintained, was as successor not to the founder of the Hasidic movement, the Baal Shem Tov, but to Shabbetai Zvi. Herzl's form of Zionism was "a messianic movement in modern garb: essentially uncompromising, its goal was to revolutionize Jewish history." (It was Buber's quasi-messianism, according to Yeivin, that was the modern reincarnation of Hasidism and that could, therefore, endanger "Herzlian messianism.") Yeivin claimed that Herzlian Zionism could

> trace its pedigree back to David Reuveni, Shlomo Molkho and Shabbetai Zvi. From the hands of these few rebels it has accepted its standard, which it should bear proudly . . . for it has but one clear and unmistakable aim: the quest for territorial Redemption, the foundation of the Kingdom for, and by, the Jewish nation on the soil of Israel.[60]

Any discussion of the role of messianism in secular Zionist political culture and in the Yishuv must take into account the complexities of the subject. Thus, for example, as argued here, the relationship between modern nationalism and the messianic ideal (or past outbursts of messianism) is one issue; and the possibly messianic character of Zionism as a movement allegedly seeking to "force the End" or attain total Redemption is another. It is one thing to use the concept of messianic tension as a definition of mass psychosis or fever and something very different to undertake a scholarly exploration of the messianic phenomenon in history. Yet another distinction is that between a messianic ideology or belief system and the more or less casual (or, more often, manipulative) use of messianic allusions or rhetoric.

I have described how Zionists in the Yishuv, despite their political differences, shared a penchant for translating a string of contemporary terms and concepts into messianic language. Thus, for example, revolution could become "Redemption"; a diplomatic triumph, "the bells of the Messiah"; a war, "the birth pangs of the Messiah"; an avant-garde, "the army of the Messiah." It is, of course, no easy task to tell when such usage was merely a question of rhetorical effect, of fashion, and when it was the outcome of a conscious and reasoned decision.

At all events, if we define political messianism as the impatient and expectant hope for a single, dramatic, all-embracing Redemption that would create a radically new world of predetermined and unchangeable shape, then the overall weltanschauung of Zionism (in particular, of its two main parties in the period discussed here) may be said to have demonstrated some, albeit essentially marginal, signs of messianism. The more extreme the group, whether on the Left or the Right, the stronger the expression of messianic themes and sentiments became. A careful distinction must, however, be made between mood, *mentalité* and even historical consciousness, on the one hand, and political ideologies, programs and activity, on the other. This latter, more operative category displayed only the very faintest traces of active messianism in the period surveyed here.

It was the eschatological idea, the longing for a totally new Jewish world to replace the old one as it disintegrated, that stimulated the Zionist ethos, particularly in the period 1917–1922. However, even then, as we have emphasized, utopian elements undoubtedly played a stronger role than messianism—at least until nationalist messianism was taken up so enthusiastically by some members of the radical Right.

The cult of redemptionism was quite incompatible (and remained in a constant state of tension) with the "realistic" political and ideological stance of the Zionist movement as a whole that, opposing any hasty attempts to bring on the millennium, preached patience in attaining its goals.

In conclusion, it should be noted that the generation of Zionists discussed here was one that lived through the violent extremes of annihilation and "Redemption." They did not, however, produce any new or original messianic ideas. It may be that their mood was simply too realistic to find consolation in dreams. But perhaps the fact that they inhabited so tangible and dynamic a world rather than an imagined world of messianic visions enabled them to find a balance between messianic mysticism and historical realism.

Notes

This paper does not deal with religious Zionism, which developed very different attitudes toward messianism than those of secular Zionism. There is also no reference to the "civic" or liberal camp in Zionism and the Yishuv, which lacked a messianic dimension.

1. See, e.g., Yosef Gorni, *Aḥdut ha'avodah 1919–1930: hayesodot hara'ayoniim ve-hashitah hamedinit* (Tel-Aviv: 1973), 17–23. Here the author discusses the atmosphere in the labor movement after the Balfour Declaration, using terms such as "messianic expectations," "messianic feeling" and "messianic-political activism." Messianic metaphor did lead some contemporaries to call those who had enlisted in the Jewish Legion "the soldiers of the Judean army" who are "realizing the messianic ideal." Equally, the struggle over the socialist nature of the Yishuv after the war was referred to, e.g., as "the war of Gog and Magog." Anita Shapira also mentions in connection with the Balfour Declaration "messianic hopes" and "a wave of messianic excitement" that, in her view, vanished during the year 1918, see "Haẓiyonut vehakoaḥ—etos umeẓiut," in Anita Shapira, *Hahalikhah 'al kav haofek* (Tel-Aviv: 1989), 41–42 and passim.

2. See Moshe Idel's new introduction to Aharon Zev Aescoly, *Hatenu'ot hameshihiyot beyisrael* (Jerusalem: 1987 [1st ed. 1956]), 10–11. Yishayahu Tishby, *Meshihiut bedor gerushei sefarad ufortugal* (Jerusalem: 1985), 52–53.

3. The majority of those who have written on the subject do not distinguish between the different and sometimes conflicting messianic ideals and expectations to be found in Jewish tradition. These, in fact, presented a wide range of messianic possibilities (i.e., different types of expectations and ways of viewing the future). Cf. Moshe David Herr, "Meshihiut medinit reialit umeshihiut eskhatologit kosmit bedivrei ḥazal," *Tarbiẓ* 54, no. 3 (1985), 331–346.

4. Avraham Shapira has found in Martin Buber's writings of the 1930s (in particular, his first lectures at The Hebrew University in 1938) ideas prefiguring those of Jacob Talmon. Buber dealt with the total nature of secular political messianism, which surrenders its coercive powers to an overwhelming political force. Talmon, however (and perhaps Buber, too), was able to reach his conclusions concerning the nature of totalitarian democracy—the inevitable result of secular messianism—on the basis not only of de Tocqueville, but also of Carl I. Becker, *The Heavenly City of the Eighteenth-Century Philosophers* (New Haven: 1932). By 1975, this book had reached its thirty-ninth edition, though it was only translated into Hebrew in 1979. It is worth noting here that Buber's outlook on culture was also total in nature. However, in his existential eschatology, the creation of a single, unified culture had to be the result of a spontaneous process rather than of pressure from an elite or higher authority. See Avraham Shapira, "Meshihiyut politit umekomah betefisat hageulah shel Martin Buber," in *Devarim lezikhro shel Martin Buber bimeleat 'esrim shanah liftirato'* (no ed. named) (Jerusalem: 1977), 51–72. Jacob Talmon's *The Origins of Totalitarian Democracy* was first published in Hebrew (as *Reishitah shel hademokratiyah hatotalit*) in 1955. The Hebrew version of the second part, *Political Messianism: The Romantic Phase*, was published (as *Hameshihiyut hapolitit*) ten years later. It would be interesting to try to analyze both the seminal effect of Talmon's work on the understanding of Zionism (and other modern ideological movements) as messianism and the ways in which his ideas were taken up and used by others. No less interesting would be an attempt to see how Talmon's view of messianism affected that of others, particularly Gershom Scholem. It would seem likely that Talmon had the greatest influence on historians working in modern history, since he dealt more with the messianic mentality than with the nature of the traditional messianic idea and its transfer to the realm of secular ideology.

5. Andrzej Walicki, *Philosophy and Romantic Nationalism: The Case of Poland* (Oxford: 1982), 240.

6. Anthony D. S. Smith, *Nationalism in the Twentieth Century* (London: 1979), esp. ch. 2, "Nationalism and the Millennium," 14–41. It should be noted that the use of traditional motifs is characteristic even of revolutionary movements. Cf. R. J. Werblowsky's comment that "also radical forms of eschatology usually try to legitimate themselves by appeal to one or more element of tradition" in his *Beyond Tradition and Modernity: Changing Religions in a Changing World* (London: 1976), 4–5. Thus, it is hardly surprising to find that use was frequently made of traditional messianic motifs in the revolutionary ideas developed within the Zionist movement. See also S. Thrupp (ed.), *Millennial Dreams in Action* (The Hague: 1972); Yonina Talmon, "The Pursuit of the Millennium: The Relation

Between Religion and Social Change," *European Journal of Sociology* 3 (1962), 125–140.

7. See Shmuel Almog, "Hameshiḥiyut keetgar leẓiyonut," in *Meshiḥiyut vee-skhatologiah* ed. Zvi Baras (Jerusalem: 1983), 419–431.

8. It is important to distinguish here between the common nineteenth-century ideas of Judaism's universal mission as well as the Judaeo-messianic views of revolutionary and missionary movements and an outlook such as that of Klausner. The latter saw in national unity and national sovereignty a condition essential both for the fulfillment of the universal messianic idea within the framework of Jewish society and for the dissemination of the Jewish national ideal among the nations.

Mission theology was thus fused with a political-nationalist outlook, Judaism with human-ity. Klausner's book was published in three parts—in 1909, 1921 and 1923. See Joseph (Yosef) Klausner's introduction to his *Har'ayon hameshiḥi beyisrael mereishito ve'ad ḥatimat hamishnah*, 2nd ed., corrected and enlarged (Jerusalem: 1927), 3–18. Klausner developed his ideology in no small measure in order to prove that the Jewish messianic ideal represented exalted utopian social ideals and, therefore, had no need of Marxism or materialist Commu-nism. He argued that, unlike that of Communism, the messianic social vision of the Israelite prophets was essentially ethical. The nationalist ideology took up the universal aspect of Israelite prophecy, which mission theology had divested of all nationalist implications, but it tended to limit its significance to Jewish national and social questions alone: its purpose became the establishment not of a new world, but of a new Jewish world. The idea of a "mission to the nations" as expressed by Herzl or Klausner (among others) came to the fore again in the 1950s, when it was taken up by David Ben-Gurion.

9. On the extremely uncertain attitude of the Palestinian labor movement toward the Bolshevik revolution, see Anita Shapira, "'Black Night—White Snow': Attitudes of the Palestinian Labor Movement to the Russian Revolution, 1917–29," in *Studies in Contempo-rary Jewry*, vol. 4, *The Jews and the European Crisis, 1914–21*, ed. Jonathan Frankel, (New York: 1988), 144–171; *idem*, "Berl Tabenkin, uVen-Gurion veyaḥasam lemahapekhat ok-tober," in *Hahalikhah 'al kav haofek*, 258–292.

10. On 27 September 1932, *Haareẓ* published an article by Shlomo Haalkushi, in which he described the "negation of the Diaspora" in Revisionist ideology as false messianism. Such attacks on Zev Jabotinsky's Revisionist movement were commonplace at that time.

11. This ambivalent attitude characterized the treatment of Sabbatianism from the ear-liest days of the Haskalah. See Shmuel Verses, *Haskalah veshabtaut: toldotav shel maavak* (Jerusalem: 1988). To the generations that witnessed the rise of popular movements, only Sabbatianism could have presented some possible parallel in Jewish history to what they had seen.

12. See the speech of Nahum Rafalkis-Nir in *Ve'idat krakov shel mifleget po'alei ẓiyon berusyah, 1907 (te'udot [documents])*, ed. with a preface by Matityahu Minc (Tel-Aviv: 1979), 152.

13. See, e.g., the discussion concerning messianic faith that took place in the German Rabbinical Conference held in Frankfurt in 1845 in *Ve'idat harabanim begermaniah bashanim 1844–1846*, intro. M. Meyer (Jerusalem: 1986), 37–45. See also Michael Graetz, "Hameshiḥiut haḥilonit bemeah hatesh'a-'esreh kederekh shivah leyahadut," in *Baras, Meshiḥiyut veeskhatologiah;* 401–418; Baruch Mevorach, *Sheelat hamashiaḥ befulmusei haemanzipaẓiah vehareformah, 1781–1819* (Ph.D. diss., The Hebrew University, 1966). The question of messianic faith in Judaism in the nineteenth century was one of the crucial questions in the controversy between the supporters of the Reform movement, of Orthodox Judaism and of secular Jewish nationalism. The nationalists were also forced to deal with the Enlightenment point of view that the messianic ideal belongs to the area of folklore and that belief in the Messiah is not one of the foundations of the faith but rather a reaction to historical circumstances—in other words, belief in the Messiah is neither realistic nor neces-sary in the age of Emancipation. See Mordechai Levin, *'Erkhei ḥevrah vekhalkalah baidiologiah shel tekufat hahaskalah* (Jerusalem: 1975), 227–231.

14. Eliezer Ben-Yehudah, *Yisrael learẓo ulelshono*, ed. Itamar Ben-Avi (Jerusalem: 1929), 221.

15. See Werses, *Haskalah veshabtaut*, 185–186.

16. Ephraim E. Urbach, *Koresh vehakhrazato be'einei ḥazal,''* *Molad* 19, no. 157 (1961), 368–374.

17. On the question of Laurence Oliphant's standing, see Shulamit Laskov's conclusions in *Habiluim* (Jerusalem: 1979), 54–71.

18. See Yaacov Shavit, "The Return to Zion in the Hibbat Ziyon Movement," *Zionism* 9 (1984), 359–372. I intend to deal with the question of the rise and fall of Cyrus as a historical symbol in modern Jewish national consciousness at greater length elsewhere. There are a number of aspects to the messianism of the Return to Zion that differed from the later prophecies to be found, e.g., in Chronicles. On the one hand, it is restorative in nature, dreaming of a past golden age, whereas, on the other hand, it contains very strong utopian elements and the vision of an entirely new world. The literature on this subject is too extensive to be summarized here. On the feeling of history repeating itself and its effect on those in this period who acted to make it come true, see Sarah Japhet, *Emunot vede'ot besefer divrei hayamim umekoman ba'olam hamaḥshavah hamikrait* (Jerusalem: 1977), 327.

19. Ahad Ha'am's essay "Be'ikvot meshiḥa" was published in *Hashiloaḥ* 16, no. 2 (1907), and *idem*, *'Al parashat derakhim* (Berlin: 1930), vol. 4. 97–100.

20. According to Ahad Ha'am, it was "people like this who once followed Shabbetai Zvi and Frank farther than Africa: [they took] a road from which there is no return. How, then, can they fail to follow Herzl to Africa in order to return from there to the land of Israel?'' "Habokhim," in *'Al parashat derakhim*, vol. 3, 200.

21. See David Vital, *Hamahapekhah haẓiyonit*, vol. 1, *Reshit hatenu'ah* (Tel-Aviv: 1978), 243, n. 5.

22. Quoted in Werses, *Haskalah veshabtaut*, 261.

23. Ibid. for a short discussion of Herzl's attitude toward Sabbatianism, 245–258.

24. See Yosef Gorni, "Hayesod haromanti baidologiah shel ha'aliyah hasheniyah," *Asufot* 10 (1966), 55–75; Jonathan Frankel, "Sefer 'hayizkor' mishnat 1911—he'arah 'al mitosim leumiyim betekufat ha'aliyah hasheniya," *Yahadut zemanenu* 4 (1988), 67–96.

25. This common interpretation of the war of freedom from Rome saw the roots of the war as not only political, but also social in nature. Thus, in its pantheon, the heroes of the Jews' struggle became heroes of the struggle for social justice, etc.

26. Berl Katznelson to Hugo Bergmann 24 August 1920, quoted in Yisrael Kolatt, "Ẓiyonut umeshiḥiyut," in Baras, *Meshiḥiyut veeskhatologiah*, 424. Katznelson, therefore, saw messianism as an attempt at radical change with unattainable goals; on the other hand, activism was a substitute, or perhaps even a synonym, for evolutionist constructivism. This latter ideology does not betray passivity of any kind, demonstrating rather a daring pioneerism that was well beyond that which might have been expected from the historical circumstances, although still remaining within the realm of the possible. Between these two extremes of messianism and activism, however, there was a gray area.

27. See Yisrael Oppenheimer, *Tenuat heḥaluẓ befolin (1917–1929)* (Jerusalem: 1982), 194.

28. See, e.g., Elkanah Margalit's attempt to distinguish between the positive utopian attitudes of the Gedud Ha'avodah and Hashomer Hazair and their members' attraction toward more dangerous millenarian utopianism, despair and nihilism (see *Hashomer haẓa'ir: mi'edat ne'urim lemarksizm mahapakhani 1913–1936* [Tel-Aviv: 1971], 17–25. Margalit examines the growth of Hashomer Hazair in an atmosphere that varied from a messianic idealism and perfectionism to bitter disappointment, disillusion, despair and even nihilism, and he discusses the themes and metaphors of both extremes. See *idem*, *Komunah, ḥevrah ufolitikah: gedud ha'avodah 'al-shem Trumpeldor beerez-yisrael: masah bemasoret haradikalism hakomunotari vehashivyoniut betenu'at ha'avodah ha'ivrit* (Tel-Aviv: 1980), 11–54; Anita Shapira, "Leshivro shel ḥalom eḥad: gedud ha'avodah 'al shem Yosef Trumpeldor," in *Hahalikhah al kav haofek*, 157–207. The Labor Battalion represents the best example of a messianic avant-garde to be found in the Yishuv, and so it is very often characterized by the terms "utopian" and "messianic," used either separately or in concert.

29. G. Hanoch, "Dorshei haḥazon," *Hapo'el haẓair*, 20 May 1927.

30. *Kehilatenu*, 1922 collection, reissued with a commentary and illustrations by Muki Zur (Jerusalem: 1988), 145.

31. *Ibid.*, 155.

32. Peretz Smolenskin, "Neḥapesah darkeinu," in his *Maamarim* (Jerusalem: 1920), 118.

33. Shapira, "Haẓiyonut vehakoaḥ," 38–42; Gorni, *Aḥdut ha'avodah 1919–1930*, 19–23.

34. Quoted in Gorni, *Aḥdut ha'avodah 1919–1930*, 18–19; Shapira, *Haẓiyonut vehakoaḥ"* 39. This is one of the best examples of messianic rhetoric being used as evidence for the existence of a collective mood.

35. In S. Ben Zion's article "El mul penei hahistoriyah," which was published in the "Shay shel sifrut" supplement to the *Palestine News* of 5 July 1918. He viewed the Balfour Declaration as "history repeating itself," and Cyrus's declaration as "the historical present."

36. Yosef Hayim Brenner, "Seridei siḥot noshanot," in *Kol kitvei Y. H. Brenner* (Tel-Aviv: 1960), vol. 2, 159–161. Brenner also saw service in the Battalions, at least from the point of view of many who did so, as following "the trumpet call of messianic Zionism," and he commented somewhat epigrammatically, "our messianic faith stems from our weakness or is even its cause; at all events, he will not come mounted on a knightly charger, our Messiah." This view of service in the Jewish Legion during the First World War as an expression of sword-bearing messianic Zionism is of course metaphorical: the Battalions were never meant to conquer Palestine and establish Jewish sovereignty there.

37. Yosef Hayim Brenner, "Ba'itonut uvasifrut," *Hapo'el haẓa'ir* 24 November 1910.

38. *Protokol hakongres haẓiyoni ha'esrim*, the fifth session of the Jewish Agency, August 1937, Jerusalem, 46.

39. David Ben-Gurion, *Zikhronot* (Tel-Aviv: 1974), vol. 4, 388. Ben-Gurion did not view the breakthrough to the partition plan, which was eventually to facilitate the establishment of a Jewish state in part of western Palestine, as a messianic event. Rather, he characterized the messianic age as being the time when there would be "a world without evil"—a contemporary reference to the rise of Nazism (*ibid.*, 294). The critics of the partition plan vilified the eagerness for the immediate establishment of a state as the "dizzy desire for a state and Shabbetai Zvi's dream" (*ibid.*, 145). Thus, any political scheme that seemed unrealistic was soon stigmatized as false messianism. On the development of Ben-Gurion's political views during the First World War, see Matityahu Minc, "'Hakonẓepẓiah hahistorit: levirur 'emdato hapolitit vehaẓiyonit shel David Ben-Gurion be'et milḥemet ha'olam harishonah lifnei haẓharat Balfor," *Ziyonut* 13 (1988), 69–88.

40. The historical metaphors used during the years of "the struggle" are surveyed in Hilda Schatzberger, *Meri umasoret beereẓ-yisrael betekufat hamandat* (Tel-Aviv: 1985), 47–69.

41. Yaacov Shavit, *Jabotinsky and the Revisionist Movement 1925–1948* (London: 1988), 322–350.

42. *Ibid.*, 143–151, and the references therein. See also Yaacov Shavit, "Uri Zvi Greenberg: Conservative Revolutionarism and National Messianism," *Jerusalem Quarterly* 48 (Fall 1988), 63–72. On the messianism of Uri Zvi Greenberg, Avraham Stern and Yisrael Sheib (Eldad), see Yosef Heller, *Leḥi: ideologiah ufolitikah: 1940–1949*, 2 vols. (Jerusalem: 1989).

43. Martin Buber, *Bein 'am learẓo: 'ikarei toldotav shel ra'ayon* (Jerusalem and Tel-Aviv: 1984 [1st ed. 1944]).

44. Uri Zvi Greenberg, "Yehudah hayom, yehudah maḥar: masa' devai, masa' gil," *Hayarden* (June 1938).

45. Uri Zvi Greenberg, "He will surely come . . ." *Hamedinah* (Warsaw: 1938).

46. Nahum Sokolow, "Journey Through Poland in 1935," in his *Watchman unto the House of Israel* (Jerusalem: 1961), 256. It is interesting to note that there was an astonishing reversal in political Zionism from the end of the First World War until the 1930s. By then, any expectations of a dramatic political breakthrough were viewed simply as false mes-

sianism. The same Sokolow who treated with derision the Revisionist political program and what he viewed as the false promises it was making had thirty years earlier reacted in exactly the same way to Herzl's vision of a "Jews' State."

47. Hayim Arlosoroff, *Kitvei Ḥayim Arlozorov* (Tel-Aviv: 1934), vol. 6, 264.

48. See Israel Ben-Shalom, "Tahaliḥim veideologiyah betekufat Yavne kegormim akifim lemered bar-Kokhva," in *Mered bar-Kokhva: meḥkarim ḥadashim*, ed. A. Oppenheimer and U. Rappaport (Jerusalem: 1984), 6–7. Ben-Shalom states, "The idea of repentance was one of the key themes in the Zealot ideology during the Second Temple period" (7).

49. In other words, Redemption can be brought about by people who are not religious, and physical redemption is a precondition for repentance. Repentance here does not mean the acceptance of the Law and all its commandments as binding but rather a religious revival—a new revelation. Sheib (Eldad) developed Klausner's dialectic argument (also propounded by Scholem in his 1934 paper *"Miẓvah habaah ba'averah"* [Redemption through Sin]) and argued that "He who comes to redeem us will somehow burst the bounds of existing religious practice, canceling various of the commandments, whether trifling or weighty . . . always with the feeling that Redemption demands some drastic action." Nationalistic messianism is not meant, however, to supersede faith or religion; it must first bring physical Redemption to the nation and only afterwards religious renewal. National renaissance, caused by the power of messianism, is an essential precondition to messianic spiritual revival. See Yisrael Eldad, "Shorshei hamaavak hadati," in his *Hegyonot yisrael* (Tel-Aviv: 1980), 144–162. Though the essay was only published in 1963, it is an excellent summary of his views.

50. Abba Ahimeir in the newspaper, "Doar hayom," 14 October 1928. This quotation has often been taken as evidence of Ahimeir's fascism; in fact, it was written in the wake of the Bolshevik Revolution. See Yosef Nedava's introduction to Ahimeir's *Brit habiryonim: ketavim nivḥarim* (Tel-Aviv: 1972), vol. 3, 7–58. Yeivin echoed these sentiments in a letter from the end of July 1932 in which he wrote that, as revolutionaries, he and his friends could not believe that the Messiah would come on a "bridge of paper." He was referring to the petition then being organized by the Revisionists in order to bring moral pressure to bear on Britain, *ibid.*, 36–37.

51. The Second Temple period is not heavily emphasized in messianic historiosophy because of the deep historical and religious feeling that it was in no way a high point in the history of the Jewish nation and could not compare to the golden age of David and Solomon. In addition, of course, there is the fact that the Jews at that time were exiled from their land. It is interesting to note that Ben-Gurion, too, though for different reasons, tended to play down the Second Temple period, preferring to emphasize the glorious period of the Israelite kingdom. Despite this, it would be accurate to say that the messianic dreams (though not the reality) of the Second Temple period have been the inspiration for modern nationalist messianism, whereas the more ancient visions became more "real" than reality itself.

52. On Ben-Gurion's 1950s polemic with Buber and Scholem, among others, and on the question of messianism, see Shapira, *Hahalikhah 'al kav haofek*, 59; and for a lengthy treatment, see Michael Keren, *Ben Gurion and the Intellectuals: Power, Knowledge, and Charisma* (De Kalb: 1983), 36–99. I do not agree with Keren's interpretation of this issue, though this is not the place to examine his approach in depth.

53. See Moshe Idel's introduction to Aescoly's *Hatenu'ot hameshiḥiyot beyisrael*, 9–10. This book and Even Shmuel's book *Midreshei geulah* were published in 1956 and 1953, respectively, and Yitzhak Baer's article, "Hatenu'ah hameshiḥit besefarad betekufat hageirush," in *Maasef ẓiyon* 5 (1932–1933). Though Scholem's essay, "Miẓvah habaah ba'averah," was published in *Kenesset* 2 (1934), his studies were published only after 1948. I have been unable to find any use made of Abba Hillel Silver's *A History of Messianic Speculation in Israel* (New York: 1927, rpr. Boston 1959) in the period discussed here. Dinur's influence was felt mostly through the lectures he gave at The Hebrew University of Jerusalem and a number of articles in which he gave expression to his Palestinocentric view of Jewish history, and in which he assessed its irrational elements. Marmorstein's articles on the messianic idea in the Tannaite and Amorite writings were published in Hebrew in *Sinai*,

vols. 5, 7 and 8 (1942–1944). See, too, J. Rabinowitz, ed., *Sinai: Jerusalem Studies in Jewish Theology by A. Marmorstein* (Oxford: 1956), 11–56, in which he argued that in the fourth century C.E., the rabbinic leadership came to the conclusion that it was no longer possible to rely on Redemption to be attained by human means, as all attempts of this kind had ended in disaster. There was no alternative in their view except to rely on the divine will and power alone. The blossoming of interest (even in religious circles) in messianism in both academic and literary contexts also belongs to a later period; see, e.g., Raphael Halevi Eisenberg, *Ḥevlei mashiaḥ bezemanenu* (Jerusalem: 1971). A thorough study of the influence of messianism and the publication of messianic texts on modern literature and historical-ideological polemic still remains to be done. Shmuel Werses's recent study (see n. 11) deals with this topic only in relation to Sabbatianism and only in the context of the very earliest days of the Zionist movement.

54. For a preliminary discussion of messianic and catastrophic themes in Polish Jewish literature in interwar Poland, see David Weinfeld, "'Al shirah 'ivrit befolin" in *'Iyunim besifrut: devarim sheneemru ba'erev likhvod Dov Sadan bemeleat lo shemonim veḥamesh shanah* (Jerusalem: 1988), 7–20; see also Chone Shmeruk, "Yeẓirato shel Uri Zvi Grinberg beyidish beereẓ yisrael uvefolin besof shenot ha'esrim vehasheloshim," in *Hasifrut* 29 (December 1979), 82–92. Shmeruk discusses the idea of the "leap forward" as expressed in the poem of the same name of 1924. This poem was later incorporated into still another, entitled *Eimah gedolah veyareaḥ*, whose central character was Shabbetai Zvi. Shmeruk also makes a number of very important points concerning both the publicistic literature of the interwar period that made use of messianic terminology and the use of messianic themes in the Jewish literature of the same period. This must, of course, be seen in the wider context of the interest of Polish historians and other writers in messianism. [On the question of messianism in the Hebrew literature of the interwar period, see Hannan Hever herein 128–158—Ed.]

55. Quoted in Werses, *Haskalah veshabtaut*, 263.

56. See Klausner's article, "Don Yosef Nasi," in his collection of historical studies, *Keshehaumah nilḥemet 'al ḥerutah*, published first in 1936 (and subsequently in a number of editions), 285. The contents of the collection had appeared previously in various contexts.

57. Joseph (Yosef) Klausner, "Ereẓ yisrael utenu'at hamahapekhah beyisrael," in *Keshehaumah nilḥemet*, 294.

58. Dinur's position is reflected most clearly in a later article, "Hatesisah hameshiḥit veha'aliyah leereẓ yisrael mimas'aei haẓlav 'ad hamagefah hasheḥorah, veyesodoteihen haideologiim," in *Lezikhro*, (Jerusalem: 1969), 75–88; repr. in *idem, Bemaavak hadorot* (Jerusalem: 1975), 237–248. See also Aryeh Morgenstern, *Meshiḥiut veyishuv ereẓ yisrael bamaḥaẓit harishonah shel hameah hatesh'a 'esrei* (Jerusalem: 1985).

59. Yehoshua Heshel Yeivin, "Minaftulei derekh hageulah," *Ha'olam* 41 (1928); repr. in *idem, Ketavim* (Tel-Aviv: 1959), 345–350.

60. *Ibid.*

Poetry and Messianism in Palestine Between the Two World Wars

Hannan Hever
(TEL-AVIV UNIVERSITY)

Was there one among the Hebrew poets active in Palestine between the two World Wars who did not touch upon messianic themes in his or her work? Uri Zvi Greenberg, Avigdor Hameiri, Avraham Shlonsky, Yitzhak Lamdan, David Shimonovitz, Yitzhak Ogen, Yehuda Karni, Yocheved Bat-Miryam, Shin Shalom and even, as I shall explain later, Natan Alterman—not one could totally escape the messianic obsession. The messianic strands interwoven into this poetry were closely linked to the Zionist politics and everyday life in Palestine as they developed during the 1920s and 1930s. Working in secular contexts, of course, the poets were drawn time and again to the language, the symbols or even the politics of messianism in their quest to bridge the gap—sometimes perceived as an abyss—between the sublime glory of the national vision and the harsh prosaic realities of the period.

Like other revolutionary and national liberation movements, Zionism transposed eschatology and millenerianism from the religious to a modern and secular sphere, seeking to implement a utopian vision as a necessary phase[1] in the historical progress toward a general salvation of mankind. However, this transference also involved transformation. In concluding his essay "Toward an Understanding of the Messianic Idea in Judaism," Gershom Scholem pointed out the two poles between which the conception of messianism has oscillated in modern Zionist discourse. On the one hand, it is clear that

> overtones of messianism have accompanied the modern Jewish readiness for irrevocable action in the concrete realm, when it set out on the utopian return to Zion.[2]

But on the other hand, "it is a readiness which no longer allows itself to be fed on hopes. Born out of the horror and destruction that was Jewish history in our generation, it is bound to history itself and not to metahistory; it has not given itself up totally to messianism."[3]

In examining the messianic themes in modern Hebrew poetry, one cannot escape the dialectical pattern thus emphasized by Scholem. The ambivalence is most readily apparent in the poetry written in Palestine during the interwar period, which witnessed extreme oscillations between far-reaching hopes and moods of profound despair. Such, for instance, was the rapid shift from the early prosperity of 1924–

1925 (the Fourth Aliyah) to the subsequent period of deep economic crisis. The short recovery was then followed by the shock of the Arab riots in 1929. The hopes aroused in some quarters by the Peel Commission were, in turn, accompanied by the existential anxiety caused by the Arab revolt of 1936–1938.

From the first, the messianic idea provoked ambivalent reactions: revolutionary self-awareness, on the one hand, and the fear that the huge gap between vision and reality could only encourage delusions and false messiahs, on the other hand. These two poles alternately attracted and repelled politicians, publicists and poets alike as they wavered between nostalgia for the Jewish messianic heritage and their fear of its practical implications.

The secular debate over messianism first began to take shape, primarily within the labor movement, in Palestine in the immediate prewar years (the Second Aliyah) and during the First World War itself. Thus, in an essay of 1909 entitled "An Irrational Solution," A. D. Gordon could state emphatically, "The Messiah's horn has not yet sounded, nor will it sound except from within the new life to be created here."[4] On the other hand, Gordon produced a qualified messianic formula that was to characterize labor culture for many years to come, "And this is our task. We must plant the ideal of Redemption and Salvation in its natural terrain; we must foster a new life here, a life of our own, and fix the center of our movement, its gravitational force, in life itself."[5] However, Gordon's ambivalence—on the one hand, seeking to reject millenarianism, on the other, reluctant to do so entirely— was not shared by all members of the Second Aliyah. For his part, Yosef Hayim Brenner wrote in 1910:

> Our people is formed by Exile and is sick; as it walks it stumbles; seven times it falls and gets back on its feet. It is for us to raise it up. Its willpower is weakening—it must be strengthened. Let us become stronger. Israel has no Messiah—let us develop the strength to live without the Messiah.[6]

To emphasize this point, Brenner could quote Rabbi Hillel's well-known antimessianic maxim, "They have no Messiah, for they devoured him in the days of Hezekiah" (Sanhedrin 99a).

Voices of yet another kind made themselves heard during the stormy optimistic period following the Balfour Declaration, when, for example, Shmuel Yavnieli called for volunteers to join the Jewish Battalions:

> In the movement of rebirth that has arisen within the people of Israel during this last generation, we see the beginning of realization of the *messianic* idea. The End [*hakez*]! Here is that magic word we have dared not pronounce, but which we do now. The end to Israel's Exile is nearing. . . . The fact that a broad ramified Zionist organization has . . . reached all the lands of exile, and has drawn hundreds of thousands of Jews under its banner—all these are harbingers of the End. . . . But the formation of the Hebrew army, that is the final clear sign that the End is in sight. Every Jewish soldier in the Hebrew camp is realizing the idea of the Messiah.[7]

But, again, this messianic enthusiasm excited by the new era also provoked vehement opposition, particularly from within the ranks of the Hapoel Hazair party. A. D. Gordon sharply attacked the call to volunteer for the Jewish Battalions and referred ironically to the coming battles as the "Redemption" and to the British as "the Redeemer." Regarding the mobilization as a "war hypnosis," Gordon strongly criticized the moral and spiritual price to be paid: "bloodshed and martyrdom for the sake of the 'Redeemer.' "[8] But for all the disagreements, there was a deep reluctance to abandon altogether the resort to messianic themes. It was precisely the elasticity of the messianic idea that made possible its powerful hold and its employment as one of the mechanisms used by the labor movement to fortify its hegemony in the Yishuv and the Zionist movement at large.

The high degree of legitimacy thus attained by the messianic idea, as well as its ambiguities and the fears that it aroused, all found direct expression in the Hebrew poetry composed in Palestine. Indeed, in no other medium did it attain such prominence. The notion of the poetic text as a modern variant of prophetic vision was not to be missed by Hebrew poetry—and the biblical prophet, after all, had often served as the harbinger of Redemption bearing news of the End of Times and the apocalpytic Day of the Lord that were to precede it. To this one might add the special sensitivity attributed to poets as being more closely attuned to the underlying realities of the day and as possessed of a privileged insight into their profound historical significance.

The question of the poet's prophetic character arose within labor literature in Palestine from its inception.[9] A. D. Gordon voiced his disapproval of the concept, declaring that the prophet would not redeem man, but instead, would only produce "arrogant verbosity, over-enthusiastic delusions, humbug of every conceivable sort—and would-be heroes of the fist, the brain or the spirit."[10] A division appeared among the poets themselves, coinciding by and large with that dividing the avant-garde from the more moderate or conservative modernists. The former, such as Greenberg, Shlonsky, Hameiri and Lamdan, tended to highlight in their poems the prophetic persona, whereas poets such as Mordechai Temkin, M. Z. Wolfowski and Levi Ben-Amitai gave voice in their poems to those who worked the soil, to the plain folk. Despite this opposition, both groups saw themselves, quite rightly, as belonging to the culture of the labor movement. Just as Gordon and Yavnieli were able to coexist in the leadership of that movement, so Greenberg and Ben-Amitai could both find acceptance as its literary spokesmen and poets.

The messianic position can thus be regarded as a radicalization and intensification of the prophetic option. The Messiah is he whose advent is announced by the prophet and who can furthermore assume the role of a savior and a legislator as well as that of a spiritual and political leader. During the early years of the Yishuv, some dreaded this vision, whereas others welcomed it. But as late as the end of the 1920s, a plurality of opinion could exist without open schism; and in that period, poetry was in this respect no different from other channels of discourse.

It seems, however, that poetry from the start allowed a higher pitch of messianic intensity. A notable example of both this pluralism and this intensity are the first two volumes of poetry published by Greenberg and Shlonsky, respectively, soon after their arrival in Palestine—both of which focused on the messianic question. The year was 1924 and both these men, two of the outstanding poets of the Third Aliyah period, now presented the first fruit of their work in Palestine: Greenberg published *Eimah gedolah veyareaḥ* (*Great Fear and the Moon*)[11] and Shlonsky,

Devai (Agony).[12] Both books are essentially collections of longer poems, and in both the concluding poems—Shlonsky's *Habrit haaḥaronah (The Final Covenant)* and Greenberg's *Kefiẓat haderekh (The Shortcut)*—deal with the question of the Messiah.

During this period both these poets produced their work as an organic part of the labor culture. Both had their books printed by the publishing house Hedim, both published ongoing work in *Hapoel hazair* and both were close, each in his own way, to the social ambience of the labor movement. Despite all these similarities, when it came to the Messiah, the positions they espoused were, in fact, no less than contradictory: Shlonsky has the Messiah perish and rejects his message, whereas Greenberg ends his book with this impassioned declaration: "Shabbetai Zvi, arise!"[13]

Shlonsky's Messiah is not an abstract figure but rather a figure whose message springs from concrete suffering and agony. Having just emerged from the tents of the *Gedud Ha'avodah* (Labor Battalion), he wrote the poems of *Devai* in the spirit of messianic ambivalence. The cautious attitude he takes vis-à-vis the messianic idea is clearly to be seen in the complicated, yet consistent, course he follows in sketching out the hopeful possibilities still remaining in the postwar modern era. After the Jewish option (Moses seeking to renew the first Covenant), the Christian option (Jesus seeking to revive the new Covenant), after Elijah (who rejects them both in the name of the individual's need of salvation) and after the traditional Messiah (the Son of David)—who makes an appearance toward the end of the poem—Job comes forward to propose the "final Covenant." He demands that all these harbingers of hope renounce the idea of a Redemption defined entirely in terms of the desirable ("Down with you, who seek Redemption for the sake of . . . !")[14] and in total disregard of the individual who opts for a message of suffering:

> Let go of man
> Let him go his suffering way, and love it, let him go and dare—
> For that is Redemption![15]

In the "Kaddish" ending the poem, the Fool mourns the traditional messianic option. But despite the elimination of the Messiah, the Son of David, the poem still retains a messianic dimension. For, as the alternative to existing versions of salvation, Job declares agony and suffering to be "the great Redemption." In the spirit of labor culture, which always distanced itself from the expectation of immediate salvation, Shlonsky places salvation or "the great Redemption" for the here and now within the context of the pioneering experience. The poem ends with a vision where two dark cliffs become the alternative tablets of the Covenant: Agony and Toil.

In the text of *The Final Covenant,* God gives his approval to Job with the affirmation, "For I have made thee a savior amongst men and bestowed the great Redemption upon thee."[16] Job explicitly assumes the role of a redeemer whose profound pessimism only strengthens him in his belief that gradual development had to replace the apocalyptic messianic event. The poem, in fact, is torn between two opposed imperatives: rejecting messianism and adopting it almost simultaneously.

On the one hand, it followed Brenner's antimessianic edict, but on the other, it also responded to the messianic tension pervading the new culture of the Yishuv.

This tense ambivalence relies to a considerable extent on the symbolism that comes to dominate the poem as a whole, turning the particular objects within it into a paradigm of themselves.[17] Thus, for instance, Job is the captain of a black ship, and black is also the color of his "good, foreign eyes." Elijah, however, is covered by a white tallith, and his shofar, too, is white.[18] Symbolism is also apparent in Job's way of developing the contradiction between the "great Redemption" and the "small salvation." Temporal metonymies confront the big with the little hand of the clock so as to form an allegorical plot contesting the traditional interpretation of time by the Messiah:

> But when time comes for vision now—
> Oh, why don't you lay your full height down on me,
> Like the big hand when it lies over the little hand—
> Upon the hour of midnight.
> Stretch yourself out on me, great God,
> For the hour is near!

To which Job irreverently responds:

> Indeed the hour is near
> When that little hand shall fall away![19]

The primary tension in these poems of Shlonsky is between their clearly symbolistic poetics and their pioneering orientation. The symbolism of the two dramatic poems "Ẓara'at (Leprosy) and The Final Covenant is traditionally associated with aestheticist leanings coupled with the refusal of any moralism or didacticism. Nevertheless, they were produced from within the context of the Yishuv, where the universal figure of Agony was readily understood as the local suffering of the pioneering avant-garde, engaging its flesh and blood in the realization of the Zionist idea. "But Shlonsky's desire for salvation," wrote the critic Yaakov Rabinovitch at the time, "is not that of a landless, abstract Jew-Man, nor merely that of an artist, but that of a man who represents those engaged in labor, building and suffering."[20] And indeed, prior to his disappearance, the Messiah communicates his vision to Job, developing the poem's symbolic pattern up until the revelation of the new Covenant:

An ancient black ship shall speechlessly move
And breath-of-unknown-mouth shall turn off the light of towers.
Masts shall crumble under the weight of sails.
Oars shall creak.
Closed-eye mariners shall row in silence
And before them two black cliffs shall loom like the tablets of the Covenant
Agony and Toil[21]

The effort to express through a network of symbols some hidden reality that underlies the concrete world finds here a spiritual medium fraught with messianic tension. The instability of the borderlines between the spiritual and the earthly, the subjective and the objective, is also manifested as a blurring of temporal coordinates. The supranatural state of perception favored by symbolism intensifies its objects, expands the limits of time and space and even neutralizes their mutual difference.[22] This antimimetic, modernistic poetics is thus able to incorporate the eschatological time dimension into the present, creating the effect of a messianic temporality.

Nonetheless, the internal tension between the symbolist poetics and its actual social implications remained. One might recall the kabbalists, who nurtured the messianic consciousness that finally erupted into political reality in the shape of Shabbetai Zvi "and never imagined that a conflict might arise between the symbol and the reality it came to symbolize."[23] In the last resort, though, it is precisely the ambiguity and lack of clarity of the symbolist figure that serves so well the ideological needs that gave rise to it. At this stage of the formation of the labor culture, symbolist poetics could still perform its ideological function of mediation, bridging the opposite poles concretizing the symbol.

Uri Zvi Greenberg's book *Great Fear and the Moon,* which closes with the long poem, "The Shortcut," is pervaded almost throughout by a powerful messianic tension. Much of the authority of the poetic speakers in this book is based on their mystical qualifications and superior knowledge of a hidden reality. Yet this mystical outlook keeps returning to the national context of the pioneering experience in Palestine. A typical example is Greenberg's conception of the Jewish Jesus who had for generations been imprisoned within the walls of Christianity, but now, as the nation is striking new roots in its land, is summoned by the poet to come join his pioneer brothers—the latter being characterized as the true representatives of the Messiah in these times:

And now my brother, come out of the monasteries, for the time has come, and
    go to *Meah Shearim* and buy a tallith, paying in gold,
That you shall take out of the coffer: the wages of having been unto them as
    mouths, as disembodied,
So that you can cover yourself and go to the Wall to pray with Jews, if you are
    ready for prayer.
Or better: buy there trousers and a shirt: *pioneer*'s clothes, and ask in Hebrew:
    which way to the Valley of Jezreel—
Jerusalem is of this earth; and they will show you the way.
Go till you come to the Valley and you shall find brothers plowing the land, you
    shall say unto them, peace *my brothers,* and they will reply: peace.
If you say: take me for the plow, they will take you; and if you work, they will
    love you as brothers, you will eat your bread in holiness.[24]

In "The Shortcut," Greenberg develops a complex narrative line ending in a quest for Shabbetai Zvi's burial place. The very title of the poem indicates clear impatience with the concept of slow, gradual progress and a preference for the miraculous breakthrough. In a sense this is an autobiographical poem, relating the story of the speaker-poet's journey from Slavic Europe to the land of Israel as itself a "shortcut." But the road here is a metaphor not only for space, but also for time. As the barriers of distance are miraculously set aside, so the early and the late become intermixed and Jewish history, with special emphasis on its martyrology, is depicted in a synchronous manner. In response to the spiritual challenge posed by the agonizing burden of pogroms and persecutions, the poem proposes the messianic solution. Now, in the messianic era, when the miraculous "shortcut" is becoming reality and the Messiah is not threatened by betrayal ("There is no longer anyone to pay the thirty pieces!"),[25] the time has come for the new Messiah to reveal himself in the guise of the pioneer-poet.

It is at this moment that the speaker identifies himself-as-poet with the figure of the Messiah. In opposition to Shlonsky's dramatization of the Messiah in *The Final Covenant,* Greenberg declares himself to be one of the four Messiahs ("Christs") who appear as guests at the dinner he prepares for the enemies of Israel. In order to lend weight to this image of the Messiah, the poet also relies on the traditional formula of the despised victim turned savior, for which purpose he relates the story of the pogrom that he and his family experienced in Lvov in 1918.

The clearly expressionist poetics employed here enables us to identify the speaker, who is also the poet, with a Messiah possessed of special spiritual qualities. ("The world is there. There is no point in repeating it," stated Kasimir Edschmid in his famous expressionist manifesto of 1917.) Greenberg's poetry is, indeed, one where the expressive comes before the mimetic, thus emphasizing the distortion of given forms. The expressionist tendency toward apocalyptic discourse manifests itself by multiplying oppositions and highlighting tension and conflict in the poetic continuum.[26] The associative composition created by the poem fuses the past and the future, the far and the near and, most important, the poet with the chain of Messiahs stretching from the distant past up until the present day. The intense presence of the expressionist speaker, with his competence in spiritual dimensions beyond perceptible external reality, motivates his special status as the harbinger of collective salvation. Having abandoned the mere registration and description of facts and having opted instead for an attempt to give radical, absolute expression to his internal subjective experience, the expressionist artist is elevated here to harbinger of a new dispensation, one where the murderer and the victim can sit together at a new (but infinitely more promising) version of the Last Supper.

The involvement of the poem with the Messiah becomes all but obsessional. And toward the end, the poet embarks once more on his quest for the Messiah who will save his people from pogroms and persecutions. He also returns to the Christian iconography of the concrete Messiah, realized in his own body:

For they have not, have no, have no, Messiah in the world!
There have been some Messiahs, woe to me knowing it! There have been some
    Messiahs, the people delivered them to the rulers. From Adam who called to
    God from the tree
To Shabbetai Zvi who defied only them . . . and bowed down to be a slave to a
    Moslem emperor!
(Woe to me, for having grown to be a man on the globe and having read the
    shame in the books of the exiled, in the very language in which I create!)
A Messiah, a Messiah for the community of Israel, who no longer knows what a
    Messiah is!

Oh, it is more bitter to me than death to feed and quench sadist-Poles, butcher-
   Ukrainians with our flesh-and-blood their life long!
Let there be a Jewish Messiah who fled the Ukraine, who escaped Poland with
   his wrath in his blood as in the heart of a volcano,
Eating with us our sulphur-like bread and drinking with us from the cisterns of
   gall!
Oh, I want no heavenly Messiah, whose body is mist and whose head made of
   onyx and who would not know our torture, our shame,
By blood and by flesh.
Who does not know of *his own flesh-and-blood* what is hunger and what thirst,
   what are sobbing children, what a screaming woman as her body is touched
   by the *trooper!*[27]

The wish is soon answered. There is an immediate allusion to the poet's being
transported to Shabbetai Zvi's burial place in Dulcine by means of a miraculous
"shortcut," which underlines once more his tendency to identify himself with the
Messiah:

There is a shortcut for the Hebrew bard who moves toward the Messiah,
   forgetting all his life beyond his flesh and blood in this world.[28]

Finally, the speaker-poet devotes the last two lines of this poem, also the closing
lines of the whole book, to a rather transparent allusion, likening the pain suffered
by "the flesh of the heavens" to that burning in his own body, thus linking himself
once more, as the "bard," to the Messiah, who (as said earlier in the poem) had
forgotten "all his life beyond his flesh and blood in this world." Greenberg develops this imagery, and in likening the messianic burning in the flesh to the "leprosy
in Job's body," he signals—by an intertextual gesture toward Shlonsky's *Leprosy*
and *The Final Covenant*—the inclusion within his messianic vision of the conflict
with the realities of the pioneering life (even though the vision was, in turn—
paradoxically—nourished by that life). But whereas Shlonsky took a reserved
attitude toward messianism, Greenberg espouses it without any reservation
whatsoever.

   Greenberg with his expressionism and Shlonsky with his symbolism thus demonstrated that an explicit, unequivocal messianism and a qualified messianic attitude
could still coexist during the 1920s. The mode of discourse developed within the
labor culture, which allowed the coexistence of these polar opposites, thus defined
the status of messianism as a rather fluid concept, lying for the most part beyond the
range of political differences. A similar tendency may be seen in essay writing,
which especially during the Third Aliyah incorporated typically messianic rhetoric.[29] The modernist poetics of Shlonsky and Greenberg, respectively, opened up
an ambivalent space wide enough to accommodate various types of messianism.
This paved the way for the public impact of the messianic poem and to an awareness
that its destructive potential would somehow have to be moderated and controlled.

   One of the pacesetters in the world of labor culture and its poetry was David
Shimonovitz. As early as 1924, he wrote:

> Messiah! Hurry up and come! From the abyss of my being
> My heart is with you, its prime wish,
> And please do not wait for a generation that is either
> All innocent or all guilty.[30]

But four years later, in 1928, Shimonovitz changed his mind. Instead of explicitly urging the Messiah to hasten, he produced a metamessianic poem, criticizing prevailing attitudes to messianism:

> And as between bottomless deep darkness and heaven's splendor
> I waver, yearning for the secret word—and lo
> With endless pain he looked at me and whispered: "How shall I appear
> When everywhere I hear: 'Let Him come and I will not see Him!' "[31]

The poem then goes on to survey various messianic preferences and the all-or-nothing attitudes that went with them: "One man intensely desires: a world like the kingdom of God! . . . and any who would add or omit anything is but a criminal and a liar"; "Yet another puts his trust only in an earthly kingdom." But all these fanatics agreed on only one thing: if these conditions could not be fulfilled absolutely, then "Let Him come and I will not see him!" This well-known phrase from Sanhedrin 92b is used here by Shimonovitz, then, to censure both the skeptical and the fanatical dissent from the basic messianic message. The Messiah is quite disgusted by this disunity, which is why he declares:

> No! I will not come, I will not come as long as I am not the essence,
> As long as I can hear: "Let Him come and I will not see him!"
> Redemption is no Redemption if not dear above all else,
> And a conditional Messiah—is no Messiah at all!"[32]

In essence, this poem is a symptom of the decisive transformation that was then taking place in the public discourse of the Yishuv. The times were those of economic crisis, of hunger, massive unemployment, more emigration than immigration—all these fanned a spirit of despair that affected even the pioneers themselves. The new Revisionist movement had advanced beyond the embryonic stage to become a notable force in the Zionist political arena. The angry criticism leveled by both the right-wing Revisionists and the radical left-wing at the mainstream labor movement for its poor handling of the crisis contributed to a state of agitation within that movement itself. A primary victim of the prevailing pessimism was the image of the pioneer, who was expected to make great personal sacrifices in the national cause. What suffered particular damage was the future-oriented, teleological strategy of the pioneer, who was expected to suffer today, postponing short-range satisfactions, in order perhaps to realize collective national projects in some far-distant future.

The two messianic attitudes rejected in Shimonovitz's poem roughly corresponded to the two poles of opinion in the Yishuv at that time. On the one hand, there were those who interpreted Zionist reality in mystical terms, thus insisting, as the poet has it, on this world as "the kingdom of God." It is quite safe to surmise that what he had in mind was primarily the radical position occupied quintessentially by Greenberg, who saw in the realization of the Zionist project a fundamental spiritual principle, a norm transcending the demands of practical judgment and the constraints of empirical reality. At the other extreme were those who trusted nothing but "an earthly kingdom," intent on restricting the pace of national salvation in order to ensure sound, even utopian, foundations. These favored a slow, gradual process of salvation, attentive to the prosaic constraints of empirical reality rather than urging the End to be obtained by force of will and depth of faith in a "Kingdom of God."

Despite his clear commitment to the labor camp, Shimonovitz here distanced himself from the credo that held socialist constructivism to be the single path to Zionist fulfillment. The intense process of politicization did not spare the Messiah. Whoever still wished, during the late 1920s, to have a place in the hegemonic discourse, was now under pressure to define his concept of messianism in far less elastic terms. Here, then, was a cultural turning point. Seeking to evade these new imperatives, and in a despairing attempt to remove the messianic category from the consuming heat of political debate,[33] Shimonovitz has his Messiah demand a Redemption "dearer than anything." Somehow he sought to preserve the place of the Messiah within the Zionist consensus in Palestine. The continued semantic collaboration between the two poles of the political spectrum demonstrates the particularly privileged status enjoyed by the concept of messianism and other related terms (e.g., "Redemption" or "harbinger") in the public discourse of the Yishuv. The use of messianic terminology by one faction did not prevent other factions from using it. In 1927, following the production of the play *The Messiah, Son of Joseph*—which provoked a lively reaction—a prominent essayist of the labor movement could still write, "Urging the End is in the air in which we live, and the exertions of the theater in this domain do somewhat express our deepest longings."[34]

Messianism, then, acted in the culture of the Yishuv as a highly charged liminal concept that can be used to map out some of the subtler nuances of ideological and political divergence. The heightened political tension combined itself with the desire to take part in the hegemonic culture in order to produce a particularly flexible discourse, which enlarged and enriched the repertoire of messianic poetry. By the late 1920s, Hebrew poetry, which stood at the forefront of the reinterpretation of messianism, had undergone a real transformation. From within the realm of labor culture there sprang new forms of political poetry.

In close proximity to the appearance of Shimonovitz's poems, Greenberg published his long poem, *Ḥazon aḥad haligyonot (A Vision of One of the Legions).*[35] This poem was essentially a virulent indictment of the leadership of the Yishuv and the Histadrut, the labor federation, for its failure to cope with the crisis. The work is constructed as a series of visions. The poetic use of vision is a characteristic device of expressionist poetics, an antimimetic form of discourse that seeks entry into the translogical essence of reality (and often into its eschatological dimension). But the eschatological tension that animated the expressionist tradition was often accompanied by an explosive apocalyptic energy.[36] Thus the final section of Greenberg's poem is essentially a dichotomous presentation of messianism and violence as two alternative directions.

About a year earlier, Greenberg had written critically of the decline in the Zionist movement, which had originally gathered "all the messianic lava of all generations and moulded it into the modern idea of a state."[37] But now, having related the terrible suffering of the pioneers under "these heavens, heavens of my ancient father, that swell as flesh in their dark agony," having singled out those few "who loyally hope for the vision that the Messiah *will* come," the poem posits messianism and violent conquest of the land as the two possible solutions:

And if these nights are not meant for pregnancy—why should the brain not light up like a candlestick,
Why should soldiers not raise torches on the mountains of Judea and the mountains of Galilee,
Why were the cannons not raised high to inform them of conquest in the great morning!
[. . .]
If not the wondrous impregnation during nights and the birth of Messiahs against burning lamplight—
Why no navy upon my Great Sea and noisy sailors with blood in their eyes:
—*Conflagration in Jaffa and fire in Haifa!*[38]

This depiction of violence as the only adequate alternative to the Messiah is a clear indication of the radical rejection of the present so typical of the messianic attitude. Preceding this prophecy of violence, there is an apocalyptic vision that envisages a salvation made possible by the restoration of Jerusalem as a royal city in the wake of catastrophic upheavals. The desire for absolute, total change here entails complete disregard for the limitations of reality and, almost as a necessary condition, a reliance on violence.

From the first, Greenberg's poem opposes messianism to the solutions characteristically advocated by the labor movement. Step by step it contests the basic assumptions of labor culture and its poetry:

Help me, O My Lord, while I lift an arm with no axe
Against fraud and fawning discourse
Among brothers in Judea—[39]

A close reading of this long poem shows it to be actually constructed as a parody of Yitzhak Lamdan's *Masadah*,[40] which has been recognized for many years as one of the major poetic works to have come out of the labor movement. Very soon after its publication in 1926, this text acquired the special status, which it has kept ever since, of a quasi-official statement of pioneer ideology. The pilgrim's wanderings to Masadah, his departure from a Europe that had rejected him, his difficulty and despair in trying to take root in Palestine and, especially (in the spirit of "despite everything" as advocated by Brenner) his heroic emergence from the sense of physical and spiritual impasse—all these were seen as typical and representative. The poem was, in fact, taken to be a sort of collective biography of the Third Aliyah generation, whose revolutionary roots had nourished a characteristically messianic ambience.

In *Masadah* Lamdan sought an ideological way out of the contradictions facing the pioneer in his confrontation with the everyday reality of life in Palestine. The image of the pioneer was most threatened at the time by the fact that he was called upon to sacrifice himself for so distant a future. The obviously decreasing willingness to tolerate present suffering and defer gratification for the sake of realizing a collective vision generated Lamdan's attempt to conclude the poem on a redefinition of temporality in pioneering discourse. Instead of a linear-progressive conception of time, situating present pain within a grand design of movement toward utopia, Lamdan now proposed a cyclical conception. His sharp awareness that, despite the hardship of the times, there was no way for his protagonist to turn back, led him to argue that desperation does not necessarily lead to a sense of finality, of a dead end, but can rather serve to open up a new beginning. The title of the last section is "Genesis" (or, "In the Beginning" ["*Bereishit*"]), and in it the protagonist declares:

> We are yet to witness the outcome of vision,
> But our eyes are already open to the discovery of a great fear:
> "Here is the boundary. From here on there are no more boundaries,
> And behind—all tracks lead to the one dead-end."
> We have finished the books of every road, year-laden
>   experience reads out
> In tears and blood
> And repeating after it we conclude:
> "Finis!" [. . .]
> Henceforth a new Book of Genesis opens on the battlement.
> And like our ancestors as they end the reading of the Torah and are about to
>   start anew—
> We will sound a roar of a new and last beginning [genesis]:
> "*Strong, strong, let us be strong!*"[41]

The centrality of *Masadah* in the public consciousness of the time seems, then, to have at least partly prompted Greenberg to react by writing *A Vision of One of the Legions* as a detailed parody. In Greenberg's work, the Messiah expected by the pioneers meets the "primeval Snake" whose soul—according to the Kabbalah of Rabbi Isaac Luria—originates, just like that of the Messiah himself, in the very root of evil. But this mystical allegory had obvious political targets. The Snake, who in the Kabbalah symbolizes the primal power of the unclean, is depicted by Greenberg as betraying his suffering brothers and suppressing the potential for salvation represented by the Messiah even in the midst of evil. The primeval Snake, then, could be easily identified as the labor leadership which, in Greenberg's eyes, was deliberately destroying every chance for the realization of his royalist messianism:

> And nightly the Divine Presence weeps
> At the threshold of the Snake's house
> And the Messiah comes to lie stupefied
> At his feet—
> He will not hear.[42]

Masadah's cyclical temporality kept both hope and despair within the space of human finitude. But in *A Vision of One of the Legions*, the only hope for progress takes the form of a superhuman, miraculous leap that is based on a mystical reading of reality. Lamdan's poem is pervaded by the characteristic ambivalence of the labor culture toward the messianic: on the one hand, the revelation of a quasi-Savior depicted in accordance with Christian messianic iconography (''and the figure has a smile even in torture, a look of consolation'');[43] and, on the other, a real fear of a messianism bound to prove false (''Why should false prophets still stand on top of altars/Prophesying Salvation, Salvation, Salvation'').[44]

Shlonsky, too, in a book entitled *Bagalgal* (*Within the Wheel*)[45] published during this same period of crisis, now attacked the vain promises of messianism. Reacting directly to Greenberg's poems, he debunked the latter's royalist fancies as grotesquely irrelevant to present harsh conditions:

> So what, if every Purim clown
> Here should mouth the name of God.
> And every *ego* riding a donkey
> Should be echoed: ''Hurrah! Messiah!''

> But woe is me, for I have seen: tricks of vision
> Do mislead my people—when it suffers hunger.
> ''Hail thee, hungry gut!'' ''Congratulations to the lean!''
> And David's Son is promised unto every womb.
> [. . .]
> I spit on every kingdom
> As the mouth of every belly screams for bread.[46]

In contrast to the conception of slow, gradual but not always steady progress, Greenberg's poem puts forward a messianic solution formulated in absolutist terms, thus establishing a wholly new rhythm, an alternative timetable, for the implementation of the Zionist vision. In order to buttress his conception of time, Greenberg launched an attack on the devices employed by labor poetry to cope with the harsh images of reality. In the fifth section of *Masadah*, ''Bide'okh hamedurot'' (''When the Campfires Die Out''), Lamdan let the man in prayer to God speak for those who were raising themselves from the depths of despair:

> Please make them patient, God, make them patient when consolation tarries!
> [. . .]
> Give strength, God, give courage to bear the suffering of this hardship.[47]

The thematics of patience and endurance as mediating between present hardship and the hope to come was a characteristic device in the ideological arsenal of labor literature that was vehemently rejected by Greenberg. He, too, like Lamdan, resorts to a direct appeal to God. But having become convinced of the betrayal of the workers' leadership, Greenberg turned the tables on the balancing and conciliatory role Lamdan had assigned to his prayer and the temporal sense it had recommended, using it instead as a vehicle for political invective:

> And wilt Thou bid me now, my Lord,
> Build a bulwark for my vision:
> So it should not be struck by a fawning gaze

> Like a lightning in windows?
> Wilt bid me be a seer
> Auguring well for Jerusalem,
> Wilt bid me be a patient one,
> Biting his own flesh all the time?[48]

The next step in this radical movement went beyond the domain of poetry. The political messianism developed in *A Vision of One of the Legions* and the call for violence stemming from it took on a nonliterary character when Greenberg joined Abba Ahimeir and Y. H. Yeivin in founding the *Brit habiryonim* (League of Thugs), the first Jewish underground organization to oppose the British. The messianic message that nurtured the league was transformed by it into an actual political program.

In his next volume of poems *Kelev bayit (House Dog)*, which came out one year later in 1929, Greenberg tried to emphasize the political consequences immanent within his literary messianism by elaborating an ideal of the poet as thug. In a poem that he defined as a "speech of the poet-thugs," the speaker there urges his fellow poets to join him in a

> League of thugs in a Hebrew fatherland
> To incense all the complacent of Zion;
> And together we will set out to fulfil our goals.[49]

House Dog broadened the political front to include an explicit confrontation with the opponents of prophecy in Hebrew poetry. In opposition to Shimonovitz, whose satires repeatedly castigated prophetic pretensions,[50] Greenberg now prefaced his book with an epigraph stating quite bluntly, "Prophecy has not deserted Israel." The poems themselves trace a trajectory for this prophetic manifesto to the book's explicit messianic purpose, spelled out in the closing poem, which is a celebration of that biblical phrase *Darakh kokhav miya'akov* "There Shall Come a Star out of Jacob" (Num. 24:17), interpreted in a midrash by Rabbi Akiva to mean, "there shall come a 'Coziva' out of Jacob," in other words, that Bar Kokhba was to be seen as the "King–Messiah" (Palestinian Talmud, Ta'anit 4:8).

On the whole, this book marked a more militant stage not only in Greenberg's politics, but also in his poetics. The efforts to find the Messiah recounted in the long poem *Besod hamashiah (In the Secret of the Messiah)*[51] included, among other things, a search for Shimon Bar-Giora, one of the Zealot leaders who ended up in Roman exile after the failure of the Great Rebellion. But a still higher form of politics, it is there suggested, is that given shape by the artist. This projection of artistic norms onto the world of political action put Greenberg, imbued as he was with his messianic faith, in close proximity to the mainstream of interwar fascist culture in Europe that displayed such fascination with the theatrical aspect of mass politics and that elevated the idea of aestheticizing the political into a veritable doctrine.

Greenberg's shift toward the political fringe was part and parcel of his intensifying political messianism. Even within Revisionism, whose ranks he joined at that time, Greenberg's messianism exceeded the accepted line. And, in thus breaking through the limits of the Zionist consensus, Greenberg marked the messianic idea with a blunt political tag that would henceforth be well-nigh impossible to discard. The radical course he took in his poetry now severely affected its public status. If poetry is normally a flexible discourse capable of absorbing tension and conflict, his tended to become a discourse with an obviously explicit political content. In this way, Greenberg's mystical expressionism exacerbated his political and cultural marginalization. In contrast, those who wished to avoid the stigma of marginality and stay within the mainstream of the Yishuv had, under these circumstances, to cling ever more closely to their vague symbolism. This poetical mode still allowed them both to disavow the extreme politicization of the messianic theme and to restrict to a minimum explicit political partisanship.

The Arab riots of 1929, which broke out at the end of August, gave clear evidence of the divisive effect of the messianic idea on the Hebrew poetry of that time. The deep sense of calamity (113 dead) soon mingled with anger at the helplessness and lack of military preparedness, for which the leadership of the Zionist movement and, specifically, the Histadrut, were blamed. The political polarization increased: while the labor parties tried to stem the tide of hatred threatening the future of the Yishuv's relationship with the Arabs and steer the high emotions into constructive channels, the Revisionists maintained a barrage of relentless criticism. Greenberg conducted a campaign of virulent propaganda against the workers' leadership. The public state of shock enabled him to proclaim all the more loudly the vital necessity of his messianic timetable.

The book he published soon after the riots, *Eizor magen uneum ben hadam* (*The Defensive Zone and the Speech of the Son-of-Blood*) included an unprecedentedly violent attack on those he considered guilty of the disaster. Greenberg's radicalization is already evident from his opening poem (the epigraph), where he affirms:

> Our God is willing and the Messiah, too, is there.
> There is a plowed field for the fatherland, and myriad youth for the army.[52]

The assertion that the coming of the Messiah was being thwarted was then used as a point of departure for a political offensive against those who were said to be responsible. Alluding to the talmudic legend about the eating of the Messiah, Greenberg writes:

> A band of fossil-hearted traitors—your leaders-misleaders,
> Eating the Messiah every day and drinking him in their goblets,
> My sacred-unfortunate motherland![53]

Greenberg's speaker even went so far as to claim for himself the authority of actual blood kinship with the casualties of the riots. In the specific context of the time, the reference to eating the Messiah and drinking his blood amounted to a farfetched, albeit figurative, realization of bodily slaughter. This expressionistic amplification, moving ever farther away from its concrete origin, rested upon imagery already introduced in the book's two previous sections, notably the image linking the pioneers, who are the spilled blood of "warring Zion," to wine likened to blood (also following the biblical metaphor of "the pure blood of the grape," [Deut. 32:14]):

> As bottles full of wine-blood in your winery
> Were your pioneers, O Zion, yearning for the Messiah!
> And I saw them break and their wine spill:
> So red, so sacred,
> So red, so sacred
> On your thresholds.[54]

This network of imagery, so obviously related to the Christian symbolism of body and blood, also suggests an analogy between the pioneers who died in defense of Jerusalem and the Messiah's self-sacrifice for the sake of the Redemption. What Greenberg did here was no less than transform the pioneering ethos. Violence, usually interpreted in that ethos as an evil to be employed only in self-defense, was now glorified as an authentic expression of strength. Greenberg made a special effort in this book to eulogize the Sicarii—the most extreme faction among the Zealots of the Great Rebellion against Rome—a people he held up, in contrast to the traditional (and allegedly passive) Jews, as the military model for the pioneers of today. He replaced the primacy of agriculture in the pioneering ethos with that of the military. Already in the poems of *House Dog,* he had declared that notwithstanding the praises he had once "said to the shovel,"

> Now I say unto you when you hold the iron
> That tills and plows your land—remember and behold: this calm iron has the
> pattern of Bar Kokhba's sword.[55]

Now, in his post-riot poems, Greenberg turned the metaphor of the pioneer's sacrifice, so often used by the labor poets, from a necessary evil into a coveted end in itself. Accordingly, his attention has shifted from the Messiah's weapons to his body, which alone could endow the pioneers' sacrifice with its full mystical significance:

> They are timber for the fire of their stake and violins for their vision,
> Indifferent to the groanings of their life, burning to ash,
> They are trumpets for the flaming joy in the fatherland.

> Thus are they prophetic soldiers and thus are they
>   kabbalists:
> *As long as the body has not dropped dead, their vision is not complete.*[56]

The more forcefully messianism was used to express the yearning for Redemption in the political arena, the more questionable it became in labor circles. Still, in order to retain the messianic dimension of their discourse, the labor intelligentsia sought flexible messianic formulae that would not compromise their political caution. One such typical solution was to distinguish nationalist and particularist from universalist messianism. Thus, writing in 1933, Ben-Gurion could assert, "In the Hebrew labor movement the historical meaning of the yearning for the Redemption has been fulfilled in all its depth and without residue, [whereas] the Revisionist filth is merely a link in the unholy chain of perversions of the redemptionist idea." In stating that normative Zionism was a messianic movement, Ben-Gurion sought to emphasize its universalistic character. In contrast, he described the Revisionists as "False Messiahs feeding on the rubbish of history . . . and now attempting to divert the movement of the people from the track of human liberation toward a 'government of blood, mud and slavery.' ''[57]

The messianic alternative posited by Greenberg can be seen, then, as a reflection of his own perceived weakness. In contrast, the labor movement, with its hegemonic self-image, had a relative advantage in the accumulation and possession of symbolic social value, especially during the late 1920s and early 1930s, and this position dictated a cautious attitude toward messianic themes. The juxtaposition of Lamdan's *Masadah* with Greenberg's *A Vision of One of the Legions* suggests that, in facing up to the challenge of the messianic narrative, the labor poets had no choice but to contest its absolutely dichotomous conception of time. One way was to reject it out of hand, to refuse in principle to accept any messianic promise, but another way was to take into account the messianic sensibility and respond to it in some measure before finally qualifying or rejecting it. This was the road usually taken by labor discourse in facing up to the messianic option, which had always also formed part, in one way or another, of its own culture. Ben-Gurion made a distinction between particularistic and universalistic messianism, whereas Lamdan tried to resolve the tension between the acceptance of the messianic sensibility and its political rejection by proposing his cyclical narrative. This complex network of tensions surrounding the messianic attitude during the late 1920s and early 1930s assigned poetic discourse a special role.

The extreme radicalism adopted by Greenberg freed him to a large extent from the need to be flexible in his poetic discourse. It was labor poetry that had to draw more heavily on the elastic potential of poetic language in order to maneuver between opposite poles. This was most clearly apparent in the writing of Avraham Shlonsky. On the one hand, his work during the 1930s seemed to remove itself from direct social involvement in the life of the labor movement in Palestine. His poetics was now oriented toward universal existential abstractions, thus marking a departure from the poetry of the pioneering ethos that he had tended to produce up until the late 1920s. On the other hand, in the period of political polarization, the literary circle in which Shlonsky moved (notably the group centered around the literary weekly *Ketuvim*) developed a clear tendency to pacifist politics. (One of the group's leaders, Eliezer Steinman, it should be noted, published a pamphlet entitled *Messianism*[58] in the year 1932 in which he launched an outright attack on the phenomenon of political messianism as it was then developing in the Yishuv.) They sought not a total renunciation of the political but rather an alternative political response.

In his introduction to a small anthology entitled *Lo tirẓah* (*Thou Shalt Not Kill*), which collected translations of antiwar poems written in response to the First World War, Shlonsky now came out explicitly against Greenberg's poetry and the political culture it represented. His direct target seems to have been Greenberg's *House Dog*. He denounced ''the mental intoxication that has spoiled the brew of poetry in Israel with its inverted notions of 'royalty' and 'vision'.''[59] Reacting to Greenberg's militaristic transformation of the pioneering ethos, Shlonsky wrote, ''The entire barracks terminology has been forced into canticles about the Messiah and the vision of the kingdom of the House of David.''[60]

In 1934, Shlonsky published *Avnei bohu* (*Stones of Chaos*), perhaps the most abstract of all his books.[61] Opponents of modernist poetics, such as Shlomo Zemach, strongly criticized this aspect of the work, which granted autonomous status to the book's linguistic texture, thus radically loosening its ties to the world of experience. In an article entitled "On the Simile," which attacked the key role assigned the metaphor by the Shlonsky–Alterman generation, Zemach focused attention, among other things, on a stanza from *Stones of Chaos* that elaborates on the emblem of Shabbetai Zvi as a "banished deer" (*"ẓevi mudaḥ"*).

> A phantom doe do we vainly pursue,
> On banished deer's horn we laid our gold,
> On a deer's horn the Explicit Name is graven.[62]

In such passages, argued Zemach, "Literature and poetry have become an arena where combinations of similes compete. One does not write, one does not think— one compares."[63] Although the modernistic metaphor has been reduced to mere verbal play, Zemach requires it to set forth "much truth and great life-wisdom,"[64] to serve the needs of statement rather than of simile. For him, these lines of verse were no more than a conceit enabling the reader to move freely from the combination "vain doe" through "deer" to "deer's horn" (according to the Hebrew idiom, to lay one's money on the "deer's horn" is to put it at grave risk). Ignoring the spiritual or metaphysical resonance of the mention of the Explicit (the Divine) Name, Zemach saw here one more merely metaphorical device. The emblem of the "banished deer" (and "deer" is, of course, "ẓevi," as in the name Shabbetai Zvi) he ignored altogether. He chose to overlook the well-known story of the Sages who, walking in the Valley of Ginossar, saw the slowly rising dawn (traditionally referred to as "the doe of dawn") and declared, "Thus is the way of Israel's Redemption" (Palestinian Talmud, Berakhot 1:1).

In sum, it is precisely what Zemach ignored that draws attention directly to a major ideological device in Shlonsky's poem. For through Shlonsky's symbolist haze, reduced nearly *ad absurdum* by Zemach's analysis, what emerges is a real critique of those who put their trust in the Messiah. Shlonsky (and here he was at one with other members of the *Ketuvim* group) was ridiculing those who would risk all on the "vain doe" of the Redemption. A reading of the entire cycle *'Al karnei haẓevi* (*On the Deer's Horn*) where this passage occurs, shows that despite the rather obvious messianic iconography and the intensive symbolism (which repeatedly suggests supernatural contexts of revelation and the restoration of the age-old faith in God), Shlonsky still anchored this messianic drama in the concrete context of the literary power struggles that were inseparable from his public persona.[65] In opposition to Greenberg's aestheticization of the political, Shlonsky, Steinman and the *Ketuvim* circle posited an alternative form of discourse aimed at politicizing the aesthetic. Whereas Greenberg sought to translate the political into the aesthetic, they invested much energy in the political dynamics of the literary life.

This blurring of the borderlines between literature and political messianism was facilitated by the semantics of symbolist poetics. Thus Shlonsky could blur the sharp political angularity of his messianic thematics, creating an ambivalent text that both responded to the messianic tension and managed to keep it within tight limits. The close affinity between the artistic perspective on reality and the symbolist tradition intensified his sensitivity to the potential power of the messianic urge. At the same time, though, his continuing commitment in principle to the labor camp limited the range of political implications that he could permit himself in his poetry. The division of labor in his reaction to messianism, relatively circumspect in his poetic practice and bluntly explicit in his nonpoetic denunciations of Greenberg, was indicative of the inner tension he had to deal with.

The poetic milieu that developed around Shlonsky and under his inspiration fostered similar patterns of response from other poets such as Avram Broides, Yocheved Bat-Miryam and Shin Shalom. They, too, distanced themselves from messianic politics while demonstrating the same reluctance to surrender messianic images. Thus Broides could write:

> There is no compensation for bereavement in great fury and lamentations.
> Salvation is in the toiling worker's palm.[66]

And, for his part, Shin Shalom in comparing the contemporary reaction to the Arab riots with traditional Jewish martyrology likewise rejected lamentation and recommended the heroic persistence of the pioneer as the proper role for the messiahs sanctifying "fields of toil."[67]

In many respects, this pattern resembled Greenberg's reaction to the riots. He, too, condemned the weeping, presenting it as cowardly and escapist. True, he himself had been tempted to find refuge in despair:

> Daily at your gates, I was herald, crying:
> Fire, fire! And all your leaders were as
> Deaf to my voice, and passed on smiling.
> Till I sank down poor and destitute
> Into the Valley-of-Sorrow-of-Life, wordless . . .
> Like one who had been bitterly lamenting the dead
> And resigned himself to the horror of the certain and will cry no more.[68]

But when the riots broke out his reaction had undergone a drastic change:

> But when the sight of blood was on the square
> And when there was smoke and the house of my tribe cried out—
> I rose up in fire and walked in blood:
> To the Stone Hall my footsteps tottered.[69]

As with the labor poets, when Greenberg rejected lamentation he was brought face to face with the messianic issue. But in his case the riots endowed the messianic dynamic with a sharply political significance. Employing an obviously political context, symbolized by the Stone Hall where the Sanhedrin used to meet in the Temple, Greenberg phrased his censure in messianic terms:

> Here they are sitting at the green table,
> The guzzlers of thy Messiah, O silenced Jerusalem![70]

In contrast to the nuanced presentation of the messianic dilemma by the labor poets, Greenberg here put forward loud and clear the option of politically radical messianism.

As the 1930s progressed, the process of political polarization accelerated. In 1933, the labor movement managed to move beyond mere cultural-ideological hegemony to gain a dominant position in the World Zionist Organization. This development aggravated the schism in the movement, and the Revisionists now broke away to form their own separate organization. That same year witnessed the murder of Hayim Arlosoroff. The widespread suspicion that he was assassinated by radical Revisionists—inspired by Greenberg, Yeivin, Ahimeir and their League of Thugs—sent shock waves of political antagonism through the Yishuv.

Greenberg was in Poland when the murder took place, but his name figured prominently in the affair as a founder and spiritual guide of the League of Thugs, members of which were soon put on trial for the crime. On his return, he met with a great deal of insult and injury, to which he reacted in a series of poems entitled *Khronikah sheḥora: Ker'a habrit (A Black Chronicle / The Rift of the Covenant).* The heat of political animosity was such that the appeal to the messianic was rapidly becoming little more than a mere tag of partisanship. The increasingly doctrinaire character of Greenberg's poetry at that time often led him, in effect, to model his political poetry on something very close to the ditty. He now abandoned the distinction he had hitherto made between the labor leadership, whom he despised and denounced, and the pioneer rank and file, whom he had admired. The rift caused by Arlosoroff's murder fortified Greenberg in his sense that as far as he was concerned,

> *The pioneering tribe has ended*
> *And the stoning tribe has begun*
> I recognize them by their flag:
> It is red.
> *Blood libel*[71]

Messianism now became for him a narrowly applied, one-dimensional political yardstick. A profound gap thus opened up between the poet and the Yishuv (even though, it must be noted, the messianic theme per se remained the subject of intense interest throughout the period, as the varied examples of Kabak, Bistritzky and Scholem amply demonstrate).[72] Greenberg could even declare that if the Messiah were to come now, he, the poet, would not be able to take part in the joyful celebration of the masses. Greenberg called on the Messiah in order to draw a single, uncompromising line of division.

In one of the poems he wrote after the murder, he denounced the internecine conflict flaring up within the Yishuv just at a time when there was a lull in the violent resistance of the Arabs, referred to by him as "Esau." For "Esau," he wrote, was only biding his time, whereas the labor movement (that "shock-haired, fine-talking, swaggering bully") is depicted as a split personality eager to resolve inner contradictions by eliminating his brother:

> He loathes the sword. . . . But if he had one, he would plunge it
> Not in the belly of murderous Esau, but in his brother's belly,
> Who believes in the Messiah and denies Marx—[73]

Greenberg collected the poems he wrote in the wake of the Arlosoroff murder trial in *Sefer hakitrug vehaemunah (The Book of Denunciation and Faith)*—surely the most virulent collection of political poems to have appeared in Palestine between the two world wars, and possibly in all of modern Hebrew literature. It included the poems he had written in the wake of the 1929 riots and the Arlosoroff affair. But the book culminated in a section bitterly denouncing the Left for its response to the Arab attacks during the revolt of 1936. Although the labor parties insisted on a policy of restraint and containment, the Right clamored for uncompromising and violent action. Greenberg reserved his most vehement words for the members of Mishmar Haemek, a kibbutz that in his estimation had failed the test of honor when it came under attack. He was convinced that what he saw as the defeatism of the socialist camp was a natural consequence of its mean materialism, its Marxist ideology:

> In Ramat-Hakovesh* which is close to Kfar Sava†
> In Ramat-Hakovesh, Marx's frightened congregation,
> Boys sitting there bear-like in the dark
> Waiting for gunfire with that special feeling . . .
>
> [. . .]
> And the sons of the kibbutz are like fatted calves.
> From Zion to Moscow they have torn open their window.
> The tree that they planted and that a Philistine burned—
> Is no grief of mine, for it is *their disgrace*.[74]

This dichotomy between the spiritual and the material served to reinforce the centrality of his messianic message. In the course of the 1930s, Greenberg acquired a preeminence within the Revisionist movement as a "seer-poet," a man "whose office and vocation is to present the vision of the Redemption as realistic and feasible." This special status undoubtedly owed much to the Polish tradition of romanticism and messianism, which was inherited both by his poetry and by the Revisionist culture as a whole.[75] The status of prophet that he had been granted, almost without reservation, within labor discourse up until the late 1920s, now came back to haunt the labor movement. As I have argued earlier, there was a direct connection between the poet's authority as a prophet and the messianic content of his work. And now, as the 1930s were drawing to a close, Greenberg explicitly linked the prophet to the Messiah:

> The Messiah will be brought by the prophet.
> Let yourself be led, O people, by the prophet!
> The prophet is always in your midst
> Summon him—and he will appear![76]

The remarkable liberty that Greenberg took with the prophetic persona in his poems was thus perceived by him as a preliminary step heralding the political emergence of the Messiah. Establishing himself as the "Seer-Poet" was but a preliminary phase designed to prepare the ground for his own apparition as the

---

*Lit. "The Hill of the Conqueror," the name of a kibbutz.
†Lit. "Grandfather's Village," a small town in central Palestine.

Messiah, who could be seen simply as a more intensive version of the prophet. Toward the end of the book, Greenberg specifically placed the three categories on an equal footing:

> I was very late in coming, I should perhaps have rather
> Been a poet and a prophet in the time of the Temple.
> Sword-girded I should have marched with *Reuveni* from the Desert to Hever;
> Or marched with *Molcho:* fire-by-fire to the fire in the square.
> Or in the land of Spain with the divine Ibn Gabirol—[77]

In *The Book of Denunciation and Faith,* the messianic pattern is reminiscent of Christian doctrine, the implication being that the Messiah has already come and that his momentary absence is to be explained only by the blind opposition of his enemies both within and without. A signal example of this motif is to be found in the poem "Beoznei yeled asaper" ("I Shall Tell It to a Child"), which relates how the Messiah was scared away by the jeering of the peddlers, who here symbolize materialism and indifference to the spiritual dimension of the national being. When the speaker asks himself where the Messiah might be at present, he suggests that the poet himself, his own body, may well have become the Messiah's dwelling place and source of food:

> Perhaps not . . . Perhaps I am his haunt: he resides in my ribs fuming and
>   raging and growling as a demon lion.
> And I tell no one else of his being in my ribs.
> And I give him *living flesh* to eat and blood that is better than wine to drink.[78]

The poem goes on to describe the diet of this hidden Messiah as being essentially aesthetic or musical in nature (albeit physiological in form):

> And I play unto him at the very deep upon a cello:
> Laments and potential prayers from my forefathers.
> And when the moon rises as the prophetic face among olive trees, I play unto
>   him at the very deep upon an organ:
> [. . .]
> Till a shiver runs ever so finely down my legs, and my cheeks and temple then
>   cave in and the eyes feel hot . . .
> And He is sobbing in my ribs.[79]

This extreme form of identification between the speaker-poet and the Messiah was, it can be argued, natural enough given the urge to subordinate the political to the aesthetic. As aesthetic norms were given absolute priority, so empirical restraints and utilitarian calculations were set aside as unworthy. The apocalyptic vision, with its expectations of ruin and destruction, became a major source of inspiration. And thus the metamorphosis of poet into prophet and prophet into Messiah came to dwell in close intimacy with ruthless violence. Or, as Greenberg put it in this statement of his *Ars poetica:*

> What is the praise of an independent people in a world of kingdoms?
> First: the miraculous power of its beautiful song.

> Second: the miraculous power of its army in the field.
> The song and the sword, never one without the other![80]

In many respects we see here the actual realization of what Steinman, for example, had predicted:[81] the violent tendency that was bound to result from a political messianism seeking to realize its kingly visions *hic et nunc*. The attainment of the Royal Sphere—in the Kabbalah this is the final realization of all the spheres—brings closer the destructive principle latent in messianism because (in Steinman's words), "For the sake of the complete Redemption, this entire world must be shattered to pieces, so that the captive sparks can be made to rise."[82]

As the apocalyptic theme became increasingly prominent in Greenberg's poems throughout the 1930s, so his critique of the present found voice in ever more violent terms. In 1928, as already noted, he concluded *A Vision of One of the Legions* by positing messianism and violence as the only two possible alternatives. But now he saw these two forces as identical:

> And I have a Messiah perhaps still far off,
> Hidden in David's sword in his sheath.[83]
> Or again:
> Your masters taught: a land is to be bought for money.
> One buys the field and drives in the hoe.
> And I say: No land is to be bought for money
> And a hoe is also for digging a grave for the dead.
> And I say: a land is to be conquered in blood.
> And only if conquered in blood is it sanctified for the people
>   The sanctity of blood.
> [. . .]
> Your masters taught: the Messiah shall come in future generations
> And Judea shall arise with neither fire nor blood.
> It shall arise with each tree, each house.
> And I say: if your generation lags behind
> Rather than force the End with its hand and its pulse
> And if it go not into fire with the shield of David
> And if its horses' stirrups go not into blood—
> The Messiah will not come even to a distant generation.
> Judea shall not arise.[84]

Even in the face of this apocalyptic creed, there were still some poets on the labor side who proved reluctant to abandon the messianic theme entirely. It is clear, however, that by now it took much more of an effort to neutralize the political potential of such poetic materials. It will suffice here to quote two examples that illustrate the difficulties involved. "The Face I'll Never See Again" was a poem written by Shin Shalom in 1936 in an attempt to cope with the sense of bereavement collectively felt by the Yishuv in the wake of the Arab revolt. His speaker, among other things, describes what had happened by recalling apocalyptic scenes in the Bible—the corpses strewn in the Valley of Jehoshaphat, for instance. These images almost necessarily suggest messianic expectations, but the poet holds back, substituting questions for prophecy:

> The stars—what are they so like?
>
> They are like myriads of eyes,
> A chain of sons and of fathers,
> Whose gaze gripped the very foundations:
> "Has a Savior come to the Valley of Jehoshaphat?
>
> Has a Savior come, or should we forever yearn,
> Without defense, deprived of wall and battlement,
> A prey to devil, to force, to annihilation—
> Is there no hope for the mourners of Zion?"[85]

The second case in point is *Eretz-Israel,* a long poem published by Yocheved Bat-Miriam in 1937. In a sort of drifting tour of the country and its scenery, the speaker unfolds a dynamic, even fluid, consciousness blurring the borderlines between spirit and matter, reality and illusion. The basic experience is a persistent effort to gain intimate closeness to, or even mystical union with, the landscapes of the motherland.[86] The mystical vocabulary that Bat-Miriam frequently uses pulls her persistently toward the question of salvation and messianism. But here the messianic energy is not deflected or obfuscated as in Shin Shalom. Rather, it forms high-tension patterns, such as the oxymoron, holding and distending it from both ends, often at the beginning and at the end of a polished quatrain:

> Prophesying in his shining dream,
> Dreamt by your chained Messiah,
> In your brood flight you extend
> My yearnings from end to end.
>
> [. . .]
>
> Embracing as a dream and closing off,
> As a vision of Redemption, threatening bereavement,
> You realize yourself and contradict
> The wondrous revelation of your mastery.
>
> [. . .]
>
> Confusion, vision and fear
> And a disappointing, impoverished glory.
> With you, like you, shines only
> The expectancy of my unredeemed despair,
>
> Footsteps echoing good tidings and Redemption,
> Light of latter days—unto your distances,
> That prophesy by signal and destination.[87]

In 1938, against the background of the political and messianic rage emanating from Uri Zvi Greenberg's recent book, Natan Alterman published his first collection of poems, *Kokavim baḥuẓ* (*Stars Abroad*). It was to wield enormous influence over the subsequent course of Hebrew poetry.

On the face of it, it would seem hardly possible to find two poets whose personalities and work diverge more widely than theirs did at that time. The pure lyricism of *Stars Abroad* would make itself heard in Hebrew poetry for decades to come, so that it might seem vain, indeed, to search the concrete detail of this great book for anything other than the lyrical. Alterman's poetry does have historical links with a variety of modernist schools and trends, but symbolism seems to be its most significant commitment in both literary practice and theory.[88] This is the clue to Alterman's defense (made in 1933) of the obscure, to his claim that there is no such thing as "the unintelligible in poetry," that literature does not "*describe* life . . . but *lives* it anew," and that "lyricism is a deliberate faking of *feelings*." And most important:

> Let not the obscure poet worry or smart over the reader's lack of reaction. The true reaction, that which is independent of actuality and the everyday, is always there; and it, precisely it, is the most secure, real and general of all. Any authentic literary work, whether it seems intelligible or obscure, is authentically felt only by the few and that only infrequently.[89]

But the trenchant tone of this article no longer stood Alterman in good stead when five years later, in 1938, he published another important statement of his views in an article entitled "The Secret of Quotation Marks." Here, too, he measured the poetic word against his symbolist yardstick. But in contrast to the ahistorical discussion in the earlier piece, his point of departure now was his concern for the fate of the poetic word at such a momentous turning point in Jewish history when the Zionist enterprise was, he felt, going from strength to strength:

> This people, so often regarded, perhaps not without cause, as the germ of decadence, division and skepticism, is at this moment, on the contrary, as sick as can be with the love of life. . . . And working so hard and devotedly to turn symbols into reality, everything real now turns into a symbol for this people.[90]

The tension experienced every day between vision and reality was disrupting the people's cognition of the real and their ability to describe it in words. Reality had become subject to "moments of great dizziness [,which] is not weakness but a dream, a confusion not of ideas but of realms."[91] The task of Hebrew poetry was, thus, "to call all these things by their names, to give an explicit name to that which it, too, cherishes."[92]

But these exigencies put poetry in a dire predicament because, in accordance with its symbolic essence, poetry viewed names as "the face of things and not their sign, the voice of things and not their appellation."[93] This sensuous attitude to words was the source of the linguistic and poetic crisis diagnosed by Alterman. Contemporary Hebrew poetry, he said, had henceforth to fight "for the true music of names, their profound, living music, [in] this time of change and renewal, a time when words carry vast spoils."[94] He saw in the contemporary reservations about big words that "moved nations and made history"[95] a symbolistic statement emphasizing the musical suggestiveness and semantic indefiniteness of words: a word should transmit its "great tunes precisely from mouth to ear."[96] Poetry, he went on to argue, had been the first to express reservations about the "big word" imprisoned within quotation marks.

This highly explicit interpretation of historical reality in symbolist terms led Alterman, almost against his will, to reveal his own attitude to messianism. For, in the overheated atmosphere of the 1930s, it was hardly possible to relate otherwise to the tension between vision and reality. And indeed, he characterized the transformation that in his view had explicitly affected the functions of the Hebrew language as a change in its messianic sensibility. The language of our people, he wrote, "in which it uttered prayers and songs for the banished deer of Izmir [i.e., Shabbetai Zvi] is now called upon to weep or sing in close embrace with the cow in the meadows of the Sharon."[97] He thus interpreted the circumspection shown by poetic language in naming contemporary realities as a form of justified caution in pursuing the task of national Redemption. For "this is no giving up, but an eager, ardent expectation. The explicit names of what is done and seen here are still within quotation marks taken from the world of reflection, of abstraction, of symbol."[98]

In other words, it is by means of his theory of poetic language that Alterman formulated a critique that is here interpreted as directed against the illusion mongers of instant Redemption. When he noted that the poem supremely "knows that all that is human and painful shall be its sustenance" or that the poem thus "fears to turn the words of prey loose" upon such things or that "nothing like poetry hates generalization and obfuscation,"[99] Alterman identified his targets on the national scene in literary terms that recall by implication Greenberg's poetic expressionism and messianic ideas.

Even into the complex composition of *Stars Abroad* Alterman inserted a poem implying reservations about the messianic potential of his own poetry. In "Beyond the Melody," he depicts pain and sorrow ("stones like tears on the world's lashes") while stressing the inadequacy of the art of poetry to give them expression:

> How should I try to wipe them away with a silken
> handkerchief?
> Above the ultimate poem trembling in their sight
> Silence sweeps round like an eagle.[100]

Thereafter the poem goes on to examine, within this framework of the relationship between art and life, two existential choices: the one faces harsh reality stoically, with humorous resignation, static and mute, based on inner contemplation. The other option is dynamic, subordinating the private domain of silent, lonely pain to the boisterous collective domain. To praise "our small and shamefaced pain" that "dwells alone like its elder brothers / The end and the heart and the autumn days"[101] may seem no more than a universal lyrical statement. But in the context of our discussion, it emerges as an implicit critique of, even a political reaction against, the excessive claims made by and for the other school of thought. For the silent, small pain is defined in opposition to the clamor of political messianism with its royalist pomp:

To keep on talking
That the well has filled up,
That the forest is aflame in the royal mantles,
But lonesome and deaf
Plowing its field
[Is] our small and shamefaced pain.

For it has no Messiah and has no flags
And silences in mourning garb watch over its candles.[102]

The poem's title, *"Me'ever lemanginah"* ("Beyond the Melody") points to the inner struggle of the small, private pain striving to find refuge from external, collective pressure—from the movement of roads

Which stand erect with music and cloud,
And walk tall, tender-powerful they walk,
Walking and rocking us in their laps.[103]

To the private realm thus stand opposed not only collective messianism and royal pomp but also, unexpectedly, music as well. This is surprising, to say the least. In this specific historical context, Alterman's abstract symbolism, with its allegiance to *l'art pour l'art* and its commitment to the primacy of music, found itself caught in a web of contradictions that were ultimately political. The symbolist primacy of music found itself face to face with a movement that, seeking to aesthetisize social reality and politics, made an equally heavy use of the musical model.[104] It would thus seem that the real dangers of the "musicalization of the political" did not escape Alterman. If *Stars Abroad* is his most refined lyrical statement, it nonetheless represented a reaction, however subtle, to the social and political context of the time. And if music is given a place of honor throughout this book[105]—indeed, an almost uniquely privileged status—Alterman still was determined to draw a clear line between himself and the mystical musicality so closely associated with the political messianism of those years and, specifically, with the poetics of its leading exponent, Uri Zvi Greenberg.[106]

As the 1930s drew to a close, then, the symbolist preference for the musical makeup of the word as opposed to its semantic import found itself confronted by harsh and immediate political facts. The symbolist affirmation of a latent mystical reality now ran the risk of being understood as a dangerous irrationalism. Its musicality without content could be seen as a sacrilization of primal drives abolishing the moral in favor of the coursing of the blood. This, in fact, was the same dilemma that Shlonsky had had to face early in his career in Palestine—the solution, too, was quite similar. But what could still take up the foreground in Shlonsky's early work had now to be placed far to the back in Alterman's text. The very fact that *Stars Abroad* was written and published during the late 1930s left its mark even on this refined *tour de force* of lyricism. Yet Alterman was not alone in taking this course. Other poets, such as Yocheved Bat-Miryam, Eliyahu Tessler, Ezra Zussman and above all, Shlonsky, each working in the tradition of quasi-symbolistic modernism, found his or her own strategies for coping with the messianic challenge.

Not only Uri Zvi Greenberg's spiritual and political presence, but also his royalist messianic ideology made itself felt through its indirect and subtle literary impact. This was yet another indication of the special complexity of his work: the more marginalized it became, the more it found roundabout ways to make its mark after all. Greenberg's poetry was, in fact, the only consistent attempt to press messianic poetry directly into the service of a concrete political party. The other messianic poetry, especially that which came out of the labor movement, sought instead a sublimated substitute for the direct political use of messianic ideas.

In his extreme radicalism, Greenberg took as his goal not to engage literature in politics, not to politicize the aesthetic, but rather to aesthetisize the political. The messianic vision was to realize itself as the negation of any present reality, liberated from any practical limitations.

The confrontation between Greenberg and Alterman, however implicit, was thus the culmination of a long process in which the role of poetry in the culture of the Yishuv had undergone repeated reexamination. The poetry of this period constituted a sort of backstage arena where the contestants kept meeting in the attempt either to settle their differences, as with Bat-Miryam's oxymoric writing, or else to develop opposition to messianic extremism as in Shlonsky's and Alterman's subtle polemics. In response to Greenberg's bold moves, Hebrew poetry had to take up explicit positions with regard to the messianic issues if it wished to maintain its privileged public status as a national medium of communication. Greenberg declared himself copiously and directly; Alterman felt that he had no choice but to voice his anti-messianic position with great circumspection and almost in secret.

Notes

I take pleasure in thanking Moshe Ron, who translated this article from the Hebrew with such unstinting expenditure of time and energy. This research was supported by the Wolf Foundation (Israel) to Promote Science and Art for the Benefit of Mankind (administered by the Israel Academy of Science and Humanities).

1. Israel Kolatt, "Ẓiyonut umeshiḥiyut" in *Meshiḥiyut veeskhatologiah*, ed. Zvi Baras (Jerusalem: 1983), 419–431. On the origins of secular messianism, see Jacob L. Talmon, *The Origins of Totalitarian Democracy* (Boston: 1955, repr. 1970).
2. Gershom Scholem, "Toward an Understanding of the Messianic Idea in Judaism," in his *The Messianic Idea in Judaism and Other Essays on Jewish Spirituality*, trans. M.A. Meyers (New York: 1971), 35.
3. *Ibid.*, 35–36.
4. A. D. Gordon, "Pitaron lo raẓionali" [1909], in his *Haumah veha'avodah* (Tel-Aviv: 1957), 93.
5. *Ibid.*, 6.
6. Yosef Hayim Brenner, "Ba'itonut uvasifrut" [*Hapo'el haẓa'ir* (24 November 1924)], in his *Ketavim*, vol. 2, (Tel-Aviv: 1960), 56–59.
7. Shmuel Yavnieli, "Divrei hameḥaivim" [1917], in his *Ketavim*, vol. 1, (Tel-Aviv: 1961), 14.
8. A. D. Gordon, "Lezikaron" [1918], in his *Haumah veha'avodah*, 401–408.
9. The notion of the Hebrew poet as prophet had become a matter of controversy because of the extraordinary status attained by Hayim Nahman Bialik before the First World War. Cf. Chone Shmeruk, "Hakeriyah lanavi (Shneor, Bialik, Pereẓ ve-Nadson)," *Hasifrut*

2 (1969), 241–244. David Frishman, "Mikhtavim 'al devar hasifrut" [letter 13, 1908], in *Kol kitvei David Frishman* (New York and Warsaw: 1930), 170–178. Joseph (Yosef) Klausner, "Yefei haruah," *Hashiloah* 23 (1911), 289–297. See also Klausner's early article, "Hayim Nahman Bialik, maamar sheni" [1903], in his *Yozrim uvonim*, (Jerusalem: 1929), 17–40.

10. A. D. Gordon, "Mitokh keriyah" [1918], in *Haumah veha'avodah*, 289.

11. Uri Zvi Greenberg, *Eimah gedolah veyareah* (Tel-Aviv: 1924).

12. Avraham Shlonsky, *Devai* (Tel-Aviv: 1924).

13. Greenberg, *Eimah gedolah veyareah*, 64.

14. Shlonsky, *Devai*, 109.

15. *Ibid.*, 108. (All the translations of verse are literal prose versions as rendered by Moshe Ron.)

16. *Ibid.*, 94.

17. Clive Scott, "Symbolism, Decadence and Impressionism," in *Modernism 1890–1930*, ed. M. Bradbury and J. McFarlane (New York: 1976), 210.

18. Shlonsky, *Devai*, 94.

19. *Ibid.*, 116.

20. Yaakov Rabinovitz, "He'arot" [1925], in *Mivhar maamarim 'al yezirato shel Avraham Shlonsky*, ed. Aviezer Weiss (Tel-Aviv: 1975), 67–68.

21. Shlonsky, *Devai*, 130–131.

22. Scott, "Symbolism, Decadence and Impressionism," 210–211.

23. Gershom Scholem, "Mizvah habaah be'averah," in his *Mehkarim umekorot letoledot hashabtaut vegilgulehah* (Jerusalem: 1974), 17.

24. Uri Zvi Greenberg, "Yerushalayim shel matah," in *Eimah gedolah veyareah*, 57.

25. Uri Zvi Greenberg, "Kefizat haderekh," in *ibid.*, 61.

26. David Weinfeld, "Shirat Uri Zvi Greenberg bishnot ha'esrim 'al rek'a haekspresionizm," *Molad* 8, nos. 39–40 (1980), 65–72.

27. Greenberg, "Kefizat haderekh," 63.

28. *Ibid.*

29. David Kena'any, *Ha'aliyah hasheniyah ha'ovedet veyahasah ladat velamasoret*, (Tel-Aviv: 1976) 35.

30. David Shimonovitz, "Bazoret" in *Shirim, sefer sheni* (Tel-Aviv: 1949), 72.

31. *Ibid.*, untitled poem, 105. The talmudic phrase "let him come and I will not see him" is understood to mean that it is preferable not to be present at the moment when the Messiah comes, since his coming will be associated with great upheavals.

32. *Ibid.*, 105–106.

33. Yitzhak Yaziv, "Mashiah ben Yosef," *Davar*, 12 August 1927.

34. See e.g., G. Hanoch, "Dorshei hahazon," *Hapoel haza'ir*, 20 June 1927. For a full-scale treatment, see Hannan Hever, *Reishit hitgabshuto shel hashir hapoliti beerez yisrael* (Ph.D. diss., The Hebrew University of Jerusalem, 1984), 354–357.

35. Uri Zvi Greenberg, *Hazon ahad haligyonot* (Tel-Aviv: 1928).

36. Walter H. Sokel, *The Writer in Extremis: Expressionism in Twentieth-Century German Literature* (New York: 1964), 2.

37. Uri Zvi Greenberg, "Mimegilat hayamim hahem," *Davar*, 18 September 1927.

38. Greenberg, *Hazon ahad haligyonot*, 30.

39. *Ibid.*, 5.

40. Cf. Hever, *Reishit hitgabshuto shel hashir hapoliti*, 273–298; Yitzhak Lamdan, *Masadah* (Tel-Aviv: 1937). References are to *Masadah* (Tel-Aviv: 1952).

41. *Ibid.*, 82.

42. Greenberg, *Hazon ahad haligyonot*, 5–6.

43. Lamdan, *Masadah*, 76.

44. *Ibid.*, 18.

45. Avraham Shlonsky, *Bagalgal* (Tel-Aviv: 1927).

46. *Ibid.*, 173; cf. Yaakov Bahat, *Uri Zvi Greenberg* (Jerusalem and Tel-Aviv: 1983), 286–287.

47. Cf. Lamdan, *Masadah*, 69.

48. Cf. Greenberg, *Ḥazon aḥad haligyonot*, 10–11.

49. Uri Zvi Greenberg, *Kelev bayit* (Tel-Aviv: 1929), 80.

50. David Shimonovitz, "Yirmiyahu . . . ," *Moznayim*, 12 April 1929; "Benei Geiḥazi," *Hapoel haẓa'ir*, 12 July 1929.

51. Cf. Greenberg, *Kelev bayit*, 3–24.

52. Uri Zvi Greenberg, *Ezor magen uneum ben hadam* (Jerusalem: 1930), 1.

53. *Ibid.*, 14. On "eating the Messiah," see herein, 129.

54. Greenberg, *Ezor magen uneum ben hadam*, 13.

55. Cf. Greenberg, *Kelev bayit*, 67.

56. Cf. Greenberg, *Ezor magen uneum ben hadam*, 7, emphasis added.

57. David Ben-Gurion, *Tenu'at hapo'alim veharevisionizmus* (Tel-Aviv: 1933), 132–133.

58. Eliezer Steinman, *Meshiḥiyut* (Tel-Aviv: 1932; dated inside 1930).

59. Avraham Shlonsky, *Lo tirẓaḥ* (Tel-Aviv: 1932), 31.

60. *Ibid.*

61. Boaz Arp'alli, "*MeAvnei bohu leKokhavim baḥuẓ*," in *Alterman veyeẓirato*, ed. M. Dorman and A. Komem (Tel-Aviv: 1989), 153–154.

62. Avraham Shlonsky (ed.), *Avnei bohu* (Tel-Aviv: 1934), 139.

63. Shlomo Zemach, "'Al hahashvaah," *Moznayim* (March 1934), 99. On this problem in Shlonsky's poetry, see Dov Sadan, "Im *Avnei bohu*" [1934], in his *Bein din leheshbon* (Tel-Aviv: 1963), 90–92. For a new perspective on this critique, placing Shlonsky in the tradition of wit poetry, cf. Dan Miron, "He'arot ḥadashot lemaḥloket yeshanah 'al sefer *Avnei bohu* le-A. Shlonsky umisevivo," *Akhshav* 29–30 (1974), 63–85.

64. Zemach, "'Al hahashvaah," 99.

65. Cf. Shlonsky, *Avnei bohu*, 137–139. Shlonsky employs the familiar biblical term "*mizmor shir*" ("A psalm and song") in his discussion of the messianic theme as a literary issue (139).

66. Avraham Broides, "Igeret," *Ha'olam*, 6 December 1929.

67. Shin Shalom, "Mitokh halehavot," *Davar*, 9 May 1929.

68. Cf. Greenberg, *Ezor magen uneum ben hadam*, 25.

69. *Ibid.*, 26.

70. *Ibid.*

71. Uri Zvi Greenberg, *Sefer hakitrug vehaemunah* (Jerusalem and Tel-Aviv: 1937), 99.

72. See esp. A. A. Kabak, *Bamish'ol haẓar* (Tel-Aviv: 1937) and Scholem, "Miẓvah habaah ba'averah," n. 23. The latter essay was first published in 1937. See also Natan Bistritsky, *Shabetai Ẓevi* (Tel-Aviv: 1936).

73. Cf. Greenberg, *Sefer hakitrug vehaemunah*, 109.

74. *Ibid.*, 138–140.

75. Yaacov Shavit, "Bein Pilsudski leMitskevich: mediniyut umeshiḥiyut barevizionism haẓiyoni (baheksher shel hatarbut hapolanit veshel zikato lefolin)," in his *Hamitologiyot shel hayamin* (Beit Berl: 1986), 23–25.

76. Cf. Greenberg, *Sefer hakitrug vehaemunah*, 91.

77. *Ibid.*, 163.

78. *Ibid.*, 38.

79. *Ibid.*

80. *Ibid.*, 164.

81. Cf. Steinman, *Meshiḥiyut*, 28–29.

82. *Ibid.*, 32.

83. Cf. Greenberg, "Yehudah hayom. Yehudah maḥar: masa' devai, masa' gil," in *Sefer hakitrug vehaemunah*, 169.

84. *Ibid.*, 163.

85. Shin Shalom, *'Olam belehavot* (Tel-Aviv: 1944), 34.

86. On the poetics and symbolism of Yocheved Bat-Miryam, see Ruth Karton-Blum, *Bamerḥak hane'elam* (Ramat-Gan: 1977).

87. Yocheved Bat-Miryam, *Demuyot meofek* (Tel-Aviv: 1942), 157–159.

88. On Alterman's symbolism, see Ziva Shamir, *'Od ḥozer hanigun* (Tel-Aviv: 1989), 81–88 and passim.

89. Natan Alterman, "'Al habilti muvan bashirah," [1933] in his *Bama'agal*, (Tel-Aviv: 1938, repr. 1975), 12.

90. *Ibid.*, 16.

91. Natan Alterman, "Sod hamerkhaot hakefulot," [1938] in *ibid.*, 29.

92. *Ibid.*

93. *Ibid.*

94. *Ibid.*

95. *Ibid.*

96. *Ibid.*, 28.

97. *Ibid.*, 27.

98. *Ibid.*, 30–31.

99. *Ibid.*, 30.

100. Natan Alterman, *Kokhavim baḥuẓ*, vol. 1, *Shirim mishekvar* (Tel-Aviv: 1961), 35.

101. *Ibid.*, 36.

102. *Ibid.*, 35–36.

103. *Ibid.*, 35.

104. On the movement from symbolism, with emphasis on *l'art pour l'art* to Fascist culture through the aesthetization of the political, cf. Walter Benjamin, "The Work of Art in the Age of Mechanical Reproduction," in his *Illuminations* (New York: 1970), 219–254, esp. 226.

105. On the symbolistic musicality of Alterman's poetry, particularly in the period preceding his *Stars Abroad*, see Dan Miron, *Miprat le'ikar* (Tel-Aviv: 1981), 101–150.

106. In another essay of 1938, Alterman employed symbolistic criteria to attack both the fascist culture in Germany and the culture of protest encouraged by the extreme Left. He warned of the danger inherent in the incitement of political passions and, more specifically, in the power of music to sweep away the masses: "'Olam vehipukho," [1938], in his *Bama'agal*, 32–38.

"The Stronger and the Better Jews": Jewish Theological Responses to Political Messianism in the Weimar Republic

Paul Mendes-Flohr
(THE HEBREW UNIVERSITY)

The false Messiah is as old as the hope for the true Messiah. He is the changing form of the changeless hope. He separates every Jewish generation into those whose faith is strong enough to give themselves up to an illusion, and those whose hope is so strong they do not allow themselves to be deluded. The former are the better, the latter the stronger.
—Franz Rosenzweig

In the midst of the Bavarian revolution of 1918–1919, a group of students at the University of Munich organized a study circle to discuss the urgent social and political questions of the day. To distinguish themselves from the right-wing *Corpstudenten*, they fancied themselves to be a *Freistudentenschaft,* and met weekly in a local bookshop.[1] In January 1919, they were addressed by Max Weber, who was soon to assume a professorship at the university.[2] In a room packed to overflowing (apparently an auditorium rather than the usual meeting place at the bookshop), Weber spoke to the enthralled students about the moral tasks and sociological boundaries of scholarship in the modern world. This lecture, delivered freely and without a pause, was recorded by a stenographer and later published under the title "Science as a Vocation." Two months later, Weber once again addressed the students on a parallel theme, "Politics as a Vocation."[3] In these now-famous lectures, the sociologist offered, in striking contrast to the heated rhetoric of the day,[4] a cold analysis of what he regarded to be the misconceived idealism of the youths then ruling the streets of Munich.

Indeed, Weber had a profound appreciation of the ideals that inspired the youths and intellectuals (some of whom he knew personally and held in great esteem)[5] who led the revolution that erupted in November 1918 and came to a brutal end in May 1919. He shared, to some degree, their conviction that—with defeat in the First World War and with the collapse of the old regime—Germany had the unique opportunity of reversing the sins of the older generation. What he objected to was the messianic enthusiasm of the students and the attendant assumption that with goodwill alone they could usher in a better, utterly just world—in which pure

159

morality would be the sole principle of governance; in which public life, free of bourgeois cynicism, would once again be suffused with spiritual and ethical meaning; in which knowledge (by which he meant science and scholarship) would cease to serve sinister, impersonal ends and be transformed into the sole instrument of personal edification and relevance.[6]

Such a vision, Weber held, was indeed noble; and yet it reflected an utter lack of understanding of the complexity and nature of the modern world. The principal error of the well-intentioned but benighted idealists, in Weber's view, was their unwillingness to accept the "disenchantment of [a] world" in which all mystery had been removed from existence by the ascendancy of reason as the fundamental ground of knowledge and social organization. Further, Weber pessimistically noted that in the rational, bureaucratic order characteristic of the modern era, "precisely the ultimate and most sublime values have [forever] retreated from public life."[7]

If meaning were to be found, it was in *pianissimo*, in the purely personal and internal realms of existence.[8] Weber concluded his first lecture with a sermonic rebuke of those who were impatient with the world as it is and thus longed for Redemption:

[For them,] the situation is the same as resounds in the beautiful Edomite watchman's song of the period of exile—the night of exile—that had been included in Isaiah's oracle: He calleth to me, . . . Watchman, what of the night? The watchman said, The morning cometh, but it is still night: if ye will enquire, come again another time (Isa. 21:11).[9]

And Weber added in a grave tone that deeply moved his audience:[10]

The people to whom this was said has enquired and tarried for more than two millennia, and we are shaken when we realize its fate. From this we want to draw the lesson that nothing is gained by yearning and tarrying alone, and we shall act differently.[11]

One is to reconcile oneself to the night of exile, forgo the hope of Redemption and fulfill the "'demands of the day' in one's personal relations as in one's vocation."[12]

Weber's association of the naive, romantic messianism of the Munich radicals with the fate of the Jews and the vain, self-defeating longing for Redemption may have been an oblique reference to the fact that so many of the young radicals were Jews. Indeed, he was troubled that Jews—among others, Kurt Eisner, Gustav Landauer, Eugen Leviné, Erich Mühsam and Ernst Toller—were playing such a conspicuous role in the Bavarian revolution.[13] Weber was convinced that the inevitable defeat of the revolution and the equally inevitable backlash would lead to the heightening of antisemitism[14]—as in fact it did.[15]

For Jewish radicals, of course, such considerations could not compromise what they regarded as a matter of principle; and, worse, they were a betrayal of humanity's hope—a hope that the philosopher of revolutionary politics, Ernst Bloch, unabashedly identified as messianic. But the revolution primed by messianic hope (according to this German Jewish philosopher) was not to be viewed as a chimerical attempt to rush the gates of paradise. It was rather a defiant refusal to accept the misery of human existence. For hope, Bloch explained, is a projection of a future that transcends existing realities; hope allows humanity to envision an alternative, happier world; hope, as such, has inspired revolutionary politics from time immemorial. Bereft of an eschatological vision and passion, a forlorn humanity would haplessly resign itself to the indignities and injustices of the established order.

Hence, for Bloch, the type of realism recommended by Weber would only serve to deny hope and to perpetuate human misery, both material and existential. Humanity would be doomed were it to reconcile itself to the disenchantment of the world. The refusal to do so was not to be construed as naive optimism; it was rather born of an unflinching recognition of prevailing evil. "The messianic," Bloch explained in *Geist der Utopie* (a volume he wrote in the wake of the horrors he witnessed during the First World War), "discerns the future precisely in the dark of the lived moment."[16] Hope is a brave confrontation with evil; it resists all temptation to deny evil's fearsome reality with the anaesthetizing categories of the sociologist and political scientist. Hope recognizes evil to be evil, as a force to be overcome if humanity is to endure with dignity.

Thus, revolutionary politics, according to Bloch, was in the first instance an angry protest against evil. But the revolutionary, he added, is preeminently an agent of hope, of a hope emboldened by what he called "a revolutionary Gnosis."[17] Painfully aware of human suffering and injustice, Bloch's revolutionary discards all illusion that the world is ruled by a benevolent, caring God, and he unapologetically assumes the Gnostic view that, as presently constituted, the world is not our home. A homeless humanity is adrift in a universe governed by satanic forces,[18] which in the modern period have tightened their grip by promoting the disenchantment of the world and the attendant cynicism masquerading as rational sobriety:

> The devil once again totally dominates us; even if one does not wish to believe in him, one sees his cloven foot, and he, the devil, absolutely undisturbed, rules us as apparently pure nothingness, as utter disenchantment [*Entzauberung*], intrinsically blocking human beings from mystery.[19]

Bloch regarded it as the task of revolutionary politics to rescue "mystery"—the misty climes in which the human spirit allows itself to hope—in order to restore to humanity the vision of the *eschaton*, the vision of a future in which one will be truly at home in the world.

Bloch thus sought to illuminate the spiritual and moral passion informing the revolutionary ethos—once defined by him as "the categorical imperative with revolver in hand"[20]—by demonstrating its fundamental continuity with the eschatological imagination. Indeed, his entire oeuvre (embracing sixteen volumes)[21] may be regarded as a sustained meditation on messianism as "the a priori of [all genuine] culture and politics."[22]

Despite his frequent reference to Jewish messianic lore and teachings, Bloch would resolutely reject the characterization of his thought as specifically Jewish. The sources of his thought were eclectic: Jewish, Christian and pagan. He recruited innumerable traditions to illustrate what he regarded to be the basic, albeit often repressed, eschatological impulse of humanity throughout the ages. Moreover, he discerned this impulse not only within religious traditions, but also in art and, above all, in music.[23] Although he did not hesitate to cite Jewish sources, they did not enjoy any particular preeminence in his writings. Certainly Bloch did not regard himself as spiritually and intellectually beholden to Judaism.[24]

Furthermore, his "revolutionary Gnosticism," with its denial of the world as God's creation (not to speak of his avowed atheism)[25] put him at extreme odds with the most fundamental theological presuppositions of Judaism.[26] There is thus a paradox in the fact that his conception of the overarching task of philosophy as developing an "epistemology of the future" seems to have been inspired by Hermann Cohen (1842–1918), a philosopher who explicitly sought to ground his work in a systematic elaboration of what he regarded to be the basic Jewish principle of messianic hope.

In July 1908, Bloch submitted his doctoral dissertation to the University of Würzburg.[27] His dissertation, which was devoted to a probing appraisal of Heinrich Rickert's theory of knowledge, was written before Bloch's adoption of Marxism and Hegelian dialectics. Yet the dissertation already displayed the rudiments of his philosophy of hope, presented in a critical *Ausandersetzung* along with Hermann Cohen's conception of hope and the future as philosophical categories.[28] Significantly, on completing his dissertation, Bloch sent a copy to the famed neo-Kantian philosopher of Marburg with a dedication: "For *Herr Geheimrat* Hermann Cohen with high esteem. Ernst Bloch."[29]

Cohen introduced the categories of "hope" and the "messianic future" into philosophic discourse, linking and explicitly developing them on the basis of Jewish sources.[30] He sought to show that the biblical, or rather, prophetic vision of a messianic future was not only the basis for, but also the most refined expression of, the Enlightenment's doctrine of progress and the moral unity of mankind.[31] To be sure, Cohen was aware of the fact that, as a collective singular, the "future"[32]—denoting a common historical experience—and "humanity"—as a moral attribute of "mankind"[33]—were unique to the modern period. But he sought to show that these concepts were also implicit in the ideational structure of biblical Judaism. Thus, as he declared in a lecture of 1907 (the year in which Bloch was working on his dissertation) "from the very first, the One God implied a mankind united in the ideal of morality."[34]

For Cohen, "messianism," which was also a term of modern coinage,[35] referred to a vision of Redemption without the mediation of God's appointed Messiah whose miraculous advent was awaited by traditional Jewry. The freeing of the conception of a messianic future from a dependence on the miracle of a personal Messiah—a Son of David dispatched by God—was typical of modern liberal Judaism, particularly as it had evolved in nineteenth-century Germany.[36] A depersonalized messianism was one of the essential tenets of Liberal and Reform Judaism.[37] Cohen argued that this transformation of the messianic concept was an immanent, dialectically necessary development within Judaism, "The ideality of the Messiah, his significance as an idea, is shown in the overcoming of the person of the Messiah and in the dissolution of the personal image in the pure notion of time, the concept of the *age*. Time becomes future and only future."[38] Cohen's conception of prophetic Judaism as anticipating the precepts of modern humanism provided a systematic, and eloquent, articulation of German Jewish liberal sensibility and what Reform and Liberal Jewish theologians referred to as the ideals of ethical monotheism.[39] Moreover, with his claim that monotheism had foreshadowed the ethical idealism of Germany's finest spirits, especially the teachings of Kant, Cohen did much to strengthen the self-esteem of German Jewry.[40] But his intention was not merely apologetic. Indeed, throughout his life he vigorously sought to guard the honor of middle-class Jewry as it sought acceptance in a world presumably beholden to liberal values.[41] Cohen was no mere liberal, however. For him, the prophetic heritage of Israel enjoined a committed concern for the poor and disinherited members of society:

> The messianic God does not represent merely a future image of world history, however. He demands—by virtue of the eternal ideas conjoined in Him—political action [in the present] and continuous, tireless participation in various concrete national tasks. It is the duty of every Jew to help bring about the messianic age by involving himself in the national life of his country.[42]

Cohen's moral-religious commitments led him to endorse socialism,[43] observing that the politics of the prophets "is nothing other than what nowadays we call socialism."[44]

For him, however, socialism was more than a moral slogan. He was sharply critical of capitalism, regarding its system of production as morally unacceptable, and he, accordingly, advocated the establishment of a cooperative economy controlled by the workers.[45] His doctrine of ethical socialism was perhaps his most enduring legacy. Basing himself on the Kantian principle that each human being must be regarded as an end-in-itself, Cohen held that a human being should, therefore, never be treated as a means or a tool by others, "The deepest and most powerful meaning of the categorical imperative is expressed in this [proposition]; it contains the moral program of a new era and the entire future world history. . . . The idea of the priority of humanity as an end becomes the idea of socialism, which defines each human as an end in itself [*Selbstzweck*]."[46]

Among Cohen's students was Kurt Eisner, the leader of the band of largely Jewish intellectuals—philosophers, poets, playwrights, pacifists and anarchists—who launched the Bavarian revolution. It was Eisner's conviction that politics could be pursued without violence. Accordingly, as an admirer had affectionately observed, "he had hoped to change Germany by kindness."[47] Eisner had studied with Cohen at the University of Marburg, being particularly drawn to the philosopher's ethical socialism, which, as he later recalled, touched him to the core of his being.[48] To the end of his life—he was assassinated by a crazed opponent of the revolution in February 1919—he remained true to his teacher's ideals of a socialism guided by the categorical imperative and the vision of the prophets.[49]

Were Eisner and his fellow Jewish revolutionaries, indeed, representatives of Judaism or, at least, of Cohen's conception of prophetic messianism?[50] To be sure, the question is more rhetorical than substantive. For one, we have no evidence that Eisner read Cohen as a fellow Jew whose message was addressed to his Jewish loyalties.[51] In his socialist writings, Cohen addressed Jews and non-Jews alike. Many non-Jews, of course, were influenced by Cohen's neo-Kantian conception of socialism.[52] Further, Eisner's Jewish comrades were apparently unfamiliar with Cohen's doctrines. If they were aware of them, they were not particularly inspired by them;[53] and there is no evidence of any other specifically Jewish teachings that may have informed their politics.[54] Yet the question of the Jewishness of the Bavarian revolutionaries—and other Jewish protagonists of the revolutions that swept Europe in the years 1917–1919[55]—was frequently raised. As Franz Kafka anxiously recorded after having overheard a conversation of German guests at a hotel dining room, "They don't forgive the Jewish Socialists and Communists a single thing; they drown them during the soup and quarter them while carving the roast."[56]

In more polite circles, the question of the Jewishness of so many prominent revolutionaries was posed in order to focus on the apparent Jewish inclination to political activism, a charge that was reinforced by the postwar upsurge of Zionism among German Jewish youth. Christian theologians suggested that the Jews' this-worldly conception of Redemption was at fault. Typical was a widely discussed essay, "Judentum und Christentum" ("Judaism and Christianity") by the highly reputed Jesuit philosopher Erich Przywara.[57] Published in 1926 in the respected and influential cultural and political monthly, *Stimmen der Zeit,* this article advanced the argument that the restless "political activism" of the Jews threatened the very foundations of a Christian civilization that was grounded in a quiet, patient faith in the saving grace of Jesus Christ. With the learned inflections of an objective scholar, Przywara maintained that the political passions of secular Jews were dialectically related to Israel's rejection of Jesus—who had brought to mankind the promise of a genuinely spiritual relationship to God—and to the consequent enslavement of the Jews' religious imagination to a this-worldly messianism.

Przywara held that the messianism of the modern secular Jew, whose humane and high ideals he acknowledged, was but a misplaced idealism. Other Christian writers were less charitable and accused the secular radical Jews of more sinister motives, linking them with the spiritually desiccated and calculating piety of the Pharisees. Perhaps the most outrageous of these critics was the novelist and cultural critic, Oskar A. H. Schmitz, who (in a special issue of Martin Buber's *Der Jude* devoted to a Jewish and Christian exchange on antisemitism) published an article with the deliberately antagonistic title "Desirable and Undesirable Jews" ("*Wünschenswerte und nichtwünschenswerte Juden*").[58] Schmitz identified the former as the Orthodox Jews "who disturb no one [and] can be most desirable fellow citizens with Aryans."[59] The undesirable Jews—deracinated and secular pacifists, socialists, Zionists—are animated by the "demonic" spirit of Pharisaism, which Schmitz defined as a sort of negative messianism. The Pharisees and their latter-day disciples, albeit irreligious, are "bearers of a messianic hope"; they view it as their task to inform the Christians that the Messiah has yet to come and, indeed, that "he must remain unreal, never to be in the here and now."[60] Hence, Schmitz concluded, "the true essence of the Pharisees is their No."[61] By insisting that Redemption must be this-worldly, the Jews, in effect, denied the very possibility of true Redemption.[62]

The challenge to Jewish scholars and religious thinkers to clarify the Jewish messianic doctrine and its relationship to political activism also came from within the Jewish community. The postwar generation of Jewish youth, particularly the Zionists among them, increasingly demanded that the Jews as a people return to history and actively seek to shape their own historical destiny in order to achieve what the more enthusiastic would call Redemption.[63] Within German Jewish circles, this problem was primarily illuminated, like so many other theological issues during the period, by Martin Buber and Franz Rosenzweig, who here, as so often, adopted radically different positions.

In striking contrast to the mood of the period, Rosenzweig taught that, by virtue of their conception of Redemption, the Jews were to remain apart from history and were to resist the temptation to participate in the perfecting of the world. The "soul" of the Jewish people, "replete with the vistas afforded by [messianic] hope, grows numb to the concerns, the doing, and the struggling of the world. . . . Its holiness hinders it from devoting its soul to a still unhallowed world, no matter how much the body may be bound with it."[64] Since their exile, Rosenzweig observed, the Jews no longer live in history—which is the affair of sovereign states[65]—but beyond it, blissfully sequestered in a spiritual reality that anticipates the Kingdom of God. The Jews' experience of time is exclusively set by the rhythms of their liturgical calendar. The fixed and elaborate pattern of prayer, commemoration and celebration of the ancient Jewish liturgy orders the year, so that each year replicates the preceding one. Jewish time is, thus, cyclical; it does not grow, it does not include or notice current events. In contrast to the peoples of the world whose life unfolds in history and whose sense of time is shaped both by current events and the fortunes that those events bear, the Jews focus their imagination and their sense of themselves as a *Schicksalsgemeinschaft,* on eternity—a time beyond growth, in which all the contradictions of history will be resolved. As Rosenzweig explained in his magnum opus of 1921, *The Star of Redemption:*

[In the circuit of its liturgical year, the People of Israel is] at its goal and knows it [is] at the goal. . . . It anticipates eternity. The future is the driving power in the circuit of its year. Its rotation originates, so to speak, not in a thrust but in a pull. The present passes not because the past prods it on but because the future snatches it toward itself. Somehow, even the festivals of creation and revelation flow into Redemption. . . . The meaning of [the eternal people's] life in time is that the years come and go, one after the other as a sequence of waiting, or perhaps wandering, but not growth. . . . And so the eternal people must forget the world's growth, must cease to think thereon. It must look upon the world, its own world, as complete. . . . As a nationality, [the Jewish people has thus] reached the point to which the nations of the world still aspire. Its world has reached the goal. . . . Because the Jewish people is beyond the contradiction that constitutes the vital drive in the life of the nations—the contradiction between national characteristics and world history, home and faith, earth and heaven—it knows nothing of war. The Jew is practically the only human being who cannot take war seriously, and this makes him the only genuine pacifist. For that reason, and because he experiences perfect community in his spiritual year, he remains remote from the chronology of the rest of the world. He does not have to wait for the world history to unroll its long course to let him gain what he feels he already possesses in the circuit of every year: the experience of the immediacy of each single individual to God, realized in the perfect community of all with God.[66]

Although indifferent to the "growth of the world," the Jews—or rather "the Synagogue"[67]—is not irrelevant to world history; indeed, the Synagogue plays a crucial role in the unfolding of history as an eschatological process. As a nation beyond history, the Jews project the image of the future, of the goal of history. As such, the Synagogue constitutes the ontological ground of the future; because of the Jews, the eschatological future is not merely a divine promise or mere utopian goal, but a concrete reality, proleptically foreshadowed in the present. The Synagogue thus embodies humanity's hope of Redemption. Accordingly, Rosenzweig evokes the ancient Hebrew benediction recited upon reading the Torah. "Blessed art Thou . . . who has planted eternal life in our midst."[68] Thus, the Jews are, indeed, an "eternal people," their eternity referring not so much to their perdurability as to their realization, within historical premessianic time, of the future Redemption.[69] Rosenzweig thus likens the Synagogue to "a star" that "must burn incessantly," its flames eternally feeding upon itself. "It requires no fuel from without. Time has no power over it and must roll past." Its eternal flame, Rosenzweig observes, marks it as a "star of Redemption."[70]

Hovering majestically above history, the "star of Redemption"—the Synagogue—beckons the peoples of the world to reach out beyond history to eternity, to a "redeemed" existence freed from the political and existential torments of history. The "star of Redemption," however, is only truly apprehended by the Church because, in regarding itself as the true Israel, it alone takes notice of the Synagogue. Despite itself, perhaps, the Church is challenged by the abiding reality of the Jews as an eternal people. The Synagogue resides where the Church knows it should, but cannot. (And here, Rosenzweig argues, lies the ultimate ground of Christian antisemitism.)[71] By virtue of its mission to the pagans, the Church enters history, associating itself with the struggles and fate of the peoples of the world. There within the bosom of history, the Church as a "supranational power"[72] is to lead the peoples of the world to Zion, to the eschatological community in which all will dwell together in common recognition of the God of Abraham, Isaac and Jacob.[73] In so doing, the Church transforms the divisive histories of the nations of the world into a "world-history" flowing along a messianic trajectory.[74]

Judaism and Christianity, according to Rosenzweig, are thus joined in a special, albeit unacknowledged, alliance. From the perspective of God's *Heilsplan*, both Covenants—the Old and the New—are valid; together, they work to bring the Redemption, the Synagogue as a metahistorical community of prayer and the Church through history. "From two sides there is . . . a knocking on the door of the future."[75]

Rosenzweig's vision of history was informed by his conviction that, on its own, history cannot redeem itself and that, left on its own, history spins upon its own directionless axis, lost in an endless cycle of wars and revolutions. This conviction began to crystallize while Rosenzweig was still a student of history at the university, and especially as he was writing his doctoral dissertation on Hegel's conception of the nation-state, which he submitted in the summer of 1912.[76] But it was later during the First World War (in which he served as a combat soldier on the eastern front) and its convulsive aftermath that Rosenzweig concluded that in order to achieve the envisioned era of universal peace and a unity of peoples, history requires a metahistorical reference, an ever-present glimpse of the paradise beyond history. Within the stormy seas of history (according to one image employed by Rosenzweig), the clear sight of land keeps the ship of humanity on course toward its destination. Significantly, he originally developed these thoughts without reference to Judaism or any other theological considerations, and, indeed, only later was he to assign a metahistorical role to Jewry.[77] Once he had done so, however, he reached the paradoxical conclusion that, for the sake of history, the Jews had to remain apart from history, resisting the allure of Zionism and political activism.

Gershom Scholem has commented that, with his doctrine of Redemption, Rosenzweig aligned himself with "a deep-seated tendency" within Judaism to deny messianism of its apocalyptic sting.[78] The traditional conception of messianism, Scholem observed, most often envisions Redemption as an apocalyptic event accompanied by a catastrophic disruption of history; accordingly, it is said, Redemption breaks into history with a cataclysmic, revolutionary force. To be sure, as Scholem acknowledged, Rosenzweig rejected "bourgeois" conceptions of progress and understood that there must be a radical disjunction between history and Redemption.[79] But Rosenzweig sought to bridge the chasm and soften the opposition between history and Redemption. His notion of an eschatological alliance between the Synagogue and the Church suggested that Redemption would be attained without any apocalyptic paroxysms. Certainly, for Rosenzweig, Jewry experiences Redemption without passing through the purgatory of an apocalypse.

One suspects that Scholem, as a Zionist, was particularly disturbed by the historical quietism sponsored by Rosenzweig's conception of messianism. For "historical passivity," Scholem contended, "is . . . hardly compatible with the deepest impulses of messianism."[80] Whenever messianic faith is a living force within Judaism, he noted, it invariably engenders an apocalyptic mood that rivets the imagination and expectations of the Jew on divine deliverance. The more intense this expectation, the greater the desire to do something to hasten the *eschaton,* to "force the End." Hence, according to Scholem, Jewish messianism is characterized by an inevitable tension between a passivity born of a pessimistic view of history and an eagerness to rush headlong into the future.[81] Although the tradition seeks to constrain messianic activism, it is, nonetheless, in Scholem's judgment, a recurring expression of messianism as a vital reality in Judaism.[82] Scholem associated Rosenzweig with Liberal Judaism and with "much more ancient" tendencies in Orthodox Judaism that have sought to deny this reality by making "a virtue of historical necessity," forbidding "the Jewish people any historic initiative, even though the alleged commandment of historical passivity [opposed] the deepest impulses of messianism and, in fact, spelled its perversion."[83]

Rosenzweig, however, actually had a profound appreciation of the apocalyptic impulse of messianism, phenomenologically, if not theologically. In various obiter dicta, he expressed a most positive regard for the apocalyptic dimension of Israel's messianic faith. But these comments are contained in his correspondence, first published in 1935. Thus Scholem had no access to them when he wrote his critique of Rosenzweig in 1930; indeed, he based his criticism of Rosenzweig's messianic doctrine exclusively on *The Star of Redemption.* In a letter to an anti-Zionist rabbi, for instance, Rosenzweig—who in his last years regarded himself as a non-Zionist as opposed to an anti-Zionist[84]—urged his correspondent to acknowledge the achievements of the burgeoning Hebrew culture in Palestine. The "dogmatic" opposition of Liberal Judaism to Zionism, he contended, was not truly religious but rather reflected the politics of Emancipation. The disingenuousness of Liberal Judaism was betrayed no less when, in opposition to Zionism, it appealed to Hermann Cohen's teaching that Redemption is in eternity, in an asymptotic, thus unattainable, future. A Jew of genuine faith, Rosenzweig averred, could not dismiss Zionism simply because of its alleged messianic pretensions:

> I can imagine that one objects to a particular present with 'You are not yet it.' How can one, however, do this out of principle for the future, and indeed for all future, without thereby destroying the future, I cannot understand. I have no idea how one can pray for something, which one holds beforehand to be impossible. . . . The prophets meant an earthly Zion of the future. The eternity, which we Jews mean, lies not in infinity [*Unendlichen*], but 'speedily' in our days. What only comes in eternity . . . does not come in an eternity.[85]

Even Hermann Cohen, Rosenzweig continued, once conceded that messianism can never be a mere asymptotic ideal. "I am still hoping to see the dawn of the messianic age," the elder philosopher had unabashedly confided to Rosenzweig, adding the traditional refrain, "and speedily in our days."[86]

Rosenzweig was even more emphatic in a gloss to one of the poems of Judah Halevi that he translated. On a joyous hymn composed by the Spanish Hebrew poet, one that sings of Israel's imminent "return home"[87] and that, Rosenzweig surmised, was written under the impact of one of the many pseudomessiahs who recurrently emerged in Jewish history,[88] he commented:

> The expectation of the coming of the Messiah, by which and because of which Judaism lives, would be a meaningless theologumenon, a mere "idea" in the philosophical sense, empty babble, if the appearance again and again of a "false Messiah" did not render it reality and unreality, illusion and disillusion. The false Messiah is as old as the hope for the true Messiah. He is the changing form of the changeless hope. He separates every Jewish generation into those whose faith is strong enough to give themselves up to an illusion, and those whose hope is so strong that they do not allow themselves to be deluded. The former are the better, the latter the stronger. The former bleed as victims on the altar of the eternity of the people, the latter are the priests who perform the service at this altar. And this will go on until the day when all will be reversed, when the belief of the believers will become truth, and the hope of the hoping a lie. Then—and no one knows whether this "then" will not be this very day—the task of the hoping will come to an end and, when the morning of that day breaks, everyone who still belongs among those who hope and not among those who believe will run the risk of being rejected. This danger hovers over the apparently less endangered life of the hopeful.[89]

In his appraisal of Rosenzweig's conception of messianism, Scholem seems to have overlooked this passage—contained in a volume published in 1927 and thus available to him when he wrote his critique of Rosenzweig—perhaps because he viewed it as nothing more than a phenomenological aperçu that Rosenzweig failed to integrate into his theology of Redemption.[90] Indeed, Rosenzweig was not saying here that the Jews *should* enter history and hasten the Kingdom. Rather, he is saying that the hope for the Kingdom, if it is real and strong—if it is truly aflame in their breasts—recurrently confronts the Jews with the temptation to enter history in order to greet the Messiah. It is a temptation, however, that is to be resisted. For Rosenzweig, the future, at least as experienced by the Jews, was to remain beyond history.

To be sure, in his later years, Rosenzweig did develop warm feelings for the young Zionists who were among his followers and co-workers. He learned to respect their commitment to Jewish spiritual renewal and came to admire the cultural achievements of the Zionist movement in Palestine. These sentiments certainly blunted any tendency he may have had to adopt an actively anti-Zionist position; indeed, as noted earlier, to distinguish himself from Jewish opponents to Zionism, he called himself a non-Zionist,[91] and looked favorably on the upbuilding of the Jewish community in Palestine.[92] He once even acknowledged in a private conversation that "Zionism is perhaps after all one of the nation's roads into the future. This road too should be kept open."[93] Yet he never endorsed Zionism as an ideology, nor did he seek to adjust his theology to accommodate this movement and its call to the Jews to return to history. For him, the Jews were to remain a metahistorical community, serving as custodians of the future and eschatological hope.

Significantly, Rosenzweig in his later years became increasingly and self-consciously apolitical, an attitude that surely served to reinforce his messianic quietism.[94] He was conservative by temperament, and looked upon the collapse of the German Empire and the abdication of the Kaiser with great grief. The revolution of 1918–1919 in particular outraged him. He decried the revolutionaries as "simpletons and peacemongers"[95] who had struck an unholy alliance with "fifteen- and eighteen-year-old do-nothings playing soldier."[96] Indicatively, he exclaimed, "I believe I'll never be a democrat again! It is as impossible as pacifism. There will always be government, and there will always be war. Freedom and peace, I regard as lying—beyond."[97] Only reluctantly did Rosenzweig accept the Weimar Republic, and undoubtedly would have regarded himself a *"Vernunftsrepublikaner"* ("a republican of reason"), a term coined by his *Doktorvater* Friedrich Meinecke when he declared, "I remain, facing the past, in my heart a monarchist, and facing the future, I become a republican of reason."[98]

In utter contrast to Rosenzweig's conservative and apolitical disposition, Buber was both a Zionist and a socialist who expressed manifest sympathy for the revolutionaries of 1918–1919.[99] His closest and dearest friend was Gustav Landauer, who played an instrumental role in all the varied stages of the Bavarian revolution. At Landauer's behest, Buber came to Munich in order to acquaint himself firsthand with the revolution. In February 1919, he spent, in his words, "a profoundly stirring week"[100] in the company of the revolutionaries of Munich.[101] He met frequently with Eisner and his comrades. As he reported in a letter to his future son-in-law, the poet Ludwig Strauss:

> The deepest human problems of the revolution were discussed with the utmost candor: in the very heart of events I posed questions and offered replies; and there were nocturnal hours of apocalyptic gravity, during which silence spoke eloquently in the midst of discussion, and the future became more distinct than the present. And yet for all but a few it was nothing but mere bustle, and face-to-face with them I sometimes felt

like a Cassandra. As for Eisner, to be with him was to peer into the tormented passions of a divided Jewish soul; nemesis shone from his glittering surface; he was a marked man. Landauer, by dint of the greatest spiritual effort, kept up his faith in him, and protected him—a shield-bearer terribly moving in his selflessness. The whole thing, an unspeakable Jewish tragedy.[102]

Buber left Munich on the morning of the day, February 21, 1919, on which Eisner was assassinated. Ten weeks later, Landauer would be brutally battered to death by counterrevolutionary troops. Buber was deeply shaken by the tragic death of his friend;[103] he viewed Landauer as a martyred idealist, a gentle anarchist who had sacrificed his life in a doomed effort to herald an era of politics without violence.[104] Buber would devote himself to honoring the memory and vision of Landauer—a man he would unabashedly eulogize as a "crucified" prophet.[105]

In his last will and testament, Landauer named Buber as the executor of his literary estate, a task that the latter faithfully fulfilled. With exemplary care, Buber issued various volumes of Landauer's writings[106] and edited two volumes of his correspondence.[107] He also published several stirring essays on Landauer,[108] and introduced his ideas to the postwar generation, especially to Zionist youth who were to be inspired by Landauer's concept of communitarian socialism.[109] Landauer's legacy also had a formative influence on Buber's own thoughts regarding the saliency of interpersonal relations in the shaping of spiritual and communal life.[110]

But one aspect of Landauer's legacy seems to have haunted Buber throughout his life: the tragedy of messianic politics. He initially sought to clarify his thoughts on the subject by way of fiction, in the form of a novel. Projected on the image of the apocalyptic struggle between Gog and Magog described in the Book of Daniel, the novel was to explore alternative ways of working for the Redemption. In a letter to Rosenzweig, dated January 1923, he apologized for not visiting him, explaining that he was preoccupied with his novel:

> "Gog" is crowding in on me, but not so much in an "artistic" sense. Rather, I am becoming aware, with a cruel clarity that is altogether different from any product of the imagination, of how much "evil" is essential to the coming of the Kingdom. In thinking about this I had a flash of insight about Napoleon, something I had previously not understood. On the Island of Elba, he once said that his name would remain on earth as long as *le nom de l'Eternal*. . . . *Nostra res agitur*.[111]

After two false starts, countless drafts[112] and more than twenty years later, Buber completed his novel, publishing it first in Hebrew in 1944[113] and then in German in 1949.[114] Both the title of the Hebrew and German captured the apocalyptic drama that was chronicled in the novel *Gog and Magog: A Chronicle*. However, that English edition, which appeared in 1958, obscured the drama by rendering the title, *For the Sake of Heaven: A Chronicle*.[115]

It was actually an anti-apocalyptic tale meant to point to the folly of attempts to usher in the Kingdom of God with one grand stroke—in the case of some of Buber's Hasidic rabbis, through theurgic prayer promoting that one last battle of "Gog of the Land of Magog." To Buber this was the road of false messianism[116] leading inexorably not only to inconsolable disappointment, but also to a nihilism, a rejection of our moral task *within* history. There is, Buber insisted, no leaping over history and the laborious—often humble and unnoticed—work of spiritual and moral transformation of society. Redemption, as Buber understood biblical and Jewish teachings, is not as the apocalyptic vision has it, "the end of history," but, instead, its perfection or, rather, the "sanctification" of the world within history.

Hence, as Buber declared in an essay of 1930, "we can only work on the Kingdom of God through working on all the spheres of man allotted to us."[117] No sphere, he emphasized, is more valid or effective than the other, "One cannot say, we must work here and not there, this leads to the goal and that does not."[118] Accordingly, Buber concluded, there is "no legitimately messianic, no legitimately messianically-oriented politics."[119] Again in contrast to Rosenzweig, Buber refused to conclude from this observation that politics was in vain, "The political sphere is not to be excluded from the hallowing of all things. The political 'serpent' is not essentially evil, it is itself only misled; it, too, ultimately wants to be redeemed."[120]

Buber identified this attitude with that of the Bible, particularly as articulated by the prophets. Indeed, he regarded the apocalyptic attitude—introduced into Judaism from Iranian religions[121]—as a fundamental perversion of the prophetic teaching of quiet, humble work of hallowing the world and thus preparing it for the messianic kingdom. The prophetic attitude—represented for Buber in the simple message of Jeremiah, "Better your ways and your affairs and I shall allow you to dwell in this place"[122]—expresses a faith in freedom, indeed, the necessity of human decision and responsibility, and thus also in history.

The apocalyptic attitude, Buber maintained, is a flight from human responsibility and history. Although sharing with the prophets a vision of the Kingdom of God, the apocalyptic message is that this Kingdom will be borne by a radical, "rupture of history" and the advent of a new aeon when, in the words of the Johannine Revelation cited by Buber, "Time will no longer be."[123] Born of a despair in humanity and history, the apocalyptic vision finds solace in an imminent Redemption initiated from beyond history and human decision. Hence, from the perspective of the apocalyptic vision, all "is predetermined, all human decisions are only sham struggles. The future does not come to pass; the future is already present in heaven, as it were, present from the beginning."[124] Publishing these reflections in a liberal German journal in 1954,[125] Buber added a parenthetical comment that many of his readers must have construed as an oblique indictment of their own failings in what was then the very recent past, "And whenever man shudders before the menace of his own work and longs to flee from the radically demanding historical hour, there he finds himself near to the apocalyptic vision of a process that cannot be arrested."[126]

Clearly unlike Scholem, Buber saw the apocalyptic attitude as essentially alien to Judaism; this, in part, was due to the fact that he defined it strictly in terms of its original expression in the Apocrypha and Pseudepigrapha, where it indisputably sponsored an eschatology that denigrates history and the efficacy of human deeds. Scholem, however, employed the concept of the "apocalyptic" in a looser sense to characterize the eagerness to anticipate a Redemption deemed imminent. Thus, the vision of an approaching Redemption beyond history—beyond the here and now—Scholem deemed to have, paradoxically, inspired the revolutionary attitude and the quest for radical change within history. In other words, Scholem understood "apocalyptic" in a broad phenomenological fashion, whereas Buber restricted himself to the ideas and moral values associated with the apocalyptic attitude. This does not mean, of course, that his interest was strictly historical or that he did not extend his purview to consider contemporary manifestations of the prophetic and apocalyptic impulse. Buber spoke, for instance, of Marx's view of the future as "an optimistic modern apocalyptic":

> In [Marx's] announcement of an obligatory leap of the human world out of the aeon of necessity into that of freedom, the apocalyptic principle alone holds sway. Here in place of the power superior to the world that effects the transition, an immanent dialectic has appeared. Yet in a mysterious manner *its* goal, too, is the perfection, even the salvation of the world. In its modern shape, too, the apocalyptic knows nothing of an inner transformation of man that precedes the transformation of the world and co-operates in it; it knows nothing of the prophetic "turning."[127]

Marx's vision of the future, Buber contended, has thus been falsely attributed to a prophetic origin.[128] Far from being a child of the prophets, Marx represented to Buber the insidious hold that the apocalyptic principle has on modern civilization— and not only in the realm of politics. Art, poetry, thought have become bound to an ethos of necessity, often bereft even of Marx's optimism, and what prevails— veiled as objectivity and *amor fati*—is an utterly lost faith in the efficacy of human moral decision and responsibility, in partnership with God, to change the course of history.

Although eschewing apocalyptic politics, Buber did, at least on one occasion, suggest that the prophetic ethos might lead one to mount the barricades in order to storm the kingdom. The occasion was a lecture that he delivered in April 1925 at a festive gathering in Berlin to mark the opening of the recently founded Hebrew University of Jerusalem. The lecture, entitled "The Messianic Mystery" ("*Das messianische Mysterium*"), was a scholarly disquisition on the Suffering Servant of Isaiah 53.[129] Buber argued at length that the anonymous servant of Deutero-Isaiah must ultimately be understood as the conscience of Israel, as the paragon of faith and responsibility before God. The Suffering Servant, he reasoned, performs his task in silence and without glory and public notice. His redemptive role is even concealed from himself. Yet the Redemption depends on him. The advent of the Messiah would be but the revelation of the mystery of the Suffering Servant, or rather the suffering servants who humbly transverse history. Hence, the mystery of the Suffering Servant becomes the mystery of the Messiah. God's suffering servants appear in history, in the "hidden history" that is "world history," the process of Redemption. It is noteworthy, Buber remarked, that Jewish tradition speaks of the Suffering Servant as the *nistarim*—those "hidden ones" especially celebrated in the Kabbalah and Hasidic lore—who by virtue of their deeds are said to prepare the secret path of Redemption.[130]

Toward the conclusion of his lecture, Buber turned to his audience and begged its indulgence if he were to descend from the plane of the academic and the conceptual to consider the implications of Deutero-Isaiah's teachings for the "reality" of Jewish and world history. This reality is characterized, Buber argued, by a tension, a creative tension between the *nistarim* and the *meshiḥiim*—messianic enthusiasts "who are all too facilely called false messiahs":

> The *meshiḥiim* are those who do not want to adapt themselves to God's unknown ways, and want to turn the everlasting task (*die allmalige Aufgabe*) into a onetime duty. The *meshiḥiim* are those who, in order to realize the Redemption, estrange themselves from the context of Redemption. The *meshiḥiim* are those who believe themselves to be the fulfillment and no longer the preparation of Redemption. These are indeed standing in the shadow of the *eved* [the Servant]—the misunderstood, the elementary misunderstood *eved*, who is [mistakenly] deemed to be the one-time Messiah, who is lifted to the position of the final, decisive *eved*. The *meshiḥiim*—mighty holy men and weak-minded and semi-scoundrels—stand in his shadow, and through them his shadow directs the hidden destiny of humankind.[131]

Buber's audience may have been somewhat baffled by this rather abstruse reference to "the reality of Jewish and world history," but his message was nonetheless clear, especially when in the closing sentence of the lecture he declared, "The hidden, true history of the world (*Weltgeschichte*) takes place between the *meshiḥiim* and the hidden servant."[132] The messianic enthusiasts—who, to be sure, number morally dubious individuals but also include persons of the most noble intentions—are animated by a genuine prophetic spirit, and, indeed, in conjunction with the more pristine servants of God, those who "hallow" the world with a silent grace, serve to quicken the Redemption.

This apparent retreat from his position that there is no messianic politics may, of course, have been but a momentary lapse; in fact, he chose not to publish the lecture and would never reiterate his approval of the *meshiḥiim* in print. But surely Buber's insistence that the messianic enthusiasts who seek to hasten the kingdom are not to be summarily dismissed as false messiahs reflected his desire to secure the proper appreciation of the idealism of the beloved Gustav Landauer and his fellow Jewish revolutionaries who dared to dream of a just world free of violence.

Notes

The epigraph by Franz Rosenzweig is from "The False and True Messiah: A Note to a Poem by Jehuda ha-Levi," in *Franz Rosenzweig: His Life and Thought*, ed. Nahum N. Glatzer (New York: 1961), 350.
I wish to dedicate this article to Ernest Frankel.

1. Karl Löwith, *Mein Leben in Deutschland vor und nach 1933: Ein Bericht* (Stuttgart: 1986), 16. The *Freistundentenschaft* was formally known as the *Freistudentische Bund*, a left-leaning liberal student group with branches throughout Germany.
2. Marianne Weber, *Max Weber: A Biography*, trans. Harry Zohn (New York: 1975), 707. Karl Löwith, who attended the lecture, gives the date of the lecture "Science as a Vocation" simply as during the winter semester 1918–1919 (Löwith, *Mein Leben*, 16). Although there is considerable confusion among Weber scholars, most now tend to follow Marianne Weber, who in her biography of her husband holds that the lecture took place in January 1919. Cf. Wolfgang Schluchter, "Excursus: The Question of the Dating of 'Science as a Vocation' and 'Politics as a Vocation.'" in *Max Weber's Vision of History: Ethics and Methods* ed. Guenther Roth and Wolfgang Schluchter (Berkeley and Los Angeles: 1979),

113–116. On the basis of his research, Schluchter himself believes that "Science as a Vocation" was actually delivered as early as November 1917 (114–115). There is no reason, however, to doubt the veracity of Löwith's report, which is given in vivid detail, although it is, of course, possible that Weber delivered the same lecture twice or had given substantially different lectures under the same title. Löwith claims that the lecture he heard was virtually identical to the printed version that was prepared on the basis of a stenographer's protocol of Weber's oral presentation. See Löwith, *Mein Leben*, 16. It may be noted that Löwith was first demobilized from the Kaiser's army in December 1917, commencing his studies at the University of Munich shortly thereafter (13). Accordingly, if we are to lend credence to his testimony that he attended Weber's lecture, it would have had to have been sometime after the November 1917 date suggested by Schluchter.

3. Marianne Weber, *Max Weber*, 707. Löwith in *Mein Leben* (17) merely notes that Weber delivered a second lecture, "Politics as a Vocation," but he does not specify the date. Contradicting the February date given by Marianne Weber, Schluchter cites a Munich newspaper that announced: "Prof. Max Weber (Heidelberg) will speak on 'Politics as a Vocation' on Tuesday, 7:30 p.m., January 28 [1919] at the Kunstsaal Steinicke." See Roth and Schluchter, *Max Weber's Vision*, 114. Schluchter acknowledges that Weber may have postponed the lecture to a later date.

4. Löwith, *Mein Leben*, 17:

> In [Weber's] statements, the experience and knowledge accumulated were concentrated; everything sprang directly from the inner self and was thought through with the most critical intellect, forcibly and intensively, thanks to the human emphasis that his personality placed on it. The renunciation of any easy solution corresponded to the acute formulation of the questions posed. He tore apart all the veils of wishful thinking, and yet everybody could not but feel that at the heart of this clear intellect there was a deeply earnest humanity. After the innumerable revolutionary addresses of the literary activists, Weber's words were a relief [*Erlösung*].

5. Weber was particularly fond of Ernst Toller, who served as chairman of the Central Council of the short-lived *Räterrepublik* proclaimed in April 1919. After the suppression of the revolution, Toller was placed on trial for high treason, and Weber voluntarily attested to his moral integrity. He also told the court that Toller was *Weltfremd*, utterly unaware of the realities of the world, and he ironically added, "in a fit of anger, God made [Toller] a politician" (Marianne Weber, *Max Weber*, 661). It is also of interest to note that in his lecture, "Politics as a Vocation," in which he delineated the limitations of a politics of *Gesinnungsethik* (an ethics of ultimate ends), Weber seems to have had in mind his young friend Toller (Roth and Schluchter, *Max Weber's Vision*. 116). Cf. Toller's reflections on the failure of the revolution:

> I have always believed that socialists, despising force, should never employ it for their own ends. And now I myself had used force and appealed to force; I who hated bloodshed had caused blood to be shed. . . . I meditated on the position of the men who try to mould the destiny of the world, who enter politics and try to realize their ideas in the face of the masses. Was Max Weber right after all when he said that the only logical way of life for those who were determined never to overcome evil by force was the way of St. Francis? Must the man of action always be dogged by guilt? Always? (Ernst Toller, *I Was a German: An Autobiography*, trans. E. Crankshaw [London: 1934], 275).

Despite the image of the revolutionaries as being youthful, not all were actually that young. Among the principal Jewish activists in the Bavarian revolution, only Toller was still in his twenties; in 1918, Kurt Eisner was fifty-one; Gustav Landauer, forty-eight; Eugen Leviné, thirty-five; Erich Mühsam, forty.

6. See Max Weber, "Science as a Vocation," in *From Max Weber: Essays in Sociology*, trans. and ed. H. H. Gerth and C. Wright Mills (New York: 1946), 129–156. On the apocalyptic mood of the supporters of the Bavarian revolution, see Arthur Mitzman, *The*

Iron Cage: An Historical Interpretation of Max Weber (New York: 1970), 225f. Also see Hanajoerig Viesel (ed.), *Literaten an der Wand: Die Münchner Räterepublik und die Schriftsteller* (Frankfurt: 1980); and Allan Mitchell, *Revolution in Bavaria, 1918–1919* (Princeton: 1965), 304–331. For the messianic rhetoric typical of the Bavarian revolutionaries, see the speech by Kurt Eisner—who served as the first president of the Bavarian Republic—at the festivities celebrating its establishment, "The world seems shattered, lost in the abyss. Suddenly in the midst of darkness and despair the sounds of trumpets ring out, proclaiming a new world, a new mankind, and a new freedom." Quoted in Stephen Lamb, "Intellectuals and the Challenge of Power: The Case of the Munich Räterepublik," in *The Weimar Dilemma: Intellectuals in the Weimar Republic,* ed. Anthony Phelan (Dover, N.H.: 1985), 140.

7. Weber, "Science as a Vocation," 155.

8. *Ibid.*

9. *Ibid.*, 128. The translators of Weber's lecture render the citation from Isaiah according to the Revised Standard Version of the Bible. I have, however, translated the citation anew in order to reflect Weber's own translation of the Hebrew text.

10. Löwith, *Mein Leben,* 149f.

11. Weber, "Science as a Vocation," 156.

12. *Ibid.*

13. For a detailed discussion of the Jews in the Bavarian revolution, see Werner T. Angress, "Juden in politischen Leben der Revolutionszeit," in *Deutsches Judentum in Krieg und Revolution, 1916–1923,* ed. Werner Mosse (Tübingen: 1971), 234–251.

14. Marianne Weber, *Max Weber,* 648f.:

Weber despised antisemitism, but he regretted the fact that in those days there were so many Jews among the revolutionary leaders. . . . He said that on the basis of the historical situation of the Jews it was understandable that they in particular produced these revolutionary natures. But given the prevailing ways of thinking, it was politically imprudent for Jews to be admitted to leadership and for them to appear as leaders. He thought in terms of *Realpolitik* and saw the danger that basically desirable political talents would be discredited in the minds of the public.

15. See Donald L. Niewyk, *The Jews in Weimar Germany* (Baton Rouge: 1980), 27f.; Saul Friedländer, "Die politischen Veränderung der Kriegszeit und ihre Auswirkungen auf die Judenfrage," in Mosse and Paucker, *Deutsches Judentum,* 50–54. On the role of Jews in the revolution in Bavaria—and elsewhere in Germany—and the anxieties this aroused in the Jewish community, see Donald L. Niewyk, "The German Jews in Revolution and Revolt, 1918–19," in *Studies in Contemporary Jewry,* vol. 4, *The Jews and the European Crisis, 1914–1921,* ed. Jonathan Frankel (New York: 1988), 41–50.

16. Ernst Bloch, *Geist der Utopie* (Frankfurt: 1973; repr. of 2nd ed. of 1918), 237.

17. Bloch, "Nachbemerkung" [1963] in Bloch, *Geist der Utopie,* 347.

18. The reference to Satan is not merely rhetorical; by hypostatizing the source of human suffering as the work of Satan, Bloch seeks to underscore that "evil" (a metaphorical term that serves to apostrophize "unjustifiable" suffering) is both fundamentally antagonistic to human nature and a power to be boldly confronted.

19. Quoted in Iring Fetscher, "Unzeitgemäss und spekulativ: Ernst Blochs 'Geist der Utopie,'" *Neue Züricher Zeitung* (weekend edition, 10–12 November 1979), 69.

20. Bloch, *Geist der Utopie,* 302.

21. Sixteen volumes of Bloch's collected writings have thus far been published by Suhrkamp Verlag of Frankfurt.

22. Bloch, *Geist der Utopie,* quoted in Fetscher, *Neue Züricher Zeitung,* "Unzeitgemäss und spekulation," 69.

23. See Ernest Bloch, *On Music,* trans. Peter Palmer, intro. David Drew (Cambridge, Mass.: 1974), 243: "Music as a whole stands at the farther limits of humanity, but at those limits where humanity, with a new language and haloed by the call to achieved intensity, to the attained world of 'we,' is first taking shape. And this ordering in our musical expression

means a home, indeed a crystal home, but one derived from our future freedom; a star, but one that will be a new Earth.''

24. Bloch's Jewishness is frequently noted in connection with his messianism, but how his ancestral faith may have influenced the development of his thought is rarely explicated. See the insightful comments by van Asperen:

> [It is difficult] to designate precisely to what extent Bloch's Jewish origin has influenced his ideas . . . Bloch certainly did not have a traditional Jewish upbringing. . . . Yet we know that as a student he counted quite a few East-European Jews among his friends with whom the questions of Jewishness were discussed. . . . Bloch at least had a conscious confrontation with his Jewishness. [To be sure, he was not a Zionist,] but he was aware of the typical contribution of Jewish spirituality. [He regarded] the Jews as the symbol of the utopian attitude. . . . [But] he states explicitly that Judaism is not an anthropological quality, but a Messianic attitude which transcends national boundaries. Thomas Muenzer showed it, says Bloch, the Rothschilds did not (G. M. van Asperen, *Hope and History: A Critical Inquiry into the Philosophy of Ernst Bloch* [Ph.D. diss., University of Utrecht, 1973], 18f.).

The question of the Jewishness of German Jewish revolutionaries and radical thinkers has exercised many. See, e.g., Rolf Kauffeldt, "Zur jüdischen Tradition im romantisch-anarchistischen Denken Erich Mühsams und Gustav Landauers," *Bulletin des Leo Baeck Instituts*, 69 (1984), 3–28; Anson Rabinbach, "Between Enlightenment and Apocalypse: Benjamin, Bloch and Modern German Jewish Messianism" *New German Critique* 34 (Winter, 1985), 78–124; and Michael Löwy, *Rédemption et utopie: Le Judaïsme libertaire en Europe centrale* (Paris: 1988). Cf. Scholem's comment that "acknowledged and unacknowledged ties to their Jewish heritage is evident [in] the writings of the most important ideologists of revolutionary messianism, such as Ernst Bloch, Walter Benjamin, Theodor Adorno, and Herbert Marcuse." (Gershom Scholem, "Reflections on Jewish Theology," in his *On Jews and Judaism in Crisis: Selected Essays* [New York: 1976], 287). Scholem's use of the term "ties" in this context is ambiguous, for he merely demonstrates parallels between "the messianic idea of Judaism" and that of the writers mentioned. Specifically, there is a tendency in the literature to regard the Jewish radicals of the Bavarian revolution and the Weimar Republic as votaries of the Jewish messianic tradition, noting that this tradition promotes a this-worldly Redemption and, accordingly, historical activism. The question of the Jewishness of the Jewish revolutionaries and radicals, however, is more complex than whether they represent (even unconsciously and by virtue of some peculiar ethnic sensibility to which they may have been heirs, often supposedly despite themselves) any particular tendency within the Jewish messianic tradition. First, why in this particular generation? How would one explain the revolutionary politics of the many non-Jews who shared the messianic vision of their Jewish comrades? My own preference is for a historical-sociological explanation of the kind reportedly suggested by Weber. See Marianne Weber, *Max Weber* (648), "On the basis of the historical situation of the Jews it was understandable that they in particular produced these revolutionary natures." For an attempt at such an analysis, see Paul Mendes-Flohr, "Jewish Intellectuals: A Methodological Prologumena," in *idem, Divided Passions: Jewish Intellectuals and the Experience of Modernity* (Detroit: 1990), ch. 1. See also Löwy, *Redemption et utopie*, ch. 3.

25. This is not to say Bloch was devoid of a religious sensibility. See Gershom Scholem, "Wohnt Gott im Herzen eines Atheisten? Zu Ernest Blochs 90. Geburtstag," *Der Spiegel* (7 July 1975), 110–114.

26. Heterodoxy per se, of course, would not disturb Bloch. He self-consciously and proudly identified with religious heretics, regarding them as the custodians of the eschatological impulse in their respective communities. But heterodoxy and heresy are positions that emerge dialectically from within a specific tradition; they bear the imprint of a spiritual and intellectual struggle with that tradition. Accordingly, heresy is to be distinguished from simply contrary opinions. In this respect, it is questionable whether Bloch's gnosticism and atheism are to be deemed Jewish heresies.

27. Ernst Bloch, *Kritische Erörterungen über Rickert und das Problem der modernen Erkennthistheorie*. Inaugural dissertation (Ludwigshafen: 1909).

28. *Ibid.*, 71–75. For a detailed discussion of Bloch's dissertation, see Paul Mendes-Flohr "'To Brush History Against the Grain': The Eschatology of the Frankfurt School and Ernst Bloch," *Journal of the American Academy of Religion* 51, no. 4 (December 1983), 636–640. In his dissertation, Bloch refers exclusively to Hermann Cohen's *Logik der reinen Vernunft* (Berlin: 1902), a purely philosophical work that makes no reference to Judaism. (Cf. Cohen's *Logik der reinen Erkenntnis*.) Yet in the preface to the first edition of the 1902 work, Cohen makes oblique but striking reference to his Jewish creed. In decrying Germany's retreat to nationalism from its earlier humanistic and universal ideals, he expresses his conviction that it is but a temporary relapse. He ascribes his "optimism" to his reassuring experience as a teacher at the University of Marburg and to his "faith in the religious truth of prophetic messianism." See "Vorrede zur ersten Auflage," in Hermann Cohen, *Logik der reinen Erkenntnis*, 2nd. rev. ed. (Berlin: 1914), xiif. In 1908 when Bloch was working on his dissertation, Cohen forcefully presented his concept of prophetic messianism in a widely reviewed essay, "Religiöse Postulate," a lecture held at the second conference of the *Verband der deutschen Juden* on 13 October 1907. (See *Hermann Cohens Jüdische Schriften*, intro. Franz Rosenzweig, ed. Bruno Strauss ([Berlin: 1924], vol. 1, 1–14). For a list of reviews of the lecture, see *ibid.*, 335. Also see Cohen's systematic discussion of the twin prophetic concepts of the future and messianism in *Ethik des reinen Willens* (Berlin: 1904), 405–411. It is reasonable to assume that at the time he wrote his dissertation Bloch was familiar with these works.

29. Cf. copy of Bloch's dissertation deposited in the Hermann Cohen Archive, Jewish National and University Library, Jerusalem, varia COH 121/B62.

30. Cohen tended to maintain a fast division between his strictly philosophical and Jewish writings. In the former, he developed the categories "messianic hope" and "future" on the basis of his idealistic method. See Nathan Rotenstreich, "Hermann Cohen: Judaism in the Context of German Philosophy," in *The Jewish Response to German Culture*, ed. J. Reinharz and W. Schatzberg (Hanover: 1985), 51–63; Paul Natorp, "Zu Cohens Religionsphilosophie," in *Cohen und Natorp*, ed. Helmut Holzhey (Basel and Stuttgart: 1986), vol. 2, 112–114, 137. Cohen's Jewish writings were collected in three volumes as *Hermann Cohens Jüdische Schriften*. For an English selection of these writings, see Hermann Cohen, *Reason and Hope*, intro. and trans. Eva Jospe (New York: 1971). Cf. Cohen's posthumous *Religion of Reason from the Sources of Judaism*, trans. S. Kaplan (New York: 1972). One important exception to Cohen's separation of his strictly philosophical and Jewish interests is his massive revision of Kantian ethics, *Ethik des reinen Willens*, in which he discussed antisemitism (*Judenhass*) as grounded in a misunderstanding of the Jews' notion of honor (*Ehre*) and their persistence as a people in the Diaspora. Jewish fidelity, Cohen argued, is not a matter of "atavism" but rather an allegiance to the prophetic mission "to prepare the union of states in the messianic idea of a united mankind" (*ibid.*, 499f.). In the same volume (399–409), Cohen also discusses in extenso the prophetic (he refrains from saying "Jewish" in this context) concept of the future and messianism.

31. See William Kluback, *The Idea of Humanity: Hermann Cohen's Legacy to Philosophy and Theology* (Lanham: 1987).

32. Jurgen Gebhardt, "Messianische Politik und ideologische Massenbewegung," in *Vom kommenden Zeiten: Geschichtspropheten im 19. und 20. Jahrhundert*, ed. Joachim H. Knoll and Julius H. Schoeps (Stuttgart and Bonn: 1984), 49–52. The emergence of the "future" as a collective singular was correlated with the crystallization of the modern concepts of "history" and "progress." Cf. *ibid.*, 50:

Future originally meant a spatial advent, the arrival of someone or something. This was the chief meaning until the seventeenth century. Only first in the early modern period does the term attain a temporal meaning, denoting also the temporal point of the advent [i.e., a future age]. It is important to note the role that the word ["future"] played in the language of the Church, the Bible, . . . where it marked but the eschatological event. It entirely corresponded to the old Latin concept of *status futurus*, which signifies the future things, the last things. . . . As a collective singular, "future" developed first in the eighteenth century out of the general concept of a future time. . . . Henceforth, it denotes the temporal space and content that follows the present time.

The concept of a future historical age, of course, could have existed *avant la lettre*, indeed, this is what Cohen endeavors to show with regard to prophetic messianism.

33. Hans Erich Bodeker, "Menschheit, Huamanität, Humanismus," in *Geschichtliche Grundbegriffe: Historische Lexikon zur politisch-sozialen Sprache in Deutschland*, ed. O. Brunner, W. Conze and R. Koselleck (Stuttgart: 1982), vol. 3, 1063–1128. Cf. H. Cohen, *Religion of Reason*, ch. 13. Cohen attributed to Kant the decisive move in rendering mankind a moral concept:

> The exact terminological meaning of the word "mankind" in Kant is, to be sure, first of all determined by opposition to the empirical man as understood in psychological and historical experience, so that mankind is equivalent to the moral rational being. However, in his terminology the term does not refer exclusively to the rational being derived from the methodology of ethics. Mankind occupies the most important position in all his formulations so that there is no doubt that it has for Kant a universal, *cosmopolitan* meaning (*Ibid.*, 241).

34. H. Cohen, "Religiöse Postulate," in Strauss, *Hermann Cohens Jüdische Schriften*, vol. 1, 6.

35. The term "messianism" was apparently first coined by the Polish-born mathematician Joseph Marie Hoene Wronski (1778–1853) to characterize a conception of absolute intellectual and political progress. See Gebhardt, "Messianische Politik," 44–46.

36. Steven S. Schwarzschild, "The Personal Messiah: Toward the Restoration of a Discarded Doctrine," in *Arguments and Doctrines: A Reader of Jewish Thinking in the Aftermath of the Holocaust*, ed. Arthur A. Cohen (Philadelphia: 1970), 521–537; Max Weiner, "Der Messiasgedanke in der Tradition und seine Umbiegung im modernen Liberalismus," in his *Festgabe für Claude Montefiore* (Berlin: 1928), 151–156.

37. See Schwarzschild, "The Personal Messiah," 526f.

38. H. Cohen, *Religion of Reason*, 249.

39. Cf. "[Hermann Cohen's] thought represents the culmination and representation in systematic form of the ideas which had become the common coin of the Reform movement in the nineteenth century" (Michael A. Meyer, *Response to Modernity: A History of the Reform Movement in Judaism* [New York: 1988], 206).

40. See, e.g., H. Cohen, "Affinities Between the Philosophy of Kant and Judaism," in *Reason and Hope*, 77–89. Cf. "Not all German Jews, of course, had an accurate idea of Kant, nor, for that matter, had all Germans. . . . But what more could [middle-class German Jews] have desired than [Cohen's] message of a sort of identity of the Jewish spirit with the doctrine of Germany's greatest philosophical genius!" Robert Weltsch, "Introduction," in *Leo Baeck Institute Yearbook* 13 (1968), viii.

41. Franz Rosenzweig, "Einleitung," in Strauss, *Hermann Cohens Jüdische Schriften*, vol. 1, xxvi–xxxi.

42. H. Cohen, "Religious Postulates" [1907], in H. Cohen, *Reason and Hope*, 49.

43. See Harry van der Linden, *Kantian Ethics and Socialism* (Indianapolis: 1988), ch. 6; and Steven S. Schwarzschild, "The Democratic Socialism of Hermann Cohen," *Hebrew Union College Annual* 27 (1956), 417–438.

44. H. Cohen, *Ethik des reinen Willens*, 559.

45. Van der Linden, *Kantian Ethics*, 221–236. Noting that Cohen's ethical socialism is to be distinguished from the reforms advocated by liberals, van der Linden reminds us (333, n. 35) that "socialists typically focus on the conditions of production, whereas [welfare] liberals typically focus on the conditions of distribution."

46. H. Cohen, *Ethik des reinen Willens*, 320, 321 (trans. in van der Linden, *Kantian Ethics*, 223).

47. Frederic V. Grunfeld, *Prophets Without Honor: A Background to Freud, Kafka, Einstein, and Their World* (New York: 1979), 123.

48. Van der Linden, *Kantian Ethics*, 303.

49. *Ibid.*, 302–307.

50. Having died in April 1918, Hermann Cohen did not witness the Bavarian revolution. Although he did not rule out "eruptive revolution" in principle when there were not other options left to resist a repressive, unjust political system (cf. van der Linden, *Kantian Ethics*, 266), it is doubtful whether he would have countenanced the actions of Eisner and his followers. With a passion and devotion equal to that with which he promoted socialism, Cohen throughout his life underscored the patriotism of German Jewry, especially during the First World War. (See Steven S. Schwarzschild, " 'Germanism and Judaism'—Hermann Cohen's Normative Paradigm of the German-Jewish Symbiosis," in *Jews and Germans from 1860 to 1933: The Problematic Symbiosis*, ed. David Bronsen [Heidelberg: 1979], 129–172, esp. 156f.) Moreover, Cohen would never have regarded any act, no matter how dramatic or far-reaching, as ushering in the *final* Redemption. The *eschaton*, he taught, lies in the absolute future that is ever-receding into eternity; messianism is, therefore, an asymptotic task.

51. Cf. David Melchior, "[Although Eisner] never left the Jewish community, Judaism and the Jewish heritage . . . meant to him as good as nothing" ("Stiefkind der Geschichte? Zum 100 Geburtstag von Kurt Eisner," *Allgemeine Wochenzeitung der Juden in Deutschland* 22, no. 7 [12 May 1967]; quoted by Angress, in Mosse and Paucker, *Deutches Judentum*, 247).

52. Among the more notable disciples of Cohen's socialism were Albert Gorland, Paul Natorp, Franz Stuadinger and Karl Vorländer. None of these individuals, who did much to disseminate Cohen's teachings, were Jewish.

53. The term "inspired," of course, is ambiguous; it may suggest that one's thought had its source or origins in Hermann Cohen or that one's thought was given added force or passion through an encounter with Cohen and his writings. In the latter case, it is conceivable that one's socialism or inclination to socialism had its origins independent of Cohen and that a Jew reading his writings on the prophetic basis of socialism may have derived from them a special sense of Jewish calling, enhancing his or her commitment to socialism. Although it is, indeed, plausible that some Jewish socialists (e.g., Bloch or Eisner) may have been so "inspired" by Cohen, we have no documentation permitting us to present this assumption as a fact.

54. Rolf Kauffeldt has sought to uncover the Jewish sources inspiring the utopian vision and political activism of two leading protagonists of the Bavarian revolution, Erich Mühsam and Gustav Landauer. Basing himself on an article by Gershom Scholem on the Jewish messianic tradition, Kauffeldt concludes Mühsam and Landauer were "beholden to this tradition" and specifically to that tendency within the tradition emphasizing that Redemption is a public, historical event and that its vision enjoins action in the here and now. "Landauer and Mühsam . . . assumed precisely the tradition of active messianism and interpreted it according to their social Utopian goal." See Kauffeldt, "Zur Jüdischen Tradition," *Bulletin des Leo Baeck Instituts*, 22. (Kauffeldt refers to Scholem's article that appeared in English under the title "Toward an Understanding of the Messianic Idea in Judaism," in Scholem, *The Messianic Idea in Judaism and Other Essays on Jewish Spirituality* [New York: 1971], 1–36.) For reasons developed throughout this article, I find this line of argumentation faulty. I shall simply note here that it is based on an imprudent reading of Scholem, isolating one element in his depiction of the complex dialectics of the Jewish messianic tradition; it is doubtful whether Scholem would have regarded political activisim of Jewish utopians as, *eo ipso*, reflecting the messianic activism of which he spoke. (See the statement, "According to some of its observers, devotees, and critics, [socialism] has in it a great deal of secular messianism. It is a moot question whether that is correct. There is an element of truth to it, but how much is a very big question" [M. Tsur and A. Shapira, "With Gershom Scholem: An Interview," in Scholem, *Jews and Judaism in Crisis*, 26].) Further, Kauffeldt bases his argument on an apodictic assertion that, as Jews, Landauer and Mühsam

had, perforce, regarded themselves as commanded by this tradition. However, an assertion, no matter how plausible, cannot be presented as evidence in the absence of compelling documentation. It is true that Landauer does seem to have taken some ethnic pride in the fact that Jews played a leading role in the Bavarian revolution. On reading an article, "The Revolution and Us," that Martin Buber published in *Der Jude* 2 (November-December 1918), Landauer urged his friend to write another article

treating the leading role played by the Jews in the upheaval. The revolution in Munich, for instance, where no one had thought of organizing on a wider scale beforehand, was prepared by seven persons: at the head Kurt Eisner . . . , two ardent young Jews [Mühsam and Toller] were his best and most tireless helpers; another ally was a well-to-do Bavarian farmer who has been blind for seven years; the other three were young workers (Letter from Landauer to Buber, 2 December 1918, in Martin Buber, *Briefwechsel aus sieben Jahrzehnten*, ed. Grete Schaeder [Heidelberg: 1973], vol. 2, 15). In the eulogy he delivered at Eisner's burial, Landauer also emphasized that the martyred revolutionary was a Jew. See Friedländer, "Politischen Veränderung der Kriegszeit," in Mosse and Paucker, *Deutsches Judentum*, 51 (n. 70).

55. In the mind of German and Jew alike, the revolution that enflamed Germany in 1918–1919 was a Jewish affair. As one antisemitic author noted, "In Magdeburg it is Brandes; in Dresden, Lipinsky, Geyer and Fleissner; and in the Ruhr, Markus and Levinsohn; in Bremerhaven and Kiel, Grünewald and Kohn; in Pfalz, Lilienthal and Heine (Quoted in *ibid.*, 51f.) Of course, the fact that Jews were also prominent in the contemporaneous revolutions in Hungary and Russia. served to reinforce the popular association of the Jews with revolutionary politics. In fact, according to the exemplary archival research of Werner Angress, among the hundreds who played a leading position in the German revolutions, we find only fifty-two Jews or individuals of Jewish descent, that is, baptized or half-Jews (Angress, "Juden in Politischen Leben der Revolutionszeit," in *ibid.*, 301–315).

56. Kafka, *Briefe, 1902–1924* (Frankfurt: 1975), 275 (cited in Grunfeld, *Prophets Without Honor*, 123).

57. Erich Przywara, "Judentum und Christentum," *Stimmen der Zeit*, 3 (1926), 81–99.

58. *Der Jude, Sonderheft 5:* "Antisemitismus und jüdisches Volkstum" (1925), 17–33.

59. *Ibid.*, 25.

60. *Ibid.*, 31.

61. *Ibid.*, 33.

62. Oskar Schmitz fails to explain, or rather does not bother to explain, how contemporary Orthodox Jews—the "desirable" Jews—manage to avoid the deleterious effects of the Pharasaic spirit. For a more comprehensive discussion of the views about Judaism and Jews that were voiced with such intensity during the Weimar Republic by Schmitz and other Christians, see Paul Mendes-Flohr, "Ambivalent Dialogue: Jewish-Christian Encounter in the Weimar Republic," in *Judaism and Christianity Under the Impact of National Socialism*, ed. Otto Dov Kulka and Paul Mendes-Flohr (Jerusalem: 1987), 99–132. For a convenient collection of Jewish and Christian exchanges in this period, see *Versuche des Verstehens: Dokumente jüdisch-christlicher Begegnung aus den Jahren 1918–1933*, ed. (Robert Raphael Geis and Hans-Joachim Kraus (Munich: 1966).

63. Martin Buber seems to have captured the mood of the postwar generation when he declared, "Youth is the eternal chance for mankind's happiness [*Glückschance*], the chance eternally offered to it and eternally squandered by it." And addressing Jewish youth specifically, he continued, "the Jewish people is deciding its fate today" (Buber, "Zion und der Jugend," *Der Jude* 3 [June 1918], 99, 102. Cf. Eva G. Reichmann, "Der Bewusstseinswandel der deutschen Juden," in Mosse and Paucker, *Deutsches Judentum*, 511–612, esp. 581–604.) A fuller appreciation of the disposition of Jewish youth in this period would require a consideration of the general spiritual agitation of postwar German society, which was marked by intense and varied utopian and radical political activities. See Michael Andrizky and Thomas Rautenberg (eds.), *'Wir sind nackt und nennen uns Du': Von Li-*

chtfreunden und Sonnenkämpfern: Eine Geschichte der Freikörperkultur (Giessen: 1989). This insightful collection of essays focuses on the German back-to-nature movement and also illuminates what the editors depict as the "mood of departure [*Aufbruchsstimmung*], the thirst for action and the pathos of belief, that reverberated in the 1920s." The editors similarly note:

> Those of the young generation fortunate enough to have returned from the inferno of the war were convinced that they were standing at a turning point in history, that a fundamental change of all values, of paradigms, was imminent. The violent ending of the nineteenth century [viz., the demise of the era of bourgeois optimism brought about by the First World War and the revolutions that followed] was regarded as the great opportunity for creating a new, better world (*ibid.*, 50f.).

64. Franz Rosenzweig, *The Star of Redemption*, trans. William W. Hallo (New York: 1970), 332.

65. Franz Rosenzweig was introduced to this distinctly German conception of history by his teacher, Friedrich Meinecke. See Alexander Altmann, "Rosenzweig on History," in *The Philosophy of Franz Rosenzweig*, ed. Paul Mendes-Flohr (Hanover, N.H.: 1988), 124ff.

66. Rosenzweig, *Star of Redemption*, 328–331.

67. In order to underscore Israel's detachment from history and its organization as principally a community of divine worship, Rosenzweig preferred to speak of the Synagogue.

68. Rosenzweig, *Star of Redemption*, 298.

69. A similar conception of a prolepsis, or spiritual anticipation, of Redemption, which one enjoys while still physically resident in the historical era, is often used to describe the Christian's experience of salvation through Jesus Christ. New Testament scholars and Christian theologians refer to this experience as realized eschatology. Within the context of Rosenzweig's polemic with Christianity, it may be argued that, by characterizing the Jewish experience of Torah and God as realized eschatology, in effect, he is appropriating what Christians had hitherto regarded to be their privileged relationship.

70. Rosenzweig, *Star of Redemption*, 298.

71. Cf. Rosenzweig's letter to Eugen Rosenstock-Huessy, undated, in *Judaism Despite Christianity: The 'Letters on Christianity and Judaism' Between Eugen Rosenstock-Huessy and Franz Rosenzweig*, ed. E. Rosenstock-Huessy (New York: 1971), 107–115, letter 11.

72. Rosenzweig, *Star of Redemption*, 329.

73. "[Through Christianity] the messianic hope, the Torah and the commandments have become familiar topics, topics of conversation among the inhabitants of the far isles and many peoples, uncircumcised of heart and flesh" (Ibid., 336).

74. For a detailed discussion of Rosenzweig's messianic conception of "world-history," see Paul Mendes-Flohr, "Rosenzweig and the Crisis of Historicism," in *idem, Philosophy of Franz Rosenzweig*, 138–161.

75. Rosenzweig, *Star of Redemption*, 350.

76. Rosenzweig's doctoral dissertation was later expanded and published in two volumes under the title *Hegel und der Staat* (Munich and Berlin: 1920).

77. For a discussion of the development of Rosenzweig's conception of metahistory and history, see Mendes-Flohr, "Rosenzweig and the Crisis of Historicism," 138–161. The roots of Rosenzweig's messianic thought lie in the Enlightenment and German idealism as much as in Judaism. With Eugen Rosenstock-Huessy and other friends, Rosenzweig shared the conviction that Europe was on the threshold of the Third Millennium prophesied by St. John on the island of Patmos. This notion goes back to Gotthold Ephraim Lessing and Friedrich von Schelling and, ultimately, to Joachim of Fiore. Cf. Altmann, "Rosenzweig on History," 125–128, and Harold Stahmer, *'Speak That I May See Thee!': The Religious Significance of Language* (New York: 1968), 109–115, 121–124. Indeed, an appreciation of Jewish messianic thought in the modern period in general, both secular and theological, cannot be divorced from this ideational context. This is not to say that Jewish messianic thought in this period is not authentically Jewish or that it merely reflects non-Jewish

thinking. The latter may, indeed, have informed the Jewish messianic imagination, thereby stimulating and triggering ideas and passions immanent within the Jewish tradition. In that case, one would speak of a dialectical symbiosis between non-Jewish and Jewish messianic thought. Of course, this may be true for all periods of Jewish thought—and not only with respect to messianism.

78. Gershom Scholem, "On the 1930 Edition of Rosenzweig's *Star of Redemption*," in his *The Messianic Idea in Judaism and Other Essays on Jewish Spirituality* (New York: 1971), 323.

79. Gershom Scholem, "Toward an Understanding of the Messianic Idea in Judaism," in *ibid.*, 15; and *idem*, "The Messianic Idea in Kabbalism," in *ibid.*, 38. The latter essay was, indicatively, first published in English under the title "Jewish Messianism and the Idea of Progress," *Commentary* 25, no. 4 (April 1958), 298–305.

80. Scholem, "Reflections on Jewish Theology," in *On Jews and Judaism*, 288.

81. Scholem, "Toward an Understanding of the Messianic Idea," in *idem, The Messianic Idea in Judaism*, 12–17.

82. Scholem's emphasis on the apocalyptic moment of messianism—he identified it as a potential source of the utopian, history-oriented passion of the Jews—would seem to have led him to regard Zionism, sponsoring as it does the Jews' return to history and utopian deeds, as a messianic movement. He, however, balked at this conclusion. David Biale explains this apparent inconsistency as stemming, in the first instance, from political rather than theological or scholarly considerations. In the mid-1920s, the right-wing Revisionist Zionists often adopted the rhetoric of messianism to promote policies that Scholem found loathsome and dangerous. He, accordingly, declared, "I absolutely deny that Zionism is a messianic movement and that it has the right to employ religious terminology for political goals." Biale notes that, in his scholarly work, Scholem endeavored to indicate the demonic forces that are often released by apocalyptic messianism. As a Zionist, his problem was, therefore, to show that the movement could tap the messianic energies of the people while pursuing a sober and rational political program. See Biale's insightful analysis, *Gershom Scholem: Kabbalah and Counter-history* (Cambridge, Mass.: 1979), 174–188; the quotation from Scholem, 177.

83. Scholem, "Reflections on Jewish Theology," in *idem, On Jews and Judaism*, 288. These remarks were made in 1974 and with no direct reference to Rosenzweig; however, they clearly apply to Rosenzweig since he represented for Scholem the most sophisticated—therefore, all the more beguiling—articulation of a messianic theology that denied the Jews the promise of living their lives on the historical level. In the same vein, Scholem undoubtedly objected to Rosenzweig's presentation of Redemption as a purely inward, spiritual experience. Scholem would regard this as a perversion of Jewish teachings, for Judaism, he insisted, "in all its forms and manifestations, has always maintained a concept of Redemption as an event which takes place publicly, on the stage of history and within the community" ("Toward an Understanding of the Messianic Idea" in *Messianic Idea in Judaism*, 1.) Although, for Rosenzweig, Redemption is experienced by the Jews in community (in the praying congregation), it certainly does not have a historical countenance; indeed, as I have noted, Rosenzweig held that, as an eschatological community, the Synagogue is a metahistorical reality. On the other hand, it should be emphasized, he taught that through Christianity, inspired by the Synagogue, Redemption would become a historical, public reality. It will be a reality, however, that is obtained not by virtue of an apocalyptic rupture in history but rather as one that gradually grows and emerges in the public weal; indeed, Redemption is a process that Rosenzweig and his Christian friends associated with the incipient emergence of the "invisible" Church of John at the beginnings of the Enlightenment (cf. n. 77).

84. Glatzer, *Franz Rosenzweig*, p. 159. Indicatively, Rosenzweig supported the participation of non-Zionists in the Jewish Agency and various projects for the upbuilding of the Jewish community in Palestine. (Ernst Simon, interview with author, 1980). On Rosenzweig's evolving attitude toward Zionism, especially as reflected in his letters and diaries, see Stefan Moses, "Politik und Religion: Zur Aktualität Franz Rosenzweig," in *Der Philosoph Franz Rosenzweig*, ed. W. Schmied-Kowarzik (Munich: 1988), vol. 2, 871–875.

85. Franz Rosenzweig to Benno Jacob, letter dated 23 May 1927, in Franz Rosenzweig, *Briefe und Tagebücher*, ed. Rachel Rosenzweig and Edith Rosenzweig-Scheinmann in cooperation with Bernhard Casper (The Hague: 1979), vol. 2, 593f.

86. Glatzer, *Franz Rosenzweig*, 351.

87. Cf. "Du schick dich an zur Heimkehr ins vielschöne Land." This line is from the poem Rosenzweig titled "The Happy Tidings" *"Die frohe Botschaft"* in his *Jehuda Halevi: Zweiundneunzig Hymnen und Gedichte Deutsch*, 2nd ed. (Berlin: 1927), 122.

88. Rosenzweig, *Jehuda Halevi*, 238. In this estimation of the circumstances occasioning Halevi's poem, Rosenzweig is following the nineteenth-century Italian Jewish scholar, Samuel David Luzzatto, whom he cites.

89. *Ibid.*, trans. in Glatzer, 350f.

90. There is also a passage in *The Star of Redemption* ignored by Scholem that indicates a profound understanding of the contemporary Jew's messianic passion to enter history. Scholem may have similarly dismissed this passage, notwithstanding its phenomenological sensitivity, as ultimately irrelevant to Rosenzweig's theology of Redemption:

> The believer in the kingdom uses the term "progress" only in order to employ the jargon of his time; in reality he means the kingdom. It is the veritable shibboleth for distinguishing him from the authentic devotee of progress whether he does not resist the prospect and duty of anticipating the "goal" at the very next moment. The future is no future without this anticipation and the inner compulsion for it, without this "wish to bring about the Messiah before his time" and the temptation to "coerce the kingdom of God into being"; without these, it [i.e., the future] is only a past distended endlessly and projected forward. For without such anticipation, the moment is not eternal; it is something that drags itself everlastingly along the long, long trail of time (227).

91. Glatzer, *Franz Rosenzweig*, 159.

92. Cf. n. 84.

93. Cited in Glatzer, *Franz Rosenzweig*, 113.

94. Forthcoming paper by Stefan Meineke, University of Freiburg, "A Life of Contradiction: Franz Rosenzweig and His Relationship to History and Politics."

95. *Ibid.*, (unpublished letter from Rosenzweig to Margrit Rosenstock).

96. Letter from Rosenzweig to his mother, 13 November 1918, in Rosenzweig, *Briefe*, 618. In the same letter (619), Rosenzweig states his political credo as "the more democracy in peace, that much less revolution and radicalism in war."

97. Unpublished letter, quoted in Meineke, "A Life of Contradiction."

98. Cited in Phelan, "Some Weimar Theories of the Intellectual," in *The Weimar Dilemma*, 26.

99. Buber did question the readiness of the revolutionaries, especially of the Spartacus party, to employ violence. See Martin Buber, "Recollection of a Death," in his *Pointing the Way: Collected Essays*, ed. and trans. Maurice Friedman (New York: 1974), 119.

100. Buber letter to Ludwig Strauss, 22 February 1919, in *Martin Buber: Briefwechsel*, vol. 2, 29.

101. For a brief memoir of the week in February 1919 in Munich in which Buber also participated in a debate with several of the revolutionary leaders at the Diet of the Bavarian Republic, see Buber, "Recollection of a Death," *Pointing the Way*, 119.

102. Buber letter to Ludwig Strauss, 22 February 1919, in Buber, *Briefwechsel*, vol. 2, 29.

103. For Buber, Landauer's murder was "a death in which the monstrous, sheerly apocalyptic horror, the inhumanity of our time, has been delineated and portrayed," quoted in Maurice Friedman, *Martin Buber's Life and Work: The Early Years, 1878–1923* (New York: 1987), 256. On the impact of Landauer's revolutionary activity and death on Buber, see the sensitive and detailed discussion, 245–258.

104. A pacifist, "Landauer fought in the revolution against the revolution for the sake of the revolution" (Buber, "Recollection of a Death," in Friedman, *Pointing the Way*, 120). "When I think of the passionate glance and words of my dead friend, I know with what force of soul he fought to protect the revolution from itself, from violence." In Buber's judgment,

his friend erred in joining the revolution, and certainly in participating in the government of the short-lived Soviet Republic of Bavaria. "I also believe that no man has ever erred out of purer motives," quoted Friedman, *Martin Buber's Life and Work,* 247.

105. As Buber stated in a memorial address:

> Gustav Landauer had lived as a prophet of the coming human community and fell as its blood-witness. He went upon the path, of which Maximus Tyrius—whose words Landauer used as the motto to his book, *Die Revolution* [1906]—said:
>
>> Here is the way of the Passion, which you call a disaster [*Untergang*], and which you [falsely] judge according to those who have passed upon it; I, however, deem it salvation, since I judge it according to the result of what is still to come.
>
> In a church at Brescia I saw a mural whose entire surface was covered with crucified individuals. The field of crosses stretched until the horizon, hanging from each, men of varied physiques and faces. Then it struck me that this was the true image of Jesus Christ. On one of the crosses I see Gustav Landauer hanging. (Martin Buber, "Landauer und die Revolution," *Masken: Halbmonatschrift des Düsseldorfer Schauspielhauses* 14, nos. 18–19 [1919], 291.)

The frontispiece of this edition of the journal reproduces a photograph in full color of the Brescia mural.

106. See Gustav Landauer, *Der werdende Mensche: Aufsätze über Leben und Schrifttum,* "edited by Martin Buber in accordance with the author's last will and testament" (Postdam: 1921); Gustav Landauer, *Beginnen: Aufsätze über Sozialismus,* "edited by Martin Buber in accordance with the author's last will and testament" (Cologne: 1924).

107. Gustav Landauer, *Sein Lebensgangs in Briefen,* ed. Martin Buber with the cooperation of Ina Britschgi-Schimmer, 2 vols. (Frankfurt: 1929).

108. See Martin Buber, *Der heilige Weg* (Frankfurt: 1919); "Landauer und die Revolution," *Masken* 16, nos. 28–29 (1919), 282–291; "Der heimlich Führer," *Die Arbeit* 2, no. 6 (June 1920), 36–37; "Errinerung an einen Tod," *Neue Wege* 23, no. 2 (February 1929), 161–165; and the chapter on Landauer in Buber, *Paths in Utopia* (London: 1949). Buber also published several essays on Landauer in Hebrew.

109. See Ruth Link-Salinger (Hyman), *Gustav Landauer: Philosopher of Utopia* (Indianapolis: 1977), 52–54; and Eugene Lunn, *Prophet of Community: The Romantic Socialism of Gustav Landauer* (Berkeley: 1973), 251–252, 271–273.

110. See Paul Mendes-Flohr, *From Mysticism to Dialogue: Martin Buber's Transformation of German Social Thought* (Detroit: 1989), 101–126; also Abraham Schapira, "Werdende Gemeinschaft und die Vollendung der Welt," afterword, in Buber, *Pfade in Utopia: Über Gemeinschaft und deren Verwirklichung,* 3rd, expanded ed. (Heidelberg: 1985), 437–439.

111. Buber letter to Rosenzweig, 18 January 1923, in Buber, *Briefwechsel,* vol. 2, 153f.

112. See epilogue to Martin Buber, *Gog und Magog: Eine Chronik* (Heidelberg: 1949), 401.

113. Martin Buber, *Gog u'magog: Megilat yamim* (Jerusalem: 1944). Aside from the last seven chapters, the novel was first published in weekly installments in the Tel-Aviv Hebrew daily *Davar* from 10 January to 23 October 1941.

114. Bloch, *Geist der Utopie.* Quoted in Fetscher, "Unzeitgemüss und Spekulativ," *Neue Züricher Zeitung,* 69.

115. Martin Buber, *For the Sake of Heaven: A Chronicle* (New York: 1958).

116. Buber, epilogue to *Gog und Magog,* 405.

117. Buber, "Gandhi, Politics, and Us," in Friedman, *Pointing the Way,* 137.

118. *Ibid.*

119. *Ibid.*

120. *Ibid.*

121. Martin Buber, *Two Types of Faith,* trans. Norman P. Goldhawk (New York: 1961), 145f.

122. Buber, "Prophecy, Apocalyptic, and the Historical Hour," in Friedman, *Pointing the Way*, 196.

123. *Ibid.*, 203.

124. *Ibid.*, 201.

125. Buber, "Prophetie, Apokalyptik und die geschichtliche Stunde," *Merkur*, 8, no. 12 (December 1954), 1101–1115.

126. Buber, "Prophecy, Apocalyptic, and the Historical Hour," in Friedman, *Pointing the Way*, 203. The delineation of the difference between the apocalyptic and the prophetic principle was one of the overarching themes of Buber's writings. In 1932 he published the first of a projected two-volume study on the biblical origins of messianic faith to be entitled *Das Kommende* (*The Coming One*). Only one volume appeared: *Kingship of God*, trans. Richard Scheimann (London: 1967); he never realized his plans to complete the second volume, but he did publish several chapters separately (see "Der Gesalbte," in Martin Buber, "*Schriften zur Bibel* [Heidelberg: 1964] 725–846). He also devoted a scholarly book-length study to "the prophetic faith" (see *idem, The Prophetic Faith*, trans. from the Hebrew by Carlyle Witton-Davies [New York: 1949]). Many of his essays are directly or indirectly informed by this theme. See Marie Natalie Barton, *The Jewish Expectation of the Kingdom According to Martin Buber* (Munich: 1967) and Avraham Schapira, "Messianismus und Erlösung in Martin Bubers Denken," in *Vom Erkennen zum Tun des Gerechten: Martin Buber (1878–1965): Internationales Symposium zum 20. Todestag*, ed. Licharz and Heinz Schmidt (Frankfurt: 1989), vol. 2, 73–85.

127. Buber, "Prophecy, Apocalyptic, and the Historical Hour," in Friedman, *Pointing the Way*, 203f.

128. *Ibid.*

129. Martin Buber, "Das messianische Mysterium (Jesaja 53): Vortrag Martin Buber bei der Berliner Feier anlässlich der Eröffnung der Universität Jerusalem, 6 April 1925." This hitherto unpublished lecture was published in the original German with a Hebrew translation and an introduction by Theodor Dreyfus in the journal of Jewish thought sponsored by Bar-Ilan University, *Da'at*, 5 (Summer 1980), 117–133.

130. Theodor Dreyfus demonstrated that the thesis propounded by Buber in "Das messianische Mysterium" served as the basis of his chapter on "the mystery of the Suffering Servant" in *The Prophetic Faith*, 202–235. Cf. Dreyfus, introduction to Buber, in *Da'at* 5 (Summer 1980), 117–119.

131. Buber, "Das messianische Mysterium," 126f.

132. *Ibid.*, 127.

Reflections on Jewish Secular Messianism

Richard Wolin
(RICE UNIVERSITY)

The past carries with it a temporal index by which it is referred to Redemption. There is a secret agreement between past generations and the present one. Our coming was expected on earth. Like every generation that preceded us, we have been endowed with a weak *messianic power, a power to which the past has a claim. That claim cannot be settled cheaply.*
  —Walter Benjamin, ''Theses on the Philosophy of History''

It seems to me particularly noteworthy that the messianic idea, the third element in that trilogy of Creation, Revelation, and Redemption, exercises unbroken and vital power even today. Creation, so closely linked to the conviction of the existence of God, has to an extraordinary extent receded or vanished from contemporary consciousness. Outside the fundamentalist minority, Revelation persists only in enlightened or mystical reinterpretations which, no matter how legitimate they may be, no longer possess the original vehemence which promoted its enormous influence in the history of religion. Yet the messianic idea has maintained precisely this vehemence. Despite all attenuations it has proved itself an idea of highest effectiveness and relevance—even in its secularized forms. It was better able to stand a reinterpretation into the secular realm than the other ideas. *Whereas more than 100 years ago such reinterpretation was still regarded as an utter falsification of the Jewish idea of Redemption and messianism—and just by the defenders of the historical school in Judaism— it has become* the center of great visions in the present age.
  —Gershom Scholem, ''Reflections on Jewish Theology''

In a celebrated essay, Isaac Deutscher offers the following depiction of a prominent Jewish personality type, the non-Jewish Jew; a figure who, especially in modern times, has been responsible for a unique and productive extension of the Jewish sensibility to the realm of secular concerns:

> The Jewish heretic who transcends Jewry belongs to a Jewish tradition. You may, if you like, see Aḥer [''the other''; Elisha ben Abuyah, a mishnaic figure and archetypal Jewish heretic] as a prototype of these great revolutionaries of modern thought: Spinoza, Heine, Marx, Rosa Luxemburg, Trotsky, and Freud. You may, if you wish to, place them within a Jewish tradition. They all went beyond the boundaries of Jewry.

186

They all found Jewry too narrow, too archaic, and too constricting. They all looked for ideals and fulfilment beyond it, and they represent the sum and substance of much that is greatest in modern thought, the sum and substance of the most profound upheavals that have taken place in philosophy, sociology, economics, and politics in the last three centuries.[1]

For Deutscher, it is not the Jewishness of the above-named thinkers that accounts for their achievements or status as intellectual innovators. Instead, in his eyes, their claim to greatness may be best understood in terms of their having made a *definitive break* with their Jewish past. Indeed, two of the first three thinkers on his list were converts to Christianity; and Freud—author of *The Future of an Illusion*—never made a secret of his equation of religion with simple superstition.

In Deutscher's estimation, therefore (and it is at this point that the selectivity of his list begins to become apparent), the aforementioned cosmopolitan intellectuals were able to achieve widespread renown and influence only insofar as they were able to transcend their own Jewishness. The source of their creativity and greatness must be explained *sociologically* and not in terms of the transposition of a religious content or sensibility to·the realm of secular affairs. Spinoza's pantheism, Heine's solidarity with the persecuted and oppressed, Marx's longing for a this-worldly transcendence of alienation—all may be explained "externally," in terms of the Jew's traditional situation on the sociocultural fringe. And thus, forced to the cultural margin, the deracinated Jew becomes a type of internationalist *avant la lettre*. In the words of Deutscher:

> They were a priori exceptional in that as Jews they dwelt on the borderlines of various civilizations, religions, and national cultures. They were born and brought up on the borderlines of various epochs. Their minds matured where the most diverse cultural influences crossed and fertilized each other. They lived on the margins or in the nooks and crannies of their respective nations. Each of them was in society and yet not in it, of it and yet not of it. It was this that enabled them to rise in thought above their societies, above their nations, above their times and generations, and to strike out mentally into wide new horizons and far into the future.[2]

There can be no arguing with the reality of the phenomenon described by Deutscher, although his analysis may, in fact, provide only a partial account of the phenomenon he seeks to explain. Similar interpretations concerning the historical uniqueness of Jewish intellectual life have been proffered often enough in the past. But precisely for this reason, it is those components of the non-Jewish Jew's experience that Deutscher *refrains from considering* that immediately pique one's interest. And, thus, one feels compelled to inquire: Can the phenomenon of the non-Jewish Jew *really* be explained without any reference at all to religious content, influences and motifs, however broadly the latter might be conceived?

Deutscher rules out, a priori, the possibility of answering this question in the affirmative. His worldview has been preformed: his own internationalism and social evolution suggest that any attempt to answer the question in a positive vein would be retrograde. In his view, it is only by freeing himself from what is specifically Jewish that the Jew truly realizes himself; in this way alone can the Jew attain the status of "humanity in general"—or what Marx referred to as "species-being."

Thus, Deutscher persists in the belief that the definitive answer to the "Jewish question" was given by Marx in his *Jugendschrift* of the same title: the self-sacrifice of Jewish identity on the altar of a socialist-utopian future. However, as the twentieth century draws to a close, can we not hear in the answer to the Jewish question adumbrated by Marx a century and a half ago more than a faint anticipation of the solution to the "minorities question" as practiced for so long in oxymoronic "socialist republics"?

Were Deutscher to have expanded his list of non-Jewish Jews to include that generation of uniquely gifted Central European apostles of messianic socialism who came of age at the time of the First World War—and here, one might single out Walter Benjamin, Ernst Bloch, Gustav Landauer, Georg Lukacs, Herbert Marcuse as well as other members of the Frankfurt School—he might have been more hard-pressed to make good his narrowly areligious explanatory scheme. More specifically, he would have been compelled to incorporate into his account factors such as the one described earlier by Scholem in "Reflections on Jewish Theology": the peculiar resilience of the *messianic idea,* which, according to the scholar of Jewish mysticism, maintained its "vehemence" insofar as it "was better able to stand a reinterpretation into the secular realm than the other ideas." For in its purest form, this Central European intellectual-type might best be described by the term Bloch applied to the sixteenth-century champion of radical social reform, Thomas Münzer, "theologian of revolution."

How does one account for the fact that the messianic idea maintained its "effectiveness and relevance" (Scholem) at this particular juncture in the history of European Jewry precisely by undergoing a fundamental modification, by being incorporated into a specific logic of *secularization?* What were the peculiar affinities between messianism, socialism and the Central European Jewish intelligentsia that brought forth this historically unprecedented synthesis of theological and revolutionary motifs? And—given the fact that the hopes for historical-messianic renewal shared by this generation of intellectuals were so brutally quashed by the coincident triumph of European fascism and authoritarian state socialism—is there any possibility that this vision of utopian fulfillment can provide succor or inspiration in our very different contemporary historical circumstances?

The social situation of Central European Jewry, so prominent in the portrait of the non-Jewish Jew sketched by Deutscher, is a factor that no analyst concerned with the phenomenon of Jewish secular messianism can afford to bypass. If one requires further proof of this thesis, one need only examine matters from the *ex negativo* standpoint of the Western European countries, in which virtually no traces of the secular messianic spirit are to be found.[3] To account for this peculiar imbalance, one must realize that, whereas the postrevolutionary promises of universal equality had gone a long way toward alleviating the plight of Western European Jews by 1914, the assimilationist dreams of Central European Jewry seemed all but dashed amid recurrent waves of increasingly virulent antisemitism. As a result, the "liberal option" for Central European Jews seemed more and more to have played itself out. The real alternatives appeared to have become either socialism or Zionism. If hopes for assimilation were futile, the only possibilities seemed to lie either in the radical political transformation of existing Central European societies—this would be a prelude to the radical transformation of the world itself—or the pursuit of a Jewish identity elsewhere.

The historical dynamic behind such thinking has been well described by Anson Rabinbach:

> In the years approaching the First World War, the self-confidence and the security of German Jewry was challenged by a new Jewish sensibility that can be described as at once radical, secular and messianic in both tone and content. What this new Jewish ethos refused to accept was above all the optimism of the generation of German Jews nurtured on the concept of *Bildung* as the German Jewish mystique. They were profoundly shaken by political antisemitism and the anti-liberal spirit of the German upper classes, which for them called into question the political and cultural assumptions of the post-emancipation epoch. Especially irksome was the belief that there was no contradiction between *Deutschtum* and *Judentum;* that secularization and liberalism would permit the cultural integration of Jews into the national community.[4]

But this explanation itself needs explaining, above all, in terms of the peculiar economic transformation experienced by the Central European monarchies in the fifty years preceding the First World War. For within this relatively brief span of time, Germany, for example (the changes were not quite as far-reaching in the case of Austria-Hungary), was transformed from a predominantly agrarian nation to one of the world's leading industrial states. Nor would these changes leave the foundations of the traditional German social structure unaffected. Whereas in 1870, for example, 70 percent of Prussian Jews lived in small villages, by 1927 this was true of only 15 percent.[5] Clearly, many Jews had taken advantage of the new opportunities for social mobility and professional advancement that had been facilitated by Germany's late nineteenth-century Industrial Revolution. At the same time, Jews increasingly found themselves blamed for changes in German society that upset the traditional balance of forces and class structure: evils of the industrialization and urbanization were attributed to "unnatural" Jewish influence. This new wave of anti-Jewish sentiment was by no means confined to instances of so-called vulgar antisemitism. It was shared by a large segment of the German conservative mandarin intelligentsia, which had suffered a decline of status and social influence as a result of the increased prestige accorded to commerce and material values in the wake of Germany's rapid economic expansion.

An important insight into the intellectual origins of Jewish secular messianism is to be found in Lukacs's preface of 1962 to his *The Theory of the Novel*. There he coins the phrase "romantic anti-capitalism" to refer to a generation of German intellectuals who, traumatized by the repercussions of rapid industrialization, nostalgically sought a restoration of precapitalist social relations. Or as Fritz Ringer has observed:

> The German academics related to the [economic] dislocation with such desperate intensity that the specter of a "soulless" modern age came to haunt everything they said and wrote, no matter what the subject. By the early 1920s they were deeply convinced that they were living through a profound crisis, a "crisis of culture," of "learning," of "values," or of the "spirit."[6]

For this generation, the distinction between *Gemeinschaft* and *Gesellschaft* popularized by Ferdinand Tönnies's 1887 classic possessed canonical status.

Lukacs retroactively characterized the legacy of his own study, written in 1914–1915:

> *The Theory of the Novel* is not conservative but subversive in nature, even if based on a highly naive and totally unfounded utopianism—the hope that a natural life worthy of man can spring from the disintegration of capitalism and the destruction, seen as identical with that disintegration, of the lifeless and life-denying social and economic categories.

His work, he continues:

> Aimed at a fusion of "Left" ethics and "Right" epistemology (ontology, etc.). . . . From the 1920s onwards this view was to play an increasingly important role. We need only think of Ernst Bloch's *Der Geist der Utopie* (1918, 1923) and *Thomas Munzer als Theologe der Revolution,* of Walter Benjamin, even of the beginnings of Theodor W. Adorno, etc.[7]

Lukacs's characterization of the romantic anticapitalist type is instructive insofar as it helps us identify some of the ambiguities of the secular messianic worldview. For one, it suggests ironically that the representatives of the secular messianic spirit mentioned in the remarks just cited (and of course, his own name should be added to the list) share a certain intellectual affinity with the German conservative mandarin intelligentsia from which they were systematically excluded. Both groups were profoundly influenced by the *Kultur/Zivilisation* dichotomy, where *Kultur* symbolized the predominance of higher, spiritual values and *Zivilisation* was associated with the crude materialistic weltanschauung of the decadent capitalist West.

Consequently, both groups tended to conflate the political and economic aspects of liberalism; the result being that the vehement denunciation of the latter frequently entailed an equally spirited rejection of the former. Because of this systematic and principled rejection of political liberalism, neither party would prove a likely candidate to come to the aid of the fledgling Weimar democracy. In both its Left and Right variants, therefore, romantic anticapitalism carried the marks and prejudices of Germany's status as a "belated nation,"[8] demonstrating an unwillingness to adapt to the demands of political modernity.

But of equal interest in Lukacs's remarks is his characterization of the worldview represented by *The Theory of the Novel*—and by extension, that of Benjamin or Bloch, for example—as *subversive;* a claim that could certainly *not* be made on behalf of the writings of the romantic anticapitalist mandarin intelligentsia. It is undoubtedly this "subversive" dimension of their thought that has made it an object of fascination to a more recent generation of critical intellectuals. For out of this sweeping and multifaceted collective oeuvre emerges a remarkably pointed and persuasive critique of capitalist civilization in virtually all its aspects.

Lukacs identifies the intellectual orientation of the secular messianic standpoint as a combination of "'Left' ethics and 'Right' epistemology." And with this verdict—despite its manifest polemical intentions—he reaches an essential insight that, nevertheless, remains undeveloped. The so-called Left ethics derived from leading contemporary theoreticians of revolutionary socialism. The point of departure was not the mechanistic Marxism of the Second International, but those exponents of "left-wing communism"—Gustav Landauer, Georges Sorel, the Dutch Council Communists—who would soon become personae non grata in the eyes of the inflexible ideologues of the Third. What Lukacs then refers to as "Right epistemology" in truth harked back to the emancipatory thrust of the Jewish "messianic idea." Only when these two factors—revolutionary socialism and the messianic idea—are conceptualized in tandem can the uniquely radical thrust of Jewish secular messianism be fully appreciated.

It was above all in the early writings of Walter Benjamin and Ernst Bloch that the idea of secular messianism was brought to fruition in its full radicality. Or, as Anson Rabinbach has observed, "there were others, of course, who embodied the new Jewish spirit, but only Bloch and Benjamin—initially without any mutual influence—brought, in varying degrees, a self-consciously Jewish and radical messianism to their political and intellectual concerns."[9]

The immediate historical sources of this secular messianic renewal were variegated. Of no small importance was the appearance in 1916 of Franz Rosenzweig's *The Star of Redemption,* which brought renewed attention to the redemptive aspects of the Jewish religious tradition. But of even greater significance was Martin Buber's enormously influential *Three Speeches on Judaism* (1909, 1911). Here, it would hardly be an exaggeration to say that Buber's emphasis on the existential and mystical components of Jewish religiosity, together with his critique of the stale convention of the rational rabbinic tradition, established the terms of debate for an entire generation of Jews interested in probing the contemporary spiritual meaning of their faith. (The direct influence of Buber's writings on the early Benjamin has been amply documented, moreover.)[10] Finally, it is known that both Benjamin and Bloch were well acquainted with the work of Franz von Baader, in whose writings the kabbalistic tradition figured prominently.[11]

The content of the Jewish messianic idea has been best described by Gershom Scholem. At its center lies a complex and fruitful tension between a restorative and a utopian dimension. Or, as Scholem notes, "The messianic idea crystallizes only out of the two of them together. . . . [Even] the restorative force has a utopian factor, and in utopianism, restorative factors are at work." And thus, the messianic idea "can take on the form of the vision of a new content which is to be realized in a future that will in fact be nothing other than the restoration of what is ancient, bringing back that which had been lost; the ideal content of the past at the same time delivers the basis for the vision of the future." Yet, although the vision of the new order receives its inspiration from the old, "even this old order does not consist of the actual past; rather, it is a past transformed and transfigured in a dream brightened by the rays of utopianism."[12]

"The world is not true, but it will successfully return home through human beings and through truth," remarks Bloch.[13] "Origin is the goal," proclaims Benjamin, citing Karl Kraus. In both of these observations, there echoes the messianic image of Redemption as a recaptured past. Yet, as Scholem indicates, this primal past—an "original leap" or *Ur-sprung*—is not something that one aims merely to restore in its pristine, original condition. Instead, the very process of conjuring forth the past in a contemporary historical setting serves to activate and release hitherto dormant, subterranean potentials that lie concealed in the past. Thus, the past is not merely recaptured, it is rendered dynamic—a *living* tradition— as a result of this fructifying contact with the secret, utopian potentials embodied in the historical present.

But the desire to realize the sublimity of the messianic idea amid the profane continuum of historical life immediately presents a dilemma of an epistemological and theological nature. For those who dwell in this continuum can have only the dimmest presentiment of the manner in which the messianic idea might apply to the realm of secular affairs; these two spheres proceed according to entirely different, mutually opposed logics. In truth, the categories of traditional logic fail us when we try to conceptualize the this-worldly significance of the messianic age. In comparison with the customary concepts of the human understanding, Redemption proves to be a category of absolute transcendence: there is no prospect of bringing about an organic transition between the historical and messianic eras. There are no (Hegelian) categories of "mediation" that would be capable of bridging the gap.

Scholem explains the absolute dichotomy between the profane and the messianic spheres of life in a vivid account:

> It is precisely the lack of transition between history and the redemption which is always stressed by the prophets and apocalyptists. The Bible and the apocalyptic writers know of no progress in history leading to the redemption. The redemption is not the product of immanent developments such as we find it in modern Western reinterpretations of messianism since the Enlightenment where, secularized as the belief in progress, messianism still displayed unbroken and immense vigor. *It is rather transcendence breaking in upon history, an intrusion in which history itself perishes, transformed in its ruin because it is struck by a beam of light shining into it from an outside source.* . . . The apocalyptists have always cherished a pessimistic view of the world. Their optimism, their hope, is not directed to what history will bring forth, but to that which will arise in its ruin, free at last and undisguised. . . . [And thus,] there can be no preparation for the Messiah. He comes suddenly, unannounced, and precisely when he is least expected or when hope has been long abandoned.[14]

Or, as Benjamin puts it in his "Theses on the Philosophy of History," for the Jews, "every second of time was the strait gate through which the Messiah might enter."[15]

The messianic idea tended to seize hold of the Jewish imagination in times of unprecedented hardship or catastrophe—such as the expulsion from Spain in 1492, in whose wake the Lurianic Kabbalah was composed. Or, as Scholem reminds us, "Jewish messianism is in its origins and by its nature—this cannot be sufficiently emphasized—a *theory of catastrophe.* [It] stresses the revolutionary, cataclysmic element in the transition from every historical present to the messianic future."[16] The neo-Kantian Ernst Cassirer would like to see in all such reliance on myth and supernatural imagery an instance of historical regression.[17] Yet it is clear that, at unusually trying moments in the life of the Jewish people, when the traditional, rational content of Judaism failed to address the people's true spiritual needs, the messianic idea provided a crucial element of cultural and religious cohesion. Through it alone could Jews render comprehensible—and bearable—historical experiences of disproportionate severity.

The proliferation of secular messianism on the eve of, and during, the First World War undoubtedly derived from an analogous historical dynamic. As hopes for Jewish equality in Central Europe were crushed, with prospects for an imminent, historical and secular solution to the Jewish question in deadlock, only a recrudescence of messianic sentiment appeared to offer new hope. The Great War itself, moreover, took on the character of a cataclysmic event that shook the very foundations of post-Enlightenment European self-confidence. The secular heirs of the messianic tradition were among those who sought to give new meaning to the legacy of optimism now in such utter disarray.

But a crucial prerequisite for the resurgence of messianic longing in a specifically secular guise was the viability of the socialist idea. For it was only with the joining of two disparate elements—the redemptive impulse of traditional Jewish messianism and the socialist belief in the imminence of a secular millennium—that the foundations of modern messianism were truly established. Those twin descendants of the Enlightenment, utopian socialism and historical materialism, were both rooted in the belief that it was possible to discern the immanent contours of a future society of freedom, solidarity and plenty.

However, theorists such as Bloch and Benjamin (as well as Lukacs, in his own fashion) were soon convinced that only an infusion of messianic thought could rescue the socialist idea from the crisis of Marxism that was so evident in the predominantly reformist character of the contemporary socialist parties. Thus, for Bloch, "[in Marxism,] the economy has been sublated, but the soul and the faith it was to make room for are missing. . . . The soul, the Messiah, the apocalypse which represents the act of awakening in totality—these impart the ultimate impulses to action and thought, and constitute the a priori of all politics and culture."[18] And, as is well known, Benjamin recommended in 1940 that historical materialism "enlist the services of theology" if it wished to be victorious.[19]

What Scholem refers to as the "revolutionary, cataclysmic element" in the transition from the profane era of history to the sublimity of the messianic future plays a prominent role in the thinking of both Benjamin and Bloch. Thus, for example, in his "Theologico-Political Fragment"—a fascinating gloss on the *Geist der Utopie*—Benjamin identifies the "cardinal merit" of Bloch's 1918 work as its having "repudiated with utmost vehemence the political significance of theocracy,"[20] since theocracy suggests that the messianic kingdom could be realized *within* the profane continuum of history. However, as Benjamin points out emphatically, "nothing historical can relate itself on its own account to anything messianic." The method of world politics, therefore, must be "nihilism": it must promote the downfall and ruination of all that is merely historical, forsaken and profane.[21] Only in this way can the path to the messianic future be cleared.

And thus, in their "revolutionary nihilism," both Benjamin and Bloch find inspiration in the doctrines of Sorel. Benjamin will praise Sorel's notion of revolutionary or "*law-creating violence*," which he contrasts favorably with the conservation idea of "*law-preserving violence*" that characterizes the modern state.[22] And in a celebrated bon mot, Bloch characterizes the ethical stance appropriate to the present age as the "categorical imperative with revolver in hand."[23]

Thanks to Benjamin's influence, the standpoint of secular messianism came to play an important role in the critical theory of the Frankfurt School. The concerted

negation of pseudoprogressive, evolutionary philosophies of history in Max
Horkheimer and Theodor Adorno's *Dialectic of Enlightenment* bears the distinct
traces of the messianic critique of the homogeneous and empty continuum of historical life. Thus, like Benjamin and unlike Marx and Hegel, their dialectical forebears, critical theorists such as Theodor Adorno and Max Horkheimer ceased to
believe in the intrahistorical prospects of Redemption. To be sure, the positive side
of the messianic idea—the effusive allegorical vision of Redemption—is lacking in
their work. Both Horkheimer and Adorno thereby show their respect for the antimessianic and traditional taboo against graven images.

However, especially in the work of Adorno, the authentically messianic strategy
of "negative theology" attains prominence. This concept suggests the unredeemed—and unredeemable—character of the profane continuum of historical life.
With Adorno, however, this idea is historicized: his notions of the "totally administered world" or the "context of total delusion" refer to a specific historical period—twentieth-century state capitalism. More important, negative theology suggests that, with the suspension of the immanent historical movement toward
freedom, the qualities of a state of Redemption can only be deduced *ex negativo*—
that is by reversing the characteristics of the degraded historical present. Only when
we realize Adorno's profound indebtedness to negative theology as a strategy of
argumentation can we appreciate the truly radical character of his cultural criticism,
its brilliant, unrelenting severity.

Perhaps the passage of Adorno's work that best betrays this covert messianic
approach is the methodological confession that appears at the end of *Minima
Moralia:*

> The only philosophy which can be responsibly practiced in the face of despair is the
> attempt to contemplate all things as they would present themselves from the standpoint
> of Redemption. Knowledge has no light but that shed on the world by Redemption: all
> else is reconstruction, mere technique. Perspectives must be fashioned that displace and
> estrange the world, reveal it to be, with its rifts and crevices, as indigent and distorted as
> it will appear one day in the messianic light. To gain such perspectives without velleity
> or violence, entirely from felt contact with its objects—this alone is the task of
> thought.[24]

Ironically, it was Gershom Scholem—who single-handedly rescued so much of the
Jewish messianic heritage from oblivion—who was often quickest to warn of the
dangers inherent in a reckless imposition of messianic perspective on the course of
secular events. As he remarked in a 1975 interview:

> I've defined what I thought was the price the Jewish people has paid for messianism. A
> very high price. Some people have wrongly taken this to mean that I am an antimes-
> sianist. I have a strong inclination toward it. I have not given up on it. But it may be that
> my writings have spurred people to say that I am a Jew who rejects the messianic idea
> because the price was too high. . . . I think that the failure to distinguish between
> messianism and secular movements is apt to trip up movements of this sort. Such a mix-
> up becomes a destructive element. The misapplication of messianic phraseology in-
> jected a false note into the minds and self-image of the devotees of those secular
> movements.[25]

The messianic idea in its modern secular guise has certainly provided a wealth of insight and illumination concerning some of the most fundamental contradictions and dilemmas of contemporary human existence. Above all, it has encouraged humanity—and not Jewish humanity alone—to confront a series of troubling existential questions concerning the irrational, the transcendent and the hopes that have been repressed and rejected by the modern predilection for scientific analysis. It would be a rationalist delusion to think that these questions would recede from human consciousness of their own accord; or that they, too, would prove pliable material for contemporary methods of social engineering. In keeping these so-called ultimate questions of human existence at the fore of modern historical consciousness, Jewish secular messianism has accorded new relevance and meaning to a variety of traditional religious preoccupations.

Nevertheless, the reservations indicated by Scholem concerning a premature effacement of the boundary separating the messianic from the historical seem well placed. As a telos transcending contemporary historical consciousness, descending on the latter suddenly from above, the messianic category of Redemption sees no compromises with the merely incremental gains of secular historical life. From this privileged, suprahistorical vantage point, all that is merely historical—customs, morality, political forms—deserves to perish. Scholem has alluded to the prominence of the "catastrophic" or "apocalyptical" character of salvation in the messianic tradition. And we have seen how both Benjamin and Bloch are attracted to the "purifying" capacities of violence. Here, moreover, there is a perfect fit between messianism and the modern revolutionary tradition as a whole as it descends from Robespierre and Jacobinism.[26]

And thus, as Scholem correctly points out, Benjamin—especially in his later writings—too readily collapsed the barrier separating religious and political concepts; a charge that, *mutatis mutandis,* could be made with respect to the other apostles of revolutionary messianism: Ernst Bloch, Theodor Adorno and Herbert Marcuse. The compelling critique of a "damaged life" (Adorno's phrase) that emerges from their work is purchased at no small cost: a potentially distorting conflation of theological and historical levels of analysis, in consequence of which the immanent trajectory of historical life tends to remain neglected and undervalued.

The problem is one that Benjamin recognized in the aforementioned "Theologico-Political Fragment," in which he wrote, "The quest of free humanity for happiness runs counter to the messianic direction."[27] But as one sees so often in the course of Jewish history, the taboo against graven images proves a difficult one to respect.

Notes

1. Isaac Deutscher, *The Non-Jewish Jew and Other Essays* (London: 1968), 26.
2. *Ibid.,* 27.
3. For example, in his excellent work, *Rédemption et utopie: Le Judaisme libertaire en Europe centrale* (Paris: 1988), Michael Löwy identifies the French thinker Bernard Lazare as "l'exception qui confirme la règle" (224ff).

4. Anson Rabinbach, "Between Enlightenment and Apocalypse: Benjamin, Bloch and Modern German Jewish Messianism," *New German Critique* 34 (Winter 1985), 78.

5. Löwy, *Redemption et utopie,* 40.

6. Fritz Ringer, *The Decline of the German Mandarins* (Cambridge, Mass.: 1969), 3.

7. Georg Lukacs, *The Theory of the Novel* (Cambridge, Mass.: 1971), 21.

8. Cf. Helmuth Plessner, *Der verspätete Nation* (Frankfurt: 1959).

9. Anson Rabinbach, "Between Enlightenment and Apocalypse," 82–83.

10. See, e.g., Richard Wolin, *Walter Benjamin: An Aesthetic of Redemption* (New York: 1982), 246.

11. For Baader's influence on Bloch, see Arno Münster, *Utopie, Messianismus und Apokalypse im Fruhwerk Ernst Bloch* (Frankfurt: 1982), 137.

12. Gershom Scholem, *The Messianic Idea in Judaism and Other Essays on Jewish Spirituality* (New York: 1972), 3–4.

13. Ernst Bloch, *Geist der Utopie* (Frankfurt: 1964), 347.

14. Scholem, *The Messianic Idea in Judaism,* 10–11, emphasis added.

15. Walter Benjamin, *Illuminations* (New York: 1970), 264.

16. Scholem, *The Messianic Idea in Judaism,* 7.

17. See Ernst Cassirer, *The Myth of the State* (New Haven: 1946).

18. Bloch, *Geist der Utopie,* 305, 346.

19. Benjamin, *Illuminations,* 253.

20. Walter Benjamin, *Reflections* (New York: 1978), 312.

21. *Ibid.,* 313.

22. See Walter Benjamin's essay, "Critique of Violence," in *idem, Reflections,* 277ff.

23. Bloch, *Geist der Utopie,* 344.

24. Theodor Adorno, *Minima Moralia* (London: 1974), 247.

25. Gershom Scholem, *On Jews and Judaism in Crisis: Selected Essays,* (New York: 1976), 26.

26. On this theme, see the recent work by Ferenc Fehér, *The Frozen Revolution: An Essay on Jacobinism* (Cambridge: 1988).

27. Benjamin, *Reflections,* 312.

The Messianism of Gush Emunim

Janet Aviad
(THE HEBREW UNIVERSITY)

There is nothing more difficult in Jewish historical research than distinguishing between the yearnings of those engaged in the prediction of impending Redemption, the position accorded them by scholars, and the actual role of those yearnings in the existential complex of history.—Israel Bartal

Gush Emunim has been characterized as a messianic movement whose radicalism stems from eschatological categories and imperatives. This image has been fostered by both journalistic reports and academic analyses of the movement. The popular conception of the settlers as fanatic messianists propelled to activist tactics and even to violence in order to advance the process of Redemption and to "force the End" was strengthened in recent years by the disclosure in 1984 of a Jewish underground, whose leaders and key members were central figures in Gush Emunim. The plan to blow up the mosques on the Temple Mount in Jerusalem in order to spur the redemptive process onward (which was conceived by, and only known to, a few underground members and which in the end was abandoned) reinforced the messianic image of Gush Emunim.

In this discussion, the conception of Gush Emunim as a messianic movement is challenged by focusing precisely on what Israel Bartal has termed "the actual role of these yearnings in the existential complex of history." My claim is that the messianic language used by some Gush Emunim leaders should not be taken as representing either an acute popular messianic mood or an ideology translated into a social force. The key to understanding Gush Emunim lies elsewhere, that is, in its ultranationalist politics.

This is certainly not to imply that messianic ideas are not part of the religious worldview that motivates the actions of the settlers or the intellectual-spiritual context within which they function. Gush Emunim must be seen as one product of the religious Zionist awakening that occurred following the Six Day Way. The victory itself and the changes in Israel's map that it engendered were understood by religious Zionists as a new stage in the advance toward full sovereignty over the land of Israel and, hence, full Redemption.

The June 1967 War, the return to Jewish patrimony over the biblical lands of Judea and Samaria and the "Redemption of Jerusalem" were perceived as vindicat-

197

ing the religious Zionist conviction that the return to the Holy Land and reestablishment of Jewish sovereignty are themselves part of the realization of messianic
processes. This belief was elaborated in books, pamphlets and articles that interpreted current political developments in religious-nationalist terms.[1]

Heightened messianic consciousness, however, does not mean, in and of itself,
that Gush Emunim is or was a messianic movement. The mere articulation of a
messianic theology does not indicate the actual force of the messianic idea in
motivating those thousands who joined the demonstrations organized by Gush
Emunim in the 1970s or who joined its settlements in the 1970s and 1980s. The
place of messianism in the overall reality of the Gush Emunim community is a
question that must be subjected not just to theological or intellectual, but also to
sociological, analysis.

A few preliminary comments on the phenomenon of messianism are thus in
order. Messianism is a broad concept, referring to a range of beliefs about the end of
history and consequent changes that will bring fulfillment and perfection to existence. Messianism is grounded upon a linear conception of time and upon an
anticipation of the dawn of a new aeon. Messianic longings, rooted in disappointment with the present, envision a total transformation in which the sufferings,
sicknesses and weaknesses of humankind will be eliminated.[2]

In Judaism, biblical prophetic hopes and predictions for Israel became messianic
ideas under the historical pressure of suffering and exile. The longing for a new
order, in which the discrepancy between God's omnipotence and Israel's plight
would be abolished, and the hope for return and national renewal provided comfort
and understanding to those bearing the burdens of exilic existence.

The political-national dimension of this vision was universalized and spiritualized
in certain periods of Jewish history. Similarly, the importance of supernatural
intervention was emphasized or reduced in different periods. The core of the messianic idea, however, remained the return of the repentant faithful to the Holy Land,
the restoration of sovereignty, the reestablishment of the Kingdom of David and the
rebuilding of the Temple. The salience of the messianic vision in religious consciousness varied throughout Jewish history, which witnessed both messianic re-
vivals and attempts to neutralize messianic forces.[3]

The rise of the Zionist movement and its achievements led Orthodox Judaism to
evaluate the contemporary national revival within messianic categories. The return
to the land, the renewal of Hebrew language and culture, the Ingathering of the
Exiles and efforts toward sovereignty—all signs of Redemption in classical Jewish
thought—raised the question of the religious meaning and status of the Zionist
enterprise.

One well-known response was the complete denial of any sacred or even positive
religious value to contemporary Zionism because the movement violated the admo-
nition against natural or human initiation of messianic processes. Another response,
that of religious Zionism, was the positive ascription of messianic concepts to
Zionism and, hence, the religious legitimation of the Zionist enterprise. This response reflects the elation felt by many religious Jews at the actual attainments of
the Zionist movement, identification with its major goals and the consequent demand that traditional symbols and categories be applied to, and absorbed by, the

national movement and the state.[4] The description of the state as "the beginning of the flowering of our Redemption" is a clear enunciation of this view.

Religious-nationalist enthusiasm and messianic rhetoric reached a new level of intensity in the wake of the Six Day War, interpreted as a miraculous and redemptive victory. The charismatic renewal that took place within religious Zionist circles after the war and the return to holy places inaccessible since 1948 found expression first in the expansion of Torah study generally. A special place in the post-1967 curriculum was held by theological works dealing with the land of Israel, the links of the people of Israel to the land and the redemptive meaning of contemporary events. This phenomenon was most evident in the Merkaz Harav Yeshiva and the institutions associated with it.[5]

Works that concretized messianic beliefs by attributing eschatological meaning to the history of modern Zionism and the state argued that the period of Redemption was indeed already in progress. One major work in which the steps are traced from the Holocaust to the Six Day War concluded, "On the basis of all this I cannot understand those who do not see this period as Redemption. What can be the meaning of these events otherwise? What other name can we give this period?"[6]

> In the upper spheres of divine providence there were plans for additional steps in the process of Redemption. . . . While the government was prepared to accept partition [of the land of Israel], God was not. For there is no power in the world that can stop the wheels of Redemption. And Redemption cannot be completed without all of the land of Israel. . . . While the government of Israel tried to dissuade Hussein from entering the conflict, God hardened his heart so that the West Bank would be liberated.[7]

Rabbi Yehudah Amital, in explaining the difficulties posed by the 1973 Yom Kippur War for those convinced of the progressive realization of messianic processes, emphasized the central significance of the Six Day War for religious Zionists:

> The question asked everywhere is, what is the meaning of the [1973] war? It is asked against the background of our certain belief that we live in the period of the beginning of the messianic process. . . . Against this background and that of the Six Day War, which taught us that war has a great goal—namely, that of the conquest of the land— two questions may be posed. First, what is the meaning of this war, since we already possess the land; second, could this war signal a reversal of the divine plan? It is forbidden to view this war as we viewed our troubles when we lived in Exile. We must see the greatness of the hour through its biblical dimension and through the messianic prism. If we have returned to breathe biblical air after two thousand years of Exile it is only because we live in the light of the Messiah.[8]

Many more citations could be adduced to illustrate the revived messianic thinking and interest that surfaced during those years. A more crucial point, however, is that the retrospective messianic interpretation of history that emerged was perfectly consistent with normative Jewish theologies throughout the generations. The transfiguration of mundane events into metahistorical signs of God's will is a key element in the premodern Jewish worldview and in traditional Jewish historiography. The historic present becomes a realm of potential cosmic meaning.

The greater exposure given to Redemption theology, however, does not necessarily indicate any change in the force of messianic ideas in daily life. If messianic awareness simply utilizes the categories and the historiographical method that are the property of all Orthodox Jews, neither going beyond religious norms nor threatening established religious patterns in the name of redemptionist activity, it remains within the parameters of conventional messianism. Conventional or commonplace messianism refers to a conception of time that assumes a progression from an imperfect present toward fulfillment in a new and perfected age, brought about through divine intervention. I suggest that the messianism of religious Zionism is indeed conventional. Further, I suggest that the messianism of Gush Emunim is also conventional, rather than apocalyptic, and that the innovation of the movement is not theological but rather political, that is, the translation of its ultranationalist values into political deeds.

To establish the context for discussion of this thesis I draw upon the distinction between conventional and acute messianism propounded by Gershom Scholem in his discussion of the role of messianism in Hasidism.[9] Although it is not possible simply to transfer Scholem's central thesis concerning the neutralization of messianism in Hasidism to Gush Emunim, Scholem's focus on the difference between acute and conventional messianism is extremely helpful in understanding the messianism of Gush Emunim.

Scholem insisted on a strict definition of the term "messianic tendencies" in analyzing the question of messianism in Hasidism, "If it means affirmation of the traditional belief, it is a truism, but if it refers to acute messianic tension in Hasidism—and this is what the controversy is about—then it is without foundation."[10] Scholem claimed that, loosely speaking, it was accurate to refer to "messianic tendencies" in describing the Orthodox belief among hasidim in the eventual coming of the Messiah but that this does not help clarify the special nature of Hasidism. He proceeded to demonstrate that messianism as "an acute, immediate force" had been eliminated within Hasidism in reaction to the overwhelming negative experience of Sabbatianism.

The messianic tendencies within Gush Emunim are not neutralized. They are, however, far from constituting that radical force that underlies the activity of a messianic movement. The messianism of Gush Emunim remains on the general utopian level and has, therefore, no immediate impact on religious doctrines or behavior, nor does it threaten social structures within Orthodoxy.

The attribution of general messianic significance to historical events is clearly not, in itself, a sign of acute messianic tension. Rather, it is a continuation of the traditional need to expand the symbolic significance of Jewish history to contemporary events. Acute or radical messianism exists when the advent of the *eschaton* is set and known. A time frame is forecast. A periodization of the stages from the present to an end-station is delineated and concrete expectations within each stage are posited in a full messianic program.

Radical messianism is characterized by a sense of living in a new aeon, that of partial realization. This stage and the plan for further messianic realization are accompanied by changes in religious behavior in the light of messianic knowledge. Such religious changes may include elements not recognized as legitimate in the premessianic era, although this is not always the case.

Acute messianism may lead to tension and conflict between the charismatic messianic leadership and the established traditional sources of authority. The religious movement or community that arises around a messianic idea or leader challenges conventional structures. If this idea is not realized and the leader fails, both the eschatological belief system and the community that arose around it are likely to collapse.

In Judaism, acute messianism has historically been linked to catastrophic events, suffering and destruction that are understood as the foreordained prelude to the great and final transformation, "Jewish messianism is in its origins and by its nature—and this cannot be sufficiently emphasized—a theory of catastrophe. This theory stresses the revolutionary, cataclysmic element in the transition from every historical present to the messianic future."[11]

When the messianism of religious Zionism, and of Gush Emunim in particular, is considered in this context, it is clear that acute messianism is characteristic of neither. First, the advent of the *eschaton* is not set in any narrow sense. All that is claimed is that extraordinary events have occurred—first through the activity of the Zionist movement, then within the framework of the state—and that other momentous changes will follow.

Assertions that "the beginning of Redemption" has dawned or even that we are in the "vestibule" or "middle of the process" are not the same thing as providing a fixed time frame for the Redemption. Indeed, such expressions, as much as they indicate a messianic consciousness, also testify to a certain vagueness.[12] Moreover, this indefiniteness increases with the passage of time. Messianic convictions of the early days of Gush Emunim in the aftermath of the Six Day War have apparently remained without concrete religious expression, at the sociological level, twenty years afterward. The study of messianic texts or doctrines—an activity that one might expect to find in a bona fide messianic movement—seems not to have caught the imagination of the Gush Emunim public, who continue to study normative religious texts. Based on observations I shall presently detail, I have not found any special preoccupation with messianic theological issues among the Gush Emunim settlers; neither can their communities accurately be described as living in active anticipation of the Redemption. They are not engaged in advancing the messianic process in any way beyond accepted or standard religious patterns and norms. Religious (as distinguished from political) behavior has not changed in response to events that are interpreted as bearing messianic significance.

I see Gush Emunim as a branch of religious nationalism whose unique significance lies at the social and political level. The movement was characterized in its first stage of development by a nationalist aspiration to settle the newly acquired areas in the land of Israel. In the second phase, Gush Emunim focused on building social institutions at the local level. Messianic rhetoric accompanied the campaign during the initial struggle to establish settlements against government and political opposition. In the subsequent period, however, messianic language and symbols have all but disappeared. The central religious interest in the settlements today, similar to that of urban Orthodox communities, is conserving or expanding the Torah order.

Moreover, Gush Emunim has attempted both to present itself as a pioneering religious vanguard and to locate itself squarely within the mainstream of Israeli politics and society. It has thus denied the radical messianic image attributed to it, claiming instead to represent the quintessential values of Zionism. It has never adopted a platform for revolutionary social action based on messianic ideology, and it has sought to discredit the only radical messianists who emerged within its midst as deviationists. Further, its own charismatic leaders have not defied the recognized rabbinic leadership of religious Zionism in the name of a new messianic norm.

Finally, Gush Emunim has not developed a theological framework in which its communities play a distinctive role. The settlements are not defined as sacred or in any way different from other religious communities. No special tension exists between the rabbis of Gush Emunim and the established Zionist rabbinic leadership on the messianic issue or its implications. Moreover, neither the belief system that underlies the existence of these communities nor their structure is endangered by a potential delay or failure in messianic expectations. The messianic element is neither acute nor central, thus the total religious framework of Gush Emunim does not depend on its fulfillment.

In emphasizing the distinction between acute and conventional messianism, as well as the distinction between messianic ideas and actual social impact, I take issue with those who have portrayed Gush Emunim as mainly a messianic movement.

The only systematic analysis of the messianic ideology of Gush Emunim is the doctoral dissertation of Gideon Aran.[13] His closely argued account of the role played by the theology of Rabbi Avraham Yitzhak Kook and its interpretation by his son, Rabbi Zvi Yehudah Kook, in the evolution of Gush Emunim is illuminating. Similarly, his account of the revival within the religious-nationalist camp following the Six Day War contributes to our understanding of the reactions to this camp. But I would argue that subsequent developments indicate the need for a reevaluation of what is central in Gush Emunim ideology—redemptionist rhetoric or nationalist politics?

Aran claims that mystical-messianic principles of faith, which he groups under the heading of "Kookism," form the basis upon which Gush Emunim is founded. Aran emphasizes the role of Rabbi Avraham Y. Kook's concept of holiness that enabled him to view secular Zionist nationalism as part of a messianic religious drama, thereby overcoming the gap between external secular reality and the internal religious perception of the meaning of Zionism and the state. Aran focuses on the significance assigned after 1967 to the land of Israel, the war and the army by religious–nationalist circles, and he emphasizes how these three elements became linked to the concept of Redemption. Aran argues that the translation of this original, mystical-messianic Kookist faith into sociopolitical realities is the unique contribution of Gush Emunim to Israeli society.

As already indicated, the Six Day War was experienced as miraculous and redemptive. It released among religious Zionists a sense of self-confidence both in their interpretation of Zionism and in their role in Israeli society. It created a new expansiveness in their efforts to transform the religious and political future of the country.

The question is whether this post-1967 spiritual revival is accurately described as a messianic-mystical phenomenon or movement. Similarly, the question arises as to the usefulness of this same messianic-mystical category when accounting for the origins and effectiveness of Gush Emunim. In both cases, sociological evidence is necessary to clarify the issues.

Aran's analysis relies on the messianic content of the rhetoric in yeshiva circles, centered in Merkaz Harav Yeshiva, during the years following the Six Day War. Affirming the reality of a messianic process in-the-making, he quotes phrases and statements drawn from the writings of Rabbis A. Y. Kook, Z. Y. Kook and their followers.[14] This is the basic evidence in Aran's thesis that Gush Emunim originated as a movement inspired by a messianic charisma. Similarly, Aran points to renewed interest in classical messianic texts within these same Kookist circles, to a proselytizing spirit and to the cultivation of a Kookist mythology that is focused on the "prophetic" insights of both Kooks as indications of the dominant influence of messianic thinking. Yet declarations that Redemption is in progress do not indicate, certainly not necessarily, the existence of a movement that actualizes messianism.[15] Aran's evidence relating to what he has called the "activization" and "actualization" of radical messianism falls short of substantiating the links among rhetoric, ideology and empirical manifestations of acute messianism.

Further, Aran has not distinguished between the conventional reading of Zionist history as sacred within traditional messianic religious categories and a radical revolutionary messianic reading. In the case of the former, new ideas are not to be expected and changes in religious behavior not demanded. Rather, in this case, the redemptive interpretation of the post-1967 period is best understood as a consistent and natural continuation of conventional religious Zionist thinking.

In short, I question the correlation between interest expressed in religious thought and the transformation of that interest into a social movement. Messianism is clearly a complex phenomenon. Messianic language may or may not reflect a fundamental shift to an acute messianism. Intense yearnings for the End of Time do not necessarily imply an immediate expectation of the End. Messianic rhetoric, especially as used by religious Zionists following the Six Day War, does not in and of itself entitle us to conclude that a wholly new religious movement, anticipating the End or working actively toward its realization, has emerged. Rather, it reveals a community, elated with victory, feeling that its worldview had emerged triumphant at last, anxious to strengthen its own institutions in the wake of the new religious revival and eager to expand its influence on public life.

I shall argue that the leaders of Gush Emunim appropriated available messianic concepts and applied them to contemporary events in ways both routine and natural from a religious-nationalist perspective. They have not, however, introduced new principles of faith, symbols or values, nor have they challenged the established religious or social order.

Gush Emunim should be viewed as a nationalist revival within the context of the diffuse messianic ideas of Rabbi A. Y. Kook and his interpreters. These inform the overall meaning given to the lives of the settlers in the same way that belief in progress informed and gave meaning to the lives of those secular Zionists who engaged in the practical activities of building a new society and state.

The innovation of the leaders of Gush Emunim was in directing the diffuse messianism, kindled by the events of June 1967, into one specific channel: settlement of the new territories. This was presented as the historic challenge and historic imperative of the generation. Redemption of the land was understood as a necessary step in a very general process of redemption; but the time frame of all the different steps was left undefined.

The intellectual construction that caught the imagination of thousands of religious youth following the Six Day War of 1967, and especially in the confused and troubled period following the Yom Kippur War of 1973, was this diffuse messianic framework joined to a commitment to one very concrete and pragmatic avenue of fulfillment. The struggle to establish settlements in the West Bank, Gaza, Sinai and Golan Heights was interpreted by the leaders of Gush Emunim as the battle to restore classical pioneering values. This time the struggle of the Jewish people was to be carried forward by the young religious nationalists, who understood themselves as waging war on the materialism, egoism and defeatism that had undermined and weakened secular Zionism. Their task was to revive the nation—as important a goal as redeeming the land.

The Gush Emunim phenomenon raises critical and subtle methodological questions. The main issue is the way one measures the valence of rhetoric (in this case messianic rhetoric) and the way one distinguishes this rhetoric from the values and ideas that determine a group's operative ideology and actions. My assumption has been that only an empirical study of a concrete community could reveal the actual significance of messianism in the life of Gush Emunim adherents, that is, the presence or absence of acute messianic ideas and sensibility that alter the religious behavior of the community. This discussion is based on such a case study, conducted in the community of Ofra.[16] Through retrospective interviews with the founders, through discussions of the present with a broad sample of all sectors of the settlers and through written questionnaire data, there emerges a picture of the force of messianic ideas and their behavioral implications—both in the past and today—that may restore some balance to our perceptions of Gush Emunim.

Ofra was the first Gush Emunim settlement to be founded in Samaria. It was founded illegally in May 1975. Its population today numbers about 215 families from heterogeneous ethnic backgrounds. Ofra is a well-established and influential settlement, widely regarded as the showcase of Gush Emunim because of its relative age, experience and the leadership roles within the settlers' movement that its members have assumed. No one settlement can be said to represent Gush Emunim as a whole, but Ofra would seem to present the values and trends common to all settlements of Gush Emunim, despite local variations.

The dominant position on messianic issues in Ofra is a conventional one. It has been enunciated most clearly by Yoel Bin-Nun, a former student at Merkaz Harav Yeshiva. The only radical messianism to have emerged within the settlers' movement that sharply contrasts with that of Bin-Nun was both articulated and acted on by another member of Ofra, Yehudah Etzion, a founder of Ofra who was a leader in the community until his arrest in April 1984 as the number two man in the Jewish underground. Etzion was tried and convicted for his role in planning the bomb attacks against West Bank Arab mayors, for executing the attack on Bassam Shaka of Nablus and for his role in the abortive plan to blow up the mosques on the Temple Mount. During his imprisonment, Etzion elaborated the messianic conception that underlay these activities. The fact that Etzion's views are regarded as a deviation in Ofra and within Gush Emunim generally reinforces my claim that nonradical messianism is more characteristic of Gush Emunim and that the main impact of the movement, therefore, cannot be explained through messianism.

It must be stated at the outset that Ofra's residents shy away from speaking about messianism—to outsiders at least. They are aware of the suspicion or stigma that the term "messianist" evokes within the general Israeli public, whose sympathy the settlers need and attempt to cultivate. The following comments of Moshe Shapira, a moderate rabbi of Ofra, indicate the problem of the "messianist" label clearly:

> The word messianic confuses rather than explains. I would eliminate it from the lexicon. I am really not a messianist. It is not a simple matter. Once I had a student who sent me a journalist from the *Christian Science Monitor* who wished to interview someone from Ofra. In those days it was like being from outer space. So I took him around and explained to him how important this hill and valley were for strategic reasons. After a time he closed his notebook. I wondered why, and then understood that he had been waiting for a fanatic, an enthusiast, who, in total messianic consciousness, was waiting for the Messiah to come any minute. This happened several times with TV programs that were canceled because I spoke of security needs and real peace. Once Dan Margalit [an Israeli journalist and television interviewer] found someone who would enunciate the slogans about being in the midst of Redemption. It was Rabbi Patron. Following this interview there was a nasty article in *Kol ha'ir* [a Jerusalem weekly], portraying us as wild fanatic messianists, as if we dictate to God in which stage we are presently found.[17]

Once the reticence is broken, however, the main theme that emerges in discussing messianism with settlers is the denial of its force in the actual political activity of Gush Emunim, in general, and in the origins of Ofra, in particular. This is expressed most clearly by Yoel Bin-Nun, an activist, teacher and guide in Gush Emunim from the movement's beginnings:

> I don't recall a single discussion when this thing [messianism] was discussed, beyond the very general background that we all had—and this was very general. It was never a factor in determining what we would do, be it a demonstration, a march or building a settlement. All of this [question of messianism] arose after Yehudah Etzion—after he left his work in the orchard. In fact, after he left Ofra. Never before had we discussed the issue of how to advance the messianic process. We did discuss how to raise the spirit of the nation.
>
> I repeat that the messianic matter was not a factor in any of our meetings or decisions. We assume that we are living in a messianic epoch and that's enough. The messianic idea provides a general motivation. But no one ever said that we should do something because we are living in the messianic period. Or the opposite—that we should not do something because we are in the messianic period and God will do it anyway.[18]

The negation is emphatic and total. Messianism is dismissed as a direct cause in determining decisions and even as a subject of theological concern. The messianism that exists within Gush Emunim, according to Bin-Nun, is that very general diffuse idea that is part of the inherited outlook of religious Zionism and that never, he asserts, became a catalyst for action.

It is also important to focus on his view of Yehudah Etzion's messianic scheme as a dangerous derailment. According to Bin-Nun, it was never a concrete issue in Gush Emunim until the discovery of the underground. Moreover, Bin-Nun claims that Etzion's involvement in messianic matters not only isolated him intellectually, but drew him away from interest in Ofra—in whose founding and growth he had played a major role, symbolized by his abandonment of the orchard he himself had planted.

Obviously, as Orthodox Jews and religious Zionists, residents of Ofra are messianists and define themselves as such. This is made clear in Bin-Nun's statement. When residents of Ofra define themselves as messianists, however, they refer to the normative traditions of religious Zionism. Residents interviewed, including rabbis and current or former yeshivah students, consistently deny the presence of extraordinary or acute messianism. Such interviews should be set against the written and oral pronouncements testifying to a messianic consciousness in the movement as a means of achieving balance in our understanding of the phenomenon. Certainly, these statements deserve to be taken as seriously as those quoted by Aran.

The routine character of the messianism endorsed is evident from a statement by one Ofra resident:

> I think that we are living in the beginning of the period of Redemption. The processes through which the land of Israel has passed in the last one hundred years are apocalyptic in their foundation. All the wars, the establishment of the state, all the news that we create in one day—something special is happening to the Jewish people. Those who deny this are Neturei Karta [an anti-Zionist ultra-Orthodox sect] who think that what has happened in the past one hundred years is the work of the devil.[19]

The term "apocalyptic" here means great, awesome, overwhelming and obviously the product of God's work in history. Something special has occurred that clearly marks the beginning of the period of Redemption. "Apocalyptic" in this context, however, has been emptied of its catastrophic elements and does not refer to the end of life as we know it, nor does it indicate a process whose precise stages are known and according to which politics or religious life is determined in a new way.

The same speaker claims that the politics of Gush Emunim is the pragmatic politics of everyday reality, governed by rational analysis and planning. In his view, this is the lesson of Zionism for the religious nationalists, a lesson firmly rejected by the ultra-Orthodox. The latter continue to hold supernatural messianic ideas, termed by the interviewee to be "irrational" and "mystical," "The haredi [ultra-Orthodox, anti-Zionist] approach is that everything is miraculous. One day the Messiah just parachutes in. There are no stages. He who grasps the process mystically, lacking all rationality, must arrive at the haredi position."[20]

The speaker distinguishes between messianic beliefs and political knowledge, asserting that the latter does not flow from the former and that it is forbidden to rely on miracles:

> No one can say with certainty that he knows what to do from the point of view of realpolitik. Modern philosophy does not accept the notion that man knows with certainty what must be done now. We *think* that there are certain goals. The question is only, how does one realize them? Thus, I believe with complete faith that the land possessed by the Jewish people will be the entire land of Israel. I believe this. But when exactly and how exactly, I do not know.[21]

The denial of precise messianic knowledge and the rejection of a distinctive messianic function for Gush Emunim is repeated by others in Ofra. Thus, Rabbi Moshe Shapira:

> Anyone who tries to put God in his pocket, who says that we are already at this point, that the Third Commonwealth has been established, that the footsteps of the Messiah can be heard in the hills and that he knows the workings of the world—I am not on the same wavelength with him. I see the whole thing as a true mixture of practice and vision. Everything we do and everything done in the Diaspora is part of the messianic process. What we do in Samaria and the prayers of the Jew in the Diaspora for the coming of the Messiah—I believe as he does. I don't believe that we dictate events. I don't say that here he [the Messiah] comes. I do believe that everything we do furthers the process, the messianic process, but we don't know the exact end.

The speaker's equation of praying for the Messiah among Jews in the Diaspora with the actions of Jews in Judea and Samaria, as well as his view that what is done today is what was always done in order to bring the Messiah, represent a clear negation of radical messianism. This negation is strengthened by total agnosticism regarding the time of the coming of the Messiah.

Shapira concludes his remarks with the statement that "Redemption is the driving force for all of us, including the secular Jews. Secular Zionism is no different from us in this."[22] If the messianism of Gush Emunim is only a driving force, analogous to the driving force that motivates secular Zionism, it is not radical messianism. Rather, it may be seen as a powerful source of energy in the progress toward the attainment of national goals.

A very clear statement of the dominant position in Ofra on messianic matters, made by another rabbi and teacher, summarily negates radical messianism:

> It is messianism in the sense that the chief rabbinate has stated that the state is "the beginning of the flowering of our Redemption." People don't feel that any minute he is coming and that I can do something for his coming tomorrow. Like Maimonides, we believe that he could come any day.
>
> There is the feeling that there has been a basic change in Jewish experience since 1948, perhaps during the past one hundred years, and people must behave in light of this change. We are no longer in Exile in the land of Israel. Sovereignty is a very basic change, in contrast to the lack of it during the thousand years of Disapora existence. This change has religious significance even though only a minority of Jews live here.[23]

Messianism has been totally neutralized here as a radical force. Sovereignty, the elimination of Exile through return to the land of Israel, is the beginning of the process of Redemption. Beyond this general orientation, no distinctive Gush Emunim messianism is presented. The forthright denial of activity to advance the messianic process in any special way and the implicit equation of those identified with Gush Emunim and of those who live in settlements with all other Jews eliminates any specific messianic role for the settlers' movement.

The task of the settlers is portrayed as that of all religious Jews: the intensification of religious life in the here and now. Now, more than a decade after the founding of Ofra, when the fundamental concern has shifted from survival to improving the inner life of the community, the issue has become the nature of religious behavior and religious attitudes.

This is, indeed, the second main theme that emerges in discussions about messianism in Ofra—the current concern with the inner religious life of the settlement and the denial of any link between this interest and messianism. Thus, "The Messiah's coming is God's business; mine is the mitzvot. I don't think that I am doing more than someone who observed the mitzvot three hundred years ago and kept the tradition alive under adverse conditions. I have the Torah and mitzvot to observe in order to be a good person. He and I are [both] hastening the Messiah." [24]

Another founder of Ofra reinforces the juxtaposition of religious piety and messianism:

> I don't know how important the messianic issue is. But actually it is simple. The religious matter is important. We live in the period between Abraham and the Messiah-King. When I take account of where I am—at the age of thirty-six—my place in the passage of time, the framework is much beyond myself. I must fulfill my role in the process from Abraham to the Messiah. There is movement, and I have a role. When the End will come depends on the behavior of the Jewish people. [25]

The meaning of "the behavior of the Jewish people" in the view of the speaker is nothing beyond the normative categories of traditional Judaism, and his own role is defined explicitly as piety:

> The main concern is heightening religious life in the settlement. Religion must be total and not just a little corner of our lives. It cannot be that we are engineers and then say our prayers after our meals. Our view of Judaism is the opposite. First we are Jews, observing Torah and mitzvot, and then we earn a living and create a state. What is my role in the world as a religious Jew? To advance myself, then those close to me and then those farther away in the subjects of Torah and mitzvot. [26]

The tension between the perceived realization of the messianic vision and the norms of ordinary religious existence has often led the "redeemed" to break out of halakhic structures. [27] Concentration on routine halakhic issues in Ofra today is itself an indication of the absence of acute messianic tension. Behavior in the settlement, both in daily religious routines and in holiday or other special observances, reveals no special messianic content and no consequent changes of religious practices. The standard liturgy has not been altered, messianic texts are not the subject of study and innovative rituals signifying messianic events or meanings have not been instituted.

One crucial point must be made regarding the concrete expression through which Gush Emunim has chosen to affirm its own brand of conventional messianism, namely, settlement of the land. It represents a full appropriation and total incorporation of the Israeli experience and of Zionist values by a key sector of the religious-nationalist population. In the words of Moshe Merhavia, who is the archetype of the *halutz* (pioneer) in Ofra, "if messianic ideology is settlement [or] the fulfillment of Zionist goals in general, then messianism exists in Gush Emunim." [28]

Insofar as settlement has become the avenue of messianic fulfillment, it subtracts from the more diffuse range of paths open in the tradition. Social justice, peace and other options are omitted from the Gush Emunim program. This constitutes a subtraction as well in terms of the range of Zionist social and political ideas.

The messianism of Gush Emunim, translated into settlement, is an imitation of

Zionism on the deepest level, adopting Zionist symbols, ideals and time frame. Thus, redemptive activity undertaken without waiting for the messianic future but through human resources, in the form of pioneering settlement, becomes both faith and calling.

Redemption is equated with the revival of the Jewish people and its achieving both political and cultural sovereignty within the land of Israel. This equation reveals that the ideology of Gush Emunim simply cloaks national goals in the garb of religious rhetoric, emptying messianism of any radical or transcendent power. Messianism merely means, in this sense, living in anticipation of a better future that, for Gush Emunim, means fuller realization of nationalist values.

The assimilation of Zionist values is evident, however, not only in settlement activity. Just as significant is the value conferred on sovereignty. The significance of sovereignty and national self-fulfillment for Gush Emunim emerges most clearly in the writings of Yoel Bin-Nun, the exemplar of the nonradical messianic trend within Gush Emunim. Bin-Nun elevates the role of the state in the redemptive process to the highest level of significance. At the same time, he projects a nativist, nationalist, restorative vision in which messianism is both emptied of its radical meaning and secularized.

Bin-Nun relies on the teachings of Zvi Yehudah Kook, the revered spiritual guide of Gush Emunim, in legitimating his interpretation of the meaning of contemporary statehood and in sanctifying the accoutrements of the modern Jewish state:

> The fight of Zvi Yehudah Kook was not primarily settling the land of Israel but two other things: raising the spirit of the nation and sovereignty. . . . First, he couldn't stand the intervention of the United States. And he rejected the depression within [Israeli] society following the Yom Kippur War, which was the opposite of the spirit that emerged after the Six Day War.[29]

No weight is assigned here either to the messianic motive or to settlement per se. The issues for Zvi Yehudah Kook, according to Bin-Nun, were sovereignty, national pride and national confidence. Settlement would be the vehicle for reviving and giving expression to these elements; therefore, the revered rabbi urged his students to settle in the territories conquered in 1967.

Bin-Nun asserts over and over again that the great revolution in the life of the people of Israel is the establishment and progressive evolution of Jewish sovereignty. It is this that constitutes contemporary Redemption. He believes that the meaning of recent historical processes is obvious:

> A simple understanding of Redemption in our day does not demand special spiritual talents nor a deep understanding of the writings of Rabbi Kook. . . . It is sufficient for a person to have open and discerning eyes to grasp the tremendous revolution that has occurred in the history of Israel, which has changed the condition of the Jewish people fundamentally—naturally, not only in the positive sense. There is no other term for what has happened except Redemption.[30]

However, in Bin-Nun's view, the process that has occurred is only partial. Progress toward full and authentic sovereignty was blocked even at the time of the establishment of the state, first by partition of the land and then by the dependence of the state on outside powers, both for recognition and ongoing economic and political support. The struggle for full Redemption is the struggle for full political autonomy. According to Bin-Nun, the question of borders is an expression of autonomy. Israel must determine its own legitimate geographical boundaries according to its own values and its own understanding of its historical rights.

The process and its advance as described by Bin-Nun is natural and pragmatic. Zionism is understood by Bin-Nun as the effort to redeem the nation through human agencies. After citing the view of Rabbi A. Y. Kook (in his *Orot. ereẓ israel*) that the meaning of Zionism is the return of the Jewish people to world history and politics, Bin-Nun goes on to argue, "He who ignores history and politics continues the Exile in his thought. The conditions for action in bringing about natural Redemption are historical and political."[31]

The natural and pragmatic character of Bin-Nun's approach to history is evident in his stress on the gradual character of the process set in motion by the Zionist movement, "We must have great patience. Historical processes don't begin or end in one day."[32] Or again, "Great things happen in our world slowly and not all at once. 'Little by little will I cast them out before you.' "[33] Bin-Nun's fundamental pragmatism, as well as the ordinary conventional character of his messianic perspective, are apparent in this statement:

> We dream of Redemption, whether we actually succeed fully or in part. Generation after generation have longed and dreamt of fulfillment. We will not cease doing so even during times of great, albeit transient, difficulty, even if the reality is only partial fulfillment. One should not negate fragmentation for practical reasons, so long as this is not taken as full Redemption.[34]

According to Bin-Nun, the End is unknown, the stages of redemptive history are open-ended, and historical processes reveal a dialectic of natural and supernatural forces in which the specific weight of each element is concealed. He rejects human efforts to "force the End" and bring about the *eschaton*. "Our understanding of Zionism as a redemptive process is based on the principle of 'slowly-slowly.' " Further, "Human attempts to skip steps in the process so as to push the Redemption ahead are a severe deviation from our beliefs and outlook. . . . Those who seek to hasten the End are those who delay the *eschaton*."[35]

The link between the neutralized messianism of Yoel Bin-Nun and the radical messianism of Yehudah Etzion is the value each attributes to sovereignty in contemporary Jewish history. Etzion, too, regards the full realization of sovereignty as the heart of the current Redemption process. Unlike his longtime friend and fellow settler, however, Etzion lives with an acute messianic consciousness and has attempted to translate his radical messianic ideas into reality.

Yehudah Etzion's thinking begins with the distinction between the existence of Israel, determined by the laws of destiny specific to the "chosen people," and the existence of other nations, governed by the laws of survival. According to Etzion, Israel must dedicate itself totally to its unique task and must constantly drive forward to its goal. A regression is seen as damaging not only in itself, but more generally to the state of holiness in the world.[36]

Most of Jewish history, in Etzion's view, has been a retreat from the Torah period when the distinctive norms and structures of Israel were established: full sovereignty, dominion over the entire land of Israel, the rule of kingship and religious courts and the Temple as the center of religious life. These constitute the ideal framework within which an authentic and pure Jewish culture could develop. For Etzion this "normative" ancient period appears harmonious and whole, characterized by faithfulness to the divine norm of destiny. Its opposite is the Exile: a loss of sovereignty, loss of the land of Israel, loss of the Temple and the degeneration of Jewish culture owing to its dilution by foreign cultures.

Throughout the exilic period, the Jewish people substituted the priority of survival for the priority of destiny, preferring to remain passive rather than penetrate beyond the obstacles in their way toward the true and destined goal. Thus, Etzion criticizes the rabbis who failed to organize a practical campaign to promote the political plans of Shabbetai Zvi. In this view, secular Zionism broke through this religious passivity and initiated the process of return to the norm of destiny. While crediting Zionism with launching the revolution, Etzion also attacks the movement and its product, the state of Israel. Both are inherently flawed because they lack proper redemptive vision and, consequently, have failed to restore the Jewish people to full sovereignty according to their destiny.[37]

Similarly, Etzion criticizes his former spiritual home, the Merkaz Harav Yeshiva, his teacher, Rabbi Zvi Yehudah Kook, and the rabbi's disciples. He claims that their sanctification of the state—a major element in the political theology of Kookist circles—hampers their capacity to criticize and act autonomously. "The state of Israel was granted unlimited and independent credit in Merkaz Harav. Its actions—even those that conflict with the model of Israel's Torah—are viewed as God's will, a revelation of His grace."[38]

From this criticism of the paralysis of religious Zionist circles today, Etzion sets out his own radical program based on the notion that the final stage of Redemption, that which fully restores the norms of Torah and destiny, must begin immediately. The plan to "purify" the Temple Mount from the "abomination" of the gentile's possession was precisely such a radical action intended to initiate the great advance. It was a necessary messianic operation—in Etzion's words, a "penetrating intervention"—in order to remove the Dome of the Rock, symbol of paralysis and the status quo.

The fact that the planned messianic act conflicted with the present laws of the state was no obstacle. In a statement prepared for his trial, Etzion said:

> I am completely aware that the sources that nurtured and pressed me to decide to do what I did don't coincide, although they do not always conflict, with the laws presently in force in the State of Israel. This disharmony will cause great suffering to me and my family. I will bear the suffering and not disavow my loyalty, which for me is paramount, to the Redemption of Israel.[39]

Etzion had charged the state itself with the task of expurgating the non-Jewish presence on the Temple Mount and doing so forthwith. "It is the possession of David, the possession of David that we are commanded to take over today. And the nation's instrument for this is, of course, the state of Israel."[40]

Given what he considered to be the paralysis of the state, the fact that the Jewish people still seemed content to settle for mere survival when true Redemption was within their grasp, Etzion was prepared to launch the process himself. He viewed the Temple Mount operation as the first step in a revolutionary process that would necessitate a total break from mere survival, peace and security:

> The purified Mount shall be—if God wishes—the ground and anvil for progress toward the next stages of holiness. As long as the Muslim Waqf is not removed from the Mount, it is as if the Jebusite king, Araunah, rules alongside the kingdom of David, and this is an unforgivable flaw in our sovereignty.[41]

The plan was foiled by the Israeli police. But ever the radical messianist, Etzion continues to plan the initiation of the final process. While in jail, he designed and projected the formation of a new radical religious movement, *Degel Yerushalayim* (Banner of Jerusalem), to carry forward the post-Zionist revolution he has envisioned. The authority of his new movement derives from the sanctity of the task it must undertake: returning the nation to Torah norms, renewing the authority of the nation itself, reestablishing the religious court of the Temple and reestablishing theocratic rule through a God-chosen king, who would expand his dominion to include all the land between the Euphrates and the Nile.[42]

Several points must be stressed in concluding this clarification of the nature of messianism within Gush Emunim. Yehudah Etzion, the genuine radical messianist who reorganized his life around a messianic agenda and acted on it, has been discredited and disavowed by the vast majority of settlers as well as by the official settler institutions. This is not to imply that an upsurge of radical messianism within Gush Emunim is impossible or even unlikely, but only to point to the movement's current response to such radical and acute messianic thinking.

Up to the present, Gush Emunim has effectively neutralized the apocalyptic elements in its messianism. Those who view this movement primarily as a messianic phenomenon take rhetoric too much at face value, given the mundane reality. The messianism of Gush Emunim, here analyzed according to the group's own self-definition, lacks sociological weight and carries little normative substance. Neither eschatological tension nor eschatologically motivated actions characterize Gush Emunim. Rather, ultranationalist values and motives are being thinly cloaked in messianic language.

Notes

The epigraph by Israel Bartal is from "Messianic Expectations and their Place in History," in *Vision and Conflict in the Holy Land*, ed. R. I. Cohen (Jerusalem: 1985), 171.

1. Surveys of theological responses are presented by Gideon Aran, *Miẓiyonut ledat ẓiyonit: shorshei gush emunim,* (Ph.D. diss., The Hebrew University, 1987), 418 ff.; Aviezer Ravitzky, "Haẓafui vehareshut hanetunah," in *Yisrael likrat hameah ha'esrim veaḥat,* ed. Aluf Hareven (Jerusalem: 1984), 135–197; Uriel Tal, "The Land and the State of Israel in Israeli Religious Life," in *Proceedings of the Rabbinical Assembly* 38 (1976), 5–11.

2. Norman Cohn, *The Pursuit of the Millennium* (New York: 1957); Yonina Talmon, "Pursuit of the Millennium: The Relation Between Religious and Social Change," *Archives européenes de sociologie* 3, no. 1 (1962), 125–148; Erich Voegelin, *Israel and Revelation* (Baton Rouge: 1958), 467–480.

3. Moshe Idel, "'Al mishmarot umishiḥiut birushalayim bamaot 16–17," *Shalem* (1987) 83–94; Zvi Werblofsky, "Messianism," in *Contemporary Jewish Religious Thought*, ed. Arthur A. Cohen and Paul Mendes-Flohr (New York: 1987), 597–602.

4. Aryei Fishman, *Hakibbuẓ hadati* (Ph.D. diss., The Hebrew University, 1975); Charles Liebman and Eliezer Don-Yehiya, *Civil Religion in Israel* (Berkeley: 1983); Eliezer Schweid, *Bein ortodoksiah lehumanizm dati* (Jerusalem: 1977).

5. Aran, "Miẓiyonut ledat," 412–423.

6. Menahem M. Kasher, *Hatekufah hagedolah* (Jerusalem: 1969), 3.

7. Yaakov Ha-Levi Filber, *Ayelet hashaḥar* (Jerusalem: 1975), 170.

8. Yehudah Amital, *Min hama'amakim* (Hebron: n.d.), 30.

9. Gershom Scholem, "The Neutralization of the Messianic Element in Early Hasidism," in his *The Messianic Idea in Judaism and Other Essays on Jewish Spirituality* (New York: 1971), 176–202.

10. *Ibid.*, 184.

11. Gershom Scholem, "Toward an Understanding of the Messianic Idea in Judaism" in *idem, The Messianic Idea in Judaism*, 7.

12. As termed in the writings of A. Y. Kook. See Zvi Yaron, *Mishnato shel harav Kook* (Jerusalem: 1974), 280–283. For Z. Y. Kook see Tal, "The Land and the State of Israel," 9.

13. Aran, "Miẓiyonut ledat."

14. *Ibid.*, 444.

15. *Ibid.*, 437.

16. The research project in Ofra was sponsored by the Ford Foundation and conducted between 1985–1987.

17. Interview with Rabbi Moshe Shapira (Ofra), 20 December 1985.

18. Interview with Yoel Bin-Nun (Ofra), 7 September 1984.

19. Interview with Yehudah Zoldan (Ofra), December 1985.

20. *Ibid.*

21. *Ibid.*

22. Interview with Rabbi Moshe Shapira (Ofra), 20 December 1985.

23. Interview with Rabbi Yonatan Blass (Ofra), 31 July 1985.

24. *Ibid.*

25. Interview with Yair Meir (Ofra), 24 October 1985.

26. *Ibid.*

27. Scholem, "Toward an Understanding of the Messianic Idea," 16.

28. Interview with Moshe Merhavia (Ofra), 28 October 1986.

29. Interview with Yoel Bin-Nun, 7 September 1984.

30. Yoel Bin-Nun, *Nekudah* no. 91 (8).

31. *Ibid.*, no. 66 (10).

32. *Ibid.*, no. 68 (7).

33. *Ibid.*, no. 53 (4–5).

34. *Ibid.*, no. 119 (12).

35. *Ibid.*, no. 73 (15).

36. Yehudah Etzion, *Nekudah* no. 75 (23).

37. *Ibid.*, no. 94 (28).

38. *Ibid.*, no. 94 (28).

39. *Ibid.*, no. 88 (24).

40. Yehudah Etzion, *Har habayit* (Jerusalem: 1985), 4.

41. *Ibid.*, 2.

42. Etzion, *Nekudah* no. 94 (28).

Essays

The Yishuv and the Jews in Europe, 1938-1945

A Current Debate: An Introductory Note

Yehuda Bauer
(THE HEBREW UNIVERSITY)

Contemporary issues inevitably affect historical debates. The history of the Holocaust is no exception to this rule. It is, therefore, hardly surprising that the role of the Yishuv and its leadership during the Holocaust has become a central issue in both topical political debates and historical writing. Ever since the so-called Kasztner trial in the 1950s, the question has been asked (primarily, of course, in Israel) whether the leadership of the Yishuv during the Second World War did everything it could have done to aid in the rescue of European Jewry.

At the Kasztner trial, the accusation was leveled against Ben-Gurion, Sharett, and others of the labor movement who were then in charge of the Yishuv's affairs that their collaboration with the British had prevented decisive rescue actions. Their representatives in Europe, such as Kasztner in Hungary, had collaborated with the Nazis, it was argued, in order to save a relatively small number of their supporters. In other words, they had betrayed the Jewish people in their gravest hour of need. It was this argument and this accusation that was part of the attack of center and center-Right political forces in Israel against the establishment of the day.

A historical debate may be tied to current issues as far as the general theme is concerned, but when it becomes influenced by current political considerations, it becomes propaganda rather than history. Hence the attempt of Israeli historians to try to examine the documentation and arrive at conclusions that are beyond the boundary of political accusations, resentments and agendas that have little to do with what happened forty-five years ago in Europe.

So far, the most important effort to deal with these problems is undoubtedly Dina Porat's book, until now published only in Hebrew, *Leadership in Crisis*.[1] Dr. Porat's overall impression seems to be that although, undoubtedly, not all the avenues were sought out and followed, the Yishuv's leadership did make a significant and consistent effort to engage in rescue efforts as best it could. She points out the objective obstacles that confronted the Yishuv—it was a small community of about half a million people ruled by an essentially indifferent (and, at times, hostile) government; and it lacked both armed forces and political clout. She also details some of the major rescue attempts that the leadership sought to engage in: the attempt to influence the Western Allies to do much more than the small Yishuv could ever dream of doing on its own; the attempt to help in ransom proposals that came from beleaguered Jewish communities in Slovakia, Romania and Hungary between the end of 1942 and mid-1944; and the ultimately unsuccessful attempt to utilize small British concessions regarding the rescue of children from the Balkans in order to have some 29,000 children as well as a smaller number of adults brought to Palestine.

Dr. Porat's book and similar efforts, mostly in the form of detailed articles dealing with different aspects of the problem, have met with hostile critiques. These are based on two main lines of thought. First, there are ultra-Orthodox Jews who argue that Zionism and Zionists were really responsible for the Holocaust, at least in the sense that they prevented rescue of the Jewish masses. According to the ultra-Orthodox argument, the Zionists' purpose was the establishment of a Jewish state rather than rescue, and they did not mind if the Orthodox masses were destroyed in the process. This version—propagated, for example, by Rabbi Moshe Schoenfeld on the basis, largely, of Rabbi Michael D. B. Weissmandel's book *Min hameizar (Out of the Abyss)*[2]—is gaining adherents even today; it is really a Jewish version of Holocaust revisionism. It does not deny the facts of the Holocaust but rather distorts the real conditions then prevailing, and it substitutes an imaginary version that by implication absolves the Nazis of the murder, placing the responsibility instead on the Zionists.

The other line of thought is informed by contemporary political considerations, such as those outlined earlier. It draws parallels between the supposed behavior of *Judenräte* and that of the Jewish, especially the Zionist, leadership in the free world. Again, the accusations, based in some cases on detailed analyses of documentary evidence, tend to argue that the leadership could have saved masses of Jews, had it only had the courage and the required vision—and had it not been disunited, factious and enslaved to the Allies. The latter, it is argued, did not merely have no wish to save Jews; they *actively* wanted not to save them.

It appears that, one generation after the event, Jews still have tremendous difficulties coming to terms with reality. The Nazis (or most of them) have died out, one-third of the Jewish people have disappeared into the abyss and again and again it is asked: Who was responsible for the elimination of the Jews in their millions? Following an ancient Jewish tradition of self-accusation ("for our sins"), it becomes clear that the real culprit was the Jewish leadership of the day. Moral blame has to be apportioned; and this, of course, prevents the real questions from being asked, namely: What were the options? What were the objective and subjective conditions? What were the motivations? And how did these change? In other words, we have yet to emerge from the world of accusations into the world of explanations.

The two discussions that follow examine, on the basis of documentary evidence, the response of the Yishuv leadership to the unfolding events of the Holocaust.

Dalia Ofer deals with the leadership's declining support for illegal immigration after the outbreak of war, and the resumption of that support as the tide of war turned in 1943–1944. The reason why support was withdrawn in 1939–1940, Ofer explains, was the hope that collaboration with Britain would do more to facilitate mass immigration to Palestine than the attempt, with little money and against insuperable obstacles, to bring in a few thousand Jews. As a result, intelligence and other forms of cooperation with British authorities were sought. Toward the end of the war, however, with the knowledge of mass destruction sinking in and the final disappointment with the British government, illegal immigration (Aliyah Bet) was considered more of a practical alternative than before.

Dvorah Hacohen, in contrast, examines Ben-Gurion's vision of mass immigration as a solution to two separate problems: that of transforming Palestine into a Jewish state with a Jewish majority and that of the rescue of Jews, at first from the intolerable conditions in Eastern Europe and later from death. The remarkable fact that emerges is just how obstinate Ben-Gurion was in persistently making detailed plans for mass rescue, despite the violent upheavals and changes that occurred in the world and among the Jewish people in the short span of years between 1938 and 1945.

The "larger" issues are not addressed directly here; but the problem is that such issues can only be evaluated convincingly if detailed and accurate research first illuminates the facts. This is exemplified in Dalia Ofer's work on immigration to Palestine in the Second World War, especially her *Escaping the Holocaust*, a major contribution to our undestanding of this complex and tangled field.[3] Other work, whether already published or being prepared for publication, will likewise advance this process. For example, Tuviah Frieling's doctoral dissertation on Ben-Gurion and the Holocaust will attempt still another view of the acknowledged leader of Palestinian Jewry and the Jewish Agency. According to Frieling, who has already published an article on the subject,[4] Ben-Gurion was directly and actively involved in all programs designed to rescue Jews. He gave priority, Frieling suggests, both to the struggle for Jewish independence (Palestinocentrism) and to rescue as the central concern of the Jewish people and the Zionist movement. Further research by other young scholars deals with the rescue programs known as the Transnistrian scheme and the Europe Plan.

There are, of course, differences of approach and opinion. But one has the feeling that, in these efforts, we are emerging from partisan and ideological arguments, which reflect the differences among different Jewish orientations, and are witnessing a scholarly effort to understand. This seems to be the only proper, or in Emil Fackenheim's terms, "authentic," way to approach the events of the Holocaust.

Notes

1. Dina Porat, *Hanhagah bemilkud* (Tel-Aviv: 1986).
2. Michael D. B. Weissmandel, *Min hameizar* (New York: 1960).
3. Dalia Ofer, *Derekh bayam: 'aliyah bitkufat hashoah 1939–1945* (Jerusalem: 1988); in English, *Escaping the Holocaust: Illegal Immigration to the Land of Israel, 1939–1945* (New York: 1990).
4. Tuvia Frieling, "Levehinat hasteriotip: Ben-Gurion veshoat yehudei eiropah 1939–1945," *Yad Vashem: kovez mehkarim* 17–18 (1987), 329–351.

Illegal Immigration During the Second World War: Its Suspension and Subsequent Resumption

Dalia Ofer
(THE HEBREW UNIVERSITY)

This essay examines the policies formulated by Zionist leaders toward immigration to Palestine during the Second World War and the factors that governed the decision-making process. Without aliyah (the Hebrew word invariably used to designate immigration in this context) Zionism could not develop and would be reduced to insignificance. However, Jewish immigration was subject to restrictions imposed by the Mandatory government, which was guided primarily by its own, not by Zionist, interests.

In the late 1930s and, in particular, during the Second World War, aliyah took on still greater significance as a means of rescuing Jews from persecution and ultimately from mortal danger. This perspective invested aliyah policy with a new ideological dimension, since normative Judaism has always considered the rescue of Jews to be both the obligation and the privilege of any Jewish body or organization. Nonetheless, the Zionist movement was still hampered by the same government limitations on immigration. The only way the movement could implement an independent immigration policy was by resorting to illegal means; but this path, in turn, involved political risks that were not inconsiderable. Thus, from the year 1938 onward, Aliyah Bet (the Hebrew term for illegal immigration) became a prime example of the effort to reconcile the needs of Diaspora Jewry, the normative imperatives implicit in Zionist ideology and political interests.

Aliyah Bet predated the 1930s; individuals and groups had attempted to settle in Palestine in defiance of the authorities in earlier periods, particularly during the last years of Ottoman rule and immediately after the First World War. It became a mass movement, however, only at that juncture when, on the one hand, a growing number of Jews found themselves forced to leave their home countries—but found that draconian restrictions excluded them from the traditional destinations of emigration in Europe and America—and when, on the other hand, a Jewish community had been established in Palestine that had as its overriding ideal the creation of a center that would provide a haven for persecuted Jews.

The Yishuv was determined to supply the tools for large-scale aliyah to Palestine, despite the authorities' restrictive regulations; and it possessed the capacity to do so to a certain extent. In response to the challenge, the Yishuv and the Jewish communities abroad created an independent aliyah movement with its own official or semiofficial organizations and patterns of activity. In defiance of the Mandatory government's immigration laws, such a movement derived its legitimization from ideological arguments.

This complex of circumstances arose twice in the history of the Zionist movement: in the years immediately before, and after, the Second World War. However, the operational and organizational methods of Aliyah Bet were first created some years before by elite groups within the Zionist youth movements, Hehalutz and Betar, that organized the ships *Vellos* and *Union* in 1934.[1] These early ventures were not sanctioned by the official leadership of the Zionist movement or the Jewish Agency Executive. On the contrary, they represented a protest not only against British restrictions, but also against the regulations concerning the selection of immigrants that had been worked out by the Zionist institutions.

The latter half of the 1930s saw the creation of a radically new political and economic situation in Central and Eastern Europe, as well as in the Middle East (the death of Pilsudski in Poland, followed by the formation of the Sanacja government; the Nazi consolidation of power in Germany; the Arab revolt and changing British policy in Palestine). As a result, aliyah policy became a major focus of political discussion. The report of the Royal (Peel) Commission in 1937 recommended partitioning Palestine into two states—Arab and Jewish. This sparked a bitter controversy within the labor movement itself, with the question of aliyah playing a prominent part in the arguments both for and against partition. Each warring faction within the labor movement sought to reinforce its own position in the Yishuv by ensuring an influx of immigrants from its own political camp. Moreover, the political struggle between the labor movement and Revisionists now intensified; the latter seceded from the Zionist Organization in 1935 and formed its own New Zionist Organization (NZO).

Under these circumstances and despite the continued disapproval of the official leadership of the Zionist movement and of the Yishuv, Aliyah Bet operations were resumed and the organizational patterns that were later to characterize it began to crystallize. Two organizations were involved at that stage in the activities of Aliyah Bet: the Revisionist movement—through its activists in the Jewish communities and members of Betar—and Hehalutz, which had the assistance of emissaries from Palestine. The immigrants, most from Eastern Europe, came mainly by sea. They assembled at ports on the Adriatic, Aegean or Black seas, then departed for the Mediterranean in specially chartered ships. On reaching the Palestinian coast they tried to land clandestinely with the help of the paramilitary forces of the Yishuv— the Haganah and the Irgun Zvai Leumi (IZL). The newcomers were then secretly dispersed among Jewish settlements, where they hid from the British authorities; the latter demanded deportation of the illegal immigrants or deducted their numbers from the official immigration quotas.

After the *Anschluss* of March 1938, conditions in Europe worsened rapidly, forcing Jews to escape without the benefit of organized help. The activists of the Aliyah Bet continually refined their methods, and their competence improved. The movement grew, soon involving more than 17,000 people from all walks of life. A number of operations were now even mounted by private individuals, without the support of official organizations. In the course of the year, as antagonism between Britain and the Zionist movement mounted, the internal political opposition to Aliyah Bet declined, although the illegal immigration organized by the Revisionists (which they generally called 'Aliyah Azmait [independent immigration]) still came under acrimonious attacks in the press of the labor movement as well as in the Jewish Agency Executive and in the leading institutions of the Mapai party. However, the legitimization of Aliyah Bet was finally accomplished in 1939 after the British government prepared and then published its White Paper of May 1939, which severely limited Jewish immigration and settlement, thus shattering all hopes for the speedy foundation of a Jewish state or national home in Palestine.

MILITANT ZIONISM AND ALIYAH BET

During 1939, Aliyah Bet shifted from the periphery of Zionist activity to the center and became an important element in the political tactics of what became known as militant Zionism (ziyonut lohemet, lit. fighting or warring Zionism), a means of resisting the White Paper policy. As early as January 1939, in anticipation of the outcome of a growing anti-Zionist trend in British policy, David Ben-Gurion planned a comprehensive political reaction on the part of the Jewish people. His plan may be described as two contiguous triangles, with Aliyah Bet as the common side. The first triangle represented the reaction of world Jewry: its sides represented (1) the Jews of America and the rest of the free world, (2) the Jews of Europe under the threat of antisemitism and Nazi rule and (3) Aliyah Bet. The second triangle represented the response of the Yishuv: its sides represented (1) Aliyah Bet, (2) armed preparation and (3) settlement.

In February 1939, Ben-Gurion visited the United States for talks with Jewish leaders and financiers concerning the preparation of resources necessitated by his new political strategy. He spoke with Louis Brandeis, the veteran Zionist leader, in an attempt to secure the latter's support for Aliyah Bet. As Ben-Gurion saw it, only the American Jews were capable of mobilizing the funds required if Aliyah Bet were to expand its operations on a large scale. On May 24, 1939, after the publication of the White Paper, Ben-Gurion cabled Solomon Goldman, president of the Zionist Organization of America:

> We must and can bring in fifty thousand Jews, one thousand a week. For that we need £7,000 per week—our part is bringing them to Palestine. Consult with Brandeis and other friends to mobilize these funds, in addition to the needs of Keren Hayesod and the Jewish National Fund. According to reliable information at our disposal, the government will not be able to prevent this aliyah. Implementation of this plan means the failure of the White Paper, an incalculable reinforcement of the Jewish position and decisive preparedness in case of war.[2]

At this time, then, Aliyah Bet was the Jewish method of national struggle. Resistance to the White Paper policy was the task of the Jewish people in general; it was not the Yishuv that was most directly injured by the White Paper, but the Jews not yet in Palestine.

> Our war is for the right of those Jews who are not in Palestine . . . and it is their war that we must wage now, not a war for the independence of the four hundred and fifty thousand Jews living in Palestine. That is the fundamental difference between our war and the war of any nation firmly rooted in its land. For a nation like that, the main thing is to throw off the foreign yoke and to that end it adopts measures and ways of war. . . .
> The purpose of our war, however, is to open the gates of the land to the masses of Israel, to the Ingathering of the Exiles, to Jewish settlement, to the realization of Zionism—*this war demands special methods and appropriate means.*[3]

For Ben-Gurion, the major resources at the disposal of the Jewish people were the pressures brought about by mounting danger, the feeling of mutual responsibility, the attachment to Palestine felt by large sectors of the Jewish people and the large communities living under democratic regimes that could extend support to their brethren in distress. These various components could be successfully mobilized only thanks to the existence of Zionism; and it was Zionism that had been building the Yishuv for years. Only under the leadership and guidance of the Yishuv could the potential inherent in the Jewish people be realized, despite the weakness of many large communities and the dangers threatening them. Zionism could not confront the British army or administration with any chance of success unless it resorted to means made to its own measure—Aliyah Bet and the settlement of the land, primarily by the new immigrants themselves.

Paradoxically, the very existence of the Aliyah Bet organization, without the approval or permission of official policy and long before the Jewish Agency Executive was willing to opt for illegal measures, now made it possible for the leadership of the Yishuv to clearly and succinctly define the methods to be employed. At the same time, however, this preexisting apparatus was not suited to the demands now to be made on it by the new strategy. The Jewish Agency Executive found itself unable to create another system; moreover, it could not even significantly modify the established organization—mainly because it had failed to raise the funds necessary to implement what Ben-Gurion termed the "Aliyah Rebellion," and, also because all such modifications were fiercely resisted by the aliyah activists.

THE REVISIONIST MOVEMENT AND ALIYAH BET

At the beginning of 1939, the NZO likewise had to redefine its position vis-à–vis Aliyah Bet (or, in this instance, 'Aliyah Aẓmait). There were many factors motivating this reformulation of the Revisionist immigration policy, some of which were related to internal political problems, others to the organizational requirements of the aliyah itself.[4] But this was not all. A major motive for rethinking the strategy to be employed was the need to prepare for the imminent struggle against Britain in light of its expected reversal of policy regarding Jewish immigration to Palestine. Parallel to Ben-Gurion's aliyah rebellion, Zev Jabotinsky demanded an "aliyah of ten thousands," in other words, a defiant aliyah of tens of thousands of Jews within a short time, mainly young members of Betar whose military training in Eastern Europe had prepared them for resistance to attempts by the British army to prevent them landing in Palestine. These Betar members, Jabotinsky believed, would constitute a force ready to fight for genuine independence.

If they were to carry out an operation on so large a scale, the NZO activists clearly had no choice but to adopt centralized patterns of supervision and organization. And by the summer of 1939, after a prolonged period of preparation, the Aliyah Center in Paris, headed by a lawyer named Shlomo Yaakobi (Yankelewicz), had completed its plans to centralize its operations, which were now to proceed in all earnest. Emissaries of the Aliyah Center conducted negotiations with various shipping agencies, which offered them numerous ships at a variety of prices. Groups of immigrants assembled in Bratislava, Poland and Romania. An office was also opened in Athens, where it was hoped that it would be easier to deal with the shipping agencies and provide assistance and supplies to the immigrant ships en route from the Black Sea.

The plans for clandestine landing in Palestine, which were coordinated with the IZL there, involved not only landing teams, but also the preparation of small landing boats. The immigrants were to be transferred to these while still outside Palestinian territorial waters in order not to risk the confiscation of the larger and more expensive ships. From January 1939 until the outbreak of the Second World War, the efforts made by the Revisionist Aliyah Center as well as those by individual members of the movement brought some ten thousand immigrants to Palestine, approximately two-thirds of all the illegal immigrants during that period.

In sum, during the summer months of 1939, before the beginning of the Second World War, the operations of Aliyah Bet as organized by the two Zionist organizations and their aliyah centers in Europe were proceeding at an unprecedented pace. Even the most vehement opponents of Aliyah Bet, such as Chaim Weizmann and Joseph Sprinzak, admitted that, given Britain's "perfidy" and the publication of the White Paper, illegal immigration was a legitimate weapon of political struggle. Many Jewish leaders in European communities—in Germany, Austria, Czechoslovakia, the Balkans, Eastern and Western Europe—directly or indirectly supported Aliyah Bet. For Jews in countries under Nazi rule, whether natives of those countries or refugees from neighboring regions, this route represented their only hope of reaching Palestine. During the months of May to September 1939, some ten thousand illegal immigrants came to Palestine.

Nonetheless, six months later, by the spring of 1940, practically nothing was left of the organizational and operational drive of Aliyah Bet. The Revisionist Aliyah Center had closed down; only a small group of activists in Bucharest was still struggling with such questions as how to honor the unfulfilled commitments of the center and what to do about would-be immigrants and refugees from Poland. The Mossad le-Aliyah Bet (known simply as the Mossad)—the very formation of which in 1939 had embodied the resolve of the Jewish Agency Executive to assume responsibility for Aliyah Bet—was now faced with a critical situation. Its staff sensed that the support they had enjoyed during the spring and summer months of 1939 had dwindled to little more than a pleasant memory; and vague rumors were afoot that the Jewish Agency had decided to terminate Aliyah Bet.

Tens of thousands of Jews all over Europe, in cities under Nazi rule as well as those that were still free, were ready to set out for Palestine. Some had made all the preparations for the journey: they had sold their property and made all the necessary payments to the Nazi authorities in order to acquire exit permits. Now, however, they had to squander their savings while awaiting departure. Others were living in temporary camps on the banks of the Danube or in the Balkan capitals. It was still possible to leave territories under Nazi rule, and Jews were, in fact, encouraged to do so in some measure.

Why, then, were Aliyah Bet operations halted, even after the outbreak of the war, insofar as the first six months of hostilities witnessed no significant change in the situation that had prompted Jews to flee Europe and choose Aliyah Bet? After the first month of the war, when the occupation of Poland was completed, fighting died down and the so-called phoney war set in. Relative calm reigned in Southern and Western Europe and in the Mediterranean region.

We shall now examine and weigh the importance of the many different factors that caused the Mossad gradually to cease operations during the first part of the war, as well as the reasons for the resumption of Aliyah Bet in 1943. And it should be noted that although the reasons for the interruption of operations by the Mossad, on the one hand, and by the Revisionist Aliyah Center, on the other, were not identical, similar factors were certainly at work for each organization. Both bodies were guided by an awareness of the political changes created by the war, by their belief that these changes could not be ignored, by their consequent inclination to direct their efforts into new channels. Likewise, the Revisionist movement would be an indirect partner to the resumption of aliyah in 1943.

During the war years, some 16,500 immigrants reached Palestine in the framework of Aliyah Bet, out of a total of 53,000 immigrants. They arrived in three waves: in late 1939 and early 1940; again, in late 1940 and early 1941; and from the spring to the fall of 1944.

THE INTERRUPTION OF ALIYAH: GENERAL CAUSES

Aliyah came to a standstill because of objective factors confronting the operations and because of subjective factors related to a reassessment of Zionist priorities in conditions of war. On the objective side, shipping agents, middlemen and seamen felt that the war made Aliyah Bet activities far more dangerous, hence less lucrative. They feared military hostilities at sea, and these apprehensions were shared by the organizers in the Mossad and the Aliyah Center. Governments were less willing to grant permits and licenses for ships engaged in Aliyah Bet, whether because of the need to mobilize vessels for the increasing war effort or because of their heightened sensitivity to potential political pitfalls. Thus, Greece, Turkey and Romania now became more susceptible to pressures brought to bear by the British government and, as a result, created various bureaucratic difficulties that could be overcome only by bribery.

In addition, the wave of refugees from Poland alarmed the Balkan and Mediterranean countries. Faced with the prospect of large alien concentrations on their soil, the Balkan governments now imposed restrictions on the transit and entry of refugees. No less acute was the fear that enemy agents might infiltrate their territories disguised as immigrants, either willingly or because their families, left behind, were being held hostage by the Nazis. The net result of all these factors was, first, that the cost of transporting immigrants skyrocketed, increasing twofold or threefold (from £7 to 10 per immigrant in the summer of 1939 to £17 to 25 in the fall of 1939 and the following winter); second, that relations with various governments and political authorities became increasingly strained—a situation that also contributed to the increased cost of immigration as it became necessary to pay larger bribes to middlemen in order to procure licenses and permits.

When the war broke out, many agents voided contracts that had been concluded with aliyah activists. Such was the case, for example, with the ship *Dora,* which had been chartered to carry passengers assembled by the Mossad from Constantza in October 1939 and which was forced to cancel its departure. A similar problem beset the Revisionist Aliyah Center in September 1939 when the owner of the *Saint Bruck* repudiated an agreement concluded in August, thus stranding Polish immigrants at the Romanian-Polish border.[5] And these are merely examples. The demand for seaworthy vessels of all kinds increased, and there was no longer any financial advantage to commissioning old ships, which had been engaged in arms traffic to Spain during the civil war and were now available. The shipowners were now eager to make quick and large profits. Costs were also driven up both by the scarcity of available vessels, as governments found the means to keep their marine fleets available at all times, and by the internal competition among the various aliyah enterprises—the Mossad, the Revisionists and the few individual entrepreneurs still active in the field.

Britain upheld the policy of the White Paper, despite the outbreak of war, and there was no sign of any concessions in regard to immigration. The British authorities continued to wield the double-edged sword of intimidation and prevention against Aliyah Bet. To deter seamen and shipping agencies, the British government enacted a series of emergency regulations. The Royal Navy redoubled its efforts to intercept and confiscate immigrant ships in Palestinian territorial waters; shipowners had to pay heavy fines in order to recover their property; and crews were arrested and brought to trial. In the attempt to cut off the immigration at its source, Britain also exerted considerable political pressures on the Balkan and Turkish governments, demanding that they forbid ships flying their flags to participate in the campaign, that they prevent the transit of refugees through their territories and that they put a stop to the embarkation of would-be immigrants at their ports.[6]

THE MOSSAD AND THE CONTINUATION OF ALIYAH BET

In August 1939 the Mossad was about to implement a far-reaching plan that involved the transportation of thousands of Jews from Germany to Palestine in cooperation with a German shipping company, Hapag Lloyd. Immigrants were to set out from the German port of Hemden and continue via the North Sea and Gibraltar to Palestine. Near the Palestinian coast, the immigrants were to be transferred to other boats outside territorial waters, thus eliminating the risk that Hapag's ships might be confiscated by the British coast guard.[7] Other plans involved refugees gathered in Hungary who were to sail down the Danube to the Black Sea.

All the aliyah activists attended the Twenty-first Zionist Congress in Geneva in August 1939, where they discussed their further plans at length. Hopes for more intensive and far-flung operations ran high, particularly in view of Berl Katznelson's supportive speech at a plenary session and repeated assurances by Ben-Gurion at meetings of both the labor faction and the Political Committee. Discussions between the emissaries and delegates of the Histadrut labor federation to the congress also encouraged increasing optimism, since there was widespread agreement that only through aliyah could the movement best continue to resist the British policies.

News of the Molotov-Ribbentrop Pact on August 23 aroused grave forebodings of imminent war, which apart from all else could sever communications between Palestine and the Diaspora. The delegates from the Histadrut and the labor movement at the congress met to discuss what the Palestinian emissaries in Europe should now do. Most of the speakers felt that they should immediately return to their posts abroad, weighing their future actions in accordance with the specific situation in their area. Opinions varied as to the future awaiting the Jews in Germany and as to the prospects of getting them out. One of the emissaries, Pino Ginzburg, believed that the Germans would no longer permit Jews to leave, but intended to intern them in labor camps and exploit them as manpower in the war effort. At the same time, he thought that the emissaries ought to return to Germany in order to continue their educational and pioneering work as long as the government permitted it. All those present agreed that it was imperative to use whatever time remained to expedite the execution of existing plans.

The aliyah activists did indeed return to their posts immediately after the rather abrupt conclusion of the congress, but a few weeks later, following the outbreak of the war, Yehudah Braginsky instructed most of them to leave Europe. Pino Ginzburg left Germany for the Netherlands: the master plan for immigration from Germany was no longer feasible and it was dangerous to stay in Germany. No aliyah emissaries now remained in the countries under the control of the Third Reich, and those still in Europe were hard put to maintain communications with the Jewish communities there or to obtain reliable information about the prospects for aliyah. The representatives of the Yishuv in Poland decided to return to Palestine; thus, by the fall of 1939, the Jewish communities under Nazi rule were left almost completely without Palestinian emissaries.[8]

At the very beginning of the war, Jewish Agency leaders informed the British government of their readiness to participate in the war effort in any possible way. Nonetheless, the basic political conception of militant Zionism had not changed: uncompromising resistance to the policy of the White Paper. What had changed was the emphasis on an element implicit in the very concept of militant Zionism—cooperation with the democracies in the war against fascism. Ben-Gurion, in explaining the nature of militant Zionism, had repeatedly invested the idea of "combat" or "fighting" with a double meaning. For example, in a meeting with youth-movement members in the spring of 1939, he had declared that militant Zionism was directed not against the people or the British Empire, but against her policies; to emphasize his meaning, he continued, "We may soon have to face a bitter world conflict, which could be crucial for the fate of mankind. And if this conflict should indeed take place, we shall all stand—together with many other nations—at England's side in battle, against Hitler and Mussolini."[9] In his cable to Solomon Goldman (mentioned earlier), Ben-Gurion referred to militant Zionism as part of the preparation for the imminent war.

After the outbreak of hostilities, therefore, militant Zionism took on new dimensions and connotations: simultaneously "with Britain and against Britain." And though this dualism had always been present, its actual meaning in terms of concrete policies now had to be worked out under very different circumstances. The practical implications of Aliyah Bet were particularly problematic. The policy of armed defense, after all, could be implemented in the context of cooperation with the British war effort, even though the Yishuv leadership and the British government had differing goals. Land could be purchased far from the public eye. The arrival of illegal immigrant boats, however, was an open affront, a tangible expression of the conflict with Great Britain.

This fact was clearly demonstrated during the very first week of the war, upon the arrival in Palestine of the ships *Tiger Hill* and *Naomi Julia*. In the violent clashes that ensued with the British coast guard there were fatal casualties among the immigrants, and the Yishuv was faced with a serious dilemma. Could the incidents be ignored, left without response? Only one month earlier, in August, David Hacohen had received instructions that the Haganah should react to British deportations of illegal immigrants by holding mass demonstrations in Haifa. Should these instructions now be canceled? The issue raised grave moral issues: Had the Yishuv's obligation to the persecuted refugees indeed changed overnight? Was the mutual responsibility of Jews the world over merely an empty phrase?[10]

The question of aliyah during the war was raised during meetings of the Jewish Agency Executive and of the Mapai leadership that sought to formulate policy with regard to the political situation: aid to the refugees who had just arrived in Romania, Hungary and the Soviet Union; and the Jewish citizens of the Third Reich who possessed immigration certificates but had been forbidden entry by the British authorities as enemy aliens. It is on the basis of these discussions that one can understand the position of the leadership toward aid and rescue operations during the early months of the war. Demands were made calling for more vigorous efforts to raise funds in Palestine for the refugees; it was suggested that use be made to that end of monetary deposits belonging to the Jewish National Fund and Keren Hayesod in the Balkans, and that contributions be solicited in the United States through the *Landsmanshaften*. Subsequently, Shlomo Lipsky went to Hungary and Yosef Barpal to Romania as representatives of the Jewish Agency, with a free hand to utilize the resources of Keren Hayesod and the Jewish National Fund. They were told to report on the nature and extent of the problems and suggest means for dealing with them.[11] Katznelson, speaking at a meeting of the Mapai Central Council, expressed a view that was prevalent in the first few months of the war:

> First of all—aliyah must go on. I don't know if people are thinking about that in this country [the Yishuv]. It might seem fantastic in time of war, but nevertheless we must

not relent. Many of those who have been dealing with it think that the whole thing has been stopped. It hasn't been stopped, it must go on. Thousands of refugees, and perhaps tens of thousands who will find themselves in the position of refugees tomorrow, will be left with no other escape. We must rescue whomever we can. If we are not going to make do with what the war gives us for nothing, but, rather, are to make plans in order to ensure gains during the war, gains in this country that will perhaps determine our fate, then we must be concerned with aliyah no less than with armed battalions. We have missed many chances, we have lost much. And we are losing every day. . . . *The gates must be opened now*—it is still possible to get out of those countries [of the Third Reich]. The Youth Aliyah, and the German training schemes [*hakhsharah*] are carrying on. There will be groups to leave there even after the war.[12]

For his part, Ben-Gurion continued to advocate a political approach to Aliyah Bet. To his mind it was still a component of militant Zionism whose educational function was now even more important because of the war.

When war broke out, the Zionist leaders felt somewhat ambivalent about the wide measure of identification with Britain's struggle expressed by the Yishuv at large. For politicians such as David Ben-Gurion, Moshe Shertok (later Sharett), Yitzhak Tabenkin and Berl Katznelson, it would be an error if identification with Britain at war were to undermine the determination to resist her Zionist policy. They believed that a decision to support Aliyah Bet would contribute to the clarification of Zionist policy as a whole, although such a decision would seem to involve inner contradictions—"together with, and against, [Britain] at the same time." Ben-Gurion articulated this approach at Mapai meetings and at the Jewish Agency Executive, suggesting that Aliyah Bet be viewed, inter alia, as a means of teaching the Yishuv when to support Britain and when to oppose her.[13] His viewpoint was buttressed and expanded by those who had already called for the continuation of illegal immigration despite the outbreak of war. Some of them demanded that as long as the Mediterranean Sea routes were open, efforts should be made to bring thousands of immigrants to Palestine, thus ensuring Jewish domination of the country after the war and the establishment of a Jewish state. As with Ben-Gurion, they, too, were looking at Aliyah Bet from a political point of view.

As a result, when some of the Aliyah Bet emissaries reached Palestine in September and October, it was decided that they should return to Europe in order to continue operations. First and foremost, the Mossad was concerned to fulfill its commitments to those groups of immigrants who had been about to embark when the war broke out; some of these were still in the Third Reich or under Nazi occupation. The Jewish Agency Executive allocated funds from its budget to bring out twelve hundred of the two thousand prospective immigrants in the Reich who were ready to leave. Further funds would be raised in the United States (an appeal had already been discussed in August at the Zionist Congress) in order to permit implementation of the many existing plans; Eliyahu Golomb accordingly left for America. As early as October, Moshe Shertok was involved in efforts to raise funds for Aliyah Bet in the Netherlands with the aim of financing the immigration of all the remaining German Jews who had fled there, in addition to those Dutch Jews who feared a German invasion.[14]

Efforts to broaden Aliyah Bet and put it on a firm basis continued throughout the fall of 1939 and during the first months of 1940. Golomb, in America, worked hard raising funds, securing support from prominent Jewish leaders and buying up options for ships; he even obtained the cooperation of the Revisionist-founded American Friends for a Jewish Palestine. All this was aimed at promoting Aliyah Bet operations and guaranteeing the necessary financial resources. Manya Shohat, sent by the Histadrut for the same purpose, made contacts both with American philanthropists and non-Zionist Jewish leaders, such as Cyrus Adler.[15]

It soon became clear, however, that this political approach was far more complex than had been expected. As early as November 13, Shertok recorded in his diary an argument between himself and Ben-Gurion concerning the British decision to refuse entry to Jewish citizens of enemy countries holding immigration certificates issued before the war. Shertok wrote:

Ben-Gurion asserted that our political future is more important than rescuing 2,900 Jews; he was willing to abandon them. I disagreed absolutely with this view. I do not believe in a conflict between our political future and bringing in thousands of Jews, which means rescuing them. Theoretically, one might envisage a decisive political victory, an opportunity not worth risking for the sake of some minor rescue or aid operation that undermines our political position. In practice, however, that is not the case. The political victory is dubious, whereas the rescue of thousands of Jews is a certainty. The mere fact that we have successfully brought in these thousands in spite of Malcolm MacDonald is a political victory in itself.[16]

This issue was only one of the many involved in negotiating with Britain about immigration and refugee relief. It was politically expedient to avoid stressing disagreement and friction; but this was impossible so long as aliyah was the most urgent item on the agenda. It is often clear that the leaders of the Yishuv did not necessarily hold different positions; the conflict was sometimes an internal one within each person who could express contradictory views at different times. One could thus hear Katznelson, Shertok, Ben-Gurion and others expressing conflicting or ambiguous positions on different occasions—sometimes even on the same occasion.

Ultimately, however, the Zionist policymakers could not in all conscience continue to support Aliyah Bet while ignoring the fact that it might compromise their position in serious discussions with Britain about the establishment of a Jewish army or other aspects of the participation in the war effort. Although this evaluation was disputed, it was underpinned by warnings that the Yishuv was not strong enough to allocate resources to both goals at once—Aliyah Bet and voluntary military service. Though this view, too, was not without its opponents, it was necessary to determine a system of political priorities as to the relations between Britain and the Yishuv. As Ben-Gurion declared at a meeting of the Jewish Agency Executive on September 17, 1939, "At the time of the White Paper we said, Jewish aliyah with or without and even against England. . . . And now, proposing a Jewish state, I say, with or without England—but not against."[17]

The impression one gets from the sparse material available about the decision-making process regarding Aliyah Bet is that no clear-cut decision was made to stop immigration. However, from December 1939 until the spring of 1940, the support that Aliyah Bet had enjoyed during the first months of the war dwindled steadily.

The subject came up for discussion several times at official meetings of the Jewish Agency Executive and in private meetings between Histadrut (and apparently also Haganah) leaders. Attention was drawn at these talks to the growing difficulties attendant on Aliyah Bet operations, and doubts were expressed about whether they should be continued.

This phase in the changing attitude toward Aliyah Bet can perhaps be called a period of doubt. The most weighty arguments against the "expedience" of the illegal immigration were economic. Aliyah exacted a high price, and Palestine was in the throes of an economic crisis brought on by the war. Some of the European markets were now closed to exported citrus and other produce, and this situation, coupled with apprehensions that the crisis might spread, created an atmosphere of uncertainty and hesitation. The Jewish Agency's income diminished because part of the money raised by the Keren Hayesod and the Jewish National Fund did not reach Palestine, and it was difficult to predict how the war would affect people's readiness to contribute. Unemployment increased and the Jewish Agency was faced with the problem of supporting the jobless. Immigrant absorption became an even more difficult task, and the various institutions engaged in resettlement, such as kibbutzim, requested more aid for each immigrant. Increasingly, appeals were addressed to the Jewish Agency Executive for funds to aid displaced persons in Europe and to help bring in owners of immigration certificates. The Mandatory government granted the Jewish Agency a large loan that enabled it to grapple with welfare needs and plan the development of new enterprises to alleviate the economic crisis.

Coupled with these economic considerations, traditional arguments against Aliyah Bet were also brought into play. Opponents blamed it for the British suspension of the legal immigration quota, which had held up the aliyah of wealthy Jews and pioneers—both needed by the country; in addition, opponents claimed, Aliyah Bet lessened the chances of economic recovery and, hence, of future increases in the number of immigrants.

No less troubling was the British argument that the Nazis would take advantage of the immigrant ships to plant spies in the Middle East and set up a fifth column; that was the only explanation, it was claimed, for their willingness to permit the departure of able-bodied Jews. This argument, though rejected out of hand by the Jewish Agency, left its mark on some of those who were negotiating with the British authorities. Weizmann and Shertok offered Britain full cooperation in collecting information and investigating suspects. They reiterated, on the one hand, that it was hard to imagine some of the immigrants could be spies; but, on the other hand, the considerable information at the disposal of the Jewish Agency concerning the Jews in Germany and the occupied countries would be made available to the British.

Shertok shared these misgivings with the Aliyah Bet activists at a meeting in Geneva in February 1940. His diary provides a summary of the meeting:

> On Sunday morning I had a long conversation with Z. A. and his colleagues [the reference is apparently to Moshe Agami, the Hebrew initial *zayin* being a slip of the pen for *mem*]. I told them of the prevailing mood at home because of the economic situation, the financial situation of the Jewish Agency, the vital necessity for some aliyah and the possibilities on that count. I explained to them that for the last few months

emphasis had shifted from resistance to the White Paper to the need to stand firm and fortify ourselves in this time of emergency, for who knows how long it will last.[18]

Shertok's talks with the emissaries in Geneva persuaded him, as he wrote in his diary, that the aliyah could not be stopped. The activists told him that Jews would try to escape from the Third Reich and the occupied countries as long as they could and that, if the Mossad failed to take up the challenge, the Revisionists and private individuals would to so—as had been the case to some extent in the previous few months. Shertok was profoundly shaken by a meeting in Geneva with Jacob Edelstein of Prague, who described the fate of the Jews who had been deported to Lublin, but who also emphasized that the Nazis were still anxious to maintain emigration.[19] Edelstein stressed that emigration was the only possible solution for the Jews of the Third Reich; it was the moral and political duty of the Zionist movement and the Mossad to make it possible.

However, Shertok failed to deliver the message clearly and unambiguously at the meetings of the Jewish Agency Executive in London and Jerusalem. Moreover, a short time later, at a meeting of the Zionist Executive in London, he said nothing of the Geneva meetings, although he did speak of the importance of aliyah in general and referred to the contribution of Aliyah Bet to immigrants since the beginning of the war. Indeed, the entry in his diary is the only evidence of his Geneva meetings. Neither did he come out strongly in support of Aliyah Bet in the spring of 1940 when Zionist policy and the work of the aliyah activists in Europe were being discussed.

The explanation for this somewhat surprising silence must be sought in the line of reasoning developed by Shertok while in Geneva—reasoning that was considerably reinforced by the events of the winter and spring of 1940. After the promulgation of the Land Regulations of February 1940, the struggle against the White Paper took a new turn, centering on activities within Palestine—the purchase of land and the planning of settlement. The Land Regulations could be circumvented within the framework of the legal system and by offering attractive prices to Arab landowners, who were ready at that time to sell their lands to Jews. This course of action met with some measure of success; despite the stringent regulations, the acquisition of land continued and new settlements sprang up. A proposal, not actually implemented, was even made to establish a special Land Department, in addition to the Department for Aliyah and Settlement, which would devise ways and means to purchase land, despite the new law.[20]

At any rate, Zionist politicians now shifted their position vis-à-vis Aliyah Bet from doubt to an actual lack of initiative. The transition to this new phase was also caused by the greater hopes for extensive cooperation with Britain prompted by appointment of the new British prime minister, Winston Churchill, who was known to be a staunch supporter of Zionism and a firm opponent of the White Paper.

At a meeting of the Jewish Agency Executive in Jerusalem on April 14, 1940, Ben-Gurion—the activist who had previously demanded a stern and uncompromising attitude toward the White Paper—declared that although militant Zionism should not be abandoned it should be given a different emphasis. He proposed a further extension of its meaning: militant Zionism, he believed, should address itself to manifestations of antisemitism among Mandatory officials in Palestine; uphold the prerogative of every Jewish child to fly the Zionist flag in Tel-Aviv; defend the right of the Yishuv to maintain an independent Jewish educational system. But where in this context was aliyah, that same aliyah that had been the overriding ideal of militant Zionism in prewar years? Ben-Gurion had this to say, "Today, aliyah is not in our hands. . . . The seas are ruled by the British navy. . . . Instead, what we need now is a militant Zionism that will strengthen and build up the Zionist movement."[21] This position won support from many of the more moderate leaders, such as Eliezer Kaplan, then treasurer of the Jewish Agency, Joseph Sprinzak, a leading member of Hapoel Hazair, who was known for his moderate views, and Werner Senator, the non-Zionist representative on the Jewish Agency Executive.

A few weeks later, a decisive discussion about Aliyah Bet took place in London. Zvi Yehieli, one of the chief Mossad emissaries in Geneva, reached the conclusion that cooperation with the organizers of aliyah in the Third Reich, even if not affiliated with the Mossad and Hehalutz, was now unavoidable. It was necessary to procure the leadership's agreement to cooperate with Berthold Storfer in Vienna, who was responsible—with the Nazi's blessing—for emigration from the Reich territories. Storfer was a Viennese businessman who had been active in 1938 in organizing the emigration of Jews from Austria through his travel agency. In 1939, he set up an independent Ausschuss für Jüdische Überseetransporte. In 1940, this office became—on Nazi orders—the sole agency for organizing Jewish emigration from the entire Reich. Zionist movement workers in Austria, Germany and Prague had reservations about Storfer. So did Mossad activists, of whom a number had known Storfer since 1938. Various attempts were made to challenge Storfer's authority, mainly by avoiding any cooperation with him.[22]

However, by the spring of 1940, Yehieli—who was aware of the great difficulties involved in organizing Aliyah Bet and who had already tried to avoid cooperating with Storfer—realized that the principle would have to be compromised. There was no choice but to come to terms with the man; perhaps, Yehieli believed, it would be possible through Storfer to fulfill the outstanding commitments of the Mossad to various immigrant groups still in Europe. Yehieli, ambivalent about his own decision, knew that such cooperation would create a serious problem for the Zionist politicians, who were afraid, among other things, that the Nazis might exploit their control of Storfer's travel agency to plant their own agents among the immigrants. This would justify the British security-based arguments against permitting Jewish immigration from the Third Reich. Nevertheless, he hoped to convince the Zionist leaders of the urgent need to cooperate with Storfer. After lengthy deliberations he was successful, though the agreement was not without reservations.

However, in the course of the discussions, Yehieli realized that the entire undertaking of Aliyah Bet was in grave danger. Kaplan stated quite bluntly that the Jewish Agency Executive had decided to discontinue Aliyah Bet. On demanding Ben-Gurion's confirmation, Yehieli was told that the Executive had not actually decided to halt operations but that it was no longer responsible for them.[23] At the same time, Ben-Gurion emphasized the great importance of bringing pioneers to Palestine by means of Aliyah Bet. The British, he said, had granted only 180 immigration certificates in the workers' quota; thus, even if they were to deduct the number of pioneers arriving under the auspices of Aliyah Bet from the overall quota, the workers' quota would not be affected. Could Yehieli have understood from all this that Ben-Gurion was nevertheless interested in continued aliyah, despite his comment on Kaplan's statement? Or was this perhaps still another manifestation of the ambiguous attitude toward the Aliyah Bet?

Failure begets failure, as the Mossad members were to discover. All but one of their undertakings during the fall of 1939 and the beginning of 1940 ended badly. In January 1940, they finally landed the immigrant ship *Hilda* in Palestinian waters. It carried immigrants who had set out in October 1939 and had been delayed at the port of Balaczek on the Romanian-Bulgarian border. It proved impossible to obtain a more seaworthy vessel than the *Hilda* for the voyage through the Black Sea and the Mediterranean. As a result, the 750 immigrants remained on the *Hilda* until January 1940, living under difficult conditions and becoming increasingly bitter. Similarly, during those same months, more than 1,500 people were stranded at the port of Sulina, Romania (these immigrants later reached Palestine aboard the *Sakariya* in February 1940), and the Revisionist Aliyah Center, which was responsible for them, was unable to send them on their way. The fate of the two groups, which were lumped together in the public eye, received extensive publicity in the international press, resulting in considerable damage to the activities of the Mossad and undermining confidence in their ability to operate after the outbreak of war.[24]

The Mossad was no more successful in finding a solution for other immigrant groups—the largest of them numbered 1,100 persons who were waiting on river boats in the Yugoslav port of Kladovo on the Danube. These immigrants had been organized for departure in November 1939 by the Hehalutz office in Vienna, under the direction of Ehud Avriel and with the blessing of the Mossad. About half of the more than 1,000 immigrants were members of youth movements and pioneers from Austria, Germany and the city-state of Danzig; among the other half were veteran activists of the Zionist movement and "unaffiliated" Jews. The group set out on its way for fear of the deportations to Lublin, although the Mossad had no ship available to carry them down to the Black Sea. Avriel and the Mossad representatives in Geneva hoped that such a ship would soon be found. However, their efforts were in vain, and in April 1940, the Kladovo group was still stranded, after a difficult, cold winter on the boats.[25]

Such failures deterred prospective supporters of the Aliyah Bet, and the activists found themselves trapped in a vicious circle that was not easily broken. A combination of circumstances—the difficulty of hiring ships and limited financial resources (resulting, among other things, from the Jewish Agency Executive's halfhearted support for Aliyah Bet) coupled with the restrictions on transferring foreign currency into and out of Third Reich territories—all this created unprecedented constraints. True, it is hard to judge whether the efforts of the Mossad would have met with greater success had more generous resources been available. However, the objective situation militated against even the best-made plans.

In November and December 1940, the problematic nature of Aliyah Bet came to the fore both in the public eye and at the political, decision-making level. The Zionist leaders had to cope simultaneously with two problems: preventing the deportation of refugees already in Palestine and successfully landing immigrants already aboard Mossad ships. The first problem arose in connection with the so-called three ships affair.

The three ships, chartered by Berthold Storfer—the steamers *Milos, Pacific* and *Atlantic*—reached Palestine in November 1940. The Mandatory government decided to deport the 3,552 passengers to the island of Mauritius in the Indian Ocean and transshipped some 2,000 passengers (all of those from the *Milos* and the *Pacific*, plus some from the *Atlantic*) to the *Patria*. The Jewish Agency Executive launched a full-scale political offensive to prevent the deportation; it failed. On November 26, the ship was sabotaged by Mossad agents with the intention of disabling it. However, the agents miscalculated the quantity of explosives needed and the *Patria* sank immediately, with the loss of 267 immigrants. The survivors, together with the group from the *Atlantic* that had not been aboard the *Patria*, were interned for some time at the detention camp in Atlit. The British authorities eventually decided to permit the survivors of the *Patria* tragedy to stay in Palestine but to deport the approximately 1,500 other immigrants from the *Atlantic* as originally planned.[26]

The Jewish Agency Executive and the Yishuv were shocked by the tragedy, which came after weeks of tension, anxiety and hopes that the deportation order would be canceled. A wave of anti-British declarations and feelings swept the country. The Jewish Agency Executive, which had been unable to avert the decision to deport the remaining immigrants from the *Atlantic*, feared a direct clash with the British authorities during the actual deportation. This, however, was carried out in secrecy on December 5. Although the immigrants themselves attempted to resist by force, there was no demonstrative protest on the part of the Yishuv. Clearly, a considerable change had occurred in the attitude of both the public and many Zionist leaders regarding Aliyah Bet and the deportation of illegal immigrants.

The second problem arose in connection with the steamer *Darien 2*, which became the subject of a heated debate between, on the one hand, those members of the Haganah and the Jewish Agency Executive responsible for cooperation with Britain in intelligence matters and, on the other hand, the activists of Aliyah Bet. *Darien 2* had been purchased by the Mossad in May 1940 after their numerous fruitless attempts to find a ship for the Kladovo group, which by then had been stranded in Yugoslavia for more than six months. In June 1940, it was decided to suspend aliyah operations in view of the dangerous situation in the Mediterranean Sea after Italy's entry into the war. A few weeks later, early in July, the *Darien 2* was handed over to David Hacohen and Yehudah Arazi, both of the Haganah, for planned use (in cooperation with Britain) in sabotage operations on the Danube.

Toward the end of the summer of 1940, it became clear that marine traffic in the Black Sea and the Mediterranean was continuing, and the Mossad decided to make another attempt to bring the Kladovo group to Palestine. As Britain was in no hurry to carry out the joint sabotage operations and had made no use of *Darien 2*, the Mossad leaders decided—with Hacohen and Arazi in agreement—to exploit the hazy dividing line between the activists of the Aliyah Bet and the intelligence men in order to restore *Darien 2* to its original function. The ship accordingly returned to Istanbul and was delivered to the Mossad agents.

Owing to various obstacles, the plan had still not been implemented by December

1940. While *Darien 2* was waiting for the Kladovo group at the port of Sulina—with 160 persons aboard—Hacohen and Arazi demanded the return of the ship, which was now needed for the originally planned sabotage operations. The aliyah activists received instructions from Palestine to deliver the *Darien 2* to Arazi and Hacohen. Arguments broke out among the Mossad agents in Istanbul, some of whom were willing to comply and relinquish the ship, whereas others refused point-blank.[27]

The loss of the *Patria,* the deportation to Mauritius and the dispute over *Darien 2* provided the background for an exchange of letters between Shertok and Weizmann in December 1940 and January 1941. These represent the third phase in the attitude of Zionist policy toward Aliyah Bet, namely, renunciation: the entire undertaking was simply dropped from the Zionist agenda. In late 1940 and early 1941, there was a danger that Aliyah Bet might hinder the efforts of political Zionism, for it stressed and gave priority to short-term at the expense of long-term goals; and the Zionist policymakers were by now convinced that it had become unjustifiable to take such a risk.[28]

Writing to Weizmann on December 17, 1940, Shertok reported on the stormy events of the few weeks since the arrival of the *Pacific* in Palestine. He described the prevalent mood in the country and the argument now raging both in public and in the governing bodies of the Yishuv about the sinking of the *Patria,* which again—but with new urgency—placed a question mark over Aliyah Bet as a whole. His conclusion, he wrote, was that the political struggle should focus on the replacement of the high commissioner. His letter made no mention of Aliyah Bet, an omission that admits one of two interpretations. Either Shertok was aware of Weizmann's negative attitude toward Aliyah Bet and was therefore reluctant to raise the subject while the Mossad was attempting to end the ordeal of the Kladovo group; or Shertok himself no longer believed it possible to achieve the goals of Aliyah Bet under existing conditions and thus ignored the subject.

Weizmann agreed with Shertok regarding the high commissioner; and he wrote that efforts had to continue regarding the practical problems on the political agenda, in particular the need to pursue plans for closer cooperation with Britain. To illustrate the degree of compromise that might be necessary to reduce the conflicts of interest between the Yishuv and Britain, he pointed to the argument about the use of *Darien 2,* and in so doing touched directly on the issue of Aliyah Bet. He had been warned, he wrote, by a British intelligence officer (probably one Colonel Simmonds, an important and sympathetic contact between Britain and the Zionist movement) that the sailing of even a single illegal immigrant aboard the *Darien 2* might have dire results for *"all their common interests"* (emphasis added). Moreover, the warning continued, such a course of action would substantiate claims that the Jews were not dependable, since in any clash of interests between Britain and the Zionists, loyalty to the latter would prevail. For the British, the incident of the *Darien 2* exemplified the contradiction between the two forms of Zionist commitment: that to Aliyah Bet and that to cooperative action in the joint war effort.

Although Weizmann contemptuously rejected this argument, he was aware of its cogency. Unfortunately, Weizmann wrote to Shertok, Zionists offering their cooperation were not considered on a par with other allies, such as the French or the

Poles. No one claimed that the latter could not be loyal allies and at the same time identify with their own national interests. The Zionists, however, were always suspect. But this was just one more manifestation of the anomalous relationship between Jews and gentiles. The only remedy for such anomalies would be the establishment of a Jewish state. That was the real goal and, to achieve it, cooperation was indispensable. Once they had opted for a strategy of joint action, therefore, the Zionists had no choice but to bow their heads and give in, even when faced with unjust and objectionable demands.

Weizmann's conclusion was quite obvious: cooperation with Britain was a sine qua non; all efforts should concentrate on that goal and anything that interfered with it—specifically, Aliyah Bet—had to be postponed. At that time, Weizmann was not alone in this position. He was supported not only by Shertok, but also by Eliyahu Golomb, who only one year before had been raising funds for Aliyah Bet.

On March 19, *Darien 2* finally entered Haifa port, with 786 illegal immigrants who were immediately arrested by the British. The Mossad, for its part, did not resume Aliyah Bet activities for some twenty months.

WHY WAS ALIYAH BET RESUMED IN 1944?

In the last two years of the war, Aliyah Bet reemerged as a combined effort of the Yishuv and political Zionism. The resumption of illegal immigration was the outcome of a process that comprised three components: comprehension of the scope and significance of the Final Solution, attempts to consolidate a rescue policy and realization of the limited and meager achievements of Zionist policy up to that time. All these factors prompted a quest for new operational targets to further the achievement of Zionist goals.

During the war, it had become quite clear that a tactical shift in Zionist policy was necessary. Participation in the Allied war effort and the projected Jewish army to fight Hitler did not materialize as hoped. By the end of 1941, it was painfully obvious that Britain would not support the establishment of a Jewish army; it was not even willing to recruit special Jewish units within the British army. Moreover, the favorable changes that had occurred in the British cabinet—the prime minister and two senior ministers were now supporters of Zionism—had not affected the inflexible White Paper policies with regard to the fundamental issues of immigration and land purchase. British leaders were primarily interested in maintaining good relations with the Arabs. Consequently, various attempts were made to bring the Arab states together under British influence. For Zionist leaders, it became increasingly obvious that the basic assumptions underlying Zionist policymaking at the beginning of the war had proved unrealistic. There was no alternative, therefore, but to adopt different political tactics.

Such a change of direction was made possible by the enhanced economic and paramilitary capacity built up by the Yishuv during the 1930s and the first years of the war—and, in tragic contrast, by the catastrophe overtaking the Jewish people in Europe. In such a situation, the basic ideological arguments heard on the eve of the war could now reemerge with renewed force: the Jewish refugee problem could not be tackled apart from the Palestine question. These arguments had immediate implications for Zionist policy.

Various governments-in-exile had promised to grant the Jews absolute equality under their regimes when the war was won. Such assurances contained an implicit threat to the Zionist argument that large-scale Jewish immigration to Palestine was the only option. In the view of the Zionist leaders, any solution that did not take aliyah into account was utterly unrealistic. As early as December 17, 1941, Shertok told Oliver Littleton:

> You must know that at the end of the war Jews will swim to Palestine. This was already the case at the end of the last war: after the pogroms against the Jews of the Ukraine, Jews crossed the Black Sea in fishing boats to get to Palestine. After all, what is happening now in Poland and Rumania, what has befallen Jewry in the Nazi countries and occupied territories is incomparably worse than what happened in the Ukraine at the end of the last war.[29]

It was the inevitability of aliyah, a result of millions pressing to reach Palestine, that would convince the Great Powers to agree to the establishment of a Jewish state in Palestine. Once again, the demand for the foundation of a Jewish state arose, for otherwise Zionism might find itself in an untenable situation after the war as well.[30] This common position enabled Ben-Gurion and Weizmann to cooperate in an effort to persuade the American Zionists to agree to their program in May 1942 in New York and later, in October, in Jerusalem. Known as the Biltmore Program, the plan called for the establishment of a Jewish state in western Palestine and reiterated that this end would solve—and be made possible by—the Jewish refugee problem in postwar Europe. Henceforth, the combination of both problems, that of the refugees and that of Palestine, would be the fundamental element in Zionist strategy.

These tactics had to contend with two stumbling blocks within the Zionist movement itself: first, there was much opposition to the idea of a Jewish state in the near future, which was motivated variously by objections to the borders of the proposed state or by other aspects of the Arab-Jewish relationship; second, there was the fear that the Jews of Europe might not necessarily want to come to Palestine after the war (until late 1942 no one had thought of asking where the millions of immigrants would come from). It was the task of the Zionist Executive to tackle these two problems. The position with respect to the first problem was clearly defined by Shertok at the Histadrut conference of April 1942. In an attempt to find the broadest common denominator shared by the various blocs within the Histadrut, he said:

> We, for our part, must be ready to demand one thing only: aliyah. That is all we need. We do not need a state, we do not need sovereignty. We ourselves are in no need of that. What we are aspiring to create here is a free life for great masses of Jews. If that is possible without a state—let there be no state; if that is possible without sovereignty— let there be no sovereignty. These are means and perhaps there are other means; they are not ends in themselves. But when the Arabs tell us: No immigration! and when the English tell us: In this situation, with the Arabs saying no, we cannot promise you immigration, we must say: Leave it to us, and we shall do it! In other words, give us control of immigration. But what does "control of immigration" mean? Control of immigration means: control of the law, control of the administration in this country, of

the entire regime in the country, of trade relations, of land for settlement, of public works. Control of aliyah means state funding; [it] means, in one word, a state. If so, we must say: Let there be a state![31]

This tactical approach, the demand for "control of aliyah" and the immediate immigration of two million (later, one million) Jews, was the declared policy of the Jewish Agency Executive until the end of the war. However, the plan was to be implemented by legal means, with the help of the Great Powers, utilizing systems of transportation that had been built up and consolidated during the war years. The model for a project of this type—mentioned during the deliberations of the Executive—was the transfer of Greeks from Turkey to Greece after the First World War. Ben-Gurion regarded this as an operation to be studied and imitated.[32]

Aliyah Bet in the last years of the war was not meant to take the place of mass immigration, nor was it expected to bring in millions of people. But it was one way of accomplishing the rescue of Jews in Europe, of reaching the remnants of Jewry and inspiring them to immigrate to Palestine and participate in the Zionist effort.

Realization of the dimensions of the catastrophe that had overtaken the Jewish people dawned on the Yishuv and its leaders in November 1942. One month before, a group of seventy-six men, women and children, Palestinian citizens who had been stranded in Europe when war broke out, arrived in Palestine as part of an exchange program. At the very beginning of the war, the Jewish Agency had requested Britain to propose that Germany permit the Palestinians to return in exchange for German nationals in a similar predicament. The negotiations, conducted through Swiss mediation, dragged on for months until a first small group of Jews reached Palestine in January 1941. Their accounts of the European situation—systematic implementation of the Final Solution had not yet begun—failed to make a deep impression on the Yishuv. The second group, however, was able to describe the destruction of Jewry at the height of the Final Solution, and the Yishuv and world Jewry were shaken to the core.

Testimony from this group corroborated news of the Final Solution that had begun to filter through to the West in the spring of 1942, and thus made possible a full awareness of the fate engulfing European Jewry. These reports were given wide publicity in the press a few weeks after the final approval in Jerusalem of the Biltmore Program, which, as noted, demanded the establishment of a Jewish commonwealth in western Palestine and which called for the immigration of two million Jewish survivors after the war. The effect was dramatic in the extreme: it now became apparent that the millions around whom the Zionist claims revolved—the same millions who were expected to knock at the gates of Palestine and "swim there" if not granted legal entry—had to a large extent already been annihilated.

A detailed examination of the effect of this information on the public and on the Zionist leadership is beyond the scope of this essay.[33] Nevertheless, it is worth noting that some voices were heard declaring that Zionism should be abandoned altogether as nobody was left to carry the movement forward to its goals. The Zionist leadership was apprehensive about the effect this viewpoint might exert on influential circles outside the movement. However, Jewish leaders in Palestine and the unoccupied parts of Europe did not subscribe to this view. On the contrary, for the overwhelming majority, the Zionist movement and the Yishuv were viewed as the only real guarantee of Jewish survival. Such terms as "remnant" and "surviving remnant," which cropped up in the Jewish Agency Executive, the Zionist Executive and other bodies during the earliest discussions of the catastrophe testify to the conviction that, despite the Holocaust, the hope of redemption was still alive.[34] Together with the other obligations of the movement, the rescue of European Jewry now became a central item on the public agenda, and the leadership had to decide where it stood in the Zionist order of priorities.

Although rescue activities did not constitute the first item on the Yishuv's agenda, Aliyah Bet was now assigned pride of place among those rescue operations that were carried out. This was not the result of a single decision adopted after reasoned discussion and consideration but rather the last stage of a process. The first factor leading to the emphasis given to Aliyah Bet was the simple fact that only aliyah could effectively extricate the Jews from the danger that threatened them. Assistance in the form of money or food parcels, for example, was certainly important, but such activities could at most postpone rather than eliminate the danger. Second, unceasing escape attempts had been made by Jews trapped in Europe, and during the last two years of the war there was a real chance to bring many out through the Balkans, in spite of German attempts to block such efforts.

The course of the war in 1943 and 1944 no longer pointed to German military victory, and the satellite countries, such as Romania, Hungary and Bulgaria, were seeking paths to disentangle themselves from the German stranglehold. One obvious way was to permit the departure of Jews, counter to Germany's intentions. The representatives of the Yishuv, and particularly of the Mossad, were aware of the situation, thanks to their contacts with the Jewish communities, and they were determined to exploit it to the full.

A third factor was the presence of Mossad representatives in Turkey from late 1941 and during 1942. Turkey served as a window onto Europe, to quote Zev Shind of the Mossad. The Mossad agents saw Jewish refugees arriving in Turkey in small sailing boats or yachts, abandoned and destitute in the quarantine section of Istanbul port and crying out for a helping hand. Since the sinking in February 1942 of the *Struma*—the refugee ship from Romania that had been towed out of Istanbul and back into the Black Sea when no legal means had been found to allow her passengers entry into Palestine—these fugitive Jews had become a symbol of Zionist impotence and of the indifference of the governments involved.[35] In response, members of the Mossad now tried to open up new routes for aliyah from the Balkans.

There was a renewed attempt to cooperate with British intelligence, which was interested in acquiring reliable information about events in the Balkans: Jewish immigrants could serve as a possible source of such information. In consequence, the Mossad set up channels of communication with Jewish communities through diplomats and diplomatic couriers, seeking to create a modus operandi that could combine British interests with the organization of aliyah. They believed (although in the final analysis this proved unrealistic) that such contacts with British intelligence would help to procure ships for the immigrants. The presence of Mossad representatives in Turkey from as early as 1941, before the extent and significance of the Holocaust had become clear, gave the Mossad an advantage over the other institutions of the Yishuv engaged in rescue operations.[36]

Finally, the influence of the official Yishuv's delegation in Istanbul must be taken into account. Discussions of the Zionist response to the Nazi extermination policy produced a decision to set up a Jewish Agency Rescue Committee with the participation of the entire Yishuv, including the Revisionists and Agudat Israel. The committee, in turn, established a mission to Istanbul consisting of representatives both of the kibbutz movements and of the Mossad who had been in Istanbul previously (endeavoring to contact their comrades in Europe) as well as representatives of various political parties and organizations such as the Histadrut. This mission was able to make permanent contact with the Balkan Jewish communities. It thus became possible to transmit information to and from Europe concerning the fate of the Jews, and various plans for aid and rescue operations were proposed. (There was a permanent center for communication with the Diaspora in Geneva; however, because of the distance, correspondence sent from there to Palestine through London and Istanbul took many weeks.)[37]

Thus, from early 1943, mutual ties were strengthened between the Jewish communities remaining in Europe and the Yishuv. The message that Zionist leaders and the youth movements in the Diaspora relayed to Palestine was one of isolation and desertion coupled with the powerful feeling that Palestine remained the only hope. They called for aliyah as the one possible solution, and now that the objective constraints had been weakened, the call became more insistent. In Palestine, too, it was believed that aliyah was possible and that it would help to bridge the abyss that had come to separate the Yishuv from the Diaspora during the long months of extermination when communications had been cut off.

These feelings were clearly expressed by Zev Shind and Eliyahu Golomb at a meeting of the Mapai leadership on January 26, 1944. In the wake of a report by Yosef Korianski of the Dror movement, who had recently arrived in Palestine from Poland, Golomb spoke of the urgent need to send aliyah emissaries to the Diaspora without further ado. If the emissaries did not reach Europe soon, while the war was still going on, Golomb stressed, it would be too late to reach the hearts of the survivors. Their bitter disappointment with the human race, with democracy and with Zionism would infect the postwar world with a permanently effective poison.[38] Only sincere and immediate efforts to liberate them from the Nazi hell and bring them to Palestine could ensure a better future for all. Thus, aliyah was now seen as essential to guarantee the survival of the Jewish people and Zionism—as the only way to reach the glowing embers of European Jewry.

In August 1943, an unidentified leader of the Mossad and the Haganah (apparently Eliyahu Golomb) had presented a document entitled "A Draft Plan for Aliyah Bet."[39] The opening section reads:

> Herewith a draft plan for the landing of 150,000–200,000 Jews simultaneously on the different beaches within the border of our country. Such a landing operation could, in our opinion, instantly solve the political-Zionist problem with which we are concerned today within six to eight months after the cease-fire. Most sections of our country's coastline are suitable for landing. Those landing should reach the Palestinian coast equipped and trained, in a large number of boats, and they should be prepared na-

tionally, morally, ideologically and militarily for the magnitude of the task they are about to perform. The entire plan is based on military principles; its success can be guaranteed only if the regulation of the operation is based entirely on the principles customary in the Or. [= Organization, i.e., the Haganah].

The document went on to present a detailed operative analysis of how to prepare implementation of the plan. Numerous passages dealt with what had to be done in Palestine: the training of one thousand seamen for the ships; the establishment of a shipping company in possession of 100 vessels, each capable of carrying two thousand people; and the assembly of many small boats in readiness for the silent and clandestine landings. The shipping company was to be set up immediately and begin commercial operations on a profit-making basis. In addition, the plan provided for the training of 250 wireless operators as well as landing teams and the establishment of absorption centers for the hundreds of thousands of immigrants. Similarly, the document laid out in detail the preparations to be made in Europe. Political contacts would have to be established with governments, with civil servants at various levels and with border police. The plan also detailed how the immigrants were to be readied and transit camps set up.

Responsibility for the execution of the plans was assigned to Palestinian emissaries (as had been done with regard to Aliyah Bet on the eve of the war). They would be charged with organizing and implementing technical matters—transportation of the immigrants, food supplies, transit permits and other necessities required prior to setting sail. But this was not all. They would also be responsible for an educational effort in the broadest sense. True, this aliyah was to be limited to people (the words "pioneers" or "youth-movement members" are conspicuously absent) whose loyalty to Zionism and "movement-consciousness" was deeply rooted. Moreover, intensive Zionist education, imbuing the immigrants with an awareness of the meaning of their mission, was of the utmost importance. The distinctions between the different trends and movements within Zionism was to be blurred, with emphasis placed on the universal goal and its broad national significance. The potential immigrants would be trained in self-defense as well as in the use of arms, which would have to be concealed from the local authorities. The purpose of this physical training was to prepare the immigrants for clashes with the British or any other forces that might try to frustrate their attempts to land. Resistance to such obstruction would be the task of a specially trained fighting force, which would also be able to enlist the aid of the Haganah.

It is most significant that this document was composed in August 1943, before the Mossad had been able to land a single ship or group of immigrants from Europe. Clearly, the idea of Aliyah Bet had a firm grip on the imagination of Mossad members, despite its meager achievements during the war years. For the Mossad, the limitations of Aliyah Bet had been caused by the lack of support on the part of the politicians. If it were now adapted to the new circumstance and vastly expanded in scope, it could become the major instrument of Zionist policy. The author of the document believed that Aliyah Bet could resolve the political problems of the movement within the span of a few months, provided the necessary efforts and resources were invested. A new element in the plan was the special role assigned to the defense forces of the Yishuv in determining its political future, thus giving expression to the power that the Yishuv had built up during the war years. The concept of the "aliyah rebellion," clearly an important component of the plan, was expanded to assume an almost literal meaning: military preparations for the realization of aliyah.

To what degree did this plan represent the policy of the entire Mossad? Was it discussed seriously? What was its influence on the decision makers? We do not know. At the very least, the document was a position paper promoting the adoption of Aliyah Bet as a key element in Zionist strategy. The author did not conceive of aliyah as a necessary response to the circumstances in Europe during the war and thereafter, though it was taken for granted that the situation created by the war and the Holocaust would make it possible to mobilize two hundred thousand young men and women as immigrants.

To our mind, however, there is an additional factor that contributed to the restoration of Aliyah Bet to its central role: its success. After a prolonged period of failure in 1943, during which not one illegal immigrant was brought to Palestine, the spring of 1944 saw the beginning of a new aliyah movement. Some forty-five hundred immigrants aboard nine ships reached Palestine, and their arrival demonstrated that the Yishuv was not totally impotent in the face of events in Europe. The immigrants had first reached Istanbul and proceeded from there to Palestine in an operation that enlisted the joint efforts of the Mossad and its delegation in Istanbul, together with other partners. But it was the efforts of the Mossad agents and delegation that inspired these other parties—among them, Ira Hirschmann, President Roosevelt's personal representative from the War Refugee Board (who had arrived in Istanbul in February 1944), and the staff of the British Consulate at Istanbul—to cooperate.[40] In this case, the Yishuv had proved able to carry its plans through to realization.

It might be argued that the success of this operation was totally dwarfed by the magnitude of the Holocaust. Moreover, it clearly did not have the potential inherent in such large-scale rescue schemes as the Europa Plan—a proposal formulated by Slovakian Jewish leaders to halt the deportation of European Jews to the East in exchange for the payment of ransom to the Nazi officials involved—or the well-known Trucks for Blood plan conceived by Eichmann that offered to stop the deportation of Hungarian Jews in exchange for the delivery of trucks and other goods from the West.[41] Nevertheless, unlike all the other schemes, Aliyah Bet did signify what the Yishuv had succeeded in doing for the Jews in Europe through its own resources; it was an expression of its perseverance and resolve in the face of innumerable obstacles.

The resumption of illegal immigration in 1943 and 1944 was characteristic of Aliyah Bet as a whole. It could never escape the tension created by the fact that, on the one hand, the leadership of the Yishuv was bound to see it, at least in part, as one among many means to achieve fundamental political goals; on the other hand, by the necessity and urgency of maintaining immigration in view of the external circumstances.

These events thus illustrate the combination and mutual interaction of the human factor—free choice—and the historical factor that narrows such choice. Aliyah Bet became a popular movement, the outcome of many of those same factors that had created Zionism itself. The leaders of the Zionist movement were not in complete control of the forces involved. Nevertheless, the scope of Aliyah Bet was largely dependent on the conscious choice and the deliberate action of Zionist policy. This was particularly evident during the first and last years of the war. The victims of the Nazi persecution in Europe looked to Aliyah Bet as their only possible means of rescue, as did Jews in the free countries of the West, who were desperately seeking ways to extend succor to their brethren.[42]

Zionist policy found in Aliyah Bet a new instrument for the furtherance of its aims. At this time, it came to represent certain needs and goals that might be defined as historical; it was only because the Zionist leadership allowed those needs to "lead" them (as Berl Katznelson put it at the Twenty-First Zionist Congress in August 1939) that it could convert these needs into drive and energy.

Notes

1. For a more complete account, see Dalia Ofer, *Escaping the Holocaust: Illegal Immigration to the Land of Israel, 1939–1945* (New York: 1990), 9–11.

2. David Ben-Gurion, *Zikhronot* (Tel-Aviv: 1987), vol. 6, 326 (entry for 24 May 1939).

3. *Ibid.,* 328 (entry for evening after Shavuot at a meeting with youth organizations).

4. Ofer, *Escaping the Holocaust,* 12–17, 69–71.

5. *Ibid.,* 43–49, 77–80.

6. For Britain's policy, see Ron Zweig, "Mediniyut veyisumah: misrad hamoshavot, hasefer halavan veha'aliyah habilti legalit leereẓ yisrael, 1939–1940," *Haẓiyonut* 7 (1982), 292–323; *idem*, "Hamediniyut habritit legabei ha'aliyah leereẓ yisrael betekufat hashoah—shelav aḥaron," *Haẓiyonut* 8 (1983), 195–244.

7. For more details, see Ofer, *Escaping the Holocaust,* 100–102; Ruth Zariz, *Haẓalat yehudim migermaniah beemẓa'ut hagirah, november 1938–1945* (Ph.D. diss., The Hebrew University, 1986), 84; testimony of Pino Ginzburg, Oral History Division of the Institute of Contemporary Jewry, The Hebrew University.

8. Histadrut Executive Committee, Geneva, 25 August 1939, Labour Archives, 39M; Pino Ginzburg to Yehudah Idelsohn, 4 September 1939, Kibbutz Meuḥad Archives 2/(Overseas) box 10, file 49; Y. Braginsky, *'Am ḥoter el ḥof* (Tel-Aviv: 1965), 245–252.

9. Ben-Gurion, *Zikhronot,* vol. 6, 327–328.

10. *Ibid.,* 364. For Ben-Gurion's position on the reaction to deportation of "illegal" immigrants, see *ibid.,* 254, 488–490 and 499 (n. 7).

11. See minutes from the Mapai Central Council, 12 September (especially Eliezer Liebenstein) and 21 September 1939 (Berl Katznelson, Aharon Zisling, Eliyahu Dobkin); Mapai Secretariat, 26 September 1939 (resolutions concerning aid to refugees from Poland and activities of Polish Immigrants Association), and 27 September 1939 (esp. Katznelson); Mapai Political Committee, 2 November 1939 (Ben-Gurion). All of the preceding documents are found in the Mapai Labour Party Archives, Beit Berl (hereafter MA) 23/39. See also minutes of the meeting attended by Yitzhak Gruenbaum, Kaplan, Dobkin, Moshe Shapira, Yosef Barpal, Shlomo Lipsky and Zvi Yehieli, 9 October 1939, Central Zionist Archives (hereafter CZA) S53/1551.

12. Mapai Secretariat, 27 September 1939, MA 23/39.

13. Jewish Agency Executive, 9 October 1939, CZA, Protocols, vol. 31 (hereafter Prot. 31); Ben-Gurion at meeting of the Mapai Political Committee, 2 November 1939, MA 23/39.

14. Moshe Sharett (Shertok), *Yoman medini* (Tel-Aviv: 1974), vol. 4, 450–456; on Golomb's mission to the United States, see *ibid.,* 468–473.

15. Eliyahu Golomb to Willard Stanton, 31 January 1940; and Stanton to Golomb, 25 March 1940, Archives of the History of the Haganah (hereafter AHH) 14/4195. Concerning options for ships, see AHH, Gustav Landauer to Eliyahu Golomb, 15 January and 12 February 1940; and Manya Shohat to Cyrus Adler, 16 February 1940. Worthy of note in this connection are contacts between Katznelson and Jabotinsky at the beginning of the war and Katznelson's full report of these contacts to the Mapai Central Council; also Katznelson's later talks with David Raziel and Zvi Lubotzki concerning cooperation between the IZL and the Haganah: these contacts stress a sense of emergency and a desire to find new channels of action in view of the war. For more details, see David Niv, *Ma'arakhot hairgun hazevai haleumi* (Tel-Aviv: 1967), pt. 3, 60–67.

16. Sharett, *Yoman medini,* 487.

17. Meeting, Jewish Agency Executive, 17 September 1939, Prot. 31.

18. Sharett, *Yoman medini,* vol. 5, 15; *ibid.,* 9–22 (report on the meeting in Geneva); *ibid.,* 23–34 (account of the economic situation in Palestine); Shertok at the Jewish Agency Executive, London, 15 February 1940, CZA. For the discussions concerning Aliyah Bet, see Yehieli Report, AHH 14/152, 21–22; and Yehudah Idelsohn's diary, 14 February 1940, Kibbutz Meuhad Archives 2/(Overseas) 23/A4.

19. The deportations were part of a German plan to concentrate and isolate the Jews in a special reservation at Nisko in the Lublin region, the final outcome of which would be their physical extermination. The first three groups, totaling about twenty-five hundred people, were sent to Lublin in October from Prague and Vienna. For more details, see H. Rosenkranz, *Verfolgung und Selbstbehauptung: Die Juden in Österreich 1938–1940* (Munich: 1978), 216–218.

20. Meeting of the Zionist Office in London, February 1940, CZA Z4.

21. Meeting, Jewish Agency Executive, 14 April 1940, CZA, Prot. 32/II.

22. Concerning Berthold Storfer, see Ofer, Escaping the Holocaust, 103–127; "The Rescue of European Jewry and Illegal Immigration to Palestine in 1940—Prospect and Reality: Berthold Storfer and the Mossad Le'Aliyah Bet," in *Modern Judaism* (May 1984), 159–181.

23. Yehieli Report, AHH 14/153. For the Jewish Agency decision to assume responsibility for Aliyah Bet, see Ben-Gurion, *Zikhronot,* vol. 6, 338 (entry for 28 May 1939), "The Executive has decided that it will now manage the affairs of Jewish immigration to Palestine."

24. Concerning the *Sakariya* and the *Hilda,* see Ofer, *Escaping the Holocaust,* 80–85, 42–48.

25. On the Kladovo affair, see *ibid.,* 49–68.

26. On the three ships affair, see *ibid.,* 31–39.

27. On *Darien 2* and the argument over its use, see *ibid.,* 55–59; and Dalia Ofer, "The Kladovo Darien Affair," in *Vision and Conflict in the Holy Land,* ed. Richard I. Cohen (Jerusalem: 1985), 218–245.

28. Shertok to Weizmann, 17 December 1940, CZA S25/1716; Weizmann to Shertok, 11 January 1941, in *The Papers and Letters of Chaim Weizmann,* ed. Bernard Wasserstein (London: 1979), vol. 20, 86–91. On the information relayed to Weizmann about the large number of immigrant ships about to set sail on Nazi initiative, see comment of Blanche Dugdale in *Baffy: The Diaries of Blanche Dugdale, 1936–1947,* ed. Norman A. Rose (London: 1973) 178.

29. Sharett, *Yoman medini,* vol. 5, 270.

30. For more details, see Yosef Heller, *Bamaavak lamedinah: hamediniyut haziyonit bashanim 1936–1948* (Jerusalem: 1985), 42–51.

31. Sharett, *Yoman medini,* vol. 5, 307.

32. CZA, Prot. 36/II (6 October 1942) and Prot. 39/I (20 June 1944 debate on Zionist policy after the war and the ways to "concretize," in Ben-Gurion's phrasing, the Biltmore Program).

33. For more details, see Dina Porat, *Hanhagah bemilkud* (Tel-Aviv: 1986), 74–101.

34. Dalia Ofer, "Minizolim le'olim: sheerit hapeletah nokhah ha'aliyah," in *Sheerit hapeletah: hakinus habeinleumi hashishi (1985),* Yad Vashem (forthcoming).

35. On the *Struma,* see Ofer, *Escaping the Holocaust,* 147–166.

36. On the views of the Mossad emissaries in Turkey in 1942 concerning refugees on ships and the situation in Turkey, see AHH 14/60 and 14/490, 14/714 (testimony of Zev Shind). For the organization of Mossad emissaries and their modus operandi in Turkey in 1942, see Ofer, *Escaping the Holocaust,* 211–217.

37. Porat, *Hanhagah bemilkud,* 213–234.

38. Mapai Political Committee, 26 January 1944, MA 24/44; Zev Shind, Mapai Secretariat, 15 December 1943, MA 24/43.

39. 12 August 1943 (unsigned document), AHH 14/628.

40. For more details, see Ofer, *Escaping the Holocaust,* 267–284.

41. On the large-scale rescue plans, see Porat, *Hanhagah bemilkud,* 309–347.

42. Dalia Ofer, ''Haha'apalah bamidiniyut haẓiyonit—bein beḥirah lekorah,'' in *Divrei hakongres ha'olami hateshi'i lemada'ei hayahadut* (Jerusalem: 1986), sec. B, vol. 2, 153–160.

Ben-Gurion and the Second World War: Plans for Mass Immigration to Palestine

Dvorah Hacohen
(THE HEBREW UNIVERSITY)

I have come to rethink Zionist issues in light of the war. We must now give up old assumptions. . . . We used to see Zionism as an historical process extending over many years. . . . In my opinion the following three principles must [now] form the basis of our politics: establishing faits accomplis, organizing for immigration, and settling two million Jews in Palestine.—David Ben-Gurion to the Jewish Agency Executive, October 6, 1942

From its earliest days, the Zionist movement was split into diverse factions and shades of opinion, dividing into the so-called political, spiritual and practical schools. Their adherents differed over the means of implementing their ideas, but all were in agreement over the ultimate goal: Zionism would transform the Jewish people socially and politically throughout the world. The rebirth of the Jewish people in Eretz Israel would both provide a physical sanctuary and transform the Diaspora mentality. However, it was the tragic dilemma of Zionism during the Second World War that its two fundamental principles—rebuilding the land of Israel and saving the Jewish people—appeared to come into conflict, with focus on one goal threatening to thwart the other.

The Zionist movement had gone through difficult periods before, but at the close of the 1930s, it seemed that the dream of creating a Jewish national home in Palestine had been shattered. The Nazis were poised to launch their war on the Jews of Europe, the backbone of world Jewry and the Zionist movement. The Yishuv faced its own crisis as Zionist leaders looked in vain to the British government for support and assistance. The new policy exemplified by the White Paper of 1939 was a particularly bitter blow for the Jewish people at this critical stage. The leaders of the Yishuv were torn between the European tragedy and the threat to their own existence in Palestine.

Some scholars of the Holocaust claim that the leadership of the Yishuv did not do enough to try to save European Jewry, concentrating instead on the effort to achieve political independence.[1] Others are deeply disturbed by what they see as the Palestinocentrism of the Yishuv's leadership, "The public, official reaction of the Yishuv in Palestine to the European Holocaust is a canker in our flesh to this day."[2] The reference is to the Jewish Agency Executive, the leading political institution in

247

the Yishuv; and in the Executive, the focus is its chairman, David Ben-Gurion, who became the foremost figure in the Yishuv leadership in the 1930s.

In attempting to explain the policies adopted during the war, scholars have emphasized the vulnerability of the Yishuv as a minority in the country, subject to foreign rule, and in possession of only limited human and financial resources.[3] In addition, until the summer of 1942, the danger of annihilation hung over the Yishuv itself. Yet a passive and helpless attitude was hardly consistent with Ben-Gurion's personality and his behavior in other crises, where he most often demonstrated boldness and a readiness to tackle difficult challenges. What is more, Ben-Gurion was among the first—perhaps one of the few—who in the very early stages of the war foresaw the extent of the catastrophe in store for the Jews of Europe.

There is ample documentation that Yishuv leaders were aware of the weighty implications of the difficult dilemmas they faced. The question of priorities in assigning resources, for example, frequently recurred in discussions of the Jewish Agency Executive and in other forums at the height of the war.[4]

One of the most extraordinary aspects of this tragic subject, and one that has hitherto received relatively little attention, is the fact that during the war years Ben-Gurion immersed himself almost obsessively in a plan that seemed hopelessly utopian at the time. This study aims to shed light on this chapter in the life of Ben-Gurion during this momentous period.

While the war raged in Europe, Ben-Gurion plunged himself into a plan to bring several million Jews to Palestine. Not even the first news concerning systematic extermination of the Jews in Europe deterred him from the issue of mass aliyah. Ben-Gurion sought in this way to revolutionize prevailing Zionist thinking, to effect a decisive change in policy and to alter operational concepts, all in the hope of finding a solution to the overwhelming crisis facing the Zionist movement and world Jewry.

In reality, Ben-Gurion had been striving desperately since 1938 to develop a radically new immigration policy that would meet two basic goals. In terms of the political struggle, he sought a way to oppose effectively the British Mandatory government and its Palestine policy. In terms of the Zionist modus operandi in the country, he wished to replace gradual growth with decisive, sweeping construction on an unprecedented and rapid scale.

Mass aliyah did not become part of Ben-Gurion's rhetoric by accident, nor was it a passing fancy. He invested intense effort over the course of several years in developing his plan. Ben-Gurion described himself as being capable of only one major undertaking at a time, and he now devoted much of his energy to the idea of bringing millions to Palestine. Moreover, this preoccupation did not end at the abstract level.

Ben-Gurion's plan seemed fantastic in its scope and, at that time (both prior to, and during, the war), virtually impossible to carry out both because of the events in Europe and the immigration policy of the Mandatory administration. Nonetheless, he set out to prove the ultimate practicability of the scheme, hoping in this way to create a political atmosphere in which Britain would be forced to change its policy. Ben-Gurion wanted to disprove the proposition that the course of events was immutable, given external political conditions. His aim was to demonstrate that conditions could be changed by new realities and that such realities could be created through the force of willpower. Ben-Gurion, in brief, believed that it was possible to subject history to the force of human will expressed through action.

The idea of Jewish immigration in the millions was not new. As early as July 1919, Max Nordau had called for a rapid and massive immigration of Jews—some 600,000 people—in order to establish a Jewish majority in Palestine as quickly as possible. Chaim Weizmann, Moshe Shertok (later Sharett) and Ben-Gurion himself had also referred on various occasions to the necessity of a massive aliyah. In addition, Zev Jabotinsky had spoken from the early 1930s on the need for a huge immigration from Europe, especially from Poland, an idea he referred to as an "evacuation" and which was adopted as part of the Revisionist movement's Ten Year Plan in 1938. Jabotinsky, who insistently warned of an impending catastrophe, conceived of mass aliyah both as a solution to the plight of those Jews suffering oppression in the Diaspora and as a means of determining the political future of Palestine. The evacuation plan called for an aliyah of 150,000 Jews a year for ten years, which at the time did not seem particularly out of step with much of the thinking in the Zionist mainstream. Finally, in the controversy over the partition plan proposed by the Peel Commission in 1937, there was almost universal agreement within the Zionist leadership on the need for an aliyah of millions.

The figure of 1,500,000 to 2,000,000 recurred in the speeches of Weizmann and Ben-Gurion to the Twenty-first Zionist Congress in August 1939. However, they, too, spoke then of the future—twenty years according to Weizmann, fifteen according to Ben-Gurion. All agreed that a figure of 100,000–150,000 immigrants per year, along the lines of Jabotinsky's plan, was reasonable.

The evacuation plan at that stage clearly depended on the cooperation of the Polish government and other European countries in persuading Britain to open the gates of Palestine to hundreds of thousands of immigrants. In light of the events of 1938 and the turnabout of the British government regarding the Yishuv, the Jabotinsky plan was rendered hopeless, especially as it was projected to continue for ten years at a time when the drums of war were already clearly audible.

The radical innovation in Ben-Gurion's proposals lay in its independence from foreign assistance: the Yishuv would rely solely on its own strength. Moreover, it was manifestly clear that the plan would have to be implemented in the face of British objections. Ben-Gurion also envisioned an immigration that was far more ambitious in scope and tempo than had originally been conceived. He spoke of an influx of 2,000,000 immigrants in the first stage, which he thought would last from one to one and one-half years—perhaps less, as we will see.

Fundamental to Ben-Gurion's thinking was the stress on mass immigration as opposed to the selective aliyah organized in previous decades by the Zionist Organization. The immigration of handpicked *halutzim* (pioneers) constituted an elitist policy aimed at youth, enlisting their ideological commitment to Zionist goals. Jabotinsky categorically opposed this policy, favoring mass aliyah instead "[to] bring poverty-stricken Jews as well as our great authors, our talented artists and all the ordinary people." He, too, however, felt that his evacuation plan should be implemented in stages, with an initial breakthrough phase to be led by a selective aliyah, "an ongoing process of choosing between the types of prospective immigrants" that would be organized according to their age and abilities.[5]

In contrast, Ben-Gurion's plan for mass aliyah called for immediate, large-scale and completely nonselective immigration. This approach met with resistance in Zionist circles, especially in the labor movement, whose ideology emphasized the decisive role of *halutzim* as the nation's avant garde. Ben-Gurion, however, had come to the conclusion that changed realities necessitated a corresponding change in policy, including that of his own party.

Whereas Jabotinsky's evacuation plan was prompted by the plight of the Jews in Poland and other European countries in the 1930s, Ben-Gurion's plan was firmly anchored in the struggle for the political future of Palestine. This, for Ben-Gurion, was identical with the future of Zionism, "In ordinary times," he said in December 1938, "aliyah needs Zionism. Now Zionism needs aliyah, or more precisely, depends on aliyah."

ON THE EVE OF WAR: THE PROPOSED ALIYAH REBELLION

The goal that Ben-Gurion relentlessly pursued was Jewish statehood, which, he believed, depended on mass immigration. He never relinquished this mission even in the midst of the worst upheavals in Europe and Palestine during the 1930s and 1940s.

He was among the very first to define the depths of the impending crisis. Following *Kristallnacht* on November 9, 1938, he warned of the great catastrophe in store, "What is happening now in Germany is not the end, it is just the beginning," he told a meeting of the Jewish Agency Executive. "Other antisemitic nations will follow Hitler's example. . . . [and] millions of Jews will face physical annihilation."[6]

Ben-Gurion first developed his ideas of mass immigration in the period following *Kristallnacht*. This period culminated with the publication of the White Paper of May 17, 1939. Designed to block the creation of a Jewish homeland in Palestine and to arrest the development of Jewish settlement, the White Paper promised the Arabs that the country would be transformed into an independent state with an Arab majority within ten years. It drastically curtailed Jewish immigration: during the following five-year period only 75,000 Jews would be allowed entry; thereafter, additional immigration would depend on Arab agreement. Jewish acquisition of land in Palestine was likewise severely restricted.

With publication of the White Paper, Ben-Gurion decided that there was no escape from the fact that Arab opposition to Zionism had become a truly national struggle that could rely on extensive support from Arab states as well as from Great Britain. Accordingly, he drew an unequivocal conclusion, "We are entering an emergency period . . . [that] demands that we take a wholly new position and put our activities on a new footing, both in constructive efforts and in militant struggle." Thus, the chapter of militant Zionism reached a new stage. Ben-Gurion advocated simultaneous action along two fronts: "constructive action," which demanded the maintenance of political contacts with the Western powers, and "militant struggle," which called for resistance to the British authorities. This demand found its expression, as war broke out, in his famous dictum, "We must help the British in the war against the Nazis as though there were no White Paper, and fight the White Paper as though there were no war."

The idea of the militant struggle developed by Ben-Gurion from late in 1938 was "not a struggle for aliyah, but a struggle [waged] through aliyah, an aliyah rebellion."[7] The principle underlying this rebellion was self-reliance.

Ben-Gurion's plan called for buying ships, creating an extensive smuggling network in Europe and organizing harbor arrangements in order to bring out thousands of Jews both openly and clandestinely. He was prepared for violent clashes with British forces should the latter attempt to prevent the ships from reaching shore or refuse the immigrants permission to disembark. Perhaps the most startling step he contemplated was "to take Haifa by force."[8] The purpose of creating incidents such as clashes between refugees and British forces, with the patent risk of casualties, was to shock British and world opinion:

> Without taking a bold, daring step toward our goal that will unite the entire Jewish people behind us and win world support, we will not be able to prevent the imminent destruction of Zionism. There is only one such possible act: an aliyah rebellion. By declaring war on Britain not with guns and bombs, not with terror and murder like the Arabs, but with a public organization of mass immigration to Eretz Israel, by bringing thousands of refugees—despite the government's order forbidding it—we will once again link the refugee question to Eretz Israel.[9]

Not surprisingly, Ben-Gurion's plan aroused intense opposition in the Zionist leadership, who feared that a public, political campaign could derail ongoing efforts to quietly smuggle small groups of Jews into the country. Among his colleagues in the labor movement, Berl Katznelson and Yitzhak Tabenkin were opposed, as were the leaders of the Haganah and the members of the Mossad le-Aliyah Bet, who were responsible for organizing illegal immigration.[10] These leaders viewed the essential task as rescuing the largest possible number of refugees without endangering their lives and without a head-on confrontation with Britain that could threaten the continuation of already organized illegal immigration efforts (Aliyah Bet). The attempts made on the eve of the war by Ben-Gurion to gain support for his plan in the United States also failed, but this did not deter him. He decided to state his case even more forcefully when the White Paper was officially published, assuming that extreme action could still bring about a change in British policy. This radical position entailed a plan for a special cadre of young illegal immigrants, those of the so-called Aliyah Gimmel, who would undergo military training and be issued weapons. Making their way quite openly to Palestine, they would attack British forces together with Haganah members already positioned on shore.[11]

Several days before the Second World War broke out, Ben-Gurion addressed the closing session of the Twenty-first Zionist Congress in Geneva:

> These terrible acts [the issuing of the White Paper and the British restrictions on immigration to Palestine] will not be negated simply by appealing to the conscience of humanity, but we ourselves, through our own willpower and strength, can negate them. . . . The White Paper has created a vacuum in the Mandate. . . . We must find

within ourselves the strength and wisdom to fill this void. We must behave as though we were a nation in Palestine . . . until we do in fact become a nation.[12]

Thus, for Ben-Gurion, the Jewish state would be created by a change in the demographic balance in the country. Whoever had the majority would create the state. In taking up the cudgels against the British and the Arabs, he meant to strike at the heart of the White Paper. Instead of halting immigration, he would organize mass immigration; instead of remaining a minority, the Jews would become the majority, leading them to statehood.

It is important to realize that Ben-Gurion based his plan for mass aliyah on the Zionist concept of Palestine as the Jewish national home, and only secondly on the situation of European Jewry. Throughout the war, Ben-Gurion remained firm in opposing those who demanded that all resources be committed to rescuing Jews in any manner that might seem feasible and that the Jews be brought to any destination that might provide even temporary shelter. He held fast to his belief that the Zionist movement alone provided the only true and lasting solution to the Jewish plight and that aliyah to Palestine was the only form of meaningful rescue. Diplomacy and dependence on the will of other nations, he believed, would not solve the problem of the Jewish refugees, nor would any partial or temporary solution.

This viewpoint encountered opposition not only among the British, but also among several of the Jewish non-Zionist organizations in the United States. The latters' position was that the question of Palestine should be kept separate from the issue of rescue. The political reality, they argued, was that Britain would not admit mass aliyah and, therefore, efforts should focus on finding alternative havens for Jewish refugees. Some also accepted the argument of the British government that Palestine, for objective reasons—its size and its absorptive capacity—could never take in all the Jews in any case.

Although the Zionists did not accept these arguments, they, too, differed over priorities: Palestine or rescue. Some agreed that the two issues be separated; they demanded that saving European Jews take precedence, even if this meant delaying the struggle for Eretz Israel.[13] But Ben-Gurion was not convinced:

> There is no greater danger to Zionism than this distinction the [British] government is making between the refugee question and that of Palestine. In ordinary times, the Zionist undertaking, the Zionist movement with its pioneering settlement activities, was merely working to make aliyah to this poor country possible. Now, when the catastrophe has taken this terrible form and has become a burning world issue, *Zionism has no political purpose* if it does not provide a definitive solution to the refugee question. Even in ordinary times [failure to meet the challenge of mass aliyah] would have been a tragedy; today, it would signify the end of the Zionist program. Separation of the refugee question from that of Palestine removes Eretz Israel from the political agenda, not only in world opinion, but also for the Jewish people.[14]

BEN-GURION DURING THE WAR:
MASS IMMIGRATION AND THE STATE

The opposition to Ben-Gurion, combined with the outbreak of the war, removed his plan from the agenda of the Zionist leadership. With characteristic obstinacy, he waited for an opportunity to bring it forward again at a later date.

The German invasion of Poland and the outbreak of the war failed to budge Ben-Gurion from his position. He was convinced that the war would alter the political map, that this was the crucial hour in which the Jewish future and the political future of Palestine would be determined and, for this reason, he believed that the Jewish people had to act rapidly and with determination. In his race against time Ben-Gurion did not pause to observe the course of the war. He turned his attention to what would happen in its wake, to a time when two main factors would influence the position of the Jews: the millions of refugees and the new political map in the Middle East and Europe. To Ben-Gurion the two issues were inextricably linked:

At the war's end the political future of Palestine will assume a critical importance. This urgency is heightened as a result of the war, since the Jewish problem is worsening. What used to be called the ''Jewish question'' was never so tragic, acute and wide-scale as it will be at the close of this war, especially after the destruction of the Nazi regime. . . . Victory alone will not solve the two bitter questions we face, or the issue of saving millions of Jewish refugees after the war. The Zionist mission is to prevent a separate solution to these two problems and to create the political conditions in Palestine to enable us to absorb a mass immigration in the shortest possible time.[15]

He foresaw that the position of Zionism at the close of the Second World War would be essentially different from that which it had enjoyed at the end of the First. Then, with the Balfour Declaration, he continued:

It seemed that we would be able to build the country at our leisure and return gradually to our homeland. Even in the countries of the worst persecution the situation of the Jews was better than now. [But] after this war we will face a radically different situation. The scope and urgency of immigration will require us to adopt untried methods, to work at a pace that will far outstrip anything we have known.[16]

Ben-Gurion's conclusion was that it would be necessary to take preemptive action by establishing faits accomplis:

After this war we should not make an effort to find the proper terminology: ''national homeland,'' ''binational state,'' ''Jewish empire'' and so forth. Our goal is to achieve the fact, not the formula. There will be no value in formulae.''[17]

As on the eve of the war, Ben-Gurion continued to reject as unfeasible all ideas of attempting to transfer Jewish refugees to other countries. He scorned any territorial solutions outside Palestine, still seeing in them an illusion, a hoax and a diversion from what was, in his view, the sole constructive course—opening Palestine to immigration:

There is no chance of absorbing mass aliyah outside Palestine. . . . If the United States and North America [as a whole] were to open their gates to the Jewish war refugees, they could, doubtless, easily absorb hundreds of thousands of Jewish immigrants. But no sane person familiar with America would believe such a thing could take place. The question remains open in all its urgency: What is to be the fate of the streams of uprooted Jews, who will have no chance of survival in some of the European (and perhaps also in Eastern [Moslem] countries)? . . . Outside Palestine, no large-scale Jewish settlement has succeeded or will succeed, even if some dream-country existed beyond the fantasies of those seeking such a territory.[18]

Those in favor of directing immigration to Palestine presented it as a clear act of rescue. In addition, they thought that the attempt to separate the issue of statehood from that of rescue was irrelevant. As Berl Katznelson, one of the key figures in the labor movement, explained:

> We must raise the banner of the solution to the Jewish question—that is, a Jewish state. I admit that, for me, the state is not the important thing. Were it possible to have a regime ensuring free immigration and settlement, I would not be carried away by the slogan [of statehood]. But after what we have experienced over the past years, we see that in this era there is no regime capable of ensuring our rights except a Jewish state. The state is a necessary means to achieve major goals for the people, not an end in itself.[19]

Ben-Gurion likewise claimed that linkage between the two issues was not a mere tactical consideration. Speaking to the Jewish Agency Executive a year later, in October 1941, he emphasized that there was an integral connection between them:

> We, as Jews, face two issues: the political future of Palestine and the rescue of millions of Jews after the war. The Zionist mission at this hour is to prevent a separate solution to the two questions. [There can be] no solution for Palestine without a solution for the people of Israel. The two issues must be combined and *a regime instituted in Palestine that will allow the absorption of mass aliyah in the shortest possible time*. To separate [the issues] denies the essence and the mission of Zionism and endangers our Jewish future in Palestine. It exposes the fleeing Jews of Europe to illusions and false adventures.[20]

In practical terms, the immigration of several million in a short period of time did not seem impossible, and Ben-Gurion was not the only one who thought of transporting millions from one country to another. The idea of a population transfer had been spoken of in some Zionist circles ever since the establishment of the British Mandate. It was also mentioned in the recommendation of the Peel Commission (1937), which raised the idea of a transfer as an appropriate and legitimate solution. In British and American diplomatic circles as well, the transfer or resettlement of large populations after the war was discussed during those years in the context of what was termed the "Jewish" or "refugee" question. At the Evian Conference in the summer of 1938, the possibility of a transfer was raised and was at the heart of German plans for a "new order in Europe."

The issue cropped up again from time to time. As no one foresaw at the beginning of the war that it would last six years, and as they could not then anticipate the Nazis' Final Solution, the question of the masses of refugees to be dealt with in postwar Europe was a concrete point in Allied discussions. True, because of the mass deportation of Jews from Central to Eastern Europe in 1940, it was feared that as many as a million Jews might be killed in the war, but that only made it more urgent to evaluate rescue and rehabilitation options for the millions of survivors expected to remain afterward.

These ideas derived added force from demographic projections made by Lewis B. Namier, the renowned British historian who was also a close aide of Chaim Weizmann. Namier foresaw the Soviet victory over Germany, with the result that Poland's border would return to the Curzon Line and one or two million Polish Jews would come under Russian rule. In addition, he predicted that between two and three million homeless Jewish refugees would remain in Europe. This led Namier and Weizmann to believe that the refugee problem would pose a significant political and moral problem for the Allies in their discussions of the postwar order. If the Zionist leadership could apply sufficient pressure on world leaders, the latter might respond positively to the demand to direct the refugees to Palestine. Weizmann even believed that the British might revise their Palestine policy and reopen the gates to mass immigration. He, therefore, maintained his contacts with British officials in the hope that these might lead to the rescue of the Jews.

Ben-Gurion was more skeptical than most of his colleagues regarding the British position. True, he did not advocate breaking off political contacts with them, but he had only faint hopes of their success. The more he discussed with British officials the chances of dropping the White Paper provisions and opening the gates of Palestine to mass immigration, the more he became convinced that salvation did not lie in that direction.

In London in the summer of 1941 to meet with Lord Moyne, the newly appointed secretary of state for the colonies, Ben-Gurion made the question of the millions of Jewish refugees the focus of his discussions. Lord Moyne suggested allotting the refugees a territory in East Prussia once the Germans were expelled in the wake of victory over Hitler. Ben-Gurion, arguing that, "the only way to get Jews to go [to East Prussia] would be with machine guns,"[21] insisted that the only real solution to the problem of the Jewish refugees was to bring them all to Palestine. He then presented his plan to absorb three million Jewish refugees in Palestine within several years. Moyne saw this as unfeasible, arguing that the country's limited economic absorptive capacity rendered such ideas impossible. Moyne had already dealt with a similar, albeit far more moderate, refugee resettlement proposal from Weizmann, who had been willing to agree to a compromise figure of 100,000 immigrants per year (whereas Ben-Gurion was adamant that millions of Jews must be brought in within the short time span of several years).

Summarizing his meetings with both Zionist leaders in a memorandum of September 1941, Moyne noted "extremist tendencies" apparent in Zionist policy, in particular the demand to bring millions of Jews to Palestine. He reiterated his view, previously stated to Ben-Gurion, that such a plan was not feasible, both in terms of the economic absorptive capacity of Palestine and in view of political considerations; Moyne claimed, for instance, that a special British army would be needed to oversee the immigration of three million Jews to Palestine. His own proposal as detailed in the memorandum was to settle Jewish refugees in desolate European areas, in South America and in Madagascar.

Lord Moyne's memorandum was discussed in the British cabinet (on October 2, 1941), but no final decision was taken at that time. The prime minister summed up the discussion, saying that after the expected Allied victory, the establishment of a Jewish state in Palestine would be an issue for the peace conference.[22]

Nonetheless, Ben-Gurion steadfastly repeated that the question of Palestine could be delayed no longer and that every effort had to be made to find an immediate solution, "not for the future, not for the next generation, as we thought before the present catastrophe, but right now."[23] "After Britain's victory," he said, "there will be *five or six million* homeless Jews in Europe. . . . Eretz Israel must be established as a Jewish state, since this is now the only means to save millions of

Jews from destruction in Europe."[24] At that time (1941), no one foresaw the full extent of the Holocaust.

During 1942, Ben-Gurion concentrated all his efforts on having his proposals adopted as the official policy of the Zionist movement. He found an appropriate forum at the First National Conference of American Jewish Organizations on May 11, 1942 (known as the Biltmore Conference, after the New York hotel where it took place). There, Ben-Gurion spoke of the immediate necessity of effecting the immigration of three to five million Jews to Palestine and the creation of a Jewish commonwealth within the framework of the postwar democratic world order.

In the meantime, Britain steadfastly refused to allow free immigration to Palestine. Weizmann applied much pressure on Churchill, who was known to oppose the White Paper, but achieved nothing. British leaders announced unequivocally that they would not consider altering their policy for the duration of the war, since such changes could alter the stability of the Middle East situation and weaken Britain's position in that region.[25]

Britain was not the only disappointment. Appeals to the Allies in the summer of 1942 and at the beginning of 1943 concerning the necessity of saving as many Jews as possible went all but unanswered. Contacts initiated with the United States, the Soviet Union and governments-in-exile (most of them in London), all ended in failure. No government was prepared to spare the resources that it would have taken to undertake a rescue program. Such was also the response of the neutral countries that were asked to accept refugees for the duration of the war. This request was accompanied by a promise that Jewish organizations, among them the Jewish Agency, would fund the refugees' stay. However, it became clear that, aside from the Allied statement denouncing the mass murder of the Jews that was broadcast on radio and printed in newspapers in the free world on December 17, 1942, there was no intention of adopting concrete and large-scale plans to rescue Jews.

The appeal to public opinion in Britain and the United States resulted in a decision in the winter of 1943 to call a conference with the participation of Britain and the United States in order to seek a solution to the refugee problem. Many viewed this decision as an opening that might herald a change in the posture of the Allies toward the Jewish refugees in Europe. But it soon became apparent that these were false hopes. Even before the committee met in Bermuda on April 19, 1943, Britain and the United States had agreed that there would be no policy change, neither in relation to the White Paper nor regarding restrictive U.S. immigration quotas. In Palestine, Jewish Agency officials had set up a committee to apply pressure on the American and British participants that prepared reports and memoranda with various proposals to be presented to the committee in Bermuda.[26] The team dealing with plans to absorb refugees in Palestine, led by Ben-Gurion, prepared a special memorandum in which it was proposed to absorb 100,000 refugees in Palestine in the space of six months—but no one paid attention to this proposal.[27] It soon became clear that the committee would produce no concrete action on the refugee issue.

The bitter disappointment over the attitudes of the Allies was expressed by Moshe Shertok to U.S. State Department officials: "What do you need Bermuda for? If you want to do something, your governments must agree; the committee is only a rubber stamp.'' Sharett received a surprisingly candid reply: ''We estimate that Hitler will not free the refugees, and if he does let hundreds of thousands of Jews go, or a million—what will we do with them? What is to be done? That will be Hitler's revenge on the Allies.''[28]

The Bermuda Conference closed following nine days of discussions held in camera. Its conclusions were that it was impossible to rescue the Jews from Nazi Germany. The participants decided not to appeal to Hitler or negotiate with him in any form. Bringing Jewish refugees to the democratic countries would only heighten antisemitism there and was, therefore, to be avoided. The White Paper could not be changed, and the logistics involved in transporting the refugees might hurt the war effort.

Linking the issue of immigration to that of Palestine seemed legitimate as long as it was still possible to speak of millions of Jewish refugees penned up in Europe with no place to go. This situation changed as the truth of the Final Solution gradually became known. The information on what was happening in the death camps was devastating, and it brought the question of rescue to the point of utmost urgency. In the search for possible avenues of rescue and finance, the Yishuv leaders established a United Rescue Committee in January 1943 with the participation of the Jewish Agency Executive, the National Council and Jewish organizations unaffiliated with the Zionist Organization. The committee was headed by Yitzhak Gruenbaum, a former leader of Polish Jewry and one of the heads of the General Zionist movement in Palestine.

Ben-Gurion took part in the Rescue Committee's meetings and was active in its activities, especially when the proposed rescue operations involved immigration to Palestine.[29] He did not head the operation, however, choosing to devote most of his energies to the struggle for Eretz Israel: meeting with Allied officials and continuing to draw up plans for the immigration of millions of Jews. When faced with the charge that the Jewish Agency was not doing enough to rescue European Jewry, Ben-Gurion replied, ''The Zionist Organization is not in a position to spearhead [such an effort], especially regarding funding.'' Criticized by his own Mapai party for the meager extent of ongoing rescue efforts and for failing to accord the rescue issue top priority, he responded that assigning chief responsibility for the task of rescue to the Jewish Agency was ''a contradiction in terms . . . [indicating] a mistaken view of the nature of the Agency and of [what was required] for rescue operations to help the Jews in Nazi Europe.'' Ben-Gurion felt that the Agency lacked

. . . overall authority over the Jewish purse and over the running of Jewish public affairs. Unfortunately there is no general organization [that has such authority]. There is the World Jewish Congress and the American Jewish Congress, the United Jewish Appeal and others. But the institution called the Jewish Agency is a Jewish organization *for the building of Eretz Israel,* and I do not want to say which is more important, to rebuild Eretz Israel or rescue one Jew from Zagreb. Perhaps it is more important at times to rescue one child from Zagreb, but these are two separate things, and confusing them . . . does no good. *The Jewish Agency must act, and I think it has undertaken to do everything possible to rescue Jews through immigration to Palestine.* That is what the Agency must occupy itself with, that is its task. . . . To rescue one more child, to look for any other means of halting the deportations, all this lies outside the Agency's proper function.[30]

Was Ben-Gurion's attitude the fruit of sheer helplessness in the face of the desperate plight of European Jews, and did he, for that reason, prefer to concentrate on an issue he could do something about? Did the Yishuv leadership refuse to acknowledge the extent of the European catastrophe? Why did Berl Katznelson and others who were especially close to European Jewry and had always been attuned to its fate not speak out more forcefully? Recent attempts to resolve these and other issues provide no satisfactory answer.[31] Ben-Gurion's own attitude is best exemplified by his stated position: by rescuing Jews through aliyah to Eretz Israel, the Jewish Agency was fully discharging its task.

The memory of opposition aroused by his early program for mass immigration prompted Ben-Gurion to formulate a new plan that entailed an independent structure that would operate under his own supervision, outside the Mossad le-Aliyah Bet. During the summer of 1942, he worked on projections of the numbers that might be involved in mass immigration and calculated the annual rate of immigrants this would entail. He had previously spoken of two million immigrants, and he believed these might be brought in over a period of eighteen months. He elaborated on this timetable, explaining his reasoning in October 1942:

> I believe that the war may not end at once but in phases. First the war with Mussolini will end, then the war with Hitler, then [the war] with Japan, which could continue another ten years. And the thing is, when Mussolini falls and the Balkans are opened, we must bring hundreds of thousands of Jews by sea to Israel.[32]

But at the same time, Ben-Gurion also continued to speak of the immigration that would arrive *after* the war, though he reiterated that time was the crucial factor in determining the fate of Palestine and the Jewish people:

> I have come to rethink Zionist issues in light of the war. We must now give up old assumptions. . . . We used to see Zionism as a historical process extending over many years. We thought at first that one thousand immigrants a year would arrive, then tens of thousands, and gradually fifty thousand. To speak of one hundred thousand a year was thought to be ambitious. We can no longer think in this fashion, and after this war . . . it is thought there will be tens of millions of uprooted people. . . . The notion of population transfers now merits consideration in America. They [the Americans] will be dealing with [postwar] political and economic planning on a vast scale, and they are prepared for this. The role of Zionism after the war will be to utilize global, government resources and to settle two million Jews at one stroke in Palestine. We must settle the younger generation of Europe here, if any survive; instead of feeding them in ghettos, we must provide them with work. . . . The role of Zionism is to transfer two million Jews immediately for the sake of future development, and together with the present Yishuv there will then be in Palestine two and a half million Jews.[33]

This plan took root in Ben-Gurion's mind and he would not give it up, despite the opposition of colleagues in the Zionist leadership and in his party and despite the skepticism of economists and settlement experts who questioned whether the projected figures were at all realistic. Ben-Gurion continued to argue the feasibility of his concept:

> Only twenty years ago, a similar transfer was carried out when almost two million Greeks were transferred from Turkey in Asia to Greece in Europe, and the transfer did not take more than eighteen months. Why should we not be able to carry out an equally rapid transfer of Jews from the ghettos of Europe to Palestine?[34]

BEN-GURION DURING THE WAR: PLANNING FOR THE IMMIGRANT MILLIONS

Early in 1941 when Ben-Gurion was about to make one of his frequent visits to the United States, he had requested Jewish Agency officials in Palestine to gather material on the absorptive potential in the country as background material to his plan for massive immigration. The rudiments of such a program were presented at a meeting of the Center for Economic Studies at Rehovot in November 1942 where Ben-Gurion challenged the economists to draw up a master plan.[35]

In assigning this formidable task to the country's leading economists,[36] Ben-Gurion sought to simplify matters by asking them to disregard political issues and questions of financing, at least at the beginning. The experts were to deal with the technical analysis and to proceed on the assumption that "there is a [sympathetic] government and there are funds." Ben-Gurion wanted them to relate their analysis to two factors: space and time. In his words, "We want to bring two million Jews to Palestine. Present me with a proposal for this: How long will it take and what is the fastest way to do it?"

The experts on economics, settlement, agriculture and demography participating in the conference were taken aback. They were not used to thinking in such terms, and they tried to dissuade Ben-Gurion from pursuing the issue, arguing that an abrupt and massive increase in population would raise serious problems of land and water resources. For those who had been familiar with earlier proposals that involved a gradual immigration over twelve or fifteen years with incremental population increases of ten percent, it was extremely difficult to come to terms with Ben-Gurion's plan for an influx of two million in only one and one-half years.

But Ben-Gurion did not yield, going so far as to suggest the possibility of bringing in one million immigrants in ten days. These immigrants, he suggested, could be housed in internment camps until ways were found to integrate them into the economy.

The experts at the meeting were astounded. "Ben-Gurion," declared one, "has oversimplified reality. He has taken [a case] of not only ideal conditions, but wholly imaginary ones." Others tried to clarify the implications of Ben-Gurion's proposal:

> Under the terms of Ben-Gurion's program, two million Jews are to come to the country. They will range in age from one to sixty. They will be hungry, weak, with no profession. It will not be possible to put them immediately to work. . . . There will be adolescents among them, and this situation will continue for more than ten years. If they are put in camps, who will take care of them?[37]

Despite these objections, some of those present were ready to take up the challenge.

Ben-Gurion was interested in preparing two analyses: one to provide an answer to the major political objection by proving the economic feasibility of absorbing millions of immigrants; the second, an operative blueprint that would investigate all options, conditions and means involved in the transportation and absorption of such vast numbers.

Toward the close of 1942 and the start of 1943, it appeared that the war might soon be over. With the defeat of the German Sixth Army at Stalingrad (February 1943), the surrender of the Germans at Tunis (May 1943) and the Allied landing in Sicily (July 1943), the Germans were surrounded and their momentum arrested. By the beginning of 1944, the gradual liberation of German-occupied areas in Eastern Europe had begun, and the Red Army was advancing steadily westward. Although the Germans still held Western Europe and planned the invasion of Hungary, the Allies were seriously discussing postwar arrangements and "reconstruction."

In Palestine, the British prepared to reopen the question of Palestine's postwar status. In March 1943, Palestine High Commissioner Sir Harold MacMichael appointed Sir Douglas Harris as reconstruction commissioner for Palestine. His duties were to submit a comprehensive plan for the country's development and economic absorptive capabilities in various fields: agriculture, industry, education and other services. MacMichael announced that, despite the large increase in urban development and industry in Palestine, the country was in essence agricultural and thus limited in its absorptive potential.

The commission, established at the beginning of 1943, was the culmination of a long series of studies and reports on Palestine initiated by the British authorities, which concluded that the Jewish demand for mass immigration had no basis in reality. The formula used time and again by the British was the "limited economic absorptive capacity" of the country—their central argument for perpetuating the restrictions on immigration. Attacking and disproving this argument was part of the goal Ben-Gurion had set himself in his own project.

In order to counter the British plan, Ben-Gurion hastened to set up his own Planning Committee. Seeking to work as expeditiously as possible, he limited the committee to himself and three others: Siegfried Hoofien of the Anglo-Palestine Bank; Emil Schmorach, head of the trade and industry division of the Jewish Agency; and Eliezer Kaplan, the Agency treasurer. These three were skeptical concerning Ben-Gurion's figure of two million immigrants. Schmorach suggested that an alternative, "realistic" plan be prepared in case Ben-Gurion's plan failed "due to a lack of the appropriate political and financial conditions." But Ben-Gurion disagreed. The only compromise he was willing to make was to divide the program into two phases; first, the rapid arrival of two million Jews and the establishment of a Jewish government; second, the more gradual absorption of another million Jews over a span of several years.[38]

In fact, however, Dr. Schmorach's plan was adopted: though Ben-Gurion remained adamant about the time factor: one million immigrants were to be absorbed within eighteen months. The committee met weekly (sometimes even more frequently). Ben-Gurion chaired the committee and participated in all meetings except when out of the country. It was decided to set up working groups in various fields of endeavor, with the full Planning Committee filling a supervisory and coordinating role. Ben-Gurion chose to handle three subjects: marine operations (ports, shipping, fishing and marine training), the wider issues of immigration and plans related to specific cities (Jerusalem and Haifa).[39] His special interest in Jerusalem stemmed from the fact that the British partition plan of 1943 had excluded it from the area of the proposed Jewish state. Ben-Gurion believed that by populating Jerusalem rapidly with significant numbers of additional Jewish inhabitants, it would be possible to force a different determination of its political status. He chose Haifa as well since he intended it as Israel's main port.

Political tensions mounted after the British cabinet affirmed a new partition plan (January 25, 1944)[40] and, in Palestine, the breakaway underground movements intensified their struggle against the British authority. As a result, relations between the different Zionist movements in the country became very tense in the spring of 1944. In April, the Jewish Agency Executive decided to bring the militant right wing Irgun Zvai Leumi (IZL) and Lehi (Stern Group) groups to heel. At the same time, the labor movement itself was splitting, as the Mapai party expelled the dissident "B" faction led by Yitzhak Tabenkin. Although Ben-Gurion and his plans now became the targets of increased criticism and skepticism within the Jewish Agency leadership, he adamantly continued to assert, "[Our] de facto decision to establish a Jewish state means [that we need to effect] the immediate transfer of such a number of Jews to Palestine that will in fact create the state and translate the decision in principle into reality."[41]

The internal conflicts and lack of certainty as to the future of Palestine—and that of the Zionist movement in general—grew out of the utter frustration and confusion that were widely felt once the extent of the Holocaust was known. An absurd situation existed in 1944: dozens of people in Palestine were laboring over an absorption program for millions of Jews from Europe, while the Nazi extermination machine was operating at full blast and killing those millions.

During that time, Ben-Gurion privately succumbed to doubt about the future of the Jewish people, Zionism and Palestine.[42] Outwardly, however, he remained firm. He did not abandon his projects for the absorption of several million people, although he reassessed the potential sources of such an immigration, turning to Jewish populations in the Islamic countries, whose potential as a source of immigration he had begun to consider in 1943. He summoned officials of the Mossad le-Aliyah Bet for a report on their activities in Arab countries and data on potential aliyah. At the same time, Ben-Gurion continued urging the Planning Committee to carry on with the feasibility study he had commissioned, and he pressed David Horowitz, the committee secretary, to submit the final report as soon as possible.

Political developments in the Middle East caused Ben-Gurion to accelerate the pace of these preparations. During 1944, as Allied victories in Europe transformed the international political atmosphere, Egypt and Iraq began to raise the issue of inter-Arab solidarity. They decided to hold an initial conference in Cairo in September 1944 and laid there the foundations for the Arab League. Established at that time, the league assigned the Palestine question a central place in its activities. It received British support; in turn, it brought increased pressure to bear on Britain to favor Arab claims in Palestine. Courting Arab political support, Britain and the United States demanded that the Jewish Agency hold direct negotiations with the Arabs. Ben-Gurion rejected the suggestion to reach a compromise based on the partition plan of the British cabinet committee. At a meeting of the Zionist Inner Actions Committee on July 5, 1944, Ben-Gurion spoke of the need for a comprehensive approach to induce Britain to accede to Jewish claims. He advocated resisting the British actively by means of mass immigration and even by a militant policy of noncompliance with the Mandatory authorities.

Ben-Gurion was convinced more than ever that "Zionism's fateful hour will arrive once the Yishuv becomes the majority."[43] With the destruction of European Jewry, the Zionist movement had had the rug pulled from under its feet. Zionism had arrived at a crisis of unprecedented proportions. The expiry of the White Paper (March 1944) and the enhancement of Arab political influence threatened to put an end to Jewish settlement in Palestine. In the decisive struggle to be waged for the country, the plan for the absorption of millions of immigrants took on the utmost urgency. This, Ben-Gurion maintained, would be the official Zionist reply to the programs devised by the British.

The master plan formulated by the Planning Committee was completed in the summer of 1944. As noted, it envisioned the transfer to Palestine of one million Jews over the course of eighteen months. The plan included subsections on organizing the transportation and embarkation of the immigrants (the boats, trains, route details and ports to be used). Detailed lists of these data were included along with notes on equipment and the number of immigrants to leave each country. Several sections dealt with the absorption process in Palestine: the number of immigrants to enter per month, refugee camps and financing. The camps were to play a major role in the absorption process and serve as the base for the physical and emotional rehabilitation that the Holocaust survivors would require. They would also provide vocational training.

It was still hoped that Britain's policy would change and, as a result, that a mass immigration of this sort might be implemented in the immediate future. In October 1944, on the eve of the American presidential elections, Roosevelt promised the leaders of the Zionist movement that, if reelected, he would act to support the creation of a Jewish commonwealth in Palestine. The Planning Committee teams continued throughout the final weeks of 1944 and the beginning of 1945 to file reports on industrial development, commerce and agriculture.

In meetings with foreign officials at the end of 1944 and during 1945, Ben-Gurion cited the plan to enable one million refugees to enter Palestine immediately as the primary goal and top priority of the Zionist movement. Asked by the Bulgarian prime minister to assess the chances for the establishment of a Jewish state, Ben-Gurion replied: "For us statehood is not simply a matter of a political act, as it is for [you]. Rather, it will result from *immigration and settlement*."[44] In his discussions with other British officials, Ben-Gurion similarly spoke of the immigration of a million Jews and the creation of the state in the same breath, terming them "the only two possible solutions" to the Jewish problem.

This position was reiterated in public appearances and in conversations with the leaders of the Zionist movement in England. He tried to convince them that "only two solutions are possible, and they must be implemented immediately and comprehensively."[45] In the United States, too, he declared, "Our chief demand is to bring one million Jews *immediately* and in a brief time period, and to do that we require a state, government, aliyah [and] financial aid."[46]

Returning to London at the end of July 1945, Ben-Gurion used his shipboard time to calculate the number of Jews remaining in Europe. The data he possessed showed that there were 11,450,000 Jews in the world altogether: (1) 550,000 in Palestine; (2) 6,000,000 Anglo-American and Latin American Jews; (3) about 3,000,000 in Eastern Europe, including 2,000,000 in Russia; (4) 253,000 in Western Europe, outside London; (5) 855,000 in Muslim countries. His conclusion: "We must bring category five in its entirety [to Palestine] as soon as possible, most of category four, all that is possible of category three, and the *halutzim* of category two."[47]

The Planning Committee had heeded Ben-Gurion's instructions to leave political and financial obstacles out of its feasibility plan. The political question clearly lay beyond the competence of the committee; however, that of financing did not. Unless it could be financed, the plan would have no practical value.

This was a complicated question, especially at a time when the country was in transition from a war to a civilian economy. The transition period was a problem that preoccupied all countries affected by the war. Palestine, however, had not suffered economically from the war; it had flourished as a result of its immense imports—far greater than ever before. The British government had poured the equivalent of almost £100 million into Palestine. Thus, the problem was not only how to maintain economic stability once this source of revenue dried up, but also how to expand the entire economic structure on a large scale so that a sudden mass influx of refugees could be absorbed.

The committee received a report on funding that questioned the feasibility of implementing the program in the space of eighteen months. It suggested that funding might be found in the form of loans, international grants and bank credit if the effort were to be spread out over a twelve-year period. But Ben-Gurion insisted on the eighteen-month time frame. To solve this problem it was suggested that reparations be demanded from Germany. This would help defray the costs of rehabilitating the refugees from Europe and settling them in Palestine. The possibility of making such a claim now became a prime factor in the committee's calculations.[48]

The war ended without any resolution of the Palestine question. Political developments on the international scene—Roosevelt's death and Harry Truman's assumption of the U.S. presidency, the defeat of the Conservatives in the British elections (July 1945), Churchill's resulting fall and the rise of the Labour Party—elicited mixed reactions of expectation and foreboding among the Jews. Europe was in the throes of the initial postwar confusion, with Holocaust survivors crisscrossing the Continent. Tens of thousands of Jewish refugees who sought to return to their former homes in Poland found them inhabited by local residents who, on numerous occasions, greeted the Jews' return with violence. More than 250,000 Jews from Eastern Europe turned to Western and Southern Europe,[49] most of them going to Austria and Germany. The idea of an armed illegal immigration (Aliyah Gimmel) was raised again.

In October 1945 Ben-Gurion presented a memorandum to General Eisenhower demanding permission for East European Jewish refugees to enter the American occupation zone. This request was granted. Reporting to the Jewish Agency Executive in Jerusalem in November 1945, Ben-Gurion explained the tactical purpose of this step, "If we succeed in concentrating a quarter of a million Jews in the American zone, it will increase the American pressure on the British—not because of the economic problem, which is not a factor for them, but because they see no future for these people anywhere except Palestine."[50]

As he thus foresaw, the displaced person camps in Germany became a burning issue in American public opinion; from then on events seemed to follow a script written by Ben-Gurion. Journalists and thousands of soldiers returning from Europe reported on the Jewish tragedy they had witnessed and on the conditions of the survivors in the refugee camps. American Jewry, through the influence of the media on public opinion and through members of Congress, called on the administration to intervene on behalf of the steadily growing number of Jewish DPs in the American zone in Germany. President Truman asked Earl G. Harrison, a representative of the Intergovernmental Committee on Refugees, to report to him on the situation in the DP camps. Harrison's report of August 1945 detailed the plight of the Holocaust survivors and proposed sending one hundred thousand Jews to Palestine. Truman turned to British Prime Minister Clement Attlee for his assent, but the British government countered with a proposal to establish an Anglo-American committee to discuss the matter, apparently believing that the committee would turn down the idea.

It now fell to the members of the economic Planning Committee to appear before the Anglo-American committee in order to present their findings on the absorptive capacity of Palestine. In Ben-Gurion's absence, the preliminary meeting of the planning committee was chaired by Eliezer Kaplan.[51] In an atmosphere fraught with tension, the committee began a feverish round of activity, holding daily meetings to prepare its presentation. It was decided to present two separate plans: one for the immigration of one million Jews ("even more, if possible"); the second a memorandum calling for the absorption of 100,000 Jews, a "first wave of immigrants," as they put it.[52]

The conclusions of the Anglo-American Committee disappointed the Yishuv leadership. True, the committee was in favor of the immigration of one hundred thousand Jews, but only as part of a program that would, in fact, limit the expansion of Jewish settlement. Nonetheless, the Anglo-American Committee's mere existence and activity marked a breakthrough in removing the issue of the political future of Palestine from the exclusive purview of British policymakers. At first the Americans, then the United Nations, were drawn in—a process that eventually resulted in the decision of November 29, 1947 to partition Palestine into a Jewish and an Arab state.

CONCLUSION

The singularity of Ben-Gurion's approach, revealed in his project for the immigration of a million Jews, did not stem from originality of thought. Many of the ideas he raised had previously been broached by others. However, Ben-Gurion bridged the gap between concept and implementation. He grasped political reality not as fixed and static but rather as a conjunction of constantly changing circumstances that obliged leaders to be always prepared to adjust their course of action. Ben-Gurion's strength—and his chief weakness, according to his critics—was his single-mindedness in pursuing his goals without regard for obstacles and regardless of bitter and tragic events. Even in the face of opposition within his own party and the Zionist labor movement, he refused to give in or compromise—he simply waited for a more propitious opportunity. He was prepared to change his tactics and seek new organizational frameworks if these would further his own aims. He saw himself as totally engaged in a mission, charged with fulfilling it without question.

Yet the question still remains: How is it possible to explain that while the gas chambers were working at maximal capacity in Europe and while every day the trains were carrying still more thousands to their deaths, Ben-Gurion could spend his time with teams of experts working out his plans for the immigration and absorption of one million immigrants? He went into the minutest detail examining ways to develop water resources and to establish new industrial enterprises. He immersed himself in exhausting discussions about which branches of agriculture should be given priority and even about which breed of sheep would provide the textile industry with the best wool.

After all, nobody was more aware—or earlier aware—than Ben-Gurion of the appalling scale of the tragedy then engulfing the Jews of Europe; but still he pressed on with his plans for a massive immigration from Europe at some unknown future date—plans that he could hardly have hoped to implement until the war was won. And how many Jews would be left alive in Europe? There is a paradox here that will in all probability never be fully comprehensible. Nonetheless, his own words from late 1943 do, perhaps, provide us with some insight, "The annihilation of the Jews in Europe means the destruction of Zionism, because there will be nobody with which to build Eretz Yisrael. What will then become of the Jewish people and its hopes; what will then be the fate of the Yishuv here in Palestine? I do not even want to think about this. It is something too terrible."[53]

Ben-Gurion here is not a man who sought to ignore the Holocaust or its meaning. Rather, he was a man struggling hard not to allow himself to be overwhelmed by feelings of helplessness, by the passivity born of despair. For the leadership to lose hope in that hour of trial would, he seems to have felt, have meant to leave the Zionist enterprise and the Jewish people without any way to move forward to the future.

With the creation of the state, Ben-Gurion set mass immigration as its top priority. He viewed mass aliyah as the most characteristic expression of the Zionist spirit, its ideological basis and source of its power. Ben-Gurion did not view the state itself as the ultimate goal of the Zionist movement. As far as he was concerned, statehood did not mark the close of an era but rather just another interim step. In a diary notation of January 8, 1949, he wrote, "The great revolution is not yet complete, and its positive role has not yet begun. In the approaching period we must lay foundations that will last for decades, perhaps centuries. We must forge the image of the state of Israel and prepare it to fulfill its historic mission."[54] And again,

"The crucial revolution is still before us. We must revolutionize the country, the people, our entire life."[55]

Ben-Gurion had in mind not only the Jewish community in Israel, but also the Jewish people in the Diaspora. To carry out such a far-reaching change in Jewish history the successes of a small population in Israel were insufficient. The creation of a tiny state on an insignificant strip of land was not the end of the road. To redeem the Jewish people and carry out a revolution in its history, it was necessary to work toward the ingathering of all Jews from the Diaspora, that is, to concentrate the majority of the Jewish people in Israel. That was his vision of the physical and spiritual salvation of his people, a vision that could not be relinquished for even a single hour. It seemed to him that the "gates of heaven" were opening for a split second; everything not achieved in that second would be lost forever.

Not everyone shared Ben-Gurion's views. Just after the creation of the state, with the onset of the large-scale immigration, voices from every side were heard calling for a limit to the immigration and a moderation of its tempo. The state was in the midst of a grim war for survival and faced dire financial and economic straits. Many warned that mass, unlimited immigration would prove too heavy a burden for the Yishuv to bear—that it would "snap the backbone of our state." Despite these nearly unanimous warnings, Ben-Gurion held fast to his decision that immigration would continue uninterrupted, and from every country from which Jews were seeking to leave. This stand aroused considerable surprise and fed speculation that Ben-Gurion simply did not understand economic problems or the logistics of immigration and absorption. But throughout, Ben-Gurion had remained consistent. In 1947, he had said, "The [prospective Jewish] state is missing one essential thing . . . Jews. As long as this lack is not minimally filled, there is no guarantee the state will survive."[56] And in 1949, he declared, "For thousands of years, we were a *people without a state*. The great danger now is that we will be a *state without a people*."[57]

Notes

1. H. Wagman Eshkoli, "'Emdat hamanhigut hayehudit beerez yisrael lehazalat yehudei eiropah (1942–1944)" (M.A. thesis, Bar-Ilan University, 1977) 4, 171–172; Zev Zahor, "Ben-Gurion vehaha'apalah," in *Yahadut mizrah eiropah bein shoah letekumah,* ed. Binyamin Pinkus (Sdeh-Boker and Beersheba: 1987), 432–433. See also Dina Porat, "D. Ben-Gurion veshoat yehudei eiropah," *Haziyonut* 12 (1987) 293–314; and Tuvia Frieling, "Levehinat hasteriotip: Ben-Gurion veshoat yehudei eiropah 1939–1945," *Yad Vashem: kovez mehkarim* 17–18 (1987), 329–351.

2. Dina Porat, *Hanhagah bemilkud* (Tel-Aviv: 1986), 99.

3. See, e.g., Yehuda Bauer, *Diplomatiyah vemahteret bemediniyut haziyonit 1939–1945* (Merhaviah: 1963); Netanel Katzburg, *Mediniyut bemavokh: mediniyut britaniah beerez yisrael 1939–1945* (Jerusalem: 1977); S. Dotan, *Hamaavak 'al erez yisrael* (Tel-Aviv: 1981); Alon Gal, *David Ben-Gurion likrat medinah yehudit: hahe'arkhut hamedinit nokhah hasefer halavan ufroz milhemet ha'olam hasheniyah, 1938–1941* (Sdeh-Boker: 1985); Yosef Gorni, *Shutafut umaavak: Hayim Veizman utenu'at hapo'alim beerez yisrael* (Tel-Aviv: 1976).

4. Dina Porat, *Hanhagah bemilkud.*

5. Zev Jabotinsky, *Neumim, 1927–1940* (Jerusalem: 1948), 83–182, 299.

6. Ben-Gurion to the Jewish Agency Executive, 11 December 1938; David Ben-Gurion, *Zikhronot,* (Tel-Aviv: 1982), vol. 5, 106.

7. *Ibid.;* see also M. Avizohar, *Haziyonut halohemet* (Sdeh-Boker and Beersheba: 1985).

8. Ben-Gurion, *Yoman Ben-Gurion,* 10 December 1938 (Ben-Gurion Archive, Sdeh-Boker); Mapai Central Council, 15 December 1938, Mapai Labour Party Archives, Beit Berl (hereafter MA); Jewish Agency Executive, 11 December 1938, Central Zionist Archives (hereafter CZA).

9. Ben-Gurion, *Yoman Ben-Gurion,* 10 December 1938.

10. On the various positions taken on this issue, see Avizohar, *Haziyonut halohemet,* 38–39.

11. Yitzhak Avneri, "'Mered 'aliyah': tokhnito shel Ben-Gurion le'aliyah bilti-legalit," *Kathedra* 44 (1987), 144–148.

12. *Minutes, Twenty-first Zionist Congress,* 18 August 1939, 348–349.

13. Menahem Kaufman, *Lo-ziyonim beamerikah bemaavak 'al hamedinah, 1939–1948* (Jerusalem: 1987); Porat, *Hanhagah bemilkud,* 179–180.

14. Ben-Gurion, *Yoman Ben-Gurion,* 10 December 1938.

15. Jewish Agency Executive, 6 October 1942, CZA.

16. *Ibid.*

17. *Ibid.*

18. David Ben-Gurion, *Bema'arakhah* (Tel-Aviv: 1957), vol. 4, 15.

19. *Davar,* 20 September 1940.

20. Ben-Gurion, *Bama'arakhah,* vol. 4, 13–14.

21. Jewish Agency Executive, 4 October 1942, CZA.

22. Katzburg, *Mediniyut bemavokh* 42–43.

23. Ben-Gurion, *Bema'arakhah,* vol. 4, 24, emphasis added.

24. *Ibid.,* 26.

25. Katzburg, *Mediniyut bemavokh,* 42–43.

26. Porat, *Hanhagah bemilkud,* 264–269.

27. *Ibid.*

28. *Ibid.,* 271 (n. 12).

29. *Ibid.,* 101–103; T. Frieling, "'Emdotav shel Ben-Gurion befarashat hazalat ha-yeladim, november 1942–mai 1945," *Yalkut moreshet* (May–June 1986).

30. Mapai Central Council, August 1943, MA.

31. Porat, *Hanhagah bemilkud,* 483–493; *idem,* "Ben-Gurion veshoat yehudei eiropah"; S. Teveth, *Kinat David: hakark'a habo'er* (Tel-Aviv and Jerusalem: 1987); *ibid.,* 428–442. [Also see Dalia Ofer herein, 239–240—Ed.].

32. Jewish Agency Executive, 6 October 1942, CZA.

33. *Ibid.*

34. From a speech delivered at the Fifth Conference of Mapai, 25 October 1942, Ben-Gurion, *Bama'arakhah,* vol. 4, 98.

35. Center for Economic Studies, 24 November 1942, Ben-Gurion Archive.

36. Among those present at the meeting were: Dr. Arthur Ruppin, Dr. A. Granovsky, Professor I. Vulcani, S. Hoofein, E. Schmorach, P. Naftali and Eliezer Kaplan.

37. Center for Economic Studies, 24 November 1942.

38. Planning Committee, 18 October 1943, Ben-Gurion Archive.

39. Center for Economic Studies meeting, 24 November 1942.

40. Katzburg, *Mediniyut bemavokh,* 121–123.

41. Jewish Agency Executive, 20 June 1944, CZA.

42. *Yoman Ben-Gurion,* 30 July 1944.

43. Zionist Inner Actions Committee, 5 July 1944: see also Fourth Zionist Conference, December 1944 in Ben-Gurion, *Bama'arakhah,* vol. 4, 193.

44. Ben-Gurion, *Yoman Ben-Gurion,* 2 December 1944.

45. *Ibid.,* 2 May and 6 May 1945.

46. Jewish Agency Executive, 20 June 1944, CZA, emphasis added.

47. Ben-Gurion, *Yoman Ben-Gurion*, 30 July 1945.

48. Dvorah Hacohen, "Hadiyunim basokhnut hayehudit 'al shilumim migermaniah be'et milḥemet ha'olam hasheniyah," *Yahadut zemaneinu* (forthcoming).

49. Yehuda Bauer, *Haberikhah* (Tel-Aviv: 1970).

50. Zev Zahor, "Sheerit hapeleitah kegoram politi," in *Maḥanot hageirush bekafrisin: yemei-'iyun beparshiyot historiyot uve'ayot yesod*, Yad Tabenkin Seminar Series (January 1987), no. 62, 23–30.

51. Planning Committee, 17 February 1946 Ben-Gurion Archive.

52. *Ibid.*

53. Jewish Agency Executive, 6 December 1943, CZA.

54. Ben-Gurion, *Yoman Ben-Gurion*, 8 January 1949.

55. *Ibid.*

56. Mapai Central Council, 3 December 1947, MA.

57. David Ben-Gurion, *Neẓaḥ Yisrael* (Tel-Aviv: 1964), 33.

A Note on the Demographic and Economic Structure of the Jewish Community in Quito, Ecuador

Tikva Darvish
(BAR-ILAN UNIVERSITY)

Yehuda Don
(BAR-ILAN UNIVERSITY)

The chief obstacle to most studies about Latin American Jewry, particularly of the smaller communities, is the absence of reliable information. Obtaining data on small Jewish minorities in Latin America is an almost impossible mission. For instance, the Jewish community in Quito, Ecuador, is not even mentioned in the important recent survey on Jews in Latin America as presented in the *American Jewish Year Book (1985).*[1]

Our purpose is to present and interpret recent information on the demographic and economic structure of the Jewish households in Quito.

The community of Quito was selected for two reasons: first, it is small and relatively accessible for investigation; second, it is still, to a large extent, a homogeneous community in which many of the methodological hazards of misinterpretation can be avoided.

We begin by describing the data source, then we suggest a demographic profile of the Jewish community in Quito. In conclusion, we examine the community's economic structure vis-à-vis the model suggested by Simon Kuznets.[2]

THE DATA SOURCE

This study is based on a questionnaire administered to *each* known Jewish household in Quito during 1985.[3] The survey includes 153 interviewees, about 90 percent of all the Jewish households in Quito, where the Jewish population was about 170 families in 1984.[4] Admittedly, the sample is small; however, because it constitutes a virtual census of the Jewish population, it is of value in permitting us to obtain a reasonably accurate image of the basic demographic and economic structure of the Jews in Quito.

DEMOGRAPHIC PROFILE OF THE JEWS IN QUITO

Country of Origin and Imigration

One-third of all the interviewed heads of households were born in Ecuador, two-thirds immigrated to Ecuador. About two-thirds of all immigrants were born in Central and Eastern Europe, namely in Germany, Austria, Czechoslovakia, Hungary, Romania or Poland. More than one-quarter of the immigrating heads of households (27 percent) were born in other Latin American countries, mainly Chile, Argentina and Columbia.

Immigration to Quito took place in two major waves that lasted a quarter of a century each. The first wave encompassed the prewar years, the Second World War and the postwar era of chaos and reconstruction in Europe. The second wave lasted from the early 1960s to the mid-1980s. More than 60 percent of all immigrants arrived in Quito during the first wave, most from Eastern and Central Europe, whereas 90 percent of the second wave of immigrants came to Quito from Latin America or Israel.

Age Composition

The age distribution of all 153 interviewees is presented in Table 1.

The age composition was relatively young, with 47.7 years as the average age, which, though higher than that of non-Jewish males in Ecuador, was close to that of the Jewish males in Israel (46.2 years as the average age). About 57 percent of all Jewish heads of households were under the age of 50, which made this small community a young one compared to others in Latin America.[5]

Table 1. Age Composition of Jewish Heads of Households in 1985

Age Group		Percentages
0–29		5.9
30–39		24.8
40–49		26.1
50–59		15.7
60–69		18.3
70+		9.2
	Total	100.0

Source: The survey.

Level of Education

The survey indicates a relatively high educational level: 56 percent of all Jewish heads of households had studied in high school, and more than three-quarters of these had obtained academic degrees; 35 percent had graduated from secondary school; and 9 percent had only finished primary school. A comparison with other Jewish communities reveals that the Jewish community of Quito is at least as well educated as the Jews in the United States (in 1970) and reached a higher educational level than that of the Jews in Switzerland (1970) and in Argentina (1960).[6]

A further indication of the advanced state of education of Jewish households in Quito is the fact that only 20 percent of those with higher education had attended universities in Ecuador and another 14 percent in other Latin American countries. About two-thirds had studied in universities and colleges in the United States, Canada and Europe.

THE ECONOMIC STRUCTURE OF THE JEWS IN QUITO

The basic model employed to investigate the economic behavior of Jews as a minority, compared with that of the majority, is that developed by Simon Kuznets. His model is applicable to what he called a small minority, that is, less than 10 percent of the overall population in a given country. The Jewish minority in Quito, of course, falls within this category as the Jewish population of Quito in 1984 numbered approximately 170 families among a total population of about 820,000.[7]

Table 2 shows the economic structures of male Jews in Quito and the non-Jews in Ecuador. Although the data concerning Jews refer to males only in the city of Quito, whereas the data on non-Jews show the total labor force in the country, we consider the comparison permissible. The population of Quito is about 10 percent of Ecuador's total population. Hence, it may be assumed that after deducting the primary sectors (specifically, agriculture and mining or quarrying) from the occupational statistics of the country the economic profile of the nonprimary sectors will, *grosso modo,* resemble the occupational structure of Quito. To facilitate comparison, Table 2 lists the occupational composition of the total Ecuadorian labor force (col. 2) together with those of the nonprimary sectors (col. 3) and of the Jewish households in Quito (col. 1).

The picture that emerges from Table 2 is well in line with the Kuznets model:

1. The economic structure of the Jews is narrower than that of the non-Jews. Although about 60 percent of all gainfully occupied Jews are concentrated in one specific area (craft and industry), only about 48 percent of the gainfully employed non-Jews are concentrated in the single most important branch (agriculture); whereas only 34.2 percent of the nonprimary sector was to be found in one category (public and community services).

2. As indicated, crafts and industry is the most prominent source of employment for Jews, accounting for about 60 percent of the total Jewish labor force in Quito. In comparison, only 11 percent of the total non-Jewish labor force in Ecuador is employed in industry. When we deduct the primary sectors, the ratio rises to 23

Table 2. Economic Structure of Jewish and Non-Jewish Males
in Quito and Ecuador (percent)

Branch	Jews (Quito), 1985	Non-Jews (Ecuador), 1981	
		All Sectors	Nonprimary Sectors Only
	(1)	(2)	(3)
Agriculture	2.7	47.6	—
Mining or quarrying	—	0.3	—
Craft and industry	60.2	10.6	23.3
Electricity and water	—	0.6	1.1
Construction	4.7	4.7	10.4
Commerce, restaurants & hotels	19.6	10.6	23.2
Transport & communication	—	2.4	5.3
Financing & business services	8.1	1.1	2.5
Public, community, personal & other services	4.7	15.7	34.2
Miscellaneous & undefined	—	6.4	—
Total	100.0	100.0	100.0

Sources: For Jews, the survey; For non-Jews, Boletin-Amario, Banco Central de Ecuador, 1985, Table 1301, 260–261.

percent. Furthermore, again in line with the characterization suggested by Kuznets, about 80 percent of all Jews employed in crafts and industry are concentrated in light industry, producing finished goods such as textiles, clothing, foodstuffs and wood and leather products.

3. Commerce comes next in importance. It absorbs close to 20 percent of the Jewish labor force. The corresponding figure for non-Jews is about 11 percent. However, after eliminating the primary sectors, 23 percent of all participants in the nonprimary labor force in Ecuador, somewhat more than among the Jews, were employed in commerce.

4. The situation in financing and business services is different. Jews preferred these occupations at a ratio of more than three to one when compared with the nonprimary, non-Jewish labor force.

5. The proportion of Jews engaged in primary activities is, as expected, quite insignificant—2.7 percent of the labor force. Even those registered as working in agriculture are, in fact, employed in administrative jobs within the agricultural sector.

6. The share of Jews in the services is, as hypothesized, very low. With 4.7 percent of all gainfully occupied, their ratio is about one-seventh of the Ecuadorian labor force outside of the primary sectors (34.2 percent).

Another typical feature of Jewish economic behavior, as spelled out by Kuznets, is the tendency of Jews to prefer independent status at work; this phenomenon is, in fact, apparent in the Jewish community in Quito. About 70 percent of all interviewed Jewish heads of households are self-employed, compared with the 40 percent of total male labor force in Ecuador in 1982.[8]

To sum up, all features of Jewish economic behavior, as formulated by the Kuznets model and substantiated later by his disciples, have been fully corroborated in the Quito study, although most other studies, including that of Kuznets, were based on studies conducted before the Second World War. The final conclusion is that the basic characteristics of Jewish economic behavior have not changed in the course of the last fifty years and, what is probably even more fascinating, the tiny and isolated Jewish community in Quito displays patterns of economic behavior that are typical of the major Jewish centers.

Notes

We owe much to Mrs. Judith Zoldan and her late husband, Steve Zoldan, for their gracious assistance in implementing the field study in Quito.

1. *American Jewish Year Book 1985* (Philadelphia: 1985), esp. 51–102; see also Sergio Della Pergola, "Demographic Trends of Latin American Jewry," in *The Jewish Presence in Latin America*, ed. J. Laikin Elkin and G. W. Merkx (Boston: 1987), 85–133.

2. Simon Kuznets, "Economic Structure and Life of the Jews," in *The Jews—Their History, Culture and Religion*, 3rd ed., ed. L. Finkelstein (New York: 1960), vol. 2, 1597–1666.

3. The names of the interviewed Jewish households were supplied by the leadership of the Asociación Beneficienia Israelita.

4. *Demographic Year Book 1984* (New York: 1986), 264.

5. Despite the biased comparison, tending to show the Buenos Aires and São Paulo figures younger than they presumably are, in reality the median age of the Quito group is lower, indicating that by comparing it with less recent statistics from Buenos Aires and São

Age Composition of Jewish Heads of Households in Quito, of Jewish Males in Buenos Aires and São Paulo (percent)

Age Group	Quito (1985)	Buenos Aires (1960)	São Paulo (1968)
30–39	29.2	29.5	22.8
40–49	30.8	25.7	28.9
50–59	18.5	27.8	24.6
60–69	21.5	17.0	23.7
Total	100.0	100.0	100.0
Average age	47.7	47.7	49.4
Median age	46.3	47.5	48.9

Sources: For Quito: the survey; for Buenos Aires and São Paulo: U. O. Schmelz and S. Della Pergola, *Hademographia shel hayehudim beargentina uvarazot aherot shel amerika halatinit* (Tel-Aviv: 1974) p. 193.

Paulo, one would have witnessed a significantly younger age composition of males in Quito than in the two large Jewish urban conglomerations in Latin America.

6. Sources for the United States: S. Goldstein, "The Jews in the United States: Perspectives from Demography" in *American Jewish Year Book 1981*, 49; for Argentina: U. O. Schmelz and S. Della Pergola, *Hademografiah shel hayehudim beargentina uvearaẓot aḥerot shel amerika halatinit* (Tel-Aviv: 1974), 5; for Switzerland: I. I. Milman, "Data on Diaspora Jewish Population from Official Censuses," in U.O. Schmelz, P. Glikson and S. J. Gould, *Studies in Jewish Demography: Survey for 1972–1980*, (New York: 1983), 94.

7. *Demographic Year Book 1984*, 264.

8. *ILO Yearbook of Labor Statistics 1986* (Geneva: 1986), 60.

The Gezerd Down Under

David Rechter
(THE HEBREW UNIVERSITY)

The disproportionate Jewish involvement in nineteenth- and twentieth-century left-wing politics in Europe, Russia and America has been well documented. Differing approaches to questions of Jewish identity—its individual, collective and political meanings—have led to a diversity of opinion regarding the relationship of this political involvement to Jewish tradition.[1]

Some have downplayed the Jewishness of at least the most notable of these radical Jews, a view that finds its most succinct expression in Isaac Deutscher's phrase "the non-Jewish Jew."[2] Jews defining themselves as international socialists, it is argued, rejected their Jewish identity as meaningless and, worse, an obstruction to revolutionary progress. Finding themselves at the margins of both their host society and their own Jewish community, they substituted political radicalism for a lost or unwanted Jewish identity.[3] An alternative approach (the "very-Jewish Jew"?) attempts to find in Jewish tradition and culture an explanation of Jewish radicalism, while a middle course is steered by those who see the Jewish attachment to the Left as primarily rooted in self-interest and sociopolitical circumstances, neither deeply embedded in, nor irretrievably alienated from, Jewish tradition.[4]

In the 1930s, Communists and the Soviet Union were seen by many Jews as their most reliable allies in the fight against fascism. This period saw a marked coincidence of interests between Jews and the Communist Left, with antifascism providing a framework within which Jews could comfortably be both Communist and Jewish. It was at precisely this time, too, that a Jewish Communist movement emerged and developed in Melbourne, Australia, a local version of the Russian and East European radical Jewish subculture.[5] From its beginnings in the early 1930s to its demise in the early 1950s, this was a small immigrant movement, at no time encompassing more than several hundred supporters in a Jewish community of some nine thousand in the early 1930s and over fifteen thousand by the late 1940s.[6] Perhaps the defining characteristic of this Australian version of Jewish Communism was its isolation from the international Jewish Communist mainstream. Influenced by, but unable to exert any influence on, the centers of European and American politics and culture, Australian Jewish Communism was typical both of Australian Jewish life and Australian Communism in general—derivative in nature and conspicuously lacking originality.

In the 1920s, some two thousand East European Jews arrived in Australia, the first time that their numbers had exceeded those of the English and Central European Jewish immigration.[7] With the gradual tightening of immigration laws throughout the decade in Europe, South America, some Commonwealth countries, and in particular in the United States in 1924, East European Jews began to look farther afield.[8] Of the two thousand who came to Australia, approximately two-thirds settled in Melbourne; among them was a small number who had been active in left-wing Jewish politics either in the Russian Empire before 1917 or in independent Poland.[9]

The East European immigrant Jews of the 1920s were predominantly tailors, peddlers and petty artisans, occupying the lower rungs of the Jewish socioeconomic ladder for the next two or three decades. By the late 1940s, Australian Jewry had experienced a marked rise in its economic status, was disproportionately represented in professional, administrative, commercial and clerical occupations, and in addition had a much higher proportion of employers than the general population.[10] The immigrants who had arrived from Eastern Europe after the First World War, while gradually establishing themselves socially and economically, retained their relatively low status until the late 1940s when there was a new wave of arrivals— the postwar refugees. Jewish Communism drew much of its support in the 1930s and 1940s from these East Europeans at the lower end of the socioeconomic scale.

In the interwar period, Melbourne Jewry comprised three fairly distinct groupings—the established and dominant Anglo-Australian Jews, the German-speaking Jews and the more recent East European arrivals. The power of the Anglo-Australians did not rest on numerical preponderance, but on control of the community's religious, social and philanthropic institutions. The 1930s saw a prolonged conflict within the Jewish community between the Anglo-Australians, on the one hand, and the East and Central Europeans on the other, with the latter demanding a broader and more intensive Jewish commitment as well as a reform of the communal power structure that would provide them with a stronger official voice in communal affairs.[11] The Anglo-Australian attitude prevalent at the time was nicely encapsulated by the comment of a prominent communal leader to the effect that, although he regarded himself as a Jew from ten to twelve on a Saturday morning, he was otherwise an Australian.[12]

For the most part, the Jewish Communists of the 1930s and early 1940s operated at the margins of this environment. Only during the middle and late 1940s was there a degree of convergence between the Communists and the political mainstream of the Jewish community, owing primarily to the perceived need for unity in the war effort and in the fight against antisemitism. The combined impact of the Cold War and the creation of the state of Israel, however, soon served to divide Jewish political life sharply, and once more the Jewish Communists found themselves on the political periphery of their community.

In January 1925, the Soviet government established the Gezelshaft far aynordnen oyf erd arbetndike yidn in FSSR (Society to Settle Working Jews on the Land in the USSR)—known as Gezerd in Yiddish and as OZET in its Russian abbreviation.[13] The notion of creating a Jewish agricultural class was not new in Soviet thinking, and it echoed a tenet of Zionist ideology: the rebuilding of the Jewish people by a return to the land. The resettlement program was proposed both as a solution to the severe social and economic dislocation of Russian Jewry and as a means of channeling Jewish national sentiment into an acceptable Soviet-style venture.

To this end the Soviet government adopted Zionist forms of rhetoric, as well as establishing its own alternative to Palestine—Birobidzhan, on the far eastern border of the Soviet Union. It was hoped that the concept of a Jewish "homeland" would attract the material and moral support of Jewish communities around the world, a hope realized by the establishment of Gezerd support organizations in a number of countries.[14] In distant Australia, with a Jewish community of some twenty-five thousand in the early 1930s, branches were established in both Melbourne and Sydney.

The Melbourne Gezerd was formed in May 1930 but did not emerge into the public eye until January 1931.[15] The intervening period was taken up with wrangling over the proposed nature and direction of the group. Initially, the aim had been to form a left-wing cultural organization akin to the Kadimah (the central cultural and social organization of immigrant Melbourne Jewry), but more open to expressions of support for the Soviet Union. Arguing for a more narrowly based Soviet-oriented organization were the Communists; their control of the Gezerd was not secured until late 1930, at which time, as one of their number later (somewhat coyly) wrote, "New people joined and ensured a pro-Soviet direction."[16]

Within a very short space of time, the Gezerd had a membership of approximately one hundred, a reading room and lending library (stocked with international Jewish, Soviet and Communist journals) and a proven fund-raising capacity, having already sent more than £50 (Australian) to Birobidzhan.[17] A Yiddish and English pamphlet was published—in a print run (so it was claimed) of several thousand copies—that appealed to the Jewish workers in Melbourne to support a campaign to "cleanse" local Jewish life of its dominant clerical and conservative influences.[18] Over the next few years, the Gezerd continued to expand at a steady, if unspectacular rate, and by mid-1933 could claim a membership of several hundred.[19] By mid-1934, the group's weekly meetings were supplemented by political economy classes and a drama circle; a number of pamphlets were published in Yiddish and English; and sufficient funds had been raised to send a microscope and X-ray machine to Birobidzhan.[20]

While the overwhelming majority of its meetings were devoted to lectures and discussions about Soviet and Soviet Jewish politics, this was not the sole concern of the Gezerd. Frequent and popular cultural evenings were held, with readings from Yiddish writers and musical performances by Jewish artists. Local politics, on the other hand, were almost entirely ignored. Over the course of the next few years, Australian Communists and left-wingers were invited (infrequently) to speak to the Gezerd, but these occasions were almost invariably arranged in order to celebrate a Soviet anniversary (that of the revolution or the establishment of Birobidzhan) or to hear an account of a visit to the Soviet Union.[21] The Gezerd's political culture was characterized throughout by an extreme narrowness. Converted in Eastern Europe to the cause of Soviet Communism—which they saw as destined to liberate not only the Jews, but all humanity—the Gezerd's leaders brought this conviction to Australia, where, isolated from the mainstream of Jewish life, their politics took on an embalmed, ritualistic quality marked primarily by pro-soviet incantations. The Soviet Union and Birobidzhan were the pivotal themes around which all Gezerd activity—meetings, discussions, lectures, fund-raising bazaars, picnics, cultural functions—was organized.

The response of the Anglo-Australian Jewish establishment to this new actor on the political stage was, at least insofar as any attention at all was paid to the Gezerd, hostile. The Anglophile editor of the community's sole English-language newspaper of the early 1930s, the *Australian Jewish Herald,* waged a lengthy war of attrition against what he called the "blustering, bumptious, swaggering demagogues" of the Gezerd, going so far on one occasion as to call for their deportation. Time and again, he labeled the group's leaders and supporters "so-called Jewish," thus setting the tone for what became the primary thrust of the establishment's attack on the Jewish Left over the next twenty years: the mutual exclusivity of Jewish and Communist commitments. This repeated insistence that the Gezerd was somehow not a Jewish organization may be seen as an attempt to marginalize the Gezerd both within the Jewish community and in the eyes of the non-Jewish world.[22]

Members of the Gezerd participated in general left-wing politics throughout the 1930s, on some occasions under the auspices of the organization. But such activity was secondary and Jewish politics remained uppermost in the priorities of most members and supporters. The Gezerd, by its very nature, and more tangibly in its (admittedly infrequent and insubstantial) contact with Soviet, French, Belgian, American, Palestinian and English branches of the society enabled its members and supporters to establish a link between the Old and New worlds. Contact with the Australian left-wing political milieu was for many members of the Gezerd perhaps the most significant or comfortable point of entry to local society, facilitating social integration and cushioning the culture shock experienced by immigrants in a new land. The degree of integration, however, into even a relatively receptive environment such as the local Left, remained limited. On the whole, the Gezerd cleaved to the familiar and did not seek incorporation into the Australian Left.

This is hardly surprising. Its vision of a Jewish future in Australia focused, after all, on the creation of a politically progressive Yiddish culture, a scaled-down version of its East European model, only incidentally adapted to the local environment. Such a commitment made merging with the Australian Communist political culture problematic. Despite a shared political outlook, the Yiddish-speaking Communists, both in their specific concerns and general ambience, were alien. They were with, but not of, the Australian Communist world.

As the only left-wing Jewish organization of the 1930s, the Gezerd housed a number of divergent political tendencies, with only the Bundists (at this stage, very few in number) unwilling to participate. Disagreements about the nature and orientation of the society were continuous and often bitter. Within the controlling group (the Communist Party "fraction"), conflict centered on the almost obsessive concentration on Birobidzhan. This, some argued, was clearly out of step with the Popular Front policies of the Communist movement in the period from 1935 until mid-1939 and invited accusations of sectarianism. The Jewish fraction of the Communist Party consisted of approximately a dozen members who met irregularly and on an informal basis throughout the 1930s. The relationship between the Gezerd and the Communist party, mediated by the fraction and like-minded members, was friendly rather than formal. Foreign groupings within the party and on the Left in general were insignificant in Australia prior to the Second World War and (with the exception of Jews and Italians) non-English-speaking immigrants were neither well organized nor numerous. Contact between the Jewish and Italian Communists was minimal; even in the postwar period there was little, if any, significant contact between, for example, the Jewish and the Italian or Greek Left.[23]

Toward the end of the decade, the horizons of the Gezerd expanded considerably. The emphasis in meetings and lectures shifted from Birobidzhan and Soviet Jewish affairs to the wider issues of war and peace, with lectures on European and even Australian politics proving popular. As the most vocal and active antifascist organization in the Jewish community, the Gezerd appealed to many of the Jews concerned about the deteriorating situation of European Jewry under fascist and near-fascist governments. Some five hundred Russian and East European Jews arrived in Melbourne in the 1930s, many of them late in the decade.[24] The Gezerd made a successful attempt to attract their support, instituting biweekly English classes in mid-1937, holding special meetings for the recent arrivals and organizing a series of lectures on Australian history.[25]

In mid-1938, the Gezerd in the Soviet Union was liquidated as part of a general government policy to restrict Jewish national life.[26] It seems unlikely that the Melbourne Gezerd knew of the demise of its Soviet counterpart, isolation in this instance working in the Australian group's favor. In any case, there could have been no question of its dissolution at this, the most successful point in its short history.[27]

By mid-1939, the Gezerd was riding the crest of the antifascist wave. It was a smaller, left-wing version of its near neighbor, the Kadimah, and its newly acquired home, the Culture House, was open daily. An active youth wing was established, a regular journal discussed and, with Jewish unity in the face of the fascist threat to European Jewry the watchword of the day, the Gezerd extended its hand to the growing number of local Bundists, establishing together the Joint Culture Committee. The committee advocated "strength in unity," attacked the forces of local Jewish "reaction," and sought to project an alternative voice in political and cultural affairs. An agenda of current issues for discussion was drawn up, including the imminent danger of world war, the position of Poland as a front-line state against Germany, the potential threat from Japan and, last, Australian "problems."[28]

In late August 1939, as the Gezerd reached the peak of its popularity, it was dealt a near-fatal blow by the Nazi-Soviet Nonaggression Pact. The pact threw the Gezerd, as it did so many on the Communist Left, into utter confusion, from which it never fully recovered. Following the initial shock and in response to the withdrawal of the Bund from the Joint Culture Committee, the Gezerd issued a statement deploring the breakdown of Jewish unity and pledging to continue the battle against Hitler and fascism.[29] Such a policy obviously contradicted the Soviet Union's new strategic position. Within the Australian Communist party leadership a similar confusion was evident, with conflicting instructions regarding attitudes to the war emanating from the party's top echelons.[30] By October or November, however, the Gezerd, like the Communist party, had settled on an antiwar line, in accordance with Comintern policy.[31]

The Gezerd, by this time, had been reduced to a mere rump, made up of the unshakeable pro-Soviet faithful, as many previous sympathizers of antifascist inclination now found their way to the Kadimah. In June 1940, the Communist party was declared illegal under the National Security (Subversive Associations) Regulations.[32] The Gezerd, although not banned, felt it prudent to go underground; for fifteen months, its activities went unpublicized and unreported.

Within a month of the Nazi invasion of the Soviet Union on June 22 1941, however, it reemerged on to the public stage, devoting almost all its energies to fund-raising in support of the Red Army and the war effort. From this time until its dissolution early in 1944, it operated from a narrow and shrinking base of support, failing to capitalize on the growing support within the Jewish community for the Soviet Union; it thus came to be regarded as a relic of a bygone era. A younger generation of Jewish Communists was already active in the Australian Communist movement, while Jewish fraction members preferred to work in broader-based groups.[33] By March 1944, Gezerd support had dwindled to the point where its general meeting failed to attract sufficient numbers to ensure continued operation.[34] The Gezerd, to all intents and purposes, was dead.

A new form of local Jewish Communism, however, now succeeded the Gezerd. Catalyzed by the wartime popularity of the Soviet Union, a Communist youth group emerged, its leaders East European-born but Australian-raised, equally at home in both the Australian and the Jewish Communist milieus. Like the Gezerd before it, this second generation of Jewish Communists saw the maintenance of Jewish culture as the key to Jewish survival in Australia, but they broadened the definition of this culture to incorporate Hebrew- and English-language activities and publications, reflecting both their broader political base and Australian roots. Among non-Yiddish-speaking Jews, too, a small but active Communist group developed— Communists of a less rigid ideological bent than those of the Gezerd, who wielded considerable (if, as noted, short-lived) power in the local Jewish politics of the middle to late 1940s.

In sum, the Melbourne Gezerd, a distant outpost of a worldwide Jewish movement, remained suspended between the Old and New worlds, isolated from both, from the one by sheer distance, and from the other by a cultural abyss. The Gezerd was not only the first Jewish left-wing organization in Australia, but also the first radical non-English-speaking immigrant group in the country's history. It both created the basis for a radical Jewish subculture in Melbourne, which flourished until the early 1950s, and paved the way for the acceptance of non-English-speaking groups into the world of Australian left-wing politics.

Notes

1. For a summary of the major explanations of the Jewish-Left nexus, see Arthur Liebman, *Jews and the Left* (New York: 1979), ch. 1; Percy S. Cohen, *Jewish Radicals and Radical Jews* (London: 1980), ch. 7.

2. Isaac Deutscher, *The Non-Jewish Jew and Other Essays* (London: 1968).

3. Robert S. Wistrich, *Socialism and the Jews* (London and Toronto: 1982), 73–75; idem, *Revolutionary Jews from Marx to Trotsky* (London: 1976), introduction; see also Nathan Glazer, *The Social Basis of American Communism* (New York: 1961), 168; Leonard Schapiro, introduction to *The Jews in Soviet Russia Since 1917*, 3rd ed., ed. Lionel Kochan (Oxford: 1978), 3–4.

4. On "very-Jewish Jews" see, e.g., Gerald Sorin, *The Prophetic Minority* (Bloomington: 1985); Hyam Maccoby, "On the Left," *Commentary* (April 1977), 78–81; George L. Mosse, *Germans and Jews* (New York: 1970), 204–207. On theories of self-interest, see Peter Y. Medding, "Towards a General Theory of Jewish Political Interests and Behaviour," *Jewish Journal of Sociology* 19, no. 2 (1977), 115–144; W. D. Rubinstein, *The Left, the Right and the Jews* (London: 1982); Werner Cohn, "Jewish Political Attitudes—Their Background," *Judaism* 8, no. 4 (1959), 312–322.

5. On this subculture, see Jonathan Frankel, *Prophecy and Politics* (Cambridge: 1981), 3 and 552; Liebman, *Jews and the Left*, 26–28.

6. Charles Price, "Jewish Settlers in Australia 1788–1961," *Australian Jewish Historical Society Journal* 5, pt. 8 (1964), statistical appendix 9a.

7. Price, "Jewish Settlers," 375.

8. Uziel Oscar Schmelz, "Migrations," *Encyclopedia Judaica* vol. 16, (Jerusalem: 1972), 1522–1524.

9. Price, "Jewish Settlers," 405. That the majority of East Europeans settled in Melbourne may explain the fact that only there did Jewish Communism take root. On the rather less developed Jewish Communism in Sydney, see David Rechter, *Beyond the Pale: Jewish Communism in Melbourne* (M.A. thesis, University of Melbourne, 1986), 52–53.

10. Price, "Jewish Settlers," 404–405.

11. The Central European refugees arrived in significant numbers in the latter half of the 1930s. There is some disagreement as to the exact number, but seven to eight thousand is a safe estimate. See David J. Benjamin, "Australia and the Evian Conference," *Australian Jewish Historical Society Journal* 5, pt. 5 (1961), 230–231; George M. Berger, "Australia and the Refugees," *Australian Quarterly* 13, no. 4 (1941), 52; Peter Y. Medding, *From Assimilation to Group Survival* (Melbourne: 1968), 150; Andrew Markus, "Jewish Migration to Australia 1938–49," *Journal of Australian Studies* 13 (1983), 18, 23. On the communal conflict of the 1930s, see Medding, *From Assimilation to Group Survival*, 33ff.

12. I. H. Boas quoted in Trevor Rapke, "The Pre-war Jewish Community of Melbourne," *Australian Jewish Historical Society Journal* 7, pt. 4 (1973), 296.

13. On the Soviet Gezerd, see Chimen Abramsky, "The Biro-Bidzhan Project 1922–59," in Kochan, *The Jews in Soviet Russia*, 64–77; Solomon M. Schwarz, *The Jews in the Soviet Union* (New York: 1951).

14. Abramsky, *The Biro-Bidzhan Project*, 71.

15. *Australier leben*, 19 May 1933.

16. *Ibid.*

17. *Ibid*, 24 July 1931, 5 February 1932, 19 May 1933.

18. *Australian Jewish Herald*, 7 January 1932.

19. *Australier leben*, 19 May 1933.

20. *Ibid.*, 3 March 1933, 19 May 1933, 18 May 1934, 28 September 1934.

21. See, e.g., *Australier leben*, 20 November 1931, 26 August 1932, 21 October 1932, 28 April 1933, 29 September 1933, 7 September 1934, 14 December 1934, 12 July 1935.

22. See, e.g., the *Australian Jewish Herald*, 24 December 1931, 7 January 1932, 26 November 1936, 23 December 1937, for such attacks. The Australian authorities, in the form of the Commonwealth Investigation Branch (the security arm of the federal government; later the Commonwealth Investigation Service and then the Australian Security Intelligence Organization) were indeed keeping track of the Gezerd. However, very little Investigation Branch archival material on Jews from the 1930s through the 1950s has survived, and much of what does exist is not available for research purposes.

23. In part, this may have been a matter of timing. As the Jewish Left declined in the early 1950s, postwar Greek and Italian migrants were only beginning to establish themselves

in their communities. See M. Tsounis, "The Greek Left in Australia," *Australian Left Review* 29 (1971), 53–60; Gianfranco Cresciani, *Fascism, Anti-Fascism and Italians in Australia 1922–45* (Canberra: 1980), 122ff; John A. Petrolias, *Post-War Greek and Italian Migrants in Melbourne* (Ph.D. diss., University of Melbourne, 1959), 255ff. The Italian Left did not become influential until the 1970s. See Janis Wilton and Richard Bosworth, *Old Worlds and New Australia* (Ringwood: 1984), ch. 8.

24. Price, *Jewish Settlers*, statistical appendix 7c.

25. *Australier leben*, 21 May 1937, 11 June 1937, 15 July 1938, 5 August 1939, 19 May 1939, 30 June 1939.

26. Schwarz, *The Jews in the Soviet Union*, 195–196; Benjamin Pinkus, *The Soviet Government and the Jews 1948–1967* (Cambridge: 1984), 13.

27. That its continued existence was not unknown in the Soviet Union is indicated by a 1943 letter from the Jewish Russian Committee of Kuibyshev to Melbourne Jewry, appealing for support for Russian Jews and citing the Gezerd as a likely source. *Australian Jewish News*, 15 January 1943.

28. *Australier leben*, 9 December 1938, 23 December 1938, 11 August 1939, 18 August 1939.

29. *Australier leben*, 22 September 1939.

30. Alastair Davidson, *The Communist Party of Australia* (Stanford: 1969), 79.

31. Kermit E. McKenzie, *Comintern and World Revolution* (New York and London: 1964), 169–177. See, for example, *Australier leben*, 16 February 1940; 22 March 1940; 19 April 1940. Topics canvassed at Gezerd meetings included "The Joy of Jews in Soviet-Liberated Poland," "Hitler's Peace Offensive," and "Phoney War."

32. Davidson, *Communist Party of Australia*, 80.

33. The younger Jewish Communists joined the Eureka Youth League. On the league, see Audrey Blake, *A Proletarian Life* (Melbourne: 1984), 73–90. In September 1941, a Provisional Committee for Jewish Work of the Australia-Soviet Friendship League had been formed, made up in the main of Jewish Communists and Gezerd members, its activity consisting largely of reporting to the Jewish community on the work of the Friendship League. For details see Rechter, *Beyond the Pale*, 73–77.

34. *Australier leben*, 17 March 1944.

Review Essays

Two Halls of Ivy and a Hybrid Hothouse: The Jews of Harvard, Yale and Yeshiva Universities

Jeffrey S. Gurock, *The Men and Women of Yeshiva*. New York: Columbia University Press, 1988. xiii + 302 pp.

Dan A. Oren, *Joining the Club: A History of Jews and Yale*. New Haven and London: Yale University Press, 1985. xiv + 440 pp.

Nitza Rosovsky, *The Jewish Experience at Harvard and Radcliffe*. Cambridge: The President and Fellows of Harvard College, 1986. iv + 108 pp.

That the university in the last hundred years has replaced the ancient Temple as a place of pilgrimage for American Jews is well attested. That the Ivy League—especially Harvard—has replaced the Holy of Holies as a place of special reverence is also well known. Although the reasons for the shift and its effects have been only partially explored, its universality is undeniable. In the United States even arch-traditionalists, who elsewhere shun universities, have sought them out. Despite Jewish enthusiasm for postsecondary education, it is clear from the three works under consideration that American universities have exhibited widely contrasting attitudes toward Judaism and its adherents. As a result, different universities have attracted different kinds of Jews with divergent views of Jewishness and its role in the public and private lives of Americans.

It should be noted at the outset that these three books are quite dissimilar; discussing them together is rather like weaving cloth of linen and woolen threads. *The Jewish Experience at Harvard and Radcliffe* appeared as a catalogue for the exhibition that marked the reopening of the Harvard Semitic Museum and was written by Nitza Rosovsky, whose husband, Henry, was the first Jew to become dean of Harvard's Faculty of Arts and Sciences. Appropriately for a catalogue, the book contains short analytical and historical essays as well as personal reminiscences and illustrative photographs. *Joining the Club,* on the other hand, is a communal history. Oren, a postgraduate fellow in psychiatry at the Yale School of Medicine when the book was published, has included much detail—which, by his own admission, many readers might consider "insignificant" (p. x)—as well as extensive consideration of some major aspects of American Jewish life reflected in events at Yale. *The Men and Women of Yeshiva* is the work of a veteran historian, who, like Rosovsky and Oren, is associated with the institution about which he writes. Gurock deals not only with American Jewish social history, but with one of the important institutions of American Jewry; and perhaps without intending it, he helps to explain the weakness of modern Orthodoxy in America.

Their differences notwithstanding, the three books weave a coherent fabric. Obviously binding them together is their common theme. Less obviously connecting them are the historical developments undergone by all three universities and the direct and indirect influences they have exerted on each other over the years. At all three schools the Hebrew Bible and language have played an important curricular role. All three were born as seminaries for the training of clergy and only gradually emerged as full-fledged universities—Harvard, the nation's oldest institution of higher learning, made the transition by the last quarter of the nineteenth century; Yale, just after the Second World War; and Yeshiva in the last twenty years. In all the institutions, traditionalists tried to prevent such development and to maintain a narrower intellectual vision and social base. At Harvard, and even more so at Yale, this meant the exclusion of Jews or the limitation of their number. At Yeshiva, where the battle is far from over, it has meant the exclusion from core programs of Jews who did not meet the school's changing standards of Orthodoxy as well as the exclusion of gentiles. (John F. Kennedy, a Harvard alumnus, is quoted by Gurock [p. 236] as wishing for Yeshiva the kind of development experienced by his alma mater, a suggestion that greatly alarmed Yeshiva's conservative elements.)

The three institutions began as male preserves and made way for women slowly and grudgingly. In 1879, Harvard consented to the establishment of an affiliated school for women (eventually named Radcliffe College), the students of which were completely integrated into Harvard College only in 1971; Yeshiva established an affiliate, Stern College for Women, in 1954; Yale succumbed to coeducation in 1969. Yale seems to have expended considerable energy looking over its shoulder in the direction of its older but more progressive brother institution in Cambridge. Eventually, it followed Harvard's leads with regard to Jews, Jewish studies and many other issues. To mark its transition from WASP social and athletic club to cosmopolitan American university, Yale offered Harvard's Rosovsky its presidency in 1977. When he turned it down, the post was accepted by another "ethnic," the late A. Bartlett Giamatti, who later became the commissioner of baseball. Yeshiva's men and women looked over their left shoulder at the Jewish Theological Seminary and over their right at the disapproving nonmodern wing of American Orthodoxy. But there, too, in more recent years, the Ivy League cast its shadow. As Harvard, Yale, Princeton and other prestigious universities began to accommodate Orthodox Jews and other minorities, students and faculty who once would have considered only Yeshiva or night school at a college in New York City now had other attractive universities from which to choose. For many, however, Yeshiva remained the most appropriate setting. In 1978, a professor of Jewish studies at Yale moved to Yeshiva to become dean of the Graduate School.

As described in these works, Harvard, Yale and Yeshiva represent a continuum with respect to Jews and Judaism. At one end of the spectrum lies Yeshiva, which was founded to enable Orthodox Jews to confront at least some of the problems posed by modernity in a setting governed by traditional beliefs and modes of learning removed from the temptations of the American lifestyle. Yale, by contrast, remained essentially inimical to Jews and Judaism until forced during the radical

1960s to break with many of its hallowed traditions, such as institutionalized anti-semitism. In between was Harvard; during the presidency of Charles William Eliot (1869–1909) it had accepted a large degree of cultural pluralism and evinced some willingness to make Jews and Judaism welcome. A measure of the difference between Harvard and Yale is the fate of their Jewish student organizations. The career of Jewish studies at the three universities also tells much about the attitudes that have dominated them.

Harvard's first organized Jewish student group, the Menorah Society, was formed in 1906. From Harvard, where the society remained active until the late 1930s, the "Menorah" idea spread to other campuses. Eliot "enthusiastically welcomed the new society as yet another aspect of Harvard's search for truth in freedom, and as a hopeful sign that the isolation of Jews at Harvard was coming to an end" (Pearl K. Bell in Rosovsky, p. 48). Eliot spoke at Menorah meetings and addressed the Student Zionist Society as well. Between 1909 and 1918, six Jewish fraternities were founded; by 1926 there were a kosher cafeteria and a students' residence sponsored by the Union of Orthodox Jewish Congregations. During the Nazi era, Jewish students—especially the Zionist Avukah group—demonstrated on behalf of European Jews and raised money for their relief. Administrators and faculty—most notably Radcliffe President Ada Louise Comstock—cooperated in these efforts and helped to bring a number of refugee students to the university. The Hillel organization arrived on campus in 1941 and by the end of the war had its own quarters. It moved to a central location in 1979 (the Torah procession was led by Dean Rosovsky and others), marking its emergence as a university community center.

At Yale, Jewish student life developed more hesitantly. The first Jewish organizations were the Yale Hebraic Club—founded in 1907 by the Woolsey Professor of Biblical Literature, Charles Foster Kent, a Christian, together with a Jewish student—and Kadimah, an off-campus, pro-Zionist group formed in 1912. Both were short-lived. A Menorah Society was organized in 1913, but had expired by 1920. Between 1917 and 1922, six Jewish fraternities sprang up. Until 1923, however, unlike the gentile fraternities that did not accept Jews, all were denied university recognition and had to exist on the fringe of legality. In 1933, at the insistence of the university chaplain's office, a Jewish counselorship was established, to be funded not by the university itself but by a Jewish alumnus under the aegis of the Union of American [Reform] Hebrew Congregations. It was housed in a campus basement opposite a lavatory. Hillel came to Yale in 1941, the same year it came to Harvard. Although the campus chaplains were generally supportive of the new organization, administrators and faculty were not enthusiastic. Students were, on the whole, unresponsive. When Rabbi Richard J. Israel assumed the Hillel directorship in 1959, one of his first major crises concerned the lighting of Sabbath candles, which students feared non-Jewish visitors to Hillel might find "annoying" (Oren, p. 221). Only in the 1970s did Hillel at Yale become a vigorous institution enjoying wide support. By then it was serving a new type of student committed to Judaism as well as students of the kind traditionally found at Yale, some of whom experienced renewed interest in Jewishness as a result of the Six Day War, and of the new respectability granted ethnicity in the United States.

Jewish studies at Harvard has had a venerable history. In the eighteenth century, the study of Hebrew was compulsory; the third oldest chair at the university is the Hancock Professorship of Hebrew and Other Oriental Languages. One of the Jews to be appointed to the faculty under Eliot was the Slavicist, Leo Wiener, author of the first comprehensive history of Yiddish literature. In 1915, Harry A. Wolfson, who was destined to become a world renowned authority on Philo and Spinoza, joined the faculty as instructor in Hebrew. It was an unusual appointment. In most American universities at that time Hebrew and biblical studies were entrusted only to Christians. Ten years later, Wolfson became the first Nathan Littauer Professor of Hebrew Literature and Philosophy, occupying a chair funded by Littauer's son, Lucius, himself a Harvard graduate; it was the first such chair in the United States.

Remarkably, Wolfson's advancement came during the presidency of A. Lawrence Lowell, best known among Jews for his attempts to institute a *numerus clausus* at Harvard during the 1920s. Wolfson's presence made Jewish studies an integral part of the curriculum and unabashed Jewishness an established, if not altogether accepted, lifestyle at Harvard. In 1970, while Wolfson was still alive, a new professorship in Hebrew and Jewish history was set up, to be followed by several others; in 1978, a major Center for Jewish Studies was founded to coordinate and promote the field. Jewish studies programs at Harvard are supported by the Harvard Judaica Collection—one of the world's great Judaica libraries, which dates back to the seventeenth century and now numbers over 150,000 volumes—and by the Harvard Semitic Museum—originally funded by Jacob Schiff.

At Yale, Hebrew and biblical studies were also prominent features of the eighteenth-century curriculum; in the last quarter of that century a compulsory freshman Hebrew course was taught by the President, Ezra Stiles, known for his contacts with the Jewish community of Newport, Rhode Island. Between 1910 and 1913, Eugene H. Lehman served as a part-time instructor in Jewish literature, the first Jew to teach such courses. In the first half of the twentieth century, however, Yale's outstanding Jewish faculty member taught medicine: Milton Charles Winternitz was dean of the medical school from 1920 to 1935 and during his tenure made it "one of the finest schools in the nation." Unlike Wolfson, Winternitz "rejected Jews, Judaism, and Jewish associations in his drive for achievement. In so doing he presented the New Haven and Yale Jewish communities with stunning evidence that the key to rising in the Yale establishment lay in becoming the 'ex-Jew' " (Oren, pp. 136–137).

Only long after Winternitz, with the arrival of Judah Goldin in 1958, did Judaic studies achieve respectability at Yale. Even then, despite the university's newfound eagerness to appoint faculty and raise endowment funds, instability characterized the field. Between 1974 and 1982, five faculty members teaching Jewish studies resigned or were released. Two of them left for Harvard. At Yale, Jewish studies have been supported by the Alexander Kohut Memorial [Library] Collection, the Yale Judaica [Monograph] Series, and, more recently, the Yale Video Archives for Holocaust Studies.

At Yeshiva, as might be expected, Jewish studies took an entirely different course. There, Judaism made up the entire curriculum of the school's first two constituent institutions, Jesibath Etz Chaim [sic] and RIETS (Rabbi Isaac Elchanan Theological Seminary); other subjects were added only in the wake of student strikes supported by major contributors. The first English instructor was hired at

RIETS in 1908, years after the school was opened. He taught Dickens to the future rabbis by translating the novels line by line into Yiddish.

Only with the arrival of Bernard Revel as president in 1915 did RIETS begin to acquire a faculty and a curriculum that resembled those of other American institutions of higher learning. Revel recruited other reliably Orthodox Jews with advanced university degrees as well as traditional Jewish learning to train his future rabbis; he succeeded in fashioning a hybrid institution that was part East European yeshiva, part modern rabbinical seminary and part American institution of higher learning. In 1922, a Teachers' Institute for training Hebrew teachers (and others not inclined toward the rabbinate) was added; and in 1928, came Yeshiva College, to provide Orthodox men with an undergraduate university education, the major component of which would be sacred Jewish studies. In the postwar era, Stern College for Women, several professional schools and the Belfer Graduate School of Science were founded. The professional schools were open to nonobservant Jews and to gentiles, both students and faculty, while maintaining an additional curriculum in Jewish studies to make them attractive to committed Jews.

For many at Yeshiva and for many of its supporters, however, such openness to the secular world, to say nothing of working closely with gentiles in Yeshiva's precincts, represented a dangerous blunder. The relatively modern curriculum of Yeshiva College caused conservatives great consternation. Consequently, even the most open of Yeshiva's faculty and administrators, such as Samuel Belkin, who served as president from 1943 to 1975—his book *Philo and the Oral Law* was published by Harvard University Press in 1940, undoubtedly with Wolfson's approval—seldom felt free to embrace secular learning with wholehearted enthusiasm. (Yeshiva's supporter, the German-born, neo-Orthodox rabbi, Leo Jung, was an exception.) Most were suspicious of modernity and retained nostalgia for the East European pietist past. As a result, Yeshiva College has yet to achieve academic distinction in fields other than Jewish studies; and even Jewish studies are subject to special constraints.

As might be expected, Harvard, Yale and Yeshiva have until recently appealed to very different sorts of Jews, although their student constituencies have also had much in common. In general, at least in the last hundred years, a university degree has been perceived by immigrants to America to be the key to economic success. A B.A. or, better still, an M.D. or an LL.B., was a one-way ticket out of the ghetto. An Ivy League degree was a Pullman ticket! From the turn of the century the children of urban immigrant neighborhoods clamored for admission to the nation's universities. By 1925, Jews constituted more than a quarter of Harvard's incoming class and 13.3 percent of Yale's (all of Yeshiva's); and many of these students came from the ghettos of Boston, New Haven and New York (Rosovsky, p. 23; Oren, pp. 40, 320).

But Harvard and Yale offered more than potential economic security. There one could hobnob with the nation's future elite and perhaps enter their charmed circle. For this, however, there was a price to be paid. At any university, other than Yeshiva, Jewish students could expect to find their religious beliefs and practices, already poorly nurtured by the fledgling American Jewish educational system, challenged and even denigrated. And immigrant parents were no match for university professors. At Ivy League schools, their lack of social graces and eagerness to climb the socioeconomic ladder characteristic of first- and second-generation Americans also counted heavily against Jews. At clubby Yale, where intellectual pursuits were often looked down on until well after the Second World War, the price was highest. University officers ensured that Jewish students and faculty would be few in number and that as many as possible would come from already assimilated families. Few Jews who cared much about their Jewishness went to Yale before the Second World War, except for those from New Haven itself. Of those who were eager to preserve a positive Jewish identity not many succeeded in that WASP pressure cooker. Self-abnegation, self-denial and self-hatred were characteristic of Jewish Yalies until quite recently.

Harvard's Jews could be subjected to similar pressures if they aspired to the life of the gentlemen's club. Leo Wiener, who intermarried and probably converted to Christianity, neglected to tell his children, among whom was cyberneticist Norbert, one fact about himself that everyone else in the Harvard community knew—he was of Jewish origin. The ambivalence of graduates, such as Bernard Berenson and Walter Lippmann, is well documented. At Harvard, however, Jews who wished to do so could easily avoid being bulldozed into assimilation. Academic achievement counted for more than it did at Yale; the administration and faculty tended to be more cosmopolitan in their outlook; and after the turn of the century opportunities existed for the positive exploration of Judaism and for involvement in Jewish affairs. Harvard attracted Jewish students and faculty eager to shed their Jewishness. It also attracted Jews prepared to struggle to blend Jewishness with a Harvard degree and upper-crust manners. Some students in the prewar era even managed simultaneous enrollment at Harvard and the Boston Hebrew Teachers' College.

In the hothouse of Yeshiva, the flowers of Judaism and Jewishness were safe. But there, too, a price was exacted for the education offered. Social comfort was achieved by limiting associations to fellow Orthodox Jews. No useful contacts with the American elite could be made. Intensive Jewish learning was to be acquired by sacrificing some of the quality of secular studies, with professional opportunities more circumscribed and economic success less assured. Yeshiva students, on the whole, cared much about being a certain kind of Jew, less about having a secular education, little at all about their standing in American society.

Happily, as the Rosovsky and Oren volumes show, times have changed. However imperfect it may be, American society is today more accepting of difference than ever before, probably more so than any other society. Social antisemitism has declined dramatically since the Second World War, and Judaism has come to be accepted as one of America's fundamental faiths. Minority groups, including Jews, have gained self-confidence and lost some of their overweening admiration for the majority culture, the shortcomings of which have become increasingly obvious. That Harvard and Yale are now most hospitable homes to both committed and lapsed Jewish students and faculty, that both offer programs of Jewish studies rivaling in quality those of Yeshiva and other Jewish institutions and that both house vibrant Jewish student and faculty communities reflects the changes that have occurred in American society in the last three decades.

Yeshiva, too, has experienced changes reflective of events in the United States, but in a different direction. Partly because some of its former constituents (those most open to the wider society?) are now being siphoned off by the Ivy League and also because of its longstanding appeal to those eager to avoid contact with the non-Jewish world, fewer and fewer of yeshiva's students come from families that value secular education highly. Students are coming to Yeshiva largely to maximize their intellectual and social isolation from a world now perceived to be threatening precisely because of its openness to Jews. In 1977, the Belfer Graduate School of Science was closed, considerably narrowing the university's scholarly horizons. Once Yeshiva's raison d'être was to provide a place for Jewish students who feared they would not be able to withstand the lures of American society or to juggle the conflicting demands of Judaism and the secular university; now, it increasingly provides sanctuary for those who reject American society altogether.

As should be evident, all three books deserve the attention of scholars and laymen. All present a positive view of their respective subjects but are appropriately critical. All are well written and researched, although the books by Oren and Gurock could have been better edited. Oren's work would be much improved if it were reorganized and shortened. Rosovsky's would be more useful if it were more inclusive. But these are no more than the minor cavils required by the reviewers' code. Together with Sherry Gorelick's *City College and the Jewish Poor* (published by Rutgers University Press in 1981), these works elucidate a significant, perhaps unique, aspect of American Jewish life. They helped this reviewer understand why, as a senior in high school (the same high school from which Wolfson had graduated many years before), he had applied to Harvard and Princeton, but not to Yale, and eventually chose Harvard.

Michael Brown
York University

The Trials and Temptations of Conversion

Todd M. Endelman (ed.), *Jewish Apostasy in the Modern World*. New York and
London: Holmes & Meier, 1987. ix + 344 pp.
Bernard Wasserstein, *The Secret Lives of Trebitsch Lincoln*. New Haven and London: Yale University Press, 1988. viii + 327 pp.

Marginal Jews in the modern period have continued to invite and excite theoretical speculation as to their unique character and unorthodox behavior and creativity. The non-Jewish Jew syndrome heralded by Isaac Deutscher is clearly a modern phenomenon that beguiles simplistic categorization, but it can possibly be synthesized as the manifestation and persistence of "Jewish characteristics" long after the individual Jew disassociated himself from, and denied, any meaningful contacts with the Jewish community. In many cases, these remarkable figures remained Jewish and saw no need to attach themselves to another religion; yet conversion was by no means completely ruled out, and significant personalities, ranging from Bergson to Mahler, chose this latter path for differing reasons and motivations.

Often, even the converted were not freed completely from the shackles of the past. Moreover, their own spiritual peregrinations and internal struggles can be construed as paradigmatic of the modern Jewish crisis. Paradoxes abound. Leading members of certain Jewish communities in Europe retained their positions even after they, or members of their immediate family, converted. Nonetheless, research into the phenomenon of conversion has seldom gone beyond the persistent interest in the classical modern case studies—Heine, Disraeli and Marx being the most prominent examples—thus neglecting an undeniably significant trend in the modern Jewish experience. The appearance of these two volumes is, thus, to be welcomed, especially as they open new perspectives into areas of great intrinsic interest.

Simon Rawidowicz—who in a wonderful phrase shrewdly designated the Jews as "the ever-dying people"—would probably have regarded the overall synopsis of conversion that emerges in these works as a confirmation of his basic thesis: no matter what the evidence shows, Jews tend to believe that their continued existence is precarious. This sense became all the more acute in the modern period. Yet the gradual openness of modern society was not simply a blanket prescription for conversion, or for what Todd Endelman calls "radical assimilation" (p. 10), as the various essays in his excellent collection on Jewish apostasy argue. All told, if the various estimates are accurate, we are speaking of approximately a quarter of a million converts by the end of the nineteenth century, and probably somewhat above that number again for our own century. Since the Second World War, however, conversion has largely been supplanted by a milder form of assimilation—indifference—though at times this attitude is accompanied by a sense of self-pride in maintaining one's original status.[1] In any event, the motivations that prompted a Gans, a Heine or the Marx and Disraeli families to leave the Jewish community rarely lead to conversion today when other forms of integration into the majority society are so readily available.

Jewish Apostasy in the Modern World does not claim to provide definitive coverage and analysis of Jewish conversion in the modern period. It originated as a seminar and later a conference in the early 1980s at New York's Yeshiva University. The intention was to cover not only apostasy, but also Christian missionary efforts, as well as some of the Jewish responses to conversion "without a hidden agenda [but] as important matters in their own right in the social and religious history of the modern period" (p. viii). The essays describe conversion in Germany, England, Hungary, Russia and the United States, some presenting an overall view, some concentrating on a particular case study. Even the narrowly focused articles, however, treat the encounter with Christianity not in the purely individualistic biographical terms to be met in Bernard Wasserstein's *The Secret Lives of Trebitsch Lincoln* but rather as a way to examine the social context within which the interaction unfolded.

Because of the lack of reliable statistics, only one of the essays attempts a purely quantitative approach (Deborah Hertz's somewhat disappointing study of Berlin in the heyday of conversion), whereas the others are, in essence, interpretative studies that refer randomly to statistical data. Certain patterns do emerge from these diversified contributions, though as the editor points out, one can hardly determine an all-encompassing thesis to explain the cause of conversion. Nevertheless, Jeremy Cohen, for example, in his article on the mentality of the medieval apostate, does show that it is possible to extrapolate certain generalizations from particular cases. By taking a close look at three prominent converts of the period (Peter Alfonsi, Hermann of Cologne and Pablo Christiani) whose individualistic roads to Christianity were marked by particular dialogues with divergent religious currents, he arrives at the conclusion that the religious factor was predominant in the Middle Ages. But this has clearly not been the case in the modern period, where the varied political and social systems have been of much more significance than has religion.

Judging from the findings of Hertz and Endelman, the image of German Jewish society as the forerunner of conversion among Jews in Western and Central Europe seems to be not completely inaccurate. Hertz upholds Hannah Arendt's thesis that the first decade of the nineteenth century in Berlin witnessed a unique wave in Jewish conversions to Protestantism, with women figuring prominently in the process, often choosing this avenue as a means of improving their social status. Hertz's piece features an elaborate analysis of statistical data originating in a genealogical research agency created by the National Socialists in 1933. Ultimately, however, this analysis brings us little closer to understanding the volcanic eruption that tore asunder ghetto mores and family traditions or the unique constellation that Berlin provided for these developments. Yet the pace of the early nineteenth-century conversions gradually died down. Indicative of changing attitudes was the metamorphosis characteristic of Heine in his later years as he began to assess anew his attachment to Jewish culture.

In his thoughtful comparative essay on German and English conversions in the period 1870–1914, Endelman reminds us that political and social antisemitism, with its accompanying atmosphere of ridicule, left a deep mark on German Jewry—tens of thousands (as many as one hundred thousand by 1914!) decided to escape their predicament through conversion. The extent of this defection prompted by expediency alone lends support to those historians who have upheld the thesis that antisemitism in the Second Reich was more than a mere cultural code but, in fact, represented a profound rejection of the Jew by German society. At the very least, this was the deep-seated perspective that prompted the Centralverein, for example, to make the struggle against apostasy into one of its prime objectives. How this situation compares to that which prevailed in the Germany of the 1930s is not discussed, but it is certainly a question worth pursuing.

In Hungary and Russia, Jews faced several periods of intensive pressure imposed by the state that brought thousands of Jews to convert. In his overview, buttressed by significant statistical detail of the problem in Hungary in modern times, William McCagg, Jr., pinpoints two major waves of conversion: the first at the time of the racial persecutions of 1919–1920 (when there were almost half—some nine thousand—as many converts as there had been since 1867) and the second during the period spanning Hitler's rise to power, the Hungarian racial laws of 1938 and the Second World War (when the number of conversions climbed to the tens of thousands). The Hungarian state structure was for a very long time far more open to the Jews than that of Germany or Russia, yet eventually it, too—through religious and later racial legislation—proved greatly responsible for the large number of conversions. Here then (as McCagg justly argues) is evidence for regarding conversion most often as a form of escape from external pressures rather than as "just the product of opportunism" (p. 159), thus following the pattern of the conversion crisis in Germany during the Second Reich rather than that of the early nineteenth century when Heine and his friends underwent baptism.

Russia, the country that saw the highest number of converts in the nineteenth century (an estimated 84,500), likewise appears to conform to the Hungarian and German models of the interwar period in that persecution was at the top of the list of causes for conversion. Although Michael Stanislawski regards "voluntary apostates" as the largest category of Russian Jews who turned to Christianity in the nineteenth century, he emphasizes that the highly repressive measures of Nicholas I accounted for tens of thousands of converts. Moreover, the voluntary apostates came primarily from among the young, impoverished and futureless Jews who turned to Christianity for momentary relief and shelter from the decaying situation of Russian Jewry under the tsars—in essence, another form of escape from oppression. Stanislawski also notes the predominance of women among the converts (an issue raised by several other authors), thus pointing to the seemingly greater difficulty that confronted Jewish women as they sought to integrate themselves into the changing Jewish society of nineteenth-century Europe.

England, as Endelman argues, presented a different context. Here, in a less centralistic and highly developed industrial state that was no more than mildly concerned with the Jewish issue, the rate of conversion was considerably lower— but not without its idiosyncratic aspects, as Benjamin Braude demonstrates in his engaging inquiry into the Palgrave family in Victorian England. Sir Francis, who became an Anglican, was not of the exhibitionist ilk of a Disraeli and neither was his son Gifford (one of four); but both showed a continued interest in Jewish matters (a remarkable letter from son to father is quoted on p. 127), in classical Judaism and in Palestine, which then held great fascination for Jews and non-Jews alike. Conversion in this case was not necessarily a final station, and Braude attunes us to the ways in which converts in the era of Emancipation often continued to struggle with the Judaism that they had apparently abandoned, in what he calls the Heine– Disraeli syndrome. (In a sense, had he been answered in the affirmative, this would have been the case with David Friedlander after his conversion in 1799.) Other examples could be marshaled to elaborate on this model, one that is not altogether distant from Deutscher's non-Jewish Jew and that constitutes one significant form of Jewish integration into the surrounding society.

Steven Zipperstein's interesting portrayal of the *maskil* Joseph Rabinovich is a case in point. In a radically different setting, in the wake of the 1881 pogroms, after having been deeply disillusioned in his search for a solution to the plight of Russian Jewry, Rabinovich converted and preached to the Jews a mixture of Haskalah ideology and newborn Christianity. Wrestling with a Jewish past that he never really left, he proposed twelve (!) articles of faith, which showed his continued belief in the superiority and uniqueness of the Jewish people.

Rabinovich was not more fortunate in bringing Jews to see the new light than were a host of different missionary groups that flourished throughout the nineteenth century. Christian missionary groups could seldom boast of a significant number of converts, even during moments of duress. At times, as Jonathan Sarna points out in his essay on the response of American Jews to Christian missions, these efforts had the reverse effect of causing Jews to rethink their community failures and compete with the missions over their constituents. He attributes to this challenge significant developments in American Jewry, ranging from improved philanthropic activity to the establishment of the Jewish Publication Society. In this view, external provocations had a positive effect on the Jewish community. As against this, though, Jeffrey Gurock brings evidence to show that the "fear" of missionaries had definite limitations. Drawing on a study of the Lower East Side in New York at the beginning of the century, Gurock documents the inability of Jewish communal organizations to develop a creative and united response to what was a concerted missionary challenge.

The Jewish religious response to the modern problem of apostasy is treated specifically in two chapters. David Ellenson provides an illuminating study of the ways in which Orthodox rabbis in Germany and Hungary confronted both apostasy and the growing decline in normative religious behavior in the nineteenth century. Analyzing their response within the nexus of adaptation to modernity, Ellenson shows that, on the whole, Orthodox rabbis moved from a position equating nonobservant Jews with converts to a more lenient stand that showed greater acceptance of

Reform and nonobservant Jews. This being said Ellenson is careful to point out the exceptions to this general development and the fact that some rabbis persisted in their categorical rejection of freethinking Jews as no different from apostates.

At the other extreme of the religious response is Benny Kraut's fascinating study of Solomon Sonneschein's encounter with Unitarianism in late nineteenth-century America. Kraut not only unravels the enigma of Sonneschein's near conversion, but penetrates to the heart of the dialogue between Reform rabbis and Unitarians. As Kraut has previously shown, the religious orbit of the two faiths was one, forcing each to define its own uniqueness of expression or else dissolve into the other. Thus, Sonneschein, who had a hand in the formulation of the Pittsburgh Platform in 1885, with its proximity to Unitarian belief, was very much in tune with leading Reform figures of his day. It was his rejection of Jewish collectivity and his willingness to leave the community that separated him from other leading Reform thinkers.

The Sonneschein episode, in my view, is significant because of the light it sheds not only on certain internal patterns of American religious history, but also on a broad and recurrent theme in Jewish life at the turn of the century that is not sufficiently discussed in this volume, that is, the increasing need felt by non-Orthodox Jews to find a minimum common denominator for their self-definition of Judaism and Jewish peoplehood. What bound together Ahad Ha'am, the Centralverein and the radical Reformers (the list is easily extended) was their open campaign against, and livid rejection of, conversion; in this, they were no less fervent than the extreme Orthodox position. The implications are clear. Especially when one is an agnostic, a believer in German nationalism or universal ethical monotheism, one must preserve a basic boundary for group identification at all costs. Conversion went beyond that line.

As can be seen, then, the essays in Endelman's collection pinpoint several predominant motivations for conversion, ranging from political oppression to convenience and even on occasion inner religious conviction (an aspect of the subject not sufficiently explored in the volume). But when it comes to looking closely at an individual's conversion and development, especially when the person involved is somebody like Trebitsch Lincoln, the stock interpretations seem to fall by the wayside. If one tries to decipher the code that brought Trebitsch (who was born in 1879) from a strictly Orthodox home in central Hungary to Christianity and later to Buddhism, one must inevitably look for psychological explanations to unravel the mystery. Bernard Wasserstein sees the root of Trebitsch's dizzy machinations as "a psychosis which, towards the end of his life, completely took control over his personality" (p. 6), though he does not necessarily offer this as an explanation for his original rejection of Judaism at the age of twenty, following his father's death. Trebitsch was one of the poor Jewish immigrants to East London whom the missionaries succeeded in coralling and baptizing.

Before us is a remarkably researched and exceptionally written biography of a figure who left no real impression on modern historical development. Wasserstein left no rock unturned in his desire to uncover the rhyme and reason of Trebitsch's life, though he himself makes no bones about the tertiary importance of his hero. He avidly pursues his treks from Hungary to England to Germany and to innumerable other destinations, showing how this lowly figure raised himself time and again from some new nadir to momentary glory or success, only then to return to his previous disarray. Here and there, Trebitsch's Jewish origins peeked through as the result of either his own design or the divinations of others, but this is not the biographer's major concern. It is Trebitsch's escapades in trying to sell himself as a double agent in the First World War as a would-be oil investor; as a participant in the Kapp Putsch of 1920; as an adviser to Chinese generals; as a Buddhist monk in Shanghai, that dominate the narrative. At times, indeed, it is hard to find the thread that connects all these varied affairs together—if one such exists! But when Trebitsch—once missionary to the Jews and once member of Parliament—is ordained in 1931 as a Buddhist monk (named Chao Kung), Wasserstein returns to the psychological dimension to explain his subject's despair of ever reaching nirvana, "Tantalised by the dim perception of this goal, and tormented by the impossibility of its achievement, his mind seesawed ever more violently between mania and depression" (p. 241).

Wasserstein's extraordinary energy and engaging wittiness in hunting down Trebitsch to every corner of the world did not suffice, it seems, and he felt compelled to add an afterword that places Trebitsch somewhere between Shabbetai Zvi and Joseph Frank—a kind of "manic messiah . . . a mirror . . . [to] the unquiet spirit of the age" (p. 290). However, these claims are not seriously worked out in the biography and are not convincingly argued. Perhaps closer attention to Trebitsch's own words would have helped clarify the internal enigma. For in the end some dimension of Trebitsch's inner life continues to remain hidden and elusive—recalling the sensation evoked on seeing Gustave Doré's "Wandering Jew."

RICHARD I. COHEN
The Hebrew University

Note

1. An illuminating example of this position can be found in the delightful memoirs of an Alsatian Jew, born a decade after the Dreyfus affair, who became a member of the Académie française in 1977. See Maurice Rheims, *The Glorious Obsession*, trans. Patrick Evans (London: 1980).

The Two Zions and the Exodus
from Ethiopia

Edward Ullendorff, *The Two Zions: Reminiscences of Jerusalem and Ethiopia.*
Oxford: Oxford University Press, 1988. 249 pp.

David Kessler, *The Falashas: The Forgotten Jews of Ethiopia.* New York:
Schocken Books, 1985, 2nd ed. xiv + 182 pp.

Tudor Parfitt, *Operation Moses: The Story of the Exodus of the Falasha Jews from
Ethiopia.* London: Weidenfeld & Nicolson, 1985. 132 pp.

Michael Ashkenazi and Alex Weingrod (eds.), *Ethiopian Jews and Israel.* New
Brunswick and Oxford: Transaction Books, 1987. 159 pp.

Called upon to name a country with which Israel shares historical ties, political
interests and cultural traditions, it is doubtful if many readers would immediately
think of Ethiopia. Yet the connections between the two countries are of an almost
unparalleled variety and historical depth. Even if one dismisses as totally legendary
the claim that the Queen of Sheba was an Ethiopian, there can be no denying the
distinctively biblical cast of traditional Ethiopian culture. The Saturday Sabbath, the
circumcision of male children on the eighth day after birth and the observance of
biblical dietary prohibitions are only a few of the customs that have traditionally
linked Ethiopians, whether Christians or Jews, to the cultural world of the Hebrew
Bible. Since the Middle Ages, Ethiopian monks have resided in Jerusalem, and
even today the Holy City remains the only site outside the homeland with a resident
Ethiopian archbishop. During the 1950s and 1960s, the shared interests of Israel and
Ethiopia—both non-Arab, non-Muslim countries "in a sea of Arabs"—encouraged them to engage in economic, political and military cooperation on a grand
scale. In recent years the vexing problem of the Beta Israel (Falasha) has simultaneously divided the two countries politically while once again highlighting the ties
that bind them together.

For Edward Ullendorff, Professor Emeritus of Semitic Languages and of Ethiopian Studies at the University of London, all of the above is, of course, commonplace. Indeed, his own research has provided some of the best scholarly documentation on the subject.[1] In *The Two Zions,* he adds a layer of personal
reminiscences to an already considerable academic contribution. During the 1930s,
Ullendorff resided in Jerusalem and studied Semitic, especially Ethiopian, languages, at the Hebrew University. In 1941, following the liberation of Ethiopia

298

from the Italian Fascists, he served in the British military administration of Eritrea-Ethiopia. At the end of the Second World War, he returned once again to Palestine, serving in the academic secretariat of the university and later in the British Mandatory government. Thus, much of Ullendorff's early adult life (as well as most of his later academic career) was linked in some fashion either to Jerusalem or to "the second Zion," Ethiopia, or to both at once. His experiences from this period form the primary basis for this book.

As Ullendorff points out in the preface, it is intended not as an autobiography, but as reminiscences. Accordingly, although the author is never forgotten in the text, he is primarily "the link, not the centre." Readers familiar with Ullendorff's scholarly writings will not be surprised to learn that his literary style is, as usual, exquisite. Indeed, there is something strangely appropriate about seeing the vanished worlds of prestate Jerusalem and prerevolutionary Ethiopia described in an English that has itself all but disappeared.

Given the richness and variety of Ullendorff's reminiscences, it is difficult to single out any one section for special notice. For readers of this journal, his description of Jerusalem and The Hebrew University in the 1930s will doubtless be of special interest. It is difficult to think of a greater contrast than that between The Hebrew University of his time, with its eight hundred students or less, and the current institution that has numbers such as those in single departments. Yet Ullendorff's comments concerning students forced to "squeeze attendance at lectures and classes into a few hours snatched from their employment" (p. 47) and a library with "many sensitive lacunae" because of "a tight university budget" (p. 48) sound all too familiar. It is similarly interesting to note that the university's practice of consulting referees abroad concerning promotions, even when local scholars are "in a much better position to form an opinion on the candidate's competence" (p. 109) also dates back at least forty years.

Much of Ullendorff's book is composed of personal portraits of illustrious figures from Jerusalem (Agnon, Buber, Scholem) and Ethiopia; the last chapter is devoted to Emperor Haile Selassie (pp. 219–238). Of those described, special mention should be made of H. J. Polotsky, today professor emeritus at The Hebrew University. Not only is Polotsky at age eighty-four one of the last survivors among the intellectual giants Ullendorff describes (pp. 81–86), he is also, perhaps more than anybody else, immediately connected to the cultural link that forms the leitmotif of this book. As an Egyptologist and semitist of world renown, it is Polotsky who has been supremely responsible for establishing the tradition of excellence in Ethiopian studies in Israel that continues to this day.

In recent years, the scholarly edifice established by Polotsky and his students, including Ullendorff, has been under attack from an unlikely source. The dramatic arrival in Israel of over half the Beta Israel (Falasha) community has turned what had long been an obscure path on the fringes of Ethiopian and Jewish history into a busy thoroughfare. Seizing the opportunity, a legion of "experts" has appeared, each prepared to offer the definitive word on the subject of Ethiopian Jewry. Ullendorff, in a notable departure from the generally gracious tone of his book, has harsh words for their efforts:

The anthropologists, comparative religionists, and students of kindred disciplines who have now descended upon the Falashas in Israel present a grave danger to the survival of genuine knowledge of the factual and traditional background and the historical antecedents of these hapless people. In the first place, nearly all these questioners are innocent of the Ethiopian languages spoken by these recent immigrants. The use of interpreters or enquiries by means of a smattering of recently acquired Hebrew are wholly unsatisfactory *per se* and do not inspire confidence either in those questioned or in the results as such. Secondly, such studies conducted away from the traditional habitat of the Falashas are virtually useless. And, thirdly and most importantly, the Falashas have very quickly learnt that full acceptance as Jews requires them to give an account of their former life in Ethiopia that approximates as closely as possible to normative Judaism— yet is far removed from reality. Some such enquiries and studies, carried out by researchers unfamiliar with Falasha languages, their original native ambience, and their religious configuration, have already appeared and constitute a grave disservice to historical truth (pp. 150–51).

Although Ullendorff mentions no specific author or book by name, one suspects that none of the other books considered here would earn his general approbation.

David Kessler's history of the Beta Israel (Falasha), first published in 1982 and reissued in 1985, was one of the first books to appear as part of the latest "discovery" of this community. It serves as an excellent illustration of the fact that scholarship, like nature, abhors a vacuum. In the absence of a first-rate scholarly history of the Beta Israel, Kessler has written an ambitious, but uneven, popular work. Whereas there can be no question that his book enables a far wider audience than ever before to grasp the essentials of Beta Israel history, it also supplies them with a generous amount of misinformation. This is particularly the case with regard to his views on the origins of Beta Israel.

Kessler, in common with Ullendorff and Tudor Parfitt (discussed later), does not view the Beta Israel as "ethnic Jews" (p. 5). In contrast to most scholars, however, he believes that Judaism reached Ethiopia not through South Arabia, but through Egypt and the Sudanic Kingdom of Meroe. Although he devotes a considerable portion of his book to arguing this thesis, virtually all his "proofs" are based on either misunderstanding or misrepresentation.

Kessler, for example, accords considerable importance to the fact that the Ethiopic (Ge'ez) Bible is translated from the Septuagint and not from the Hebrew (pp. 18, 50). Yet it is difficult to understand how this can be said to offer any support for his thesis. Scholars are unanimous in believing that the translation of the Bible into Ge'ez was primarily the work of Christian translators. Certainly, the Beta Israel do not have their own translation of the Bible but rely on that of the Christians; in some cases, even using manuscripts that are Christian in origin. The crucial point, the implications of which Kessler totally fails to grasp, is that despite the use of a primarily Greek *Vorlage,* a significant number of Jewish Aramaic loanwords and Hebraisms appear in the text. These, not the use of the Greek, are the clearest evidence of early Jewish influences on Ethiopian culture.

No less problematic is Kessler's attempt to posit a historical connection between the Beta Israel and the ancient Jewish community of Elephantine (near modern Aswan). Elephantine Judaism was, according to Kessler "remarkably reminiscent" of that of the Beta Israel (p. 44). Given our extremely limited knowledge of the religion of Elephantine and the fact that the religion of the Beta Israel almost certainly assumed its present form in Ethiopia over the past five hundred years,[2] it is difficult to understand exactly how one would go about determining similarities and what, if any, significance these would have historically. However, even if we, for the moment, ignore this vexed methodological question, several points argue against Kessler's position. Undoubtedly the strongest parallel between Elephantine and Ethiopian religious practice concerns the performance in both groups of sacrifices by a priestly religious elite. Even here, however, it must be admitted that important differences exist; whereas in Elephantine a hereditary priesthood sacrificed in a temple, among the Beta Israel a nonhereditary priesthood sacrificed on an open-air altar.

Nor is this the only difference. The attitudes toward the Sabbath presented by the two communities are, for example, a study in contrast. In Elephantine, the Sabbath "appears to have been honored more in the breach than in the observance,"[3] whereas among the Beta Israel it is observed with tremendous respect and great rigor. Moreover, the Beta Israel's rules of Sabbath observance as well as many other features of their religious life are strongly influenced by the *Book of Jubilees*, an apocryphal work composed in the middle of the second century B.C.E., long after the Elephantine community had ceased to exist. Thus, the Sabbath as observed by the Ethiopians can scarcely be said to have resembled that in Elephantine.

Similarly, although Kessler discreetly ignores the subject, it is difficult to find support for his thesis in the clear evidence of religious syncretism in the Elephantine cult. Although there can be little question that Yahu (Yahweh), the God of Heaven, was the primary focus of the religious attention of the Jewish garrison at Elephantine, homage was rendered to other gods as well. As Bezalel Porten notes, "There is evidence for this devotion [to the gods] on both the individual and communal level."[4] Needless to say, polytheism does not appear among the Jewish influences that reached Ethiopia.

Although the remainder of Kessler's book is not nearly as reckless as his discussion of origins, errors abound. Many can be directly attributed to his lack of familiarity with the requisite source languages for scholarly research on Ethiopia. His claim (pp. 4, 47) that the term "Falasha" is an ancient name indicating that the Jews of Ethiopia were "exiles" from the Holy Land is, for example, totally untenable in light of the fact that it was not applied to the community prior to the fifteenth or even the sixteenth century. Similarly, although there can be no denying the importance of the chronicle of Sarsa Dengel as a source of the history of the Beta Israel, the text is written in Ge'ez, not Amharic (p. 127). Perhaps most important, Kessler's innocence of the relevant languages leads him almost automatically to an overreliance on the writings of the Scottish explorer, James Bruce, for historical detail (pp. 52–56, 79, 86, 94, etc.). There can be little question of the major role Bruce played in the modern "discovery" of Ethiopia, but as a source of historical knowledge, he leaves much to be desired.[5]

Kessler makes no attempt in the second edition of his book to examine events after 1982. Thus, the task of recounting the story of the dramatic exodus from Ethiopia of more than half the Beta Israel community is left to his compatriot and occasional collaborator, Tudor Parfitt.[6] Parfitt, a lecturer in Hebrew literature at the School of Oriental and African Studies in London, was in the Sudan gathering material for a Minority Rights Group report on the Falashas at the time of Operation Moses. He, thus, had a unique opportunity to observe the dramatic events of the period and succeeded in a matter of months in publishing his account of this episode. Because his was the first of what was to become a steady stream of books on the rescue of the Beta Israel, Parfitt was able to lay claim to the most obvious title for his work (preempting later and less fortunate authors).[7] Given the speed with which he was able to produce his book, it is inevitably more journalistic than scholarly in character and should be evaluated accordingly. Despite the absence of references (and an index!), making a careful assessment rather difficult, it appears, on the whole, to present a clear and reliable outline of the main details of the rescue operation.

Parfitt begins his book with a short survey of Beta Israel history (pp. 8–15). This is undoubtedly the weakest section of the book, for it is characterized by a disturbing tendency to repeat the errors of previous authors, including Kessler's overdependence on Bruce (cf. pp. 8, 11, 12). Accordingly, we are told (p. 8), "those Ethiopians who had accepted Judaism and refused to embrace Christianity were persecuted," but no documentation of any kind exists on this point, and it appears highly unlikely this was true prior to the sixth century. The Tigrean kings of Aksum are said to have been Amhara (p. 9), and King Yekuno Amlak, it is claimed, was "determined to destroy the power of the Falasha." This latter point finds no support in the contemporary sources and appears very dubious given the king's other more pressing problems. Perhaps most unfortunately, Parfitt follows the common trend in writings about the Beta Israel that depicts their existence in Ethiopia as little more than an unrelieved series of wars, pogroms and massacres.

Turning to the more central portions of the book, numerous small errors mar the narrative. Ovadia Hazzi (p. 25) is presumably Hezzi Ovadia; Simha Barhani (p. 55) is Zimna Berhane; Moshe Bar Yehuda (p. 40) is Moshe Bar Yuda. On a more serious level, it is difficult to understand in what sense the Ethiopian People's Revolutionary Party can be characterized as "violently anti-Zionist" (p. 29), and the Beta Israel's problems with the Israeli Chief Rabbinate have turned out to be far more durable than Parfitt (pp. 128–130; cf. Kessler, p. xiii) or perhaps anyone else anticipated.

No history of Operation Moses or the events surrounding it would be complete without the consideration of the role played by the numerous pro-Beta Israel pressure groups that were active from 1974 onward. There can be little question that these groups, most notably the American Association for Ethiopian Jewry (AAEJ) and the Falasha Welfare Association (FWA), played a vital role in educating the Jewish and Israeli public and in pressuring successive Israeli governments to act on behalf of the Beta Israel. There is perhaps no greater testimony to their tenacity and ultimate success than the fact that, by the early 1980s, the issue was no longer if Ethiopian Jewry should be helped, but how and at what speed.

Having said this, it must be admitted that the role of these groups, particularly the militant AAEJ, in the 1980s is the subject of considerable controversy. By that time, so much distrust had accumulated between the AAEJ leadership and the Israeli government that little room existed for cooperation. The direct involvement of the AAEJ in rescue attempts further exacerbated these tensions. In Parfitt's opinion (pp. 55–61), the AAEJ's contribution in the buildup to Operation Moses was primarily negative—their bungled rescue attempts and failure to recognize the genuine shift in Israeli policy detracted attention from vital, in some cases life-or-death, matters. Needless to say, the AAEJ and their supporters do not share this view.[8] Scholarly analysis of Operation Moses will in the future have to clarify this issue.

Just as Kessler makes no attempt to examine the aliyah of Ethiopian Jews in any detail, Parfitt was forced by time constraints to defer an analysis of their experience in Israel. There has been no shortage of authors willing to fill this gap. In the wake of Operation Moses, the study of the Beta Israel became something of a growth industry. At one point in 1986, no less than fifty researchers claimed to be involved in studying one aspect or another of the lives of the fifteen thousand Beta Israel in Israel.

Originally published as a special double issue of *Israel Social Science Research* (vol. 3, nos. 1–2) in 1985, the volume of Ashkenazi and Weingrod was reissued in 1987 with the addition of one article. Although the editors state that several of the articles have been revised, this is readily apparent only with regard to their introduction. The remaining articles retain the original page numbers, typographical errors and inconsistencies.

Indeed, as is so often the case with collections of papers, *inconsistent* seems to be a key adjective appropriate here. In this case, it describes not only the system of transliteration from Ethiopian languages and the details of many bibliographical references but, most important, the level of the papers. At the upper end of the scale we find Chaim Rosen's important discussion of the "core symbols" of Ethiopian identity (pp. 55–62). Through the presentation of a series of opposing concepts that appear in Amharic, Rosen succeeds in throwing considerable light on the values and behavior of Ethiopian immigrants. Similarly informative is Shoshana Ben-Dor's analysis of the Beta Israel's unique pilgrimage festival, the *Sigd*, which marks the renewal of the Covenant (pp. 140–159). Beginning with the earliest mentions of the holiday in medieval Ethiopia and continuing through the observation of the festival in Israel in recent years, Ben-Dor examines the manner in which the festival has changed in response to the varying political and social circumstances.

Unfortunately, not all the articles in the volume are as successful as these two. Stanley M. Newman's essay (pp. 104–111) on Ethiopian Jewish absorption and the Israeli response is a case in point. While decrying the use of stereotypical generalizations about Ethiopians who "don't know how to hold a pencil," the article abounds in such sweeping statements about Israelis ("School principals, school psychologists, counselors and teachers all tell the same stories of Ethiopian school-children. . . . An almost unanimous concern exists over body odor"). Commenting on the policy whereby most Ethiopian immigrants had their names changed when they arrived in the country, Newman writes, "The motivation behind it may be more closely related to *Israeli prejudice* than to the 'official' explanation that name changes aid in the assimilation process" (p. 109; emphasis added). He then suggests that consultations with Ethiopian leaders might have led to a more informed decision. In fact, this particular policy was strongly supported by veteran Ethiopians consulted on the matter.

Toward the end of his article, Newman notes (p. 111) that the Ethiopians "have been able to speak in one voice on their own behalf." Anyone even vaguely familiar with the divisiveness and infighting that have characterized so much of their political activity in Israel (cf. Ben-Dor's essay, p. 153) can only wonder what he must have been thinking of. Similar questions arise with regard to Jeff Halper's lengthy analysis (pp. 112–139) of absorption policy, the main thrust of which is to argue that, despite claims to the contrary, the "mistakes of the fifties" are being repeated in the absorption of the Ethiopians. The Ethiopians, he argues, are apparently destined to become part of the "'second Israel,' Jews of Middle East background who are found by and large in the working classes" (p. 112). One of the four major errors cited by Halper is "the 'channeling' of immigrants to the margins of society." Concerning the Ethiopians he writes, "Beta Israel immigrants are channeled, like their counterparts of the mid-1950s, into peripheral development towns" (p. 132).

Yet even a superficial examination of the absorption plans reveals this statement to be demonstrably false. According to the Ministry of Absorption's "Master Plan for the Absorption of Ethiopian Immigrants," large numbers of Ethiopians were to be settled in urban areas. Haifa, Jerusalem, Petah Tikva, Netanya, Holon, Bat Yam and Beersheba alone were scheduled to house more than 25 percent of all Ethiopian immigrants, with a similar number in such places as Rishon Lezion, Rehovot, Ashdod, Ashkelon, Hadera and Nahariya. Indeed, close to 40 percent of all immigrants were listed to be settled in the central region of the country. In fact, however, by the summer of 1988 it had become clear that the main problem was not so much *where* the Ethiopians were settled, but *whether* they were settled at all. Four years after Operation Moses, a combination of government mismanagement and immigrant selectivity meant that more than 40 percent of the Ethiopians were still residing in absorption centers.

More helpful and less polemical in tone are the articles of Raphael Schneller (pp. 33–54) on nonverbal communication; Gadi Ben-Ezer (pp. 63–73) on cross-cultural misunderstandings; Michael Ashkenazi (pp. 85–96) on information exchange; Tamar Dothan (pp. 87–103) on children's adaptation patterns—all of which indicate the complexity of the situation and the tentativeness of their findings. Given the fact that most of these articles were first written in 1985, less than a year after Operation Moses, one can only regret that the authors were not given the opportunity to revise their contributions in order to take into account the ongoing changes in the lives of the immigrants and in absorption policy.

The crucial question with regard to the absorption of Ethiopian immigrants appears not to be whether the authorities are repeating the "mistakes of the fifties" but rather, have they been quicker in identifying the mistakes of the 1980s? To determine this, it will be necessary to build on the foundations laid by the best of these studies through a series of long-term analyses of immigration policy and its consequences. Only then will it begin to become clear if the Beta Israel's journey from the "second Zion" has taken them to the Promised Land or the "second Israel."

STEVEN KAPLAN
The Hebrew University

Notes

1. Edward Ullendorff, *Ethiopia and the Bible* (London: 1968).

2. Steven Kaplan, "'Falasha' Religion: Ancient Judaism or Evolving Ethiopian Tradition," *Jewish Quarterly Review* (July 1988), 49–65.

3. Bezalel Porten, *Archives from Elephantine* (Berkeley: 1968), p. ix, quoted in Kessler, *The Falashas*, 42.

4. Porten, *Archives*, 174.

5. Cf. Richard Pankhurst, "Problems About Bruce's History of the Zagwe Dynasty," *Quardeni di studi etiopici* 6–7 (1985–1986), 86–92.

6. David Kessler and Tudor Parfitt, *The Falashas: The Jews of Ethiopia*, The Minority Rights Group, Rpt. No. 67 (London: 1985).

7. Cf. Louis Rapoport, *Redemption Song: The Story of Operation Moses* (New York, 1986); Ruth Gruber, *Rescue: The Exodus of the Ethiopian Jews* (New York, 1987); Claire Safran, *Secret Exodus* (New York, 1987).

8. In response to Parfitt's book, *Operation Moses,* Nathan Shapiro, president of the AAEJ, sent a letter on 27 November 1985 to editors offering a preview of the book and pointing out various errors of fact that it allegedly contained. In actuality, at least on historical and cultural matters, Parfitt appears more reliable than Shapiro. The letter concludes, "I wish to emphasize that Parfitt's book is more than an attack on the AAEJ, *it is an attack and an insult against the community of Ethiopian Jews in Ethiopia and Israel.* . . . If you wish to review it, we hope you will note its inadequacies and inaccuracies" (emphasis added).

The "New Historians" and the Establishment of Israel

Benny Morris, *The Birth of the Palestinian Refugee Problem, 1947–1949*. New York: Cambridge University Press, 1987. xx + 380 pp.

Ian Pappé, *Britain and the Arab-Israeli Conflict, 1948–1951*. London: Macmillan, 1988. xxi + 273 pp.

Avi Shlaim, *Collusion Across the Jordan: King Abdullah, the Zionist Movement, and the Partition of Palestine*. Oxford: Clarendon Press, 1988. x + 676 pp.

The trouble with revisionist historians is that only too often they attempt to read history backwards. Occasionally, as in the present instance, they seek to read the present into the past. They thus attribute present difficulties to the mistakes of an earlier day and assume that recognition of past error will summarily provide the key to solving current problems. Revisionism, however, can be wrong on two counts. For one thing, history evolves forwards not backwards, and putting the clock back does not alter the facts or necessarily furnish a solution. Events in the interim may make earlier errors, if such they were, completely irrelevant to resolving current difficulties. Furthermore, and this is crucial, the revisionist assessment of past mistakes may itself be flawed. Even in the light of newer and more complete documentation than was previously available, it may emerge that there is no basis for revising history, except in the minds of the revisionists themselves.

These thoughts are brought to mind by the three books reviewed here. At least two of them, the works of Shlaim and Morris, are outright revisionist. Shlaim candidly states that his is "a revisionist history which differs very sharply, and on many important points, from the pro-Zionist as well as the pro-Arab histories on this subject" (p. viii). Morris does not reveal his revisionist bent in as categorical a manner. However, in a series of articles that have followed the publication of his book, he has described his work as being one of the "new" histories that "significantly undermine, if not thoroughly demolish, a variety of assumptions that helped form the core of the old history" dealing with the Arab-Israeli dispute (*Tikkun*, November/December 1988, p. 21). Morris's polemical writings on the subject have provoked a vigorous reaction (led especially by Shabtai Teveth, biographer of Moshe Dayan and Ben-Gurion), and the result has been a vast new literature assessing Israel's role in the origins and durability of the Palestinian problem. To be more specific, the thrust of the revisionist thesis is that this problem—in all its current intensity and dimensions—is a product of deliberate and misguided Israeli actions and that the sons of Israel today are suffering from the sins of their fathers at the time of the establishment of the state of Israel in 1948. In short, the Palestinian problem is peculiarly a consequence of Israeli commission or omission. Nothing else, it would appear, contributed to the tragedy of the Palestinians as much as Israeli malfeasance. Palestinian homelessness, Palestinian statelessness, the Palestinian refugee problem, and, implicitly, even Palestinian terror, including the *intifada*—all are to be laid at Israel's doorstep.

This is not a new thesis. It is, in fact, a thesis that has been propagated by the Palestinians and the Arab world ever since the Palestinian problem arose. What is new is that historians, ostensibly objective, interpret the facts on the basis of recently opened archival materials, and reach similar conclusions. The charges are serious and the analyses that lead to these charges warrant careful scrutiny to determine whether they are borne out by the written record or whether they are not merely a reflection of the writer's predilections. Is there more assertion than fact in the charges leveled against Israel?

Before proceeding to examine the case for the revisionist thesis and the strength of the evidence adduced, it is appropriate to comment on an underlying assumption of the thesis: that if the U.N. partition plan of 1947 had been implemented as originally envisioned, peace and tranquility would now reign in the Holy Land. This is a facile belief, itself dependent on a further crucial premise, that the Palestinian Arabs would have been content with a part of Palestine and would have foresworn hostility both to the Jewish state and an internationalized Jerusalem, as prescribed by the partition resolution. In the event, of course, neither the Palestinian Arabs nor the neighboring Arab states were ready to tolerate the emergence of either entity in 1948, and the hostility manifested then has not waned over the years. Indeed, it has only waxed stronger as revealed by the text of the so-called Palestinian Declaration of Independence announced in Algiers in November 1988, which is little less than a summons to arms against Israel. Regardless, then, of the strength of the evidence regarding Israeli complicity in the plight of the Palestinians, any assessment that assumes a rosy outcome in the absence of this alleged "complicity" seems quite misplaced or, at least, highly speculative.

Shlaim and Morris, respectively, deal with the central facets of the Palestinian problem—the failure of the Palestinians to attain statehood in 1948 and the creation of the refugee problem in the same year. Pappé, on the other hand, focuses on these two issues from the perspective of British policy in the period 1948–1951. All three authors draw heavily on original material in British, American and Israeli achives. (References to Arab sources are, of course, notably absent, and this, in itself, raises serious questions about their conclusions.) The factual material assembled in these three works handsomely enriches our knowledge of the factors that operated in the formative years of the Arab–Israeli dispute. The books are veritable treasure houses of information about the events that transpired and the personalities involved. Morris and Shlaim both write in a superb style and their accounts are fascinating, if disturbing. Moreover, the printed page in each case is a pleasure to peruse. Unfortunately, the Macmillan Press was not as kind to Pappé. Although his study also contains keen insights, it unfortunately suffers from a lack of careful editing. More editorial attention would have improved the work considerably. Further, the lack of a running head for the Notes to identify the pages in the text to which they relate is most frustrating. Macmillan, with just a little more investment, could have produced a far more attractive volume.

Shlaim states his thesis on the very first page of his magnum opus. In 1947, "clandestine diplomacy" between the Hashemite Kingdom of Jordan and the Zionist Yishuv produced "an explicit agreement" to divide Palestine between themselves and thus frustrate the emergence of an independent Arab state in Palestine. This "explicit agreement," which was ostensibly sealed at the secret meeting of November 1947 between King Abdullah and Golda Meir, "laid the foundation for mutual restraint during 1948" in the military sphere "and for continuing collaboration in the aftermath of the war." Thus, Palestine would be partitioned, but not as envisaged in the U.N. partition resolution. A Jewish state would emerge; and Transjordan would expand to include the area assigned for the creation of a local Arab state. This "unholy alliance" (p. 121) between Amman and Tel-Aviv represents the "collusion across the Jordan" in Shlaim's title.

A further "accomplice" to the "crime" was Great Britain, which encouraged Abdullah to enlarge his kingdom by gaining control of the West Bank and by ultimately annexing it to his territory. The alternative of an Arab state in part of Palestine headed by its archenemy, Haj Amin Al-Husayni, the former mufti of Jerusalem and collaborator with Nazi Germany, it was believed, would threaten all British interests in the Middle East. Such a state would forever remain unstable and would endanger Britain's most reliable ally in the region, Transjordan. Abdullah's annexation of the West Bank was, thus, a convenient way of strengthening Transjordan and forestalling the rise of a troublesome entity in the area.

But the key focus of Shlaim's charge is the imperialist nature of the two conspirators: King Abdullah and the Zionist movement. From the very beginning, each entertained expansionist designs. In 1897, when Herzl at Basel proclaimed the Zionist goal of a Jewish state, Palestine was inhabited by half a million Arabs and some 50,000 Jews. "But in keeping with the spirit of the age of European imperialism, the Jews did not allow these local realities to stand in the way of their own national aspirations" (p. 2). According to Shlaim, "[in a sense] violence was implicit in Zionism from the start" (p. 10). In this connection, he quotes the extremely anti-Zionist book by David Hirst according to which "in any true historical perspective the Zionists were the original aggressors in the Middle East, the real pioneers of violence, and the Arab violence, however cruel and fanatical it might eventually become, was an inevitable reaction to theirs." Thus, Zionism, from its very birth, was tainted by sin in Shlaim's opinion.

And Abdullah, although his birth was hardly a sinful event, was guilty of pursuing his own ambitious dream of reestablishing a Hashemite Empire in the Fertile Crescent. Mindful of the tragic loss that his father had endured in the Arabian Peninsula when he was defeated by Ibn Saud, Abdullah was intent on reviving the glory of the past by gaining control of the area of Syria, Transjordan and Palestine. This fantasy led him not only to conspire with the Jews, but to actually "weaken" the Arab front by restraining his forces in the confrontation with the Zionist enemy. According to Shlaim this "played a major part in the eventual loss of Palestine" (p. 2). Abdullah held clandestine meetings with Zionist leaders even before and during the Second World War. He saw in them a vital force that could help him consolidate his kingdom throughout Greater Syria. His respect for Jewish enterprise, Jewish money and Jewish military prowess induced him to seek an accommodation with the Zionists and to enlist them as an ally in the pursuit of his ambitions. This was the basis of the conspiracy, of the collusion, that would allow each of the two parties to realize its own territorial goal at the expense of Palestinian statehood.

Several points need to be noted before analyzing the substance of the "conspiracy." Shlaim's account of the rise of Zionism reveals little or no appreciation of the key motive inspiring the Zionist enterprise—the desire to resolve the problem of Jewish homelessness, which had led to countless centuries of persecution and suffering at the hands of Christian and Moslem nations and had culminated in the horrors of the Holocaust. Even before that catacylsmic event, the international community of states, recognizing its own complicity in the age-old Jewish problem, had acknowledged the need for a political solution and had therefore confirmed the Balfour Declaration. The claim of the Jewish people to their ancestral home— which had largely lain waste for centuries—was thus given international sanction. The events of 1939–1945 added a note of urgency to the entire debate and spotlighted the magnitude of the crime committed against the Jewish people by Britain when, capitulating to Arab threats, it slammed shut the doors of Mandatory Palestine in the face of the Jewish masses fleeing Hitler's gas chambers. International endorsement of the Jewish claim to its ancestral home was now reconfirmed by the U.N. partition resolution. This critical background is sadly missing from the Shlaim account, which barely notes the Holocaust or its impact upon Jewish consciousness or upon the consciousness of the international community.

Another item that Shlaim (and Morris) blithely pass over is the enormous cost to the Yishuv of Israel's War of Independence. This first round of the Arab–Israeli dispute resulted in 6,000 deaths (not casualties, as Shlaim would have it). Which means that, on top of the frightful cost of the Holocaust, the Jewish people lost fully one percent of its 600,000 population in Mandatory Palestine. It is worth recalling that neither Britain nor the United States came close to losing that percentage of its population in the Second World War. Only Russian losses in that conflict stand comparison. The enormity of the cost to Israel is a factor to be taken into account with regard both to the savagery of the conflict and to Israel's determination to ensure for itself defensible borders that would make it less vulnerable to Arab aggression in the future.

In this connection, it should be noted that a considerable portion of the losses were sustained in clashes with the Transjordanian Arab Legion, in particular in the environs of Jerusalem. To this day, Jerusalemites relate accounts of the battles in which they participated while repelling the Legion's attacks on the city. It is well known that a Transjordanian tank attack was halted only at the very edge of the Israeli-held western sector of Jerusalem. Only the resolute defense of the city by the Israeli forces prevented its conquest by Abdullah's Legion. The Israeli-held half of Jerusalem was under siege from the Arab Legion for months. There were daily civilian casualties as a result of the bombardments and sniper fire that rained in indiscriminately from east Jerusalem. Food and water were strictly rationed because the Legion, supported by Palestinian irregulars, ambushed every convoy on its way up to Jerusalem. Privation and suffering were the lot of fighters and civilians alike until a side road was laboriously constructed through the mountainous approaches to the city. Residents of Jerusalem will be astonished to learn that they had endured the torment of shellfire and severe scarcity during a period of phony war.

It is, thus, of little wonder that Yigael Yadin, chief of staff of the Israeli army, subsequently denied that Ben-Gurion's actions in the War of Independence had in any way been guided by a hidden agreement with Abdullah to exercise mutual restraint. Ben-Gurion's repeated attempts to dislodge the Arab Legion from Latrun confirm how remote any thought of such an "agreement" was from his mind. Likewise, his proposal to the cabinet in August–September 1948 to drive the legion back over the river Jordan and to occupy the entire West Bank, together with east Jerusalem, completely undermines the "conspiracy" thesis. (His proposal was rejected by the Israeli cabinet, to Ben-Gurion's dire regret.) The fact is that Abdullah and Golda Meir never did achieve an agreement, and Abdullah made it quite clear that the die was cast for war. Significantly enough, Shlaim omits the text of any Abdullah–Meir agreement from the collection of documents in the appendixes. There simply was none. These circumstances establish quite clearly that the collusion in the title is a misnomer.

But what is particularly surprising is that the author himself acknowledges as much. It is worth quoting Shlaim at length because, in this extract, he categorically rejects the allegation of "collusion" between Ben-Gurion and Abdullah:

> There was no collusion between the socialist leader and the feudal warlord: the contact was severed in May and it was not renewed until four months later. Hence, the most that can be claimed is that during the latter part of this period there was a tacit understanding between the two rulers to avert a major collision between their armed forces. This tacit understanding was based on perceived interests that the two had in common and which neither shared with their Arab partners-opponents. And it was this perceived interdependence or overlap of interests that led each ruler independently to exercise a measure of self-restraint in relation to the other.
>
> The distinction is not purely semantic. "Collusion" presupposes a direct and explicit agreement and it carries the connotation of a shabby and secret deal. "Tacit understanding," on the other hand, can issue from mutual mind reading, leading to awareness that cooperation between adversaries can work to their mutual advantage but without any direct contact or explicitly formulated plan of action. The difference between the two is small but significant. For if there had been collusion between the Zionist leader and the Hashemite monarch, how is one to account for the fierce fighting that took place between their respective armies in the central front? Surely the whole point about collusion is that it enables politicians to avert a head-on clash and limit the bloodshed. A tacit understanding, by contrast, is much more vulnerable to miscalculation by the policymakers and confusion on the part of their subordinates (p. 235).

On the same page, Shlaim also quotes, approvingly, Yigael Yadin's dismissal of collusion as a myth.

Given this frank acknowledgement that there was no collusion between Abdullah and the Zionists, how is one to explain the choice of title and the manner in which Shlaim presents his key thesis at the beginning of his book? It is difficult to understand what possible purpose all this can serve unless it is to tarnish Israel's name by attributing the failure to establish a Palestinian state in 1948 to Jewish machinations interacting with the vile ambitions of a devious Arab monarch.

But the fact is that the Yishuv never conspired to deprive anyone of statehood. The Yishuv only conspired to establish a Jewish state in peace. It endeavored at all costs to avoid the horrors of war and had no desire to interfere in the fate of the Arab sector of Palestine or the proposed Arab state so long as those in charge were ready to tolerate the establishment of a Jewish state.

If the mufti had proclaimed that he had no claims on the area allotted the Jewish state, no doubt the Yishuv would have collaborated with him in a peaceful implementation of the partition plan. But on the morrow of the General Assembly vote of November 29, 1947, Arab bands began to prey on Jewish property, Jewish lives and Jewish interests. The mufti proclaimed a fight to the finish and not only mobilized his own Palestinian forces but summoned the neighboring Arab states to dispatch their armies into Palestine to destroy the nascent Jewish state. The mufti and his followers were not geared to establish an Arab state in all of Palestine, or even in part of it, and they were not prepared to countenance a Jewish state at all. Under such circumstances, how can it be said that it was the Yishuv that aborted the birth of an Arab state? The Palestinians themselves, in 1948, forestalled the birth of their own state, vacating the front to the neighboring Arab states, and, above all, to Transjordan. Their hostility to a Jewish state was so complete that they drowned their own national ambitions in the flood of aggression that they unleased against the Jewish state. The Palestinian leaders thereby decreed the fate of the Arab sector, propelling it in a spirit of blind hatred into a war that would bring in its wake destruction, desolation and diaspora.

Recognition that war has consequences brings us to a consideration of Morris's book, which again seeks to pin the blame upon the Jews and upon Israel—this time for the tragedy of the Palestinian refugee problem. According to Morris, although there was no premeditated or systematic scheme to expel Arabs, Israeli army commanders, especially in the later stages of the war, took action that promoted a mass exodus of the Arabs from the areas in which they resided.

Before considering the strength of his evidence and whether Israel was indeed a primary factor in producing the flight of the Palestinians, it is again important to stress that in considering this problem it is impossible to overlook the responsibility of the Palestinian leadership for the outbreak of hostilities and for the consequences that flowed from it. War has consequences, and if the initiation of belligerence is a criminal act, as the Nuremberg trials confirmed, then that leadership stands convicted of causing its tragic outcome. Morris fails to take sufficient account of this basic fact in attributing the blame for the creation of the refugee problem.

But Morris himself is led to conclude that "the Palestinian refugee problem was born of war, not by design, Jewish or Arab" (p. 286). Israel, he agrees, did not initiate, plan or foment the flight of the Arabs. Numerous factors were at work, not least "the major structural weaknesses of Palestinian Arab society" (p. 286) and the Arab fear "that the Jews, if victorious, would do to them what, in the reverse circumstances, victorious Arab fighters would have done (and did occasionally, as in the Etzion bloc in May) to defeated Jews" (p. 288). These underlying conditions produced a "psychosis of flight" that led to a mass stampede.

Early Israeli reaction was to attempt to stem the flight. Only afterward, when the conflict expanded with the intervention of the Arab states, did security considerations sometimes lead to a change in Israeli tactics. As the front line between Jews and Arabs moved forward, steps were taken to ensure that the local populace not serve the enemy as an outpost of resistance behind the Israeli lines. "Cleansing the territory" became the only means of fighting a sustained war with five Arab armies. Thus, the very nature of the conflict brought in its wake a policy of banishment. The Arabs first fled spontaneously. Their flight was subsequently also prompted by the Israeli forces acting out of security considerations. As the conflict grew in viciousness and in expanse, nationalist motives also became a factor. If the Arabs were, indeed, the enemy in the full sense of the word, then there was no place for large numbers of them in the Jewish state. Their very aggression had produced a situation in which their ability to remain in a Jewish state as loyal citizens was no longer tenable. Morris fails to appreciate that the progressive stages of the Arab flight followed automatically from the nature of the war that the Palestinian leaders and the Arab states unleashed against the Jewish state. In this case, attribution of fault, like charity, begins at home.

Morris dismisses as a myth the popular claim that Palestinians were exhorted in radio broadcasts from the Arab Higher Committee (in Palestine) and the Arab states to evacuate their homes until the battle was over (pp. 129, 290, but cf. pp. 59, 66 and 84). He claims to have examined all the records of contemporary Arab broadcasts that were monitored and to have found no sign that the Palestinians were urged to flee (see especially his article in *Tikkun*, p. 99). And, very possibly, there is no such mention in the monitored broadcasts. However, the fact remains that the Arab refugees themselves *did believe* that they were advised to leave and *acted* upon that advice. This is made evident by contemporary reports from British diplomats who met with the refugees. Thus, a visit to Gaza by one such diplomat produced the following comment, "But while they express no bitterness against the Jews . . . they speak with the utmost bitterness of the Egyptians and other Arab states. 'We know who our enemies are,' they will say and they are referring to their Arab brothers who, they declare, persuaded them unnecessarily to leave their homes" (FO 371/75342/XC/A/4991).

Alongside the above quotation a Foreign Office official penned a query: "Did they?" This brief comment only highlights the fact that it is largely immaterial if the Arab states did or did not actually encourage evacuation. What is important is that the refugees acted in accordance with such a belief and subsequently felt extremely bitter for having acted on the basis of what they regarded as bad advice.

Morris's book, as the title denotes, focuses upon the *origins* of the Arab refugee problem. However, the political importance of that problem lies in the fact that, even today, more than forty years later, it has still not been resolved. The question arises: Were any opportunities missed in the first few years after the establishment of the state of Israel in 1948 of finding a solution to the refugee problem and of bringing about a peaceful settlement of the Arab–Israeli dispute? Each of the books under review addresses this problem. Once again, Israel finds itself placed in the dock, this time to be charged with sabotaging, or at least with willfully squandering, the opportunities to resolve the key issues in the dispute.

Thus Shlaim, in reviewing Israel's endeavors to reach an agreement with Egypt at Lausanne in 1949, is led to conclude that Israel was not flexible enough. The Egyptians were represented by Abdel Monem Mostafa; Israel was represented by Eliahu Sasson and Reuven Shiloah. Shlaim sums up the negotiations:

> What Mostafa's lecture to Sasson and Shiloah showed, and in this respect there was no fundamental difference between Egypt and the other Arab states, was that in 1949 the Arabs did recognize Israel's right to exist, they were willing to meet face to face to negotiate peace, they had their conditions for making peace with Israel, and Israel rejected those conditions because they were incompatible not with her survival as an independent state but with her determination to keep all the territory she held and to resist the repatriation of the refugees (p. 488).

It is not difficult to refute this charge. Once again Shlaim himself, as with the charge of collusion, demonstrates that it is baseless. Just a few pages before the above quotation he notes that "the Israelis were outraged to discover the full extent of Egypt's territorial claims in Palestine, not least in view of the repeated public declarations that Egypt had no territorial ambitions of her own in Palestine and had only intervened to uphold the rights of the Palestinian Arabs" (p. 485). What were the Egyptians asking for? Merely "to hold on to the Gaza Strip, to extend the area of the strip in the south and in the north, to extend Egypt's border to the Dead Sea in a line that would include Majdal and Beersheba, and to attach to Egypt the southern Negev" (p. 486). The spirit underlying these demands was revealed by Mostafa in a talk with the Americans when he indicated that "in order to regain the confidence of the Arab world and bring lasting stability to the Middle East, America had to ensure that the state of Israel would not be large, nor powerful, nor overpopulated with Jews." Egypt, he explained "would not feel secure if on her border in the Negev there were to be three or four million Jews, all educated, all enterprising, all imbued with the spirit of self-sacrifice" (p. 487).

Thus Shlaim himself documents the fact that the Arab states were ready to recognize Israel only if it would consent to shrink to a ministate by awarding them territory in return for their belligerency in a land where they had no claims or title. Israel was asked to surrender the Negev, its access to the Gulf of Eilat, and its riparian rights on the Dead Sea in order to satisfy the avaricious appetite of its belligerent neighbors. The parable of the fox and the lamb comes readily to mind. The ministate that the Arabs sought for Israel would have been hopelessly vulnerable in later rounds of the protracted Arab–Israeli dispute. Arab demands for territory at the expense of the diminutive area awarded Israel under the partition plan and their obstinate insistence on the return of *all* the refugees reveal the full extent of Arab designs against Israel and their resolve to annihilate it at the first opportunity.

It is likewise baseless to charge Israel with responsibility for the failure of negotiations to conclude a Jordanian–Israeli nonaggression pact in 1950 or for the failure of a Palestinian state to emerge in the West Bank in 1949–1950. Shlaim himself shows that Israel went to extraordinary lengths to facilitate the conclusion of the nonaggression pact, but that its efforts were frustrated by internal opposition within the Hashemite state and by external opposition to Jordan's policies from the Arab states. King Abdullah was compelled to beat a retreat at the last moment (pp.

540–549). And the Palestinian option, as Shlaim himself makes clear, was a mirage from the start:

> On their own, in the aftermath of the Palestine disaster, the Palestinians could not create a viable state, let alone an independent state. Only in cooperation with Israel and, in the final analysis, only if Israel were prepared to use her own army to expel the Arab Legion from the West Bank could such a state be formed, but then it could have been nothing more than a satellite. (p. 509)

As Pappé correctly points out:

> It is noteworthy that no one talked about the Palestinian problem at that time (1948–51). There was a clear distinction between the question of Palestine's future, namely, the territorial problem as well as the question of sovereignty, and the question of the refugees' future, that is the humanitarian aspect of the problem. The main implication of such an approach was that the Palestinians were not regarded as a nation or as a people who could constitute a side in this dispute. The main reason for this approach was the attitude of the parties involved in the conflict towards the concept of an independent Palestinian state alongside a Jewish state. Such a state as offered by the UN resolution of November 1947 had been ruled out by all the parties prior to the war in Palestine. Most of the Arab states and the Arab Palestinians demanded a unitary state in Palestine, whereas Transjordan, with the consent of the British and the Jewish Agency, contemplated the annexation of the areas allotted to the Arab Palestinians in that resolution. During the bilateral and multilateral negotiations which followed the Palestine war, the Arab governments tended to accept the principle of partition without recognising the Jewish state. In fact, each Arab country suspected the other of conspiring to annex the territories allotted to the Palestinians (pp. 74–75).

And as for resolving the refugee problem, it is quite clear, as Morris amply demonstrates, that the Arab states were not intent on finding a solution to the problem. They preferred to preserve the issue intact—with all its poignancy, tragedy and festering animosity—as a potent weapon in their campaign to destroy Israel. Israel was in a catch-22 situation. It could not accept the refugees back en masse without destroying itself demographically as a Jewish state. And yet it could never prevail on the Arab states to adopt resettlement in Arab lands rather than repatriation to Israel as their basic guideline. Thus, Israel was simply not in a position to influence Arab policy. It could not accept the refugees nor could it cede territory without endangering itself.

Manifestly, the Arab refugee problem could only be resolved if it were treated as a case of population exchange. Such exchanges had taken place on numerous occasions in the aftermath of the First and Second World Wars. The Arab–Israeli conflict of 1948 was a subsequent outcome of those two conflicts and the population movements that followed the Palestine war could have been treated in accordance with accepted procedures. This, indeed, is how British diplomats in the Middle East viewed the development, as contemporary documents demonstrate. These diplomats, including the consul in Jerusalem, Sir Hugh Dow, the ambassador to Amman, Sir Alec Kirkbride, and the ambassador to Lebanon, Mr. Houghton-Boswell, referred to the Arab flight as the "silver lining" on the dark clouds of war. The demographic imbalance would willy-nilly be improved. (It is a pity that Morris does not quote them at length.)

But fecklessly, the British and American governments failed to press for a program of resettlement. As Pappé says, the problem was treated as one "which called for temporary relief rather than an overall solution" (p. 212). Failure to provide permanent homes and gainful employment fostered the growth of a ruthless terrorist movement. The refugee problem, as noted earlier, was a tragic consequence of Arab aggression. Israel could not be blamed for adhering to a policy on this question, as on the territorial question, which was designed to forestall future Arab attempts to eliminate the Jewish state.

It is self-evident, then, that Israel was not remiss in 1948 in pursuing policies, both externally and internally, that maximized its ability to survive as an independent sovereign Jewish state. It owes nobody an apology for surviving. It has a claim on the land as of right and not by sufferance. It would have been entitled to employ whatever tricks were at its disposal to defeat its enemies, who were sworn to destroy it. In fact, though, not tricks but hard-won battles, fought at enormous cost, enabled it to prevail and to preserve its Jewish identity. In the wake of the war and the undiminished Arab resolve to destroy the Jewish state, Israel was not only entitled, but compelled, to take steps that would deter future Arab aggression.

In light of the foregoing, one can only ask, in all fairness, what do the revisionist historians want? It has been amply demonstrated, as Shlaim himself says, that there was no collusion; as Morris acknowledges, there was no preconceived plan to expel Arabs; as Pappé agrees, there was no plan to forestall the emergence of a Palestinian state. If all this is true, then what is the aim of the "new historians"? What have they added to our knowledge? The answer, it appears, is that modern Israel, willy-nilly, was born in sin. The Christian notion of "original sin" is stamped on the state of Israel like the mark of Cain, never to be erased. But even if the charge were true, of what significance is all this? Surely many states, such as the United States itself, with its imperial policy of Manifest Destiny, were born in sin, yet this does not mark them for eternity. The answer is supplied by Morris when he questions Israel's claim to an "untarnished image" (p. 1). He elaborates on this point in his article in *Tikkun:*

> If Israel, the haven of a much-persecuted people, was born pure and innocent, then it was worthy of the grace, material assistance, and political support showered upon it by the West over the past forty years—and worthy of more of the same in years to come. If, on the other hand, Israel was born tarnished, besmirched by original sin, then it was not more deserving of that grace and assistance than were its neighbors.

Here Morris reveals himself not as a historian but as a polemicist, as one who has an axe to grind. If he had contented himself with writing history by recounting the facts and analyzing them, his stand would have been dignified and his conclusions would command respect. But when a writer candidly reveals that the "original sin" that he and his colleagues have discovered is a reason to cut Israel down to size today, to cease treating it as something special, to reduce financial and political support for the country, then one sees a strange motive inspiring the writing of this "new history." The aim, quite clearly, is to attribute blame for the plight of the Palestinians—their refugee status and their failure to attain statehood—to Israeli malfeasance in 1948, and to suggest that the wrongs of 1948 can be rectified in 1990 by restoring to the Palestinians today their robbed nationhood. This, supposedly, requires a more "even-handed" approach by the international community of states, and especially by the United States. This is the thrust of the approach of the "new historians."

But if this policy goal is their proclaimed aim, then their historiography is, at best, suspect. There is a clear measure of a priori thinking in their research and writing. Finally, and more important, as they themselves demonstrate, the charges against Israel are quite unsupported by the evidence. This only leaves us with something of a mystery. Why do gifted historians engage in such a disjointed form of writing or, at the least, a disjointed manner of drawing conclusions?

SHLOMO SLONIM
The Hebrew University

Vienna, the Habsburg Empire and the Jews

William O. McCagg, Jr., *A History of Habsburg Jews 1670–1918*. Bloomington: Indiana University Press, 1989. 289 pp.

Hillel J. Kieval, *The Making of Czech Jewry: National Conflict and Jewish Society in Bohemia, 1870–1918*. New York: Oxford University Press, 1988. 279 pp.

François Fejtö, *Requiem pour un empire défunt: Histoire de la destruction de l'Autriche–Hongrie*. Paris: Lieu Commun, 1988. 437 pp.

E. M. Lilien, *Briefe an Seine Frau 1905–1925*. Ed. Otto M. Lilien and Eve Strauss. Königstein/Ts.: Jüdischer Verlag Athenaum, 1985. 301 pp.

Steven Beller, *Vienna and the Jews 1867–1938: A Cultural History*. Cambridge: Cambridge University Press, 1989. 271 pp.

George E. Berkley, *Vienna and Its Jews: The Tragedy of Success, 1880–1980s*. Cambridge, Mass: Abt Books/Madison Books, 1988. 421 pp.

Hilde Spiel, *Vienna's Golden Autumn, 1866–1938*. London: Weidenfeld & Nicolson, 1987. 248 pp.

Sigurd Paul Scheichl and Edward Timms (eds.), *Karl Kraus in Neuer Sicht*. Munich: Edition Text + Kritik, 1986. 255 pp.

Edward Timms and Naomi Segal (eds.), *Freud in Exile: Psychoanalysis and Its Vicissitudes*. New Haven and London: Yale University Press, 1988. 310 pp.

Peter Gay, *Freud: A Life for Our Time*. New York: W. W. Norton, 1988. 810 pp.

Robert Knight (ed.), *"Ich bin dafür die Sache in die Lange zu ziehen:" Die Wortprotokolle der österreichischen Bundesregierung von 1945 bis 1952 über die Entschädigung der Juden*. Frankfurt: Athenaum, 1988. 287 pp.

The Jews of the Habsburg Empire formed the second largest Jewish community in Europe before 1918. On the eve of the First World War, there were approximately 2.25 million Jews in the immense territory between the Carpathians and the Alps that constituted the heterogeneous multinational Danubian state, compared to just over 500,000 Jews in Germany, 250,000 in England and some 80,000 or 100,000 in France. Since the mid-nineteenth century, the various Jewries that made up the Habsburg domains found themselves confronted with acute and extraordinarily complex problems of modernization, religious and cultural identity as well as national-political orientation. The awakening of the nationalities in East Central Europe in the course of the century—a development that came to threaten the very survival of the supranational Habsburg state—was especially dangerous and perplexing for the Jews of the empire whose stability and prosperity was increasingly bound up with that of the dynasty itself.

Tragically, as the history of Central Europe would subsequently demonstrate, the collapse of the dynasty irrevocably unhinged the sociopolitical and psychic equilibrium in that part of the world, destroyed its cultural unity, helped unleash the Nazi juggernaut (thereby opening the way to the destruction of European Jewry) and brought Stalinist totalitarianism into the heartland of European civilization. Thus, the causes of the dissolution of the Habsburg Monarchy, a question long-debated by historians, remain of some importance for literally millions of people still living out the tragic consequences of the dismemberment that took place in 1918.

For François Fejtö, a well-known Hungarian-born historian and journalist who has lived in Paris for the past half-century, the empire did not collapse for internal reasons: it was eliminated from the map of Europe by Allied decision makers, encouraged and even manipulated by the exiled Czech leaders, Masaryk and Beneš, whom he describes as *"deux génies de la propagande."* In the name of national self-determination, they persuaded the Western Allies that an independent Czechoslovak state, free of German and Russian tutelage, could become the focus of *Mitteleuropa,* a delusion cruelly unmasked by events twenty years later. Yet, like Romania, Yugoslavia and Poland, Czechoslovakia was in reality a multinational successor state acting as if it were a homogeneous, unitary nation-state. In many ways, it was even less equipped than the Habsburgs to handle minority problems.

Fejtö believes that Vienna in the closing years of the monarchy was in any case moving toward federalization and that national separatism could have been contained by countervailing centripetal forces had it not been for the Allied victory and determination to dismantle Austria-Hungary. Apart from the Czech intrigues and the Allied belief that Vienna had become an instrument of, rather than a barrier to, the Prusso-German *Drang nach Osten,* there was also an ideological factor that Fejtö emphasizes—namely, the influence of international Freemasonry.

He argues that especially in France (but also in Italy) Freemasonry acted as the spearhead of militant, anticlerical republicans determined to liberate "oppressed nations" in Eastern Europe and fulfill the legacy of the French Revolution. In this ideological context, Catholic Austria was misleadingly perceived and stigmatized as a bulwark of the "clerical, retrograde spirit" and as a "prison-house" of the suppressed peoples of East Central Europe whose national rights had to be restored. Fejtö's arguments on this score tend to be highly circumstantial and somewhat dubious, but he has opened up an interesting line of inquiry.

Fejtö does not discuss Habsburg Jewry at any length (some ten superficial pages are devoted to Jewish assimilation and antisemitism), but at the head of his final chapter, there is a quote from the Galician-born Jewish intellectual, Manès Sperber, which might have served as an epigram for William McCagg's highly idiosyncratic account of the subject. Sperber writes, *"Quelque chose de supranational nous lie: le résidu que nous portons en notre âme de l'ancienne Autriche"* ("Something supranational links us: the residue that we carry in our soul from Old Austria"). This remark might apply to the common cultural heritage within the melting pot of nationalities shaped by Habsburg rule, a legacy that owed as much to the cosmopolitan Jewish leaven as it did to the German language, that irreplaceable *lingua franca* of the Dual Monarchy. But McCagg also seems to argue that the supranational culture linked the Jewries of the empire into a truly distinctive whole, despite the amorphous character of the Habsburg cultural-political experience and the very different levels of modernization and development that the various Jewish communities had undergone. This is certainly a challenging proposition, and one cannot but admire the sweeping boldness with which McCagg sets about trying to make his case.

It is, after all, no easy task to take on the entire Habsburg Jewish experience, from Vienna, Bohemia and Hungary through to Galicia, Bukovina and Trieste. Moreover, to embark upon such an immense undertaking without a knowledge of Hebrew or Yiddish is particularly problematic, not to say an act of calculated chutzpah even for someone of McCagg's linguistic skills and familiarity with the region. The negative consequences of this unfamiliarity with internal Jewish history and its sources are apparent when he deals with topics such as Frankism, Hasidism, the Galician Haskalah, Jewish Reform and also in the short shrift given to the leading Viennese Rabbis (Adolf Jellinek and Moritz Güdemann get a single reference each!). The internal politics of the Viennese *Israelitische Kultusgemeinde* and the discussions within the Austrian Israelite Union (accessible to the author as they were conducted in German) are by and large disregarded as, more surprisingly, is the rise of political Zionism and the intense controversy it aroused. (Herzl, for example, receives a mere paragraph—as does Nathan Birnbaum, the founder of Austrian Zionism—while the development of Jewish nationalism in Galicia, although mentioned, is only superficially analyzed.)

On the other hand, McCagg's panoramic sweep does permit him to concentrate on empirewide developments and to compare the effects of modernization on traditional Jewish communities in different parts of the monarchy. The impact of Magyarization and neology in Hungary; the effect of Josephinian policies in Bohemia; the vignettes of peripheral communities in Trieste and Bukovina; and the emergence of an ennobled Jewish elite in Vienna before 1848—each subject is particularly well done. But the author's claim that all this must change our perception of the "Habsburg all-Empire bourgeoisie" (whatever that actually means) can scarcely be sustained by the evidence.

The notion that leaders of the *Kultusgemeinde* set the tone for Viennese society as a whole during the 1860s and 1870s seems to me, for example, a bizarre exaggeration. So, too, does the author's strange argument that in 1848 the bourgeois Jews of Vienna *won* (achieved) emancipation but as members of the Habsburg middle class they were defeated. Curiously enough, McCagg sees the Viennese rising of 1848 as a "Judeophile" revolution (in my view, it can more properly be regarded as a seed plot of modern antisemitism!) that created dangerously optimistic illusions about the gentile environment and encouraged Jews to persist in their mistaken belief that more assimilation would lead to more emancipation. This sounds like good "Zionist" doctrine (indeed, McCagg frequently emphasizes and at times overstates the theme of national self-denial among Habsburg Jews). But why blame Jewish self-delusions on 1848? In fact, real Jewish emancipation only came in 1867 (a far more important date in Habsburg Jewish history than is suggested in this book) after nearly two decades of reaction—by that time the memory of 1848 had decidedly faded.

Altogether, McCagg's handling of Viennese Jewish history seems shakier than his accounts of Hungary, Bohemia or even outlying parts of the empire, and this is especially apparent in the closing section of the book entitled "The Catastrophes, 1875–1918." (Surely they didn't begin that early?) Karl Lueger's Vienna is hardly mentioned; the rise of populist antisemitism and the Jewish response is evoked in the sketchiest of terms; there is virtually no reference to the massive Jewish role in late Austro-Hungarian culture, above all in Vienna and Budapest. Nor are any reasons for these omissions provided. This is a pity because for all its faults and weaknesses, this is a valuable, thought-provoking and occasionally brilliant book based on extensive reading and wide-ranging knowledge that now and then offers flashes of real insight deserving of more detailed investigation by historians.

Hillel Kieval's account of the transformation of Bohemian Jewry in the closing decades of the Habsburg monarchy employs a similar terminology to that of Mc-Cagg ("urbanization," "demographic change," "integration," "modernization" and "ethnic nationalism" are key categories) but in style and temperament is almost antithetical. This is a very sober, professional and scholarly study, well organized and structured, carefully focused on its subject and ascetically avoiding any kind of speculative judgment. Its major theme and claim to originality is its description and analysis of the rise of the Jewish movement that sought to promote assimilation into the Czech culture and nation. The clash between this rising trend and the rival options of German cultural assimilation or, alternatively, of Jewish nationalism, form the core of the book. They are set against the background of a postemancipatory, industrializing society split down the middle by German-Czech national antagonism, arguably the most intense of all the ethnic conflicts that ravaged the Habsburg monarchy in its last years.

Kieval emphasizes that the advocates of Czech Jewish assimilation mostly came from the countryside, had themselves gone to Czech-language gymnasia and aimed at a fusion of Czech culture with Jewish values. They believed that Czech patriotism rather than loyalty to Vienna or to German culture was the best guarantee for Jewish emancipation, and they strove in particular for a *linguistic* realignment of Bohemian Jewry. Although a minority trend among Czech Jews before 1914, Jewish patriots had, in fact, achieved their goal by the turn of the century as Jews began to switch from German to Czech schools and to declare Czech their "language of everyday use." As the author points out, this dramatic change coincided with the disintegration of German liberalism in fin-de-siècle Prague, and the rise of Czech national extremism and a militant Czech antisemitism that has often been underestimated by historians. However, the paradox of mounting antisemitism in Prague around 1897 *and* the growing use of Czech by the Bohemian Jews, although addressed, is never fully elucidated in the book.

Zionism in Prague, which also forms a major theme in Kieval's study, may, in fact, be seen as a logical response to the inhospitable nature of both the German and the Czech national movements to Bohemian Jews at the turn of the century. Affirming Jewish national identity clearly offered a way out of the impasse in which the Jews were exposed to attack as "agents" of either German or Czech interests!

But Prague Zionism also had a distinctively ethical and humanist character that found expression in Martin Buber's immensely influential "Three Addresses on Judaism," with their summons to a rebirth of Jewish spiritual creativity and their emphasis on the transformation of the self as the harbinger of national redemption. Nowhere more than in Prague around 1910 did the romantic, irrationalist, anti-positivist Zionist credo espoused by the Viennese-born, Galician-educated and culturally Germanized Buber find such an enthusiastic response, though it was one that was necessarily confined to a small circle of younger Jewish intellectuals.

The heartland of Zionism in the Austro-Hungarian Empire was not, of course, to be found in cities such as Prague, Budapest or Vienna (though the latter in Herzl's day was the center of the World Zionist Organization) but rather in peripheral areas such as Bukovina and, above all, among the *Ostjuden* of Galicia. The letters to his wife of the Galician-born Ephraim Moses Lilien (1874–1925)—the leading Jewish graphic designer of his day and the first major artist to offer his services to the Zionist movement—strikingly illustrate the spontaneous sense of Jewish peoplehood that underlay so much of this East European Zionism.

Coming himself from a deprived, underprivileged background, Lilien's social and national instincts encouraged him to see in Zionism a necessary and natural reaffirmation of Jewish pride and group consciousness. Writing from Berlin in July 1905 he tells his future wife, "I saw the fate of my people, and its distress has also become my own. Not because we are brothers in faith [*Glaubensbrüder*] but because we are ethnic brethren. We are a people, a race. We, all of us, rich Jews and poor, educated and ignorant, have *one* past."

Lilien's strong sense of *Stammesbewusstsein* and his belief in the organic continuity of Jewish history and *Volkstum* (which led him to unequivocally condemn assimilation as national "suicide") drew him to Buber and his Austrian Zionist friend Berthold Feiwel, with whom he collaborated in founding the Berlin-based *Jüdischer Verlag* in 1902. At this time, he was closely linked to Weizmann's Democratic fraction, and it was out of this involvement that in 1905 he became a member of the committee to establish the Bezalel School of Art in Jerusalem. Lilien taught there in 1906 for several months and visited Palestine again, in 1910, 1914 and 1918—the last time as a lieutenant in the Austro-Hungarian Army toward the end of the First World War. His impressions from the Holy Land are vividly recorded in some of the letters, and the text is illustrated by crisp, elegant line drawings (mainly in india ink), etchings, portraits and *Jugendstil* designs that often illustrated the biblical scenes and motifs that became Lilien's trademark as an artist.

It would be difficult to find a sharper contrast to Lilien's worldview than that espoused by his Viennese Jewish contemporary, the satirist Karl Kraus, who probably detested *Jugendstil* aestheticism, orientalist romanticism and Zionist ideological mystifications in about equal measure. Kraus had no more time for self-consciously Jewish art than he did for *Ostjuden* or for what he once sardonically referred to as "oriental enclaves in Western civilization." Jewish themes are by and large absent from the published proceedings of the London symposium on Kraus organized by two well-known specialists in the field, Edward Timms and Sigurd Paul Scheichl. However, this collection of papers, which focuses on the relation between language and experience, contains a number of insights useful to any study of Jewish identity in fin-de-siècle Austria. In the first place, our attention is drawn to a theme once formulated thus by Kraus's Bohemian-German Jewish contemporary Fritz Mauthner, "Indeed, I don't understand how a Jew who was born in one of the

Slavonic lands of the Austrian empire could avoid being drawn into the study of language.'' Kraus's commitment to language as a mirror of society, ethics and the world was, of course, more emotionally charged than a mere concern with the ''study of language'' might suggest.

For Kraus, the decline and then the collapse of Austria-Hungary and of the civilization he cherished was reflected above all in the corruption of the word. His strength lay in his relentless exposure of that corruption, even though as a Jewish intellectual he was cut off from ready access to political power and would remain permanently distrustful of institutions, ideologies and party politics. Yet, ironically enough, this assimilated Jew, for all his radicalism and moral intransigence, was ardently attached to the aristocratic elitist values of an older pre-1848 Austria, at least as long as the monarchy existed. Only following its collapse did the fiercely individualistic Kraus begin to be drawn into the orbit of the Austrian Social Democrats, though he remained decidedly critical of their revolutionary commitments and political style.

Kraus was even more hostile to psychoanalysis, though in many ways he had been pursuing a project parallel to that of Freud by different means. As Jewish insider-outsiders appalled by the hypocritical morality of a repressive bourgeois society, both Kraus and Freud fought for sexual enlightenment, for the deconstruction of clichés, conventional wisdoms and established truths and both felt intuitively that European civilization was embarked on a course of self-destruction. In that sense, the writings of Kraus and Freud can be read as barometers uniquely sensitive to the sickness of late bourgeois Central European culture and to the unresolved dilemmas of Jewish assimilation.

Peter Gay's monumental biography of Freud, written in engaging, lucid prose and infused with a strong belief in the psychoanalytic project, eschews, however, any Austrocentric approach to his subject matter. For all the careful scholarship that stands behind this book (and the research is impeccably thorough) this is essentially a celebratory work full of reverential admiration for its hero, though not without the gently ironic reproof or the occasional critical aside. Freud's flirtations with hypnosis, his personal experiments with cocaine, his love affair with his sister-in-law, his alleged plagiarism, his abandonment of the seduction theory of neurosis and his authoritarian leadership of the psychoanalytic movement are all dealt with (though the more controversial of these issues are relegated to the bibliographical essay at the back of the book). So, too, there is a description of Freud's complex relationship with his daughter Anna (whom he analyzed for more than three years), who was never to marry, and who became in Gay's own words ''his most precious claim on life, his ally against death.'' Gay goes into these and other episodes in scholarly detail, yet the net effect is, strangely, one of evasiveness as if he feared to probe too far into Freud's family life and intimate personal relations.

Thus, his hero's ambivalent ties to his mother, his conservative views on women (morally and intellectually inferior!) and his ambiguity about his own Jewishness are discussed but subtly downplayed. Indeed, Professor Gay appears to dismiss with a disconcerting blandness the notion that psychoanalysis had any Jewish origins at all. Equally surprising is the lack of attention given to Freud's sexual identity and to his disenchantment with his own marriage, especially in the light of his earlier, ardent courtship of Martha Bernays. Finally, we get no clear sense of where Gay stands on the touchy question of the status of psychoanalysis as a science, a claim that has increasingly been discredited in recent years, without necessarily diminishing the personal stature of Freud as a discoverer, liberator and mythmaker of the unconscious.

But how Jewish was Freud and to what extent was this fact important in the life of the hero? Professor Gay tends to stress above all the scientist and the atheist in Freud, the man of the Enlightenment, the last of the *philosophes* (perhaps most evident in his embattled rejection of institutionalized religion) at the expense of any deep-rooted allegiance to his Jewish roots. There is no analysis in depth, for instance, of what Freud might have meant when writing of the "irresistible" attraction exerted by Jews and and Judaism; of the "many dark emotional powers, all the mightier the less they let themselves be grasped in words, as well as the clear consciousness of inner identity, the secrecy of the same mental construction." Gay disposes of such statements by a casual reference to Freud's belief (taken from Lamarck) in the inheritance of acquired characteristics. But the explanation is as unconvincing as the author's efforts to divorce Freud from his Viennese cultural background. For without the environmental influences, without the peculiar viciousness of Viennese antisemitism, without the clericalism and bigotry or the resistance of the medical and academic establishments, neither Freud nor psychoanalysis would have become what they did. Nor was this simply a matter of defiance and self-preservation in the face of a hostile environment. Freud clearly valued his Jewishness and maintained his ethnic self-identification in remarkably consistent terms over a period of at least sixty years.

An interesting counterweight to Gay's minimalist approach in these matters is provided by Ivar Oxaal's essay for the volume on *Freud in Exile* (edited by Edward Timms and Naomi Segal). Without rigidly embracing a deterministic form of ethnic maximalism, Oxaal does suggest that, sociologically speaking, it was highly probable that Freud and his psychoanalytical circle would be mostly Jewish under Viennese conditions. Sander L. Gilman, in another essay in the same book, argues that the embattled position of psychoanalysis within a medical science still riddled in the nineteenth century with racist assumptions resembled that of the Jews in a hostile gentile world. As a Jewish outsider, Freud had "to use the status of science to overcome the stigma of race" and to try and explain such phenomena as bisexuality or "male menstruation" as a sign of universal development rather than a specific sign linked to racially inferior Jews.

The essay by Ritchie Robertson provides yet another viewpoint on Freud's Jewish identity by treating his *Moses and Monotheism* as a work of imaginative literature inspired as much by Goethe as by biblical scholarship. Robertson rightly points out that Judaism for Freud was a traumatic neurosis (like other religions) but at the same time, more intellectually and morally advanced than its rivals. Thus, it was more adapted to a scientific age of rationality. However, Robertson also notes that *Moses and Monotheism* is Freud's most Nietzschean work. The authoritarian charisma of the Egyptian-born Moses rather than a process of rational inquiry successfully imposed monotheism on the Jewish people. But Freud still remained a rationalist in reaffirming Jewish identity as an act of choice rather than an unalterable birthright or destiny.

We are, thus, once again brought back to the question of whether there was anything specifically "Jewish" in the involvement of intellectuals such as Freud in late nineteenth-century secular, positivist culture. Was their commitment to science, reason and enlightenment not shared by educated Germans (and most other cultured Europeans) as Peter Gay would certainly argue? Does it make any sense, therefore, to speak of a distinctive culture of Austrian Jews between 1867 and 1938 as Steven Beller does in his new book? How, indeed, is one to define a Jew in the Austrian, and especially in the Viennese, context?

Beller disposes of this last question rather cavalierly by simply deciding that anyone of "Jewish descent" or even of partially Jewish descent is to be considered as a product of Jewish assimilation and, hence, must count as a Jew. He even contends that "the presence in the family past of Jewish ancestors was liable to mean that one started with a view of the world which was substantially different from that of others who were not of Jewish descent." Thus, we are treated to extensive discussions of the "Jewishness" of such extremely marginal "Jews" as Hugo von Hofmannsthal and Ludwig Wittgenstein, which seems decidedly ethereal and divorced from reality. (For Wittgenstein, the case can perhaps be made but not in the way it is here).

Beller begins his book with lists and percentages of Jews in fields such as psychology, philosophy, political and social thought, legal theory, literature, theater and operetta, music and art. There are few surprises here because the lists simply confirm that Jews dominated (or were proportionately "overrepresented") in fin-de-siècle Vienna's cultural elite. Next he produces figures for the Viennese gymnasia that again confirm what we already knew from Marsha Rozenblit's earlier study, namely, that the educated liberal bourgeoisie in Vienna was predominantly a Jewish bourgeoisie.

The novelty is that from this quantitative base Beller seeks to prove that the fact of being Jewish had a major impact on the attitude of Jewish individuals in the cultural elite to their work "and hence on that work itself." This thesis is much more problematic because as Beller realizes, there were not a few Austrian gentiles such as Hermann Bahr, Adolf Loos, Oskar Kokoschka, Robert Musil, Georg Trakl or Schoenberg's gentile disciples, Webern and Anton Berg, who held views virtually identical to those of the assimilated Jews he investigates. The author, in order to circumvent this difficulty, is forced into some bizarre, not to say silly, assertions. Thus, he rhetorically asks: "How many writers from Vienna who were not Jewish traveled across Europe?" The significance of this remark escapes me. According to Beller, cosmopolitan gentiles were in any case exceptional [sic] or else influenced by a "Jewish" outlook because they had Jewish wives! (This is not the only instance where Beller appears to fall victim, despite himself, to a quasi-racial methodology for the most philosemitic of reasons!)

More pertinently, Beller argues against Carl Schorske that the Jews were not simply a special case within Vienna's liberal bourgeoisie. They *were* that bourgeoisie, the missing "Protestant" middle class in a Catholic Austrian setting. Beller also has some interesting insights into the process of assimilation itself, writes well about the crisis of modernism and is useful on the specific values that he believes the Viennese Jewish intelligentsia to have embodied. Unfortunately, however, much of this discussion is vitiated by the ethnic maximalism the author insistently espouses—an approach that constantly runs the risk of appearing to be naively reductionist and determinist in presenting anything of interest in Viennese culture as an essentially "Jewish" phenomenon.

The danger is all the greater when, as in Beller's book, there is virtually no discussion of the organized Jewish community and of its religious, communal or political options. Thus, we are given a cultural history of Viennese Jews in which they are present only as deracinated individuals whose identity is unclear and whose relation to the larger Jewish context is entirely nebulous. The net result is not surprisingly *unhistorical* and, indeed, except for the mid-1890s, refers to the external events that affected and influenced Viennese Jewry in a remarkably vague, offhand manner.

Hilde Spiel's lavish and elegantly produced coffee-table book generally avoids the pitfalls of treating the Jews in isolation from Austrian society and politics. Though this is not a scholarly work, it is a highly readable and instructive introduction to the Viennese cultural world that was brutally extinguished in 1938. Herself a product of that environment and familiar with many of its dramatis personae, Hilde Spiel is able to faithfully reproduce much of its atmosphere and texture. Thus, she captures, with a sure touch, the polarities in the cosmopolitan Viennese character— the deceptive gaiety of German-Austrian *Gemütlichkeit,* Slavic *Weltschmerz,* alpine naivete, Italian elegance, the Spanish obsession with death and the intellectual refinement of emancipated Jews.

It is the liberal Jewish bourgeoisie who, in her account, provide the ethical seriousness, the rationalism and the commitment to high culture that shook the Viennese out of their easygoing hedonism, their mindless malice and gloomy fatalism. At the same time, as befits the author of an earlier study of Fanny von Arnstein and the Jewish salons, Spiel clearly identifies with the established, thoroughly assimilated, old-Viennese families of Jewish origin who were so important as patrons of Vienna's modern culture. Particularly revealing is the way she agrees with the verdict of the English observer Henry Wickham Steed (editor of the *London Times* and its foreign correspondent in pre-1914 Vienna—by no means himself immune to antisemitism) that "the Jews of Vienna would have ceased to be exposed to anti-Semitism were their ranks not swelled every year by thousands of newcomers from Galicia and Hungary." This misleading assumption, still heard today in certain milieux, echoes in a remarkable way the irritation of the late nineteenth-century Jewish establishment in Vienna with the *Ostjuden* who were allegedly spoiling their chances of full assimilation.

Such foibles aside, Hilde Spiel honestly admits that she would rather not have distinguished between Jew and non-Jew, and this adds poignancy to her concluding plea with its veiled reference to the Waldheim affair. It is worth quoting in full:

> In writing this account of a great cultural epoch, I would have preferred not to have to point out which among the men and women who helped to create it were of Jewish descent. What they themselves would have wanted was to be accepted simply as Austrian poets, painters or composers. This was and still is a Utopian wish. For that reason one may do well to rouse the collective memory and stress the fact that it was due to a unique moment in history, to an unrepeatable symbiosis, that Vienna's great era came about. To profit from it in retrospect, as the city now does, would seem to oblige

its inhabitants to pay more than lip-service to the memory of its banished or murdered Jews, and to respect those few left of the same faith who still trust them to the extent of once more living in their midst.

The pertinence of these remarks seems all too obvious in the light of recent developments in Austria. The election of Waldheim, the accompanying exploitation of an antisemitic discourse by the Austrian People's party, the successes of the extreme right-wing Freedom party and the insecurity felt by Vienna's tiny Jewish community today, all point to the difficulty that Austrians have in overcoming their past. Their evasiveness in dealing openly with the Nazi legacy, their inability to uproot endemic popular antisemitism and to face their moral responsibility toward the Jews have paradoxically focused the world's attention on their failings as never before. It was, therefore, almost inevitable that a book such as George Berkley's massive indictment of the Austrian character and, in particular, Vienna's treatment of the Jews would appear at this juncture in time.

There is, of course, a great deal to condemn in Austrian behavior, though whether this should be the historian's main task is more than debatable. However, Professor Berkley is a political scientist by training, and this is his first foray into the field, a fact that explains much about the book he has written. Based mainly on interviews and a précis of secondary sources (sadly, it must be said that the borrowings occasionally border on plagiarism), devoid of proper footnotes and any pretence of objectivity, the study, nonetheless, has a certain grim coherence sometimes lacking in more scholarly works. The thesis is disarmingly simple—to quote the Austrian Jewish satirist, Alfred Polgar—"The Germans make good Nazis but lousy anti-Semites. The Austrians make lousy Nazis, but what first-class antisemites they are!"

In other words, this study sets out to prove that the Austrians were always more committed and passionate antisemites than the Germans and that Vienna's Jews were from the beginning living in a fool's paradise of self-delusions and self-deception. Evidence for such assumptions certainly abounds, as it does for the subsidiary thesis that Viennese Jews were simply too successful for their own good, almost inevitably breeding gentile envy and hatred as a backlash against their competitive drive. So, too, there is much to support the contention that in 1938 the Austrians behaved even more brutally than the Reich Nazis toward the Jews. Carl Zuckmayer's evocation of the *Anschluss* sums it up succinctly, "The netherworld had opened its gates and vomited forth the lowest, filthiest, most horrible demons . . . a torrent of envy, jealousy, malignant craving for revenge."

Nor has Berkley invented anything in his description of postwar Austrian meanness toward Jewish Holocaust survivors, reflected in the haggling and foot-dragging over restitution claims. This shabby affair and its antisemitic undertones have now been fully covered by the British historian Robert Knight, who has reproduced all the relevant documentation from cabinet protocols of the Austrian government between 1945 and 1952 together with a valuable introduction and footnotes. This confirms what was long-suspected—namely, that the Austrian government sought by various maneuvers and delays to avoid paying any financial compensation to the Jews. It also actively discouraged their return to Austria and in common with public opinion was highly susceptible to stereotyped anti-Jewish thinking—all of which reinforces the main thrust of Berkley's thesis.

Nevertheless, Berkeley's exposure of Austria's antisemitic face ultimately becomes tiresome, unbalanced and even self-defeating. There is no attempt at nuance, at understanding the deeper issues raised by Central European antisemitism or the assimilationist dilemmas confronting the Jews. Thus, the Jews are condemned at different times for lacking in pride, for not uniting against the enemy, for having failed to conciliate their enemies or for having stayed in Austria rather than emigrating to Palestine—even though these criticisms are self-contradictory and obviously made with the benefit of hindsight.

Berkley's lessons from the past also strike the present reviewer as more than dubious. Thus, we are told that "the less Jewish a Jew becomes, the more may his very Jewishness imperil him," as if this is a universal truth. Next we learn that a Jewish community will not be able to protect itself "unless it is first a community," and finally we are left with the speculation that had the Viennese Jews been unified and negotiated an agreement with the Catholic Church in the 1930s, they might have been better off.

Unfortunately none of these assumptions has any historical basis. In fact, the Jewish leaders in Vienna understood the antisemites much better than Professor Berkley realizes; in the end it made no difference. Moreover, the author seems to have forgotten that the Nazis massacred the Orthodox, the traditional, and the committed Jews with the same cruel efficiency as they dispatched the spineless "assimilators," the indifferent, and the "*konfessionslos.*" Nor, in the final analysis, did the structure of the Jewish community, its level of organization or its internal unity substantially affect the fate of the Jews.

The history of Viennese Jewry is a fascinating and tragic story, but it is best written by dispensing with the comfortable clichés of omniscient condescension toward those trapped in events over which they had relatively little control.

ROBERT S. WISTRICH
The Hebrew University

Book Reviews

POLITICAL AND COMMUNAL HISTORY

Shirley Berry Isenberg, *India's Bene Israel: A Comprehensive Inquiry and Source-book.* Berkeley and Bombay: Judah L. Magnes Museum/Popular Prakashan, 1988. 443 pp.

In the preface to her long-awaited book, Shirley Isenberg explains that her aim is to provide a comprehensive and documented account of the Bene Israel in India, a synthesis of anthropology and historiography, which will serve as a sourcebook and point the way to future research, particularly for the pre-British period. She has succeeded admirably. The product of many years of meticulous research in primary sources from several countries and a close analysis of secondary materials and interviews, this book is truly a compendium of knowledge about the Bene Israel.

The largest of India's three Jewish communities, the Bene Israel once numbered more than 20,000 at its peak in the early 1950s. Although the community in India has now dwindled to about 5,000 as a result of emigration, there are approximately 25,000 to 28,000 people of Bene Israel extraction in Israel today, and this book is indeed a fine exposition of their history and culture set in their Indian context.

The book is divided into three parts: the origins and early history of the Bene Israel; the community in the nineteenth century; and its development in the twentieth century. In the early chapters, Isenberg summarizes the Bene Israel's own traditions and then proceeds to carefully examine various theories of origin that would place their arrival in the Konkan, on the western coast of India, anywhere from the eighth century B.C.E. to the sixth or seventh century C.E. The discussion shows how some theories have developed based on the holidays that the Bene Israel did and did not observe in the past, explores the possible role of the Radhanites in their discovery or even ancestry, and presents relevant material from the Indian letters found in the Cairo Geniza. Although she refrains from drawing a definite conclusion as to when the Bene Israel arrived and from where, Isenberg seems to believe that their presence in India goes back to before the fifth century C.E. The problem, as she indicates, is that the earliest definitive documentation on the Bene Israel consists of seventeenth-century *sanads* granting hereditary rights, which she reproduces in an appendix. The author urges a systematic search of all relevant archives, documents, village records and genealogies for further information about the Bene Israel. She also suggests that excavation (so far refused by the community) of the Navgaon mounds, the traditional burial site of the earliest immigrants, might shed some light on their origins and early history.

There are two thoughtful chapters on the early relationships between the Bene Israel and the Cochin Jews, in which Isenberg asserts that the Yemenite influence in the Bene Israel liturgy came through the community's contacts with synagogues and hazans in Aden, not just from the Cochin Jews. A related appendix analyzes a controversial problem of dating: when was Samaji Hassaji (Samuel Ezekiel Divekar, the founder of the first Bene Israel synagogue in Bombay) released from his status as a prisoner-of-war of Tipu Sultan in the eighteenth century? (The notes to this appendix are erroneously placed with those of the following one.)

Isenberg's long-term interest in the influence of Christian missionaries in reviving and enhancing the Jewish knowledge and observances of the Bene Israel is reflected in her very informative chapter based on mid-nineteenth-century mission reports and journals. She is most appreciative of the role of Reverend John Wilson, the Scottish missionary, in promoting secular and religious (including Hebrew) education among the Bene Israel and reproduces in an appendix his rarely found account of the community—written in 1838–1839. The missionaries, as she emphasizes, were singularly unsuccessful in the achievement of their primary aim: the conversion of Bene Israel to Christianity.

Isenberg offers an excellent description of the unique *malida* observance of the Bene Israel, "an auspicious ceremonial offering accompanied with an invocation for the presence and blessings of the prophet Elijah." *Malida* is a mixture of coconut, raisins, nuts, cardamom, rose water and sugar, offered with rice or wheat cakes and fresh fruit. In discussing this and the celebration of holidays in general, the author displays her extensive knowledge not only of Jewish customs, traditions and rituals, but also of those of the Hindus. Explaining those Bene Israel customs that are not common to other Jewish communities, she argues that although they had been assimilated from local folk customs, their incorporation did not imply Bene Israel participation in Hindu or Muslim worship.

In a section on synagogues in the nineteenth century, Isenberg mentions, "Baghdadis were still acting on their belief that Bene Israel did not qualify as part of a minyan" (p. 148). Actually, in the late nineteenth century, Bene Israel *were* being counted in Baghdadi minyans; the exclusion seems to have begun in the early twentieth century and ceased (as Isenberg herself points out) around 1927. Other topics covered in the nineteenth-century section include arts and letters, castelike patterns emerging within the Bene Israel community itself and in its relationships with the Baghdadis; Bene Israel names, occupations and homelife; H. S. Kehimkar and the Israelite School; Bene Israel in the Konkan and beyond it. Isenberg concludes that, despite an initial spurt in education and improvement in their financial condition during the first half of the nineteenth century, the Bene Israel did not continue to progress "as a significant urban community" in the latter half. She attributes this to a slackening of school attendance, a lack of an entrepreneurial spirit that might have produced wealthy merchants or entrepreneurs, intracommunal schisms and an uprooting from traditional rural patterns when the Bene Israel moved to Bombay. Their search for security led them to accept lower-level government employment.

In an interesting account of village life in the twentieth century, based on vignettes drawn from interviews with elderly Bene Israel now in Israel, Isenberg stresses the modus vivendi the rural Bene Israel established with their non-Jewish neighbors as well as their adherence to "their own old way of Jewishness," with the synagogues as the focal point of their religious life. Discussing occupations, she includes a valuable table listing the number and percentages of Bene Israel and Baghdadis employed by the E. D. Sassoon and Company mills in Bombay in 1943, although the figures given for the percentages of each group seem too high.

Writing about the Bene Israel Conference and the All-India Israelite League, two organizations that functioned primarily between 1917 and 1927, she aptly points out that although the lists of resolutions of both groups were "always long and well-meaning [responding to the needs of the community], the actual achievements of these two bodies were disappointingly few." She might, however, have mentioned that the rivalry between these two organizations stemmed partly from previous factionalism within the community over the control of communal institutions, such as the synagogues and schools, and was reflected in the rivalry between the periodicals (which became organs of either the conference or the league) at the time.

In discussing Bene Israel in India's independence struggle, Isenberg correctly observes that they were characteristically apolitical. There were exceptions, however, and she devotes an interesting section to the Bene Israel advocate David Erulkar and his fight throughout his multifaceted career for the cause of Indianization. (J. B. Israel's changing political views, particularly on Jewish communal representation, would also have been a worthwhile subject to explore.) Isenberg analyzes fairly the motives behind the emigration to Israel of the Bene Israel who, despite the ambivalence of some, from 1919 onward periodically formed short-lived Zionist organizations of their own that were in touch with emissaries from Palestine. However, many of the chapters in this (and earlier sections) are extremely short and might have been combined for a more effective, less choppy presentation.

It is in the broad range of demographic data and appendixes that the real strength of this work as a sourcebook lies. Isenberg has compiled summaries and synthesized tables by comparing and supplementing figures given in government censuses, gazetteers and works by nineteenth- and twentieth-century authors. Although, as she says, the tables relate to Indian Jews as a whole rather than to the Bene Israel alone, just the work done in bringing together and synthesizing these statistics is invaluable. Her appendixes reproduce primary and secondary materials that are otherwise quite inaccessible, including some prepared by Rebecca Reuben and the late J. B. Israel as well as Isenberg's own translations from the Hebrew of Solomon Reinemann's mid-nineteenth-century references to the Bene Israel.

Some twenty photos (with long captions), three excellent maps, glossaries of both Indian and Jewish terms and clear writing add to the attractiveness and usefulness of this volume for both specialists and the general reader. It should occupy a central place in the growing literature on the Jews of India.

JOAN ROLAND
Pace University

David Goldberg and John Rayner, *The Jewish People: Their History and Their Religion*. New York: Viking, 1987. xiii + 401 pp.

Paul Johnson, *A History of the Jews*. London: Weidenfeld & Nicolson, 1987. x + 644 pp.

When Johnson's book first appeared, critics quickly made the point that it belonged to a category of Jewish literature long and wisely forsaken by Jewish historians— that of the one-volume history of the Jews. One cannot help feeling that the critics were right, particularly so nowadays.

Only a person unfamiliar with the subject matter would venture on such a task. Moreover, Johnson's range of secondary sources, though impressive, is limited to works in English. Where these are lacking, as in the case of Byzantine Jewry, there is little Johnson has to say. The book is also curiously unbalanced in view of its time scale—about two-thirds of the book deals only with the last millennium of Jewish history. In other words, the millennia from the biblical period to the early Middle Ages are crammed into about two hundred pages. There is little about social or economic conditions, except for moneylending in the Middle Ages and the film industry in the twentieth century.

In essence, what Johnson has done is string together (especially for the modern period), a number of biographical sketches of illustrious Jews with some linking historical narrative. What holds all this together is some sort of unconscious framework that depicts the Jews as a subversive force, sometimes rational, sometimes irrational. They are said to have rationalized money, for example, in the early period of capitalism (the fifteenth and sixteenth centuries). In the twentieth century, irrationalism takes over. Thus Walter Benjamin is said to have argued:

> Most forms of knowledge were relativistic creations, and had to be recast to ensure proletarian or classless truth. The irony of these brilliant but destructive insights was that, whereas Benjamin saw them as scientific historical materialism, they were really a product of Judaic irrationality—his was the old tale of how intensely spiritual people, who can no longer believe in God, find ingenious substitutes for religious dogmas.

For all that, Johnson writes well, has a flair for description and narrative that undoubtedly make this an interesting work. I see it as an eminently suitable gift for a studious barmitzvah boy in the hope that it would stimulate his curiosity and lead to higher things.

If a one-volume history of the Jews is a suspect project, what is one to say of a single volume that aims to combine the history of the Jews with that of their religion? The work of Goldberg and Rayner does not emerge too unfavorably from a comparison with Johnson's. It suffers admittedly from the same lack of balance in overemphasizing the modern period. But it is more modest overall and, in a simple, unpretentious style, some dozen chapters take the reader from the biblical beginnings to "Statehood and Recovery." So much for Part I. The three other parts deal, respectively, with the literature of Judaism, the theory of Judaism and the practice of Judaism. The weakest part is undoubtedly that dealing with literature from the Talmud onward. It is little more than a catalogue of illustrious sages, commentators and writers with their dates—far better to have omitted it entirely than to be so cursory.

The two authors are practicing Reform rabbis, and this is readily discernible throughout the book. But their affiliation does not obtrude in any one-sided way and they present their own viewpoint with careful regard to that of mainstream Orthodoxy.

The tone, at least in the historical section, is one of pronounced optimism. They identify with the victory of emancipation:

> The struggle for emancipation having been long since concluded—although sporadic manifestations of economic, social or professional antisemitism still occur in even the most enlightened countries—the Jew has steadily been acclimatised to the language and *mores* of his chosen environment. It is only the devoutly Orthodox who remain apart, in order to preserve their distinctive way of life.

This confidence is a little difficult to share, especially as one feels that recent events have made it impossible ever to recapture the same enthusiasm with which our ancestors welcomed the values of Emancipation. It may be that it is "only the devoutly Orthodox who remain apart," but not only does that minority seem to be increasing relative to the rest of Jewry, but their response to events by way of "withdrawing" may perhaps prove more positive and sagacious than those who trust in the permanence of past values. In fact, Goldberg and Rayner also talk of a "spiritual vacuum" that has largely been filled by identification with the state of Israel, so that those who do not "remain apart" seem to have little to offer by way of religious sustenance.

This book lacks the sparkle (as well as the occasional wrongheadedness) that characterizes Johnson's and one cannot be so confident that it will stimulate the reader's curiosity. But, in a sober manner, it will undoubtedly introduce the reader to the main features of Jewish history, beliefs and practice.

LIONEL KOCHAN
Oxford

Oskar Mendelsohn, *Jodenes Historis i Norge gjennom 300 ar.* Volume 1, Oslo: Universitetsforlaget, 1969. 698 pp.; Volume 2, Oslo: Universitetsforlaget, 1986. 664 pp.

The Jewish community of Norway has never counted more than fifteen hundred members, and with the exception of the period 1910–1942, the number has been less than one thousand. Oskar Mendelsohn's history of this community is, comparatively speaking, probably the largest of its kind. This has made possible a tremendous wealth of detail, which sometimes makes for rather heavy reading.

A clear presentation of the material together with a useful, analytic table of contents and good indexes of persons and subjects, however, make it possible for readers with special interests to find what they are looking for. The references (mostly included in the text in volume 1 and given in a conventional scholarly apparatus in volume 2) are ample. The author has worked his way through immense amounts of archival materials and has read vast quantities of newspapers and other periodicals.

The first volume covers the period up to the German occupation of Norway in 1940, whereas the second spans the years 1940–1980 (with some of the data going as far forward as 1985).

Analytically, the work can be seen as divided into four parts, of which the first deals with the "prehistory" of Norwegian Jewry. The second describes the foundation and the history of the two communities of Oslo and Trondheim up until 1933. The emphasis here is on the inner life of the communities, but there is also material on their relationship with the surrounding society. The main difference between Norwegian Jewry and many other communities was, for obvious reasons, the absence of a conflict between an older, established group of more or less assimilated Jews and newer immigrants from Eastern Europe.

The third part, presented in the last chapter of volume 1 and the first half of volume 2, deals with the Holocaust. The number of Jewish (and other) refugees from Central Europe who were allowed to settle in Norway was very limited, and the debates they engendered were very similar to those familiar from other countries.

Occupation and deportation took a heavy toll, leading as they did to the death at the hands of the Nazis of 759 people (some 42% of the Jewish population). Only 25 of those deported survived. Almost 1,000 Jews escaped to Sweden; a few others made their way by sea to England where they joined the Free Norwegian forces; and a small number were left in Norway. In a short but very important chapter, the author weighs the degree of responsibility of the German occupation authorities as against that of the collaborationist Quisling government. It is to be regretted, however, that the strictly Norwegian focus, which the author has maintained throughout his work, prohibited him from bringing a comparative perspective to bear on this problem.

The last part of the work describes the reconstruction and inner life of the communities after the war, lists practically all books of Jewish interest published during this period and summarizes press discussion of issues of concern to the Jews, particularly the state of Israel and the Middle East conflict.

Apart from the section on the Holocaust, it is perhaps the first part of the work that could be of greatest interest to non-Norwegians. Jews were only sporadically authorized to visit Norway during the period when the country was united with Denmark. In 1814, however, the Norwegians were able to frame their own constitution, which remained in force even when the country formed a confederation with Sweden, from 1814 to 1905. The constitution was liberal—but the Jews were explicitly prohibited not only from living in, but even from visiting, the country. The main argument in favor of this clause was economic, built on the images current at the time of the Jews as usurers and predators, but religious prejudice also played an important part.

This exclusionary clause was discussed intermittently in the following years, but it was not until 1837 that a sustained campaign to abolish it started, largely owing to the commitment of one man, the poet Henrik Wergeland. He was a patriot, raised to venerate the constitution, but he was also a liberal who felt that the clause on the Jews was alien to the spirit of the constitution. As a result of his initiative, the parliament voted on an amendment in 1842, but the bill did not obtain the two-thirds majority required. Wergeland—who died in 1845—and his friends continued their campaign. The bill was introduced again without success in the parliamentary sessions of 1845 and 1848; it was finally carried only in 1851.

A comparison of the four votes reveals interesting differences. In 1842, a large majority of the deputies representing the cities voted for the amendment, whereas most of the farmers were against it. In 1848, the situation was reversed: the majority of the farmers voted for the amendment, but now the city representatives were opposed to it. In the small minority who were still opposed to the amendment in 1851, there was only one farmer. It is true that in 1842 most of the city representatives were officials, whereas in 1848 and 1851 they belonged to the commercial and industrial class, but it is undeniable that the climate of opinion in Norway had undergone a major change.

Jodenes historie i Norge gjennom 300 ar will remain the standard reference on the history of the Jews of Norway. Further research might provide new insights into particular issues, but it is unlikely that it would compel major revisions in the broad panorama painted by Oskar Mendelsohn.

Svante Hansson
Paris

Richard John Neuhaus (ed.), *Jews in Unsecular America.* Grand Rapids: Wm. B. Eerdmans, 1987. 120 pp.

This small volume consists of four essays and a report of the dialogue between the authors and a group of theologians, philosophers, social policy specialists and ethicists of diverse religious and political backgrounds. Milton Himmelfarb's brief opening contribution—a series of propositions presented in rapid-fire fashion— suggests that whereas American Jews are somewhat ambivalent about a number of domestic social welfare programs, they continue to be staunchly opposed to any breach in the wall separating church and state.

But even here there seems to be something of an inconsistency in American Jewish attitudes and values. Himmelfarb points out that although they are so vociferously opposed to teaching about religion in the public schools, as indicated in Steven M. Cohen's 1984 survey of American Jewish attitudes, more than half of the American Jewish respondents favored such teaching in *Israel's* public schools. As I have indicated elsewhere, the paradox goes even further than suggested by Himmelfarb. It relates not only to an apparent discrepancy with respect to religion in public schools in the United States and Israel, but to much broader issues of religion and politics as well. In Cohen's survey of 1986, for example, there are rather specific data on issues within the realm of religion and state that indicate that most American Jews were neither disturbed by, nor particularly concerned about, the whole issue of religion and state in Israel.

It is no surprise to read that America's Jews are strongly opposed to the Moral Majority. What is more surprising is that at least half of those Jews surveyed stated that they did not believe that the decline in religion in American life had contributed to a decline in morality.

In contrast to the assertion that they are (in Charles Silberman's phrase) "a certain people" who have virtually reached complete equality in American society, most American Jews disagree with the notions that "antisemitism is not currently a serious problem for American Jews" and that "virtually all positions of influence in America are open to Jews."

To offset the dominant viewpoint of American Jews during the second half of the twentieth century, Himmelfarb concludes his piece with a quote from Naomi Cohen's seminal book on German Jews in the United States between 1830 and 1940, *Encounter with Emancipation (1984)*. Naomi Cohen emphasizes that those German-American Jews desired a country in which the government would treat all religions equally and that the very idea of a state divorced from religion was a notion "as abhorrent to Jews as it was to most Americans." This shift in the American Jewish conception of religious liberty is precisely the subject systematically analyzed in Jonathan Sarna's article in the volume under review.

Sarna provides a brief historical survey of the alternatives that American Jews have posed to counter the idea that America is a Christian country. He shows that until the mid-nineteenth century Jews did not oppose bills that discriminated against atheists because they believed that America should, in fact, be a religious country, though not a specifically Christian one. During the latter part of the nineteenth century, however, a growing number of Jewish spokespersons, especially Reform rabbis, argued for the separation of church and state, demanding that the state per se must be legally agnostic. That position grew into a consensus that lasted until the 1960s.

Today there is no longer a universal consensus because of new dilemmas. On the one hand, there is the historically valid concern that nondenominational religious practice will sooner or later become Christian. On the other hand, some Jews fear that secularism will lead to assimilation. America's Jews still have not come up with the ideal resolution to this dilemma.

This basic theme sets the stage for David Novak's article. He enumerates the different types of American Jews and their respective attitudes to American society. He argues that "religious" Jews—by that he means those Jews, not necessarily Orthodox, who define Judaism and their relation to America in religious rather than cultural terms—are not faced by the dilemma suggested by Sarna. Novak points to the traditional Jewish understanding that non-Jews are obligated to observe the seven Noahide Laws of universal morality and that Jews have a "mission," not necessarily to convert non-Jews, but to encourage and assist them in being more religious *within the context of their own monotheistic religions*. He, thus, cites a responsum by the late Rabbi Moshe Feinstein, the noted halakhic authority who supported prayer in public schools. Novak finds it ironic that stereotypes of religious Jews depict them as being extremely insular, concerned only with themselves and oblivious to the larger society. As Rabbi Feinstein's responsum shows, however, traditional Jews do retain a concern for the moral and spiritual life of the larger society.

Marvin Wilson surveys the changes in Christian perceptions of Jews as well as the changes in Christian-Jewish relations in America. He briefly sketches the history of a relationship that can, at best, he suggests, be characterized as stormy, although significant improvements have taken place since the end of the Second World War. For evangelicals, in particular, one dilemma is that, in many cases, they continue to believe that it is their duty to attempt to convert everyone, including Jews. But Wilson sees change here as well (although a resolution adopted at a subsequent major conference of evangelical leaders does cast some doubt on his optimism in this respect). On the other hand, evangelicals have often been strongly supportive of Israel. In the final analysis, he concludes, the key to change is "Christian repentance," the first step of which involves confessing one's sin and acknowledging one's failure. The extent to which the church seriously engages in this process will determine the character of future Christian–Jewish relations.

These and related issues are touched on in Paul Stallsworth's account of the dialogue in which the main participants responded to each other, and in which many others also took part.

The book will capture the interest of anyone concerned with the issue of religion in the United States, in general, and what it means to be Jewish there, in particular.

CHAIM I. WAXMAN
Rutgers University

Wolfgang Plat (ed.) *Voll Leben und voll Tod ist diese Erde: Bilder aus der Geschichte jüdischer Österreicher.* Vienna: Herold Verlag, 1988. 342 pp.
John Bunzl, *Der lange Arm der Erinnerung: Jüdisches Selbstbewusstsein heute.* Vienna, Cologne, Graz: Böhlau Verlag, 1987. 141 pp.

In March 1938, Austria became part of Hitler's empire. Fifty years later official Austria made its first large-scale attempt to reconsider the events that had followed Austria's annexation to Nazi Germany: Austrian enthusiasm for its "return" to the German Reich and the vicious, cruel persecution and destruction of the Austrian Jewish community. These issues are not only moral questions: they impinge on Austrian identity and self-understanding.

Officially, Austria is defined as "Hitler's first victim." This definition was canonized by the Allied powers in the international treaty of 1955, which gave Austria its independence as a neutral state. However, in Austrian self-understanding it is not quite clear whether the Allied powers defeated Austria as part of Nazi Germany and consequently imposed ten years of occupation or whether they liberated Austria from a seven-year occupation by Hitler's Germany. Austria's current president, Kurt Waldheim, still pronounces his conviction that he defended his home country when serving under the Nazis in Yugoslavia and receives popular acclaim for so doing. On the other hand, Austria never felt the need to pay reparations ("Wiedergutmachung") for the persecution and material dispossession of the Austrian Jews, because Austria, as such, was no longer in existence when these happenings occurred.

This ambivalence shapes Austria's attitude toward its Jews, those of the past and those of the present. In the wake of Kurt Waldheim's election campaign, hitherto politely hidden antisemitism became acceptable once again. This present threat concerned the Jewish community in Austria more than the question of past guilt. Nevertheless, both issues are, in reality, closely connected: the unwillingness to accept responsibility for crimes committed in the Nazi era feeds dislike and hatred of the Jews who, for their part, question this theory of injured innocence.

The new wave of open antisemitism caused sincere soul-searching among part of the Austrian public (and, of course, among most of Austria's Jews). After two years of sharp, painful and often embarrassing discussion of Austria's past guilt and present antisemitism, the commemorations of 1988 came, perhaps, almost as an anticlimax. But it should be noted that the sudden rise of public interest in these issues has led to the publication of the relevant historical documents on a large scale. In 1988, Austria remembered not only the Anschluss of 1938, but also the fact that historical amnesia had characterized the Second Republic for some forty-five years. The books that we are to discuss here are both examples of the attempt to reintegrate the Jews into Austrian history. They describe the position of the Jews in Austria in the past, but also reflect their position in the present.

Voll Leben und voll Tod ist diese Erde: Bilder aus der Geschichte jüdischer Öster-reicher is a collection of essays written by authors from different fields: journalists, historians, political scientists, theologians. The book was published as background information to a four-part television documentary produced by the Austrian national network. The occasion of this series was the fiftieth anniversary of *Kristallnacht*— the first large-scale pogrom against Jews in Germany and Austria by the Nazi regime on November 9 and 10, 1938. The main impetus for the project however, was provided by the "new" antisemitism that erupted in 1985. This fact led to the introduction of an apologetic note, quite blatant in the film, less obvious in the book.

Jewish and non-Jewish authors from Austria and Israel describe the valuable contributions made by the Jews to Austrian history from the Middle Ages until the establishment of the Second Republic in 1955. In the preface to the book, Alfred Payrleitner, a well-known Austrian journalist, expresses the conviction of the team of authors that providing information about the importance of Jewish involvement in Austrian history is the best way to fight antisemitism. Two young political scientists from Innsbruck, Andreas Maislinger and Günther Pallaver, provide a case study of antisemitism without Jews in their home province of the Tyrol, where anti-Jewish folklore is still very much alive.

Critical notes and studies of this type mark the book off from the "official" Austrian attempts to "cope with the past." On appropriate occasions, politicians and public figures stress the loss Austria has suffered by the destruction of its Jewish community—a loss inflicted on Austria, they stress, by the Nazis. In this way, Austria tries to do justice to the historic role of its Jews and still maintain its image as "Hitler's first victim." The book before us, though, shows that the loss Austria suffered was, in part, self-inflicted and clearly desired by a large section of the population. It places the history of the Jews within the Austrian context, a part of

Austrian history, but avoids the temptation to paint a harmonious picture of the Austrian Jewish symbiosis. This historical relationship is analyzed here as one of constant tension and ambivalent interdependence.

Walter Grab and Klaus Lohrmann have written articles that provide an effective survey of the history of the Jews in Austria from the Middle Ages to modern times. They each explain how important Jewish financiers were at times to the rulers; how hated Jewish moneylenders and tax collectors became to the general public; and how the status of the Jews fluctuated between "privilege" and expulsion in accord with the estimate of their own interests made at any moment by the powers-that-be. The book stresses the influence Jews had on the making of Austrian history and analyzes the effect of general historic trends on their fate.

A very impressive article by Nikolaus Vielmetti describes the establishment of the modern Jewish community. The author shows that the character of the community was shaped both by the changing attitudes of the Jewish people in Europe in the nineteenth century—secularization, religious reform—and by the necessity to struggle against far-reaching political and legal restrictions.

The Viennese community remained Orthodox, making relatively slight concessions to the times in the form of German sermons and prayer books in both German and Hebrew. This approach corresponded to the conservative tendency both of the Jewish community and Austrian politics in general. The approach embodied in the book—studying the development of Jewish life in the broader framework of Austrian history—is most fruitful (although it must be said that even this volume is not completely free of apologetic elements). Pursuing the dual purpose of serious research and the refutation of age-old prejudice, it fortunately is not only well intended, but also very informative and well written.

The book closes with a series of portraits of Jews who were persecuted, expelled and murdered by the Nazis that is preceded by an impressive scholarly survey by Jonny Moser of the events that marked the Nazi destruction of the Jewish community. However, the book does not limit its interest in this area to the period of the Second World War alone; it also describes specific examples of the abortive attempts made by Jews to obtain justice after the war, be it the conviction and punishment of the Nazi murderers or the restitution of stolen property.

In 1945, the primary aim of Austrian politicians of all camps was to reach a broad consensus of opinion in support of the emergent democratic system. They thus made a clear-cut decision in favor of the social and political reintegration of former Nazis at the expense of the Jews. In postwar Austria, Jews were not welcome; their claims, moral as well as financial, were considered to be detrimental to the construction of the Second Republic. This fact is only now, with great caution, being brought to the attention of the public.

In his contribution, Simon Wiesenthal commemorates two of his friends, later among the group that refounded Jewish communal life in Vienna, who managed to survive the war in that city; but he also stresses the fact that two of those who helped save them were gentiles, subsequently honored in Israel. Wiesenthal tries to draw a line between his claim that Austria has still not done justice to its Jews, the living and the dead, and his belief in the decency of at least some individuals. Herein, perhaps, lies an answer to those who ask how Jews could have resettled in postwar

Austria. Answers, however, are beyond the scope of this book. At the most, it shows possible ways to better understanding and a more peaceful coexistence than those characteristic of the past eight hundred years.

Jewish Consciousness Today, is the subtitle of John Bunzl's book *Der lange Arm der Erinnerung: Jüdisches Selbstbewusstsein heute.* The author, a political scientist who specializes in Jewish and Middle Eastern affairs, presents a concise and very critical discussion of the major historical events and ideologies that have shaped the consciousness of the modern Jew. Although his discussion includes certain aspects of Israeli society, his main focus is on Central Europe, particularly Austria. Bunzl uses his professional skills to sketch an intellectual history that is personal but not merely subjective, and he can thus make a valid claim to be representative. Beneath his scholarly approach, the reader feels the author's personal involvement—his search for an intellectual, social and territorial home.

Bunzl describes the development of modern Jewish consciousness, arguing, along familiar lines, that the price demanded of the Jews for the grant of emancipation was their secularization and their assimilation. Only in a secular society could the Jews be accepted as equal citizens without converting to Christianity, but "enlightened" ideologies also sought the gradual disappearance of the Jews within a supposedly universalist "mankind." However, the Jews never quite paid this price. Even secular and acculturated Jews maintained and developed a distinct Jewish consciousness that was shaped both by their "enlightened" views and by their memory of the Jewish past.

In the case of Austria, the acculturated and westernized Jewish communities became the strongest supporters of the "Austrian" idea in the multinational Habsburg Empire during the age of growing nationalism. However, Zionism and Jewish nationalism developed in reaction against the national frictions and growing antisemitism characteristic of the empire in its last decades.

For their part, the "enlightened" ideologies, liberalism and socialism, could offer no solution to the Jewish question other than their increasingly embattled assimilationism. Bunzl exposes a major weakness in the Social Democratic movement, the fact that the socialists underestimated antisemitism, treating it as a by-product of the class struggle and that after 1934, and even to this very day, Nazism has been all but equated with the Austro-Fascism that destroyed the labor movement four years before the Anschluss. This misinterpretation of historic events affects more than its attitude toward the Jews, it also impedes an objective assessment of the First Republic and of Austria's attitude to the Nazi regime. Bruno Kreisky's willingness to form a coalition government with a party led by a former member of the S.S. as well as his pronounced indignation at the Jewish criticism of Austria's past and present constitute, in Bunzl's view, more a true reflection of socialist ideology than of Jewish self-hatred. Bunzl's critique of socialist ideology is of particular interest, coming as it does from an insider. Socialism is one of the author's intellectual homes, but he cannot completely identify with it because of his Jewish consciousness. His analysis is thus critical, although not unsympathetic, and it demonstrates a profound knowledge of the problems involved.

Zionism and Israel are similarly treated as of the greatest significance, but cer-

tainly not beyond reproach. Again the author draws a distinct line between legitimate criticism and superficial condemnation. This section of the book is understandably the most personal one. Bunzl argues that the trauma of the Holocaust has
become an obstacle on the path to peace in the Middle East. The profound distrust
of the Arab world is not only the result of the bitter experience acquired in the
Middle East, but also a reaction to the European past. The author is convinced that
peaceful Jewish–Arab coexistence is possible and that more should be done by
Israel to achieve it. Despite his strong sympathies with Israel, he still claims that the
Diaspora has the right to criticize the Jewish state as well as to develop its own
independent Jewish way of life. The very rigid Israeli demands on the Diaspora to
maintain an unquestioning loyalty lay too heavy a burden on Jews who consider
themselves a concerned opposition. It is not that the author is unaware of the
problems involved in criticizing Israel in the Diaspora, especially in Austria. Non-
Jewish criticism, after all, has in recent years often compared Israel's policy in
Lebanon and the occupied territories to Nazi atrocities, and by putting the Holocaust
on a level with the wars fought by the Jews has sought (implicitly and even
explicitly) to whitewash Austria and Germany. Nevertheless, the author insists on
the legitimacy of Jewish criticism, especially in internal Jewish discourse, but also,
with due care, even in the public arena.

Kurt Waldheim's election campaign and the new wave of outspoken antisemitism
are placed by Bunzl in the larger context of postwar Austrian history. The insinua-
tions of a Jewish conspiracy against Austria made by the Waldheim camp, which
served as an excuse for overt Judeophobia, demonstrated yet again that there is no
willingness to understand, let alone accept, the particularity of the Jewish collective
consciousness, now shaped, too, by the experience of the Holocaust. Nevertheless,
Bunzl maintains his belief that the real home of the modern Jew can only be built by
Jews and non-Jews together—in the Diaspora as well as in Israel.

The books discussed here both, in their different ways, seek to bridge the gap that
still separates the Jews from their Austrian environment. They provide no answers,
but do present a clear and objective picture of the place occupied by the Jews in
Austria, in both the past and the present.

ELEONORE LAPPIN
Institut für Geschichte der Juden in Österreich

Shimon Shamir (ed.), *The Jews of Egypt: A Mediterranean Society in Modern
Times*. Boulder and London: Westview Press, 1987. 304 pp.

Although a great deal has been written on Egyptian Jewry of the Hellenistic and
medieval periods, studies of the modern era are still all too rare. (Indeed, the very
subtitle of this volume is clearly intended to call to mind one of the classic studies of
the earlier period, S. D. Goitein's magisterial work based on the Geniza documents,
A Mediterranean Society.)[1] Hence, this collection of fourteen papers presented at a
conference held at Tel-Aviv University in 1984 is a welcome addition to the avail-

able literature. Several of the contributors to this volume are themselves the authors of some of the few full-length monographs that do exist on Egyptian Jewry during the nineteenth and twentieth centuries (most notably Gudrun Krämer and Jacob Landau).

As is often the case with conference volumes, there is some unevenness among the contributions. A few pieces are unusually brief (one of five pages, two of six, and one of seven). Several of the chapters seem rather cursory; for example, Michael Winter's "Egyptian Jewry During the Ottoman Period as a Background to Modern Times" (pp. 9–14), Maurice Mizrahi's "The Role of the Jews in Economic Development" (pp. 85–93), or Jacques Hassoun's "The Traditional Jewry of the Ḥāra" (pp. 169–173). There is a manifest disequilibrium between these brief pieces and some of the lengthy and detailed studies, such as Shimon Shamir's "The Evolution of the Egyptian Nationality Laws and Their Application to Jews in the Monarchy Period" (pp. 33–67), which closely examines the question of how the prosperous Jewish community of Egypt's so-called Liberal Age could end up with a majority of stateless individuals and prove to be so weak and marginal. This subject has been discussed by others before, but never at such length. Shamir concludes by pointing to the irony that in considering their Jews as unassimilable and by making most of them stateless, the Egyptian authorities unwittingly were "endorsing the premises of Zionism, which they so strongly opposed and which a great part of the Jewish community itself had hardly adopted as yet" (p. 62).

Another detailed piece of work is Zvi Zohar's "Lowering Barriers of Estrangement: Rabbanite-Karaite Intermarriage in Twentieth-Century Egyptian Halakha" (pp. 143–168). As he has done in other publications, Zohar demonstrates the creative ways in which Egyptian rabbinic authorities dealt with halakhic problems in modern times. Another superbly well-documented item is Thomas Mayer's "The Image of Egyptian Jewry in Recent Egyptian Studies" (pp. 199–212). This important but depressing study reveals the generally low standards of veracity in Egyptian studies, both popular and academic, on topics of local Jewish history. Mayer's findings are not new to readers of Arabic; however, they are not as well known as they should be to others.

Gudrun Krämer provides a valuable sketch of Jewish participation in Egyptian politics in her brief contribution, which is a succinct extract from her pioneering dissertation *Minderheit, Millet, Nation? Die Juden in Ägypten, 1914–1952* (pp. 68–82).[2] Krämer shows that, with a few exceptions, Egyptian Jews coupled their traditional political quietism with genuine loyalty to the monarchy in the decades that followed the First World War. She also argues—rightly to my mind—that Arabo-Islamic nationalism in the late 1930s and 1940s pushed the Jews and other minorities to return to their own ethnic roots and that during the Second World War Zionism succeeded in making significant inroads among the middle class, particularly among the youth. As in other Arab countries, any active participation in the Egyptian nationalist movement was limited to a few intellectuals.

Another outstanding contribution is that of Nurit Govrin, who, in her stimulating survey of the writings of exiles from the Yishuv in Egypt during the First World War, examines how they described their encounter with the local Jewish community (pp. 177–191).

This collection is introduced by an excellent preface that reviews the subjects and scope of the individual contributions and sets them into a contextual whole. This introductory *vademecum* and the organization of the articles by themes (Ottoman Background, Political Community, etc.) helps the volume to achieve a greater unity than many other published conference proceedings. In addition to the editor's preface and the individual contributions, there are valuable appendixes that constitute nearly one-third of the entire text. These include the Portuguese chronicles discussed in Jacob Landau's contribution; the French text of the 1929 Egyptian Nationality Law; the hitherto unpublished correspondence of Ya'qūb Ṣanū' (Abū Naḍḍāra) discussed in Shmuel Moreh's essay; and the rare Judeo-Arabic and Arabic texts of the Sēder al-Tawḥīd and Megillat Purim Miṣrayim.

The publication of this book marks a significant expansion of the available literature in English and a good summary of the state of current research on Egyptian Jewish history and culture.

Norman A. Stillman

State University of New York at Binghamton

Notes

1. Berkeley and Los Angeles, 1967–1988, 5 vols.
2. Wiesbaden, 1982.

Sydney Stahl Weinberg, *World of Our Mothers.* Chapel Hill: University of North Carolina Press, 1988. xxiv + 325 pp.

Several years ago at a conference on Jewish history at Brooklyn College, Irving Howe was challenged to explain the male chauvinism inherent in the title of his monumental work, *World of Our Fathers,* and to justify devoting so minuscule a proportion of his book directly to women. He replied that "without mothers there could be no fathers." This retort, although somewhat insensitive, was on the mark in terms of the dedication to family held by the vast majority of Jewish women in the immigrant generation.

In her work of consciously "compensatory history," using primarily the oral histories of forty-six Jewish women, most of whom arrived in the United States between 1912 and 1925, Sydney Stahl Weinberg often makes essentially the same point about the dedication to family. Much recent scholarship (e.g., Virginia Yans-McLaughlin, Kathleen Neils Conzen, Victor Greene and especially John Bodnar) suggests that all immigrant groups, albeit with some variations, subordinated the needs of individuals to the benefit of families. Sociocultural history helped shape the way different groups sought to sustain family strength (Poles and Italians emphasized houses and land, whereas Jews put the stress on "good jobs" and education), but the family was primary and one was expected to trim self-aspiration when necessary. This was true of all immigrants, including Jews, but particularly of women.

In the East European shtetl in the late nineteenth and early twentieth centuries, "wives were central to the family's emotional and economic well-being," (p. 19) and from a young age working-class and middle-class Jewish daughters were expected to take on serious responsibilities within the home and sometimes in the workplace as well. Modernization in Eastern Europe meant that young Jewish women would be increasingly exposed to urbanization, industrialization and secular education. Many developed an improved self-esteem and heightened expectations. And many, especially those who moved to the cities of America, "were less accepting . . . than their mothers had been at their age" (p. 40).

But even in New York, which "seemed to breed a new assertiveness," home and "family remained the center of women's concern" (p. 127). According to Weinberg, young women who contributed household or outside income to aid in the education of a brother or who "minded the store," achieved a feeling of competence in helping provide for their families and in the authority they possessed within the home. Weinberg does not romanticize the Jewish family. Indeed, as regards the old country, she follows Joshua Rothenberg's lead in "demythologizing" the shtetl. One daughter reflected the memories of many when she said:

> I didn't get affection. Trouble is the parents did not have the time. There was a lot of work. Already they had three smaller children [who] . . . were always crying. And it was such a pity—my mother was always cursing and angry, and she was frustrated— working very hard. And my father was free. He did not feel anything the way they now teach men to share, to help (p. 31).

Weinberg also demystifies the immigrant kitchen, so sentimentalized by male writers—that is, by Jewish sons. Henry Roth and Alfred Kazin have given us remarkably moving portraits of mothers in kitchens, nourishing families with food and love. For daughters, however, the kitchen—the central focus of the household— was often a place of unremitting drudgery. "Whether or not they had a paying job, girls were expected to assist with the housework" (p. 153). Cooking, cleaning, ironing, helping with the younger children and assisting in the piecework that was a mainstay of so many households meant long hours of toil in the kitchen. Yet it was in the same kitchen that deep psychological and emotional attachments were made between mothers and daughters:

> Mothers could offer little useful advice to daughters on how to behave as young single women, but they set important examples in understanding how to approach life, care for a family's physical and psychological needs, and relate to people. . . . As members of a generation that emphasizes self-fulfillment, we might not easily understand the satisfactions of those who lived their lives for and through others. It seems clear, though, that these immigrant daughters were profoundly affected by mothers' examples of service and self-sacrifice, and like their mothers, if efforts were rewarded by an appreciative family, they learned to achieve satisfaction from such a life (p. 148).

Young immigrant Jewish women with individual aspirations repressed by parents and culture nonetheless developed strong bonds to both and "many patterns of decision making followed the ones women had learned in their parents' homes" (p. 223). Where daughters differed from their mothers, however, was in their ability to limit their families. By having fewer offspring they hoped to avoid the decisions their parents were forced to make in taking children out of school and sending them to work. These complex and resilient daughters of the shtetl and of the impoverished Jewish neighborhood determined "that their daughters as well as their sons would get the education and other advantages, that they had been denied by poverty" (p. 224).

This is the kind of material that is often absent from other works and that makes Weinberg's study so valuable. However, although it does give one—even a man—a sense of what it must have been like to be a Jewish immigrant daughter, mother or sister, the work does not advance a more analytical understanding of the dynamics of the lives of women, particularly in the larger world. Once the women get to America the historical context virtually disappears.

The family and kitchen were obviously central in the lives of most immigrant women, but many, including a majority of Weinberg's sample, did have experience outside the home—at school and at work. The labor movement, however, gets little attention, despite the fact that this was an arena in which an important minority of immigrant Jewish women did achieve satisfaction outside the home. Here, as in other places, the results are skewed by Weinberg's idiosyncratic sample. We never learn very much about Weinberg's principle of selection, but she makes "no claim to scientific methodology." Most of her women came to America after 1912, many in the 1920s, which is late in the era of mass immigration. Thus, they came into a very different economic and political context from the 1890s and early 1900s, the decades of labor militancy.

Weinberg's "free-flowing interview" style elicits marvelous chunks of memory, but it may have stood in the way of asking more pointed questions or following up on other important matters. Although all the women identify as Jews, for example, one is never quite sure of the emotional and behavioral content of that Jewish identity. We learn little about how women perceived their non-Jewish contacts at work or school or whether they experienced antisemitism. Relations between men and women in the workplace and in the unions, questions of class consciousness, feminism, Zionism and the Holocaust also go unexplored.

When Irving Howe wrote *World of Our Fathers,* he really meant fathers, but he also really meant "world." Weinberg's book offers up a small, important slice of the world of our mothers, but we are left waiting for much more.

GERALD SORIN
State University of New York at New Paltz

SOCIAL SCIENCES, SOCIAL HISTORY AND POLITICS

Harry J. Ausmus, *Will Herberg: From Right to Right.* Foreword by Martin E. Marty. Chapel Hill: University of North Carolina Press, 1987. xviii + 242 pp.

In many ways the trajectory of Will Herberg's life (1901–1977) is representative of many other twentieth-century American radicals. He was a firm supporter of the .

Bolshevik Revolution as a young man, but as a Lovestonite he was booted out of the party in 1929. He remained a man of the Marxist Left and wrote political pieces for labor and radical periodicals until about 1940. Then followed a transitional period in which Herberg shifted from political to religious modes of thought, all the while denying that he had changed politically and glossing his shift by paying obeisance to everyone's favorite Cold War theologian, Reinhold Niebuhr. Finally, the neoconservative movement of the 1950s attracted him and favorable references to Whittaker Chambers and Edmund Burke began turning up in his articles (in the course of his lifetime, he wrote more than six hundred articles, in addition to three books). He ended his active intellectual and political life as a regular contributor to William Buckley's *National Review* and as a purveyor of a testy sort of conservatism that disapproved of Martin Luther King and civil disobedience while supporting the war in Vietnam.

But there is another, more interesting Herberg: the lay theologian (of a neo-Orthodox bent) and student of American religion trapped by now in an all-too-predictable paradigm from which he was ready to be released. In this incarnation, Herberg staked out a position astride the three great American religious communities. As the story goes, he almost converted to Catholicism; his religious mentor and confessor of sorts was the Protestant, Niebuhr; and he remained a Jew, though eventually teaching at Drew, a Protestant seminary in New Jersey. His first book, *Judaism and Modern Man* (1951), was an attempt to forge a Jewish religious stance that avoided the liberal vacuities of Reform Judaism and the hidebound traditionalism of Orthodoxy. He was powerfully influenced by Franz Rosenzweig and Martin Buber; and his emphasis fell on historicity, eschatology and the existential nature of the biblical faiths as opposed to the search for transcendence and ontological foundations characteristic of the Greek and "oriental" modes of theology and religious life. To Herberg, Judaism and Christianity were complementary rather than opposing traditions, with the newer religion being God's way of involvement in the gentile world. Put another way, to be antisemitic was to be anti-Christian.

Herberg's other major work was a piece of religious sociology, *Protestant, Catholic, Jew* (1955). In this influential book, he offered historical sketches of the American experience as undergone by each religious community and then went on to assert that in addition to their common adherence to a kind of civil religion (Herberg named this the American Way of Life) Americans of native and immigrant backgrounds retained their allegiance to the traditional biblical faiths. Thus he postulated two modes of American religiosity—civil and biblical. Though Herberg was nothing if not eclectic in his theological and religious sympathies, he was decidedly unsympathetic to the quasi-religious tenor of the American Way of Life.

All this points generally to what is perhaps the central theme of Herberg's life and thought—a deep hostility to idolatry, that is, to absolutizing any historical institution, practice, theory or value. As he grew older, this hostility took the understandable, though not inevitable, form of an obsession with totalitarianism as the quintessential form of political idolatry. In addition, he constantly attacked the refusal of secularism to recognize the importance of, or need for, the religious dimension in modern life.

Indeed, Harry Ausmus argues in his short and rather disjunctive conclusion that the political and the religious Herberg were pretty much the same person: "Metaphysically speaking, Herberg made no substantial change at all, except for adopting explicit ethical precepts that were decidedly lacking in Marxism" (p. 213). The problem is that I read this passage to say precisely that there *were* substantial change(s) in Herberg's positions. What else could "adopting explicit ethical precepts that were decidedly lacking in Marxism" mean? Because Herberg could find no final or firm values in history and no warrant that they would ever be realized, Ausmus concludes with the surprising charge of "covert nihilism" against Herberg. This is an important challenge to, among other things, Protestantism in general and Herberg's deep hostility to idolatry in particular. But Ausmus does not develop the point enough to clarify his argument. As a result, the reader is more likely to feel ambushed than enlightened by it.

In fact, the problem with Ausmus's study is not his delineation of Herberg's political and religious vision. That is admirably clear, if repetitious. It is rather that he adopts such a narrow focus and limits himself unduly. He sneers at psychological analysis of his subject; but some such approach might have helped us gain a sense of Herberg the man and explain what Ausmus would see, I suppose, as merely a superficial deconversion to conservatism. On this topic, John Diggins's work on Herberg in *Up From Communism* (1975) is neither confronted nor even mentioned. Nor does Ausmus deal at all with the extensive literature since the mid-1960s on the theme of civil religion. There is no evidence that Herberg ever responded to Robert Bellah's famous essay on the topic, nor does Ausmus discuss John M. Cuddihy's *No Offense* (1978), which is relevant to Herberg's and Bellah's work.

Finally, I confess puzzlement at Herberg's apparent avoidance of the Holocaust and its implications. Though he wrote several pieces on Israel in the late 1940s and early 1950s and occasionally discussed antisemitism, neither the Holocaust nor the Eichmann trial seems to have engaged his interests or energies. This is particularly striking in Herberg's case because it was precisely after the horrors of the death camps were revealed that he embraced (via Rosenzweig, as did Niebuhr) the theological position that Christianity and Judaism were, in Niebuhr's words, "two religions with one center, worshipping the same God, but with Christianity serving the purpose of carrying the prophetic message to the gentile world."

RICHARD H. KING
University of Nottingham

Joel Colton, *Léon Blum: Humanist in Politics,* 2nd ed. Durham: Duke University Press, 1987. 484 pp.

This work by Joel Colton, first published in 1966, undoubtedly remains the best comprehensive presentation of Léon Blum as an individual and as a political figure from the time of the Dreyfus affair through the interwar period and, finally, to Vichy. The author displays an admirable command of Blum's literary and journalistic activity, his political writings and the chronology of political and social events in which Blum was intimately involved. He guides the reader accurately through a fascinating array of confrontations: internal conflicts, involving strikes, for example, or the opposition to the Socialist and Communist parties; and external crises, such as the threat of war engendered by the rise of fascism or the tragic events of the Spanish civil war. In spite of the recent publication of other biographies and studies devoted to Blum, Colton's book probably remains the best reference work on the subject.

Nevertheless, the brief text added to this second edition is somewhat disappointing in that it deals only with a comparison between the experiences of Blum and François Mitterand; it would appear that Colton is only partially acquainted with the variety of new works that have already been devoted to the socialist experience under the current president of France. Colton would have done better, perhaps, to return to Blum's political activity per se in order to provide—to a greater extent than he originally did—a more comprehensive theoretical interpretation of that activity in relation to the party system, the nature of the state, the particular character of capitalism, the role of the intellectuals in the articulation of social struggles and the parliamentary system. Not one of these questions, which are so vital to an understanding of Léon Blum's particular arena, is really to be found in Colton's work: he remains faithful to the model of scholarly, Anglo-Saxon biographies, deliberately resisting all systemization. The reader who seeks a better understanding of an epoch, however, will regret this reticence, which somewhat restricts our understanding of an essential period in contemporary French history.

Furthermore, Colton's treatment of the crucial question of antisemitism is no more than cursory. This is a dimension one would wish to see dealt with more extensively in his book. In a work of 484 pages, fewer than 20 are devoted to the Jewish dimension of Léon Blum's life or to the violent antisemitism launched against him. All too quickly, the author glides over Blum's Judaism, professed explicitly from adolescence to the end of his life. His activities on behalf of Zionism are merely alluded to, giving the mistaken impression that Blum expressed his "sympathy" for the Jewish national renaissance only at the end of his life. In a word, this otherwise masterful book strikes one as astonishingly reticent about the fact that Léon Blum was a socialist Jew whose role reflected the importance of Jews in the ranks of the emancipatory republic. This entire, vital dimension of Blum's personality is relegated to the backburner, when it could have served as part of the context of Blum's career. The case of Léon Blum somehow resembled that of other state Jews (as I would call them) so numerous in postemancipatory modern France.

The other side of the coin, the incredible antisemitic resentment unleashed against Blum's presence at the head of government, is barely and only indirectly mentioned. A mere few lines are devoted to the improbable hatred displayed by Charles Maurras, Léon Daudet (whose name appears only once, though his attacks against Blum as a Jew were an almost daily occurrence), Henri Béraud and many others: there is almost nothing on *l'Action française, Gringoire, Candide, Je suis partout, Le Charivari, L'Emancipation nationale* and the extensive national and local press in which the most scurrilous antisemitism was voiced against Blum without respite; a few lines on the epithet *"Karfunkelstein,"* but nothing on the many other antisemitic slurs, nothing of the sexual antisemitism that circulated so constantly, hinting, variously, at Blum's alleged Don Juanism, homosexuality or effeminacy. This theme is an essential aspect of the rejection of Blum on the part of the *francité*.

Similarly, we find nothing on the theme of wine and the local antisemitism that developed in the wine-growing region of Aude that Blum represented as a deputy and whose archives and press are never cited; nothing on the violent incident that erupted in connection with Blum when Dormoy dared compare a Jew to a Breton; nothing on the Catholic antisemitism that surfaced both in Paris and in the provinces, especially in Alsace, after Blum's attempt to transform the school system and secularize it.

Finally, Colton all but ignores the frenzied antisemitism that developed both in France and in Algiers after the Blum–Violette decrees, which are not mentioned but which were proposed to alleviate somewhat the colonial character of the electoral system in Algiers; and he ignores the antipathy (Jewish antisemitism) of various Jews who opposed the Blum "phenomenon." One may cite numerous examples of the anti-Jewish animus that was expressed against Blum: in the Chamber of Deputies, rallies and conventions, in theaters, songs, parades. All this is constantly downplayed as are antisemitic manifestations in the Socialist and Communist parties.

The special theme of Blum's Jewishness and of antisemitism cannot be treated systematically and in detail in a book that seeks to render an account of Blum's overall activity in a historical context rife with critical events. Yet its omission somewhat mars our comprehension of the history of France preceding and heralding the cruel Vichy era. Its inclusion would have enriched the analysis of this dimension of French society so laden with dramatic consequences.

PIERRE BIRNBAUM
Université de la Sorbonne

Geoffrey Wigoder (ed.), *Contemporary Jewry: Studies in Honor of Moshe Davis.* Jerusalem: Institute of Contemporary Jewry, The Hebrew University, 1984. 269 (English) + 162 (Hebrew) pp.

Moshe Davis has had a career rich in intellectual initiative. The extensive bibliography of his writings compiled by Rivka Demsky for this tributary volume reminds us that Professor Davis was among the very first to attempt an academic account of American Jewish religious development. His pioneering study *The Emergence of Conservative Judaism* appeared in 1963 and is in no danger of losing its status as a classic of American Judaism. Calling upon historical research skills of an enviable sort as well as upon an unusual sociological *Verstand* and, perhaps even more striking, a vibrant imagination (a sine qua non in any significant scholarly endeavor), he has been able to establish a new, multifaceted discipline or amalgam of disciplines: *Yahadut zemanenu* (contemporary Jewry).

Perhaps no century equals our own in its impact on the "Jewish street," an impact both calamitous and constructive. To undertake the exploration of the unprecedentedly tangled twentieth-century Jewish experience—to do this now, while memory is reasonably fresh and data have not been lost, so that there may be some fruitful coordination of the multifarious research efforts under way in modern Jewish studies—this is a grand vision. Of course, future scholars will have to shape the deeper perspectives that only the passage of time permits, but they will have a promising foundation on which to develop their interpretations of the changes this century has wrought in Jewish communal structures, sensibilities, patterns of behavior, Jewish identity and Jewish fate.

In the current festschrift, colleagues, students and friends have dedicated to Davis two dozen essays (sixteen in English, eight in Hebrew) mostly on various aspects of nineteenth- and twentieth-century Jewish life and related topics; for instance, studies of post-Holocaust Jewish-Christian relations and late nineteenth-century Judeophobic philosophizing. Readers will find in the volume notable essays on homiletics; Americanization; America-Holy Land connections; Hebrew and Yiddish; Zionism; interfaith understanding or the lack thereof; North American, Soviet and Polish Jewry; demography and social psychology; antisemitism; and the Holocaust.

So conglomerate a volume with such a distinguished roster of contributors is not easily reviewed—but perhaps it will be helpful to mention at least a few of the essays that focus on the American scene. Menahem Kaufman's account of the late and highly gifted Arab nationalist thinker and historian, George Antonius, offers a remarkably well-documented discussion of an early attempt to recruit American support for anti-Zionism. Antonius's exertions might have proven more fruitful for the Arab cause had the American entry into the Second World War not insured that his connections with the pro-Nazi grand mufti of Jerusalem would sabotage his appeal.

Shulamit Nardi's reflections on "Yiddish in American Zionism" reminds us how early twentieth-century American Zionist spokesmen (e.g., Bernard G. Richards, Louis Lipsky, Maurice Samuel and Meyer Weisgal) found *mameloshn* Yiddish rather than the "arcane and distant" Hebrew a natural medium in which to elicit Jewish and Zionist sympathies. Lloyd P. Gartner's contribution illuminates a distinctive question in American Jewish studies: how contemporary historians have seen the Jews of New York City as a Jewish group and as an American group as well as how these historians view the relations between the Jews and the city. He devotes particular attention to the work of Moses Rischin, Arthur Goren, Jeffrey Gurock and Deborah Dash Moore.

Michael Brown probes the complicated yet unmistakable shift in Canadian Zionism: "the Americanization of Canadian Zionism." He argues that what was once an aliyah-minded community continues to "manifest almost universal pro-Israel sentiment, but take(s) every opportunity to hold up [its] own country as an alternative center of Jewish life."

The world of contemporary Jewry reflected in these essays is very much a man's world; it is also a pity that the festschrift pays such scant attention to the arts and to scientific achievement, but no collection of this type can hope to be all-inclusive. In this instance, there is surely far more reason to be grateful for what is offered than severe about what is omitted. And evident in the collection is a certain largeness of spirit—appropriate enough in a tribute to Moshe Davis: for example, the rescue from oblivion of both an unsung Holocaust hero, a Jewish partisan in Nazi-occupied Eastern Europe, and of a Christian Lebanese spokesman for Arab nationalism and anti-Zionism.

In its range and depth, the festschrift suggests how right Davis has been to conceive of contemporary Jewry as an interdisciplinary enterprise. The collection is vivid testimony to the global perspectives he has consistently championed in his leadership of the Institute of Contemporary Jewry. Withal, both in its English and its Hebrew sections, it is a pleasure to read. Congratulations are due to everyone who has had a hand in this impressive work.

Stanley F. Chyet

Hebrew Union College, Jewish Institute of Religion

Michael Löwy, *Rédemption et utopie: Le Judaisme libertaire en Europe centrale.* Paris: P.U.F., 1988. 264 pp.

Michael Löwy's new book *Rédemption et utopie,* dealing with the libertarian Jews of Central Europe, is of great interest. The introduction relates the personal aspect of the book: he was born in Brazil; his parents came from Vienna; he studied and undertook research in São Paulo, Tel-Aviv and Manchester; he has lived in Paris for the past twenty years. He is in search of his historical and cultural roots that are part of the culture of East and Central European Jews, a spiritual world that has been destroyed.

In the introduction, the author develops the key concept that, in his view, uniquely identifies the giants of the Jewish intelligentsia educated in Central Europe under the old regime. Among them were religious thinkers with anarchistic tendencies such as Martin Buber, Franz Rosenzweig, Gershom Scholem and Leo Lowenthal; defenders of a negative utopia such as Franz Kafka; religious-libertarian atheists such as Gustav Landauer, Ernst Bloch, Georg Lukacs and Erich Fromm; and figures who defy simple categorization, such as Walter Benjamin and Bernard Lazare. The author claims there is a common denominator that characterized them all, and he uses the term *"affinité elective"* (adopting the term *"Wahlverwandtshall"* from Weber's study of the Protestant ethic). In considering the applications of this concept, Löwy finds instances of it in medieval alchemical doctrines and in Goethe.

Applying this thesis to the illustrious group of Jewish intellectuals who form the target of the study, Löwy seeks out the affinities that linked Jewish messianism and libertarian utopianism. In doing this, he argues that he is also furthering the sociological analysis of the Jewish intelligentsia in Central Europe, thus making it possible to understand the common ground shared by groups and ideas traditionally viewed as antithetical. Within a sociocultural framework, Löwy develops persuasive explanations for the sources of the rebellion against the modern state and capitalism, which, in the cases under consideration, he sees as a product of the synthesis between German romanticism and the Jewish messianic tradition.

Lowenthal and Buber, he contends, viewed the Jewish settlement of Palestine as a shining example of socialist utopia in practice. He seeks to comprehend the split among "religious anarchists" into a faction that strove for the communal realization of the Zionist dream in Palestine (such as Buber) and another faction that viewed the Soviet revolution as the fulfillment of utopia. In fact, even in Buber's writings, we find a metaphoric allusion to this dilemma: "Moscow or Jerusalem."

Redemption, according to Löwy, appears in the Jewish intelligentsia's ideology as correcting the world, "*tikkun 'olam*" in kabbalistic terminology. This is a Jewish German synthesis, despite Scholem's denial of its Germanic roots and Lukacs's denial of its Jewish roots. The urge for salvation and the redemption of the world was expressed in the rebellion against the old authorities, in the yearning for community, for libertarian socialism, in short, "a continuing spiritual revolution." The author clearly connects such views and actions with the prophetic vision, viewing such figures as Ernst Toller and Walter Benjamin as "prophets unarmed," at times helpless and even suicidal. However, he emphasizes the great influence they exerted after their death and their continued relevance today, even if theirs is "the history of the losers," to use Walter Benjamin's expression.

We cannot examine at length the term "*affinité elective*" as thus applied by the author; but it should be noted that this concept serves him as the link between various sociological or cultural patterns that cannot be traced to one common and causal link and that cannot be subsumed under the term "influence" in the traditional sense. There is an attempt here to enlist a Weberian concept in order to explain a specific phenomenon, for which the historical Marxist explanation is inadequate. The term he coins, *affinité elective*, is an affinity that includes a sense of reciprocal attraction, creating new phenomena as they blend into one another. It is taken as understood that we are dealing with separate and distinct elements that, nevertheless, possess mutual gravitational force. And this attraction exerts itself under certain sociological conditions that, in turn, can either amplify or arrest it.

This is only the tip of the iceberg of this complex, fascinating argument. We hope soon to see this book, which is both so interesting and relevant, in Hebrew and English translations.

Avraham Yassour
University of Haifa

Ruth Dudley Edwards, *Victor Gollancz: A Biography.* London: Victor Gollancz, 1987. 782 pp.

This is a sprawling biography of an emotional, complex, maddening, indefatigable publisher and left-wing public figure who provided through his firm, and especially through the Left Book Club, an important medium for the dissemination of libertarian and socialist ideas in interwar and postwar Britain.

As his biographer amply (perhaps too amply) demonstrates, Gollancz was a man of contradictions. He was a freethinker who refused to publish Orwell's *Animal*

Farm on the grounds that an attack on the Soviet Union during the Second World War was a luxury Britain could not afford. He was a socialist egalitarian who accepted a peerage. Most curious of all, he was a proud Jew who proclaimed his deep belief in the Gospels of Christ.

This last facet of his life is a persistent theme in this biography. The portrait of Gollancz in his early years shows him deeply embarrassed by his Jewishness and determined to do everything to escape from it. But the pervasiveness of "civilized" antisemitism in British culture and the Nazi seizure of power eventually brought Gollancz to see the futility of his flight from his origins. The breaking point came in the Second World War when he realized the enormity of the disaster European Jews were facing. The result was a nervous breakdown, after which he spared neither time nor effort on behalf of the rescue of the survivors.

His return to the fold did not preclude his ongoing insistence on the compatibility of Jewishness with an acceptance of the teachings of Christ as true. He was never baptized, and he refused to admit that his ecumenism was both philosophically impossible and positively insulting to those who took seriously the teachings of both faiths. But Gollancz was never one to consider the civilities of polite discourse. He was a gadfly, ready to take up whatever unpopular causes his conscience directed him to address. He spoke out against anti-German sentiment in postwar Britain. He worked for Arab refugees in the late 1940s and worked against capital punishment (including the sentencing to death of Eichmann) in the 1950s and 1960s. He both annoyed people and made them think in equal part.

His legacy is difficult to measure. His firm is still highly respected, but without the distinctiveness of its early years. His liberal socialist faith has fewer and fewer adherents in the age of Thatcher. His cultural ecumenism seems as remote as ever. In retrospect, Gollancz appears to symbolize the convictions of a bygone age, one in which left-wing politics had intrinsic appeal and in which enemy and ally were clearly distinguishable. His was the voice of the Labour victory of 1945. Edwards argues (p. 399) that his "colossal influence on a vital election remains unmatched in twentieth century political history." This is doubtful, but it is still true that in his publishing and public work, Gollancz helped bring British socialism out of the shadows of the interwar years. At the end of another period of mass unemployment and Conservative hegemony, is there anyone able to do the job today?

J. M. WINTER
Pembroke College, Cambridge

Michael R. Marrus, *The Unwanted: European Refugees in the Twentieth Century*. New York and Oxford: Oxford University Press, 1985. 414 pp.

As Michael R. Marrus reminds us in this landmark book, there was no refugee *problem* before the twentieth century. There have of course been *refugees* throughout history, but they generally had little problem finding a place of refuge. Able-bodied citizens were considered an asset, not a liability; the unwanted of one society were the enrichment of another (as the Ottoman Sultan Bajazet said in welcoming Jews expelled from Spain in 1492). Even the term "refugee" had no general meaning, being applied only to those who fled France following the revocation of the Edict of Nantes in 1685.

"Refugees" became known as such and were seen as an international problem only in the course of the nineteenth century. By the last two decades of the century, a large surge in the number of the displaced led states to begin closing their doors to newcomers. This new restriction on entry was reinforced by the same nationalistic currents that forced refugees out of their native countries of origin in the first place. The result of this cycle of expulsion and exclusion was the refugee crisis of the twentieth century, aptly termed by Marrus "a radically new form of homelessness" or a "new variety of collective alienation" (pp. 4, 13).

The story has been told before, but never so well. Without pontificating, Marrus provides a spare but powerful chronicle of displacement and international indifference. He focuses on Europe and on the middle decades of this century, the heart of the refugee crisis, though implications for other areas and more recent years could be drawn. The understated style of the book serves to reinforce its strength as a telling commentary on one of the great tragedies of our time.

Inevitably, much of the story of refugees in the twentieth century is a Jewish story. The era of forced mass movements began with the Jewish exodus from Eastern Europe before the First World War, which—though it might not qualify as a refugee movement by restrictive contemporary legal definitions—was "perhaps the greatest population movement of postbiblical Jewish history" (p. 27). International efforts to cope with the refugee crisis of the 1930s were weakened by the perception that it was, after all, a Jewish problem. And in the wake of the Second World War, the survivors from the Holocaust posed a refugee issue of unprecedented intensity. As Marrus says, "the experiences of these Jews made it impossible for them to think and behave like other displaced persons. A vast gulf of agony and humiliation yawned between them and the rest of humanity" (p. 332).

But the Jewish aspect cuts even more deeply. To reread the historic account is to be reminded what a central role British policy toward Palestine played in keying the mean-spirited international response to refugees in the late 1930s. Before the British clamped down on entry into Palestine in 1936, as the high commissioner for refugees, James MacDonald, put it, "The daily grace in the High Commissioner's office was 'Thank God for Palestine'" (p. 163). After the clampdown, British opposition to any increase in Jewish immigration contributed greatly to the weakening of international refugee rescue efforts, in particular to the emasculation of the Evian Conference of 1938 and the Bermuda Conference of 1943. Even at that later date, with the Nazi mass murder of Jews a well-known fact, the British still worried that the Nazis "may change over from the policy of extermination to one of extrusion, and aim as they did before the war at embarrassing other countries by flooding them with alien immigrants" (p. 264).

As this illustrates, there was a clear causal link between the highly restrictive immigration and refugee admission policies of the late 1930s and the very occurrence of the Holocaust. Marrus, as others before him, documents Nazi efforts to force Jewish emigration, which continued until after the invasion of Russia:

"Scholars have sometimes failed to appreciate the zeal with which the Germans pursued their earlier emigration objectives and the radical redirection implied by the genocidal program begun in the midst of the Barbarossa campaign'' (pp. 230–231). It is hard to escape the conclusion that, had more doors been open, the Nazis might never have developed their demonic designs.

Though Marrus devotes little space to current refugee policies, the implications are not difficult to draw. The current international definition of refugees—people with a ''well-founded fear of persecution'' on racial, religious or similar grounds— would not cover many of the most desperate cases in the book, just as it does not cover many in distress today (those fleeing violence or war, economic disaster, nondiscriminatory tyranny). The attempt to deprive Soviet Jews of legal status as refugees in U.S. law, whatever the motives behind it, looks most shortsighted in historical perspective.

Though Europe has generated relatively few refugees in recent years, the number of the displaced elsewhere has grown to a magnitude not far removed from that reached by Europe at the peak of its crisis. Observers speak of a gathering refugee crisis in the Third World; although Marrus (p. 370) cites a figure for 1983 of 7.9 million refugees (narrowly defined) worldwide, more recent estimates range as high as 15 or 16 million. As in the 1930s, this challenge has triggered a retrogression in the international response to the refugees as a snowballing impulse to restrict their entry sweeps through nations fearing a massive influx of the ''unwanted.'' Books such as Marrus's eloquent narrative are essential tools to make us aware of the human costs exacted by the surrender to such fears.

ALAN DOWTY
University of Notre Dame

Maurice Isserman, *If I Had a Hammer . . . The Death of the Old Left and the Birth of the New Left*. New York: Basic Books, 1987. 259 pp.

Events during the first years of the Cold War shattered what remained of the American Left. So complete was this destruction that when a new generation of radicals emerged in the 1960s it appeared to them as though little connection existed between the ''old'' Left that had been destroyed in the 1950s and the ''new'' Left emerging in the 1960s. In recent years, a number of younger historians (many of whom are veterans of the rise and fall of the new Left) have begun to piece back together the history of the old Left, especially after 1945. In the process, they are attempting to find the connections between radical generations and to ascertain where their own political lives fit into the larger patterns of American radical history.

A number of the shards of this shattered portrait have been restored by Maurice Isserman in *If I Had a Hammer . . . The Death of the Old Left and the Birth of the New Left*. Isserman offers four detailed case studies of radical movements during the 1950s, linking them both backward and forward in time. His earlier work,

Which Side Were You On?: The American Communist Party During the Second World War (1982), traced the history of the American Communist party in its most popular period. Buoyed by the American wartime alliance with the Soviet Union and the attempts of Earl Browder to redefine the CP as a "political association" that would join a progressive coalition of New Dealers, socialists and other progressives, the party grew to its largest membership in 1946.

Isserman's new book takes up the story from there, with the first chapter charting the collapse of the party as it suffered external and internal traumas. The anti-Communist hysteria that swept postwar America led to the jailing of party leaders under Smith Act indictments, the purging of Communists from the CIO and the pervasiveness of a national anti-Communism that seeped into everything from Hollywood and academe to the State and Justice departments. The revelations made in 1956 by Nikita Khrushchev about the crimes of Joseph Stalin delivered the final blow, and the party was never able to recover.

Yet as Isserman points out and as American leftists knew at the time, the Communist party had been the most successfully organized radical movement in recent American history, and a great many individuals had passed through it. They remained a radical constituency waiting to be reorganized—to become a new Left. Several individuals tried. The second and third chapters deal with attempts to forge a new movement by Max Schachtman, on the one hand, and Irving Howe and *Dissent* magazine, on the other.

The chapter on Schachtman is fascinating insofar as it follows the personal career of one American leftist, but when one looks at the numbers of individuals involved in this movement its importance diminishes. Schachtman was one of the handful of radicals who tried to carry the torch of the Left in this politically barren period. But his perspective was always limited. After thirty years of internecine bickering, the veterans of the old Left still thought and fought in the style of past decades. Even the few new converts of the era, such as Michael Harrington and David MacReynolds, found themselves caught up in the agendas of the past.

Irving Howe came out of the world of younger radicals of the 1930s. Once a Trotskyist and a follower of Schachtman, Howe attempted to carry the banner of democratic socialism while most of his fellow New York intellectuals moved to liberalism or even conservatism. Isserman is especially good at showing how Howe continually tacked to the near-Left side of the political mainstream, maintaining his legitimacy as both a radical and a contemporary American intellectual. Howe's position in foreign affairs is a good example. Non-Communist radicals had called for an independent "third camp," an alternative to the Americans and the Soviets. The liberal anti-Communists took a hardline ("I choose the West") position. Howe and *Dissent* argued for "critical support" of the United States, a "second-and-a-half" position.

Isserman's initial premise that *all* connections between the old Left and the new were obliterated in the 1950s is partially belied by the subsequent history of Howe and *Dissent*. This is not the story of unknown connections but of intense antagonisms. Howe has since written that he "overreacted" to the new Left, becoming "harsh and strident." His attacks on the emerging radicalism demonstrate how bound he was to the battles of the past. Howe and Lewis Coser characterized the very earliest stirrings of the new Left (in 1961!) as "New Styles in Fellow-Traveling.'' (Howe's second career as a literary critic would set him at odds with the artistic side of the counterculture that grew later in the decade. Although not part of Isserman's province, this served to reinforce Howe's hostility to the actions of the young.)

The American Left has talked about itself for so long that it is understandable why anyone writing about this period would choose to analyze Howe and Schachtman. As veterans of the 1930s, they stood on guard constantly and conspicuously to fend off Stalinism or deviationism, and ever argued their own brand of radical purity. This set of American radicals kept themselves front and center in the history of the American political Left, often obscuring other radical movements.

Isserman breaks out of these constraints in his fourth chapter, and it is the most important part of his book. It is likely that he worked backward from the 1960s rather than forward from the 1930s when he came to deal with the peace movements of the late 1950s. Many of the activists in the peace camp would later become the older radicals most comfortable in the Left of the 1960s: David Dellinger, Dorothy Day, Bayard Rustin, A. J. Muste and even Paul Goodman. Whereas Irving Howe was "harsh and strident" and "overreacted," David Dellinger became one of the Chicago Seven.

It is easy to see how campaigns aimed at banning the atomic bomb could mesh with the antiwar campaigns over Vietnam. But there was also something qualitatively different about these radicals. Like the young new Left that followed, they did not come out of, and did not seem to care about, the ideological battles of the past. In 1980, Irving Howe told the *New York Times* that the disputes of the 1930s and 1950s "for many of us . . . made people what they are today." These disputes did not "make" the new Left. When the young encountered this mentality, it both surprised and exasperated them.

Isserman recounts briefly what James Miller has described in great detail in the early chapters of his book on Students for a Democratic Society (SDS) entitled *"Democracy is in the Streets": From Port Huron to the Siege of Chicago* (1987). After drafting the Port Huron Statement, the SDS leaders faced an inquisition from their sponsoring organization, the League for Industrial Democracy. They were charged with being "soft on Communism" by Michael Harrington and others. Even though tempers ultimately subsided, this proved a crucial moment in the generational division.

Later in the decade, Irving Howe and Philip Rahv, founding editor of *Partisan Review*, engaged in a name-calling exchange in the letters column of the *New York Review of Books*. Each accused the other of being miffed that the young leftists had not turned to him for guidance. This incident occurred after the cutoff point of Isserman's study, but it reveals much about the difficulty faced by these older radicals. The events of the 1930s and 1950s had made the older radicals what they were. There had been periods of economic catastrophe and radical optimism followed by a decade of witch-hunting and radical retrenchment. When a new Left emerged in the 1960s, built, as the Port Huron Statement makes clear, on a new set of presumptions about American society, these older radicals found themselves out of step with the new rhythm. The moral credo of the pacifists proved more adaptable than the neosocialist realpolitik of the ex-Communists.

Maurice Isserman has added to our ability to reconstruct movements and individuals driven off the political stage by the domestic side of the Cold War. He sketches in the connections between the "death of the old Left" and the "birth of the new Left," but in the end he reveals as much about the limits of the relationship as about the ties that bind. Some of what made the new Left "new" was its disinterest in many of the issues of the old Left. That disinterest led to differing perspectives, political disputes and often outright hostility. As a result, these two phases of American radical history remained distinct, sharing more issues than they understood but never achieving the kind of organic development that would have made each a more powerful force in American life.

ALEXANDER BLOOM
Wheaton College

Edward Tivnan, *The Lobby: Jewish Political Power and American Foreign Policy.* New York: Simon & Schuster, 1987. 306 pp.

The blurb on the dust jacket of this book proclaims its theme to be "a substantive issue in American politics and foreign policy—the role that a part of the American Jewish community plays in influencing U.S. policy in the Middle East." In fact, there are large areas of this policy with which Mr. Tivnan does not deal: Iran, Syria, the Lebanese quagmire, to name but a few. What the author has done is to investigate the role and impact of "the Lobby"—the American Israel Public Affairs Committee (AIPAC).

Mr. Tivnan believes that AIPAC has become "an obstacle to peace in the Middle East," and his major argument for so concluding is that it has been too successful in discouraging genuine debate within the American Jewish community about the effectiveness and worth of the policies of successive Israeli governments. This is a serious issue, a most legitimate subject for academic inquiry and popular argument. To be thoroughly aired it requires an informed and impartial analysis both of Israeli foreign policy as well as the support given to that policy by American Jews. Mr. Tivnan is able to provide neither.

His own personal view of the matter seems clear enough. He apparently believes that the Palestine Liberation Organization (P.L.O.) is a moderate and moderating force committed to negotiating with the Israelis for a reasonable settlement ("land for peace") of the so-called Palestinian Arab question. The Likud-dominated governments of Israel in recent years do not, in Mr. Tivnan's view, want a reasonable settlement, and these have been bolstered in their intransigence by the activities of AIPAC, which has the effrontery (one might almost say chutzpah) to employ sophisticated lobbying techniques to encourage blind support for Israel from non-Jews and Jews alike—to the detriment of world order, the tranquility of Israel itself and the interests of the U.S.

In arguing thus, the author betrays a lamentable ignorance of Islamic politics, a subject that is, in any case, never discussed in his book. A root cause of Arab–Jewish hostility in the Middle East is the Islamic belief that a state of affairs in which any part of the realm of Islam is dominated by Jews (or, indeed, by any non-Muslim group) is intolerable. Palestine (including, of course, Jerusalem) is part of this realm. Therefore, it is the duty of all faithful followers of the Prophet to help destroy the Jewish (sometimes described as the Zionist) state.

When the late President Sadat journeyed to Jerusalem to address the Knesset, the imams in the mosques of Cairo offered consolation to the masses by explaining that only the tactics had changed, not the strategy. The same is true of the P.L.O., founded (it should be well noted) before the reconquest of Jerusalem, Judea and Samaria by the Jews in the Six Day War. The "Palestine" that the P.L.O. was established to "liberate" did not comprise the territories of Judea, Samaria or Gaza, which (it will be recalled) were already in Arab hands between 1948 and 1967. A Palestinian Arab state could have been proclaimed in these territories at any time during this period. Such a proclamation was never made, nor would it have been reasonable to expect any follower of Islam to have acquiesced in such a proclamation, for such acquiescence would have been tantamount to acceptance of Jewish rule over part of the Islamic realm.

I daresay that one could find—and that Mr. Tivnan has found—individual Muslims who genuinely accept the legitimacy as well as the reality of the reestablishment of a Jewish state. Purely for the sake of argument, I shall even admit the possibility that Mr. Arafat is a reformed gentleman, a man of peace. The fact is, though, that the vast, the overwhelming majority of the adherents of Islam do not accept the view that it was right to reestablish Jewish statehood in Palestine. They are affronted by the Jewish flag flying over Jerusalem, just as they were when it first flew over Tel-Aviv. It is for this reason, among others, that Israeli politicians across a wide spectrum are right to tread with the utmost caution in any dealings they might have with the P.L.O., and it is for this reason, among others, that AIPAC supports this extreme caution.

Indeed, AIPAC has not been selling "a neoconservative version of the American Jewish community to the White House and Congress" with which "literally millions of American Jews disagree." Mr. Tivnan does that community a major disservice in suggesting that this is what has happened (pp. 263–264). "The much discussed metamorphosis of American Jews into Republicans [the author declares] has yet to occur." This may well be the case, though it is worth remembering that in 1980 Reagan won more than 40 percent of the Jewish vote. However, even if it were true that the Jewish vote had remained overwhelmingly Democratic, it would, nonetheless, be dangerous to infer, therefore, that American Jews were compromisers or appeasers when confronted by the Middle East.

What Mr. Tivnan has done is to present his own wishful thinking as if it were established fact, and his own blinkered vision as if it were reality in the round. Had he done this with style, one might have felt in a forgiving mood with regard to his arguments. In fact, the book is sloppily written, full of sentences without verbs and pseudo-intellectual jargon. Its use, without explanation, of American terminology (e.g., "op-ed-page pieces," [p. 247]) is a confession that his book is addressed to an exclusively American audience; but I doubt that many American Jews will give the work more than a passing glance.

GEOFFREY ALDERMAN
Royal Holloway and Bedford New College
University of London

RELIGION, THOUGHT AND EDUCATION

Eliezer Berkovits, *Mashber hayahadut bimdinat hayehudim (Crisis of Judaism in the State of the Jews)*. Jerusalem: Reuven Mass, 1987. 141 pp.

Eliezer Berkovits, an eminent modern Orthodox theologian and halakhist, here presents his conception of the secular-religious conflict in Israel and its deeper implications, both personal and public. His main contention is that both the religious and the secular ways of life and thought have suffered the impact of our period, its tragic events and its declining ethical culture. The result is a dangerous spiritual and moral impoverishment. In the secular camp, Berkovits observes materialism, egoistic individualism and alienation from the Jewish people and from Jewish forms of identification. His discussion of the secular culture concentrates on what he considers its highest representative elite: the kibbutz movement. Making abundant use of the severe self-criticism in this movement, which reflects its sense of spiritual and moral decline, he documents his claim that the revolution of the first generation against the Jewish religious inheritance, which actually sustained their pioneering social-national enterprise, now serves to impoverish the subsequent generations.

In the religious camp, Berkovits observes primitivism; narrow-mindedness; halakhic fossilization, especially with regard to the problems of governing a Jewish state; a cowardly reluctance to confront the positive achievements of modern science, technology, philosophy and the arts; and a lack of moral sensitivity. He blames these phenomena mainly on the tragic effects of the Holocaust and on the negative impact of a secularism in decline.

The conclusions are obvious. Berkovits recommends a deep reorientation in Israeli education. The secular school system should place more emphasis on the rabbinic tradition, the fullness of its literary achievement, its symbols and norms; whereas religious education should be more open to the world and to the whole Jewish people, thus seeking to develop a greater moral sensitivity.

The author is a profound thinker and a fine writer. The strength of his book lies in its simplicity and clarity of exposition, on the one hand, and in its prudent use of rabbinic sources, on the other. And with regard to the modern Orthodox public, he may well achieve his goal, namely, to convince his readers of the urgent need to redirect religious education along the lines that he recommends. He makes effective use of the traditional idiom familiar to that audience and appeals to its sense of responsibility as part of the Jewish people (*klal yisrael*).

However, one may be forgiven for having doubts about his chances of convincing the secular public. In the first place, his discussion, though demonstrating fairness with regard to secular sensitivities, is on the whole one-sided. Thus, he quotes prolifically from secular educators who admit the existence of a spiritual crisis, but he does not pay due attention to the variety of secularist worldviews that have been developed by some eminent contemporary thinkers as alternatives to his traditional concept of a Jewish society within a Jewish state. More important, he does not try to empathize in depth with the experiences that inform and shape the existential inclinations of a young secularist in Israel toward Judaism and its religious content.

It would seem that the author's views are based mainly on opinions shaped within the Ashkenazic community in the prestate and early state period; thus, he does not take into account the great shift in the nature of Israeli secularism as it was reshaped by the mass immigration from Arab countries and by the more recent experiences undergone by Israel. Indeed, in this context, we should note that even from the religious point of view Berkovits attaches a disproportionate attention to the old problem of the relationship between science and faith, trying to convince his readers of what is, in fact, taken for granted by most religious educators: namely, that there is no danger in a full scientific education. In contrast, he fails to confront the really disturbing issue of the status to be assigned to "secular," as against "holy," studies when it comes to teaching the humanities; they are, after all, often seen as two competing alternatives that demand primacy and exclusivity in order to attain high levels of achievement and creativity.

Nonetheless, Berkovits's attitude is positive both in its critical analysis and in its practical suggestions, and we should wish him and his followers success in their attempt to bridge dichotomies and to guarantee that Israel functions as a Jewish state. But this crucial goal requires a deeper and more comprehensive intellectual effort if it is to exert the influence it seeks on the Israeli educational system.

ELIEZER SCHWEID
The Hebrew University

Stephan F. Brumberg, *Going to America, Going to School: The Jewish Immigrant Public School Encounter in Turn-of-the-Century New York City.* New York: Praeger, 1986. xvi + 282 pp.
Alan Wieder, *Immigration, the Public School, and the Twentieth Century American Ethos: The Jewish Immigrant as a Case Study.* Lanham: University Press of America, 1985. vi + 117 pp.

Stephan F. Brumberg and Alan Wieder, in their books on New York City and Cleveland, Ohio, share a generally positive view of the public school's influence on the East European Jewish immigrants. Drawing on the literature of educational and immigration history and on personal interviews with "representative" (Brumberg, p. 266) or "prototypical" (Wieder, p. 8) Jewish immigrants, they conclude (in Wieder's words) that "the American dream and melting pot are not myth, but rather reality" (Wieder, p. 106). Both express the hope that lessons gleaned from the public school experience of immigrant Jews might benefit more recent immigrants and racial minorities so that public schools can function as a ladder of educational and social mobility.

An authority on the methods by which public schools transmit cultural values and mediate among different ethnic, racial and religious groups, Brumberg has written a detailed and well-documented study that is supplemented by period photographs. He attributes the rapid educational assimilation of Jewish immigrant children from the late 1880s until the First World War to a confluence of positive factors: personal ambition, family encouragement, societal support and the opportunity for schooling.

Brumberg points out that the children of Jewish immigrants "arrived at the doorsteps of the public schools with their bookbags already laden with a richly textured and highly varied bundle of experiences, attitudes, values and world views" (p. 51). They were influenced by the Jewish Enlightenment, which had spread from Germany through Galicia and into Russia, where the Haskalah stressed "rationalism in religion," vernacular languages and secular studies (p. 38). Moreover, when the onslaught of pogroms in Russia and the problems prevalent in the Austro-Hungarian Empire spurred the great emigration, at least two-thirds of the East European Jews entered the United States as skilled workers, "the highest proportion of any immigrant group" (p. 47).

These immigrants chose public school education for their children. By 1917, more than 277,000 were in New York public schools, whereas a tiny minority of only 1,000 went to *yeshivot;* in all, less than one-fourth of Jewish schoolchildren received religious instruction. In the Pale of Settlement in Russia, only 3.5 percent had studied in government schools, whereas almost all received instruction at *cheder* or Talmud Torah. In New York City, "the educational world of the Jews had been turned on its head," Brumberg concludes (p. 190). Yet Jewish education did succeed in carving out a "complementary relationship with the existing schools" (p. 197), and the Jewish community contributed to the education of the nonschool population through libraries, evening classes and free lectures for adults.

There were, he emphasizes, three aspects to the "encounter" between Jewish immigrants and the public schools. One side was formed by the New York City Board of Education and the public schools, representing the predominantly white Anglo-Saxon Protestant establishment; and a second by the more than 1.5 million East European Jews, almost 27 percent of the population by 1920, who made New York City "the largest Jewish city in the world" (p. 200). "The established Jewish community, largely German in background but also including old Sephardic families" was "the vital link" between these two groups (pp. 200–201).

Of the board's primary goals, "basic scholastic preparation emphasizing literacy in English"; "acculturation"; and use of "the schools to facilitate and rationalize socio-economic stratification" (p. 143), only the first two were shared by the immigrants. As they learned English, students were taught values and proper behavior: American morality and ethics, "conceptions of American beauty and 'taste,'" "civic virtue," hygiene and proper grooming (pp. 76, 127). Despite its "absolutist and rigid . . . definition of American culture," Brumberg recognizes that the educational system allowed immigrants "to share" the "American patrimony" (p. 223). But although Jewish immigrants accepted American educational methods and values, they rejected the vocational program (the Gary Plan) that was added in 1914 with the endorsement of German Jewish social reformers since it made "stratification a manifest function of schooling" (p. 112).

In studying the reactions of immigrant Jews to the public schools, Brumberg draws on interviews with twenty-six men and women, born between 1887 and 1911 in the United States, Russia and Austria-Hungary; of these, four are gentiles, twenty-two were educated in New York City public schools, and nine became public school teachers. Reporting that their teachers were "strict disciplinarians," they nonetheless, remembered with "fondness and pride" the elementary schools they attended (p. 125). Jewish teachers also became "the very models of Americanhood" to their students (p. 138).

Among his interviewees "there was near-unanimous consensus that the schools were largely unbiased," probably because of "an implicit 'gentleman's agreement' to keep proselytizing out of the classroom—political as well as religious—so that the public school could be acceptable to all citizens of the City" (p. 218). Because of this consensus, Jews, unlike Catholics, did not create a parallel, parochial school system from elementary school through university. (Catholics resented what they felt was the Protestant bias of school boards and teachers.)

Brumberg's "contemporary speculations" are relevant to public schools today, which, unlike those of eighty years ago, have divided goals: one for middle-class and one for racial minority students. Lessons derived from the immigrant Jewish experience could help to guide today's schools. They should work with "established elements of an immigrant community" (p. 221) and "develop special curricula for the newly arrived immigrant children" (p. 222). Moreover, educators "must strive to become knowledgeable concerning the cultures of the children they serve" and should include these cultures in the curricula "for *all* students, not just a subcultural minority" (p. 222).

Like Brumberg, Wieder hopes that by tracing "the progress of the early twentieth century Jewish immigrant," he will help us to "better understand the mass society in which we live" (p. 6). He, too, aims at encouraging the public schools to accept racial minorities, particularly, blacks "into the American ethos" (p. 106).

After reviewing much of the literature on the subject, Wieder finds the arguments of both public school advocates (Ellwood Cubberley) and their critics ("revisionists" such as Michael Katz) inconclusive. As a result of his interviews with more than thirty Cleveland Jews, who had immigrated to the United States between 1895 and 1923, he concludes that the public schools "were neither great educational utopias nor did they inflict harm on immigrant children" (p. 98). The summaries of thirteen interviewees form the most interesting part of his study. Seven of them completed grammar school, five are high school graduates, but only one went on to finish college. Of their twenty-seven children, however, twenty-five graduated from high school, eighteen became college graduates and five went on to graduate study. And of their thirty-five grandchildren, all had already graduated or expected to graduate from high school, twenty-eight had completed four years of college and five pursued advanced degrees. This very small sample thus suggests that educational achievement beyond grade school level occurred only in the second and third generations.

Two of the thirteen commented on the way in which "steamer," or special English classes, helped newly arrived immigrant children adjust to regular classes. For Rae Sherman and other immigrant women, "neatness, correct grammar and written language in general appear to be the ticket out of sweatshop piecework" (p.

76). For Sarah Greenbaum, "the Jewish concept of the teacher as a rabbi was transferred to the public school teacher" (p. 78); a few remembered some teachers as "condescending and anti-semitic" (p. 86). Yet "the greater part of the immigrant experience in the public school was a good one," says Wieder (p. 98).

In its present form, his book is only a promising beginning. Omitted from his limited bibliography are such useful sources as the annual reports of Cleveland's superintendent of education, census data, and the *Reports of the Immigration Commission* (The Dillingham Commission) 61st Congress, 3rd session, Senate Document #747 (1911; reprinted in 1970).

Wieder never explains why he chose Cleveland. According to the 1920 census, Cleveland—about one-eighth the size of New York City—had a Yiddish- and Hebrew-speaking population of 30,383, constituting 5.5 percent of the city's population. A comparison of ethnic-group distribution by school level in Cleveland indicates that for Russian Jews, who were 5.7 percent of the pupils, primary education was both important and economically feasible but that native-born whites and German Jews were three times as likely to attend high school. Wieder makes little effort, however, to study either the different groups of Jewish immigrant children in Cleveland or its public school system.

Although Wieder's interviewees provide interesting oral memoirs, his book needs more substance and smoother writing. Those seeking solid information, intellectual context and an excellent analysis of the Jewish immigrant's experience in the public schools should consult Brumberg's study on New York City.

MARCIA G. SYNNOTT
University of South Carolina

Yoel Florsheim, *Medinat yisrael—ḥevrah yehudit?* (State of Israel—A Jewish Society?). Jerusalem: Reuven Mass, 1986. 135 pp.

This book should attract readers interested in the sociopolitical problems of Israel as well as those whose concerns are with the strictly religious issue. It constitutes a rare attempt by a modern Orthodox scholar to deal with these problems from both metahalakhic and halakhic points of view. Florsheim adopts a theoretical halakhic approach to modernity and seeks to prove it superior to secular assumptions by undertaking a detailed and realistic examination of, and suggesting viable solutions to, some of the most disturbing dilemmas that confront Israeli society. Obviously, the tenor of his philosophy is apologetic, but the attempt to prove his argument by a logical discussion of the issues aimed to convince the nonreligious (as well as the religious) reader endows this book with depth, openness and intellectual credibility.

An honest apology always contains an element of self-criticism. And Florsheim admits that, when measured against the norms of behavior prevailing in the country, Israeli Orthodox society does not differ from its secular counterpart. It shares the same realities and faces the same unsolved problems, unquestioningly adopting secular and unsatisfactory modes of conduct. The result is that the religious community has not developed, as it should have done, the potential of its own halakhic approach. The inevitable result has been an erroneous approach to, and even the neglect of, halakhah itself, even though in Orthodox thought it constitutes a total discipline that should inform and guide all private and public aspects of human life. Thus, the halakhah as practiced by the Orthodox today is flawed when measured against its own ideal. It rests content with existing norms, avoids new decisions and has not developed the new halakhic models of thought needed to cope with modernity, in general, and with the realities of a Jewish state, in particular.

Florsheim does not make do with admonitions alone. He himself develops some new halakhic models and applies them quite convincingly in his chapters on, for example, democratic society and private rights, the status of women, the welfare state, the freedom of trade-union conflict and the place of a non-Jew in a Jewish society. From a practical point of view, these chapters are the most rewarding and we recommend that they be read closely. However, as the main goal of the author was to prove his metahalakhic theories and to demonstrate how the "State of the Jews" that we now have can be replaced by a truly "Jewish state," we will concentrate here solely on this broader issue.

In contrast to the secular democratic approach, the halakhic method is characterized according to Florsheim by the following qualities. First, it is based on an *objectively* true knowledge of the nature of man, his destiny, duties and rights and on an absolute authority, whereas the secular approach is subjective, poorly defined and thus, necessarily relativistic. Second, although even in halakhic terms there is a valid distinction between the moral commandments, which are not to be enforced by the courts, and the civil laws which are so enforced, halakhah in its entirety is all-encompassing, normatively precise and decisive in morally binding, no less than in legally binding, commandments. Moreover, it has its *religious* sanctions against moral transgressions, whereas the secular approach merely recommends moral "values" while lacking a system of spiritual sanctions.

And, finally, halakhah is based primarily on the concept of human *duty,* not on that of human right, although it maintains clearly that our duties toward our fellowman are his rights and that his duties toward us are our rights, whereas the secular approach is based solely on the concept of rights, defining the rights of others as the limits of our own rights and vice versa. It follows that responsibility for our fellowman, including material help when needed, is, according to the halakhah, an obligative and precisely defined moral commandment that includes the duty of every man to care for his own existence and well-being. According to the secular approach, as understood by Florsheim, all these duties are no more than recommended values. In one place, he goes so far as to suggest that according to the "gentile," or Christian, morality, which informs secularism, there is no duty to aid a suffering fellowman—help in such cases is only "allowed," or recommended, not demanded.

These differences, the author claims, make halakhah inherently superior in its greater capacity to reach objectively just, decisive and realistic solutions to every evolving social problem; to inspire a voluntary and positive response to its norms, which can thus be applied more efficiently and successfully; and to achieve the necessary balance between the demands that every individual makes on society and the demands he has to make on himself.

Thus far, Florsheim doubtless sounds convincing to his fellow Orthodox scholars, who may therefore well follow him in trying to develop his important recommendations on the basis of their shared halakhic creed. However, it would seem that even a believing Orthodox Jew, once he presents himself as an objective and open-minded thinker, could be expected to demonstrate much more precision and empathy in the presentation of humanistic and secular conceptions. For the sake of a clear-cut argument, Florsheim tends to present the humanist secular approach in ways much too abstract, generalized, simplified, one-dimensional and, above all, unified—as if there is only one secular moral philosophy underpinning the legal system and the ethical code in a democratic society. He himself admits that the Orthodox community has silently adopted as its own many secular laws and moral values; moreover, his own thought makes it quite clear that he, too, has been deeply influenced by humanistic morality (especially in his relation to the status of women and non-Jews in Jewish society), though he does not overtly state as much. In such a context, one would expect him to admit more knowledge of the diversity of opinions, tensions and complexity characteristic of secular ethical thought. Thus, he should have noted that the concept of a primary ethical duty and of moral absolutes are central to some influential humanistic teachings, especially those from which modern Jewish Orthodoxy eventually profited in the development of its meta-halakhic theories. One might also have expected him to be more careful in repeating such prejudiced opinions about Christianity (unfortunately typical enough of Jewish Orthodoxy) as the aforementioned view that it does not demand human solidarity with sufferers.

Again, Florsheim himself grants that, in spite of the halakhically binding character of moral norms, the Orthodox community in its entirety complies nowadays only with what is considered a halakhic law, whereas in terms of social ethics, it has adapted itself entirely to "secular" behavior. But surely this admission should have prompted him to think more critically not only about the nature of Orthodox society generally, but also about the validity of his claim that the halakhic conception of moral obligation is more effective than the secular and that there is a qualitative difference between the halakhic and the nonhalakhic view of law and morality. After all, it can hardly be said that the superiority of the one ethical system over the other has been pragmatically proved, a fact to which we will immediately return because of its far-reaching significance.

If his argument was meant to convince the nonreligious and the non-Orthodox as well as the Orthodox Jew, Florsheim should have taken more into account the need to reinforce his belief that the religious view of human nature, destiny and justice is truly ("objectively") objective—since the secular philosopher will tend to argue that it is in fact most subjective precisely because it claims to be objective, to be informed by an absolute divine revelation. Indeed, Florsheim's own conviction that it is essential to develop halakhic models through the application of autonomous human ethical and juridical thinking, clearly requires the modification of his own oversimplified, authoritative argument. In order to convince the unconvinced, he would have to present an answer to the secular contention that the religious claim to possess absolute, objective knowledge of human nature and of ethical principles must be limited for the sake of human autonomy; that religion, if it asks an organon of human reasoned criticism, is bound to become tyrannical.

But from the practical point of view, which for Florsheim is rightly a matter of principle, the fact that the Orthodox community has adopted secular assumptions and values should have aroused far more concern than is revealed in his book. When proposing to apply halakhic moral norms to modern society in a modern state, one should inquire whether there is something in the nature and reality of such a society that renders these norms hard or even impossible to apply. I would here suggest that what in the past made the moral norms of halakhah as binding as its laws was not the power of religious sanctions, which today seems to be entirely lacking, but rather the fact that a congregational community can frequently be most effective in defining and applying moral norms—as even secular, idealist communities such as the kibbutz and the moshav have demonstrated. A congregational community has its own ways to impose ethical behavior on its members, applying an interpersonal and interfamiliar system of moral punishments and rewards (as can be observed even today in closed religious congregations that do not apply the same norms in their relationship to the wider society around them). Thus, in the abstract, Florsheim may be right in his claim that some of Israel's severest problems could have been effectively solved by a congregational type of ethics, but the irony, of course, is that most of these problems themselves result from the deep crisis of congregational life that, in turn, is the product of a society dominated by the modern state.

The assumption throughout the book is that all the complex problems of Israeli society result from applying the wrong conceptual tools to modern issues and that, therefore, once we change tools, all our troubles will be duly solved. This may well represent the typical approach of a talmudic scholar, but it is, surely, too formalistic to be effective. We here in Israel are facing a deep structural crisis of society. And unless we apply our theoretical and practical thinking directly to the problem of renewing congregational structures that can support human solidarity and reciprocity even within the Jewish state, there will be no basis upon which to apply some of Florsheim's well-meant and—in principle—even realistic suggestions.

We must then sadly conclude that until the author shows us a practical halakhic way both to build a new social congregational society for the masses within the organizational framework of the state and also to solve the problem of relations between state and society, his belief that a day will come when all the Jews in Israel voluntarily opt for halakhah as their guide to life will remain just one more dream.

ELIEZER SCHWEID
The Hebrew University

Harvey E. Goldberg (ed.), *Judaism Viewed from Within and from Without: Anthropological Studies.* Albany: State University of New York, 1987. x + 352 pp.

The anthropological studies collected in this volume cover a heterogeneous range of subjects that involve a number of Jewish settings and communities. The volume is divided into three parts, each containing three articles. The first part deals with the development and meaning of central texts and rituals in historical contexts; the second and third parts examine contemporary expressions of Judaism in America and Israel, respectively. Even within a given section, the articles differ widely in their subject matter, but in his general introduction, epilogue and other contributions to the book, the editor has skillfully shown that all the articles relate to a number of key themes. In fact, this is a rare specimen among books of collected articles: an integrated work in which the editor takes a major role in providing background and shows how the articles can be interpreted to complement each other in the development of general theses.

In his introduction, Harvey Goldberg notes that there has been little contact between anthropology and Jewish studies but that recent developments in the two disciplines have made possible a mutually beneficial linkage. He argues, for example, that anthropologists are now less prone to impose inappropriate conceptual frameworks, such as the evolutionary approach familiar from their own society, and have come to emphasize more the need to understand cultures in their own terms. Thus, anthropologists interested in Judaism are more ready to analyze it "from within" and to focus on its specific patterns, and this approach can link them with scholars in Jewish studies. Anthropologists will continue to be interested in comparisons, but Goldberg emphasizes the importance of attention to the special characteristics of a given cultural context or tradition. He expands this theme in his epilogue where he writes that all humanity faces certain basic issues, but the ways these issues are defined differ. He argues further that different traditions relate to the same grand dichotomies, such as good and evil or chaos and order, but that some dichotomies are more central to a given culture than to others.

Analyses that compare Judaism to other religious traditions would be highly relevant to Goldberg's arguments, and I was somewhat disappointed that the contributors rarely attempt such comparisons. The "from within" perspective of contributors is also evident in their lack of attention to the wider social and cultural contexts of the Jewish issues they analyze. A summary of the wider contexts is provided by Goldberg's introductions, but these sections are mostly potted history and are not part of the anthropological or sociological analysis that remains, for the most part, at the micro or case-study level. Goldberg warns against a reductionism that describes cultural phenomena as simply derived from their social contexts, but some readers may find that the predominant tendency of most contributors to limit their analysis to specific cultural issues goes too far in the other direction.

In his discussion of the particularity of the Jewish religious tradition, Goldberg emphasizes the central importance of the study of sacred texts and their influence on ritual and daily life. Among some poststructuralists, a focus on texts provides an opportunity for an objectivist analysis that distances itself from the many interpretations and meanings assigned to those texts by the actual participants in the culture. Goldberg, however, appears to prefer a hermeneutic approach with its emphasis on the meanings intended by the authors of the texts and on those understood by the audiences. He, thus, seeks to avoid two extreme approaches to the study of texts: on the one hand, the analysis of the text as having a single meaning; on the other, the view of the text as infinitely malleable with its meaning depending entirely on the reader. Texts are to be understood as providing a recognizable particularity within a religious tradition, but they are also open to a range of interpretations and thereby allow innovations in ritual and behavior.

The structural continuity of the Jewish tradition over a long time span and amid great social change is demonstrated in Goldberg's own article, in which he analyzes meanings of the Torah scroll in a range of different settings. He writes that the enduring structure is not only shaped by the classic texts that are selected and interpreted by members of the society, but also by the widespread rites and customs that are interwoven with the texts. The meaning on which he focuses is the symbolic linkage of the Torah scroll to procreation. This linkage is an "open-ended" one so that "given certain central values and conceptions within traditional Jewish thought, there is a potentiality of this association being made, and remade." A complex analysis of particular symbolic relationships is provided, but Goldberg tends to hedge around the question of whether members of the society intended or were conscious of these interpretations. This type of symbolic analysis is often ambiguous about the relative contributions of participants and anthropologists in the recognition and creation of meanings, and this problem makes itself especially felt when Goldberg links his analysis to such structuralist themes of Claude Lévi-Strauss as the opposition between nature and culture.

Other contributors vary in the extent to which they emphasize conscious symbolic creativity—deeper meanings, as in the structuralist approach—or explanations in terms of cultural forces or changes in social structure. At the level of explanation, the two other articles in the historical section provide an interesting contrast. Zvi Zohar's paper on the consumption of sabbatical produce in biblical and rabbinic literature is a complex analysis in many ways, but his explanation of religious change is a fairly straightforward one. It is based on the presumed motives of sages in responding to their understanding of the social and religious needs of the Jewish community in changing circumstances.

Samuel Cooper's highly ingenious analysis of the laws of mixture is more ambiguous concerning the analytical status of meanings and explanation. Cooper argues that the "force of custom" created a convergence of codes that dealt with prohibited mixtures of milk and meat, wool and linen, grape and grain. One side (milk, wool, grape) represents life; the other side (meat, linen, grain) represents destruction. The items in the death category, unlike the life category, have both sacred and profane expressions, and they have to undergo transformation before they can become part of everyday life.

This summary gives only a bare indication of the richness of Cooper's analysis, but I was left uncertain about the analytical status of the oppositions. Cooper writes that the force of custom and tradition imposed a coherent configuration on the law and that custom expressed the opposition of life and death even when the law did not. This formulation appears to give this opposition a status outside the cultural system that responds by giving it symbolic expression. But why does the cultural system deal with this opposition and not others? Cooper writes that life and death are metaphors "to describe the structure of the oppositional system." This implies that there is a structure that is contentless until the cultural system applies metaphors. The problems here are hardly solved when Cooper writes that his research is "only intended to demonstrate the level of consistency," not "the meanings of the oppositions." What is meant by "meaning" here? Surely the analysis of the structural oppositions is at the level of meaning, even if it is only the scholar who has made that meaning apparent? Or is the level of meaning, perhaps, even deeper than the structure of oppositions? Or is the reference simply to the meanings as understood by the members of society themselves that, as Cooper suggests, vary historically. The problems here regarding the relationships of the "force of custom," the structure of oppositions and the levels of meaning are very perplexing.

Structuralism and the anthropologist's search for deep meanings are less evident in the papers on Judaism in contemporary America and Israel. Here the emphasis is on the cultural innovation of participants, but symbolic creativity is analyzed within settings that differ in the extent to which the sacred texts constrain and direct the creativity. Two papers, one by Barbara Myerhoff on members of a senior adult center in Venice, California, and the other by Tsili Doleve-Gandelman on ceremonies in Israeli kindergartens, deal with relatively secular contexts in which traditional sacred texts hardly constrain the innovators. Myerhoff's beautifully written piece describes how the senior adults endeavored to overcome their "severe invisibility" within the society by means of a parade and a collective mural in which they presented their history and culture to the outside world. As in the case of the modern educators who shape the kindergarten celebrations in Doleve-Gandelman's article, the symbolic activity of participants appears to be almost entirely on a conscious level, and the role of the anthropologist is to conceptualize in more general terms the symbolic innovations and reinterpretations.

The article by Yoram Bilu on the role of dreams in the development of a pilgrimage site among Moroccan Jews in Israel is concerned with a traditional setting, but the constraints on the symbolic creativity here are mainly nontextual forms of popular religiosity. However, as Goldberg points out, the textual tradition does penetrate popular religiosity; the images in some dreams may be understood against the background of biblical references, and the dreams themselves are often written down and utilize forms associated with sacred texts. A community with a greater textual orientation is that of the Bobover hasidim in Brooklyn, New York, but as Shifra Epstein shows in her article on their Purim plays, creativity and individualism is permitted and even encouraged as long as they remain within the framework of tradition. The Bobover follow the texts of "great tradition" Judaism during Purim, but they also have their "small tradition" Purim play in which they give expression, through ritual inversion and oppositional themes, to their society, its boundaries and their interaction with outsiders.

The articles by Riv-Ellen Prell on gender in an American Jewish community and by Menachem Friedman on the haredim (ultra-Orthodox) in Israel provide an interesting comparison. Both deal with innovations within settings in which participants emphasize the need to retain the sacred tradition and its texts. Here the similarity ends. Prell deals with a havurah whose members wish to remain traditionally observant (they do not change the texts or ritual) and yet simultaneously to achieve gender equality in their religious setting. An absorbing account of the use of humor during the services of Simhat Torah shows how they fail. Prell demonstrates that a balance of innovation and tradition does not appear possible when the aim is to change a fundamental category of the tradition, such as gender. In comparison,

Friedman shows that innovation is successful when a community concentrates its efforts on strict interpretations of the traditional texts.

More than the other contributors, Friedman locates his analysis of cultural change within the social context. The contemporary ultra-Orthodox community and its adoption of stricter halakhic standards is shown to have developed when, following the destruction of the traditional East European communities, there emerged a new religious framework, a "voluntary community," that encouraged competition in degrees of stringency and intransigence. Of particular importance was the development of a new type of yeshiva that, unlike the locally based yeshivot of the past, is a totalist institution cut off from the norms and customs of the family and local community. The yeshiva students see themselves as part of a learned elite called upon to uphold the tradition of codes that has come to triumph over the more compromising tradition anchored in the daily life of the local community.

Friedman's article is a welcome contribution by a sociologist in an excellent collection of mainly anthropological papers. Hopefully, the book will encourage further research in the sociology and anthropology of Judaism.

STEPHEN SHAROT
Ben-Gurion University of the Negev

Frederick E. Greenspahn (ed.), *The Human Condition in the Jewish and Christian Traditions*. Hoboken: Ktav, 1986. 258 pp.

This volume consists of papers delivered at symposia of the University of Denver's Center for Judaic Studies that give an analysis of the Protestant, Catholic and Jewish views of different aspects of the human condition. Noted theologians of the three faiths respond to the following subjects: human nature, sin and atonement and eschatological hopes.

In the first section, R. L. Kress describes the Catholic understanding of human nature. In his treatment of the nature of man in the Old Testament, I found a most faithful rendition of the traditional Jewish view. Richard L. Rubenstein, whose paper is entitled "Human Condition in Jewish Thought," speaks only briefly of the rabbinic notions of good and evil and of human freedom. His main concern seems to be to explain why so distinctive a vision of the human condition evolved among the Jews. His thesis, reminiscent of Nietzsche, is that some of the most distinctive concepts of Judaism, such as Exile and Redemption, the institution of prophecy, kingship, messianism, the doctrine of the two inclinations and the severity of the Jewish attitude toward idolatry "are [all] consequences of the echo of Jewish political powerlessness and impotence." The inference that Rubenstein draws from this is that although the Jewish view of the human condition may have been rational and appropriate for the Jewish people in the light of their "sociopolitical situation," their mistake was to suggest that their view could be a path of redemption for all mankind. While all the other contributors engage in theology, using the criterion of cognitive truth, Rubenstein gives us questionable sociology in a relativistic mode.

In presenting the Catholic view, Robert Kress uses the effective existential approach that starts with the question: "What is man?" If man is the question to which God is the answer, then we may never fully grasp the answer unless we fully appreciate the question. We cannot take it for granted that man should exist. For why should the world and human beings exist at all? It is unfortunate that, except for Abraham Heschel, few Jewish theologians have cultivated this approach. This is probably because we tend to identify with Moses rather than with Abraham, that is, we start with the *Jewish* religious experience rather than with the *human* condition.

In an excellent paper on "Sin and Atonement in Judaism," Michael Wyschograd points out that sin is a religious not an ethical category and constitutes a break in the relationship between God and man that requires remediation. This is in contrast to that Protestant tradition in which, as Langdon Gilky tells us, "all atonement is the work of God and of God in Christ, no act of ours, no amount of merit, not even the level of our perfection, can make atonement." More than an act of disobedience, sin is an attempt "to unthrone God by making man into a God-like creature." Wyschograd goes on to show how contemporary Jewish notions of sin and atonement tend to be distorted by a largely unconscious "dialogue" with secularism, on the one hand, and Christianity, on the other. Jewish theology strives to maintain a proper balance between the ubiquity of sin, on the one hand, and optimism in the ultimate victory of the good, on the other. Although Judaism affirms the reality of human freedom, God remains in control of history and man's ability to frustrate God's plan for His creation is limited.

Steven S. Schwarzschild's paper on Jewish eschatology contains a very learned discussion on the relationship between messianism and resurrection. However, his attempt to interpret the Jewish belief in the Messiah as enjoying "eternal futurity" ("The Messiah will always not yet have come unto all historical eternity") is clever but not very convincing. Schwarzschild gives adequate attention to Jewish messianism as an ethical force and is properly sensitive to the complex dialectic of grace and ethics in Jewish eschatology.

Writing on "Eschatological Hope in Protestant Tradition," Clark H. Pinnock describes how the coming of the Kingdom in Protestant orthodoxy became eclipsed by an almost exclusive concentration on the personal salvation of the individual rather than on the transformation of the world at the historical level. In recent times, however, "futurist" eschatology has ceased to be theology's "foster child" and, in Pinnock's view, stands near the beginning of its development in the work of such theologians as Oscar Cullmann and Wolfhart Pannenberg. A Jewish theologian could have no quarrel with his conclusion: "The Biblical story has to do not only with what happens when I die or with man's efforts to build a world of peace and justice . . . it is an affirmation about the finale towards which all history moves . . . it is about the fulfillment of the purposes of God according to which He created the world in the first place."

This work brings into sharp focus the comparative emphases of the Jewish and Christian traditions on the most fundamental religious themes and is a valuable contribution to contemporary theology.

SHUBERT SPERO
Bar-Ilan University

Werner Kraft (ed.), *Briefe an Werner Kraft/Gershom Scholem*. Afterword by Jorg
  Drews. Frankfurt: Suhrkamp, 1986. 165 pp.

This volume of letters to the poet Werner Kraft enables one to learn much about the
young Scholem during the time he was a student and setting forth on his intellectual
trail. We meet him before he had become deeply versed in Kabbalah. The book
shows him immersed to an unusual extent in his studies, with a real zest for work
and broad interests in different fields: language, mathematics, literature. It also
reveals the concern of Scholem for Kraft (on whose behalf he was ready to make
great efforts); and, last but not least, it relates the interesting chapter of Scholem's
hostility to the German army.

The revolutionary character of Scholem in his attitude, both to his father and to
Germany, was described by him in his autobiography *From Berlin to Jerusalem* and
receives further corroboration in this work. Both books demonstrate his strong,
fearless antiauthoritarian attitude: a youth not afraid to oppose his father and leave
his home as well as ready to reject compulsory army service. Scholem's stance was
a rare exception in German Jewish history. Werner Kraft, to whom I talked before
writing these lines, suggested that Scholem appears to have resembled his father
both in character and talents.

In June 1917, the young Gerhard (Gershom) was inducted into the army; he
refused, however, to follow orders in the army camp and pretended to be psychotic.
One could not make out what had happened to him. Scholem, as Zalman Shazar
once told me, screamed constantly without stopping; he refused to look anybody in
the eye, lest it distract from his impersonation of a madman. He was guided, so he
later related, by intuition, as he had never read a book on mental illness. He was
finally declared unfit and released from the army as incurable. Whether the whole
thing was, in fact, rationally planned or whether he succumbed to some kind of
crisis, is not completely clear. Werner Kraft suggested that the army physicians
were probably Jewish and so more lenient toward him. On being discharged, he
went to study in Jena and Bern.

Politically, Scholem as an ardent Zionist was not on the German side in the War;
he thought that a British victory would be of advantage to the Jewish cause. In one
of his later writings, he gave expression to his strong anti-German sentiments and to
the feeling that Germany had treated its Jews unjustly.

When I asked Werner Kraft (alert at ninety-two years of age) how Scholem could
have written him letters from the army hospital if he was constantly screaming,
Kraft retorted that he must have pretended to be suffering from the kind of mental
disease in which the periods of sickness were interspersed with periods of normal
behavior. Interestingly enough, it should be mentioned that, years later, Scholem
ascribed to Shabbetai Zvi a disease of that sort.

He wrote to Kraft on July 14, 1917, two months after he was inducted:

> My state of health is, unfortunately, not good, because of terrible stress due to the
> struggle against the environment. I do have a chance to improve my health [though],
> since I have in the meanwhile been exempted from active duty and am working in the
> postal service, which is easier, until I go to the center for nervous disorders. The will to
> health may perhaps not help me as much as at other times, because another will is

stronger still. In a different environment my nerves would easily find that equilibrium, which here naturally has been upset (pp. 14–15).

Can we learn from this passage that he really was under great nervous strain? Be that as it may, he wrote to his friend on August 11 that the doctors had decided to release him shortly from army duty.

It remains an open question for me whether Scholem's rejection of the war was specifically related to Germany and its superfluous involvement in the First World War or whether he was committed to a general rejection of army service. I was his student when I met Scholem on the street in 1948 and was a soldier mobilized by the Haganah (Jerusalem was besieged and subject to heavy shelling by the Jordanians). To my surprise he expressed an attitude similar to that which had guided him in Germany. He was sorry that we students were serving in the army and had discontinued our studies; he remarked, "in the army they only take advantage of you."

Following his discharge in the First World War, he wrote to Kraft, "I consider my dismissal a victory for the intense efforts that I have made and that have cost me a great deal" (p. 21). As to the fact that the psychiatrist considered him unbalanced, he merely commented that it did "not mean much," and he added, "Besides, as far as the war is concerned I really *am* insane."

In the letters Scholem sought to imbue his friend with the resolve to reject the army. Thus, he could write, for example, "The spiritual center [in Palestine] is stronger than might, and there exists for us no other way, no other weapon against injustice and disorder than by overcoming it through concentration upon that center" (p. 25). He enumerated the evils of the army to Kraft and asked him why he did not want to stand up against it. What kind of weakness was holding him back? The army certainly did not need his compassion.

According to Scholem's statements in these letters, then, it was Zionism that led him to oppose Germany. He may, however, also have been affected by the strong hostility to the war of his brother Werner, who became an ardent Communist. The two of them formed an unusually strong opposition to their father, who, like most German Jews, was a good German patriot. In the Scholem family, the revolt of the younger generation was extremely strong. But in contrast to his brother and father, Scholem, of course, rediscovered Judaism.

Kraft, for his part, was weak. He served in the army, although he was extremely miserable as a soldier. He was sent to serve as a sanitary orderly in an army hospital for soldiers suffering from shell shock and hysteria. He found the army utterly objectionable; was afraid that he might not survive the war and, at times, he even contemplated suicide.

"You seek to remain mute," wrote Scholem, "but don't do that. Don't be silent. Silence will kill you, because you will be alone with your misfortune. *But I can suffer with you and I insist on my right to do so*" (p. 44). Or, again, "I consider it my great good fortune that I can stand by you and I will not desist."

In those years, they were friends with Walter Benjamin and, together, they formed a triangle. Benjamin is often mentioned in the letters and his thoughts are discussed. Yet if one compares Scholem's relationships with Walter Benjamin and with Kraft, one sees that his relations with Benjamin were more complicated and did not reveal the same devotion. As Kraft told me, Scholem was attracted to, but also afraid of, Benjamin—intimacy with so complicated a man could have destroyed his own life. It was probably out of this fear that Scholem appeared selfish in his letters to Benjamin. Scholem did not go out of his way to help Benjamin come to Palestine. It appears as though he could never fix a date for Benjamin's visit: Scholem was always very busy with his research. No doubt the difference in the correspondence depended on the different character of the recipient. (See, *Walter Benjamin—Gershom Scholem: Briefwechsel,* [1980].)

Scholem discovered Judaism early in life, and, for him, it meant East European Jewry, the Hebrew language and Eretz Israel. During the First World War, he encouraged Kraft to involve himself in the Judaism that he himself had discovered, one that had something of a folk character rather than being based on philosophies or ethical theories. East European Jews had come to play an important role in his life; he felt that he could talk to them and that they shared similar interests (p. 105). Scholem now developed his great admiration for Agnon. Whether the East European Jews could reciprocate such feelings is another question.

Parallel to his interest in the East European Jews was his passion for the Hebrew language, which he made enormous efforts to learn. Languages and the philosophy of language played an important role in his life, and this was true above all of Hebrew and its classics. In those years, he worked hard on the text of the Bible, its meaning and its translations (as well as on translation from Hebrew in general). "Judaism," he wrote to Kraft, "begins and ends with Hebrew" (p. 65). So great were Scholem's talents and so broad his interests that even at this early stage of his life he seemed like some giant, going his lonely way that he could share with no one.

Two great Jewish contemporary thinkers are mentioned in this volume, Hermann Cohen and Martin Buber. One might expect that Buber, with his penchant for myth and mysticism, would emerge as Scholem's favorite, whereas the aged Cohen, the Kantian who had no truck with such matters and attacked pantheism, would be alien to him; but the opposite was true. One finds a very harsh tone marking his references to Buber. He considered Buber inauthentic, whereas he was full of admiration for Hermann Cohen.

It is a well-known fact (as described in *From Berlin to Jerusalem*) that Scholem strongly disagreed with Buber regarding the Jewish attitude to the First World War. He was furious that Buber, a leading Zionist, had emerged as a war enthusiast. But here in the letters to Kraft we learn how critical he was of Buber's work on mysticism and of his ideas on "realization" as developed in *Daniel* (p. 50). He accused Buber of intellectual sterility and of borrowing from others, whereas silence for Scholem constituted the highest category of language. Buber, in his view, used his pen too much.

The relationship between the two, it appears, was complex and, for all his criticism, Scholem did take Buber seriously, visited him occasionally, participated in his quarterly, *Der Jude,* and admired the fact that Buber did not bristle if criticized. Nevertheless, it was Hermann Cohen whom he saw as the great man and the great Jew who had returned to faith. On Cohen's death in 1918, he wrote to Kraft that never had he "felt such a sadness over a person—and I hardly knew him.

How Jewish Cohen was I only experienced last winter; I would have never believed it'' (p. 80). Scholem attended some of Cohen's lectures delivered for Der Hochschule für Wissenschaft des Judentums after the aged philosopher had left Marburg to teach Judaism and philosophy at that institution. ''Cohen,'' concluded Scholem, ''will, in a superior sense, be my model.''

Life constantly surprises; reading this volume one would have never guessed that the writer of these letters would one day become the greatest scholar of Kabbalah in our century.

RIVKA HORWITZ
Ben-Gurion University of the Negev

Joel Ziff (ed.), *Lev Tuvia/On the Life and Work of Rabbi Tobias Geffen*. Newton, Mass.: Rabbi Tobias Geffen Memorial Fund, 1988. lxi + 200 pp.
Ronald Kronish (ed.), *Towards the Twenty-first Century: Judaism and the Jewish People in Israel and America/Essays in Honor of Rabbi Leon Kronish on the Occasion of his Seventieth Birthday*. New York: Ktav, 1988. 341 pp.

In recent years, increasing attention has been given to the history of the Orthodox rabbinate in America, and with good reason. Because this group claimed to represent Jewish tradition and was accepted as such by many immigrants, these rabbis had an impact on the immigrant experience even when they could not influence immigrants and their children to follow their example. Perhaps just as significant is the process by which immigrant rabbis from Eastern Europe adapted to American realities.

One of the more impressive rabbis who came to America in the beginning of the twentieth century was Rabbi Tobias Geffen. After arriving in the United States in 1903, he took rabbinical positions with a number of communities until he came to Atlanta, Georgia, in 1910. There he served as rabbi until his death at the age of ninety-nine in 1970. This memorial volume put out by his descendants serves not only as a fitting memorial to a beloved rabbi, but also as a very useful source for American Jewish history.

The English section of the book consists of two major parts—articles written by family members about different aspects of his life and career and translated selections from his writings. The descriptions of the day-to-day family life of a rabbi in the South are very revealing and reflect a reality quite different from the relatively well-documented life of New York Jewry. Perhaps the most interesting of these materials are the translated selections from Rabbi Geffen's diaries, which he kept regularly. The topics range from the rabbinical to the meteorological and include almost everything in between. This diary, even in excerpted form, is of historical interest not just for the information it contains but for the insight it provides into what the author felt was worth noting (and not noting) at the time.

The Hebrew section (sixty pages) consists mainly of homiletical material previously published elsewhere. The one legal responsum (also translated into English) is of interest because it deals with the kashrut of Coca Cola. It turns out that not only was Rabbi Geffen given access to the secret formula of Coca Cola but that he convinced the company to change a problematic ingredient for a kosher one!

The appendixes include a bibliography of works by and about Rabbi Geffen and, perhaps more important, a detailed catalogue of his papers held at the American Jewish Historical Society in Waltham, Massachusetts. Unfortunately, Rabbi Geffen's autobiography, privately printed in 1951, was not republished here.

Editors and authors of memorial volumes usually have warm feelings toward the individual so honored and the family members who edited and wrote many of the articles in this book make no secret of the deep affection and respect they have for Rabbi Geffen. However, the fascinating career that they have documented and the revealing primary material they have organized—often translated into English but not "touched up"—should make this book of value to a wide circle of readers interested in American Jewish history.

The volume of studies in honor of Rabbi Leon Kronish is very different in nature. Although there is ample reference to the honoree and his manifold activities, the essays in the book are devoted more to the issues of interest to him. After an opening essay by Elie Wiesel entitled "On Teaching Peace," the volume is divided into three main sections. The first deals with the future of Israel; the second deals with the future of American Judaism, and is introduced by a transitional essay by Ronald Kronish (son of the honoree and editor of the volume) on Israel and the Diaspora. The last section of the book consists of a number of articles written by Rabbi Kronish himself over the course of years.

Any book that devotes itself to the future is by definition easily dated; obviously, with the course of time and the passage of events, some of the predictions will be borne out but many more will be rendered irrelevant. Gradually, the book will lose some of its usefulness as a guide for planning and thought. On the other hand, the reflective essays of which this volume is composed are a good source for an understanding of the present.

True, they hold no surprises. Most are written by well-known figures whose views are no secret. However, as a group, they provide insight into the ideologies that motivate an important segment of contemporary Jewish activists. For this purpose, not only the original and thought-provoking, but also the less exciting, are of value. This is a useful sourcebook for those interested in contemporary Jewish thought.

Among the more interesting papers are Irving Greenberg's essay, "Toward a Principled Pluralism," which deals with the complex issue of cooperation and dialogue among the different branches of the Jewish community; and Paula Hyman's short piece on "Jewish Studies and the Jewish College Experience," which raises important questions on the functions, real and anticipated, of academic Jewish studies today. A similar question is raised, in a very different context, in Ephraim Shapira's "'Living with the Bible': Feasibility or Deception."

SHAUL STAMPFER
The Hebrew University

Levi Meier (ed.), *Jewish Values in Bioethics*. Philadelphia: Human Sciences Press, 1986. 195 pp.

Of all subjects in the field of ethics and philosophy, none is of greater public interest than medical ethics. Subjects such as those related to the inception or termination of life are of universal interest; the array of new issues resulting from technological advances are more fascinating than science fiction; and the dilemmas are often heartrending. The field, if judged by the number of publications, journals and symposia, has burgeoned incredibly over the past few decades.

The present volume is a useful introduction to Jewish medical ethics for the layman. The editor, Rabbi Dr. Levi Meier, the chaplain of the Cedars Sinai Medical Center in Los Angeles and a practicing psychotherapist, has assembled a series of public lectures in medical ethics given at the hospital. Because of the nature of the material, each chapter is necessarily relatively short and simply written at a popular level. The authors include most of the familiar faces in the field: Immanuel Jakobovits, Fred Rosner, David Bleich and David Feldman. But the editor has broadened the base of the book and the subject matter considerably by the inclusion of several distinguished scholars not normally classified as specialists in medical ethics.

Irving Greenberg's challenging and thought-provoking essay, the longest in the book, provides a valuable perspective on the philosophy of Judaism, in general, and the role of medicine and the physician within this context. And Emanuel Rackman's discussion of the halakhic process describes his minority, maverick position within the Orthodox rabbinate, one that many of his colleagues reject as being more in line with that of the Conservative movement.

The tragic Holocaust experience is one that cannot be ignored by any serious thinker in the field. The editor wisely included two moving pieces by Elie Weisel and Victor Frankl that are particularly relevant to the relationships between physician and patient.

The editor himself draws upon his practical experience in opening and closing the volume. All in all, the volume provides the layman with an easily readable and valuable introduction to the field of Jewish medical ethics.

SHIMON GLICK
Ben-Gurion University of the Negev, University Center for Health Services and Sciences in the Negev

Paul Mendes-Flohr (ed.), *The Philosophy of Franz Rosenzweig.*, Vol. 8, Tauber Institute for the Study of European Jewry Series. Hanover, N.H., and London: University Press of New England, for Brandeis University Press, 1988. x + 260 pp.

This book of essays by distinguished thinkers, some of whom knew Rosenzweig personally, adds up to an imposing and significant presentation. In his introduction,

Paul Mendes-Flohr sets the tone of the book with his assertion that "both ideationally and spiritually there is a continuity between his [Rosenzweig's] deep involvement in the philosophical tradition of German Idealism and his later theocentric affirmation of Judaism." At the same time the volume makes clear Rosenzweig's departure from Hegel, who erred in ascribing an ontological status to history. For history, according to Rosenzweig, is not the unfolding of being but the discrete act of man. Convinced that traditional philosophy could not proceed beyond Hegel and his conflation of reason and the history of philosophy, Rosenzweig strove for a new mode of philosophizing in speech-thinking (*Sprachdenken*), which combines time and the spoken word with the uniqueness of truth.

Mendes-Flohr thus ushers in a group of essays, most of which were selected from a philosophical symposium held in Jerusalem in 1980 on the fiftieth anniversary of Rosenzweig's death. Gershom Scholem's essay on *The Star of Redemption*, however, is from a memorial address he gave in 1930. In it, Scholem points out that even after Rosenzweig freed himself from the spell of Hegel's philosophy, it left its impress on him for a long time, as the form and inner style of his masterpiece *The Star of Redemption* testify. Reiner Wiehl supplies the necessary counteremphasis by pointing out in his essay that "experience" in Rosenzweig's "new thinking" freed itself from the spell of scientific thinking. Abundance and multiplicity now have priority over unity, the new and unique over the universal, contingency over necessity and law.

Nathan Rotenstreich in his essay on "Rosenzweig's Notion of Metaethics" introduces a welcome note of criticism by pointing out that Rosenzweig did not give due attention to the societal aspect of human existence, as a result of which his whole exposition of the position of man is inadequate. Rosenzweig's entire anthropological approach is characterized by an attempt to make self-enclosure so radical that only revelation and divine miracle can open man to dialogue. As a result, Rosenzweig's primary presentation may well be tainted by the general bias of his system. Rotenstreich also cautions against classifying Rosenzweig as an existentialist *tout court;* in Rosenzweig's view, the whole scope of existence is yet to unfold, while existentialism includes the broader coordinates of existence at the very beginning of its analysis.

A signal contribution to this volume is Bernhard Caspar's essay on "Responsibility Rescued," in which Caspar ties Rosenzweig's concept of responsibility to the absolute character of the other that calls and affirms me, to the disappointment that reveals to me the otherness of the other, to the criterion of truth as its ability to establish a bond between persons and to the direction of responsibility toward the absolute. In his essay on "Rosenzweig and Hegel," Otto Poeggeler points out, "Despite all his criticism of Buber's dialogical principle, Rosenzweig replaced the I that dialectically disposes of ideas by the dialogue of Thou and I that leads respectively to revelation and Redemption."

In his penetrating essay on time and the eternal in Rosenzweig's view of history, Alexander Altmann lays bare, without criticizing, the truly awful dualism in which Rosenzweig relegates the Jew and Judaism to an eternity beyond history and worldly creativity. But at the end of his essay Altmann states that Rosenzweig's history hovers between time and eternity in such a way that "one fails to see how the final day can be reached with the Jew eternally at the goal and the Christian eternally on the way.''

Another important essay in this book is Paul Mendes-Flohr's ''Franz Rosenzweig and the Crisis of Historicism,'' which points out that Rosenzweig's conception of a necessary dialectic between metahistory and history emerged from a protracted struggle with the dilemma of historical relativism. Rosenzweig vigorously rejected the idea of historical progress, yet passionately affirmed growth and even perfection in time.

The most surprising essay in this book is that of Moshe Idel in which he points out that *The Star of Redemption* clearly offers us a version of the Lurianic Kabbalah, placing the idea of *tikkun* (the mending of the world through the reunification of God with the exiled sparks of the divine) at the center of Jewish religious experience and making the keeping of the commandments the key to achieving the unity of God. Also of note is the essay on ''The Concept of Language in Rosenzweig's Thought,'' in which Rosenzweig's friend and biographer, Nahum N. Glatzer, points out a paradox in Rosenzweig's relation to speech that is entirely absent, one notes, in that of Martin Buber:

> From Rosenzweig's explanation one gains the impression that *The Star,* which uses the new method of speech-thinking, is indeed concerned with the word exchanged between human beings, with human speech that awakens the I in a fellow human; that in its view dialogue is an interhuman dialogue and love more than a simile and metaphor. But when we go back to the text of *The Star,* we are confronted with the fact that word, speech and language take place in the sphere between God and man; that it is God who awakens the I in the human person; that language in most instances is the language of prayer and hymn addressed to the Godhead; and that love is a sacred state communicated to man in revelation and answered by man in sacred devotion.

MAURICE FRIEDMAN
San Diego State University

Michael A. Meyer, *Response to Modernity: A History of the Reform Movement in Judaism.* New York: Oxford University Press, 1988. 494 pp.

Modernity transformed all aspects of Western culture in the nineteenth century. The American and French revolutions challenged traditional notions of authority and the promise of freedom, equality and individualism radically altered Western consciousness. The economic developments that accompanied the political revolutions contributed to massive population movements, which, in turn, destabilized traditional patterns of social organization and undermined the idea that morality and religion are eternal verities. The transformation of Europe both by those who welcomed the change and those who regarded the change with horror demanded a response.

What did religious reform mean in the context of the dynamic transformation of Western culture in the nineteenth century? Although all Western religions were affected by modernity, Judaism faced special problems. The corporate and consensual nature of Judaism made it especially vulnerable to the promises of modernity.

Judaism lacked both the authoritarian controls of Catholicism, which checked the extreme aspects of modernity, and the radical individualism of Protestantism, which was so compatible with modernism.

Meyer has set himself an ambitious goal in his latest work, *Responses to Modernity: A History of the Reform Movement.* In it, he seeks to encompass the institutional, intellectual, political and social aspects of the Jewish response to modernity in global terms. The volume is comprehensive and encyclopedic, but it does not present either new research or a startlingly novel thesis. Instead, it is a survey and synthesis of previous studies of the Reform movement. Meyer concentrates on description rather than engaging in the analytical discussion the subject calls for.

Following the usual pattern prevailing in descriptions of the Reform movement, Meyer examines in some detail the conditions in Germany. He retells the story of the founding of the Hamburg Temple, the preparation of new prayer books and the eventual institutionalization of mixed seating. What emerges from this account is how conservative and limited were the innovations in German Reform.

The contrast is most dramatic when the author relates the history of the Reform movement in North America. From the very beginning, the lay leadership of American synagogues responded radically to the conditions facing them in the New World. In contrast to Germany, Austria and France, the United States did not have a state religion or a ministry of religion to oversee and enforce communal unity. In America, religions have been treated simply as voluntary associations, thus the unity of a religious community has always been in jeopardy. Nonetheless, the Reform movement achieved greater unity in America during its early life than it had in Europe. For almost fifty years, Jewish immigration to America was homogeneously German. German Reform provided rabbinic, intellectual and spiritual leadership to American Jews. Unity disintegrated with the arrival of the great masses of Jewish immigrants from Eastern Europe.

Meyer also describes the development of the Reform movement in France, Austria and Italy as well as offering a glance at its growth in South America, South Africa, Canada and Israel. What emerges from this global survey is that Judaism has taken on the color of the religious and political institutions dominant in the host culture. In Catholic Austria, Reform was more conservative than in Protestant Germany and developed forms that were analogous to those of the Catholic Church; in Germany, the models were found in Lutheranism.

In his opening chapter, Meyer tries to define the Reform movement in terms of the evolution characteristic of Judaism over the centuries: change in Judaism is not a new phenomenon. He notes that all the elements we associate with Reform, including the organ (introduced in the Prague synagogue), antedated the beginnings of the movement in Germany in the nineteenth century. Meyer tries to account for the difference between these prior changes and the transformation that he identifies specifically with Reform. His solution to the problem of definition rests in the provocative distinction between reforming Jewish life and reforming Judaism. Presumably, this means that changes were made in Jewish practice prior to the nineteenth century, whereas after that time the goal was to reform Judaism itself. However, this is not a viable distinction. Changes in practice transform Judaism, and the reform of Judaism transforms practice.

But more serious than this problem is the fact that the distinction masks the most potent aspect of modernity—the intellectual lure and power that made it a corrosive force with regard to Judaism.

Jewish thinkers have always been attracted to their intellectual environment. Historically, Judaism has appropriated non-Jewish elements and transformed them into Jewishly relevant concepts and values relevant to Judaism. What distinguishes the Jewish response to modernity from traditional Jewish borrowing is that for modern Jews the standard of acceptability and respectability derives much more from external models than from traditional Judaism. In the contemporary world, Judaism accommodates itself to the assumptions and values of modernity.

That Judaism lives in symbiosis with the host culture in the Diaspora is virtually axiomatic. In light of this, there is a need for more comprehensive conceptualizations of the problem of cultural encounter and transformation. As Jacob Neusner points out repeatedly, there is no such thing as autonomous Jewish history, but only Jewish history in the context of national or continental history. Meyer does not adequately detail the diversity of the various historical contexts and does not address the frameworks within which the responses to modernity find their rationale. There is no discussion of the meaning or dynamics of modernity with its promise of freedom, equality and individualism.

The most serious omissions are those of the relationship between secular and religious authority. Meyer touches on the tension between the demand for personal decision and communal unity, but only within the context of Judaism itself. Even here, however, he ignores the problematic nature of religious authority in a cultural context that promises personal freedom and civil liberty.

Reform views itself as an attempt to blunt the impact of modernity. But as Meyer shows, Reform thinkers were as entangled in the canons and values of modernity as the vast majority of educated Jews (and most Christians). It is a moot point whether Reform has saved Jews for Judaism. If it has (as is probably true in America), it does so at great cost. Reform Jews in the nineteenth century self-consciously cut their ties with tradition. In so doing, within a generation or two, they no longer knew what had been reformed. In America, the Reform movement is coming to realize that the need to reappropriate the tradition is necessary for religious survival and for an authentic life within the milieu of modernity.

BERNARD ZELECHOW
York University

ISRAEL AND ZIONISM

Asher Arian and Michal Shamir (eds.), *The Elections in Israel 1984*. Tel-Aviv: Ramot, 1986. 300 pp.

The Elections in Israel 1984 is the fifth book in a series that Asher Arian began editing after the 1969 general elections. Although the first four books in the series—

covering the elections of 1969, 1973, 1977 and 1981—were edited solely by Arian, this time Michal Shamir of Tel-Aviv University also took part.

The series should be regarded as a major contribution to the field of electoral studies in Israel. A number of other major works on elections and voting behavior in Israel have been published since the series began, and even during the 1960s. Nevertheless, the Tel-Aviv series has given Israeli research in this field a sense of continuity that was previously lacking.

The present volume consists of fourteen articles, divided into six sections. Arian and Shamir are responsible for the introduction and the epilogue, respectively. Uriel Ben-Hanan (The Hebrew University), Benny Temkin and Gideon Doron (both Tel-Aviv University) deal with the economics of Israeli elections. Efraim Torgovnik (Tel-Aviv University), Ilan Greilsammer (Bar-Ilan University) and Hanna Herzog (Tel-Aviv University) focus on competing political parties. Nadim Rouhana (Van Leer Institute), Joseph Ginat (Haifa University), Ehud Sprinzak (The Hebrew University), Gershon Shafir and Yoav Peled (both Tel-Aviv University) investigate polarization among Jews and Arabs; articles by Nurit Gertz (Tel-Aviv University), Yael Yishai (Haifa University) and Michael Keren (Tel-Aviv University) are included in a section entitled "Rhetoric and Opinion."

As is the case in most edited volumes, the papers differ considerably in their theoretical and methodological approaches as well as in their analytical depth and scholarly value. And again, as is common in such collective efforts that cover electoral campaigns in other countries (e.g., Howard Penniman's "At the Polls" series), the selection of subjects covered by the various contributors tends to be arbitrary.

Thus, there is an article about the Kach list and two articles concerning the Arab voters but no single article is fully devoted to either of the two major contestants— the Alignment and the Likud. Those involved in the campaign management of these two parties may rightfully claim that the descriptions included in some of the articles are not completely accurate.

Nevertheless, Arian should be congratulated for his ongoing endeavor as manifested in this important and unique series. One must also commend Michal Shamir for her collaboration on this volume and possibly on the coming 1988 volume. The collection should be recommended to any student of the Israeli political system. One hopes that many volumes on future elections will follow with even more impressive contributions.

ABRAHAM DISKIN
The Hebrew University

Eliezer Ben-Rafael, *Status, Power and Conflict in the Kibbutz.* Avebury: Aldershot, 1988. 166 pp.

This book is in very many ways as difficult as it is important to read, especially for the English-speaking student of the kibbutz. It is important because it assembles an impressive battery of subjective evidence concerning the politics of kibbutz life, as the title of the book indicates. The author reports on several different research projects that share an essentially emic perspective, namely, one based on the subjective perspectives of the kibbutz members themselves—itself a welcome contribution to the sociology of the kibbutz. The data encompass 627 subjects from twenty-nine kibbutzim, on the basis of which, among other things, the author is able to generate multidimensional subjective status profiles; an analysis of conflictual occurrences in forty-three kibbutzim; and a data set of biographical profiles of executive incumbents in sixteen kibbutzim. Out of all this data, the reader receives an account of perceived status and power differentials in kibbutzim, along with some understanding of their operation and their consequences.

But having said that this work is important to read, we are left with the major difficulty, namely, the theoretical interpretation of this rich mosaic of data. The issue is that there does not seem to be a consistent overall interpretation but rather a collection of typologies and antinomies that are problematic in their own right and especially so in concert.

To be more specific, it has to be said, first, that the whole book is poorly served by a weak translation from the Hebrew into what is often simply not idiomatic English. Second, the conceptual paradigm of the book, the API (the authority-prestige-influence dimension), which is supposed to play the analytic role that SES (socioeconomic status) plays in the stratification analysis of modern society at large, appears to this reviewer as an inadequate superimposition on the data. Third, the theoretical significance of the work as a contribution to general stratification analysis seems to be, at least in some degree, overstated. Fourth, and this is really the most regrettable point, these methodological claims obfuscate the real theoretical insights that do appear in the book and that, in fact, are a natural outcome of the data analysis as presented by the author. The concept of decollectivization, coined by Ben-Rafael, predates much contemporary discussion in the kibbutz media today of the limits of the collective as opposed to the members—limits that have become manifest during the current socioeconomic crisis with which the kibbutz movement is grappling.

From the data the author presents, we receive unquestionable evidence that the contemporary heterogeneous multigenerational kibbutz has structurally distributed power and status differentials. That is to say, at any one time there are those who have more power and status than others, there are conflicts and in the conflicts there are winners and losers—and some are more often winners than others. The author chooses to find an explanation for these phenomena in the antinomy between the "egalitarian ethos" and the "meritocratic philosophy" of the kibbutz or, elsewhere, in the contradiction between the "spirit of democracy" and the "spirit of capitalism" where capitalism, as he sees it, stands for progress (p. 147).

It is difficult to see why these theoretical concepts were necessary at all in the exposition (just as it is not clear to what extent the API index, once expounded, is actually used in the author's own empirical analysis), unless the point is to assert that the stratification process in the kibbutz, as elsewhere, is both unavoidable and irreversible. Stemming as it does from a subjective perspective, this viewpoint seems to this reviewer to be unnecessarily deterministic as well as an unwarranted reification of the kibbutz structure. It is unwarranted because of its theoretically based insistence that the differentials in power and status among members are the genetic outcome of a social class structure. The task facing the contemporary kibbutz is not the abolition of its latent class structure, but the maintenance of its collective social order. Indeed, Ben-Rafael's own discussion of the dynamics of social conflict certainly lends plausibility to this alternative interpretation.

Ben-Rafael discusses what he calls the "usurpative" process, wherein through conflict, interest groups get a bigger share of the collective pie, itself normatively defined, than they apparently "ought" to. Here the interpretation is ambiguous, since it is difficult to know from the analysis just which interpretation of the common good is the sociologically appropriate one: that of the kibbutz institutions, which by definition identify their will with the common good and are, therefore, being usurped, or that of the usurpers, who are pursuing their legitimate (or illegitimate?) interests. However, rather than discussing this interest-group perspective in isolation, it would have been more useful, both theoretically and empirically, to have linked it to the analysis of decollectivization. Such an approach would have made it possible to understand the differentials in status and power among members, as shown in Ben-Rafael's data, as well as their institutional consequences for the kibbutz. Whether these processes and theories have implications for the larger society or for sociological stratification theory is best left for the reader to judge.

DAVID MITTELBERG
University of Haifa

Mitchell Cohen (ed.), *Class Struggle and the Jewish Nation: Selected Essays in Marxist Zionism by Ber Borochov*. New Brunswick: Transaction Books, 1984. 218 pp.

Ber Borochov died in Kiev on December 17, 1917, a respected party leader, brilliant theoretician and renaissance man who left unfinished work in diverse fields. As Mitchell Cohen's selection of Borochov's work indicates, the chief effort of this Marxist Zionist was his attempt to ground Zionist ideology in the materialistic approach to history, an important issue for the Jewish intelligentsia in Russia at the beginning of this century. However, this is not the full extent of Borochov's achievements.

Borochov joined the Russian Social Democratic Labor party at age 19, in Ekaterinoslav, but was never an ardent disciple of any of that party's leaders or factions. In 1901, he was expelled for his Zionist leanings, despite his active role in strengthening Zionism's Marxist underpinnings.

The Poale Zion party, of which Borochov was a founder and leader, was an interesting phenomenon within both the Zionist subworld of Eastern Europe and the international socialist movement. The editor's introduction provides an able historical survey of the period, describing the crystallization and development of Borochov's ideas.

Borochovism was multifaceted, and students of the subject cannot ignore any of its aspects. Its principal feature was Borochov's attempt to consolidate what Cohen calls Marxist Zionism. He went to great lengths to define the "materialistic basis" that had underpinned Jewish national existence during its two thousand years of exile. In this he was opposed to Karl Kautsky—who regarded Judaism essentially as a religion—as well as to Lenin and Stalin—who denied the possibility of a Jewish national revival. Similarly, he denied the sociological validity of the other theories of Jewish assimilation. His main ideological target in Jewish politics was the Bund, the Jewish Social Democratic party. Borochov's nationalist theories are outlined in his essay, "The National Question and the Class Struggle." This important milestone in Borochov's thought was a response to those in the socialist camp who denied the existence and unity of the Jewish people; it is comparable in its sophistication and caliber to the work of Kautsky, Karl Renner, Otto Bauer and others who addressed the national problem from the Marxist perspective.

Borochov's intellectual prowess and originality of thought stood him in good stead when he challenged the regnant Marxist dogmas of his day (he denounced Georgy Plekhanov's deterministic methodology and supported Bogdanov's empiromonism). His concept of the "conditions of production" provided Borochov with the basis to explain the separate development of nations and ethnic groups during the period of modernization and capitalist growth. He described the nation as an entity in its own right, shaped by the processes of historical change. He therefore understood the continued existence of the Jews as a people in the Diaspora, their emigration patterns and, finally, the process that was bringing them to territorial concentration in Palestine as the manifestation of objective social forces. (Further examination is required to pinpoint exactly what he meant, in different contexts, when he referred to such deterministic or "stychic" processes.)

Though he was not identified as a proponent of socialist "constructivism" in Palestine and was totally ignorant with regard to the Arab question, some of his views still have a contemporary relevance meriting further study. Interest in Borochov's writings (including the appearance of this English translation) is of more than a historical-academic nature. Borochov, after all, was a spokesman for the "realistic," as opposed to the chauvinistic variety of nationalism that so often is seen as the "normal" road for nations to tread.

Lyuba Borochov, his wife, recounts that when they once stayed at Liège, in Belgium, Borochov had the occasion to discuss with Lenin the synthesis of Zionism and socialism. Lenin said jokingly, "That would be sitting in two chairs; actually, not on two chairs, but in the space between them." This troubled Borochov and remains troubling, if we consider the anomalous position of the Jews in Soviet Russia to this day.

Mitchell Cohen's collection demonstrates evidence of thorough research, and it is to his credit that he has included new translations as well as updated material. The collection is certainly representative and includes articles from the years 1905 to 1917, a glossary including biographical data and the names of parties and terms essential for understanding of the subject. The introduction is a knowledgeable survey of the different phases in Borochov's life and his struggles. I am in agreement with Cohen's conclusion that "Borochov's legacy is thus that of a theorist and political figure who insisted on asserting the particular needs of his people without negating the internationalist spirit. This internationalism refused to be self-denying" (p. 32). Similarly, I agree that the controversy over the communal settlements in Palestine was to a certain degree a reflection of "the ongoing dispute between Marxist and anarchist models for reshaping society" (p. 28). However, I doubt that Cohen has said the definitive and last word on the development of Borochov's ideas toward the end of his life.

AVRAHAM YASSOUR
University of Haifa

Mitchell Cohen, *Zion and State: Nation, Class and the Shaping of Modern Israel.* Oxford: Basil Blackwell, 1987. 322 pp.

Where did the Israeli labor movement go wrong? What unseated the Israeli Labor party, which (together with Sweden's SAP) held the longest record of uninterrupted rule in the West? What turned the promise of an egalitarian, idealistic "society of workers" into the reality of a bureaucratized, elite-dominated and deeply stratified society in which political discourse is dominated by the categories of *nation* and *state,* instead of *class?* These are significant, albeit not exactly new, questions in the literature on Israel in political science and related fields. And Mitchell Cohen is well qualified to take them up again. Although he is not an Israeli but an American Jew, he is no casual observer from afar. His command of sources is impressive and extends to original research in Israeli archives.

In answer to the question, "What went wrong?" *Zion and State* puts forward, in essence, three central claims. First, although the volume is by no means a polemical tract, it places the locus of the labor movement's decline firmly within the ideological sphere. The labor movement is said to have "de-ideologized" itself by jettisoning an extraordinary socialist potential in favor of the state-centeredness (state "reification") known in Hebrew as *mamlakhtiyut.* Second, Cohen sees in this transformation of "political culture" the key to both the labor movement's success *and* its eventual collapse. Historically, Mapai could not have attained the leadership of the Zionist movement without compromising its class character. It fought off the Revisionist challenge by internalizing the Revisionist premise that "the nation and the state were and should be entities above class." The irony is that in the realities of post-1967, Jabotinsky's heirs could make a stronger claim than the labor movement to be the true representatives of this ideology. Third, it follows that Cohen dates the socialist fall from grace—the rise of *mamlakhtiyut* and the delegitimization of the labor movement's claim to privileged status—to the 1930s rather than to the period after 1948. By implication, this casts doubt on the validity of other interpretations of why *mamlakhtiyut* triumphed—for instance, the view that Ben-Gurion exploited the instruments of statehood to neutralize the labor Left or, alternatively, that in order to draw the mass immigration of Middle Eastern origin into Mapai, the party of labor was impelled to decouple itself from laborism.

Substantively, *Zion and State* is subdivided into three main sections. The first (the least integrated with the central theme of the volume) contains a survey of the literature on nationalism and a historical overview of emergent Zionism as an idea and a movement. In the second part, the core of the book, Cohen traces the rise of the labor movement in Palestine and within the Zionist movement worldwide. His principal focus is on the confrontation between labor and Revisionism, both at the level of ideas and in terms of substantive political developments. The final section of the volume documents the political consequences of sovereignty, including several case studies of how labor movement institutions were "nationalized" and subordinated to the state. Overall, although the book is relatively long and detailed, it is well written and clearly enunciates its central thesis. If for no other reason than the absence in the English language until now of a political history of the Israeli labor movement on this scale, Cohen has made a worthwhile contribution. For those familiar with the Hebrew-language literature, however, the book breaks little or no new factual ground. The opinion of the informed reader must therefore rest on the validity of Cohen's interpretation of what went wrong. This reader was not convinced.

To make the claim that socialism was eclipsed by nationalism in the Israeli labor movement means necessarily to raise complex and contested issues, which *Zion and State* unaccountably sidesteps. An obvious problem in this context is whether the weltanschauung embraced by the leaders and mainstream followers of Mapai and the Histadrut ever truly reflected, in Cohen's words, "radical class politics." The "constructive" socialism of labor Zionism may have been revolutionary in a number of respects, but it was also marked by two rather unsavory departures from socialist principle. First, it rejected class solidarity between Jewish and Arab workers; instead, it opted for national exclusivity, a working partnership between the Jewish labor movement and the Jewish middle class, including the bourgeois elements that dominated the Zionist movement. And second, it developed a socioeconomic system based, in part, on enterprises owned de jure by the workers (i.e., by the Histadrut) but not controlled by them de facto. Cohen never faces up to these contradictions, nor to the question they inevitably raise of whether the failure of the labor movement to fulfill its socialist promise was a *structural* inevitability. His book is also very meager in describing the concrete content of the radicalism and "anticipatory socialism" that he claims to have discerned in the pre-*mamlakhtiyut* labor movement; and it is not specific concerning the transition to socialism, which (Cohen believes) represented a real alternative path that Israeli politics and society could have followed. In these respects, *Zion and State* is hardly more persuasive than the standard self-conception of its own history developed by the labor movement itself. This is not what we expect from a volume billed by its author as a "critical interpretive analysis."

The idea that *mamlakhtiyut* killed socialism in Israel actually has a long history. It is the core of what might be called "the Mapam version of history," a view that has been expressed in systematic scholarly works as well as in ongoing political debates. (In this connection, the absence of any reference in Cohen's book to the work of Henry Rosenfeld or Gadi Yatziv is surprising, particularly on the part of an author otherwise so well informed.) Cohen's contributions to this school of thought are worthy, but not startlingly new. At the theoretical level, he defines *mamlakhtiyut* as state "reification" and "fetishism." Empirically, Cohen stresses the historical fact that Mapai turned away from socialism before rather than after statehood (despite the contrary belief of some naive observers). The argument is couched in terms—Mapai's embrace of "segmented pluralism," elsewhere known as "consociationalism"—that are again well entrenched in the literature, as is the case in the work of Dan Horowitz and Moshe Lissak.

A related and far more damaging omission is the failure to develop an *analysis* of why Mapam and the more radical movements to its left were unable to steer Mapai toward the socialist and movement-oriented politics that Cohen, echoing their critique, retrospectively champions. In contrast, even though there is not much new to be said about the historic failure of the Revisionists (as shown by Cohen's treatment, which is inferior, for example, to the prior work of Lilly Weissbrod, also passed over in *Zion and State*), the Revisionist challenge is the subject of nearly three whole chapters. One would hardly have known from reading this book that according to Walter Laqueur, for example, in the period of the Third Aliyah, there was a time when "it seemed likely that a substantial part of the urban workers would desert Zionism and join the Communists" (*A History of Zionism,* 1972, p. 306). The fact that in the 1940s there was a real possibility that Mapai would be pulled sharply to the left by Mapam and its predecessors is at least awarded three pages, but Cohen does not tell us why this potential was not realized.

My final note of reservation concerning Cohen's work is more subjective in that it involves a disagreement with his choice of theoretical perspective. Politics are sometimes analyzed as a system of power, sometimes as an arena in which deeper sociological and economic forces receive expression. Cohen, however, has chosen to treat the voluntaristic realm of ideas and the dominant personalities (Ben-Gurion and Jabotinsky) who formulate them as the core of political culture and thereby of politics. Most significant, class is treated as an ideal rather than as an analytical point of departure for historical analysis. Consequently, the reader emerges without any sense of how politics in Palestine and in Israel have been shaped by political economy. Thus, for example, the weakness of the Jewish working class in the labor market of Mandatory Palestine; the compatible economic interests of the workers and of the very sizable petite bourgeoisie in the Yishuv; and the fact that Jewish capitalists had fragmented interests and were partly overshadowed in the economic realm by "national capital," appear to this writer at least to provide clues indispensable to understanding the rise to political dominance of Mapai. The other dimension of analysis pointedly neglected in *Zion and State* is the conflict between Zionism and the Arabs, tellingly described in the volume's preface as a subset of "Zionist foreign policy," and specifically excluded from its terms of reference. Here, too, we might have expected a critical, Marxissant study such as Cohen's to pay attention to political economy.

To illustrate, a strong case can be made (as a recently published book by Gershon Shafir suggests) that it was the economics of competition between penniless Jewish settlers and Arab laborers that propelled the former into the arms of the Zionist movement. The *halutzim* set in motion the political dynamics that would lead to the formation of Mapai and to its imperative quest for control of the Zionist institutions that subsidized their existence in Palestine. The labor movement discovered early in its history the benefits of defining its conflict with the Arabs in national terms, and its leaders repeatedly exploited the politics of the national conflict as a successful means of mass political mobilization and competition with political rivals.

In this connection, although many would agree with Cohen that labor itself paved the way for the ultimate triumph of its historic enemies on the Right, I doubt whether this development is to be explained primarily by the banal idea that a nonsocialist *mamlakhtiyut* opened up an ideological vacuum ready to be exploited by Menahem Begin. Instead, labor's "reification" of *the national conflict*—specifically, of territorial expansion, settlement and "security"—was what opened the way to the remarkable ideological success of "neo-Zionism."

MICHAEL SHALEV
The Hebrew University

Naomi W. Cohen, *The Year After the Riots: American Responses to the Palestine Crisis of 1929–1930.* Detroit: Wayne State University Press, 1988. 210 pp.

The dispute over Jewish services at the Western Wall that had begun on Yom Kippur of 1928 reached its climax after Tisha B'Av the following year (15 August 1929) with a widespread Arab attack on Jewish settlements and communities in Jerusalem, Hebron and Safad. The toll of these riots was 133 Jewish dead and 339 wounded. The British police and army were unprepared to handle the situation, in spite of early warnings that Arab riots were in the making. During the first critical days of the violence, the British were mainly passive. Only the quickly improvised intervention of the Haganah in Jerusalem prevented further massacre.

The bloody "events" of 1929, as the pogrom was called in the Yishuv, involved much more than a local religious dispute about the control of the Western Wall. Growing Arab nationalism, on the one hand, and the rise of the right-wing Revisionist party, on the other hand, contributed to the tense atmosphere. Furthermore, the gradual British retreat from support for the establishment of a Jewish National Home in Palestine led the Mandatory authorities to abandon its balanced policy, turning more and more in favor of the Arabs. This trend encouraged Arab extremists.

The riots of 1929 reinforced this development, bringing about a clear reversal in Britain's Palestine policy. The Passfield White Paper of 1930, based on the recommendations of the Shaw Commission and the Hope–Simpson report, was not favorably disposed to the Zionist enterprise, which it described as dangerous to the Arab economy. The White Paper seriously restricted Jewish immigration and settlement. Before the riots, the anti-Zionist position was mainly supported by officials in the Colonial Office and the Foreign Office; now it became the official policy of the British government. The events of 1929–1930 intensified the political debates in the Yishuv between the labor movement, the Revisionist camp and the Brith Shalom group, focusing the discussion on Jewish attitudes toward the Arabs, the role of Great Britain and settlement strategies. Zionist defense policy was also subjected to a thorough examination, the outcome of which was the establishment of the Irgun Bet, an organization independent of, and rival to, the Haganah.

The causes of the riots in 1929, the growing British alienation from Zionism, the reaction of the Yishuv, the foundation of the Irgun Bet, the political upheaval in the Zionist movement after the publication of the Passfield White Paper—all these have received due historical attention. Scholarly works have dealt extensively with the period. However, although the attitude of Franklin D. Roosevelt to the Holocaust and to the Jewish refugees and the role of Truman in the events that led to the establishment of the state of Israel are by now well researched, American reactions to the riots of 1929 are virtually unknown. That gap in American Jewish history has now been filled by Naomi W. Cohen's book.

Although the U.S. government had registered its support of the Balfour Declaration and even though eight American citizens had been killed and fifteen wounded in the riots of 1929, the Hoover administration refused to intervene, maintaining the course of noninvolvement that dominated American foreign policy in the 1920s. As a matter of fact, isolationist policy was a good pretext for State Department officials, who tended to oppose the Zionist program anyway, to urge the administration not to impose American influence on the situation in Palestine.

Several factors contributed to this American diplomatic approach. Zionism as a national movement had been regarded as harmful to American investments in the Ottoman Empire. Powerful Protestant missionary societies in the Middle East, whose sympathies lay with the Arabs rather than the Jews, were influential in American opinion. Secretary of State Robert Lansing opposed President Wilson's support of the Balfour Declaration on the grounds that many Christians would resent "turning the Holy Land over to the absolute control of the race credited with the death of Christ" (p. 19). State Department officials sometimes depicted Zionists as arrogant Communists. And there were certain antisemitic impulses at work in American anti-Zionism.

One of the key individuals who prompted the State Department to adopt anti-Zionist arguments was Paul Knabenshue, the American consul-general in Jerusalem. In one of the most original and interesting parts of this book, Naomi Cohen carefully examines Knabenshue's prejudices as revealed in his correspondence with State Department officials; this is now in the National Archives. The American consul excused Arab violence on the grounds that the Jews had sparked them off by "provocative acts." "Every impartial student realizes," he reported, "that the Arabs were more or less driven to such action in defense of their rights" (p. 33). He accepted the Arab case that the Western Wall belonged to the Muslims and Jews had no rights there. As though influenced by the *Protocols of the Elders of Zion,* his reports depicted Zionism as the cause of a united wealthy international Jewry; and he explicitly backed British and Arab arguments that blamed the Jews for everything. "In a sense, of course the Jews are always responsible, for they generally bring troubles upon themselves. If they were not, they could not be attacked" (p. 33). From time to time, he was consulted by his colleagues in Washington, D.C., and his advice was sought and accepted by department officials.

In addition to such anti-Zionist sentiments and to the policy of noninvolvement, maintaining good relations with Great Britain was also a factor in Secretary of State Henry Stimson's refusal to pressure the British with regard to its Palestine policy. And finally, the idea that involvement on the Zionist side could potentially damage American interests in the Arab world still retained its hold.

To put pressure on the administration to side with the Zionist cause, American Jewry needed unity, leadership, an efficient and energetic lobby and funds. Unfortunately American Jewry lacked these resources. In a detailed examination of the various Jewish groups, the author, an authority on American Jewish history, analyzes the ideological and personal differences and rivalries that prevented unified action.

Particularly controversial was Judah L. Magnes's plan, formulated with the help of John Philby, a pro-Arab British official. A member of Brith Shalom, Magnes supported a binational state in Palestine, shared by the Arabs and the Jews, in which a single parliament would be elected on the basis of universal suffrage. The rights of the Jewish minority would be protected by the veto power of the British high commissioner. Taking into account the rights and demands of the Arab population, Magnes preferred Ahad Ha'am's concept of Palestine as a spiritual center to the idea of a Jewish national home, which he considered to be unworkable. Magnes's one-man diplomacy significantly undercut Zionist influence in America and in England.

Cohen concludes that the efforts of American Jewry to influence Great Britain "were little more than exercises in futility." Deep internal differences and rivalries not only prevented "any show of serious determination, but . . . prompted England to plan on using Jewish divisiveness to its own advantage" (p. 174). Lack of a decisive united campaign certainly contributed to the failure to influence the administration and the American public. The goal was probably unattainable, but the author clearly voices her judgment that "for opportunities overlooked, or mishandled, in the critical year that followed the riots, American Jewry were largely at fault" (p. 177).

American Jewry's failure to neutralize hostile elements in the State Department and the public, and the question, "What could have been done?" remind us of the recent polemic over the role played by American Jewry during the period of the Holocaust. Cohen helps us to see more clearly that the same basic shortcomings that characterized Jewish activity in the Nazi period were already evident in 1929–1930: hopeless divisiveness, political timidity and the unrealistic hope that an enlightened public would support the humanitarian cause of the Jews. Although the author admits that Jews were powerless in the 1940s to change Franklin D. Roosevelt's attitudes, as they were too weak to influence an anti-Zionist State Department and an antisemitic public, she maintains, nonetheless, "If unqualified success was unattainable, perhaps the severity of the outcome could have been mitigated, concessions extracted, or compromises negotiated" (pp. 176–177).

It seems that here the author leaves the solid ground of historical fact, entering the risky area of speculation. A method that suggests the various options that might have been taken up is highly controversial and has led to criticism of certain Holocaust historians, in particular. It might be wiser simply to state the facts, leaving speculation to the reader.

This is an interesting, well-written scholarly book that discusses, with authority, a neglected period. As a prologue to the 1930s, it enables us to better understand the role played by American Jewry during the Holocaust.

HAIM GENIZI
Bar-Ilan University

Yehuda Eloni, *Zionismus in Deutschland, von den Anfängen bis 1914. Schriftenreihe des Instituts für Deutsche Geschichte, Universität Tel-Aviv,* no. 10. Gerlingen: Bleicher Verlag, 1987. 570 pp.

Zionist historiography has in recent years tended to deal with the various branches of the Zionist movement separately, viewing them as integral parts of the Jewish communities in which they functioned. The picture of the Zionist movement that has emerged from these studies is a colorful one reflecting the different patterns of development dictated by local conditions in each country and its own particular role in local Jewish life as well as its attitude toward the world Zionist movement.

The Zionist movement in Germany has been examined in a number of studies, which (like that of the book being reviewed) focus on the period from the establishment of the World Zionist Organization by Herzl until the First World War—the period when German Zionism played a central role in the world movement. These studies, in particular those of Jehuda Reinharz and Stephen M. Poppel, have succeeded in shedding new light on the role played by Zionism within German Jewry and in proposing explanations for the very formation of a Zionist movement in Germany. These questions have also been dealt with in studies on German history, such as that of Moshe Zimmerman; in more general studies concerning the formation and early years of the Jewish national movement, such as those of Jacob Katz and David Vital; and in studies of the social history of German Jewry, such as those of Steven Aschheim and Jack Wertheimer.

There remain, however, a number of central issues relating to the period before 1914 that have not yet been subjected to serious analysis—most prominently, perhaps, the role played by German Zionism in the formation and development of the world movement. Yehuda Eloni's book is the first and only comprehensive monograph to have been published on the history of Zionism in Germany before 1914 (assuming, of course, that the "inside" history written in the 1950s by Richard Lichtheim, one of the leaders of the German Zionist movement, cannot be considered a historical study). Eloni's work is, indeed, a very complete and factual account of the events involved in the movement's formation and activities in the period before the First World War. However, it succeeds to only a limited extent in being the definitive work on this subject.

The book is divided into two sections. The first, consisting of ten chapters, is arranged chronologically and covers the emerging national revival in the nineteenth century; the activities of the Hovevei Zion in the 1880s, the organization of the movement during Herzl's time, the "language war" in Palestine (Hebrew vs.

German); and events of the period immediately preceding the First World War. The second, shorter section, discusses in detail various specific topics, such as the Mizrachi, Zionist youth movements and communal activities (*Gemeindepolitik*).

Eloni's primarily chronological approach is one of the book's weaknesses. This is because the discussion of many issues that require in-depth analysis in and of themselves is scattered among different chapters in the chronological section. As a result, the issues either do not receive the treatment they deserve, or do not receive it in the right place. Perhaps the most striking example occurs in the seventh chapter, entitled "On the Activity of German Zionists in the World Zionist Organization," which covers only the specific period of the ninth Zionist Congress (1909) without dealing at any length with such major issues as the Uganda debate. Another case in point is the chapter dealing with the move toward radicalism, which gives only superficial treatment to the questions of the Ostjuden and the relationship of German Zionism with the Zionist labor movement. Even the leadership struggle between the Berlin and Cologne branches, which is described in some detail as being of importance in the organizational development of Zionism in Germany, is scattered among many chapters; thus, it is not adequately analyzed, and the sociopolitical questions involved are largely ignored.

On the other hand, the analysis of those topics with which the book does deal at various points is so pedantic in its emphasis on organizational matters, so minutely detailed and so burdened with lengthy quotations, that it is very difficult to follow. The benefit that might have been derived from such detailed, chronological treatment is diminished as well by the lack of adequate indexing.

Eloni does not address issues raised by modern historiography, and he refers to theses developed by other scholars neither in the copious notes nor in the bibliography. Thus, for example, in the chapter on the forerunners of Zionism, Eloni writes as if nothing had been written before on the subject. He likewise totally ignores the issue of why those people who turned to Zionism before the First World War did so, and gives little sociological analysis of the membership in the movement (though he does provide interesting statistics on the regional variations in the movement's support).

Another problem is the minimal historical context. For example, the author's discussion of the Mizrachi in Germany is based neither on any analysis of its origins in general nor on any comparative analysis of its unique development in Germany. As a result, he can provide no definitive answers concerning the question of what German Zionism's role was in the development of the world movement. Finally, despite his discussion of the relations between the Zionists and their opponents within Germany, no significant picture of the place filled by Zionism in German Jewish life emerges. Eloni places his book in a kind of vacuum, ignoring any context at either the historical or the historiographical level.

All of these problems are reflected in the book's critical apparatus and appendixes. Though the author uses a broad range of sources, including German archival material from the Foreign Ministry and state and municipal archives, the bibliography is strange and unwieldy. Ignoring the most important studies in the field, it does list all the articles from the contemporary press quoted in the notes (this list alone covers some seventeen pages). Another failing is the lack of a subject index.

It would seem, then, that the Institute of German History at Tel-Aviv University decided to include this book among its publications mainly to present German readers with a factual survey of the history of the Zionist movement in Germany. However, sound advice and judicious editing would have been invaluable in helping the author demonstrate his great expertise in this subject in a more useful and readable fashion.

HAGIT LAVSKY
The Hebrew University

Sergio Itzhak Minerbi, *Havatikan, erez hakodesh vehaziyonut 1895–1925 (The Vatican, the Holy Land and Zionism 1895–1925)*. Jerusalem: Yad Yitzhak Ben Zvi Institute, 1985. 256 pp.

The emergence of political Zionism in the nineteenth century added a new dimension to the two-thousand-year-old conflict between the Church and the Synagogue. On scriptural grounds the Holy See was bound to oppose the return of the Jews to Zion, believing as it did that the destruction of the Temple and the dispersion of the Jewish people were the penalties for their crime of deicide. So long as the Jews refused to embrace Christianity, they were condemned to perpetual wandering and unrest. Their return to the Holy Land would run counter to this doctrine, and the Church would, therefore, have no choice but to discourage it. The question of the Holy Places (for which the Zionist leaders were willing to admit extraterritoriality) was only part of the problem; when Theodor Herzl visited the Vatican in January 1904, he was made aware of the doctrinal gulf that separated Catholicism from Judaism. "As long as the Jews deny the divinity of Christ," Cardinal Merry del Val told him, "we certainly cannot make a declaration in their favour." Pope Pius X himself was equally blunt, "The Jews have not recognized our Lord, therefore we cannot recognize the Jewish people." When Herzl objected that he was not asking for the Holy City, but only for the "secular land," the Pontiff replied, "We cannot be in favour of it."

Thirteen years later, when the British were set to conquer Palestine, it seemed for a moment that things had changed. While asking the Zionists to keep clear of an area well beyond the Holy Places (including Nazareth, Tiberias and Jericho), both the papal secretary of state (Cardinal Pietro Gasparri) and the Holy Father himself (Benedict XV) told Nahum Sokolow that his movement need fear no opposition from the Church. The former affirmed that the Holy See wished the Jews well in their attempt to build a "Jewish kingdom." The latter expressed himself in even warmer terms: "The return of the Jews to Palestine was a miraculous event . . . yes, yes—I believe that we shall be good neighbours." On the same occasion, Cardinal Gasparri gave the impression of preferring Great Britain to France. It was in the light of these assurances that Weizmann felt justified in claiming that "the highest Catholic circles" saw no objection to the establishment of a Jewish National Home in Palestine (May 20, 1917).

It soon became clear to all concerned, however, that the papal authorities were having second thoughts on the subject. When Weizmann himself called on Cardinal Gasparri in April 1922, he found him not only unsympathetic but hostile. In the following month, a Vatican memorandum was presented to the League of Nations that, although not opposing the Mandate as such, argued that Articles 2 and 4 (the key articles ensuring the establishment of the Jewish National Home) contradicted the Mandatory concept as defined in the League of Nations Covenant because they seemed designed less to serve the interests of the indigenous population of Palestine than to lead in time to ''an absolute preponderance of the Jewish element in the economic, administrative, and political field to the detriment of other nationalities.''

The Vatican also found unacceptable the proposal in Article 14 of the draft that a Commission for the Christian Holy Places examine rights to the Catholic Holy Sites and insisted that voting power in such a commission be exclusive to Catholics. Weizmann explained that the Zionists ''were completely uninterested in this problem''—that they ''fully realized it to be something to be settled between the Christian powers and the Vatican'' and that ''if these could not reach a satisfactory agreement among themselves, it was no fault of [the Zionists].'' His disclaimers, however, fell on deaf ears; Cardinal Gasparri evidently believed that ''the Zionist Organization was, in some obscure fashion, a branch of the Palestine Government, and 'could use its influence' if it chose.'' The opposition of the Vatican to Britain's ''Zionist'' policy was given an additional impetus by the appointment of a Jew, Sir Herbert Samuel, to the post of high commissioner in Palestine.

Given its doctrinal hostility to the Zionist movement (which was apt to spill over into outright antisemitism), its disapproval of Zionist conduct in the Holy Land and its tendency to put part of the blame for British policy toward the Catholic Church on the Zionist leadership, the Holy See could not but support the Palestine Arabs in their struggle against the Jewish National Home. Monsignor Luigi Barlassina, who served as Latin patriarch in Jerusalem throughout the period of the British Mandate, played a key role in this tacit alliance between Roman Catholicism and Arab nationalism. (It is worth bearing in mind in this connection that most Christian organizations in Palestine were—and are—to a greater or lesser extent anti-Zionist and pro-Arab).

Although the Vatican attitude toward Zionism has been consistently negative (save for a brief interlude during 1917–1918), its motives have always been exceedingly complex. Sergio I. Minerbi, author of several valuable monographs on Italy and Zionism, has put us in his debt by presenting a dispassionate and convincing analysis of the numerous and conflicting factors that have gone into the making of that policy. His book is grounded in an exhaustive study of the published sources and extensive research in British, French, German, Belgian, Italian and Israeli archives; its value is further enhanced by well-chosen illustrations and a comprehensive bibliography.

His conclusions are predictably pessimistic. Although there were (and are) pro-Zionist as well as anti-Zionist currents within the Catholic Church, the former have had little effect on the policy of the Holy See. And although relations between the Jews and the Curia have improved since the Holocaust—the Church universal at the

Second Vatican Council absolved the Jews in 1965 from the charge of deicide—the conflict between Zionism and Catholicism remains unresolved. There have been official contacts between the popes and Israeli leaders, but the Holy See still persists in its refusal to establish diplomatic relations with the state of Israel, as the author notes in his concluding sentence, "All we can do is to hope that progress towards peace in the Middle East will bring about a normalization of relations with the Vatican, despite the theological obstacles which the Church has not yet overcome."

MEIR MICHAELIS
The Hebrew University

Amos Perlmutter, *The Life and Times of Menachem Begin.* Garden City, N.Y.: Doubleday, 1987. xi + 422 pp.

This is not the first biography of Israel's sixth premier. Several works on Begin's life have appeared before this book: some pure propaganda, others journalistic and a few short academic studies of Begin as the Irgun underground commander, opposition leader and prime minister.

However, Perlmutter is the first scholar to write a comprehensive biography of Begin, combining great knowledge with colorful, fluent writing skills. He portrays Begin as "Israel's most influential prime minister next to Ben-Gurion." At the same time he sees him as a tragic figure who stepped down leaving a torn nation to his warring successors (p. 394) and as a man who combined a gift for political pragmatism with an unbending belief in Eretz Israel, a streak of hero worship and military romanticism (p. 319).

Perlmutter says that "this particular portrayal of the life of Menachem Begin is intended as a political biography, not a personal one" (p. ix). It is by no means self-evident, however, that this is sound, since it is doubtful whether one can distinguish at all between personal and political aspirations or between personal outlook and political ideology. In the case of an ideological leader such as Begin, the connection between the two aspects of his thought is of a special interest. It is impossible to adequately understand his attitude to Germany, for example, without taking into account his memories of his childhood during the First World War or of his experiences during the Second World War. More than that, it is impossible to understand what motivated Begin in deciding on military operations against the P.L.O., including the Lebanese war, unless due weight is given to the fate of his family in the Holocaust; and this is no less true of his decision to bomb the Iraqi nuclear reactor. Perlmutter himself notes that a knowledge of Begin's experience in Lithuania when that country was annexed to the Soviet Union and subsequently as a prisoner in Stalin's Gulag are necessary to understand his approach to the Soviets.

Another methodological problem relates to the sources Perlmutter selects and uses. The book is based mainly on secondary sources, including background briefings by politicians, journalists and academicians. Perlmutter uses Begin's autobiographical books, *The Revolt* and *White Nights,* which describe his activities before the establishment of Israel and on occasion he also quotes from Begin's writings and Knesset speeches in the 1950s and the 1960s. But the media still serves as the major source of information, and no primary source from Begin's time in government is used to prove significant factual arguments.

This modus operandi inevitably produces mistakes. For example, the author provides a colorful, detailed story of Begin's last day in office. He writes that he announced his intention to resign in September 1983 (in fact, he did so a month earlier, in August) and "named Foreign Minister Yitzhak Shamir his successor" (p. 15). A few pages later, however, he writes that Begin did not inform the cabinet at the last meeting he chaired of his intention to step down (pp. 22–23). But, in fact, Begin did precisely that, announcing his intention to resign at the cabinet meeting of August 14, 1983—the last meeting he chaired—in accordance with the Basic Law on the subject. Moreover, he was never ready to nominate, or recommend, any successor, explaining this position by the demands of democracy, "No democratic leader should influence the nomination of his successor," he reiterated many times. And, indeed, it was the Central Committee of the Herut party that nominated Shamir. Begin did not participate in the meeting at all because he had already secluded himself at home.

According to Perlmutter, "By November 14, [1982] he [Begin] had already made up his mind, irrevocably [to step down]." On this day, his wife, Aliza, died in Jerusalem while he was on an official visit to the United States (p. 19). But the Begin enigma cannot be solved so easily. Perlmutter provides no evidence to prove that Mrs. Begin's death was the primary cause of the resignation nor, indeed, that the decision was made on November 14, 1982—nine months before he in fact stepped down. Why did he wait so long before acting accordingly? We are not told.

Describing Begin's last day in office, the author gives a list of the newspapers his hero read on that particular day, "ending with the Herut weekly, *Min haareẓ*." Such a publication never existed. At that time Herut had a monthly bulletin called *Be'ereẓ yisrael*.

These and other factual errors should be corrected if a second edition is published. More of a problem is created by the structure of the book. The longest section is the first, which describes Begin's years in Poland, 1925–1942—some one-third of the whole book. Perhaps these proportions reflect the amount of work the author invested in the research and in the writing. Indeed, the early part of the biography includes more primary sources than the rest of the book. Here we find, for example, an exchange of letters at the beginning of the war between Begin and a leader of the Revisionist party in Israel. From the way that Begin talks of the Anglo-French war against Germany, it seems that he did not assign the Jewish people a role in the war at the time (ch. 8).

However, the amount of research invested in this early period of Begin's political career cannot change its historical relevance. Seen in historical perspective, those years in his life were of only a preparatory significance, whereas the truly important story began later. Yet the Polish period takes up 128 pages, while his period as prime minister, including the peace treaty with Egypt, are given only seventy-three pages. To his five years as the Irgun commander, Perlmutter assigns 110 pages.

This is no arbitrary choice but rather reflects Perlmutter's assessment of the man. In a closing "Assessment of Begin," he writes that Begin, "may well be remembered strongly—for the Revolt and for Camp David, but in many ways his most remarkable achievements may have been his political survival and that of the Herut Party that he created and the legacy and ideology of Jabotinsky and Betar, which he kept alive." One may agree or disagree with this judgment, which reflects the author's own list of priorities. But from a broader perspective, it seems that it is an unbalanced assessment. The changes Israel underwent during Begin's term in government have been of the greatest political, social and cultural significance. The peace treaty with Egypt, the West Bank settlements, the grounding of foreign policy on ideological principles and historical memories, the destruction of the Iraqi nuclear reactor, the "war of choice" in Lebanon, the strategic cooperation with the United States, the legitimization of the non-Zionist Agudat Israel as a coalition partner and of religiosity in public policy and political behavior and, last but not least, the social and political emancipation of Sephardim—all made a real, a remarkable, change in Israel.

Perlmutter correctly notes one of the sources of the change, "Begin was Israel's first prime minister to represent the classic Diaspora European Jew, whose route to Israel was entirely different from the early settlers" (p. 11). This, certainly, is a fundamental aspect of Begin's personality. During his rise through the ranks of the Betar movement in the Poland of the 1930s, during his command of the Irgun underground in the 1940s, and, again, during his political leadership in opposition and in government, Begin was a Jewish, rather than merely an Israeli, leader. His Jewish identity, which was formed by education, ideology and experience, provides a key to understanding his politics and policy-making. It goes far to explain the religious tendency that took shape within his ideology as well as the policy he conducted. Not only domestic decision-making, but security and foreign policy, too, were influenced strongly by that identity. Almost every decision, whether relating to the future borders of Israel or to nuclear doctrine, resulted from it.

A systematic study of Begin's ideology would require a searching analysis of Jewish nationalism as he understood it. He saw nationalism as rooted in the traditional religious sources of Judaism, a fact that led him to adopt the Orthodox position on such issues as "Who is a Jew?" on the one hand, and to base his vision of Eretz Israel on religious sentiments, on the other hand—the sacred patrimony that modern Israel should never relinquish.

The contradictions between such an approach and the realpolitik he had to administer as a prime minister led him to make ideological innovations in order to find a compromise between his sense of pragmatism and his devotion to ideology. This aspect of Begin's leadership still awaits exploration. The complexity of the relationship between ideology and policy-making, which characterized the Begin era, deserves more attention than it is given in this book—a book that has already attracted attention among the students of the subject.

ARYE NAOR
Jerusalem

Avraham Schweitzer, *Israel: The Changing National Agenda*. London: Croom Helm, 1986. 174 pp.

Some books can be evaluated and reviewed immediately on publication, but some are best reviewed only after a lapse of time. The books in the latter group need a longer perspective to enable adequate evaluation. Volumes that contain collections of extemporaneous articles, reflective essays, operational theories, social and political predictions or all of these elements belong to this latter category.

Schweitzer's book definitely belongs in this class; hence, the present review is not too belated. For in fact this book is a longish essay that, at best, may be termed as reflective in nature. It also clearly aspires to predict grand political developments and changes in Israel.

The book starts with a brief attempt to analyze the extremely complex questions pertaining to the growth and demise of the political ideologies that inspire the various political camps. But as it moves along, the first section winds up with a highly subjective review of the entire political and economic history of the Jewish state. It is true that this historical review attempts to focus on the successes and, more specifically, on the failures of the labor camp, which for many years served as the first and only hegemonic power in Israeli politics. But the analysis, which is interspersed with a number of historical digressions, is not very clear about the legitimate question Schweitzer poses, namely, how and when did Labor "exhaust its program?"

When dealing with major issues such as this, which are at the very heart of the political process, it is not enough (even in a reflective essay) to produce vague and general statements such as this, "Sometime between 1960 and 1965 the coalition led by Mapai had exhausted the voters' patience, having worn out its political substance and accomplished the national agenda with which it was identified" (p. 76). The clarifications that follow this statement are neither comprehensive nor very convincing.

Similarly, the explanation of how the Likud emerged as a major political force in Israel, finally winning victory in the famous 1977 election, is very general and impressionistic. Schweitzer attributes that victory mainly to the desire of the Israeli public for a "more straight-backed posture vis-à-vis the gentiles—not only the Arabs—and the coalition headed by Menachem Begin looked like promising precisely this" (p. 80). The ensuing discussion of the Likud period—far shorter than that to be found in the first part of the book, and based on the author's assumption that the Likud hegemony is a transitory phenomenon—rests on rather conventional analyses and suffers, like many other more journalistic accounts of this phenomenon, from a lack of depth and breadth.

Most questionable, however, are the very basic assumptions of the author that constitute the main gist and message of the book. Schweitzer assumes that the Likud is a party without a history, that it was totally and singularly identified with Menachem Begin and that after Begin's resignation and withdrawal it lost all chances for resurrection. He claims that sooner than anybody expected—especially after the failure of the war in Lebanon—the Likud exhausted its ideological vitality; that it is incapable of shaping the national agenda; that its supporters, especially Oriental Jews, are deserting it as they come to realize its profound inadequacies; and that the internal controversies in the party are bound to lead to its further deterioration.

Contrary to Schweitzer's analysis, developments since the publication of his book have definitely demonstrated that the nation is still split down the middle with regard to expansionism and the annexation of the territories; that there has not been a mass defection from the Likud camp; that, over the years, the Likud has succeeded in creating a solid base in Israeli society; that, despite the withdrawal of Begin, the mediocrity of Shamir and the controversies among the Likud's leaders, the party's supporters have not been perturbed. And, most important, the author's wishful thinking that the Israeli public is turning its sights inward and is ready to tackle internal economic and domestic social issues has not materialized. In fact, the situation is such that unless a solution to the Israeli Palestinian conflict is found, national attention and the national agenda will continue to concentrate on this existential problem. Therefore, the Likud will maintain a central position in the political system and, no less than the Labour party, will determine the national agenda.

With regard to the foreign policy arguments presented in this rather long essay, it is highly questionable whether Israel can afford to leave the conflicts with Syria and Jordan unresolved and concentrate, in preference, on a very gradual solution of the Palestinian issue. Rather, it would seem that this assumption, which is intended to justify the author's plea for a turning inward, neglects two fundamental factors: first there can, in all probability, be no gradual and piecemeal solution to the Palestinian issue, and second, the Palestinian issue is essentially and inseparably connected to all other aspects of the Arab–Israeli conflict.

Finally, a short note on the basic concept underlying this book. Without going into complex explanations, it should be noted that though "the national agenda" (which is regarded by Schweitzer as the essence of politics) is a very important aspect of the political process, it is by no means the most fundamental variable shaping major developments nor, therefore, can it be used in itself to predict future processes. At best, it is only what is known in the jargon of the social sciences as an intermediate variable.

GABI SHEFFER
The Hebrew University

David Shipler, *Arab and Jew: Wounded Spirits in a Promised Land.* New York: Times Books, 1986. xvii + 599 pp.

The Arab–Israeli conflict is mainly a struggle over the political control of territory. Most Arabs, especially most Palestinian Arabs, have wanted as much of the land as they can possibly get. So have most Jews. Precisely because Palestine, or the land of Israel, is "a promised land" for each people, compromise, literally a "*com*bined *promise,''* is the only basis for a political settlement. David Shipler's study of "wounded spirits in a promised land" is a detailed sampling of the ignorance, stereotypes and personal suffering that make moving toward a compromise extraordinarily difficult.

Shipler is so impressed by the weight of accumulated fears and distortions that he sees it as the decisive obstacle to peace. Neither Arab nor Jew, writes Shipler, "can truly see the other through the veil of grief and anger." They will not find peace, he maintains, "in treaties, or in victories. They will find it, if at all, by looking into each other's eyes."

Shipler was the *New York Times* bureau chief in Israel from 1979 to 1984. The montage of interviews, observations, and vignettes that he provides reads very much like a collection of essays and human-interest articles that might have appeared in the *Times* daily edition or its Sunday supplement. Moving through topics such as terrorism, religion and nationalism, Shipler establishes the mutual "aversion" that, he says, most Jews and Arabs have for one another. The bulk of the book is then devoted to the negative images they have of each other that have been produced by sustained and bloody conflict and fostered by segregation, ignorance and a mutual sense of victimization. The last part of the book, on "interactions," ranges from romantic evocations of the Sinai landscape and Bedouin culture to the torture of Arab suspects by the Israeli "secret police," the frustration of Arab Israelis at the refusal of their fellow Jewish citizens to accept them as equals and the efforts by some brave and tolerant souls in each community to make human contact with one another.

Shipler's survey of attitudes is an effective introduction to the varieties of personal pain associated with a political dispute spanning generations, such as that between Arabs and Jews. This human face of the conflict is usually missed by the media with its compulsive attraction to violence and its focus on narrowly defined diplomatic achievement. Nor is it to be found in most scholarly studies, which tend to focus on a search for long-term trends or for structural shifts. Shipler's empathy with the victims of hatred, including the haters themselves, is apparent. So is his skill as a writer and storyteller. If his occasional shift into the first-person voice is sometimes jarring, it nevertheless reminds the reader of the particularity of the view being expressed and the emotional engagement necessary for this kind of writing. Shipler's descriptions of anti-Arab Israeli humor, of viciously antisemitic Arab propaganda, of gratuitous violence meted out to innocent people by Israeli soldiers and policemen, of the abuse and torture of Palestinian prisoners, of the atrocities committed against Israeli POWs by the Syrians or of the countless humiliations to which the most loyal of Israeli Arabs are subjected in the normal course of their lives will help even hard-boiled analysts of Arab–Israeli affairs to discover that their capacity for outrage has not been exhausted.

The book's shortcomings will be more apparent to the trained observer than to its intended audience—the general public. Despite some fascinating portraits of unusual Israelis (his discussion of Jewish–Arab married couples and their offspring is particularly interesting), Shipler's main sources are limited and conventional. They are the standard, English-speaking "talking heads" who live in the Jerusalem area and are familiar to viewers of the network news and readers of the *New York Times*. For wise and personalized commentary on the ugliness of particular incidents or the meaning of disturbing statistics, Shipler quotes at length from interviews with David Hartman, Meron Benvenisti and Danny Rubinstein. On the Arab side, he quotes equally generously from interviews with Jamil Hamid, Raja Shehadeh and Ibrahim Kareen.

Throughout the book, there is an admirable attempt to achieve balance. But in his systematic effort to do so, Shipler sometimes blurs the issues he seeks to illuminate. To balance the wealth of material available to show Jewish insensitivity, bigotry and malice toward Arabs, he must move back in time and well beyond the borders of the "promised land." Although most of his Jewish examples of prejudice are easily culled from Israeli Jewish life in the late 1970s and early 1980s, Shipler's evidence for anti-Jewish sentiment among Arabs and for examples of Arab cruelty to Jews comes overwhelmingly from the 1950s and 1960s—and from Egypt, Syria, Lebanon and Saudia Arabia, rather than Palestine. That this may reflect the realities of power more than the distribution of evil among the two peoples is perfectly plausible. But it would have been better, in this reviewer's opinion, to have acknowledged this imbalance and discussed its implications rather than ignore it.

There are also some places in the book where Shipler's own limitations as an observer are apparent. His discussion of the Koran, and of Islam in general, evinces a personal distaste for, or at least relative ignorance of, the Muslim tradition and its interpreters. After quoting approvingly Rabbi Hartman's description of the biblical tradition as containing "deep intolerances," lacking "pluralism" and capable of being honestly used "to expel the Arabs from every inch of this territory," Shipler uses an Egyptian cleric's characterization of the Jewish god as "obsessed with his people," as a "'country' man whose world ended with his tribe . . . a regional tribal, separatist god . . .'' as evidence of Muslim antisemitism.

Elsewhere Shipler finds it shocking that neither Arabs nor Jews, in a meeting to discuss terrorism, blinked an eyelash at one woman's distinction between violence against Israeli Jews in the occupied territories as legitimate and violence against Israeli Jews within the Green Line as illegitimate. "Nobody in the room," he comments, "challenged her fine distinction between innocents dying on one side or the other of an imaginary line." In view of the importance of preserving a distinction between the occupied territories and Israel proper if a territorial compromise is ever to be achieved, the author's shock shows considerably more about the quality of his political analysis than it does about the callousness of Israelis and Palestinians.

Lacking an historical introduction, *Arab and Jew* cannot be recommended as the optimal first book on Arab–Israeli affairs. Yet for those with a general sense of the conflict it provides a fair, accurate and highly readable account of how complex and resistant to improvement is the struggle over who will rule and who will live in the twice-promised land.

Ian S. Lustick
Dartmouth College

Ehud Sprinzak, *Ish hayashar be'einav (Each One Does as He Sees Fit: Illegalism in Israeli Society)*. Tel-Aviv: Sifriyat Poalim, 1986. 183 pp.

Ehud Sprinzak's slim but riveting book illuminates one of the less pleasant aspects of Israeli society. The author describes and analyzes so-called meteorological phenomena, that is, topics of popular conversation that everyone seems to be convinced are "acts of God" and as such not amenable to change in the ordinary way. In Sprinzak's view, however, it is not only possible, but essential to change these norms. The first step, which he takes here, is to make us more aware of what is involved.

The focal point of the book is what Sprinzak calls the "illegalism in Israeli society." Illegalism, as he sees it, is not mere lawbreaking. It is an overall cultural concept based on the attitude of the government and the public to the legal system and revealed in our civil behavior. In essence, this term denotes the blatant mockery of the legal system by both leaders and citizens (p. 23) that vitiates the spirit, if not the letter, of the law. Illegalism expresses itself in four primary forms: an ideology that justifies breaking the law, violent extraparliamentary activity, political corruption and political patronage.

In Israel, according to Sprinzak, law and order may be the basis of society, but illegalist behavior is readily apparent in the political arena. Furthermore, fundamentally instrumental attitudes to the law and scorn for the idea of a regime based on law and order have become deeply rooted in the culture and politics of the society since its earliest pioneering days (p. 18).

A survey of Israeli politics indicates the historical causes of this phenomenon, which can be summarized as, "everyone does as he sees fit." Sprinzak traces it back to the Diaspora, where, as a persecuted minority, Jews lived under governments that were usually arbitrary, inconsistent and untrustworthy.

Likewise, Zionist settlement and defense policy in Mandatory Palestine was inimical to the development of legalistic tendencies. The multiplicity of public bodies for various strata of the Yishuv, the internal legal systems that undermined the judiciary, "protekzia" (patronage), and the rather cavalier approach to the allocation of funds (contrary to rules of proper organization and control)—all these are the legacy of the Mandatory period.

Moreover, no formal constitution was adopted by the nascent Israeli state and thus Israel politics again missed a chance to tread the path of legalism. In the decision not to adopt a constitution, the author sees evidence that party interests took precedence over the concept of a state governed by law.

The 1950s, too, provided ample opportunity for the growth of illegalism: the waves of mass immigration, the economic crisis and the black market, the unskilled public administration, an almost omnipotent ruling party—all these made legalism a remote concept in Israel. The norm of "live and let live" settled permanently in the corridors of power. The "pragmatism" prevalent in the post-Ben-Gurion era (Pinhas Sapir was its most prominent representative) encouraged the attitude of "each one does as he sees fit."

Throughout the book, Sprinzak repeatedly finds fault with the duality of Israeli politics. On the one hand, the state was administered in all respects as a society of law, with no ideology of illegalism. On the other hand, alegal or illegal behavior flourished, characterized by corruption at the top, weak observance of the law and the reluctance of the political system to deal with lawbreaking by extraparliamentary groups. The author raises the specter of past scandals that were shunted to the back of the national memory: the case of the Autocar factory, for example, or "the Israel Company." The corruption exposed in these affairs was not a result of individual avarice but rather of the system that identified the good of the state with the good of the party and its leaders. Illegalism did not stop at the top; it infiltrated the public at large, whose scorn for the law has become notorious.

Illegalism, claims Sprinzak, is a general phenomenon, not restricted to any particular political camp. The rise of the Likud to power in 1977 did not contribute to an improvement, and very much remains to be corrected in cases of public corruption and political appointments. Again, in the author's opinion, Gush Emunim represents a blatant example of extraparliamentary illegalism, mainly because of its ideological justification of lawbreaking. From the Elon Moreh affair and the violent opposition to the evacuation of Yamit only a short distance remained, he argues, to the terrorist underground that he sees as a branch of Gush Emunim. (In criticism of Sprinzak's argument here, it has to be stressed that there is a large nucleus within the movement that strongly opposes violence and demands that it be replaced by persuasion.)

The author's final conclusion is more optimistic than his analysis. He believes the political history of the state attests to a gradual reinforcement of legality (p. 148), attained mainly by legislation and judicial rulings. Despite the rise in violent extraparliamentary activity, other factors, such as the weakening of party hegemony and the growing professionalism of government administration, have contributed to some curtailment of illegalism. Sprinzak also proposes several operative measures: the adoption of a formal constitution, educational campaigns in the school system and the enlistment of public and academic institutions to advance the causes of legality and legalism.

It is to be hoped that Sprinzak's will not remain an isolated voice, but will inspire, as the author hopes, wide academic, educational and public activity.

YAEL YISHAI
University of Haifa

Emmanuel Wald, *Kelalat hakelim hashevurim: dimdumei ha'ozmah hazevait vehamediniyut hayisraelit, 1967–1982 (The Curse of the Broken Vessels: The Decline of Israel's Military and Political Power 1967–1982)* Tel-Aviv: Schocken, 1987. 240 pp.

Dr. Emmanuel Wald was an NCO in the Golani Brigade (elite infantry) before he left to study systems analysis in the United States. Back home with a Ph.D. in his pocket, he was assigned to a position in the manpower branch of the Israeli army that carried the rank of lieutenant colonel. Unable to forge a working relationship with his superiors, he was transferred to the War Academy (Mikhlala Lebitahon Leumi), where he wrote the study under review. His inability to work with his superiors (as his enemies say) or his radical criticism of the military (as he himself claims) at one point caused him to be denied access to the official sources he needed. To get at them, he resorted to rather unorthodox means and was caught *in flagrante delicto*. The affair, which could have led to a court-martial, ended in his final separation from the army. The so-called Wald Report was discussed by the General Staff, though not for twelve hours as its author had demanded. Later, it was published in a "civilianized" form, that is, without much of the data and documentation on which it had originally rested. Its strongly worded criticism of the Israel Defense Forces (IDF) gave rise to a storm of publicity that, as is wont to happen in such cases, ended up by dying down.

In essence, Wald's argument is simple. Never during its history did Israel develop a coherent strategic, as opposed to a tactical-operational, doctrine. This did not matter much before 1967 when it was a question of protecting the country's existence. However, it became glaringly obvious in the aftermath of the Six Day War, which left the country's political-military leadership wondering what to do next. The absence of a coherent top-down doctrine made it impossible to review the operational, tactical and technical challenges facing the armed forces in depth. Instead, the IDF at these levels grew autonomously, so to speak. It added more of the same, using its enormous social prestige to rebuff even the little outside criticism to which it was subject. The results were already obvious during the war of 1973 when Israeli organization, doctrine, and staff work were found to be faulty in many ways.

Again, the lessons were not learned. The very size of the military establishment and the resources put at its disposal compared to those of everybody else made it like a boat with an enormous keel, impossible to steer. Unwilling to think things through at the top, the IDF continued to focus on the lower levels of war. By 1982, while still built around the tank and the fighter bomber as it had been in 1967, the Israeli army had become one of the most heavily armed forces in history. It had also accumulated vast layers of administrative and logistic flab (this is one of the few places where Wald supplies facts to support his claims, though his interpretation of them is not necessarily correct). The flab may have been one reason why, for all that the military advantages were entirely on its side, the IDF in Lebanon proved surprisingly heavy-handed and clumsy. The magnificent performance of the air force alone excepted, many of its objectives were achieved belatedly or not at all.

This is the thesis. How well does it stand up to criticism? Academically the book is a ragtag. Wald ranges far and wide over the shortcomings of the IDF with respect to organization, doctrine, training and command. He provides precious little detailed documentation in support of his allegations; this situation may be due, in part, to the sanitized form in which the study was published, but it often seems to result from the author's failure to do his homework and use even those sources that are available. More seriously still, in the case of all events prior to 1982, the study is but a brief sketch. It offers few examples in support of its claims, sometimes to such an extent that it reads like mere ranting. With respect to the war of 1982 itself, Wald goes into greater detail and indeed this is probably the best part of the book.

Yet Wald fails to mention several important factors that contributed to the IDF's uncertain performance: the political game of hide-and-seek, for example, that was being played inside Begin's government (even though this could well have been presented as one part of the problems the author discusses) or the orders issued within the IDF to advance cautiously in order to save casualties. Finally, one may question whether Wald's fundamental criticism—the absence of a coherent military-political doctrine at the top and the failure to develop it downward—is not overdrawn. After all, few countries during the twentieth century can claim to have had such a doctrine, whereas the example of those that did (such as Nazi Germany) is hardly encouraging. Wald approaches the subject from his point of view as an academic systems analyst. Perhaps he puts too much emphasis on planning as opposed to day-to-day improvisation in response to the environment and enemy moves—a course that, some would argue, is the only one realistically open to a politician.

This having been said, and looking back from the perspective of mid-1989, reading the book with all its shortcomings leaves one with the uneasy feeling that Wald may well have been right. His basic claim, that the absence of a politico-strategic doctrine will cause the military sector (particularly one that swallows as much of the state's resources as does the IDF) to follow its own momentum, seems to rest on solid fact. At a lower level, some of Wald's criticisms appear to have been conceded in a halfhearted way by the present chief of staff. For example, General Dan Shomron has been reported as saying that the army had far too many high- and medium-level officers. On another occasion, he spoke out in favor of "a small jolly army," presumably the opposite of the top-heavy, ponderous, gold-plated machine that Wald accuses it of being.

By way of a personal impression, it is enough to watch the hundreds upon hundreds of uniformed bureaucrats emerging from the *Kiryah* (the Israeli Pentagon) at the end of each working day to suspect that the IDF is no longer the lean, mean fighting machine it was in 1967. With the *intifada* adding to its troubles and sapping its moral fiber, one may only hope that a better work than Wald's be written on the subject, that people pay attention to it and that the points the author raises will not be put to the test of war anytime soon.

MARTIN VAN CREVELD
The Hebrew University

Walter F. Weiker, *The Unseen Israelis: The Jews from Turkey in Israel.* Jerusalem and Lanham: The Jerusalem Center for Public Affairs, Center for Jewish Community Studies/University Press of America, 1988. xii + 131 pp.

This work, in itself, is the result of a welcome initiative. The history of Ottoman and Turkish Jewry has, after all, been the object of relatively little study until now. As for research on the Turkish Jews in Israel, it has been little and far between. It is a fact (to restate the idea in the title of the book of Walter F. Weiker) that their "invisibility" within Israeli society has certainly not served to attract the interest of scholars. But the truth is that, Turkish studies aside, works of this type can also contribute to a deeper understanding of the highly heterogeneous Israeli society.

Who are these Jews from Turkey? What do they represent in this society? The author attempts to answer these questions through the use of sociological methods, combining interviews (seventy-five in number) and statistical data. However, the image that emerges is somehow unfocused and lacks definition. A more rigorous interpretation of the important information gathered could have led to more significant conclusions. Nonetheless, some key themes do emerge.

The book also contains a chapter on the history of the community in its original context, the Ottoman Empire. Certainly, Weiker does not pretend to be a historian. Nevertheless, it would have been more salutary if he had provided some solid information rather than clichés. A number of recent works have thrown new light on the history of these Jews, descendants of the exiles from the Iberian Peninsula, and their utilization would have prevented some of the errors. An article in the *Encyclopaedia Judaica* devoted to the Jews of the Ottoman Empire is not sufficient even for a simple introduction (see the bibliography, p. 18, no. 2). Some of the numbers, dates and other data in the book have to be corrected.

The years of the mass immigration immediately following the founding of the state of Israel (1948–1949) saw the arrival in the country of about 30,000 Turkish Jews. Following crises and changes of the regime in Turkey, new waves of emigration would follow periodically. But, unfortunately, the author does not provide information on the total number of Turkish Jews in Israel.

He presents us, then, with a social group demonstrating a solid communal identity, but invisible to the Israelis. Weiker attributes this phenomenon to the fact that Turkish Jews constitute a middle group between the two most important ethnic elements in the country, the Euro-American and the Afro-Asian groups. Data on their age of marriage, rates of fertility, levels of education and vocations all corroborate his hypothesis. Turkish Jews are well integrated into Israeli society. They do not pose problems, hence they are not perceived by the surrounding society. Turkish Jews do not make enough noise to be noticed. This trait translates itself into a limited participation in the social and political life of the country.

The author finds additional reasons for this invisibility, the guiding principle of his work. However, it might have been more productive to emphasize the past of this group in their country of origin. Turkish Jews are Jews of silence, a silence that in Turkey was the price for their security and well-being. Their relatively autonomous mode of organization and the fact that they did not participate actively in the surrounding society confined them in the social and political arenas to the communal sphere, the main principle being to be as little noticed by the outside world as possible. Such behavior is also to be found among the Turkish Jews in France who began arriving in that country, especially in Paris,[1] from the beginning of this century. In this respect, Weiker is justified in constructing his book around this central idea.

He studies four areas where Turkish Jews are concentrated: Yehud, near the Ben-Gurion airport; Bat Yam (which one can call little Turkey); Levinsky Street in the south of Tel-Aviv; and certain areas of Jerusalem (Mamillah, Yemin Moshe). The first of these quarters, Yehud, is relatively lower class and is the home of the

Turkish Jews who arrived immediately after 1948; Bat Yam is more middle-class; Levinsky Street constitutes a major economic center for the community; and last, in Jerusalem, the Turkish Jewish population is made up mostly of professionals and intellectuals. The author does not forget the more recent immigrants, coming from prosperous backgrounds, who have concentrated in Herzliya and Ramat Aviv. He presents a diversified picture, quite representative of the community as a whole.

The author attempts to analyze the specificity of these different areas in the series of interviews he conducted in a mixture of Turkish and Hebrew, throwing in some English and French (as he writes). A lack of knowledge of Turkish Jewish society sometimes leads him to errors. Nowhere does he question the veracity of the interviewees. Hence, the somewhat fanciful image of Turkey is never analyzed in terms of myth. One of the interviewees, arriving in Israel in 1968, claims to have worked for several European newspapers in Ladino (p. 47). One has to ask where such newspapers existed in Europe. Another recounts having fled Izmir in 1944 toward Palestine with the help of the Alliance Israélite Universelle. But one knows that the latter was not operational in the community beyond the 1920s and that in 1944, given the situation that prevailed in occupied France, it was surely not in a position to help. The list of such slips is a long one. One should perhaps ask why the interviewees provided such information. Is this just the result of a dimming memory? Nevertheless, all this does not detract substantially from the general image that the author tries to present.

With this book, Weiker wanted to fill a lacuna. He ran the risks of the pioneer. But it is impossible to ignore the fact that the work would have benefited from tighter argument, better documentation and a more methodical approach. And it would have gained further from a conclusion and an index.

Esther Benbassa
Centre national de la recherche scientifique (CNRS)

Note

1. On Turkish Jews in France, see Annie Benveniste, *Le Bosphore à la Roquette* (Paris: 1990).

Yael Yishai, *Land or Peace: Whither Israel?* Stanford: Hoover Institution Press, Stanford University, 1987. xxii + 265 pp.

Yael Yishai has written an important study of the domestic constraints that have hindered and the supports that have facilitated Israeli policy toward the territories occupied in the Six Day War of 1967. Yishai's focus on the domestic factors involved in the evolution of Israeli policy on this issue between 1967 and 1982 involves a detailed analysis of the relevant political parties, interest groups and public opinion.

Her conceptual focus is on policy, behavior and capacity, and it is guided by three main theoretical assumptions held by the structuralist-functionalist school of political analysis. Political input consists of supports and constraints. The degree of equilibrium between supports and constraints determines the capacity of decision-makers to legislate and act. In general, equilibrium is determined by the amount of influence exerted by the actors involved in the input process. Their influence derives from organization and from political and ideological proximity to the point of decision-making. By proximity is meant direct or indirect representation on, or access to, the authoritative institutions of decision-making and the ability to exert effective influence on those institutions.

Although this approach provides a clear focus for the presentation and analysis of the data, it ignores additional perspectives that would have shed important light on the subject. For example, Yishai claims in her preface that "Israel's stance is not based on paranoia but on the need to confront genuine enemies." Clearly, no objective observer would deny that Israel confronts real enemies. However, there are important differences in evaluating the extent and nature of the perceived threats, as well as the relative dangers posed by the alternative territorial policies. Whereas Yishai indicates that various interest groups and parties perceive the nature of these threats in dramatically different ways, she fails to stress sufficiently how much these perceptual differences (or degrees of paranoia) are related to their opposing stands on territorial policy.

Her approach essentially ignores the important implications of such psychological and cultural factors. I suggest that a key to understanding the ideological positions on this issue lies precisely in the relationship between the psychological perceptions of threat and the cultural perceptions of the "other" that, in turn, are related to temporal perceptions of the past as myth or history.[1]

In her first substantive chapter, Yishai sketches the development and evolution of "the authoritative policy," dividing the period under discussion into several phases. She concludes that in the first period (1967–1970) the tendency was to make clear distinctions between the various territories. In the second stage (1970–1973), the Gahal block, led by Menahem Begin, withdrew from the coalition when the government appeared to accept the idea of a withdrawal on all fronts at some time in the future as indicated by Security Council Resolution 242. The period 1973–1976 is characterized as one of partial withdrawal from principles and territories—the main change being the acceptance of the notion of "peace in stages." Golda Meir and her successor, Yitzhak Rabin, signed agreements for the separation of forces with both Egypt and Syria and, in addition, an interim agreement with Egypt. Yishai characterizes Menahem Begin's policy in his first phase as prime minister, from 1977–1979, as one of full withdrawal on a single front: back to first principles. And the period 1980–1982 served to reaffirm the principle of non-withdrawal on other fronts: the annexation of territories.

In her second chapter, Yishai outlines the implementation of settlement policy. She discusses the ideological origins of the policy, the socioeconomic infrastructure of the settlements and the political process involved. Here, again, she divides her narrative into periods.

From 1967–1969, the government was resolute in establishing settlements only on the Golan Heights. From 1970–1973 it continued to concentrate settlement in areas deemed vital to Israel's security, now including not only the Golan, but also northern Sinai and the Jordan Valley. The establishment of Kiryat Arba in the Hebron area was a model that characterized the expansion of settlements into initially unauthorized areas in 1974–1976. During this period, the leaders of the new right-wing religious movement, Gush Emunim, expertly exploited serious divisions within the government—particularly the rivalry between Rabin and Peres—to achieve important victories.

The expansion of authorized settlements in "Judea and Samaria" (accompanied by the use of these biblical terms for the West Bank) became a top priority of the Likud governments in the period 1977–1982. Whereas at first Gush Emunim took the initiative and had to continue to pressure the government, during the latter part of this period, Begin's government moved with unprecedented vigor to settle the West Bank—even while it was evacuating the settlements in Sinai in accordance with the Camp David agreement.

Chapter 3 is devoted to political parties. Yishai focuses on the role of factional input and deals primarily with the Labor party. Her discussion of factional activity is limited to only one of the three main factions, Ahdut Ha'avodah, and to other groups established to promote strategic settlement in the territories. This creates a certain inbalance in her analysis, and her tendency to ignore earlier studies of the Labor party leads to errors. For example, she states that, after the October War of 1973, "The Galili Document was scrapped and replaced by a scheme known as the Fourteen Principles" (p. 92). In fact in a most divisive meeting of the Central Committee on December 5, 1973, in which Pinhas Sapir and Golda Meir uncharacteristically attacked each other's positions in public, Sapir prevented a vote on the status of the Galili Document and declared that everyone should remain with his own "torah."[2] Yishai's assertion that the downfall of the Labor government may have been caused by the victory of the dovish posture is a serious oversimplification. The role of the other parties takes up less than three pages.

The author's analysis of the hawkish constraints focuses on the Land of Israel Movement and Gush Emunim. Here, in contrast to the previous chapter, her analysis does take into account earlier and important scholarly research. She argues that both these groups challenged government policy and presented an alternative line of their own.

Yishai's characterization of the organization of Gush Emunim is confusing. At the top of page 119, she claims, "the Gush did not institutionalize," but at the foot of the same page, we read, "the Gush institutionalized reluctantly." She then proceeds to describe significant levels of institutionalization with the creation of several auxiliary organizations mislabeled here as branches; and she states that "the institutionalization of the Gush was accompanied by growing isolation" (p. 123). Finally, Yishai suggests that organizational proliferation was one of the four causes of the movement's decline. She mentions the involvement of some Gush Emunim leaders in the Jewish terror organization in only a single sentence and fails to consider that this phenomenon might have been in part a reaction to the institutionalization of what had initially been a highly charismatic movement.

In the fifth chapter on the dovish groups, Yishai claims, "the 1973 October War did not produce a more dovish mood'' and that the leadership was not urged to alter its course or policies. In the opinion of this reviewer, she is simply wrong here.[3] It is true, however, that the dovish sentiment—produced in many Israelis by the dramatic failure of strategic depth to prevent war—failed to find tangible political expression. In this respect Yishai is correct.

The most important movement discussed by Yishai is Peace Now, and her discussion is particularly important both because it is one of the first to appear in English and because it is based on original research and interviews. Yishai concludes that Peace Now was considerably less influential than Gush Emunim. Given her focus and standards of measurements, this is certainly accurate. However, the contributions of a movement such as Peace Now are more significant when viewed through other conceptional lenses.

Professor Yishai's discussion of public attitudes in her sixth chapter is a useful review of relevant public opinion polls. However, her interpretation tends to exaggerate the degree and permanency of hawkish views. Her claim that ''the possibility of a change in Israel toward more dovish attitudes on the territories is therefore remote'' (p. 193) was revised in her postscript when she had to account for a significant trend toward moderation by 1985. In fact, Yishai's book fails to convey the picture of a polarized Israeli society as it is today and as it has been for the past decade. She only uses the term ''polarization'' once—on the penultimate page of her postscript.

The strength of Yael Yishai's study is its focused analysis of evolving Israeli policy toward the territories. However, the narrowness of the conceptual approach precludes adequate consideration of the social and cultural forces that cannot be ignored when it comes to answering the question posed in her subtitle—''Whither Israel?''

MYRON J. ARONOFF
Rutgers University

Notes

1. Myron J. Aronoff, *Israeli Visions and Divisions: Cultural Change and Political Conflict* (New Brunswick: 1989).
2. Aronoff, *Power and Ritual in the Israeli Labor Party* (Assen: 1977), p. 151.
3. Ibid., 96.

ANTISEMITISM, HOLOCAUST AND GENOCIDE

Yitzhak Arad, *Belzec, Sobibor, Treblinka: The Operation Reinhard Death Camps,* Bloomington: Indiana University Press, 1987. viii + 437 pp.

The first generation of Holocaust scholars has almost completed its honorable task. It has pioneered the way to solving the awesome methodological and philosophical

problems associated with the writing of genocide history, a constant struggle as the book under review illustrates.

This volume is, without exception, the most extensive scholarly work to date on the institution of the death camp; it examines, in particular, three such camps erected with the express purpose of annihilating the entire Jewish population of the so-called General Gouvernement: the Nazi-occupied territories of central and eastern Poland. In pursuit of his goal to expose in full detail the genocidal machinery—the death factory—Yitzhak Arad has faithfully scoured the extant sources that survived the indiscriminate ravages of war and the Nazis' systematic determination to destroy every clue of their crime, be it the death camps and their records, the mass graves or the surviving victims, lest their memories were to make possible a historical reconstruction of the Nazi deeds. Throughout his study, Arad weaves the testimonies of survivors, a constant viva voce, into his clinical but always humane and humanistic analysis of these three terrible places where in 1942–1943 (for almost twenty-one months) the mass production of death, the extermination of the Jewish people, was the exclusive activity.

Nothing escapes Arad: the planning, the chief strategists and administrators of genocide, the construction of the camps, the mass transportation of the victims, the techniques of assembly-line killing, the excruciating specifics of human suffering, "life" in the death camps, resistance and escape—and the outside world: the Catholic Church, the peasant countryside and the Polish underground. It is a laudable effort and a commendable reference work.

And yet Arad's work is flawed, perhaps seriously. To begin with, mention must be made of minor though not entirely unimportant points. There are, unfortunately, far too many German language infelicities, such as missing umlauts (p. 15); misspellings (*"Umschlogplatz"* [p. 6], and *"Aschkolonne"* [p. 176] instead of *Umschlagplatz* and *Aschekolonne*); garbled singulars and plurals (*"Ausweise"* instead of *Ausweis* and *"Fahrplananordnung"* instead of *Fahrplananordnungen* [pp. 61, 125]; grammatical errors (the third person singular or plural *"sie"* instead of the second person *Sie:* the former meaning "she," the latter the formal "you"; and *"Endlich is der Judenstadt fertig"* instead of *Endlich ist die Judenstadt fertig* [pp. 116, 184]); as well as crucial mistranslations: *"Umsiedlersonderzüge"* as "special evacuation trains" (p. 96) instead of *resettlement* trains, so crucial a term for capturing the Nazi use of terminology as camouflage.

Mention has to be made, too, of the fact that there are photographs whose origins remain without reference (pp. 94, 156, 182, 185, 187 and 323). Are the first three from the Kurt Franz Album? The generally poor quality of the photographs make identifications questionable, for example, in the case of the very blurred faces of (supposedly) Stangl and Franz (p. 93) in contrast to their snapshots (p. 185). Is no one identifiable in the much clearer group picture (p. 182)? Where was it taken? How does one know they are "members of Operation Reinhard"? Holocaust photographic evidence, in particular, must be applied cautiously. How, by the way, does one know that the pile of shoes (p. 156) are from Belzec? The reader and student deserve to know sources and to learn why they have been interpreted in a particular way.

Again, it is hard to understand why there is only one map and why that is hand-drawn and less than useful (p. 132). The book should have included a full-scale geographical component, with clear maps to locate Belzec, Sobibor and Treblinka in the General Gouvernement, in prewar Poland and in Eastern Europe. How else can the uninitiated reader learn *where* these tragic events took place and, for example, from *where outside* the General Gouvernement the tens of thousands of Jewish deportees had been brought? (They had been transported from Theresienstadt in the West, for example, and from Lida, Minsk and Vilna [Vilnius] in the East.) Nor would it have hurt to have provided a scale (in meters) for the three diagrams of each death camp, located respectively on pages 35 (Sobibor), 39 (Treblinka) and the last, curiously, on page 437 (Belzec).

This latter point leads one to more serious flaws of organization as well as omission and interpretation. At first glance, the book is a neatly organized work of forty-six chapters, divided into three parts. But this proves to be a false impression. Many chapters should have been combined into one coherent unit: for example, chapters 3 to 5 on camp construction, 6 to 8 and 18 to 19 on deportation, 33 to 36 on resistance in Treblinka and 37 to 41 on resistance in Sobibor. Some chapters are misplaced. Chapters 14 (''Jewish Working Prisoners'') and 15 (''Women Prisoners'') interrupt the development of the central theme of Part I (''The Extermination Machine'') and would have been better placed in Part II (''Life in the Shadow of Death''). Chapters 45 (''Operation *Erntefest*'') and 46 (''The Liquidation of the Camps'') do *not* belong in Part III (''Escape and Resistance''); similarly chapter 43 (''Reports about the Death Camps in Polish Wartime Publications'') should have served as an epilogue. As for chapter 20 (''Extermination of Gypsies''), it rightly belongs in an appendix because the Gypsies were not formally a part of Operation Reinhard.

In the appendixes, too, there are problems. Appendix A contains a reconstructed list of the deportations of Jews from the General Gouvernement alone. But why were not the known transports from Western, Central and Southern Europe included, as well as those from the U.S.S.R.? These constituted an integral part of Operation Reinhard, regardless of how it was defined by its Nazi architects. A very incomplete, nonalphabetized list in Appendix B records the fate of some individual Nazi criminals, but this section ought to have incorporated the material in chapter 24 (''Portraits of the Perpetrators''), which as it now stands makes a strange opening chapter for Part II. To be of some use, this appendix should have been fully updated: the notorious Kurt Franz, for instance, is left in 1965, condemned to life imprisonment. What has happened to him since?

There is no appendix that focuses on the problems involved in calculating the number of victims, a major lacuna in a book about genocide. Scattered throughout Arad's book are some data, but he does not come to grips with the crucial problem of totals. On page 44, he speaks of 2,284,000 potential victims in the General Gouvernement; Appendix A adds up to another total; page 165 speaks of 1.7 million victims from that region, leaving out the ''tens of thousands'' transported from outside the General Gouvernement: from Salonika to Vilna; from Danzig (Gdánsk) to Minsk. There are, besides, in the various Holocaust sources widely differing estimates by Germans and Poles as well as by the Western historians who specialize in the field (e.g., Alexander Donat and Raul Hilberg).

No author should be taken to task for not doing what he did not set out to do. And yet there are two topics that deserve to be brought up. One is the question of Majdanek: though technically not a part of "Operation Reinhard," the camp played an integral if not primary role in the total history of Belzec, Sobibor and Treblinka. Arad admits as much in chapter 45; he classifies it as a death camp (p. 132) alongside the other three. Majdanek's omission strikes one as unjustified, reflecting again a slavish acceptance of the bureaucratic definition of Operation Reinhard used by the Nazis.

The second omission is the Demianjuk trial in which Arad served as an expert witness. While "Ivan the Terrible" plays a small role in the book, an appendix could have provided an opportunity for an essay on what light the trial (which began as the book was being finished) sheds on our understanding of Operation Reinhard and its sundry methodological, philosophical and interpretive problems.

There are other questions raised by the text but not resolved by the author. For example, we are told that "all the [Jewish] prisoners who had worked in the extermination area" were killed in order to destroy potential witnesses; how, then, did Abraham Kszepicki, a member of one of these Kommandos and the author of a vital testimonial, survive? We are also told that Odilo Globocnik's claim that Hitler visited Operation Reinhard's headquarters (p. 102) was false; yet Arad's counterclaim (p. 103) remains without supporting evidence. The Treblinka uprising is dated by Arad in chapter 35 as having taken place on August 2, 1943; yet according to the Polish underground in its weekly report of August 13, 1943, the event took place on August 3 (p. 357). Unfortunately, there are far too many similar issues, both major and minor, strung throughout the book, that are left unresolved.

This intense criticism of a serious and important scholarly work written by a member of the first generation has been undertaken in order to focus attention on the responsibility to fundamentally upgrade Holocaust research, a task that now devolves on the emerging second generation of scholars. It is they who must meet the challenge and surpass the high standards set by those who came before them, among them Yitzhak Arad.

They may indeed have to overcome powerful taboos—studying the Holocaust *in context*—in order to add depth to their research. One example springs to mind in light of Arad's study. It was among the aims of Operation Reinhard to recruit manpower from among the millions of Soviet prisoners of war held by Germany. It is not enough to say simply that the S.S. selected Ukrainians to form special SS auxiliary units; it should, rather, also be emphasized that this step was well thought out in accord with the Nazi racial policy toward the Slavs as *Untermenschen*. In the scheme of Nazi genocidal practice, Ukrainians were seen as potentially useful in a *temporary* sense only. Ethnic Russians, however, were initially targeted (after Jews and Communist "commissars") for rapid wholesale extermination. The overwhelming majority of the more than two million Soviet POWs who were deliberately starved to death behind barbed wire in open fields during the bitter 1941–1942 winter were ethnic Russians, *not* Ukrainians. It would be of benefit, in future, to place the Holocaust in the broader framework of the genocidal design that inspired the Nazis in Eastern Europe. But that is a task for the second generation freed from the understandable inhibitions of the first. It would make Operation Reinhard that much *more* a crime against humanity and certainly no less a Jewish tragedy.

HENRY R. HUTTENBACH
The City College of the City University of New York

David Engel, *In the Shadow of Auschwitz: The Polish Government-in-Exile and the Jews, 1939–1942*. Chapel Hill and London: the University of North Carolina Press, 1987. xii + 338 pp.

The attitude of the Polish government-in-exile toward the Jews has been described in previous studies, but the book by David Engel is the first of such scope and ambition. The author has combed the archives in Israel, Great Britain and the United States (as well as interviewing two key figures in the book, Edward Raczynski and Jan Karski). A vast quantity of published material—the contemporary press, articles and books—in Polish, English, Hebrew, Yiddish, German, French and even Portuguese supplements the use of the archival sources. The result, however, is only a partial success.

Engel opens his book with a chapter concerning the situation of Jews in Poland before 1939 that is based mainly on secondary sources. His assertion that these problems are important for understanding the period 1939–1945 is true, but his analysis is superficial and burdened with mistakes, some more important, some less. A review is not the proper place to enumerate obvious misinterpretations; I can only mention as an example that the anti-*shechita* law of 1936 was introduced not by the government (pp. 27–28), but, on the contrary, against its considered opinion. Much more important is the presentation of the National Democratic ideology as typical of Polish society as a whole. Engel does not see differences between the changing Polish cabinets and presents their national policy as almost uniform. The attempt to build up a general picture of the Jewish situation prior to the Second World War is, in effect, a failure.

The next four chapters—based on primary sources—are devoted to relations between the Polish government and the Jewish politicians until the autumn of 1942. The merit of these chapters lies in their thorough analysis of the discussions, arguments and misunderstandings on both sides. The opinion that the nationalists had an important influence on the Polish government is not a discovery. The detailed presentation of events, however, is most instructive and explains the reasoning that lay behind the decisions and declarations as well as the apprehensions, the hopes and (especially important) the illusions of the politicians, whose scope for taking effective action was so limited. Both the Polish and the Jewish leaders abroad were dependent on the Big Powers, above all on Great Britain. They tried to win these powerful partners to support their plans and ideas. They could not do much more.

Both Jews and Poles were burdened with the memories of prewar conflict and sometimes with old stereotypes. Mutual lack of confidence was often the underlying cause of the controversies. Engel makes it possible for the reader to understand the dilemmas and difficulties faced by the Jews and the Poles in exile and to appreciate the differences between, and within, both camps. In the light of this analysis, I doubt if Polish and Jewish representatives were capable of finding a common solution to the points at issue. Their additional handicap was limited knowledge of what was going on in occupied Poland.

The irony of history (the author does not underline this) is that the main differences between the Jewish and Polish politicians were related to their views on future relations between Poles and Jews in independent Poland. The genocidal policy of the Nazi regime and the political realities in Poland after 1944 would, in retrospect, render these quarrels pointless.

One of the most interesting parts of the book is the analysis of Polish-Jewish relations in the Soviet Union. Engel describes the contrasting attitudes of the different Polish officials and, justly, notes the anti-Jewish stance adopted by some of the military men. This led to conflicts; it remains an open question whether, and to what extent, this situation was expected and accepted (or maybe even provoked) by the Soviet regime. This problem is discussed incidentally.

The cases and problems analyzed here could be expected to create a general picture of Polish policy; this, however, is a weak point of the book. Whereas the author often excels in his detailed study of the events and reveals a complex picture of real life in individual cases, the general view is oversimplified, limited to a depiction of the Polish government as anti-Jewish or, at least, as largely indifferent to the Jewish fate. Engel quite often accepts at face value, without any critical analysis, the data that is in accord with his thesis, and he sometimes constructs complicated suppositions based on scarce or doubtful information.

In February 1940, for example, the Polish government-in-exile received the detailed report concerning Polish-Jewish relations in occupied Poland (delivered by Jan Karski). Engel is right when he indicates that the opinions expressed there on the behavior of the Jews under Soviet occupation "represented an unwarranted extrapolation from a fundamental kernel of truth" (p. 61) when he criticizes this part of the report. Somewhat later, however, he himself accepts without any critical analysis that part of the report where Karski described and condemned Polish hostility to the Jews in generalized and undifferentiated terms (pp. 62–63). Such a duality is contrary to the proper methods of historical analysis. Differences in the wording used by the press in the reports on the liquidation of the Warsaw ghetto in autumn 1942 are used to argue that the Polish government tried to suppress the information about the tragedy of Polish Jews (pp. 188–193). The analysis is ingenious, but it seems that the author simply does not know anything about the practical side of putting information into a newspaper. Almost all the discrepancies enumerated in the book can be explained as a result of shortening the original, much longer report; some of the actual misunderstandings were probably caused by sheer haste (a normal state of affairs in all newspapers). The passage about the death of Professor Franciszek Raszeja, introduced in the much more tragic information about the liquidation of the Warsaw ghetto, was probably not the result of political premeditation. It may well have been included to indicate to Polish readers that all the people living in the Warsaw ghetto were being brutally murdered.

The question of why the news of the mass deportations and murders was not released immediately can be explained without complicated suppositions. In 1942, it was very difficult to believe that in Europe, in the twentieth century, the extermination of a whole nation was possible. Even the people living in the Warsaw ghetto did not believe in this possibility at first. Yitzhak Levin, who received the news from the Polish consulate in New York (probably on September 3, 1942) and communicated it to Rabbi Stephen Wise, writes that Wise had doubts, in spite of similar information received from London. (The relevant article, published in *Biuletyn Żydowskiego Instytutu Historycznego* 1977, no. 1, is not quoted by Engel). Only after several weeks, following the receipt of further corroboratory evidence, did Wise accept the report as true. Even now, almost fifty years later and after the publication of thousands of studies and documents, one is often astonished by the naivete of questions asked in good faith by some people (especially in America) who have lived their lives far away from the scene of the Jewish tragedy.

Engel considers that the words of Wladyslaw Sikorski, who on October 29, 1942, promised that Polish Jewry would "benefit fully from the blessings of the victory of the United Nations, in common with all Polish citizens," were "rather ironic" in light of the information then in possession of the Polish government (p. 197). I am inclined to believe that quite a different interpretation is the correct one: at that moment Sikorski still did not understand the full significance of the reports coming from Poland.

Perhaps Engel is right in his views on the Polish government-in-exile. The methods he uses to argue the case, however, often undermine confidence in these conclusions. In contradiction to his generalized statements, I finished the book with a much better opinion of the Polish politicians in London than before. I hope that in the second volume of his study, Engel will formulate his general conclusions with more caution and argue them with the same skill that he demonstrates in analyzing particular cases.

JERZY TOMASZEWSKI
Warsaw University

Shimon Huberband, *Kiddush Hashem: Jewish Religious and Cultural Life in Poland During the Holocaust.* Ed. Jeffrey S. Gurock and Robert S. Hirt. Trans. David E. Fishman. New York and Hoboken: Ktav and Yeshiva University Press, 1987. 474 pp.

The study of the Holocaust, which focused in the immediate postwar years mainly on the German role (anti-Jewish policies, war criminals) has subsequently become increasingly diversified. Since the mid-1950s, attention has also focused on the part played by the occupied nations as well as by Germany's allies in determining the fate of the Jews; on the attitudes of the governments in the free world and of the international organizations, such as the Catholic Church and the Red Cross; and on the Jewish response as manifested, for example, in the Jewish councils or in Jewish resistance.

In spite of the enormous progress that has been made in the last forty years, a great deal of moralism (the tendency to look for the "good" men and the "bad" men) still clings to many studies. However, particularly during the last decades, a body of research has begun to emerge that applies the normal standards of historical research to the ways in which Jewish society functioned under the conditions of extreme crisis.

Simultaneously, general historiographical developments have proved to be most dynamic. As the branches of social and economic history have flourished, interest in so-called daily life has grown; thus, everyday routine and the problems of the common man have become a major focus of interest.

The influence of this daily-life historiography has in recent years encouraged some scholars involved in Holocaust research to pay close attention to the ways in which the Jews in ghettos, in communities that were not ghettoized and in concentration camps actually lived. One of the subjects that has, thus, become a focus of interest is the daily life of religious Jews under Nazi domination. The simultaneous and rapid development of oral history combined with the willingness of many Holocaust survivors to record their memories now, after many years of silence, have supplied the social historian with many new sources of information. A most welcome contribution to the literature available in English in this field is provided by this publication of the writings of Shimon Huberband.

Rabbi Huberband (born in 1919), a historian, writer and poet, lived in Piotrków Trybunalski until the early stages of the war in 1939. When his family was killed in a German bombardment, he moved to Warsaw. There he plunged into research and joined the underground Oyneg Shabbes archives headed by Dr. Emanuel Ringelblum, who considered him a brilliant worker. Huberband was even awarded a cultural prize in the ghetto for his achievements. He continued his historical research under incredible conditions of hunger and overcrowding. In August 1942, he was deported to Treblinka together with more than 250,000 other Warsaw Jews. In the Treblinka death camp he perished.

Huberband was a very sensitive observer, and he possessed a keen social consciousness. This explains his precise, detailed and thorough descriptions and studies of Jewish daily life in occupied Poland, particularly in Warsaw. Huberband wrote, among other things, about wartime folklore, the extortion of money from Jews by Jews, the moral suffering and moral decline of Jewish women, a women's labor camp, the need to rescue Jewish cultural treasures and the destruction of Jewish communities. But his main field of interest was religious behavior in all its facets and the daily life of religious Jewry in particular. Consequently, he called his main study *Kiddush Hashem (The Sanctification of God's Name)*. His fields of interests—daily life, women's history, religious Jewry during the Holocaust—show that he was forty years ahead of his time.

A collection of his writings was translated and published in Hebrew in 1969 by Yad Vashem; the collection was edited by J. Kermish and N. Blumenthal. The lag of eighteen years between the Hebrew and English editions may seem strange.

However, a close reading of the new edition suggests that it was worth the wait. The original Yiddish text has been translated into very readable English by David E. Fishman, and the book has been edited by Jeffrey S. Gurock and Robert S. Hirt of Yeshiva University. The Hebrew edition was used as a starting point for the introduction and notes; however, substantial alterations and additions have been included. First, the somewhat clumsy Hebrew introduction has been abridged and, consequently, improved. Second, some nearly illegible parts of the original text, left out in the Hebrew edition, were deciphered and now appear in the English version (p. 213). Third, some additional writings, deciphered since the Hebrew appeared ("Gallows" and "A Photo Gallery in the Ghetto") have been added, and one article on general Jewish history, which has no bearing on the Holocaust, has been omitted.

However, the main contribution of the English edition is the altered arrangement of the chapters into four main parts (with an internal logical sequence of paragraphs): 1. autobiographical materials, 2. daily life and death in the Warsaw Ghetto, 3. Jewish religious life in Nazi-occupied Europe, 4. the destruction of East European Jewry. As a result of this new arrangement—the outcome, no doubt, of considerable thought—the *fragments* written by Huberband have become a whole, a real *book* with coherent progressions and contours. Consequently, Huberband's *Kiddush Hashem* can now be considered a handbook for both scholars and students. Some minor printing errors (of which the gravest is the sentence that his father "descended from bakers," instead of bankers [p. xxi]) do not diminish the achievement of this edition.

The translator and the editors have presented to the world of learning the superb achievement of one of the many Jewish scholars cut down by the Nazi madness.

DAN MICHMAN
Bar-Ilan University

Sharon R. Lowenstein, *Token Refuge: The Story of the Jewish Refugee Shelter at Oswego, 1944–1946*. Bloomington: Indiana University Press, 1986. 246 pp.

In August 1944, a total of 982 people (among them 872 Jews) were gathered together from refugee camps in Allied-occupied Italy and brought to the United States where they were interned at Fort Ontario, a centuries-old former army camp in Oswego, New York. There they remained until early in 1946, when they were naturalized as American citizens and released.

Largely forgotten, the story of the shelter has been revived during the past decade as a result of the recent conversion of Fort Ontario into a historical museum and park and in the wake of recently organized nostalgic reunions of former refugees. The biggest reunion was organized by Ruth Gruber who, as special assistant to Interior Secretary Harold L. Ickes, had accompanied the refugees from the port of Naples, remained with them during their first few weeks at the camp and returned to visit them at frequent intervals. Gruber gave a personal account of those years in her book, *Haven*.[1]

Although Sharon R. Lowenstein's book, *Token Refuge*, came out three years after Gruber's (and Lowenstein acknowledges Gruber's work), it is the product of meticulous independent research first undertaken years before. A scholarly yet human account, it presents the establishment of the Oswego shelter from three angles of perspective. The politicians and men of the Roosevelt administration viewed the shelter as a temporary haven for refugees who would be returned to Europe at the end of the war. The refugees saw the shelter as a first step in their permanent settlement in the United States as full-fledged citizens. And we, looking back with the author, in order to judge both of these viewpoints retrospectively, perceive the shelter from a third angle—as a microcosmic reflection of the attitudes that shaped policy toward the Jewish victims of the Holocaust. The book appears at a time when Roosevelt is being called to account by historians for his callous approach to the Holocaust. In this respect, Lowenstein is no exception, as the title of her book clearly suggests.

Fortunately, responsibility for the Oswego shelter fell into the hands of the two cabinet members who were most sympathetic to the plight of the refugees—Secretary of the Interior Harold L. Ickes and Secretary of the Treasury Henry Morgenthau, Jr. More specifically, the War Relocation Authority (WRA), which directly administered and managed the shelter, was part of the Interior Department, whereas the War Refugee Board (WRB)—which brought the shelter into being, recruited and selected the refugees and retained responsibility for overall policy—belonged to the Treasury Department.

As the author reminds us, Roosevelt's establishment of the WRB in early 1944 came in response to a stinging "Report to the President" issued by Morgenthau and his aides, which castigated the State Department for quashing efforts to rescue European Jews. From the outset, however, as Lowenstein points out, Morgenthau's position on the WRB was deliberately weakened, for Roosevelt made sure to appoint Secretary of State Cordell Hull and Secretary of War, Henry L. Stimson, as the other two members of the three-man board. Like Roosevelt, these men had only marginal sympathy for plans to rescue the Jews of Europe.

Despite general cooperation by the WRA and the WRB, Lowenstein demonstrates that the two government bodies basically differed in their attitudes toward the refugee shelter. Ickes's WRA was against restrictive camps in general—even for Japanese Americans and certainly for refugees from Hitler. It favored allowing the inmates easy access to the outside world and pushed for the early closing of the camp and the admission of the refugees as immigrants under the existing quotas. In contrast, Morgenthau's WRB was for stringent enforcement of confinement conditions and the return of the refugees to Europe at the end of the war, in keeping with Roosevelt's original plan. The WRB officials were not being inexplicably harsh; they argued that thousands more might be saved if it were demonstrated that the refugees were not being admitted in circumvention of U.S. immigration laws.

Roosevelt's original commitment to return the refugees at war's end took on new meaning after his death. Ickes favored admitting the refugees as immigrants, but Morgenthau continued "to insist on faithful adherence to Roosevelt's wishes," feeling that "any violation of his 'promise' to the dead Roosevelt would mean 'I could not sleep with my conscience.' " "The refugees," notes Lowenstein, "did not know that the benefactor for whom they deeply grieved was responsible for the restrictions against which they chafed'' (pp. 119–120). Eventually, the refugees were naturalized, but they remained in suspense—and in confinement—until eight months after the war ended.

Token Refuge is a well-balanced book that examines its subject both politically and sociologically—each to an equal degree. Its first three chapters are devoted to the political background leading to the establishment of the shelter and the government decisions that determined shelter policy. In addition, three chapters at the end are devoted to the political maneuvering that finally led to the closing of the shelter and the naturalization of the refugees.

In contrast, the core of the book is devoted to the refugees themselves—their recruitment, expectations and experiences at the shelter. Lowenstein expresses the basic irony of the American ''shelter'' as seen through the eyes of the arriving refugees:

> Nothing made as much of an impact on the entire group as did the six-foot chain-link and barbed wire fence that awaited them at the fort. It contradicted everything that America represented. All felt shock and anger but none more so than the nearly 60 percent who had eluded internment entirely in Italy or had lived there under ''free internment'' restrictions, having only to report daily to local police. They now faced imprisonment that had not even been imposed upon them ''by an enemy'' (p. 47).

Once settled, most of the refugees learned to cope with their confinement. Now, however, they faced a problem of a different sort. The refugees were a mixed group in many ways: divided as they were by national origin, degree of religious observance, age, attitude to the work ethic and general temperament. The issue now was how to live with one another. And once this problem had been met and overcome— for better or for worse—the real challenge became apparent: how to live meaningful lives in such an unnatural environment. The book's interesting narrative style, interspersed with engaging anecdotes and well-documented information, gives us a good picture of life at the shelter. In addition, eight tables and five appendixes provide detailed statistics about the refugees as a group.

A fascinating epilogue tells the individual stories of about one-third of the refugees: their backgrounds, their experiences in Europe and at the shelter, their subsequent lives as U.S. citizens and their retrospective thoughts about the shelter. The former refugees' recollections about the shelter are as varied as their individual personalities, but they are revealing nonetheless. The following is a sampling:

> ''Quarantine . . . fence . . . zoolike . . . very beautiful people in Oswego . . . a big waste of time . . . Oswego delayed us during our prime years, but it was not like a concentration camp'' (p. 101).

> ''It was an abomination. The U.S. Government owes us compensation for that imprisonment'' (p. 170).

> ''One of my most wonderful experiences'' (p. 182).

> ''It was a mixture of pain, disappointment, frustration and only faint hope that we might remain in the United States'' (p. 180).

> ''Today I know we had it very good'' (p. 183).

"The most important thing is the fact we were taken to America . . . one of the greatest gifts imaginable" (p. 187).

"We saved ourselves [before being taken to America; Oswego] doesn't wash [America's] hands clean (p. 168).

The refugees were grateful to be in America, but they didn't owe their lives to the Oswego shelter. They had already been on safe territory in Allied-occupied Italy before they embarked for the United States.

Despite wishful thinking on the part of the rescue advocates, "the Emergency Refugee Shelter remained a unique and solitary act of tokenism. It served neither as a prototype for additional havens nor as a model for a new approach to immigration" (p. 160). Indeed, until recently, the shelter had been all but forgotten, except by those who lived through the experience. It is good that the story has now been retold. As Lowenstein points out, the story of these refugees "makes more immediate the loss of six million and offers a tantalizing glimpse into what might have been" (p. 1).

Bernard Marinbach
Jerusalem

Note

1. Ruth Gruber, *Haven: The Unknown Story of 1,000 World War II Refugees* (New York: 1983).

Robert Wistrich, *Hitler's Apocalypse: Jews and the Nazi Legacy*. London: Weidenfield & Nicolson, 1985. viii + 309 pp.

No one who writes on antisemitism can be accused of tackling a simple issue or one limited in scope. To be sure, this does not deter many authors, and works on the subject are not in short supply. We pay attention to these works, however, in fits and starts, depending on the state of the Jew and the Jewish state in the world. The ineptitude of President Reagan, German Chancellor Helmut Kohl and their public relations experts in planning "Bitburg Sunday" (May 5, 1985) gave rise to great concern, and caused a new generation to rethink the significance of *Shoah* on the fortieth anniversary of the Second World War. Similarly, the attitude of the Roman Catholic Church to Kurt Waldheim; the beatification of Edith Stein (Sister Teresa, the famous nun converted from Judaism, who was killed in the death camp at Auschwitz in 1942); and the building of convents at concentration camps focuses attention on Christian-Jewish relations and suggests, perhaps, that the Church is determined both not to forget the victims of the Holocaust and also to forgive the agents of Nazism. The decision of the Church has done more than upset many Jews. It has also provided a brief glimpse into the Vatican's psyche and demonstrates how far the Church must travel from *Nostra Aetate* in order to establish rapprochement with the Jewish people.

The resolution declaring Zionism to be racism, introduced at the Women's Conference in Mexico (sponsored by the United Nations) and subsequently accepted by the General Assembly in 1975, provoked Robert Wistrich to reflect upon renewed fears of antisemitism; his book seeks to go beyond the usual categorical definitions to a more illuminating cultural analysis. By learning what makes anti-Zionist sentiments fashionable in the West and in the Third World, we may eventually be able to counteract them. His title suggests that while Hitler and his ilk were defeated in 1945, Hitlerism was not. The Second World War, in his view, was launched not as a conventional war but as an eschatological battle to destroy the Jews and usher in the Aryan millennium. Arab nationalism and the Islamic fundamentalists have declared holy war (*Jihad*) against the state of Israel, thus (he suggests) resuscitating virulent and age-old antisemitic hatred. And the systematic campaign of "anti-Zionist" propaganda by the U.S.S.R., the longest of its kind in the twentieth century, has promoted "an image of the Great Russian nation as representing the forces of light combating the dark powers of 'international Zionism,' and seemed to be aimed at preparing the ground for their own Soviet-style 'Final Solution' of the Jewish question."

For the author, the study of modern, political and ethnic hostility to the Jews necessitates a historical and textual approach. The discourse of antisemitism, symbols and text constitutes an important leitmotif throughout his book. No single text is going to turn an entire society into a Nazi Germany or bring on a second Holocaust. But if such a development were to recur, it would be as the result of discourse and ideology. It is this supposition that justifies Wistrich's critical appraisal of various writings, a commitment that takes him from classical fin de siècle Viennese antisemitism and the *Protocols of the Elders of Zion* to current left-wing anti-Zionism. It is through the power of symbols and texts that the Nazi legacy can live on. Or, as President Ronald Reagan noted (ironically, the remark came shortly after his controversial laying of a wreath in the Military Cemetery at Bitburg, where a number of S.S. members are buried), "the one lesson of the Second World War, the one lesson of Nazism, is that freedom must be always stronger than totalitarianism, and that good must always be stronger than evil."

Of course, the stereotype of Evil, perennially treated melodramatically in the media, is Adolf Hitler—swaggering, sneering, barking out his murderous commands. What is thus lost is the meaning, the lessons and the very sense of what is meant by *Shoah*, with its sui generis planet of murder camps supported by millions. Perhaps this is partly because the world has been trembling on the verge of apocalypse since 1945; partly, because genocide is a real threat in Africa, Asia and South America; partly, because there is always a profound urge to cover up, to deny, to consign to history's oblivion the practice of Evil (which includes the Soviet gulag and Stalin's policies that cost Russia tens of millions of lives).

But the Holocaust is absolute; and its consequences have entered the fabric of the Jewish present and the Jewish future. Therefore, historical research is essential—

above all, in this era when many are indifferent, when some deny the Holocaust altogether and still others make use of it in anti-Jewish propaganda (e.g., the portrayal of Israel as a Nazi state engaged in a policy of extermination against the Palestinians). What is clear is that the world community is at a point where it is about to lose the very meaning of the Holocaust—not only because we cannot really understand a past suffered by others, but also because it is now employed as a metaphor for the horrors of the past and present, which diminishes, relativizes and finally dismisses it. And the ultimate disrespect, as Wistrich points out, is the twinning of the Nazi swastika and the Star of David as joint symbols of genocidal fascism.

Wistrich brings freshness to the study of antisemitism, both the old and the new. His well-structured chapters on Hitler's politics of either/or, for instance, or on Christianity's teaching of contempt, compel the reader to rethink accepted cliches. Moreover, he is harsh in his analysis of Palestinian sympathizers who talk of ''Israeli Nazism'' and right-wing Israeli leaders who misuse the *Shoah* for political ends. ''Not every act against Israel is a continuation of the Holocaust. Not every condemnation of Zionism is an expression of latent or manifest antisemitism.'' Commendably, the author, even though employing academic language, seeks to address the educated public, not simply the scholar. The book's captivating imagery brings home to the reader the realization that Hitler's vision of apocalypse retains its threat.

ZEV GARBER
Los Angeles Valley College

Zbyněk Zeman, *Heckling Hitler: Caricatures of the Third Reich.* London: I. B. Tauris, 1987. 128 pp.

This book is a further addition to the latter-day proliferation of publications dealing with every possible aspect of the immensely fascinating Third Reich, and in this case the considerable expertise of the author in the field of Nazi propaganda has contributed to a profusely illustrated and well-balanced volume. Many of the best-known caricatures—by David Low, Karl Arnold and T. T. Heine—can be encountered here once again. This is a well-wrought collection for students studying Nazism for the first time, and in this respect no censure, I believe, is appropriate. It will also prove handy for teaching purposes or, alternatively, as a present, since it is not overly expensive.

The volume will, however, disappoint those who would like to benefit from the homework done by the author by tracing some of his illustrations—he does not supply readers with precise data as to the origins of each and every caricature, thus making it very difficult to ascertain copyright and authenticity. What may have originated as a device to streamline the volume may thus serve as a liability and make it difficult for scholars to reap greater benefit from it. Precisely because the close to two hundred caricatures are such successful examples of propaganda, it would have been worthwhile to have numbered them consecutively and to have identified them by means of a list of some sort.

Another drawback is the failure to identify the precise dates of those caricatures that appeared in newspapers and journals. Some of the specimens in the book appear to have been culled secondhand. Pictorial sources have too often not been accorded the scholarly care that is bestowed as a matter of course on written sources; it is a pity to encounter an established authority treating his subject matter in this rather cavalier fashion.

The text is written in a manner to please laymen, but one sometimes wonders if the author has kept up with recent and not-too-recent scholarship. Thus, for instance, Zeman ignores the studies of Henry A. Turner and repeatedly refers to the financing of Hitler by big business, a theme favored at the time by caricaturists on the Left, as if it were a matter of undisputed fact. The repeated partiality of the author for this type of reasoning does not increase his credibility. On the contrary, it indicates that up to a certain degree he is held captive by his subject matter. The idea that big business financed Hitler is a clear instance of propaganda getting out of hand, of caricaturists following a dogmatic party line and thereby helping delude both the public at large and two generations of historians about the true nature of the Nazi movement and the secrets of its success. The Nazis won the streets thanks to superior organization, discipline and dedication at the grass roots level and with very little funding from the business world. Greater sophistication in the interpretation of the source material should have been employed.

Last but not least, the author of this review has always felt a bit uneasy about admitting John Heartfield within the fold of caricaturists. His work is pure propaganda and does not allow for the ambiguities and subtleties of true caricature. The artists of *Simplicissimus* do prove, contrary to some opinion, that the Germans did possess a sense of humor of sorts; Heartfield, the typical party hack, did not.

HENRY WASSERMANN
The Open University of Israel

Susan Zuccotti, *The Italians and the Holocaust: Persecution, Rescue and Survival.* London: Peter Halban, 1987.

In his second book of memoirs—*La Tregua (The Truce,* 1963)—Primo Levi recalls that Olga, a Jewish refugee from Yugoslavia, found temporary peace in ''paradoxical Italy, officially antisemitic.'' He was right. As far as treatment of the Jews was concerned, wartime Italy was indeed a paradox. Italian Jews could be arrested and imprisoned for no apparent reason in their own country, whereas their rulers did everything in their power to protect them in German-occupied areas. Italian synagogues were sacked with impunity, yet Jewish relief agencies were permitted to collect funds abroad and aid refugees. Jewish Fascists were punished for the crime of not being ''Aryans,'' but some of their anti-Fascist brethren from abroad found a haven in Italy. In most of Europe, the Holocaust appears to be a one-dimensional picture of hunter and prey, of victimizers and victims. In Italy the behavior of Jews and gentiles alike spanned the full range of human possibility, from active resistance to spontaneous collaboration. In the words of Susan Zuccotti (née Sessions), an American gentile with an Anglo-Saxon background, "The Holocaust in Italy was a twisted legacy—a blend of courage and cowardice, nobility and degradation, self-sacrifice and opportunism. In contrast to other countries, perhaps, the worthy behaviour outweighed the unworthy, but the horror was none the less real."

Dr. Zuccotti has written an account of this "twisted legacy" because she was determined "that the story of the Holocaust be told and retold, that we who were young then shall not forget, and that new generations of children like our own shall learn, reflect, and try to understand the inconceivable." The result of her determination is a piece of scholarly research that may fairly be described as the best general introduction to this subject available in English. It is based on the ample documentary material on file at the Centro di documentazione ebraica contemporanea (CDEC) in Milan, on diaries and memoirs written by Italian Jews over the past four decades and on personal interviews with survivors. Good use has also been made of the secondary literature on Italian Jewish history and demography. Zuccotti's chief purpose is to assess the conduct of the Italians—Fascists, anti-Fascists and non-Fascists—toward the Jews during the Second World War and to place it in the context of gentile conduct throughout Europe.

Mussolini's racial policy, unlike Hitler's, did not aim at the physical extermination of the Jews; all he wanted was to remove them from the mainstream of Italian life and, if possible, from Italy altogether. After the Italian armistice of September 1943, however, he lost control of the anti-Jewish crusade he had initiated five years earlier, Hitler having decided to treat the ill-starred Fascist Social Republic as conquered as well as occupied territory. But although the Final Solution of the Jewish question was extended to Italy immediately after Pietro Badoglio's surrender to the Allies, well over four-fifths of the "non-Aryans" on the peninsula succeeded in eluding the grasp of Himmler's myrmidons. Catholic Italy thus shares with Protestant Denmark the distinction of saving the highest percentages of Jewish lives.

At the trial of Eichmann after the war, it was stated by Hulda Campagnano, a Jewish witness from Florence, that "every Italian Jew who survived owed his life to the Italians." No student of the Holocaust in Italy would disagree with this tribute to the Italian people, least of all Dr. Zuccotti. Even so, she rightly insists that there was another side to the picture. After all, antisemitism was imposed on the Italians by Mussolini, not by Hitler; from October 1938 to July 1943, Italian Jewry was persecuted and humiliated by the Fascists, not by the S.S.. Nor should scholars indulge in facile generalizations about the Italian national character. Does the fact that so many Italians rescued Jews imply that Italians generally are more compassionate and altruistic than other people? Certainly not. On the contrary, despite their international reputation as a warm and immensely humane people, Italians are not known for their civic virtue or charity sometimes associated with altruism.

Similarly, the focus on Jewish survivors and courageous rescuers should not distract attention from one "equally critical phenomenon," namely, the effusively antisemitic Italian press (there was no other press in occupied Italy), the informers, the prison guards whose cruelty to political prisoners was exceeded only by their cruelty to Jews and, finally, those politicians who decreed that Jews should be interned, even though they knew internment would ensure deportation.

Did the Holocaust in Italy begin with the German occupation in 1943 or with the Fascist race laws in 1938? Zuccotti thinks it may have begun "with the dictatorship itself"; perhaps it began "when the first black-shirted thug truncheoned his victim or administered the castor oil." Hence Fascism, like Hitlerism, was an absolute evil, despite its more moderate attitude toward the Jews. On this point, Zuccotti would appear to agree with Piero Caleffi, a veteran anti-Fascist and a survivor of Mauthausen, who wrote in 1955, "Consciously or not, the Fascists had been the originators of the extermination camps."

Like most students of the subject, Zuccotti has no doubt that, but for the establishment of Mussolini's puppet republic, many more Italian Jews would have survived the Final Solution. Given the manpower shortage of the S.S. in Italy, Fascist cooperation in the liquidation of nearly seven thousand Italian Jews was essential. Even so, the Germans regarded Il Duce's anti-Jewish policy as woefully inadequate. To the Fascists the Jews were "foreigners" and "enemy nationals" for the duration of the war; to the S.S. they were "subhumans" and permanent enemies of "Aryan humanity." For the Fascists, temporary internment was an adequate solution; Hitler and Himmler would not accept anything short of physical extermination.

Zuccotti denies that Fascist legislation was designed to take the wind out of the sails of the Germans, affirming that Mussolini and his henchmen were indifferent to the fate of the Jews. On this point, her analysis is open to criticism, for it fails to take into account the fact that the main objective of the Fascist leaders was the restoration of Italian sovereignty; since Hitler's policy of genocide constituted an open infringement of that sovereignty, they were bound to resent it, whatever their feelings about the Jews. Moreover, even the Fascist Jew-baiters—men such as Roberto Farinacci and Giovanni Preziosi—never went so far as to call for the extermination of the Jews. Mussolini himself, in a talk with his German medical adviser in February 1944, declared that he was "not an antisemite" and that Hitler's treatment of the Jews "did not redound to Germany's honour." But although it is true that Il Duce was too much of an Italian to approve of the Final Solution, it is equally true that he and his underlings helped to create the conditions in which the Holocaust in Italy became possible.

Inevitably there are controversial judgments (about the attitude of the popes for example) as well as a very few factual inaccuracies. Augusto Segre was born in 1915 (not in 1918); Dante Almansi served as vice-chief of police under Emilio De Bono in 1923–1924 (and not until the promulgation of the racial laws); Renzo Ravenna, far from being a veteran *squadrista,* was not even a member of the Fascist party at the time of the March on Rome (he served as mayor of Ferrara from 1926 to 1938); when Mussolini fell from power, Giovanni Preziosi fled to Croatia (not to Germany). These minor errors, needless to say, do not in any way detract from the validity of Dr. Zuccotti's account. *The Italians and the Holocaust* is a solid piece of historical scholarship and a significant contribution to our understanding of the Holocaust in German-dominated Europe. It is also the work of a "righteous gentile." It is a book that deserves and will attract a wide readership.

MEIR MICHAELIS
The Hebrew University

Ronald W. Zweig, *German Reparations and the Jewish World: A History of the Claims Conference.* Boulder and London: Westview Press, 1987. xi + 198 pp.

It is many years since the study of the Holocaust ceased to concentrate exclusively on Nazi-occupied Europe and turned its attention first to the role of the West during the Second World War and then, at a later stage, to the fate of the survivors and their children. Nana Sagi's book *German Reparations*[1] represented a conspicuous landmark in this broad advance of historical scholarship. Her study, in contrast to the autobiographic and journalistic treatment of reparations habitual until then, was based on systematic research, although she was still hampered by the archival statutory limit.

Ronald W. Zweig, a staff member at the Tel-Aviv University Institute for Research of Zionism, has followed the path pioneered by Sagi, but has had access to archives previously closed. Permitted to mine the original documents, he has succeeded in writing a persuasive historical record of the Conference on Jewish Material Claims Against Germany (in short, the Claims Conference). Created in 1951 by the major Jewish organizations of the world, it was saddled with the task of seeking reparations from the Federal Republic and later with the distribution of that money.

Zweig's is a concise book. A master of brevity, he has been able to condense the description of major developments into a few pages (although some of the most important episodes may one day form the subject of full-length monographs).

The book opens with a summary of the situation facing European Jewry after the Holocaust and describes the early requests for reparations—an unfortunate term, as Zweig admits. Only with the fourth chapter does the author turn to the core of his topic: the negotiations with West Germany and the establishment of the administration of the Claims Conference. In the next three chapters, the reader is provided with a meticulous description and analysis of various programs executed by the Claims Conference. These chapters are largely filled with *querelles juives*. As Zweig points out repeatedly, much money was at stake. Money meant both power and material benefits. There never was a shortage of candidates for both.

Nevertheless, the Claims Conference succeeded in establishing programs for the benefit of the survivors, for the individual Jewish communities and for the Jewish people at large. A little-known detail is revealed when Zweig demonstrates that the Jews of Moslem countries also gained direct support from the money given for the survivors of the Holocaust (pp. 74, 75). The eighth and last chapter (conclusions apart) demonstrates that the Claims Conference in its final stages was filled with a real sense of historical mission, taking upon itself to establish the Memorial Foundation for Jewish Culture, and thus transcendating the present.

This book is a monument to Nachum Goldmann, that great Jewish statesman of international stature who was never understood, still less liked, by the small men of the Israeli Zionist establishment. A flamboyant cosmopolitan with a historical perspective and with real compassion for the suffering Jewish masses, Goldmann was a towering personality who in dealings with Germany surpassed all the other Jewish politicians of his time. The only man to match Goldmann in modern German Jewish annals was Konrad Adenauer.

In his desire to tell a fast-moving story, Zweig ignores various episodes that deserve more detailed treatment. One such chapter, here ignored, was the constant (and fascinating) struggle between the Jewish Agency—staffed by the Ha'avarah (Transfer) veterans—and the government of Israel over the claims from Germany. (Incidentally, most of the government officials involved were, likewise, Jews from Germany.) Furthermore, neither of these institutions was willing to give due weight to the various organizations representing German Jewry. The constant nagging that characterized the relations between these different bodies, the certain coolness toward the *Ostjuden* who made up most of the survivors, the widespread sense of discrimination and dissatisfaction—all make up an unfortunate story that Zweig prefers to ignore. It is enough to mention that one of the incentives for setting up the Claims Conference was Adenauer's puzzlement in the face of the competing Jewish claimants seeking to negotiate for the Jews. The avalanche of men and organizations eager to represent German and world Jewry flabbergasted Adenauer, and his feelings of exasperation had already reached Goldmann in the summer of 1951.

Of the three forms taken by German reparations—payments (*shilumim*) to Israel, the global contribution to the Claims Conference and the personal indemnities—only the first two have been the subject hitherto of historical research. The indemnities are still awaiting their historian.[2] When German negotiators "exaggerated" in 1952 by setting the total sum of the personal indemnities at eight billion German marks, they were corrected by Goldmann, who put the estimate at six billion. Yet Zweig uses the up-to-date figure of eighty-five billion (p. 155), a fantastic sum that nobody expected in 1952. Certainly, the indemnities and their impact deserve extensive inquiry.

German Reparations and the Jewish World is a welcome contribution to modern Jewish historiography.

YESHAYAHU A. JELINEK
Beersheba

Notes

1. Nana Sagi, *German Reparations* (Jerusalem: 1980).
2. Two new books deal with indemnities in general: Christian Pross, *Wiedergutmachung: Der Kleinkrieg gegen die Opfer* (Frankfurt: 1988); and Ludolf Herbst and Konstantin Goschler (eds.), *Wiedergutmachung in der Bundesrepublik Deutschland* (Munich: 1989).

LANGUAGE, ART AND LITERATURE

Lewis Fried (ed.), *Handbook of American-Jewish Literature: An Analytical Guide to Topics, Themes, and Sources*. Westport: Greenwood Press, 1988. 540 pp.

American Jewish literature over the past several decades has attracted the attention of both the general reader and the academic critic in America and abroad. Despite the wealth of material on the subject, most studies and assessments of individual writers or works do not place them in the context of any larger framework or literary tradition. Lewis Fried's attempt to provide such an overview in this collection of essays is welcome. According to Fried, the purpose of the volume is "to acquaint the general reader with the major subjects and themes of American-Jewish literature, and to renew the scholar's familiarity with this material and its interpretation." Achieving a balance between the needs of a general audience and those of more specialized academic readers is a difficult task, but this collection does offer partial rewards to both groups.

To Fried's credit, he has included a great variety of genres in his total concept of American Jewish literature: prose fiction, poetry, drama, literary criticism, theology, ideology, autobiography and historiography. Moreover, he has broadened the scope of the discussion by including three long essays on Yiddish writing in America, an essay on the fiction of the Holocaust and a comparative study of German Jewish and American Jewish literature. Each essay includes a basic bibliography and suggested further readings. The only major oversight is that there is no chapter devoted to documenting the Jewish presence in the field of literary or cultural periodicals and in literary academic life. As a result, a general reader would come away from this volume without realizing the impact made by such periodicals as the *Menorah Journal,* the *Partisan Review* or *Commentary,* or the contribution of intellectuals and critics such as Lionel Trilling, Philip Rahv, Harold Bloom, Geoffrey Hartman, Leslie Fiedler and Alfred Kazin, who have done so much to shape the entire field of American literary study.

The strongest essays in the collection are those that either explore a subject that is not normally represented in surveys of American Jewish literature—such as Hannah Berliner Fischthal's review of American Yiddish literary criticism and Saul Friedman's discussion of Holocaust historiography—or those that argue a position strongly, such as Kathryn Hellerstein's essay on women poets in Yiddish. Hellerstein not only raises the question of whether these women constitute a separate tradition and canon within Yiddish literature, but she also sheds light on the male critical tradition in Yiddish letters and the causes for the exclusion of these women poets. In general, the group of essays about Yiddish literature is among the best in the volume. Friedman's essay is also provocative, as he passionately defends Raul Hilberg's controversial history *The Destruction of European Jews* and harshly criticizes Lucy Davidowicz's much-lauded work *The War Against the Jews.*

A collection of essays of this nature, mapping the terrain of a particular field of knowledge, is most successful when it is self-aware, when it tests and questions the very categories that it sets out to document: in short, when the parameters are not taken for granted. This can be achieved in a variety of ways. Asher Milbauer does so by being personal and anecdotal in his essay on the image of Eastern Europe in American Jewish writing, recounting how, after his emigration from Russia, he came to realize to what extent that country had been depicted symbolically as "the land of the Pharaoh." Gershon Shaked is the only one of the contributors to ask the central question most directly: "What is Jewish literature in non-Jewish languages?" Is the Jewish element genetic, thematic, linguistic or semiotic? His interesting comparison of German Jewish and American Jewish fiction explores the problem of dual identity from a fresh vantage point.

Unfortunately, not all the essays have this self-conscious edge, and some slip into the trap of summarizing plots and themes of works without any criteria for the selection of the texts other than some unexplained consensus about their place in the canon. David Fine's essay on "American Jewish Fiction from 1880–1930" is an example of this type of essay, which, although informative, remains ultimately too encyclopedic to be memorable. Sanford Marovitz's analysis of images of America also rarely rises above plot summary, and he fails to use the existing tradition of self-definition in American literature and criticism in evaluating how American Jewish writers have dealt with the subject.

The worst offender in this respect is Bonnie Lyons's essay that identifies American Jewish fiction since 1945 by the presence of *Yiddishkayt,* a term she identifies with a set of such themes as man's mixed moral nature, antiromanticism, the centrality of the family, intellect and spirit. These and other equally vague terms, after all, are applicable to the entire tradition of the Western novel. To support her thesis, she occasionally cites only one work, and often it is by Bellow. Lyons has nothing to add to Malin and Stark's landmark essay of 1964 on the subject, which employed categories too general to be useful, but was nonetheless pioneering in its attempt to define what has been barely recognized as a distinct body of literature. Nothing is gained by repeating this exercise in 1988.

The volume is unified by the various contributors referring to the same authors and works from different perspectives, yet the canon remains rather traditional (with the exception of contributors such as Hellerstein, who makes a point of challenging its exclusivity). It is ironic that only in the contribution by a European critic—Sepp Tiefanthalter's essay on the German reception of American Jewish literature—is there mention of important but less canonic American writers, such as Raymond Federman. As a handbook, this collection will undoubtedly prove useful to the student of American Jewish literature, particularly those essays that provoke the reader to confront some of the major questions in the field as opposed to those that lull him into torpor with plot summaries and well-worn truisms.

HANA WIRTH-NESHER
Tel-Aviv University

Grace Farrell Lee, *From Exile to Redemption: The Fiction of Isaac Bashevis Singer.* Carbondale: Southern Illinois University Press, 1987. 129 pp.

In the publisher's promotional material for *From Exile to Redemption,* I. B. Singer is reported to have said, "Grace Farrell Lee understands me better than I understand myself." Given Singer's almost legendary disdain for literary criticism and critics, the quotation should be read sardonically. That the publishers (and, apparently, the author herself) regard it as an endorsement underscores the limitations of this book.

Despite comments about the importance of fiction and language, Ms. Lee is more interested in Singer as a modern philosopher than as a writer. Echoing a line in *Passions,* she begins with his questions about "why a man is born and why he must die'' and proceeds to answer the existential dilemmas raised by Singer's novels and stories. Illustrating the uneasy balance between the religious and secular presented in the fiction, she considers Singer's views of exile and redemption, the old and the new, the personal and the communal. Although she casts a wide net by invoking such terms, both her analysis of specific texts and the book's primary arguments are disappointing. Singer, she maintains, connects exile from the self to a much more profound exile from religion and God; he transforms religious and communal terms into secular and personal ones. Finally, and rather anticlimactically, she concludes that Singer views Redemption and transcendence in the modern world as dependent upon the willingness to have faith in ''the profound consolation of love'' and ''the community of two.''

Ms. Lee sees Singer's sources in the Bible, Kabbalah and Jewish folklore, but she presents an uneasy and unconvincing mixture of these sources. Like many critics of Singer's fiction, she can neither read the Yiddish originals nor do justice to the religious sources she claims are central. But the most disturbing part of this book is that it is a book at all. Her reading of Singer might have justified an essay or article, but cannot sustain a book-length study.

ANITA NORICH
University of Michigan

Recently Completed
Doctoral Dissertations

Gary A. Abraham   University of Pittsburgh, 1987
"Max Weber and the Jewish Question: A Study of the Social Outlook of His Sociology"

Abraham Ben-Jaacob   The Hebrew University, 1989
"*Hagirat yehudei bavel lehodu vehishtak'utam bah*" ("The Immigration of the Iraqi Jews to, and Their Settlement in, India")

Marcia Drezon-Tepler   Columbia University, 1985
"Interest Groups and Political Change in Israel"

Joseph Elichai   The Hebrew University, 1989
"*Tenu'at hamizraḥi befolin hakongresait 1916–1927*" ("The Mizrachi Movement in Congress Poland in the Years 1916–1927")

Esther Enoch   The Hebrew University, 1989
"*Masoret 'Agnon vehamodernah basiporet ha'ivrit shel shenot hashishim*" ("The Agnon Tradition and Modernity in Hebrew Fiction During the 1960s")

Gila Fatran   The Hebrew University, 1989
"*Merkaz hayehudim ha'Uzh'—irgun meshatfei pe'ulah o irgun haẓalah?*" ("The Jewish Center in Slovakia [Ú Ž]: An Organization of Collaboration or Rescue?"

Moshe Halevi   Tel-Aviv University, 1989
"*Maks Nordau—haguto haẓiyonit ufo'alo batenu'ah haẓiyonit*" ("Max Nordau—His Zionist Philosophy and His Activity in the Zionist Movement")

Iwona Irwin-Zarecka   University of California, San Diego, 1987
"On a Memory Note: The Jew in Contemporary Poland: A Study in the Construction of Collective Memory"

Sharon Kaplan Jaffe   University of California, Los Angeles, 1987
"The Immigrant Journey in Twentieth-Century Jewish-American Fiction"

Allan Laine Kagedan   Columbia University, 1985
"The Formation of Soviet Jewish Territorial Units, 1924–1937."

Naomi Liron   University of California, Berkeley, 1987
"Cynthia Ozick. The Self-Subverting Artist"

Avraham Maapil   The Hebrew University, 1989
"*Iẓuv hemeẓiyut basiporet ha'ivrit shel S. Yizhar*" ("The Depiction of Reality in S. Yizhar's Hebrew Fiction")

Doron Niederland The Hebrew University, 1989
"*Defusei hagirah shel yehudei germaniyah (1918–1938)*" ("The Patterns of
Jewish Emigration from Germany [1918–1938]")

Haim Peles The Hebrew University, 1989
"*Hahityashvut hadatit beerez yisrael beshenot ha'esrim vehasheloshim*"
("The Religious Settlement Movement in Palestine in the 1920s and 1930s")

Andrew Ritchie University of California, Berkeley, 1987
"Adapting to Abundance: Eastern European Jews and Urban Consumption in
America, 1880–1914"

Eli Shaltiel Tel-Aviv University, 1989
"*Pinhas Rutenberg umanhigut hayishuv, 1919–1942*" ("Pinhas Rutenberg
and the Yishuv Leadership, 1919–1942")

Robert Moses Shapiro Columbia University, 1987
"Jewish Self-government in Poland: Lodz, 1914–1939"

Peter Shaw The Hebrew University, 1989
"*Historiyah hevratit shel hakehilah hayehudit beodesah 1871–1900*" ("A
Social History of the Jewish Community in Odessa 1871–1900")

Michael Charles Steinlauf Brandeis University, 1988
"Polish-Jewish Theater: The Case of Mark Arnshteyn, A Study of the In-
terplay Among Yiddish, Polish and Polish-Language Jewish Culture in the
Modern Period"

Sara Strassberg The Hebrew University, 1989
"*Tefisat haadam ezel A. H. Gordon veharav Kuk*" ("The Concept of Man in
the Thought of A. D. Gordon and Rabbi Kook")

Bradford Towne University of Utah, 1987
"Population Structure and Anthropometric Variation Among the Habbahi
Yemeni Jews (Israel)"

Yitzhak Yanai Tel-Aviv University, 1989
"*Haideologiah hahevratit shel mapai leor mediniyutah bamedinah uvahista-
drut bashanim 1948–1953*" ("The Social Ideology of Mapai in the Light of
Its Policies in Government and in the Histadrut, 1948–1953")

Yosef Zuriely The Hebrew University, 1989
"*Mibe'ayot hahinukh shel yaldei hateimanim beerez-yisrael (1882–1948)*"
("Issues in the Education of Yemenite Children in Palestine [1882–1948]")

STUDIES IN CONTEMPORARY JEWRY, VIII

Edited by
Peter Medding

SYMPOSIUM

**A New Jewry? America Since the
Second World War**

Anthony Smith, The Question of Contemporary Jewish Identity

Review Essays

Marcus Arkin on the German-Jewish economic elite

Aharon Klieman on the Israel–Jordan relationship

. . . Plus reviews and a listing of recent doctoral dissertations

Note on Editorial Policy

Studies in Contemporary Jewry is pleased to accept manuscripts for possible publication. Authors of essays on subjects generally within the contemporary Jewish sphere (from the turn of the century to the present) should send two copies to:

Studies in Contemporary Jewry
Institute of Contemporary Jewry
The Hebrew University
Mt. Scopus, Jerusalem, Israel

Essays must not exceed thirty-five pages in length and must be double-spaced throughout (including indented quotes and endnotes). Reviews must not exceed one thousand words per book. Unsolicited material should be sent no later that April 1. Further information may also be obtained by fax: 011–9722–322–545.